C000182637

STUDIES IN EARLY MODERN CULTURAL,
POLITICAL AND SOCIAL HISTORY

Volume 23

BRITISH TRAVELLERS
AND THE ENCOUNTER WITH BRITAIN,
1450–1700

Studies in Early Modern Cultural, Political and Social History

ISSN: 1476-9107

Series editors

Tim Harris – Brown University
Stephen Taylor – Durham University
Andy Wood – Durham University

Previously published titles in the series
are listed at the back of this volume

BRITISH TRAVELLERS AND THE ENCOUNTER WITH BRITAIN, 1450-1700

John Cramsie

THE BOYDELL PRESS

First published 2015
The Boydell Press, Woodbridge

ISBN 978-1-78327-053-8

The Boydell Press is an imprint of Boydell & Brewer Ltd
PO Box 9, Woodbridge, Suffolk IP12 3DF, UK
and of Boydell & Brewer Inc.
668 Mt Hope Avenue, Rochester, NY 14620-2731, USA
website: www.boydellandbrewer.com

A catalogue record for this book is available
from the British Library

The publisher has no responsibility for the continued existence or accuracy of URLs for
external or third-party internet websites referred to in this book, and does not guarantee
that any content on such websites is, or will remain, accurate or appropriate

This publication is printed on acid-free paper

Typeset by
Frances Hackeson Freelance Publishing Services, Brinscall, Lancs

Printed and bound in Great Britain by
TJ International Ltd, Padstow, Cornwall

Contents

List of Illustrations

Acknowledgements

This book is a story of many journeys. It has occupied my attention from the undercroft café of St Giles Cathedral in Edinburgh to the Vieux Porte Montreal, from state parks along the Minnesota north shore of Lake Superior to Professor Java's in Albany NY, and eclectic, inspiring places in between. People throughout have supported and encouraged me in their unique, invaluable ways. My gratitude is heartfelt and lasting to those whose names are not here.

I appreciate the generous funding of the Humanities Faculty Development Fund and History Department Tracy Fund at Union College. For permission to quote from and reproduce archival materials and images, I thank the British Library, Cambridge University Library, the Henry E. Huntington Library, the Mary Evans Picture Library, the National Library of Scotland, the National Library of Wales, and ProQuest. The NLS and NLW have earned my warmest regard. The staff in Edinburgh and Aberystwyth made sure that the morning trudge upstairs and uphill, respectively, promised a good day's work in the most knowledgeable and pleasant surroundings.

At Boydell, I have benefited from the expert handling of Michael Middeke, Megan Milan, and their unsung colleagues. Many, many thanks. I am grateful to Boydell's anonymous reader for a welcome view from outside the forest and the trees. I have benefited from many lively conversations with Peter Sowden and Tim Harris. This is not the book they signed me up for, but I can never repay their interest in this one. Tim has been a great friend since we met in his Folger Institute seminar and I am fortunate to number him among my close colleagues. John Guy offered a kind dose of encouragement at just the right time. My gratitude to John now stretches over more than twenty years, for bringing me to St. Andrews to work with him in the 90s and his continuing friendship since. I am sorry my undergraduate teacher, Stanford Lehmberg, died before this book came out. One of our last conversations concerned this project and I would like for Stan to have read it. Portions of this book have benefited from the scrutiny of friends and colleagues at successive Medieval and Renaissance Scottish Languages and Literature conferences in St Catharines, Ontario (2005), Padua (2011), and Bochum (2014). I am especially grateful to Roger Mason for arguing with me about John Lesley's *Historie*, pointing me toward the Blaeu atlas of Scotland, and sharing various essays on George Buchanan's *Historia* before publication.

My travels in Britain over more than twenty years have constantly energized my work as a historian. They have been filled with memorable meetings and remarkable people. As a traveller, I earned three particular debts in writing this book. Thanks to Jill and Rob Inglis at Thorntons (formerly) in Linlithgow, for

ix

superb porridge and evening conversation, for directions to the canal path and time to think about the day on my walk to the station, and for bringing alive Linlithgow Palace and Falkland. Thanks to Hilary and Clive Davies at Bodalwyn in Aberystwyth, for constant humour, for helping with the basics of Welsh, and for memorable evenings watching the Six Nations and Wales versus the All Blacks. Finally, thanks to Stephen Alford and Max Fletcher, the oldest and dearest of friends, for journeys through Shropshire, Cambridge and the Fens, the Lake District, Abbotsford and the Scottish Borders, and Northumbria, especially Holy Island, Warkworth Castle, Barter Books in Alnwick, and a ruddy, salt-sprayed Guy Fawkes Night at Low Newton by-the-Sea.

That I am any kind of traveller is thanks to my wife Cynthia. Our most remarkable journey to date has been to China – much too long in coming. Barely off the plane in Hong Kong, we found ourselves bound for Nanchang, a teeming clash of ancient teahouses and venerable mah-jong players, Soviet era bathroom-tile architecture, and turbo-capitalist hucksterism. In that exciting city of hot food and hotter weather we became adoptive parents to one of the province's renowned 'spicy Jiangxi girls'. This book is for Jingmae Marie Cramsie, who gives me so much more to think about than work and takes me on the journeys that only an imaginative, artistic, and determined child can. 'Baba loves Jing Jing, yes indeed.'

Schenectady
3 March 2015

Introduction:
A New Encounter with
Early Modern Britain

Roger Williams, the founder of Providence, penned *The Hirelings Ministry None of Christs* in 1652. He wrote at the close of the religious wars that had pitted the peoples and churches of Britain and Ireland against one another since 1637. Williams denounced the incomplete conversion of souls to the Gospel of Christ with racial imagery: 'although the holy Spirit of God, in every Nation where the Word comes, washeth white some Blackamores, and changeth some Leopards spots, yet the bodies and bulks of nations, cannot by all the Acts and Statutes under heaven, cut off the Blackamores skin'. We might think Williams bemoaned the state of grace in the American colonies, but he had in mind the complacent reformers who trumpeted the 'great and mighty conuersions of whole Nations, England, Scotland, French, Dutch, &c. from Popery to be good Protestants'. As a promoter of Independency, the freedom to seek God outside a 'state' church, Williams drew a direct contrast between the established churches of the Old World and the spirituality of the New: 'This mine eyes have often seen among the thousands of wild, yet wise Americans ... utterly uncapable of Formes and Ministers (or Officers) of Christian Worship, while yet in their naturally and worldly capacities ... made spirituall and heavenly, by the holy Spirit of God.'[1]

The Protestant churches in Britain and Ireland compiled a dismal missionary record in the Isles. According to Williams, 'as an eminent Person lately spake (upon occasion of a Debate touching the Conversion of Indians) we have Indians at home, Indians in Cornwall, Indians in Wales, Indians in Ireland'. They desperately needed the true Gospel to stop them being 'turned forward and backward as the Weather-cock' by this or that established church. Williams contended that 'it is not the will of the Father of Spirits that ... any Towne or Parish (so called) in England, Scotland, or Ireland, be disturbed in their worship (what worship soever it be) by the ciuill sword' acting for a state church.[2] The answer for the peoples of the Isles, 'Indian' or otherwise, lay with the Gospel

---

[1] Roger Williams, *The Hirelings Ministry None of Christs* (WING W2765; London, 1652), pp. 13, 18–19.
[2] Williams, *Hirelings Ministry*, p. 13.

fervour and Holy Spirit that fed those wild, yet wise Americans, openly professed in free assemblies by women and men who sought the Son of God.

Roger Williams presupposed that the Britain he wrote about was a multicultural one. He recorded ethno-cultural complexity at home within and among 'three Nations', encounters with Amerindians in the Atlantic world, and religious distinctions that spanned Europe and the Americas.[3] Williams also expected his readers to understand these multicultural nuances, even pejorative ones like Cornish Indians with its obvious resonance of heathenism. His travels at home and abroad were intended to vouch for these descriptions, insights, and arguments.[4]

In a figurative sense, Williams' journey began two centuries earlier. While many Britons lived and died near their birthplaces, the roads and byways of medieval Britain were home to an eclectic and surprisingly large collection of travellers. Some of them, like Gerald of Wales in the twelfth century or John of Fordun in the fourteenth, took to the roads intent on describing their countries and fellow inhabitants. The Atlantic voyages that began in the fifteenth century did not so much inaugurate a European fascination with discovery and humanity as give new encouragement to old interests. Ethnography – the study of humanity itself – occupied travellers and regimes as much as commercial gain, religious fervour, or dreams of empire. Medieval travel, European voyages in the Atlantic, and the drive to study humanity propelled British travellers into a new encounter with Britain in the Tudor and Stuart centuries. Travellers' journeys and narratives uncovered, recovered, and fashioned the multicultural Britain that was Williams' starting point – and ours.

*　*　*　*　*

A more curious or stylish title for this book might have been taken from the famous Tudor traveller John Leland. Leland wanted to make known to Henry VIII and the world a realm 'payntid with his natives coloures'. He intended to chronicle and celebrate how the peoples of England and Wales came to settle the towns and villages, valleys and mountaintops they called home, record the marks they left in the landscape, and celebrate the noble histories and complex cultures they created. In short, Leland sought to capture how they became the people that he met and came to know through his travels. Madness seized Leland's mind before he accomplished this life's work, but dozens – eventually hundreds – of Britons shared the same passion to tell the stories of their island and its people.[5] The individuals studied here include actual travellers as well as armchair

---

[3] Williams, *Hirelings Ministry*, sig. A4a

[4] Williams, *Hirelings Ministry*, p. 13.

[5] Unless otherwise indicated, I use the terms Britons and British simply to identify the inhabitants of Britain.

travellers and those who blurred the boundaries between them. Their letters, diaries, journals, and histories range from the epic, poignant, and matter of fact to the exotic, preposterous, and hateful; the sources include actual and imaginative narratives and those which combined both elements.

Multicultural Britain presented itself to travellers in three related ways. Today we would call Britain an immigrant nation, built by centuries of encounters, interactions, and exchanges among a succession of migrant groups and ethnic communities. Tudor and Stuart travellers read this in their histories, marked it on the landscape, and rubbed up against its vestiges in contacts with fellow Britons. Second, travellers might associate cultural complexity with distinct ethnic groups related to ancient migrations – e.g. Picts, Norse, Saxons – or national and supranational labels more familiar to us: Scottish, Welsh, English, Irish, British. Finally, travellers took in a remarkable and fascinating number of ethno-cultural markers: physicality and appearance, dress and adornment, food and drink, economic livelihoods and environmental relationships, education and language, oral and literary cultures, religion and belief systems, political practices and warfare, social structures and relationships, artefacts and monuments, families and gender, customs and manners, temperament and humour. Inevitably, immigrant Britain, ethnic groups or nations, and the focus on cultural markers interacted or layered on top of one another. Travellers explained and interpreted human variety in relationship to climate and topography, Classical models of civility and barbarity, the process of degeneracy, the Old Testament origins of nations or 'races', social evolution from nomadism and hunter-gathering through intensive agriculture to commercial society (stadial theory), or – more often – some ad hoc and inconsistent combination of these.

For Thomas Palmer, writing in 1606, the nature of a people was one among the key topics for investigation in journeys abroad. Travellers should begin with five questions: 'whether the people bee ciuill or barbarous ... free or seruile ... religious or profane ... warlike or effeminate ... of what condition of bodies, and disposition of mind.'[6] Natural temperament or discipline might explain a people's civility or barbarity, but Palmer implied a certain geographic determinism in classing the people of 'Africa, America, Magellanica, and those of Northeast Europe and Asia, by nature barbarists'.[7] Travellers could mark civility and barbarity through 'gesture, apparel, decencie, conuersation, diet, feeding, giuing of honour, and all other actions of the people of a countrey'.[8] In all this travellers should note well the marks of civility that might instruct their own nations: 'For proofe whereof behold how the English, Scottish, French, Italians, & Spanish which are the most reformed & courtlike people, are tainted with

---

[6] Thomas Palmer, *An Essay of the Means How to Make Our Trauailes, into Forraine Countries, the Most Profitable and Honourable* (STC 19156; London, 1606), p. 60.

[7] Palmer, *Trauailes*, pp. 60–1.

[8] Palmer, *Trauailes*, p. 61.

some blemish of barbarousnesse, the which of other heathen nations they might learne to reforme.'[9] Palmer contrasted the charitable treatment of strangers by 'African heathen Negros' in a long list of civil and barbarous qualities among nations. He included the similarities between Scottish nobles who, in times past, 'leuie[d] the Virginitie' of local maids and a group of Bengalis who never married a woman that had not been similarly treated by 'some white Christian or Mawhometan'.[10]

While this book focuses on the recovery of travellers' encounters, it is important to emphasize a second theme with Palmer's tract in mind. Travellers' experiences, conceptions, and descriptions of cultural complexity were simply too varied to fit tidy categories and I have deliberately avoided creating a schema for them or prescriptive definitions of the peoples they encountered. Wide-ranging curiosity drove them. Like Kathleen Wilson and Graham Robb (among others), I reject the understandable but distorting search for dominant patterns in travellers' experiences or predictable, defining characteristics of particular nations, regions, or ethno-cultural groups.[11] Robb in particular offers a salutary warning in his account of France and the French from the *ancien régime* to the Great War. He writes, 'Beyond the squares, the monuments and the rooms of state that form the backdrop of most French history lay a world of ancient tribes and huge vacant spaces.'[12] Locality and particularity predominated in the *pays* (micro-provinces): 'Brittany would have to be subdivided several times before an area could be found that meant something to the people who lived there. ... Local identity consisted ultimately, not in ethnic origins, but in the fact that a community happened to be where it was rather than somewhere else.'[13] Even with an enviable wealth of evidence, Robb rightly emphasizes that 'nearly all the distant figures mentioned in travellers' accounts, who might have dispelled false impressions with a few words and gestures, are just dots in the landscape'.[14] Those distant figures hold the key to recovering the cultural complexity of France, to describing 'the lives of the inhabitants ... and the exploration and colonization of their land by foreigners and natives', such that '"France" and "the French"' would mean something more than Paris and a few powerful individuals'.[15]

There is good reason to think that the peoples of the three 'nations' occupying Britain possessed stronger ethno-cultural identities than Robb's dots on the

---

[9] Palmer, *Trauailes*, p. 62.

[10] Palmer, *Trauailes*, pp. 62, 65.

[11] Kathleen Wilson, *The Island Race: Englishness, Empire and Gender in the Eighteenth Century* (Abingdon, 2003), pp. 3–4, 7.

[12] Graham Robb, *The Discovery of France: Historical Geography from the Revolution to the First World War* (New York, 2007), p. 9.

[13] Robb, *Discovery of France*, pp. 25, 49.

[14] Robb, *Discovery of France*, p. 107.

[15] Robb, *Discovery of France*, pp. xvi–xvii.

French landscape, even in the Tudor and Stuart centuries.[16] Still, Alan Everitt and Joan Thirsk looked beneath the expanse of England to uncover the diverse social topographies, farming regions, and local economies they termed the *pays*.[17] Reflecting on more than two decades' work on England's *pays*, Everitt reiterated that

> Differences in local patterns, in rural economies, in industrial origins, in parish typologies: these do not exhaust the historical diversity of provincial society. They are enough to suggest, however, that whereas we normally think of England as a single community, a unitary society, it is also legitimate to think of it as an amalgam of different societies all at varying stages in their evolution, all influencing each other, yet all developing in their own way, moving forward at different periods and at different paces, so that one finds older societies co-existing, often with equal vigour, alongside the new.[18]

Maps of early modern Scotland and Wales can be similarly marked and divided.[19]

Where Everitt brilliantly illuminated the complexities of landscape, society, and economy, this book emphasizes cultural complexities. It probes beneath familiar national labels or traditional ethnic identities by focusing on the diverse and disparate experiences of travellers with multicultural Britain. For example, travellers understood full well that Britain's history was a history of migration, conflict, settlement, and cultural exchange both outwith the island and within it. Travellers read it in the landscapes they traversed or studied. Familiar labels like English or Scottish or Welsh meant only so much either to travellers or those they encountered, especially when accounting for people's origins or in the immediacy of local contacts and experiences. It is convenient to talk of nations, kingdoms, and the evolution of Britons, but the peoples of Tudor and Stuart Britain sometimes betrayed a very modern ability to accommodate a multi-layered sense of cultural complexity and identity: part *pays*, part nation, part

[16] See R.R. Davies, *The First English Empire: Power and Identities in the British Isles 1093–1343* (Oxford, 2001), pp. 113–71; Davies, *The British Isles 1100–1500: Comparisons, Contrasts, and Connections* (Edinburgh, 1988); Davies, *Domination and Conquest: The Experience of Ireland, Scotland and Wales 1100–1300* (Cambridge, 1990); Davies, *Lord and Lordship in the British Isles in the Late Middle Ages* (Oxford, 2009); Margaret T. Hodgen, *Early Anthropology in the Sixteenth and Seventeenth Centuries* (Philadelphia, 1964); John Kerrigan, *Archipelagic English: Literature, History, and Politics 1603–1707* (Oxford, 2008), pp. 1–90; Colin Kidd, *British Identities before Nationalism: Ethnicity and Nationhood in the Atlantic World 1600–1800* (Cambridge, 1999); Kidd, *The Forging of Races: Race and Scripture in the Protestant Atlantic World, 1600–2000* (Cambridge, 2006); Ania Loomba and Jonathan Burton, eds, *Race in Early Modern England* (Houndmills, 2007); Roxann Wheeler, *The Complexion of Race: Categories of Difference in Eighteenth-Century British Culture* (Philadelphia, 2000).
[17] Alan Everitt, *Landscape and Community in England* (London, 1985), pp. 14, 41–2; Francis Pryor, *The Making of the British Landscape: How We Have Transformed the Land from Prehistory to Today* (London, 2010), pp. 381–3.
[18] Everitt, *Landscape and Community*, p. 6.
[19] Pryor, *Making of the British Landscape*, pp. 304–14, 355–73, 390–400.

something else, much of it accompanied by silences and ambiguities. Within the broader brush strokes, I hope to mark the distant figures on the Tudor and Stuart landscape, even if so often it is impossible to paint their native colours in depth or detail.

This book makes a final point: Tudor and Stuart travellers found nothing incomprehensible in a Britain that was simultaneously multicultural and what we would characterize as overwhelmingly 'white'. This is not to reject concepts of colour, attitudes about racial difference, and the imaginative importance or real presence in Britain of people from Africa, Asia, or the Americas.[20] However, travellers' narratives establish the pervasiveness of multicultural mentalities and habits of thought like Thomas Palmer's or Roger Williams' before the presence of large numbers of Black, Jewish, and Asian migrants changed the demographic character of Britain. Multicultural Britain began long before post-colonial migration, a fact with social and political implications for contemporary Britain that will be explored in the conclusion.

This story of British travellers and their 'discovery' of multicultural Britain is a vital but curiously unexplored one.[21] It is certainly not for lack of interest in travel or British travellers abroad.[22] Indeed, Richard Hakluyt began collecting and publicizing accounts of English voyagers in the reign of Elizabeth I to spur overseas exploration and expansion. Recent books illustrate how 'cosmopolitan Britons' embraced cultural practices well outside their experiences at home.[23]

---

[20] Peter Freyer, *Staying Power: The History of Black People in Britain* (London, 1984); Ania Loomba, *Shakespeare, Race, and Colonialism* (Oxford, 2002/2009), pp. 22–74. Miranda Kaufmann's study of 'Black Tudors' is forthcoming from Oneworld Publishers; http://www. mirandakaufmann.com/history.html.

[21] The study of travellers in pre-Independence Ireland has not been neglected. For example, Nicholas Canny, *Making Ireland British 1580–1650* (Oxford, 2001); Andrew Hadfield and John McVeagh, eds, *Strangers to That Land: British Perceptions of Ireland from the Reformation to the Famine* (Gerard's Cross, 1994); Wilson McLeod, *Divided Gaels: Gaelic Cultural Identities in Scotland and Ireland c. 1200–c.1650* (Oxford, 2004); Patricia Palmer, *Language and Conquest in Early Modern Ireland: English Renaissance Literature and Elizabethan Imperial Expansion* (Cambridge, 2001); William H.A. Williams, *Tourism, Landscape, and the Irish Character* (Madison, WI, 2008).

[22] Edward Chaney, *The Evolution of the Grand Tour* (London, 1998); Nicholas Dew, 'Reading Travels in the Culture of Curiosity: Thévenot's Collection of Voyages', *Journal of Early Modern History* 10.1&2 (2006), pp. 39–59; Brian Dolan, *Exploring European Frontiers; British Travellers in the Age of Enlightenment* (Houndmills, 2000); Dolan, *Ladies of the Grand Tour* (London, 2002); R.W. Frantz, *The English Traveller and the Movement of Ideas 1660–1732* (reprinted; Lincoln, NE, 1967); Mary C. Fuller, 'Making Something Fit of It: Questions of Value in the Early English Travel Collection', *Journal of Early Modern History* 10.1&2 (2006), pp. 11–38; Andrew Hadfield, *Literature, Travel, and Colonial Writing in the English Renaissance 1545–1625* (Oxford, 1998); Antoni Maczak, *Travel in Early Modern Europe* (Oxford, 1995); John Stoye, *English Travellers Abroad 1604–1607* (revised edition; New Haven, 1989); Sara Warneke, *Images of the Educational Traveller in Early Modern England* (Leiden, 1995).

[23] Among many books published since the year 2000, Colin G. Calloway, *White People, Indians, and Highlanders: Tribal Peoples and Colonial Encounters in Scotland and America* (Oxford,

With a focus on early modern geography, antiquarianism, anthropology, and the explosive investigation of the natural world from the mid-seventeenth century, scholars have recovered the dedicated, often passionate exploration of British origins and the island's complexity.[24] Reversing the gaze, we find Turkish and Moorish travellers for whom Britain was a land to be discovered.[25] Europeans and a growing number of global travellers too pursued their fascination with Britain by journeys there, from the future Pope Pius II's travels in Scotland and England to the Enlightenment Europeans who made Britain part of their 'grand tour'.[26]

We know a good deal, then, about the cultural encounters of British travellers abroad and the travellers who treated Britain as a land to be discovered. This book brings together these two vital topics. It recovers the purposeful discovery and rediscovery of Britain's cultural complexity by its own peoples. Britons eagerly did at home precisely what those who journeyed to the Ottoman Empire and Asia or explored the Americas and Africa did.[27] They travelled to 'unknown' lands, encountered cultural complexity, attempted – or not – to understand the peoples they met, and explained or constructed those experiences and insights

2008); William Dalrymple, *White Mughals: Love and Betrayal in Eighteenth Century India* (Harmondsworth, 2003); James Ellison, *George Sandys: Travel, Colonialism and Tolerance in the 17th Century* (Woodbridge, 2002); Alison Games, *The Web of Empire: English Cosmopolitans in an Age of Exploration 1560–1660* (Oxford, 2008); Maya Jasanoff, *Edge of Empire: Lives, Culture, and Conquest in the East 1750–1850* (New York, 2005); Gerald MacLean, *The Rise of Oriental Travel: English Visitors to the Ottoman Empire, 1580–1720* (Houndmills, 2004); MacLean, *Looking East: English Writing and the Ottoman Empire before 1800* (Houndmills, 2007); James Mather, *Pashas: Traders and Travellers in the Islamic World* (New Haven, 2009).
[24] Frank Emery, 'English Regional Studies from Aubrey to Defoe', *Geographical Journal* 124.3 (1958), pp. 315–25; Adam Fox, 'Printed Questionnaires, Research Networks, and the Discovery of the British Isles, 1650–1800', *Historical Journal* 53.3 (2010), pp. 593–621; Michael Hunter, *John Aubrey and the Realm of Learning* (New York, 1975); T.D. Kendrick, *British Antiquity* (London, 1950); Stan Mendyk, *'Speculum Britanniae': Regional Study, Antiquarianism, and Science in Britain to 1700* (Toronto, 1989); Rosemary Sweet, *Antiquaries: The Discovery of the Past in Eighteenth-Century Britain* (London, 2004); Stuart Piggott, *Ruins in a Landscape: Essays in Antiquarianism* (Edinburgh, 1976); E.G.R. Taylor, *Tudor Geography 1485–1583* (London, 1930); Taylor, *Late Tudor and Early Stuart Geography 1583–1650* (London, 1934).
[25] Nabil Matar, *Islam in Britain 1558–1685* (Cambridge, 1998); Matar, *Turks, Moors and Englishmen in the Age of Discovery* (New York, 1999); Matar, ed., *In the Lands of the Christians: Arabic Travel Writing in the 17th Century* (London, 2002).
[26] P. Hume Brown, ed., *Early Travellers in Scotland* (reprinted Edinburgh, 1973); Malcolm Letts, *As the Foreigner Saw Us* (London, 1935); Norman Scarfe, *To the Highlands in 1786: The Inquisitive Journey of a Young French Aristocrat* (Woodbridge, 2001); Clare Williams, *Thomas Platter's Travels in England 1599* (London, 1937).
[27] The big picture of world discovery and exploration into which Britain fitted is captured by William Cunningham, *The Cosmographical Glasse, Conteinyng the Pleasant Principles of Cosmographie, Geographie, Hydrographie, or Nauigation* (London, 1559), Preface and pp. 6, 72–5.

in written narratives.[28] It erases the false distinctions between home and abroad (later, between imperial metropole and colonial periphery) that have influenced studies of British travellers literally since Hakluyt's *Principal Navigations* deliberately excluded voyages of discovery near home. Consequently, it does not analyse travellers and immigrants who came from outside Britain, including Muslims and continental Europeans. Instead, the book emphasizes how the age of discovery became in Britain an age of self-discovery. The focus on Britain would not be everyone's choice. In her account of Victorian travellers and national identity, Marjorie Morgan explained, 'I did not want to confine the study to travel within Britain, because I believe ... that nations are forged both from within and from outside national borders.'[29] However, what follows will reveal the difficulty of meaningfully defining within and without, given the cultural complexity of early modern Britain.

The idea of discovering multicultural Britain in the Tudor and Stuart centuries might trouble traditional historians who see in it anachronism. For the great scholar-traveller William Camden, writing in the 1580s and 1590s, multicultural Britain began when the island's first inhabitants journeyed across the land bridge that would one day become the English Channel. Others joined them and over the centuries the Gaels, Picts, Scots, Welsh, and Cornish eventually emerged from these communities of 'Britons'. With Romans, Angles, Saxons, Jutes, Norse, and Normans they spent the next millennium creating, contesting, and reshaping the cultural mosaic of Britain. When Camden set out to write *Britannia* and took to the roads and footpaths to discover it at firsthand, those complex cultures guided and informed his epic journey into the past and its contemporary reality.

Multicultural best defines an island that is home to the influences and legacies of many cultures over almost the entirety of human settlement there. It is a statement of fact, not political correctness. Unfortunately, no early modern term quite captures Camden's and other travellers' encounters. In medieval usage 'complexion' referred to the collection of qualities that defined one's nature, while 'complex' and 'complexity' both became ways of identifying the composite nature of something, including humans.[30] One thirteenth-century Scottish poet commented on 'qualiterque Britannia stirpe multi-gena variatur' or how 'Britain

---

[28] Examples of individuals engaged in projects of discovery at home and abroad like Robert Boyle or William Petty are noted in Frank Emery, 'The Geography of Robert Gordon, 1580-1661, and Sir Robert Sibbald, 1641-1722', *Scottish Geographical Magazine* 74.1 (1958), pp. 6-8; Emery, 'A Map of Edward Lhuyd's Parochial Queries in Order to a Geographical Dictionary', *Transactions of the Honourable Society of Cymmrodorion* (1958), p. 43; Fox, 'Discovery of the British Isles', pp. 596-8.
[29] Marjorie Morgan, *National Identities and Travel in Victorian Britain* (Houndmills, 2001), p. 4
[30] A useful discussion is Wheeler, *Complexion of Race*, pp. 2-45.

becomes different with a lineage of mixed peoples'.[31] I therefore typically use multicultural or cultural complexity or, when appropriate, ethnicity.

I have divided the story into three parts around select sets of travellers: John Leland (1503–52), two near-contemporary Scots, John Mair (1467–1550) and Hector Boece (1465–1536), and their sixteenth-century successors in the first part; Fynes Moryson (1565–1630) and his seventeenth-century contemporaries in the second; and lastly, William Camden (1551–1623) and the team of travellers led by Bishop Edmund Gibson who revised his *Britannia* in the 1690s. These travellers' reputations are well established, but their backgrounds, particular journeys, and literary remains make it possible to free them from pigeonholes that obscure their unique and multi-layered encounters with Britain. For example, typing Camden as an English antiquarian, saddling Leland with an epitaph like 'the father of English History', or locking them into particular phases of antiquarianism defies their acute awareness of the cultural complexity to be found in their journeys. Focussing only on the 'main' travellers would produce too neat a story. That is why journeys and narratives by several dozen contemporaries richly contextualize them. These 'supporting' travellers bring crucial diversity and depth of experience and this study would be incomplete without them.

Studies by Barbara Korte, Esther Moir, Ian Ousby, and Richard Trench aimed for similar breadth.[32] Stan Mendyk's *Speculum Britanniae* (1989) covers the most ground and my book takes an interest in many of the same individuals, from Leland through Gibson's team. Mendyk masterfully examines the evolution of the chorographic tradition (the study of regions, counties, and localities) among primarily English travellers and writers. The antiquarian and topographic impulses of Camden, William Lambarde, John Norden, William Burton, and the like evolved into or joined with an emphasis on precision and systematic examination of the natural world. After the mid-seventeenth century, the natural rarities described in Joshua Childrey's *Britannia Baconica*, the 'scientific antiquarianism' of John Aubrey, or the natural histories of Robert Plot and John Morton (among others) all demonstrated an empirical turn influenced variously by Francis Bacon, Samuel Hartlib, the Royal Society, and others.

What Mendyk's account lacks is an interest in cultural complexity as approached here. Richard Carew (Cornwall c. 1602), George Owen of Henllys (Pembrokeshire c. 1603), and Edward Lhuyd (Wales from the 1690s) number among the travellers that our studies share. For Mendyk, Carew's ethno-cultural descriptions of the Cornish are of less importance than establishing him

---

[31] Walter Bower, *Scotichronicon*, ed. D.E.R. Watt (nine volumes; Aberdeen/Edinburgh, 1996–2000), IX, pp. 62–3.

[32] Barbara Korte, *English Travel Writing from Pilgrimages to Postcolonial Explorations* (Houndmills, 2000); Esther Moir, *The Discovery of Britain: The English Tourists 1450–1850* (London, 1964); Ian Ousby, *The Englishman's England: Taste, Travel and the Rise of Tourism* (Cambridge, 1990); Richard Trench, *Travellers in Britain: Three Centuries of Discovery* (London, 1990).

within the history of chorography or a particular kind of antiquarian interest.[33] Mendyk's analysis shares nothing with Owen's sustained interest in the cultural complexity of Pembroke, with its Welshries, Englishries, Irish immigrants, and the long history of settlement, interaction, and exchanges that marked the county. Instead, Owen's topographic and geographic descriptions become part of describing the empirical engagement with the natural world.[34] Despite recognition of Lhuyd's interest in comparative linguistics, he emerges foremost as a 'regional natural historian' who shared the antiquarian interests of 'natural scientists' and made a particular contribution to the development of palaeontology and archaeology.[35] Mendyk's focus follows that of Frank Emery, whose 1958 articles (and others) on regional studies emphasized natural history and the influence of the Royal Society, though with a strong British perspective grounded in Wales.[36] Finally, Mendyk's contention that 'the English situation typifies the whole' and a late chapter briefly surveying the work of Robert Sibbald, Martin Martin, and James Wallace strike a jarring, Anglocentric note.[37]

The emphasis on geography, natural history, anthropology, antiquarianism, or the creation of useful knowledge too often separates the likes of Carew, Aubrey, Lhuyd, William Nicholson, and others from their interest in Britain's human complexity. It need not. Rosemary Sweet's *Antiquaries* reminds us that the antiquarian label need not conjure up genealogical pedantry, obsessive collection of coins and bric-à-brac, or a backward-looking devotion to Classical remains.[38] Adam Fox in 2010 widened the perspective to British and Irish 'research networks' built around printed questionnaires.[39] More recently, Fox explained that John Aubrey or Thomas Machell betrayed 'a fascination with the evidence of former times preserved in the memories and practices of the people', especially the cultural complexity of a locale like Westmorland and its people, customs, manners, and history.[40] Rich, insightful, and constantly instructive, these studies point us toward the need to adopt a Britain-wide perspective, reconsider prescriptive definitions, and deliberately focus on cultural complexity in its own right.

---

[33] Mendyk, '*Speculum Britanniae*', pp. 68, 77–8.
[34] Mendyk, '*Speculum Britanniae*', pp. 205–6.
[35] Mendyk, '*Speculum Britanniae*', pp. 147, 150, 205–11.
[36] Emery, 'English Regional Studies', p. 315.
[37] Mendyk, '*Speculum Britanniae*', pp. 4, 213–28.
[38] Sweet's is a complex and nuanced appreciation of eighteenth-century antiquaries and their researches across Britain and Ireland that 'fit less neatly with the requirements of our teleological frameworks.' Sweet, *Antiquaries*, p. xv and generally.
[39] Fox, 'Discovery of the British Isles', p. 594.
[40] Adam Fox, 'Vernacular Culture and Popular Customs in Early Modern England: Evidence from Thomas Machell's Westmorland', *Cultural and Social History* 9.3 (2012), p. 330 and generally.

Lastly, travellers are not the whole story. The primary sources here are printed texts and, to a lesser extent, manuscripts. Some are conventional travel narratives, like the accounts of John Taylor or Fynes Moryson. Others are the works of travellers who ranged far (Camden) and near (Carew), but are not strictly conventional accounts. They may have features of travel narratives, contain information derived from first-hand journeys, or demonstrate the influences of travel or travel reading. Some travellers revealed their interest in multicultural Britain in works that on the surface are about neither travel nor cultural complexity. Then there are the works of armchair travellers and non-travellers like William Harrison or Robert Sibbald for whom travel, encounter, and cultural complexity are nonetheless important concerns. Many texts and narratives outlived their authors. We must recover the history of those texts and the readers who experienced multicultural Britain via them. Reading between the lines of texts and being attentive to production and consumption are essential.

Travellers, their contemporaries and readers, and surviving texts are the threads woven together to reconstruct the discovery of multicultural Britain between 1450 and 1700. This book has been a joy to write, but it required reconciling four competing demands: chronology, individual travellers and narratives, diverse geographic spaces, and a complex mix of topics. It follows a broadly chronological pattern. However, I divided the story into three distinct parts, hoping to avoid an endless parade of travellers stretching from 1450 to 1700. In each part I typically devote individual chapters to the spaces inhabited by the three nations and the peoples within. I have balanced the organizational value of this for readers against my criticism of focussing on nations. The different travellers, topics, and connections (noted and implied) among the nations give each chapter its own character.

Finally, let me briefly explain what this book is not. I am conscious that these travellers represent a select set that do not open the experiences and insights of 'ordinary' Britons in the way Morgan achieved using the relative abundance of narratives from the Victorian period.[41] To reach those Britons here would require a very different approach to cultural complexity via the techniques for community reconstruction or the analysis of folklore and oral cultures. Scholars have already undertaken such work to good effect.[42] London has naturally

---

[41] Morgan, *National Identities*, pp. 5–6.
[42] Carl B. Estabrook, *Urbane and Rustic England: Cultural Ties and Social Spheres in the Provinces, 1660–1780* (Manchester, 1998), pp. 192–252; Judy Ann Ford, 'Marginality and the Assimilation of Foreigners in the Lay Parish Community: the Case of Sandwich', in *The Parish in English Life, 1400–1600*, ed. Katherine L. French, Gary G. Gibbs, and Beat A. Kümin (Manchester, 1997), pp. 203–16; Adam Fox, *Oral and Literate Culture in England 1500–1700* (Oxford, 2000); Adam Fox and Daniel Woolf, eds, *The Spoken Word: Oral Culture in Britain 1500–1850* (Manchester, 2002); Matthew Hammond, ed., *New Perspectives on Medieval Scotland 1093–1286* (Woodbridge, 2013); Andy Wood, *The Memory of the People: Custom and Popular Senses of the Past in Early Modern England* (Cambridge, 2013).

attracted increasing attention.[43] Despite this, for some readers I will not have given London its due. If one could choose a single location in which the encounter with cultural complexity became routine, it would be that unique gathering of peoples along the Thames. London was – is – remarkable for the concentrated encounters among a diverse, complex, shifting population of Britons (and those from further afield). But it was not alone. My view away from London is designed to avoid a traditional metropolitan bias. Ideally one should bring the different investigative strands together – as Robb did with *The Discovery of France* – but I have chosen to focus on travellers and cultural complexity across a broader canvas.

I am not a practitioner of literary criticism or cultural studies. I benefit from the insights of my colleagues in those fields, but I am by training and inclination an archival historian.[44] I subject travellers' narratives to critical scrutiny as texts shaped by diverse motives and biases, home to complicated and sometimes conflicting mentalities, open to obvious questions about reliability and veracity, and produced in particular cultural, political, and material circumstances.[45] But this

---

[43] Jacob Selwood, *Diversity and Difference in Early Modern London* (Farnham, 2010) is the outstanding example. Other relevant work on London with greater or lesser attention to ethno-cultural groups and encounters includes Paul Griffiths and Mark S.R. Jenner, eds, *Londinopolis: Essays in the Cultural and Social History of Early Modern London* (Manchester, 2000); Imtiaz H. Habib, *Black Lives in the English Archives, 1500–1677* (Aldershot, 2008); Scott Oldenburg, *Alien Albion: Literature and Immigration in Early Modern England* (Toronto, 2014); Nigel Goose and Lien Luu, eds, *Immigrants in Tudor and Early Stuart Britain* (Brighton, 2005); Randoph Vigne and Charles Littleton, eds, *From Strangers to Citizens: the Integration of Immigrant Communities in Britain, Ireland and Colonial America, 1550–1750* (Brighton, 2001); Katharine W. Swett, '"Born on My Land": Identity, Community, and Faith Among the Welsh in Early Modern London', in *Protestant Identities: Religion, Society, and Self-Fashioning in Post-Reformation England*, ed. Muriel C. McClendon, Joseph P. Ward, and Michael MacDonald (Stanford, 1999), pp. 249–63.

[44] I have benefited from David Abulafia, *The Discovery of Mankind: Atlantic Encounters in the Age of Columbus* (New Haven, 2008); Benedict Anderson, *Imagined Communities* (London, 1983/1991); Hartmut Berghoff et al., eds, *The Making of Modern Tourism: The Cultural History of the British Experience, 1600–2000* (Houndmills, 2002); Homi K. Bhaba, *The Location of Culture* (London, 1994); Felix Driver, *Geography Militant* (Oxford, 2001); Jas Elsner and Joan-Pau Rubies, eds, *Voyages and Visions: Towards a Cultural History of Travel* (London, 1999), pp. 1–56; Stephen Greenblatt, *Renaissance Self-Fashioning: From More to Shakespeare* (Chicago, 1980); Greenblatt, ed., *New World Encounters* (Berkeley, 1993); Harry Liebersohn, *The Travelers' World* (Cambridge, MA, 2006); Said Manzurul Islam, *The Ethics of Travel: From Marco Polo to Kafka* (Manchester, 1996); Mary Louise Pratt, *Imperial Eyes: Travel Writing and Transculturation* (London, 1992); Edward Said, *Orientalism* (London, 1978); Said, *Culture and Imperialism* (New York, 1993); Anthony D. Smith, *The Ethnic Origins of Nations* (Oxford, 1986); Justin Stägl, *A History of Curiosity: The Theory of Travel 1550–1800* (Amsterdam, 1995).

[45] The issues are surveyed in Daniel Carey, 'Compiling Nature's History: Travellers and Travel Narratives in the Early Royal Society', *Annals of Science* 54 (1997), pp. 269–71 and generally; Daniel Woolf, *The Social Circulation of the Past: English Historical Culture 1500–1730* (Oxford, 2003), pp. 300–7.

book remains an analytical narrative by a historian rather than a highly theorized study written chiefly for members of a particular academic sub-field.[46] I have, therefore, aimed for clarity and accessibility. I typically avoid jargon, specialist terminology, or dense theory and historiographic analysis. Readers will normally find the scholarly infrastructure of the book in the references and bibliography, and I have endeavoured to wear them lightly in the text outside the conclusion. I suggest, imply, or prod readers with my findings rather than browbeating them with my arguments. I want this book to be a fresh, spirited conversation with readers about the Tudor and Stuart period as seen through the eyes of British travellers.

* * * * *

Chapter 1 explains how the so-called 'Age of Discovery' inaugurated by Portuguese and Spanish explorers in the fifteenth century set the stage for a new – meaning, at first hand – encounter with multicultural Britain. Travel was a regular feature of the medieval world but what David Abulafia calls the 'discovery of mankind' in the Atlantic propelled a new European determination to study and understand humanity in all its detail and complexity. Britain became part of the geography of travel and discovery in this expanded view of humanity. In these same years, ethnography acquired a more systematic character and agenda, aimed at detailing cultural complexity and, ultimately, categorizing humanity itself. Roger Barlow and Andrew Boorde were among those in England who first brought travel, discovery, and ethnography together. Britain's place in the evolution of travel, discovery, and ethnography sets the stage.

Chapter 2 reconstructs the particular Tudor imperial gaze that shaped John Leland's travels and literary projects. Leland found his way to virtually every corner of England and Wales. Leland's original fascination had been with elevating the status of Britain's literary worthies dating back to Antiquity. By the time his travels ended in the 1540s, Leland had developed an even grander agenda. He took his cues from Henry VIII's exalted ideas of imperial kingship and break with the Church in Rome. Likening Henry to Charlemagne, Leland promised to compose a county-by-county description of the Tudor emperor's dominions of England, Wales, and surrounding islands. The notebooks of Leland's travels, his celebrated *Itinerary*, show him deeply attuned to cultural complexity in the past and its persistence before his eyes. He crossed into and through some of Britain's unique cultural zones: lowland England proper, the former lands of the Danelaw stretching through Lincolnshire and Yorkshire, the North of England and the Anglo-Scottish Borders, Devon and Cornwall, the English Channel communities, and Wales. He also found pious lessons for the

---

[46] For example, Andrew McRae, *Literature and Domestic Travel in Early Modern England* (Cambridge, 2009).

church's new supreme head in the bricks and mortar and devotional legacies of an ancient British Christianity free of papal corruption. Leland sought the essential first-hand information that Henry needed to rule a multicultural Tudor *imperium* at a time of dramatic political and religious upheaval.

Chapter 3 turns to Leland's Scottish counterparts and their readers. The Stewart monarchs also governed a kingdom that owed its foundation to multiple migrations and long, complex cultural interactions. Histories written between the fourteenth and sixteenth centuries opened with topographic and ethnographic descriptions that explained this past. Based at least in part on their own travels and following the lead of John of Fordun (c.1340s) and Walter Bower (c.1440s), John Mair (1521) and Hector Boece (1527) crafted new histories that responded to demands for the careful scrutiny of cultural complexity. The next generation of fellow travellers read the accounts of Leland, Boece, and Mair and recast the peoples of Britain for a variety of political and cultural purposes. The establishment of Protestant national churches played a central role. In Scotland's case, the Englishman William Harrison contributed English translations of Boece's description and Mair's history to Raphael Holinshed's *Chronicle* (1578). Harrison, an exemplary armchair traveller, embellished Boece's original to portray the Scots as a credulous, superstitious people who did not meet his standards for reformed Protestantism in the 1570s. As if anticipating Harrison's translation, John Lesley, the Bishop of Ross and partisan supporter of Queen Mary, produced a unique Catholic reading of the Scots. Lesley focussed on the noble (ethnographic) qualities of the ancient Scots revealed by Mair and Boece and emphasized these as the defining features of the highlanders (and borderers) who stood ready to liberate their fellow Scots from the heresy of the lowland Presbyterian Kirk.

Chapter 4 examines how national rivalries, religious plurality, and undertones of Anglo-Protestant imperialism encouraged some travellers to align confessional and ethnic identities in their narratives. Especially from the 1570s, they crafted visions of godly nations that clashed with the cultural complexity of Boece or Leland. George Buchanan, Queen Mary's arch-nemesis, wrote the history of political unrest and disputed successions so that they became the expressions of an ancient Scottish republicanism: Mary's removal from power by her Protestant lords was only the latest legitimate exercise of the Scottish people's unique right to sack monarchs who failed the public good and true religion. Harrison read Leland's descriptions avidly and his 'Description of England' for Holinshed had some of the flavour of the multicultural Tudor *imperium* through which Leland travelled. However, Harrison's evangelical bent turned Leland's accounts of ancient religious piety into English superstition that mirrored his treatment of Boece's Scots. John Stow and William Lambarde joined Harrison in debating the religious practices that defined the English nation. They too used Leland's first-hand experiences for their own ends, yet did so in ways that, for a biographer in 1772, showed why Leland was 'justly stiled the Father of English History'. The multicultural views of Leland's travels had been confined to an Anglocentric box. Still, despite the best efforts of rulers, clerics, writers, and local actors after mid-century, cultural complexity could not be so easily suppressed or configured along abstract or normative lines. These travellers and their accounts highlight the unsettled and competing experiences and perspectives among British travellers. Their struggles and accommodations typified a multi-layered sense of cultural complexity and identity.

* * * * *

A systematic, first-hand approach to ethnography – part of the broader systematization of knowledge – and the development of the travel narrative genre affected the encounter with multicultural Britain in the seventeenth century. Book Two looks at Stuart Britain through the eyes of the traveller-ethnographer. These travellers identified distinct peoples who inhabited Britain and recorded the characteristics that defined them. However, the ethnographic gaze could simultaneously seek out cultural complexity and systematize it around reductive, abstract markers and labels. It might not acknowledge the history of migration and settlement that was the starting point for, say, Leland's understanding of multicultural Britain. The 'immigrant history' of Britain might have a very different meaning for these travellers: a past that was distinctly past and led by some kind of inevitable progression to the birth of the English, Scots, or Welsh nations. The particularity of the *pays* might disappear in the defining qualities of a nation or hard-to-shake assumptions about its people. Our entrée to this engagement with multicultural Britain comes through perhaps the most celebrated English traveller of the period: Fynes Moryson.

Moryson travelled extensively in continental Europe and the Middle East during the 1590s before embarking on travels in Britain and a stint in Ireland during the Nine Years' War. He travelled with an explicitly ethnographic gaze and betrayed real passion for cultural discovery. Moryson left behind a well-known narrative, his *Itinerary* (1617). It was the first part of a two-volume comparative ethnography based on descriptions of the topography (broadly defined), polity, religious practices, and nature, customs, and manners of the people for each land he visited. Britons were to be lined up for comparison alongside their neighbours in Europe and the Holy Land. Moryson peddled his share of second-hand stereotypes, but the *Itinerary* is still read because so much of what he wrote was grounded in first-hand experience. Those 'foreign' journeys equipped him to discover multicultural Britain. However, Moryson's *Itinerary* included only a basic county-by-county topographic overview of Britain along with descriptions of diet and apparel. He cribbed the topographic details directly from Camden's *Britannia*. How do we explain this surprisingly unoriginal description of Britain? Ironically, travel lay at the heart of Moryson's difficulties.

The 1617 *Itinerary* broke off in the middle of describing the different polities. Moryson prepared the continuation volume for publication in the 1620s. The second part of the 'Itinerary' exists only in manuscript. Except for an unpublished transcription with editorial analysis by Graham Kew, it remains little studied. I bring together the two halves to shed new light on Moryson's encounter with Britain. As he completed the second part, Moryson decided to drop the British chapters entirely and write a separate British ethnography. No printer took on the second volume and Moryson never composed the British ethnography. What went wrong? Moryson undertook a massive comparative ethnography that depended on and, indeed, promoted itself because of travel and encounter. Unable or unwilling to undertake dedicated journeys of discovery at home, Moryson abandoned his British ethnography. He could not conceive of accounts that relied only on armchair travel or a cursory familiarity with Britons. Absent his own first-hand experiences, Moryson's complete 'Itinerary' could not stand out from the 'big beasts' in the marketplace (Camden's *Britannia* and John Speed's *Theatre of the Empire of Great Britain*) or meet the expectations for first-hand experience among readers.

What can be salvaged from Moryson's failure? A good deal, actually. First, Moryson wrote a stop-gap account of the customs and manners of the English for the unpublished 'Itinerary'. Much of the detail reflected Moryson's own experiences of his native people, albeit melded to a good dose of conventional wisdom about the 'English'. Reading between the lines of the manuscript 'Itinerary' proves fruitful. Throughout, Moryson made cross-cultural comparisons between England and the other lands he visited. They carry us out of Britain and we inevitably learn more about the island's continental neighbours than about the English. Still, this is not a wasted or superfluous journey. The comparisons reveal much about Moryson's experience and understanding of the English that is not otherwise accessible. Moryson interrogated the English in these embedded comparisons. They complicate the pro-English chauvinism typically attached to him.[47] Further, Moryson's comparisons are ubiquitous in more than a thousand folio pages. For Moryson, then, to experience and describe virtually any people was an opportunity to study oneself. His ethnographic framework and practice of cross-cultural comparison defied the too-often parochial gaze of his contemporaries. Finally, it challenges contemporary scholars who create a false dichotomy between Moryson's travels and cultural encounters in and outwith Britain. This close reading is the focus of Chapter 6.

One longs for Moryson's 'lost Britain', for first-hand descriptions animated by a keen eye and cultural curiosity. Moryson made only a fortnight's journey to Scotland, reaching Falkland Palace in 1598 for a glimpse of his future king, James VI. His journeys into Wales had one purpose, onward passage to Ireland. His cannot be the ethnographic gaze by which we encounter Scotland and Wales in the seventeenth century. Instead, we can imaginatively recover Moryson's undiscovered Britain through the journeys of other travellers. These stand-in

---

[47] For example, Anna Suranyi, *The Genius of the English Nation: Travel Writing and National Identity in Early Modern England* (Newark, DE, 2008).

Morysons too showed a passion for travel, undertook deliberate journeys of discovery, and did so determined to write ethnographic descriptions.

Chapter 7 follows them to Scotland. When James VI became the first flesh-and-blood ruler to unite Britain and Ireland in 1603, he transformed the Anglo-Scottish boundary. Travellers seized the opportunity to experience and test what they had only read or learned at second and third hand from descriptions in Holinshed, Camden, Speed, and the like. John Taylor and Anthony Weldon were Moryson's real contemporaries. Taylor's curiosity and determination to discover Scotland and its peoples opened up a broader canvas and more complex ethnography of lowland, highland, and the middle grounds between them than the crabbed Weldon, whose brief journey inspired nothing but loathing for a caricatured and stereotypical Scottish people. James Howell, William Brereton, and those who travelled after Moryson's death in 1630 encountered Scotland throughout decades of tumultuous religious and political change. Brereton's journey across Britain and Ireland has a *fin de siècle* quality, travelling through Charles I's kingdoms at the moment when the deceptive, artificial calm of his personal rule disintegrated. From the standpoint of the Welshman Howell and English travellers, the destruction of the Caroline regimes and execution of Charles accentuated ethno-religious differences. These fractures and an oppressive Restoration monarchy encouraged broader cultural hostilities. Thomas Kirke must be the poster child for a certain kind of English encounter with Restoration Scotland. Every ethnographic marker provided an opportunity to fashion the most negative observations right down to the prickly hair of hogs and the practices of Scottish washerwomen. Fifteen years earlier, John Ray carried with him into Scotland the great mid-century interest in natural history, part of what we know more familiarly as the 'scientific revolution'. The rich topography and the close association of the Scots with their environment would make Scotland an incomparable destination for those determined to discover and understand anew the natural world.[48] Some travellers reveal Scotland much as Moryson might have found it, while later ones highlight the evolution of travel and the encounter with multicultural Britain.

Chapter 8 takes us to the lands of the ancient Britons, Wales and Cornwall. Thomas Churchyard travelled to Wales (c.1587) determined to sing the praises of Elizabeth's loyal subjects in verse. Camden's colleague George Owen (1603) wrote a history of Pembrokeshire that captured its dynamic ethno-cultural past. Owen's near contemporary, the Cornishman Richard Carew, published his *Survey of Cornwall* in 1602. In it, Carew revealed a cultural sensitivity and acuity that surely rivalled Moryson's. Carew and Owen scrutinized their neighbours across an impressive range of ethnographic markers. They documented the complexity to be found in the *pays* or beneath national labels. War and the

---

[48] Fredrik Albritton Jonsson, *Enlightenment's Frontier: The Scottish Highlands and the Origins of Environmentalism* (New Haven, 2013).

scientific revolution also affected later encounters with Wales and Cornwall. The wars of the three kingdoms inflamed ethnic hatred. Conflict hardened national identities such that the New Model Army determined to deal with the 'strangers' who plagued England and English dominance in Britain.[49] Anna Trapnel, the charismatic witness to the 'imminent' arrival of the fifth monarchy and the rule of Christ, turned against the religious conservatism of the Cornish during her journey to preach among her fellow religious radicals in the 1650s. By contrast, John Taylor found the religious traditionalism of the Welsh refreshing as he undertook one last journey in 1652. The Restoration cleric William Richards could not contain his bigoted strand of Tory Anglicanism when he penned the grim, racist *Wallography* (1682).

What, then, of Moryson's 'undiscovered Britain'? This is something of a tease. Moryson's Britain is there to be discovered only by reading between the lines of his surviving works or as an imagined journey. We can identify what it would almost certainly have dealt with and cautiously suggest that Moryson would have rendered his ethnographic descriptions with significant depth and cultural sensitivity. Whether they escaped the reductive qualities of national labels is another matter. We fill in a good many gaps in Moryson's travels and experiences by joining his ambitions to the actual journeys of other seventeenth-century travellers in Britain. Yet none of them travelled or wrote on the canvas Moryson proposed to. He aimed to encounter and master multicultural Britain in its entirety. He failed. Only William Camden could claim to have accomplished something remotely like a unified account of multicultural Britain built on first-hand experience. Camden's *Britannia* closes out the book.

*   *   *   *   *

Britannia stands as the most storied attempt to create a single-volume account of Britain and its peoples. Camden completed an ethnographic history of the peoples who migrated to and settled Britain from the earliest fables right through to James VI. Founded on devoted scholarship and first-hand experience by Camden and his collaborators, *Britannia* became the established account after its first publication in 1586. Plenty of ink has been devoted to Camden's antiquarianism, while the Tudor historian Geoffrey Elton spectacularly mischaracterized *Britannia* as a general survey of England.[50] By contrast, I deliberately explore the book's multicultural perspectives and how later travellers engaged with its account of Britain.

Chapter 9 analyses Camden's settlement narrative, an intense story of migrations and conflicts, encounters and exchanges among Picts, Scots, Romans,

---

[49] Mark Stoyle, *Soldiers and Strangers: An Ethnic History of the English Civil War* (New Haven, 2005).

[50] G.R. Elton, *England Under the Tudors*, 3rd edn (London, 1991), p. 434.

Saxons, Danes, and Normans. Here was the story of Britain as an immigrant nation four hundred years before, say, Robert Winder's *Bloody Foreigners* (2004). By the time of *Britannia*'s final editions in 1607 (Latin) and 1610 (English), Camden found in this history reason to call for the unity of hearts and minds so desperately sought by King James when the Stuart monarchy absorbed the Tudor dominions. Unity might develop through a shared Protestant faith, as James hoped. For Camden it stood the best chance through an understanding of Britain's shared multicultural past – and future.

The settlement of Britain set the stage for Camden's topographic and anti-quarian descriptions. Camden laboured over successive editions, stating quite plainly that the story of Britannia's peoples must evolve. Only regular travel and rediscovery would capture that evolution. Experience taught him this lesson. Camden never travelled to Scotland or Ireland and made only limited journeys in Wales. No one appreciated Camden's point better than Bishop Edmund Gibson. By 1695, readers could choose from the many more travel narratives in print or manuscript, thanks to the kinds of travellers studied in Chapters 7 and 8. Gibson knew he had to make good the limits of Camden's travels and respond to changing expectations. Gibson embarked on an ambitious project to publish a revised edition of *Britannia* for a new generation of Britons. He recruited well-qualified experts and tasked them to compose corrections and additions that would follow each of Camden's original chapters like endnotes. The last three chapters study Camden's original account alongside the interven-tions of travellers a century later. Gibson's *Britannia* thus becomes the story of the encounter with multicultural Britain at the end of the seventeenth century.

Chapter 10 begins with Gibson's collaborator for Wales, Edward Lhuyd. The Shropshire native and Keeper of the Ashmolean Museum added an abiding fas-cination with linguistics and natural history to his conscientious decision to make his own journey through Wales. Those few months' travelling inspired Lhuyd to plan an independent account, combining a complete natural history of Wales, a dictionary-etymology of the 'British tongue', and a cultural comparison of the Britons in Wales with their relations in Ireland, Scotland, Cornwall, and Brittany. Given his thoughtful additions to *Britannia*, the information he later sought by circulating parochial questionnaires, and surviving correspond-ence, there is no doubt Lhuyd would have produced a detailed ethnographic description of Wales. But Lhuyd died before completing this project. What he left behind tells us nonetheless that interests which moved Camden and his followers – topography, antiquities, the origins of Britain's peoples – had been joined by comparative linguistics, a systematic approach to natural history, and fully developed ethnography. Lhuyd's career endorsed Moryson's foresight and revealed what made Camden's *Britannia* incomplete after a century of travel and encounter in Britain, Ireland, and overseas.

Chapter 11 turns to Scotland. Seventeenth-century Scottish travellers and scholars surpassed the discoveries of their predecessors. Timothy Pont, James Balfour of Denmilne, and Robert Gordon of Straloch amassed first-hand experiences or actively collected descriptions from local informants throughout the country. These travellers laid the foundation for the most significant account of Scotland in the seventeenth century: the forty-some maps and ethno-topographic descriptions of Scotland in Joan Blaeu's multi-volume *Atlas Novus* c.1654.[51] These Scots laboured with a deep sense of patriotism, but the expensive Latin folio edition of the 'Scottish Atlas' worked against a wider impact. Partly for this reason, Robert Sibbald, the Geographer Royal in Edinburgh, conceived of an even more elaborate 'Scottish Atlas'. He took time out from this project when Gibson commissioned him to revise Camden's Scottish chapters. Sibbald did not undertake a new journey through Scotland. Instead, Sibbald stood on the shoulders of those earlier travellers while acting as the focal point for a vast network of informants.[52] Sibbald knew his own mind and deviated from Gibson's instructions, writing instead what were essentially competing chapters to Camden's own rather than a series of corrections and additions. Camden may have described Scotland as 'a great kingdom' after the accession of James VI and I, yet his account still left it a poor relation and weak neighbour. Sibbald set out to redefine Scotland, to erase the stigmas of poverty, weakness, and violence and to establish it on an equal footing with its neighbours in the pages of *Britannia*. Yet Sibbald's was a limited achievement exploring the cultural complexity of the Scottish people. His additions do not achieve anything like the distinction of Lhuyd's for Wales, and scattered through Sibbald's papers are local reports that attest to the cultural vibrancy of the Scots that never found a place in *Britannia* or his own – ultimately failed – 'Scottish Atlas'.

Chapter 12 examines the complex revision of Camden's chapters about England. One of Camden's lasting legacies had been the encouragement of county historians. A century later they could be called on to explain the cultural landscape in England. None of these individuals or a single point of view could possibly do justice to the cultural complexity of England and its people. *Britannia* tells us much about what Camden and his collaborators, along with Gibson and his, made of that complexity at either end of the seventeenth century. We see them regularly grappling with the nature of a county or region's people. Thus Jonathan Trelawney self-consciously drew the Cornish boundary at the Tamar, in contrast to Camden. Coming full circle, Hugh Todd separated Cumberland and the borderers from Scotland with remarkable zeal at a time when the Union of crowns was almost a century old; for Camden, who lived on both sides of that Union, the Borders were nothing if not a meeting ground of peoples and cultural traditions. Despite shifting views of England's cultural complexity and an increasingly Anglocentric and imperial reading of *Britannia* by the 1690s, the

---

[51] Roger A. Mason, 'From Buchanan to Blaeu: The Politics of Scottish Chorography, 1582–1654', *George Buchanan: Political Thought in Early Modern Britain and Europe* ed. Caroline Erskine and Roger A. Mason (Farnham, 2012), p. 42.

[52] Charles W.J. Withers, *Geography, Science, and National Identity: Scotland since 1520* (Cambridge, 2001), p. 80.

contributor who wrote of England's 'motley breeds' perhaps best captured the tone of Camden's (and Gibson's) *Britannia*.

The closing reflection will address the broader implications of recovering multicultural Britain in the Tudor and Stuart period. In particular, I will consider the implications for the New British History, the established approach to cultural complexity in the Tudor–Stuart period. I will also examine the importance of a deliberately multicultural approach to British History in light of recent debates about the National Curriculum in England and the history curricula in Wales and Scotland.

BOOK I

Britain in the Age of Discovery

1

Travel, Discovery, and Ethnography in Early Modern Britain

Llandaff cathedral stands inside a green oasis on the banks of the River Taff, sheltered from the busy routine of Cardiff, Wales' modern capital. Here on 15 March 1188, Baldwin of Forde, the archbishop of Canterbury, preached the cross to an assembly of English and Welsh subjects. The devout Baldwin was well into a six-week mission through Wales to inflame the soldiers of Christ to take the cross and join the crusaders in the Holy Land. Baldwin's entourage of Welsh princes and clerics included Alexander, archdeacon of Bangor and Gerald, the canon of St David's, perhaps 'the most talented scholar and churchman in Wales'.[1] Alexander fulfilled a vital role. Baldwin knew no Welsh and it fell to Alexander to translate. At Llandaff, the task required double translation: Latin to Welsh and Latin to English. The task on that spring day in March may have been made easier by a feature of the assembly Gerald noted in his narrative account, a *Journey Through Wales*. The Welsh and English stood on opposite sides of Baldwin, yet 'from each Nation many took the cross'.[2]

Gerald recorded Baldwin's tour in his diary. He set to work almost immediately upon returning home to compose a narrative account. He finished the *Journey Through Wales* in 1191 and began work on a second account in 1193. This became the *Description of Wales*. Where the first book recorded Gerald's encounters with Wales and its mix of peoples – Welsh, English, Normans, Flemings – the *Description* stands as one of the finest ethnographies between Herodotus and the end of the seventeenth century. Gerald's accounts stand out for their quality, but they are remarkable for another reason. Almost no travel narrative that describes encounters among the peoples of Britain in such depth, detail, or ethnographic precision can be found until the Tudor and Stuart period. This chapter explains how the legacies of medieval travel, European voyages in the Atlantic, and the drive to study humanity propelled British travellers into a discovery and rediscovery of multicultural Britain in the Tudor and Stuart centuries.

---

[1] Gerald of Wales, *The Journey Through Wales* and *The Description of Wales*, trans. Lewis Thorpe (London, 1978/2004), p. 27. Hereafter I cite the *Journey* and *Description* by their separate titles, but all references are to the Thorpe translation cited here.

[2] Gerald, *Journey*, p. 126.

Medieval travellers

Britons always travelled.[3] For all the later talk of a safe sceptr'd isle, war hardly spared a generation in medieval Britain. Soldiers impressed throughout the Isles turned the North of England and lowland Scotland into killing zones in the fourteenth century. The Welshmen of Owain Glyn Dŵr's army came from all parts of Wales and were met by English levies and the armed might of the Anglo-Welsh border lords. Perhaps as many as ten thousand Scots made their way to ports in Fife, Lothian, and elsewhere to fight for France in the Hundred Years' War. The English empire in France pulled its own soldiers, colonists, and adventurers to Dover and other Channel ports. They included Glyn Dŵr, who burnished his military credentials against the French. Some of them returned to take up arms in the Peasants' Revolt or, decades later, the Wars of the Roses. Henry Tudor arrived in the land of his Welsh forefathers in his unlikely bid for the throne. He landed at Milford Haven in 1485 and led his forces to Market Bosworth by way of the Welsh coast, turning inland at Machynlleth, entering England via Welshpool and Shrewsbury, on to Stafford, Lichfield, Tamworth, and the crown.[4]

Soldiers and sailors, kings and usurpers, along with pilgrims and priests, chapmen and merchants, bards and players, students and journeymen, clerks and judges, labourers and vagabonds, outlaws and spies encountered the cultural complexity of Britain at first hand in their journeys. Some travelled for its own sake, their imaginations alive with images of marvellous places and exotic people, notebooks ready to create a lasting record.[5] Gerald's *Journey Through Wales* still invites the interest of students by juxtaposing the gritty reality of accompanying Baldwin with the Welsh shepherds who shouted to one another across the peaks of Merioneth and mystical tales that Gerald could not entirely discount without diminishing the power of God to effect the impossible. The ambitious and imperial-minded John Hardyng spent three years in Scotland at the behest of Henry V,

---

[3] Norbert Ohler, *The Medieval Traveller* (Woodbridge, 1989), pp. 143–245; Jean Verdon, *Travel in the Middle Ages* (South Bend, IN, 2003); Ian D. Whyte, *Migration and Society in Britain 1550–1830* (Houndmills, 2000), pp. 22–8, 63–4; Anna Suranyi, *The Genius of the English Nation: Travel Writing and National Identity in Early Modern England* (Newark, DE, 2008), pp. 15–35.

[4] R.R. Davies, *The First English Empire: Power and Identities in the British Isles 1093–1343* (Oxford, 2000), pp. 22–30, 54–88, 172–84; Nicholas Canny, *Europeans on the Move: Studies in European Migration, 1500–1800* (Oxford, 1994), pp. 76–7; Glanmor Williams, *Owain Glyndwr* (Cardiff, 1993/2005), pp. 20–5 and 63–9.

[5] For example, A.D. Carr, 'Inside the Tent Looking Out; The Medieval Welsh World-View', in *From Medieval to Modern Wales; Historical Essays in Honour of Kenneth O. Morgan and Ralph A. Griffiths*, ed. R.R. Davies and Geraint H. Jenkins (Cardiff, 2004), pp. 35–44. Christian K. Zacher, *Curiosity and Pilgrimage: The Literature of Discovery in Fourteenth-Century England* (Baltimore, 1976) examines the imaginative power of curiosity in literary travel, with some relevance to the interests of genuine travellers.

searching for evidence to support renewed claims of English suzerainty. Writing his *Chronicle* in old age, Hardyng composed a verse itinerary of the country which took in the 'good corne lande' of the North-East before it gave way to the 'mountaynes, drye mosses and wete / Wher the wild Scottes do dwell'.[6]

These are rare works and, as Robert Bartlett has explained, Gerald's *Journey* and *Description* are the most remarkable.[7] The *Journey* bears closer attention. Gerald reworked the *Journey* at least three times between 1191 and 1214. Baldwin and the cause oftentimes appear as minor actors. The *Journey* really owes its shape to Gerald's unending fascination with his native Wales. Not long after completing the first draft, Gerald paired his chatty, anecdotal *Journey* with another work, the *Descriptio Cambriae*, which he completed in 1193 or early in 1194.[8] According to Gerald, he set out 'in this short treatise to write a *Description of Wales*, my own country, and to describe the Welsh people, who are so very different from other nations'.[9] Gerald divided his *Description* into two books. The first described Wales and the notable qualities of the Welsh, while the second explored their failings. Between them, Gerald's *Journey* and *Description* offered manuscript readers three exemplary works: a travel narrative, a topographic description, and a complex ethnography.

The *Journey* certainly conveyed an exotic and colourful sense of Wales. When a woman unsuccessfully attempted to buy her husband's freedom with a bell once belonging to St David, 'God took vengeance on them' and burned the entire town 'except the wall on which the handbell hung'.[10] A vivid sense of the journey comes through. On the way to St David's, Baldwin's party crossed the Newgale Sands. There, twenty years before, a tremendous gale had scoured the shoreline to expose tree trunks 'standing in the sea with their tops lopped off, and with the cuts made by the axes as clear as if they had been felled only yesterday ... and the wood of the tree-trunks shone like ebony'. For Gerald, these had been felled 'at the time of the Flood, or perhaps a little later'.[11] The question preoccupied later travellers.[12]

Bangor to Caernarvon found Gerald at his descriptive best:

> Our road led us to a valley, where the going was hard, with many steep climbs up and down. We dismounted from our horses and proceeded on foot, in intention at least rehearsing what we thought we would experience when we went on our pilgrimage to Jerusalem. ... The Archbishop sat himself down on an oak-tree, which had been

---

[6] P. Hume Brown, ed., *Early Travellers in Scotland* (Edinburgh, 1973), p. 20.
[7] Robert Bartlett, *Gerald of Wales 1146–1223* (Oxford, 1982), pp. 187–210.
[8] Gerald *Journey*, pp. 40–4, 49–50.
[9] Gerald, *Description*, p. 211.
[10] Gerald, *Journey*, p. 79.
[11] Gerald, *Journey*, p. 157.
[12] Alexandra Walsham, *The Reformation of the Landscape: Religion, Identity, and Memory in Early Modern Britain and Ireland* (Oxford, 2011), pp. 377–9.

1 'The Summit of Snowdon, North Wales' (c. 1850). Reproduced by permission of the National Library of Wales.

completely uprooted and overturned by the force of the winds, for he needed to rest and recover his breath.[13]

As if the 'alps' of Snowdonia were not impressive enough, at the top of Snowdon itself Gerald found two lakes, one with a floating island 'which moves about and is often driven to the opposite side by the force of the winds' and another filled with eel, trout, and perch all missing their left eye.[14]

Gerald lived the reality of medieval Britain's ethnic mosaic and carried it naturally into his narratives. He served the Angevin regimes of Henry II and his sons, Richard and John. In 1183 and again in 1185, Gerald participated in the Angevin conquest of Ireland. The experience shaped his *Topographia Hiberniae*, a history and topography of Ireland completed by the time of his journey to Wales in 1188.[15] He subsequently recorded the conflicts between the Welsh and the kings of England with their motley collection of subjects and agents, Anglo-Saxon, Norman, Angevin, English, even Welsh. Brecknock brought to mind the Norman Bernard de Neufmarché. He first seized it 'from the suzerainty of the

---

[13] Gerald, *Journey*, p. 184.
[14] Gerald, *Journey*, pp. 194–5.
[15] Gerald of Wales, *The History and Topography of Ireland* trans. John J. O'Meara (London, 1982), pp. 12–15.

28

Welsh' and married Nest, the 'daughter of Gruffydd ap Llywelyn, who for so long had oppressed all Wales by his tyranny'. The abbey of St John the Baptist came to grief from a host of factors, 'the boundless extravagance of the English ... uncontrolled ambition, [and] the ever-growing vice of ingratitude' among them. The most recent outrages were the work of 'Ranulf Poer, Sheriff of Herefordshire ... although Henry II, King of the English, was the real instigator'. Henry II was not alone in plaguing the Welsh: 'William Rufus, the son of King William the Bastard, and the second of the Norman Kings in England, penetrated far into Wales in his own day.' The Welsh of Brecknockshire were no prize either: 'The natives of these parts are much given to implacable quarrels and never-ending disputes ... and shed their blood freely in internecine feuds.'[16]

All was not conflict. According to Gerald, Wales enjoyed a time of peace under the great clerk king Henry I, though he was not an unqualified blessing for the people of Pembroke. The Flemish were 'sent there by Henry I, King of the English, to colonize the district'.[17] It was they who brought 'the strange habit' of boiling the meat off the shoulder blades of rams and reading their indentations. For Gerald, they were people 'highly skilled in the wool trade, ready to work hard and to face danger by land or sea in pursuit of gain, and, as time and opportunity offer, prompt to turn their hand to the sword or the ploughshare'. More often than not, though, these 'brave and robust people' took up the sword against their Welsh neighbours. The rocky, barren, windswept land about St Davids, devoid of woods, rivers, and pastures, therefore became a land lying 'between two hostile peoples who are constantly fighting over it'. If 'only Wales could find the place which it deserves in the heart of its rulers, or at least if those put in charge locally would stop behaving so vindictively', then the Welsh and Flemish could learn to live side by side as neighbours and not as colonizers and colonized.[18]

Britain and Ireland were alive with legendary sites and miraculous stories. There are powerful reminders of just how far Gerald lived on the other side of the religious upheavals that would sweep away the old faith and the monastic orders in the sixteenth century:

> In the deep vale of Ewias, which is shut in on all sides by a circle of lofty mountains and which is no more than three arrow-shots in width, there stands the abbey church of Saint John the Baptist. ... The church is constructed on the very spot where once there stood the humble chapel of Saint David, the Archbishop, which was adorned with woodland moss and wreathed about with ivy. It is a site most suited to the practice of religion and better chosen for canonical discipline than that of any other of the monasteries in the whole Island of Britain.[19]

---

[16] Gerald, *Journey*, pp. 88, 96, 98, 109, 169.
[17] Gerald, *Journey*, p. 141.
[18] Gerald, *Journey*, pp. 141–2, 161.
[19] Gerald, *Journey*, pp. 96–7.

Gerald reported that God brought an entire monastic field to ripeness a month early, just as the food ran out.[20] On an island near Anglesey, a plague of small mice arrived to ravage the food supply any time the hermits fell out, and departed as soon as harmony returned.[21] A boy in Llanfaes who 'tried to steal some young pigeons from a nest in St. David's church' spent three days with his hand stuck fast to the stone he had leaned on. A similar fate befell an evil woman who literally licked up offerings from a church altar in Bury St Edmunds. Her 'lips and tongue stuck fast to the altar' for all to see for the better part of a day during her false devotions.[22] Neither medieval Wales nor England could be read as anything but superstitious lands in all this, but 'darkest Wales' found it a much harder stereotype to shrug off when we think of Roger Williams' lament about the unredeemed Indians of Wales.

Gerald felt it necessary to defend his *Description*. Determined to 'extol in my writings and adorn with all the flowers of my rhetoric those rugged countries, Ireland, Wales, and Britain', Gerald answered those who said he 'should not squander on such insignificant themes the gifts which God has given me'.[23] Gerald's preface treated Archbishop Stephen Langton to a spirited rejection of insular thinking:

> Distinguished writers have composed and published admirable histories of other countries. I have been inspired to think it may be a useful and praiseworthy service to those who come after me if I can set down in full some of the secrets of my own native land. ... It is a tale as yet untold, I have worked hard at it, and it will cause pleasure to my own relations and my countrymen.[24]

This might have been the agenda for any number of Tudor and Stuart travellers.

Just whom did Gerald have in mind as his countrymen? Gerald's 'mixed Welsh and Norman blood and his Marcher sympathies put a millstone around his neck' when it came to advancement in the Angevin regime.[25] However, this background equipped him 'to write the innovative topography and ethnography' that was the *Description*.[26] Gerald chose a logical starting point. Wales became one of the last refuges for the Britons 'when the Saxons first occupied the island, and they have never been completely subdued since, either by the English or the Normans'. For as long as anyone could remember Wales had been divided into three, Gwynedd (north), Dyved (south), and Powys (middle), thanks to the Brutus-like division of the kingdom among the three sons of Rhodri Mawr. Dozens of subdivisions and disputes followed that only the 'Welsh bards, singers,

---

[20] Gerald, *Journey*, pp. 126–7.
[21] Gerald, *Journey*, pp. 187, 190.
[22] Gerald, *Journey*, pp. 83–4.
[23] Gerald, *Description*, p. 212.
[24] Gerald, *Description*, pp. 212–13.
[25] Bartlett, *Gerald*, p. 185.
[26] Bartlett, *Gerald*, p. 212.

and jongleurs' knew by heart, along with Rhodri Mawr's descent from Adam by way of Aeneas. Rhodri's Wales once included present-day Shropshire – 'now occupied by the English and the Normans' – three great royal places (Dinevor, Aberffraw, Pengwern), and, later, cathedral sees at Llandaff, Bangor, St Asaph, and a purported metropolitan see at St David's.[27] Flat fields and the coastline made Cardiganshire and Dyved particularly attractive. Gwynedd and her rich soil were well protected from nature's elements, in contrast to the rugged and wild lands of Merionethshire. The mountains of Snowdonia could supply all the herds of Wales with pasture, while the fantastically productive Anglesey could do the same with grain.[28]

The peoples of Wales sprang from these diverse social and topographical foundations. Evidently Welshmen vied for bragging rights over who spoke the best Welsh. Was it the better-articulated speech of the Welsh heartland of Cardiganshire or the more carefully pronounced and preserved speech of Gwynedd, 'for that area has far fewer foreigners'? In Gerald's view, speakers in Brittany and Cornwall probably spoke what was closest to the 'original British speech', just as the Devonians and West Country English probably preserved that language's original better than the 'northern regions ... greatly corrupted by the Danish and Norwegian invasions'. Otherwise, he would not judge.[29]

One thing above all else defined the Welsh. They were a warrior people, 'ready to take up their weapons and willingly sacrifice their lives', esteeming 'it a disgrace to die in bed, but an honour to be killed in battle'. They cherished freedom, and no wonder, 'for these are the descendants of "The sons of Aeneas who fought for liberty"', according to Gerald's reading of Virgil. These fierce, agile warriors 'have not hesitated to fight without any protection at all against men clad in iron, unarmed against those bearing weapons, on foot against mounted cavalry'. The Welsh were 'given neither to gluttony nor to drunkenness', spent 'little on food or clothes', ate a plain modest meal that included flatbreads, and routinely defied the cold. The Welsh slept in 'a communal bed, stuffed with rushes, and not all that many of them' covered with a 'stiff harsh sheet, made locally and called in welsh a "brychan"'.[30] And, they frequently beat the odds, as Henry II attested in words probably contrived by Gerald: 'In one part of the island there is a race of people called the Welsh who are so brave and untamed that, though unarmed themselves, do not hesitate to do battle with fully armed opponents.'[31] Like many fringe peoples, these Welsh were wild and untamed, a feature surprising to Gerald, considering that 'the wild animals in

[27]   Gerald, *Description*, p. 223.
[28]   Gerald, *Description*, pp. 220–30.
[29]   Gerald, *Description*, p. 231.
[30]   Gerald, *Description*, pp. 235, 237.
[31]   Gerald, *Description*, p. 234.

the island are not particularly fierce, whereas the Welsh show no signs of losing their ferocity'.[32]

The Trojan connection distinguished the Welsh from their English neighbours. Unlike the Welsh, neither the English nor the Saxons from whom they originated possessed 'great boldness in speaking and great confidence in answering'.[33] The English seemed servile by nature and lived in an oppressive, hierarchical feudal society that traded a bold spirit of liberty for the guarantee of a 'minimum of social and political order'.[34] The English inherited the cold nature of the Saxons that matched their ancestors' German climate. By contrast, descent from the Trojans marked the Welsh physically and temperamentally. Having been 'transplanted from the hot and arid regions of Anatolia', they kept 'their dark colouring ... their natural warmth of personality, and their hot temper, all of which gives them confidence in themselves'.[35] How remarkable indeed would be the transformation of British notions of skin colouring and human nature in the centuries after Gerald.

The air of muck and decay did not hang about these people of the so-called Celtic fringe. Both men and women cut their hair short, close to the scalp, and men sported only moustaches for facial hair. Both took great care with their teeth, more so than in any country Gerald had visited, 'constantly cleaning them with green hazel-shoots and then rubbing them with woollen cloths until they shone like ivory'. The Welsh were also 'quicker-witted and more shrewd than any other Western people'. Welsh intellectual life appealed to Gerald's literary side:

> In their lawsuits, official speeches, and civic addresses they use almost all the devices of public speaking ... In their narrative poems and their declamations they are so inventive and ingenious that, when using their native tongue, they produce works of art which are at once attractive and highly original ... they delight in alliteration, and especially that which links together the initial letters or syllables of the words.[36]

A lively tongue made the Welsh the equal of the English. Gerald thought it remarkable that 'the Welsh and the English, so different from each other and so antagonistic, could ever consciously agree about the rhetorical device'.[37] The Welsh deserved their reputation as great wits who 'make the most droll comments ... [and] love sarcastic remarks, and libellous allusions, plays on words, sly references, ambiguities and equivocal statements'.[38]

Gerald's interests extended to musical traditions and embraced exchanges among the Welsh, Scots, and Irish as a cultural community centred on the Irish

[32] Gerald, *Description*, p. 235.
[33] Gerald, *Description*, p. 245.
[34] Bartlett, *Gerald*, pp. 200, 196–203.
[35] Gerald, *Description*, p. 245.
[36] Gerald, *Description*, pp. 238–40.
[37] Gerald, *Description*, p. 241.
[38] Gerald, *Description*, p. 243.

Sea.[39] He cribbed his *Topography of Ireland* in the process and that account gives a nice flavour of his sensitivity toward cultural complexities:

> One should note that both Scotland and Wales, the former because of her affinity and intercourse, the later as it were by grafting, try to imitate Ireland in musick and strive in emulation. Ireland uses and delights in two instruments only, the harp, namely, and the timpanum. Scotland uses three, the harp, timpanum, and the crowd [viola]. Wales uses the harp, the pipes, and the crowd. They also use strings made from bronze and not from leather. In the opinion, however, of many, Scotland has now not only caught up on Ireland, her instructor, but already far outdistances and excels her in musical skill. Therefore people now look to that country as the fountain of the art.[40]

The Welsh shared their broken choral harmonies with another cultural community: 'In the northern parts of Great Britain, across the Humber and in Yorkshire, the English who live there produce the same symphonic harmony when they sing.'[41] Gerald noted too that this was not a tradition typical among the English, once again suggesting that the Norse influence in the Danegeld might provide the answer.

As someone within the Angevin establishment and a traveller comfortable moving between Wales, Ireland, and England, Gerald could write a description of the Welsh that punished them for their faults and sang their praises. As a self-described 'serious historian' Gerald felt this was his duty even if the 'natural propensities of the Welsh may well have been corrupted and changed for the worse by their long exile and their lack of prosperity'. Unfortunately, for example, a Welsh promise or oath was not worth much, 'for their minds are as fickle as their bodies are agile'. Indeed, they were positively deceitful, ready 'to perjure themselves to their own convenience and for any temporary advantage'. That said, their laws had stood the test of time, with one exception: 'It is the habit of the Welsh to steal anything they can lay their hands on and to live on plunder, theft and robbery, not only from foreigners and people hostile to them, but also from each other.'[42] Hospitality and open doors evidently coexisted with a hunger for land so powerful that the Welsh would move marker stones, dig up boundary ditches, or bring lawsuits, arson, and murder to bear on those whose land they coveted. The ancient custom of partible inheritance among sons did not help matters, nor did fosterage, which created stronger bonds among foster brothers than with one's own. Among the Welsh one dared not offer accommodation to a visitor poorer than oneself. At the first sight of 'affluence' theft and demands knew no bounds.[43] Welsh hospitality came with a price, then.

---

[39] Bartlett, *Gerald*, pp. 205–6.
[40] Gerald, *Topography of Ireland*, p. 104.
[41] Gerald, *Description*, p. 242.
[42] Gerald, *Description*, pp. 255–7.
[43] Gerald, *Description*, pp. 260–2.

There was also a hidden side to the Welsh reputation as fierce defenders of liberty.[44] Welsh soldiers may have been quick to fight and ferocious in joining battle, but the first reverse quickly turned ferocity into confusion and retreat. For Gerald, Lucan's description of the Germans was apt for the Welsh: 'In the first onslaught they are more than men, in the second they are less than women.' How, then, had the Welsh defended their great redoubt for so long? Defeated on the battlefield, they melted into the countryside and carried on a guerrilla war of ambushes and night attacks. 'In a single battle they are easily beaten,' according to Gerald, 'but they are difficult to conquer in a long war, for they are not troubled by hunger or cold, fighting does not seem to tire them, they do not lose heart when things go wrong, and after one defeat they are ready to fight again and to face once more the hazards of war.'[45]

One vice had profound implications for the Welsh: 'It was because of the sins, and more particularly the wicked and detestable vice of homosexuality that the Welsh were punished by God and so lost first Troy and then Britain.' However, homosexuality ended long ago in Wales, according to Gerald. The Welsh confidently predicted that their atonement would relieve Britain of its foreign occupiers and return the island to its native sons and daughters, the restored Britons. Gerald would have none of this 'illusion'. Having forsaken homosexuality was no penance 'when we see them still sunk in sin and in a deep abyss of every vice – perjury, theft, robbery, rapine, murder, fratricide, adultery, incest' and all manner of wrongdoing. The Welsh may have learned something from the English and Normans about 'how to manage their weapons' and been able to loosen 'the yoke which once weighed so heavily upon them', but this recovery was no sign that Merlin's prophecies were about to come true.[46]

Gerald closed the *Description* with a curious discussion of how the Welsh could be conquered and, in turn, how they could turn back any conqueror. Experience in Ireland obviously shaped Gerald's analysis. Much of what he wrote came verbatim from the *Topographia Hiberniae*, with Wales and Welsh simply substituted in the text. The core problems 'causing the ruin of the Welsh people and preventing them, generation after generation, from enjoying prosperity' mimicked typical English diagnoses of Ireland's inveterate ills: the absence of primogeniture (in favour of partible inheritance in Wales and communal ownership in Ireland), the destruction of stable patriarchal-familial relationships by fosterage, and the curse of political fragmentation because of an inability to loyally serve one king.[47] If the Welsh hoped to escape permanent subjugation, they must adopt something of Norman-French military tactics, unite behind 'only one prince and he a good one', and exploit their natural fortress.[48] It is no simple

44 Bartlett, *Gerald*, pp. 196–203, 206–8.
45 Gerald, *Description*, pp. 259–60.
46 Gerald, *Description*, pp. 264–7.
47 Gerald, *Description*, p. 273.
48 Gerald, *Description*, pp. 273–4.

matter to pin down Gerald's political sympathies, with Angevin imperialism, Welsh independence, heroic resistance under a modern Welsh Arthur, or some form of incorporative union that respected Welsh identity and culture.[49] Gerald thought he knew what the final outcome would be, though: 'Whatever else may come to pass, I do not think that on the Day of Direst Judgement any race other than the Welsh, or any other language, will give answer to the Supreme Judge of all for this small corner of the earth.'[50] It was not a bad prediction.

The discovery of humanity

Few medieval travellers left accounts like Gerald's, but that had begun to change by the end of the fourteenth century.[51] British travellers built on medieval movements between Europe and the North Sea, North Africa, and, thanks to the 'decisive influence' of Marco Polo's account, Asia.[52] Atlantic voyages of discovery gave a new impetus to acquire first-hand knowledge of humanity, near and far. By venturing far into the Atlantic, 'European horizons were vastly enlarged' by nothing less than the 'discovery of mankind – of the variety and range of human activity and expression'.[53] Explorers and travellers determined to 'scrutinize this foreign world, to perceive it in all its empirical qualities – and to write home about it in meticulous detail'.[54] Empirical scrutiny and thoroughness became benchmarks for travellers at home and abroad, whether for purposes of exploration, colonization, or simply the mastery of knowledge.

The impact of Spanish and Portuguese discoveries upon English imaginations is usually timed to the second half of the sixteenth century, with the voyages of Martin Frobisher or Francis Drake and the discovery narratives compiled in Richard Hakluyt's storied *Principal Navigations, Voyages and Discoveries of the English Nation*.[55] The renowned William George Hoskins, who enlightened two generations with his *Making of the English Landscape* (1949), wrote of an Elizabethan

---

[49] Bartlett, *Gerald*, pp. 185, 212.

[50] Gerald, *Description*, p. 274.

[51] Jan Borm, 'Defining Travel: On the Travel Book, Travel Writing and Terminology', *Perspectives on Travel Writing*, ed. Glenn Hooper and Tim Youngs (Aldershot, 2004), pp. 13–26; Mary B. Campbell, *The Witness and the Other World: Exotic European Travel Writing, 400–1600* (Ithaca, 1988), pp. 1–11; also Stan Mendyk, 'Early British Chorography', *Sixteenth Century Journal* 17.4 (1986), pp. 459–81.

[52] Campbell, *Witness and the Other World*, pp. 15–162; Andrew Hadfield, ed., *Amazons, Savages, and Machiavels: Travel and Colonial Writing in English, 1550–1630* (Oxford, 2001), p. 4.

[53] David Abulafia, *The Discovery of Mankind: Atlantic Encounters in the Age of Columbus* (New Haven, 2008), p. xiv; Canny, *Europeans on the Move*, pp. 9–25.

[54] Barbara Korte, *English Travel Writing from Pilgrimages to Postcolonial Explorations* (Houndmills, 2000), p. 30; Helda Quadflieg, '"As mannerly and civill as any of Europe": Early Modern Travel Writing and the Exploration of the English Self', in *Perspectives on Travel Writing*, ed. Hooper and Youngs, pp. 27–40.

[55] Korte, *English Travel Writing*, p. 31.

discovery of England beginning in the 1570s, when 'almost suddenly the notion was born that all around us was this unknown country; and maps, descriptions, and histories, poured forth for the next three hundred years'.[56]

The impulses for discovery actually came together in England well before this. They met in the person of William Botoner (or Worcestre, as he is better known), the son of a prosperous Bristol denizen and her saddler husband. Grammar school in Bristol and further study at Oxford prepared Worcestre for twenty years' service to John Fastolf. His eclectic literary projects and interest in travel became full-time pursuits after Fastolf's death in 1459. The greatest journey Worcestre chronicled took him from Norwich in August 1478 through East Anglia to London, on to Salisbury, Castle Coombe, Tintern Abbey and the Welsh borders, passing back through Bristol, on to Devon and Cornwall and St Michael's Mount before the long return journey to London. He confined his travels in 1479 to Anglia and London. A more ambitious journey to Glastonbury, by way of Oxford and Bristol, capped his travels in 1480.[57]

We know them as *Itineraries*, but Worcestre's notebooks are just that, eclectic and fragmentary aids to memory written on 'folded sheets of paper' carried with him on his travels: mileages and distances, lists of river crossings and castles, a day-by-day diary, the measurements and adornments of churches, lists of saints and noble genealogies, tomb epitaphs, 'information' from local denizens, and extracts from authorities like Gildas or Gerald of Wales.[58] We cannot be certain what Worcestre intended to accomplish with his notebooks – perhaps a study of English antiquities – but the *Itineraries* consistently reveal an eagerness to discover even the most rudimentary details of Britain or turn an ear to a well-informed contact. For example, in 1477, Worcestre met with an unknown Scotsman and obtained basic details of the lordship of the Isles and the Orkneys, information about the wellsprings of the Tweed, Annan, and Clyde rivers, and historical tidbits. The men and women of Ross venerated St Duthac above all others, King Arthur kept the round table at Stirling Castle, and one Robert Hacon, 'a seaman among the fishers of Cromer town, was of English birth and the first to discover the country of Iceland by accident'.[59] Such matters jostle for attention.

The journey to Bristol in 1480 found Worcestre in a distinctly British frame of mind. He spent time excerpting notes from a chronicle belonging to John Burton of St Thomas church. The result was a revealing rudimentary ethnography:

> According to the differences of climate men differ in their features, the colour and temperaments of their bodies and spirits; hence we see the Romans serious, the Greeks

[56] W.G. Hoskins, *Provincial England: Essays in Social and Economic History* (London, 1963), p. 210.
[57] Antonia Gransden, *Historical Writing in England II c. 1307 to the Early Sixteenth Century* (Ithaca, NY, 1982), pp. 327–32; Nicholas Orme, 'William Worcester', *Oxford DNB* at www.oxforddnb.com.
[58] Gransden, *Historical Writing in England II*, p. 332.
[59] William Worcestre, *Itineraries*, ed. and trans. John H. Harvey (Oxford, 1969), pp. 5–7.

fickle, the African shifty, and the Gauls fierce by nature and bolder in temper. We see that the nature of the climate acts not by necessity but by a certain inclination or disposition, etc ... Also note that the tendency of the spirit is much influenced by the body's complexion, when the doctors diagnose that one is jovial, sad, or wanton, or of some other humour. But these judgments are repeatedly true in that in most men the reason yields to the passions, and by them is led astray though not of necessity, inasmuch as reason has rule over the passions.[60]

Nature and nurture each played their part. Climate worked on complexion and temperament to produce dispositions toward certain characteristics, but reason possessed the capacity to deflect if not tame the 'tendency of the spirit'. The early 'English' evolved into an amalgam of the peoples with whom they interacted and from whom they 'learnt': ferocious Saxons, effeminate Flemings, and hard-drinking Danes. Worcestre went on to describe the bounds of Britain, betraying a distinct affection for Geoffrey of Monmouth's *Historiae Regum Britanniae* and a perennial bit of English indifference to the complexity of Britain: 'England, largest of the islands, is 800 miles long from Totnes in Cornwall [Devon] to Caithness in Scotland, and 300 miles wide from St. David's in Wales to Canterbury in Kent.'[61]

Bristol, the maritime gateway to Europe, Ireland, and the Atlantic remained in Worcestre's blood. His notebooks include a list of Arabic terms used for the parts of the astrolabe and the astronomical sightings taken with it.[62] Just as practical-minded, Worcestre composed a gazette of the islands that dotted Britain and Ireland and took particular interest in Man and the Western Isles. His survey of the Baltic Sea community could only have come from contacts with merchants and traders. Riga and Reval grew up in the Polish province of Livonia, rich with copper, iron, gold, and silver. In the unnamed Russian province that neighboured Livonia 'there live many heathens as well as Christians, and there are abundant wax, skins, and ____ forests' as well as gold and silver. No wonder the rich merchants of Novgorod – long ago saved from the Livonian Knights when the brittle ice of Lake Peipus gave way beneath them – could afford to gild the church belfry in gold. Stockholm hummed with trade and the English merchant house boasted doors and gates 'gilded over latten and copper in honour of the merchants'.[63] Events in far-off Danzig even resonated with English religious politics. When one monk in Danzig refused to help 'the Lollards of the country of Prague' that occupied the city, they seized the monk and 'on "Haynesburg" Hill half a mile away, like Brandon Hill outside Bristol, they set him against the fire spitted upon a spit made of a fir-tree by the Cathari (heretics)'.[64]

[60]   Worcestre, *Itineraries*, p. 323.
[61]   Worcestre, *Itineraries*, pp. 325–7.
[62]   Worcestre, *Itineraries*, p. 241.
[63]   Worcestre, *Itineraries*, pp. 193–5.
[64]   Worcestre, *Itineraries*, p. 307.

Robert Hacon's 'discovery' of Iceland was not a lone notice of Atlantic exploration in the decade before Columbus. According to Worcestre's intelligence, 'he who wishes to sail to the island of Brazil' must set course by the Great Blasket. Worcestre had a personal interest in Atlantic exploration. His sister Joan married a second time, taking the Bristol burgess John Jay as her husband. An eighty-ton ship owned by John Jay Jr – whether Joan's stepson or son is unclear – sailed for Brazil by way of final provisioning on the west coast of Ireland in 1480. Under the command of John Lloyd, 'the [most] competent seaman of the whole of England' in Worcestre's opinion, the ship spent nine months at sea before storms forced it to turn for home and seek safe haven in Ireland. Worcestre's gazette of the Canary Islands, Azores, Cape Verde Islands, and two dozen more 'off Africa' should not, then, surprise us.[65] Worcestre had all the instincts of a discoverer: his interests in the discovery of England or the lands of his fellow Britons joined with Atlantic voyages of discovery.

Travellers after Worcestre fashioned a culture of travel, discovery, and empire that took in Ireland, Northern Europe, and both sides of the Atlantic. Scotland and England were not untouched. Some of those ten thousand Scots who found their way to service in France during the Hundred Years' War must have included 'Highland "galloglass" ... active in Ireland in the late thirteenth and fourteenth centuries, founding mercenary dynasties there'. Scottish pedlars actively traded in both Denmark and Poland by the 1490s, setting the stage for significant permanent communities like the merchants who controlled the trade between Danzig and Scotland.[66] James IV (c.1500) granted a licence to John Barton to prey on Portuguese shipping to 'redress' certain wrongs and the prize cargo apparently included certain 'More lassis'. The 'black people at James's court were often involved in entertainments' and these Atlantic contacts may have encouraged his 'obsession' with building a proper Scottish navy.[67]

Scottish monarchs met their subjects at first hand long after their Tudor cousins settled down in their circuit of palaces in the Home Counties and Thames Valley. The political culture demanded personal contact with Scotland's kings and queens. James III came to grief for many causes, but at least one reason why he 'happenit to be slain' after the Battle of Sauchieburn had to be the air of aloofness that surrounded a monarch who clung to Edinburgh. By contrast the battle's victor, the future James IV, regularly rode the judicial circuits into the localities, travelled into the Highlands and Borders, accompanied two major expeditions to the Western Isles as a minor, embarked on his naval programme, and displayed a remarkable level of piety, to judge by his many pilgrimages.[68]

---

[65] Worcestre, *Itineraries*, p. 309, 373–7.

[66] Canny, *Europeans on the Move*, pp. 77–8.

[67] Louise Olga Fradenburg, *City, Marriage, Tournament: Arts of Rule in Late Medieval Scotland* (Madison, WI, 1991), pp. 250, 258.

[68] A.D.M. Barrell, *Medieval Scotland* (Cambridge, 2000), pp. 170–81; Norman MacDougall, *James IV* (East Linton, 1997), pp. 42–4, 102–16, 180–9, 196–8, 229–38.

Well travelled, James IV evidently recorded the linguistic divide between Gaels and Scots in Nairn.[69] Alexander Lindsay's famous *Rutter*, a pioneering set of maps and navigational instructions for the entire Scottish coast, enabled James V to do his father one better. The king and his court 'circumnavigated' the realm in 1540, including the Shetland Islands. Equal parts military-judicial expedition and pleasure cruise, the regime burnished its high-flown imperial pretensions.[70] Just nine years later, Donald Monro's voyages through the Western Isles produced one of the earliest ethnographies of Scotland's maritime possessions.[71]

Neither Scotland nor England cut into the Iberian lead in the New World, but the adventurers and schemers who angled for sponsorship from the Tudors stoked an English passion for discovery. Bartholomew Columbus could not gain Henry VII's support for his brother's project in 1490-91 – that ultimately came from the king and queen who would fatefully match Katharine of Aragon with Prince Arthur and, later, Henry VIII. The Italian Zuan Caboto (John Cabot) was another matter. Cabot exploited the interest Bristol merchants had in Atlantic exploration, especially their determination to lay claim to new fishing grounds. Armed with broad-ranging patents from Henry VII, Cabot sailed from Bristol in 1498 on what he hoped would be the beginning of a permanent colonial enterprise in Newfoundland. He never returned, but Cabot's voyages paved the way for the rise of the Bristol fishery and the formation of a Newfoundland trading company. Cabot's son Sebastian undertook his own voyage to North America in 1508. He may have discovered the entrance to Hudson's Bay before returning to England and serving the new king, Henry VIII, in a very different capacity as a cartographer during the 1512 campaigns in France.[72]

Discovery became entangled with imperial ambition in Scotland and England. Henry VIII's imperial gaze expanded to match his self-image, but it did not initially include a maritime *imperium* that might rival his Spanish in-laws. He determined at first to cut a grand figure on the European stage, in imitation of England's greatest warrior-prince, Henry V. The Tudor Henry invaded France and occupied Tournai in 1513 and proclaimed his imperial achievement with a new issue of coinage that sported a closed crown, symbol of closed or entire sovereignty. Goaded by republication of the *Debate of the Heralds*, which celebrated French royal independence and denigrated English monarchs as papal vassals, Henry even set his eyes on becoming Holy Roman Emperor, until Cuthbert Tunstall reminded the king that he needed to be a German subject. Henry

---

[69]   Adam Fox and Daniel Woolf, eds, *The Spoken Word: Oral Culture in Britain, 1500-1800* (Manchester, 2002), p. 13.
[70]   Jamie Cameron, *James V: The Personal Rule 1528-1542* (East Linton, 1998), pp. 228-48, 336-8; Jane E.A. Dawson, *Scotland Re-formed 1488-1587* (Edinburgh, 2007), pp. 146-8.
[71]   Reprinted in Martin Martin, *A Description of the Western Islands of Scotland*, ed. Charles W.J. Withers and R.W. Munro (Edinburgh, 1999).
[72]   D.B. Quinn, *England and the Discovery of America* (New York, 1974), pp. 73-102, 119-28.

took solace in the purported imperial status of the English crown.[73] This claim, massively researched and elaborated by the king's humanist think-tank in the late 1520s, became the foundation for the break from Rome and the Reformation Parliament's full-blown declaration of the Henrician *imperium* in the 1530s. The imposition of a uniform system of English common law and administration on Wales as well as the reconstruction of the lordship of Ireland as a kingdom in 1541 served the notions of unchallenged royal authority and the practicalities of security for a regime gone rogue in European eyes. The promotion of a 'reformed' *Anglicana Ecclesia* also aimed to give substance to the king's *imperium*.

With a plate so full, Henry, his counsellors, and intellectuals at court might be forgiven for not devoting more time to launching England on an Atlantic *imperium* – to seize with the eyes, let alone take physical possession, as Grotius described it in 1633.[74] However, before marriage and succession came to dominate Henry's thoughts, he entertained a secretive proposal from Sebastian Cabot. Having 'defected' to the Habsburgs in 1513, Cabot returned to England in 1520 with a project to find a north-west passage. The 'discovery' of the Pacific ocean across the Darien isthmus in 1513 made it unlikely that a westward passage to China, Japan, and the Spice Islands would be found in the mid-latitudes. Ferdinand Magellan embarked in 1519 to discover a 'south-west' passage to Asia for Spain. Cabot hoped to jump horses and return to England permanently with a commission to find a parallel passage across the top of the world. Henry, Cardinal Wolsey, and the council signed on, but hostile scepticism from London merchant companies sent Cabot back to the employ of Charles V.[75]

Henry's eclectic interests still turned periodically to exploration, discovery, and maritime empire. He maintained at least ephemeral connections to three voyages on either side of Cabot's project: John Rastell's attempted exploration of North America in 1517; John Rut's path-breaking survey extending from Labrador to the West Indies in 1527; and Richard Hore's curious 'combination of a sight-seeing and exploration tour' to Newfoundland in the company of 'gentlemen from the Inns of Court and Inns of Chancery who wished to see the New World'.[76] Until Rut's failure to find the North-West Passage in 1527, cartographers, projectors, and those with an interest in voyages of exploration found some support and encouragement from Henry.[77] The impulse for discovery and the encounter with humanity could be found throughout England and Scotland

---

[73] John Guy, *Tudor England* (Oxford, 1988), pp. 104–7.

[74] Anthony Pagden, *Lords of All the World: Ideologies of Empire in Spain, Britain and France c. 1500–c.1800* (New Haven, 1995), p. 82.

[75] Quinn, *Discovery of America*, pp. 144–7.

[76] Quinn, *Discovery of America*, pp. 184, 189.

[77] Quinn, *Discovery of America*, pp. 160–91; James A. Williamson, *The Voyages of the Cabots and the English Discovery of North America under Henry VII and Henry VIII* (London, 1929), p. 280.

long before Richard Hakluyt expressed disappointment with the results in the late sixteenth century.[78]

The study of humanity

Journeys of discovery focussed attention on ethnography, the deliberate study of human complexity at home and abroad. Like the Bartons, who brought black women to the court of James IV, early English adventurers transported Amerindians to Europe as exotic specimens. Hakluyt's version of Robert Fabyan's *Chronicle* connected Cabot to the arrival of 'three savage men' in England and their presentation to Henry VII. 'They were clothed in beastes skinnes, and ate rawe flesh, and spake such speech that no man coulde understande them,' wrote Fabyan, 'and in their demeanour like two brute beastes, whom the king kept a time after.' Two years later, Fabyan hardly recognized these Newfoundlanders, 'apparelled after the manner of Englishmen ... I coulde not discerne from Englishmen, till I learned what they were'.[79] English dress might have been enough to confuse Fabyan, but letters patent granting rights of exploration and trade in 1501 and 1502 made blunt distinctions. The patentees received power to 'find, recover, discover and search out any islands, countries, regions or provinces whatsoever of heathens and infidels ... unknown to all Christians'.[80]

The Stewarts understood at first hand the cultural complexity of their subjects, but they could also thank the learned among them. For Scottish intellectuals, Paris beckoned. It drew John Mair, who left his farming parents behind in the 1490s for, first, Godhouse College in Cambridge, and then the Collège de Ste Barbe and Sorbonne. Mair cultivated his humanity through history, philosophy, and theology and became a prolific teacher and writer during a fifty-year career that spanned appointments in Paris, Glasgow, and St Andrews.[81] One small portion of Mair's commentary on Peter Lombard's *Sentences*, his *In Secundum Librum Sententiarum*, turned to the legitimate foundations for 'Christian rule over pagans'. For Mair in 1510, Aristotle offered crucial guidance with respect to the newly discovered Amerindians: they were 'by nature slaves'. Mair's opinion joined an Iberian political debate that involved Juan López de Palacios Rubios, whom Ferdinand I tasked in 1512 to consider the legal and ethical foundations of the New World Spanish empire: 'Like Mair, Gregorio, and Mesa, he assumed the answer to the question of whether or not the Indians might legitimately be conquered and enslaved lay in the nature of the Indians themselves.' Not a little of what defined their 'nature' for Palacios Rubios lay in the ethnographic

---

[78] For travel and the rise of English cosmopolitans, see Alison Games, *The Web of Empire: English Cosmopolitans in an Age of Exploration 1560–1660* (Oxford, 2008), pp. 17–46.
[79] Williamson, *Voyages of the Cabots*, p. 37.
[80] Williamson, *Voyages of the Cabots*, pp. 57, 47 respectively.
[81] Alexander Broadie, 'John Mair', *Oxford DNB* at www.oxforddnb.com.

descriptions of the Amerindians that he digested in composing his brief for the king.[82] Mair and Rubios's arguments absolved the conquerors of wrestling with the Amerindians' legal status; they assigned the Amerindians to a category of (lesser) peoples that would be further defined and expanded by first-hand travel and ethnography during the next two centuries.[83]

The Amerindians thus informed the study of humanity for a Spanish civil lawyer and a Scottish intellectual who scrutinized his own people in the next decade. A century later, John Speed's *Theatre of the Empire of Great Britaine* (1611) would characterize the ancient Britons 'as a barbarous lot who dye themselves, wear long hair, and practice "diabolical superstition" as religion' and thus 'draw a comparison between these primitives and contemporary American Indians'.[84] Hakluyt, Richard Eden, Walter Raleigh, Thomas Harriot, and John White had scrutinized and reported on Amerindian societies in the intervening years, paving the way for Speed.[85] John Aubrey later drew parallels with Amerindians and their encounters with Europeans in the Atlantic. When Edmund Waller wondered in 1666 if Salisbury plain had always been an open expanse, Aubrey mused,

> In Jamaica, and in other plantations of America, e.g. in Virginia, the natives did burn down great woods, to cultivate their soil with maiz and potato-rootes, which plaines were there made by firing the woods to sowe corne. They do call these plaines Savannas. Who knows but Salisbury plaines, &c. might be made long time ago, after this manner, and for the same reason?[86]

Unrest in Massachusetts in 1676 prompted Aubrey to write that 'the descent which the Indians lately made on the New England-men for want of walled Townes. So the Romans were served by the Britons: which occasioned them to build Cities; and all our City walles were built by them: the Saxons knew not how to builde with stone.'[87]

The gentlemen from the Inns of Court and Chancery in Hore's 1536 expedition apparently encountered a party of Eskimos on the south coast of

---

[82] Anthony Pagden, *The Fall of Natural Man: The American Indian and the Origins of Comparative Ethnology* (Cambridge, 1982), pp. 51.

[83] Pagden, *Fall of Natural Man*, pp. 38-41, 156-98. See also Ulrike Morét, 'Gaelic History and Culture in Mediaeval and Sixteenth-Century Lowland Scottish Historiography' (Ph.D. thesis; University of Aberdeen, 1993), pp. 60-2 for discussion of Mair's sense of primitivism and contrasts with those of his contemporary Hector Boece; Dr Morét's thesis is available at no cost via the British Library EThOS service at http://ethos.bl.uk/Home.

[84] Stan Mendyk, *'Speculum Britanniae': Regional Study, Antiquarianism, and Science in Britain to 1700* (Toronto, 1989), p. 82.

[85] T.D. Kendrick, *British Antiquity* (London, 1950), pp. 122-5; Andrew Hadfield, *Literature, Travel, and Colonial Writing in the English Renaissance 1545–1625* (Oxford, 1998), pp. 85-133.

[86] John Aubrey, *The Natural History of Wiltshire*, ed. John Britton (London, 1847), p. 10.

[87] John Aubrey, *Monumenta Britannica or A Miscellany of British Antiquities [Parts One and Two]*, ed. John Fowles and Rodney Legg (Boston, 1980/81), pp. 436-7.

Labrador. Oliver Dawbney, aboard the *Trinity* and destined for prosperity in the Barbary Coast trade, claimed to have 'willed them [his fellow passengers] to come up if they would see the natural people of the countrey, that they had long and so much desired to see ... and upon the viewe they manned out a ship-boat to meet them and take them'. The Eskimos wisely returned to shore: 'our men pursued them into the Island, and the Savages fledde and escaped: but our men found a fire, and the side of a beare on a wooden spit'. They also found 'a boote of leather garnished on the outward side of the calfe with certaine brave tailes, as it were of rawe silke, and also found a certaine great warme mitten'. The men took these curiosities back to the *Trinity*, but they might have done better to take the roasted bear. They ran out of provisions. One man evidently murdered and braised a shipmate before the company tricked a French fishing vessel out of its own craft and sailed for home. Members of the French crew later arrived in England to demand recompense. Henry VIII heard out both sides, took pity on his countrymen for their distress, and then compensated the French.[88] Whether the king also heard of the encounter with the Eskimos is unknown. He might have been interested enough to ask, assuming that the 'native chief' purportedly brought back and presented to him at Whitehall by William Hawkins in 1530 or 1531 sparked a lasting curiosity about the Amerindians.[89]

John Rastell's response to his own failed voyage in 1517 indicates that there was more to all this than curiosity. A serious interest in cultural complexity animated travellers. Rastell, who married Thomas More's sister Elizabeth, put his humanist education to work as a lawyer alongside Christopher St Germain in the Middle Temple, and as a moderately successful printer after 1510. Along with More's life of Pico della Mirandolla, Rastell published his own play, *A New Interlude and A Mery of the Nature of the .iiii. Elements*, in 1520. Rastell intended that this, the first play in English, would contrast commonweal and virtue with private interest and present this classic humanist debate for vernacular readers. The New World of America – as Rastell, here, first defined it – played a vital role. He worried that the prospects for private gain would supplant the disinterested commitment to the discovery and possession of the New World. He no doubt had in mind the failure of his own expedition, when the crews of his two ships mutinied, abandoned Rastell in Waterford (where he wrote the *New Interlude*), and made a tidy sum selling their provisions in Bordeaux.[90]

Rastell used the character of 'Humanity', its teachers 'Studious Desire' and 'Experience', and their foils 'Sensual Appetite' and 'Ignorance' as mouthpieces to report 'Of certeyne poynt[es] of cosmography ... and of the new founde landys

[88] Quinn, *Discovery of America*, pp. 184–9; Williamson, *Voyages of the Cabots*, pp. 113, 268–71.
[89] Franklin T. McCann, *The English Discovery of America to 1585* (New York, 1952), p. 59.
[90] Cecil H. Clough, 'John Rastell', *Oxford DNB* at www.oxforddnb.com; Andrew Fitzmaurice, *Humanism and America: An Intellectual History of English Colonisation, 1500–1625* (Cambridge, 2003), pp. 28–32.

and ye maner of ye people.'[91] Encouraged by Humanity, Studious Desire collects Experience, who confirms that

> Ryght farr syr I haue rydden & gone
> ¶And seen straunge thynges many one
> In affryk / europe and ynde
> Bothe est & west I haue ben farr
> North also and seen the sowth sterr
> Bothe by see and lande
> And ben in sondry nacyons
> with peple of dyuers condycyons[92]

Taking up a map, Studious Desire asks Experience to locate the realm that is 'callid e[n]gla[n]de / Somtyme brettayne I vnderstonde'.[93] Experience seamlessly knits Britain within the rest of Europe and the Atlantic:

> Syr this ys ynglande lyenge here
> And this is skotla[n]de yt[that] Ioyneth hym nere
> Compassyd a boute euery where
> with the occian see rownde
> And next from them westwardly
> Here by hym selfe alone doth ly
> Irelande that holsome grounde
> ¶Here than is the narowe seey
> To Calyce and Boleyne the next wey
> And flaunders in this p[ar]te
> Here lyeth fraunce next hym ioynynge
> And spayn[e] southwarde fro[m] the[e]s sta[n]dynge ...
> And northwarde on this syde
> There lyeth Iselonde where me[n] do fyshe
> But be yonde that so colde it is
> No man may there abyde
> ¶This See is called the great Occyan[94]

Rastell praised Henry VII's initial attempts to take up a civilizing mission among people with customs and manners so different from the English:

> And what a great meritoryouse dede
> It were to haue the people instructed
> To lyue more vertuously
> And to lerne to knowe of men the maner
> And also to knowe god theyr maker
> whiche as yet lyue all bestly

---

[91] John Rastell, A New Iuterlude and a Mery of the Nature of the .iiii. Element (STC 20722; London, 1520), sig. A1b; the printed text is faint in many places.
[92] Rastell, A New Iuterlude, sig. B7b–8a.
[93] Rastell, A New Iuterlude, sig. B8b.
[94] Rastell, A New Iuterlude, sig. B8b–C1a.

> For they nother knowe god nor the deuell
> Nor neuer harde tell of heuyn nor hell
> wrytynge nor other scripture ...
> ¶Buyldynge nor house they haue no[n] at all
> But wodes / cot[is] / and cauys small
> No merueyle though it be so
> For they vse no maner of yron
> Nother in tole nor other wepon
> That shulde helpe them therto[95]

As though it should have been a simple matter, Experience laments the feeble efforts to extend English dominion into this great ocean. The natives lacked knowledge of God and the Devil, writing, buildings, and iron tools and weapons. Experience indicted their pagan subsistence by rehearsing the great natural and material resources they failed to exploit.[96] For Rastell, exploration would reveal the complexity of humanity and pave the way for its moral and material progress. For the Amerindians or bestial, cunning peoples yet to be encountered, perhaps this meant the imitation or imposition of English customs and manners, especially commercial ones. If so, the fascination with the Americas that Rastell shared with his brother-in-law led to rather different literary ends.

Thomas More and Rastell lived in London when the Amerindians brought home by Bristol merchants were 'paraded up and down Cheapside' and Cabot's voyages were a favourite topic of conversation. More's *Utopia* (1516), which relied heavily upon the account of Vespucci's voyages in the *Cosmographie Introductio* (1507), recounts the fictional voyage of Raphael Hythloday to the New World with Vespucci.[97] At the heart of More's discussion of the island republic of Utopia lay a fictional ethnography. Hythloday described an ideal society that banished the devastating, corrupting influences of material gain. The Utopians lived in fifty-four cities evenly distributed across the landscape, identical in language, customs, institutions, and laws. Particular subjects included topography, cities, officials, occupations, social relations, slavery and criminal justice, warfare, religions. Hythloday's travels through Utopia juxtaposed a host of other social practices and beliefs with shortcomings in More's England.[98] We do not know if Henry VIII read *Utopia* or whether his association with More or letters patent supporting Rastell's 1517 voyage encouraged an interest in the details of exploration and ethnography. It did serve such a purpose for the Edwardian regime: in 1556 Protestants published 'a mass market translation to drum up investors for a voyage of exploration to China and the East Indies in which several privy

---

[95] Rastell, *A New Iuterlude*, sig. C2a
[96] Rastell, *A New Iuterlude*, sig. C2b.
[97] John Guy, *A Daughter's Love: Thomas and Margaret More* (London, 2008), pp. 97, 108-9.
[98] Thomas More, *Utopia*, ed. Edward Surtz (New Haven, 1964), pp. 59-152.

councillors had bought shares'.[99] *Utopia* certainly influenced imaginative travel literature well into the eighteenth century.[100]

One work that combined ethnography and discovery reached Henry late in life. The Bristol merchant Roger Barlow translated and significantly augmented Martin Fernandez de Enciso's *Suma de Geographia* and presented it to the king in 1541. Barlow's 'Brief Summe of Geographie' added descriptions of certain parts of Britain, Ireland, and the Atlantic islands to Enciso's original. Enciso-Barlow's ethnography was not particularly sophisticated or systematic in dealing with familiar regions.[101] Barlow's descriptions assumed familiarity with Britain and Ireland. Wales and the Welsh occupied a tiny thumbnail sketch: 'This contrey is well inhabited and aboundant of corne catall and al maner vitalles. The people be goodlie men and valiant and cruel to ther enemyes. ... Upon this cost [the north Bristol channel] and also throughout all the principalitie of wales the people be very actyve in feates of armes, good horsemen and bowemen.' The English in the south-east deviated only slightly from this formula, being 'of good and honeste conversation, true and faythfull to their frendis and cruell to ther enemyes'. Rapidly moving north to Berwick, 'scotlande hathe plenty of vytail and corne but not so abundant as is the realme of englande, for this lande is in many places steryll. The people be tall men and hardy but unfaythful of promesse.' Finally, the Irish offered a stark duality. Tudor magistrates might not agree that the people of the Dublin Pale and coasts were 'quyet and obedient to ther kyng' but they would not dispute that the Gaels in the countryside 'liveth by stelyng and robbyng as sylvages' and did nothing to exploit the land's potential, having 'alwaies contention and warre among them selfes'.[102] Barlow could not garner support for publishing his 'Geographie' and readers interested in Britain or Ireland may not have missed these superficial nostrums or homogenous stereotypes.

The deliberate study of humanity in all its complexity forced travellers to confront fluid, complex, and shifting conceptions of ethnicity (and race). Medieval readers variously interpreted William of Malmesbury's use of *gens* in his *Gesta Regum Anglorum* to mean people, nations, nationality, race, tribes, blood, stock, family, or multiple and hybrid ethnicities. What gave peoples their unique ethnic identity might result from 'geographical determinism' that quite literally shaped their bodies and minds or a unique culture, particularly as it related to customs and manners, language, or law.[103] Travellers might notice some or all of these in attempting to understand cultural complexity, and their descriptions inevitably varied in focus and emphasis. Thus John of Fordun's fourteenth-

---

[99]   Guy, *Daughter's Love*, p. 272.
[100] Campbell, *Witness and the Other World*, pp. 211–17.
[101] Roger Barlow, *A Brief Summe of Geographie*, ed. E.G.R. Taylor (London, 1932), p. 41.
[102] Barlow, *Summe of Geographie*, pp. 45–50.
[103] Robert Bartlett, 'Medieval and Modern Concepts of Race and Ethnicity', *Journal of Medieval and Early Modern Studies* 31.1 (2001), pp. 42–7.

century *Chronica Gentis Scotorum* or *Chronicle of the Scottish Nation* described 'the Scots as a nation (*natio*) but a nation composed of two races (*gentes*)' defined by languages and customs that had in-built qualities of civility and barbarity.[104] When Walter Bower created his *Scotichronicon* out of Fordun's *Chronica* in the fifteenth century, he appended the anonymous 'Liber Extravagans', a verse description of Scotland that predated both him and Fordun. The unknown writer remarked on 'qualiterque Britannia stirpe multi-gena variatur' or how 'Britain becomes different with a lineage of mixed peoples'.[105]

Writers found nothing incomprehensible in a Britain that was simultaneously multicultural and home to robust kingdoms and nations. For example, travellers did much to record fragments of 'dialect, proverbs, traditional tales and many other aspects of vernacular culture from communities across England, Scotland and Wales'. They traversed 'a series of palpably distinct cultural environments' cutting 'across any sense of common national identity' in a way that ensured 'a high degree of variety not only between the constituent parts of the British Isles but also within them'.[106] Local and regional dialects permeated Britain. For Thomas Jones in the late seventeenth century 'there was a closer affinity between Welsh and Hebrew than there was between the Welsh spoken in Gwynedd and that in south Wales'. A seventeenth-century Scottish contemporary, James Kirkwood of Dunbar, commented on the variety of local lowland accents and the variety of dialects among Gaels that 'instantly identified the origin of the speakers and abruptly made them unintelligible to others'.[107] Thomas Palmer's 1606 treatise for travellers emphasized the polyglot character of English, with borrowings from its island neighbours, Ireland, and European tongues. It might be that 'euerie language in his owne Countrey is most honourable, and equally ancient' even 'though it be a deriuatiue *quoad tempus*, but not *quoad perfectionem*'.[108] An English-speaking traveller from London to Scotland in 1704 lost his linguistic bearings by the time he reached Lincoln, writing that 'I think the comon people of Lincolnshire speake more corruptly and awkwardlye then the comon people of any other county of England that I were ever in.'[109]

Throughout his literary life (1656–97), John Aubrey used aborigines and indigenous or indigenæ to label the ancient Britons and their contemporary descendants, including a local informant in Ramsbury Hundred,

---

[104] Bartlett 'Concepts of Race and Ethnicity', pp. 47–50.
[105] Walter Bower, *Scotichronicon*, ed. D.E.R. Watt (nine volumes; Aberdeen/Edinburgh, 1996–2000), IX, pp. 62–3.
[106] Fox and Woolf, *Spoken Word*, p. 30.
[107] Fox and Woolf, *Spoken Word*, p. 14; also Lloyd Bowen, 'Fashioning Communities: The County in Early Modern Wales', in *The County Community in Seventeenth-Century England and Wales*, ed. Jacqueline Eales and Andrew Hopper (Hatfield, 2012), pp. 90–4.
[108] Thomas Palmer, *An Essay of the Means How to Make Our Trauailes, into Forraine Countries, the Most Profitable and Honourable* (STC 19156; London, 1606), p. 56.
[109] *The North of England and Scotland in MDCCIV* (Edinburgh, 1818), p. 17.

north Wiltshire.[110] He titled one set of notes the 'Nature and humours of the Aborigines'.[111] Aubrey gave distinctive qualities of mind and body to the commons of North Wiltshire and Gloucestershire, the Downs of South Wiltshire, the borderers of Herefordshire, Shropshire, and Montgomeryshire, Norfolk, Scotland, Yorkshire, Devon, Somerset, and Kent. Wales and the Welsh were divided along various lines of topography and character. Aubrey typed the Welsh generally as black-eyed and dark-haired. The civil, hospitable, but self-interested north Welsh exceeded their southern neighbours in subtle wits. Dissemblers filled Glamorganshire, while the litigious took to Brecknockshire. Soil quality (literally) and topography played a critical role for Aubrey.[112] He questioned 'if the Natives (Aborigines) of One Country being transplanted to another, will not after some Generations degenerate according to the Nature of the Soile?' Aubrey trotted out the old canard of degenerate Englishmen who became 'as lazy as the Irish' after just a handful of years in the island.[113]

In medieval Europe, plurality became 'a sign of political maturity and power that a ruler governed several peoples'.[114] Plurality of customs, peoples, and topography underpinned 'pretensions to imperial power and titles' among Carolingians and Ottonians as well as Anglo-Saxon and 'Scottish' kings.[115] Aethalstan and Edgar among those Anglo-Saxon kings claimed a unique kind of *imperium* among their fellow lords and kings in Britain – Welsh, Cornish, Northumbrian, Hiberno-Scandinavian, and Scottish. It receded only as the intensive, coercive, self-consciously English authority of *rex Anglorum* supplanted the extensive and culturally complex lordships that embodied the claim to be *rex totius Brittannie*.[116] In Wales, neither territorial integrity nor political sovereignty worked to produce a 'common Welsh identity'. Instead, Welshness depended on 'law customs, language, mythology, and borders', especially the ethno-legal borders that emerged between the law of Wales (Wallia), the law of the Anglo-Norman marcher settlements (Marchia Wallie), and the law of England.[117] When

---

[110]   *Wiltshire. The Topographical Collections of John Aubrey*, ed. John Edward Jackson (Devizes, 1862), p. 312; Aubrey, *Natural History of Wiltshire*, pp. 10–12.

[111]   John Aubrey, *Three Prose Works*, ed. John Buchanan-Brown (Carbondale, IL, 1972), pp. 313–14.

[112]   Aubrey, *Three Prose Works*, pp. 345–6.

[113]   Aubrey, *Three Prose Works*, p. 314.

[114]   R.R. Davies, 'The Peoples of Britain and Ireland 1100–1400 I. Identities', *Royal Historical Society Transactions* 4 (1994), p. 11.

[115]   R.R. Davies, 'I. Identities', p. 11. See also Davies, 'The Peoples of Britain and Ireland 1100–1400 II. Names, Boundaries and Regnal Solidarities', *Royal Historical Society Transactions* 5 (1995), pp. 1–20; Davies, 'The Peoples of Britain and Ireland 1100–1400 III. Laws and Customs', *Royal Historical Society Transactions* 6 (1996), pp. 1–3.

[116]   George Molyneaux, 'Why Were Some Tenth-Century English Kings Presented as Rulers of Britain?', *Royal Historical Society Transactions* 21 (2011), p. 90.

[117]   R.R. Davies, 'The Identity of "Wales" in the Thirteenth Century', in *From Medieval to Modern Wales*, ed. Davies and Jenkins, pp. 48–9, 51–6; also Bronagh Ní Chonaill, '"The

Edward I and Henry VIII set their sights on the mastery of Britain they intended to subordinate their island rivals and local elites to an English crown that asserted an undisputed right to a lost British *imperium*. Only a puny emperor boasted of ruling over a single homogenous people, and those that did either practised a kind of linguistic-political expediency or simply defied the classical and medieval reality of multi-ethnic polities.[118] Tidy nations might have been hard for medieval and early modern Britons to comprehend.

Literary encounters

Encounters with humanity occurred during real journeys. They also took place in the minds of would-be travellers when they read.[119] Tudor and Stuart intellectuals believed in God and revered the Classics. Authorities like Thucydides, Polybius, Xenophon, Strabo, Livy, Caesar, and Tacitus confronted readers with human complexity.[120] Herodotus set the standard, even if the scope and spirit of his ethnographic inquiry lost something in the centuries before its fragments resurfaced in the fifteenth century.[121] With his empirical sense, first-hand travel, and local research, Herodotus is not unfairly vaunted as the first historian or ethnographer, despite also peddling dubious information that encouraged later descriptions of human monstrosity and barbarity.[122] Herodotus met his share of impressive and repulsive peoples in his journeys. What made his *Histories* compelling lay in his instinctive ethnography:

> Herodotus approached the task of describing manners and customs with a fairly definite idea of what constituted a culture, and a fairly specific set of questions for evoking details from informants. The criteria which separated one group from another and gave individuality to his descriptive portraits were common descent, common language, common religion, and the observance of manners in smaller details of living, such as dress, diet, and dwellings.[123]

Many descriptions in the *Histories* are ethnocentric, taking Greece as the essential frame of reference. Yet Herodotus suggested that lands and peoples at a distance – Ethiopia or the Arabs – might offer many things 'fine and rare',

Welsh, you know, are Welsh": the Individual, the Alien, and a Legal Tradition', in *Nations in Medieval Britain*, ed. Hirokazu Tsurushima (Donington, 2010), pp. 75–85.

[118] Bartlett, 'Concepts of Race and Ethnicity', pp. 50–4.

[119] Ania Loomba, *Shakespeare, Race, and Colonialism* (Oxford, 2002/2009).

[120] Donald R. Kelley, *Faces of History: Historical Inquiry from Herodotus to Herder* (New Haven, 1998), pp. 19–74, 130–61; Peter Burke, 'A Survey of the Popularity of Ancient Historians 1450–1700', *History and Theory* 5.2 (1966), pp. 135–52.

[121] Margaret T. Hodgen, *Early Anthropology in the Sixteenth and Seventeenth Centuries* (Philadelphia, 1964), pp. 28–9.

[122] Herodotus, *Histories* (New York, 1910/1997).

[123] Hodgen, *Early Anthropology*, pp. 22–3.

rather than simply deviant or undesirable from a narrowly Greek perspective.[124] The ethnographies also reconstructed the peoples whom the Persians conquered or incorporated in their imperial heyday, a kind of literary riposte on behalf of the Lydians, Egyptians, Ethiopians, 'tribes of Indians', Arabs, and Scythians.[125]

Herodotus' ethnographic descriptions attracted British readers, attentive to topography, physiognomy, language, spiritual practices and folklore, livelihoods, and all sorts of manners both ordinary and fantastic. Fordun and Bower credited Herodotus with reporting that 'the land of the Scots is not inferior even to the soil of Britain itself'.[126] Perhaps Herodotus and Atlantic discovery impacted on More's thinking in *Utopia*, finding on the exotic margins a race with many fine customs and practices worthy of respect, even emulation.[127] Richard Carew 'naturally and easily' cited Herodotus and other classical authors in his iconic *Description of Cornwall* (1602).[128] Here too was the quintessential Classical story of a multi-ethnic *imperium*. The Greek general Xenophon took up the subject a generation later when he composed the *Cyropaedia*. His account of Cyrus the Great as a model empire-builder became a 'best seller' among humanist readers. The message of Herodotus or Xenophon would have been clear: imperial regimes needed ethnography to help make sense of the cultural complexity of their peoples and territories. John Leland certainly understood as much when he travelled the Tudor dominions for his master, Henry VIII.

Herodotus' ethnography found its way into *De Proprietatibus Rerum*, Bartholomaeus Anglicus' encyclopaedia of 'properties' compiled from Greek, Arabic, and Jewish sources in the 1230s. The properties described include the ethnic features of peoples throughout the world, from Ethiopia to India to Britain. The ancient inhabitants who came to Scotia marked 'diverse figures and shapes on their flesh and skin' with iron pricks until by 'meddling with Englishmen, many of them have changed the old manners of Scots into better manners for the most part', leaving only the 'wild Scots and Irish ... to follow their forefathers in clothing, in tongue, and in living'.[129]

John Trevisa translated *De Proprietatibus* in 1398 and Wynkyn de Worde made these potted ethnographies available to English readers in 1495. A decade earlier Trevisa produced an English translation of Ranulf Higden's already widespread *Polychronicon* or universal history.[130] In it, Higden's 'contribution to

---

[124]   Tim Rood, 'Herodotus and Foreign Lands', in *Cambridge Companion to Herodotus*, ed. Carolyn Dewald and John Marincola (Cambridge, 2006), pp. 297–8.

[125]   Rood, 'Herodotus and Foreign Lands', pp. 293–4; Herodotus, *Histories*, pp. 273–80.

[126]   Bower, *Scotichronicon*, I, p. 183.

[127]   F.J. Levy, *Tudor Historical Thought* (San Marino, CA, 1967), p. 69; Kelley, *Faces of History*, p. 152.

[128]   A.L. Rowse, *Tudor Cornwall* (New York, 1941/1969), p. 423.

[129]   Ania Loomba and Jonathan Burton, eds, *Race in Early Modern England* (Houndmills, 2007), p. 65.

[130]   John Taylor, 'Ranulf Higden', *Oxford DNB* at *www.oxforddnb.com*.

the ethnology of the English people was more notable, for the last section of his *descriptio* of England, which dealt with language, customs, and character' included a view of the English that emphasized 'regional distinctions'.[131] The fifteenth-century Warwickshire antiquarian John Rous – and through him, John Leland – owed some of his interest in 'social customs' to Higden's description.[132] Such works stood as sober competition to the hodgepodge of monstrous races, exotic ethnographies, the biblical descent of humanity, and origin myths in the wildly popular travels of John Mandeville, first published in English in 1496.[133]

The 'obscure German Hebraist' Johannes Boemus naturally drew heavily on Herodotus and other classical authors in his *Omnium Gentium*. He sought to provide a useful comparison of polities and 'make accessible to the ordinary reader an already not inconsiderable body of knowledge concerning the variety of human behavior, to arrange it on a broad geographical plan, with the geographical features subordinated to the ethnological, and to use the printed page, as others had employed the "cabinte de curiosités," for assembling and exhibiting the range of human custom, ritual, and ceremony'.[134] The *Omnium Gentium* became a hit upon its publication in 1520. Reprinted in 1536, Boemus' universal ethnography turned into the *Fardle of Factions* in its 1555 English edition.[135] Classical authors dominated, despite the existence of eye-witness accounts of the New World, including Aristotle's explanation for the skin colour of non-Europeans coming from the 'black seed' of the father.[136] Tacitus' ethnography of the 'barbarian' Germans also proved popular among humanist readers who wanted to grapple with the complexity of the New World and study early Europeans. William Camden became such a reader as he imagined and wrote *Britannia*.[137]

The Bible contributed a babble of voices, the genealogical origins of human races, and openings for pernicious definitions of human difference associated with black and white, slave and free, evil and good.[138] In two deeply learned and persuasive studies, Colin Kidd has worked to recover biblical concepts of race and ethnicity in the early modern Atlantic world against crude assumptions of its

---

[131] Chris Given-Wilson, *Chronicles: The Writing of History in Medieval England* (London, 2004), p. 133.
[132] Gransden, *Historical Writing in England II*, p. 324.
[133] Loomba and Burton, *Race in Early Modern England*, pp. 51–74.
[134] Hodgen, *Early Anthropology*, p. 131.
[135] Hodgen, *Early Anthropology*, p. 137.
[136] Loomba and Burton, *Race in Early Modern England*, pp. 82–3; also Hodgen, *Early Anthropology*, p. 137.
[137] Kelley, *Faces of History*, pp. 159, 184.
[138] Loomba and Burton, *Race in Early Modern England*, p. 65.

effects on cultural differences and biological racism.[139] For Kidd's early moderns, the Bible provided the foundation for the study of humanity:

> Thus, scripture dictated that beneath the world's ethnic diversity there was a web of family relationships. ... Early modern Christian anthropologists did not immediately presume an unbridgeable gap between the white European self and the non-European Other, but were led by scriptural imperatives to explore how the Other might fit with the knowledge of the dispersion of peoples found in Genesis 10 and 11 ... [140]

Consequently, peopling Britain or 'the New World was first and foremost a theological conundrum, and only secondarily an ethnological question which might be settled on its own term'.[141]

Despite the excavation of these biblical–theological impulses, Kidd admits that the theological conundrum encouraged the study of comparative ethnology – 'culture, beliefs, languages and appearance' – between Amerindians and Europeans even if it was less for its own sake than for 'fitting Amerindians within the permitted parameters of sacred history'.[142] By contrast, I am concerned precisely with how Britons engaged with ethnographic markers regardless of the schema of biblical origins or sacred history into which they did or did not fit cultural complexity. Travellers and first-hand encounters with complexity question attempts to marginalize Britons' multicultural interests. More simply put, Kidd's sources and interests may lead to only part of the early modern engagement with ethno-cultural complexity in Britain.[143] This book takes the reader on a different, sometimes parallel journey.

The encounter with Britain

Thomas More contemplated a devout life among the Carthusians of the London Charterhouse before admitting that he lacked the necessary discipline. Fifteen years later, as More embarked on *Utopia*, Andrew Boorde, a teenager hailing from Borde's Hill in Sussex, joined the Charterhouse. Boorde gave up meat and women – perhaps – for thirteen years but finally sought release from his vows in 1528. Medicine called him, and he travelled through the medical schools of continental Europe, on and off until 1534. While More languished in the Tower, Boorde fell in with his nemesis, Thomas Cromwell. Cromwell dispatched

---

[139] Colin Kidd, *British Identities Before Nationalism: Ethnicity and Nationhood in the Atlantic World 1600–1800* (Cambridge, 1999), pp. 9–72; Kidd, *The Forging of Races: Race and Scripture in the Protestant Atlantic World, 1600–2000* (Cambridge, 2006), pp. 54–78.

[140] Kidd, *Forging of Races*, p. 58.

[141] Kidd, *Forging of Races*, p. 56; Kidd, *British Identities*, pp. 61–4, 75–9, 290.

[142] Kidd, *Forging of Races*, p. 62.

[143] Michael Braddick's *State Formation in Early Modern England c. 1550–1700* (Cambridge, 2000), pp. 287–313, 340–78 finds a Britain defined by religious plurality and cultural particularism beneath the abstractions of national labels.

Boorde to take the pulse of European political opinion toward the Henrician revolution. Two weeks before More ascended the scaffold, Boorde described the long queue of Continental enemies to the king's proceedings.[144] When Boorde returned to England in 1535, he composed an itinerary of his European travels, parts of which were topographical and ethnographic. Boorde lent the itinerary to Cromwell, who lost it. Under cover of a medical practice in Glasgow, Boorde fed Cromwell useful intelligence about the Scots in 1536 and 1537, later writing that 'my scyences & other polyces dyd kepe me in fauour, that I dyd know theyr secretes'.[145] More European travels followed and Boorde embarked on a minor literary career from his new digs in Montpellier about the time of Cromwell's fall. In 1542 Boorde wrote his *First Book of the Introduction of Knowledge*, finally published in 1547.[146]

Boorde's interest in travel and medicine fed his intention to describe the 'notycyon & practes of Physycke in diuers regyons & countres', but he opened with an ethnography designed to capture the 'naturall dysposicion' of the peoples he encountered.[147] Boorde started each chapter with a wry address in verse from a typical native. He then answered with observations designed to interrogate the stereotypes.[148] His native Englishman proclaimed a love for fashion, a fickle attachment to serious learning, and an insufferable, mean arrogance built on an abundance of all things and the apparent freedom to act unhindered by others. Boorde called Englishmen to embrace true learning and virtue, abandon pride, and make good on a natural disposition and situation that rivalled or outshone 'any other lande and nacion that euer I haue trauayled in'.[149]

Boorde was attuned to Britain as a cultural crossroads, even if he betrayed an Anglocentric reading of its complexity consistent with the imperial ambitions of Henry and Cromwell:

> In England, the Walshe tongue is in Wales, The Cornyshe tongue in Cornewall, and Iryshe in Irlande, and Frenche in the Englysshe pale [of Calais]. There is also the Northern tongue, the whyche is trew Scotysshe; and the Scottes tongue is the Northern tongue. Furthermore, in England is vsed all maner of languages and speches of alyens in diuers Cities and Townes, specyally in London by the Sea syde.[150]

Sensitivity to cultural complexity did not translate into tolerance when Boorde mouthed a typical Cornishman in his 'apendex' to the English chapter:

---

[144] Elizabeth Lane Furdell, 'Andrew Boorde', *Oxford DNB* at www.oxforddnb.com.
[145] *The Fyrst Boke of the Introduction of Knowledge made by Andrew Borde*, ed. F.J. Furnivall (London, 1870), p. 137, hereafter cited as Boorde, *Introduction*.
[146] Furdell, 'Andrew Boorde'.
[147] Boorde, *Introduction*, p. 116.
[148] For a narrowly English reading of Boorde's work see Cathy Shrank, *Writing the Nation in Reformation England 1530–1580* (Oxford, 2004), pp. 27–49.
[149] Boorde, *Introduction*, pp. 118–22.
[150] Boorde, *Introduction*, p. 120.

Iche cham a Corynshe man, al[e] che can brew;
It wyll make one to kacke, also to spew;
It is dycke and smoky, and also it is gyn;
It is lyke wash, as pygges had wrestled dryn.
Iche cannot brew, nor dresse Fleshe, nor vyshe [fish] ... [151]

Boorde found Cornwall 'a pore and very barren countrye' with nothing but fish and tin to its credit. The bilingualism of the land did not commend it, divided between 'naughty Englyshe ... [and] Corynshe speche', with most people not even speaking a word of the former. Even so, Boorde gave a passable lexicon of basic Cornish words.[152]

According to Boorde's stock Welshman, laziness, bare legs, singing, an addiction to roasted cheese, genuflecting to the Virgin Mary, and plucking a harp with horsehair strings qualified one to join the race. So too did the familiar play on Welsh patronymics and the tradition of proud lineages: 'I am a gentlyman, and come of brutes blood; My name is, ap Ryce, ap Dauy, ap Flood. ... My kyndred is ap hoby, ap Ienkin, ap goffe.' Boorde noted the real north–south topographic divide in Wales and spotted the 'waste & wast ground ... maryses, & wylde and high mountaynes'. Boorde claimed to have personally disproved that a cup or napkin dipped in St Winifrede's well would bring out water with drops 'redyshe like bloude'. From there, Boorde's ethnography fashioned the Welsh into a 'reude and beastlye people' whose consumption of milk and whey and poor, bare lodging reminded him of the people of Castile and Biscay. Iberia (and the Catholic Church) came to mind again when Boorde described the 'folyshe wordes' and lamentations for the dead he witnessed in Ruthin and elsewhere. An early kind of commodity futures trading – they sold their lambs and wheat a year in advance – numbered among the stupid things the Welsh did. Speech and manners too varied between North and South Wales, but the Welsh as a whole ultimately manifested both positive and negative qualities. They could be hardy, strong, and 'goodly men', with many 'louynge and kyndharted, faythful & vertuous' among them, but others proved to be 'lyght fyngered' and lecherous, with 'bastards openly knowen; and many prestes sonnes aboundeth in the countre.'[153]

All this might set the Welsh apart from the Tudor heartlands, but Boorde's Welsh lexicon betrayed regular contacts: 'who so wyll lerne to speake some Welshe, Englyshe and Welshe foloweth. And where I do not wryte true Welshe, I do write it that euery man may rede it and vnderstand it without any teachynge.' Even so, Boorde peppered his practical Welsh with cultural stereotypes that followed from the ethnography. He envisioned that a request for the best lodging in town being met with the response, 'At Iohn ap Dauy ap Ryse house.' 'Wyfe!

[151] Boorde, *Introduction*, p. 122.
[152] Boorde, *Introduction*, pp. 123–5, 128.
[153] Boorde, *Introduction*, pp. 125–8.

hath preestes wyues in Wales?' might be met by an indignant 'Hold thy peace! they haue no Wyves now.' Requests for meat, bread, and drink might be right for Cornwall, but the (English) traveller needed a different command in Wales, 'Mayden, come hether, and gyue me some roste cheese!' The traveller could expect to be told 'Tarry a lytle, man, and you shall haue enowgh.' Curiously, Boorde returned to more innocuous phrases for travellers to Ireland.[154] Not so Scotland, where Boorde spent more than a year gathering intelligence for Cromwell. He offered a few loaded phrases in pidgin Scots-English:

> What contryth man be ye? ...
> I es a gewd falow of the Scotland blewd ...
> Than haue you plenty of sowes and pygges ...
> A pygge is good meate. A gryce is gewd sole.[155]

'For as much as the Scottish tongue and the northern Englyshe be lyke of speche', Boorde passed over anything more.

Boorde's description of the English essentially took in 'lowland' England, while Scotland too featured a north–south divide: 'In Scotlande they haue two sondry speches. In the northe parte, and the part ioyning Ierland, that speche is muche lyke the Iryshe speche. But the south parte of Scotland, and the vsuall speeche of the Peeres of the Realme, is lyke the northern speche of England.'[156] Scottish monarchs and travellers after James V increasingly looked on this linguistic divide as more than geographic; it betrayed a cultural divide between lowland civility and highland barbarity.[157] Boorde captured this attitude as well as any in the period. One part of Scotland lay next to England, the 'other parte of Scotlande is a baryn and waste countrey, full of mores, lyke the land of the wylde Irishe. And the people of that parte of Scotland be very rude and vnmanered & vntaught.' Still, lowland Scotland and its inhabitants were nothing to brag about. Lowlanders would 'gnaw a bone, and cast it into the dish again', they served fish and flesh roasted and sodden with gravy, and proffered an abundance of oatcakes. The borderers were worse, living in poverty and penury, occupying houses shared between people and animals thrown up in a few hours, and robbing and stealing to subsist.[158]

Boorde brought together the three intellectual currents that powered the early modern encounter with multicultural Britain: the passion for attentive and broad-ranging travel, self-conscious journeys of discovery, and the study of human complexity, of ethnography. Among the English, he never achieved the

---

[154] Boorde, *Introduction*, p. 129, 134–5.
[155] Boorde, *Introduction*, p. 138.
[156] Boorde, *Introduction*, p. 138.
[157] Roger Mason, 'Civil Society and the Celts: Hector Boece, George Buchanan and the Ancient Scottish Past', *Scottish History: The Power of the Past*, ed. Edward J. Cowan and Richard Finlay (Edinburgh, 2002), pp. 95–119.
[158] Boorde, *Introduction*, pp. 136–8.

lasting recognition afforded Leland's journeys, while the Scots scarcely seem to have noticed the travels of the one-time Glasgow doctor and spy. Boorde's fate tells us something about just how his impulse to capture the cultural complexity of the known world collided with the realities of travel, discovery, and ethnography. Boorde anticipated that his punchy blend of verse and narrative would work against him with serious readers:

> Of noble England, of Ireland and of Wales,
> And also of Scotland, I haue tolde som tales;
> And of other Ilondes I haue showed my mynd;
> He that wyl trauell, the truthe he shall fynd.
> After my conscyence I do wryte truly,
> Although that many men wyl say that I do lye ...

Travellers always attracted scepticism: had they really witnessed what they claimed to have seen, and did they get the details right? The nonsense of Mandeville's *Travels* eventually fell by the wayside, though slowly. John Norden, the meticulous surveyor famous for county mileage tables, found the tomb in St Albans Abbey belonging to Mandeville, 'whose trauayles in forraine regions and rare reports, are at this time admired through the world'.[159] Still, fantastic descriptions and comprehensive claims inevitably fell to empirical pressure.[160] Boorde surely anticipated some of this when he pleaded the truth of his far-flung descriptions.[161] These are questions we must continue to ask of our early modern sources, ever on the look-out for well-intentioned and self-serving travellers eager to enlighten and persuade, naïve and duplicitous informants, patrons and printers with complex, opaque interests, readers all too happy to impart their own meaning on the experiences and texts of others.[162]

Boorde perhaps sensed another problem. Cultural complexity, especially that of newly 'discovered' humanity, demanded thoroughness from travellers. Boorde's *Introduction* did not fit the bill. Even those as well travelled as Boorde faced real practical constraints in meeting standards for meticulous detail and description. Time, resources, geography, and the rigours of travel limited the scope for first-hand encounters with humanity and the careful scrutiny of its complexity by any one individual.[163] Translated, published, and dedicated to Walter Raleigh at the instigation of Hakluyt in 1589, Albrecht Meyer's guidelines

---

[159]   John Norden, *Speculis Britaniæ Pars The Description of Hartfordshire* (STC 18637; London, 1598), p. 10.

[160]   Justin Stägl, *A History of Curiosity: The Theory of Travel 1550–1800* (Amsterdam, 1995), pp. 1–94.

[161]   Boorde, *Introduction*, p. 144.

[162]   Miri Rubin, 'What is Cultural History Now?', in *What is History Now?*, ed. David Cannadine (Houndmills, 2002), pp. 86–9, and the essays Rubin notes in James Clifford and George E. Marcus, eds, *Writing Culture: the Poetics and Politics of Ethnography* (Berkeley, 1986).

[163]   Ohler, *The Medieval Traveller*, pp. 3–140; Atoni Maczak, *Travel in Early Modern Europe* (Cambridge, 1995), pp. 4–182.

for 'Gentlemen, merchants, students, souldiers, marriners, &c.' of 'whatsoeuer particular thing shall be seene, learned, offered, obserued, and described in any Region' set a daunting standard for observation, one that Fynes Moryson would reiterate in the seventeenth century.[164]

A universal history after Herodotus or even Polybius was impossible even with a lifetime in which to travel.[165] It could only be a collaborative work or a grand synthesis of others' travels and descriptions. Edward Grimstone translated one such work in 1615 as *The Estates, Empires and Principalities of the World*, by Pierre D'Avity (1613).[166] The English folio edition numbered more than twelve hundred pages and described the world's polities, including the customs and manners of their peoples. According to D'Avity's preface, whatever satisfaction he felt in his great work, 'I will giue much more to those that shall labour to make it perfect; for that in my opinion it is not yet fully finished, and that any man may adde something dayly vnto it, for that from time to time they haue more certaine aduice from all parts, specially from those countries which haue not been much frequented, either by reason of the distance or for their barba-rousnesse.'[167] When the armchair traveller Samuel Purchas took up Hakluyt's mission to compile travel accounts of lands outwith Britain, he confirmed the impossibility of anything but a collaborative approach to the monumental task of describing the complexity of humanity.[168] From William Camden to Robert Sibbald to Edward Lhuyd, collaborators would never be hard to find for projects designed to examine the complexity of Britain, from its peoples to its flora, fauna, landforms or the like, in the Tudor and Stuart centuries.[169]

For cultural and political reasons as well as these practical limits, some travellers made kingdoms, nations, or 'peoples' the boundaries for their journeys of discovery and descriptions of humanity. John of Fordun 'wrote back' against Edward I's imperial designs and depredations. John Mair celebrated Scotland's history and its people in order to advocate for an Anglo-Scottish dynastic union of equals. Hector Boece sang a patriotic hymn to the Scottish nation and stroked the lofty Renaissance pretensions of James V. But each of them travelled and wrote with the intent to chronicle the history of an independent Scotland and

---

[164]   Albrecht Meyer, *Certaine Briefe, and Speciall Instructions for Gentlemen, Merchants, Students, Souldiers, Marriners, &c. Employed in Seruices Abrode* (STC 17784; London, 1589), title page, sig A3b and B1a.
[165]   John Burrow, *A History of Histories* (New York, 2008), pp. 23, 66–71.
[166]   Hadfield, *Literature, Travel, and Colonial* Writing, pp. 105–6.
[167]   Pierre d'Avity, *The Estates, Empire and Principalities of the World* (STC 988; London, 1615), sig. A4a
[168]   Hadfield, *Amazons*, p. 37; Campbell, *Witness and the Other World*, pp. 217–22, 255–66.
[169]   Adam Fox, 'Printed Questionnaires, Research Networks, and the Discovery of the British Isles, 1650–1800', *Historical Journal* 53.3 (2010), pp. 593–621; Charles W.J. Withers, *Geography, Science and National Identity: Scotland Since 1520* (Cambridge, 2001), pp. 69–111; *Life and Letters of Edward Lhuyd*, ed. R.T. Gunther (Oxford, 1945).

the complex peoples subject to the 'King of Scots' and now crowded in under that label.[170] They might spar with English and Welsh writers about Brutus and English claims to British suzerainty, but Scotland bounded their projects. Leland too had his master's British dominions in his sights with his planned 'Civil History' of England and Wales. For British travellers, then, the natural bounds of travel and ethnography might take in Britain and Ireland, or the respective realms of the Stewarts and Tudors, perhaps even the individual four nations (England, Wales, Scotland, and Ireland).

Interest in cultural complexity inevitably complicated neat bounds. Travellers in Britain could not help but discover that upon 'closer examination what seem to be "national" units dissolve into a number of distinctive cultures with their own perception of the past, of social status ... or religion and of many other aspects of life'.[171] Language compromised the boundaries of Boorde's four nations. The phrase guaranteed to produce the best roasted cheese might only be needed in Wales, but Boorde must have realized by the time he counted his way to three in four 'different' regions that there was some kind of linguistic affinity among Britons: tray (Cornwall), try (Wales), tre (Ireland), dre (Scotland).[172] The drive to comprehend such peoples thoroughly and completely eventually pushed many travellers to discover and study 'manageable' spaces. Some still aimed for a larger canvas, like Fynes Moryson or Edward Lhuyd, who spent five years on the road and engaged scores of collaborators and subscribers for this massive dictionary of the British tongues. But grand projects often proved fraught or brought their architects to grief. In England and Wales especially, travellers instead made individual counties the focus of their journeys and study. William Lambarde's *Perambulation of Kent* set an impressive standard in 1576, followed by Carew's *Survey of Cornwall* (1602) and George Owen's study of Pembrokeshire (Wales) in 1603.[173] The Scottish archives are littered with manuscript histories of burghs and counties composed during the seventeenth century, some at the behest of noble patrons and others reflecting the interests of local experts like Robert Gordon of Straloch.[174]

The traveller who most welcomed this kind of specialized discovery and description was Camden. After several editions had made their way through the press, Camden freely admitted that his iconic *Britannia* would never be a complete or thorough description of Britain (and Ireland) and its peoples until

---

[170] Matthew H. Hammond, 'Ethnicity and the Writing of Medieval Scottish History', *Scottish Historical Review* 85.1 (2006), pp. 16–20.

[171] Hugh Kearney, *The British Isles: A History of Four Nations* (Cambridge, 2006), p. 9.

[172] Boorde, *Introduction*, pp. 123, 128, 133, 138.

[173] Andrew McRae, *God Speed the Plough: The Representation of Agrarian England 1500–1600* (Cambridge, 1996), pp. 231–61.

[174] *Geographical Collections Relating to Scotland Made by Walter Macfarlane*, ed. Arthur Mitchell and James Toshach Clark (three volumes; Edinburgh, 1906–1908); Withers, *Geography: Science and National Identity*, pp. 40–56.

a legion of travellers combed the local countryside and encountered its residents across generations. With his global horizon, d'Avity called out to a would-be Leland and Boece to improve his accounts of individual nations. Yet Camden had already made the same call, for the same reason, to his fellow travellers to discover Britain in all its parts and its peoples in all their complexity. The editions of *Britannia* completed during Camden's lifetime would never have been as rich without a team of collaborators, especially concerning the North of England and Scotland.[175] For Camden, the exploration of Britain and its peoples must be constantly pursued and renewed in order to capture the changing face of humanity. Yet even here, in the county and local histories that Camden sought, the cultural complexity that travellers encountered made drawing ethno-topographic lines difficult. Both Carew and Owen learned this lesson when they studied Cornwall and Pembrokeshire.

When Thomas Hearne first began publishing Leland's *Itinerary* in 1710, he reflected on just these issues. According to Hearne, Britain's literary worthies left few descriptions of the island. They might record ecclesiastical and political affairs in some detail, but 'as to a Survey of it, they contented themselves with general and loose Accounts, such as that which stands at the beginning of Bede's Ecclesiastical History; a Description very slight and mean if compar'd with the other Excellent Performances of that Great Man'. Because of their 'confinement', the monks who became the keepers of Britain's history 'were incapacitated for travelling and making such Observations as were absolutely necessary for a just and faithful Description of the Isle'. Gerald of Wales proved a notable exception with his descriptions, an achievement that resembled that of Herodotus. However, Gerald filled his accounts 'full of fabulous and incredible Relations, agreeable to the Humour of the Age', especially descriptions of 'strange Animals and Customs'. Leland was Hearne's point of departure.[176] Leland and his contemporaries inaugurated a new encounter with Britain. Britons moved and engaged with one another in person and in texts for another two hundred years. They engaged the grand abstractions of Britain and its nations alongside the gritty reality of diverse localities and enclaves of peoples seemingly lost in time. We begin with John Leland's journey through the Tudor *imperium*.

---

[175] Angus Vine, *In Defiance of Time: Antiquarian Writing in Early Modern England* (Oxford, 2010), pp. 85–108.
[176] *The Itinerary of John Leland the Antiquarian* (nine volumes; Oxford, 1710–12), I, pp. i–v.

2

Travels through the Empire of Henry VIII

Henry VIII fancied himself a cultured king and accomplished thinker with a talent for theology. The king sought the company of learned men and married three women – Katherine of Aragon, Anne Boleyn, and Katherine Parr – who stimulated his intellect, collected books, and patronized writers and preachers. Like jewel houses, the libraries at Westminster, Greenwich, and Hampton Court held the king's precious books, codices, and manuscripts.[1] Only with difficulty could Henry move his great body, racked by obesity and leg ulcers, to be among them. Four volumes of Britain's literary worthies, from the Romans to the Tudors, guided Henry through some of the authors on his shelves, books rescued from the monastic communities that the king's religious policies had decimated. Alongside great poets and writers stood centuries of British, Saxon, and Norman kings, from whom Henry traced his lineal descent. Their lives and achievements, recounted in the three great tomes of 'De Nobilitate Britannica', ornamented the young Tudor dynasty. The realm that Henry would leave his son Edward lay before him in a great 'Civil History' called 'De Antiquitate Britannica'. In this Tudor *Domesday Book*, the king studied the English and Welsh shires, minutely described. Henry found the crowning glory cast in silver, a magnificent relief of Britannia carefully designed to echo the fabled silver tablets of Charlemagne and stroke the king's imperial vanity.

Or so went the fantasy penned by John Leland in his 'Newe Yeares Gyfte' for the king in 1546.[2] He promised Henry the books and 'quadrate table of silver' that would give literary and visual substance to the Tudor 'worlde and impery of England'.[3] Beginning in the mid–1530s, Leland spent a decade travelling in order to establish the physical, cultural, and historical reality of the Tudor *imperium*. He made good on the king's commission to search out monastic

---

[1] James P. Carley, ed., *The Libraries of Henry VIII* (London, 2000), pp. xxiii–lxvi.
[2] Leland's friend John Bale published the New Year's Gift with his own commentary as *The Laboryouse Iourney [and] Serche of Iohan Leylande, for Englandes Antiquitees* (STC 15445; London, 1549). The version referenced here is reprinted in John Chandler, *John Leland's Itinerary: Travels in Tudor England* (Stroud, 1993), pp. 1–15.
[3] *The Itinerary of John Leland*, ed. Lucy Toulmin Smith (five volumes; Carbondale, IL, 1964), I, p. xli, hereafter cited as Leland, *Itinerary*.

libraries and bring their 'monumentes of auncyent wryters' to the welcome light of day, helping to uncover the records of the ancient Christianity of the Britons before it succumbed to the corrupting influences of the papacy.[4] Monastic visitations and British 'hystoryographers' spurred travel with an expansive gaze:

> I was totallye enflamed wyth a loue, to se throughlye all those partes of thys your opulent and ample realme ... I haue so traueled in your domynions both by the see coastes and the myddle partes, sparynge neyther labour nor costes by the space of these vi yeares past, that there is almost neyther cape nor baye, hauen, creke, or pere, ryuer or confluence of ryuers, breches, washes, lakes, meres, fenny waters, mountaynes, valleys, mores, hethes, forestes, woodes, cyties, burges, casteles, pryncypall manor places, monasteryes, and colleges, but I haue seane them, and noted in so doynge a whole worlde of thynges verye memorable.[5]

A glorious literary past, evidence for the primitive church in Britain, the historical accomplishments of ruling dynasties, and a grand topographical description would cast a brilliant reflection on Henry VIII and the Tudor *imperium*. Henry's philosophy of *imperium* or imperial kingship asserted the king's unchallenged authority in temporal and spiritual matters within his dominions. The peoples of England, Wales, and Ireland were the subjects of a Tudor emperor, one with lofty political and religious ambitions and an eye for the territory of his neighbours in Scotland and France. Leland's literary ambitions outlived Henry, just. The king died shortly after New Year 1547. Edward VI's regime nursed imperial designs at least as thoroughgoing within Britain and Ireland, but within months of the young king's accession Leland descended into some sort of madness that prevented him from meeting his literary promises. He finally died in April 1552. Edward followed in August 1553. Their deaths brought down the curtain on a particular Tudor imperial moment.

Many arguments have been made on Leland's behalf because of his projects and publications. By turns he invented systematic fieldwork and antiquarianism, discovered England, constructed 'a sense of, and pride in, national identity', suppressed 'any sense of a geographically, culturally, or politically divided realm', and sought to preserve an English past and identity in a time of 'rapid cultural change'.[6] These positions tend to pigeonhole Leland the traveller and a broader perspective is needed, especially when it comes to Leland's encounter with the cultural complexity of the Tudor dominions. For Leland and the Henrician regime, the Tudor imperial project was consciously 'British' (and European) in both cultural and geographic terms. They sought to recreate the British *imperium*

---

[4] For the *Antiphilarchia*, see James P. Carley, 'John Leland', *Oxford DNB* at www.oxforddnb. com; Cathy Shrank, *Writing the Nation in Reformation England 1530–1580* (Oxford, 2004), pp. 68, 79.

[5] Chandler, *Leland's Itinerary*, p. 9.

[6] Chandler, *Leland's Itinerary*, p. xxi; Shrank, *Writing the Nation*, pp. 69, 71, 86, 103; John Scattergood, John Leland's *Itinerary* and the Identity of England', in *Sixteenth-century Identities*, ed. A.J. Piesse (Manchester, 2000), 62.

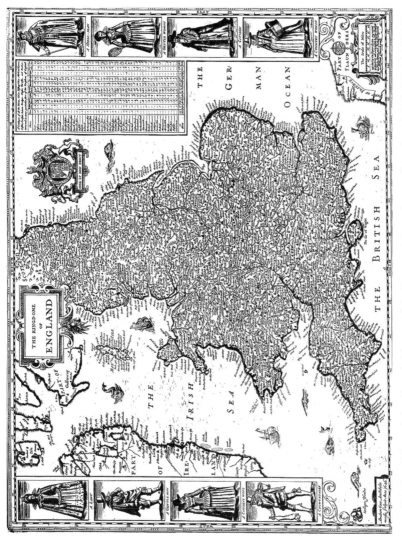

of Brutus for the Tudors and master it by cultural, political, religious, and, in the case of Scotland, military means. This ambition focussed Leland's travels and his encounters with the Tudor *imperium* and its peoples. Leland's travels and reading of the landscape recreated the migrations and interactions of peoples who populated Britain from its Celtic origins to the birth of the Tudor dynasty in Wales. He crossed into and through some of Britain's unique cultural zones: lowland England proper, the former lands of the Danelaw stretching through Lincolnshire and Yorkshire, the North of England and the Anglo-Scottish Borders, Devon and Cornwall, the English Channel communities, and Wales. Alive to the cultural complexity found in those spaces, Leland's description of the Tudor *imperium* certainly would not have been an England writ large, had madness not stilled his pen. Ironic indeed for a traveller fated to become the 'father of English History' for eighteenth-century readers – and their modern descendants. For now, the quest to understand Leland's Tudor imperial gaze begins with his formative years.

John Leland and Tudor intellectual life

Leland joined the bright minds that added learning and artistry to Henry VIII's court. He could thank some luminous figures, his adopted father Thomas Myles, the second Duke of Norfolk, Cardinal Wolsey, and the king. Myles sent Leland to St Paul's School. There he joined in the *studia humanitatis* under the supervision of the great humanist William Lily, the headmaster appointed by Dean John Colet. Leland's fellow pupils included future patrons: William Paget, Antony Denny, Thomas Wriothesley, and Edward North. Leland took his B.A. at Christ College Cambridge in 1522 and tutored the young Thomas Howard until Norfolk's death in 1524. By his own account Leland afterward proceeded to Oxford, thanks to Henry VIII. Finding the atmosphere oppressively conservative, Leland embarked for study in Italy and France. He settled in Paris, evidently with the financial support of the king and patronage from Wolsey. Leland remained in Paris until 1529 and returned to a royal chaplaincy and an absentee rectorship (Pepeling in Calais) in 1530. He successfully navigated the fall of Wolsey and the rise of both Anne Boleyn and Thomas Cromwell. During the mid–1530s he catalogued the holdings of monastic libraries – the commissioners for dissolution not far behind. Leland preserved an uncertain number of books and manuscripts by taking personal possession of them and directing others to the king's libraries. However, his call to systematically collect and preserve the works as a national resource fell on deaf ears.[7] His home travels ended in 1545 and Henry sent Leland to France to acquire seeds, grafts, and fruit trees in 1546. Leland's descent into madness came in 1547 and his brother

---

[7] D.R. Woolf, *Reading History in Early Modern England* (Cambridge, 2000), p. 180.

took him into custody in 1551. Death in 1553 finally released Leland from the demons that haunted his mind.[8]

Leland saw himself as a poet, and his poetry suggests that the years in France inspired and nurtured most of his mature intellectual qualities.[9] From the first he sought out the best humanists and poets, naming in one poem Guillaume Budé, Jacques Lefèvre D'Etaples, Paolo Emilio, and Jean Ruel as the 'perfectly educated men' he 'diligently attended'.[10] These men adorned 'the school on the Seine' and Leland implored Thomas More's servant Richard Hyrde to join him there, where 'perpetual spring holds sway in the wide fields'.[11] Hyrde answered Leland's call, as did his schoolboy friend William Paget.[12] The Seine moved Leland to pastoral delights. No wonder he responded to the lands through which he travelled and composed a figurative travel narrative in the Thames river poem *Cygnea Cantio* (1545).[13] Besides Horatian eloquence, Leland acquired the skills of archival scholarship. He learned, in his words, the ability to 'dig out from the deep shadows many manuscripts of the ancients' and return decayed works to their full glory.[14] Leland's journeys into the monastic libraries brought this talent to fruition.

Just as Lily had at St Paul's, the examples of Lascaris and François I's royal librarian, the incomparable Budé, nurtured Leland's 'feeling for the ancient world, for manuscripts, for legal history, for antiquarian studies in general'.[15] Jean Lemaire de Belges and Robert Gaguin introduced Leland to the *rhétori-queurs*, patriotic poet-chroniclers whose medieval studies celebrated the royal house, chivalric ideals, and the unrivalled eminence of Charlemagne.[16] Lemaire de Belges popularized the claim for the Trojan origins of the French in his *Illustrations de Gaule*, elevating France's cultural heritage above that of Rome's and Italy's with the direct link between Gaul and ancient Troy.[17] Gaguin's *Compendium de Origine et Gestis Francorum* proved notable in England

[8] Carley, 'John Leland'; Carley, 'John Leland in Paris: the Evidence of his Poetry', *Studies in Philology* 83.1 (1986), pp. 7–12; Chandler, *Leland's Itinerary*, pp. xi–xvi; T.S. Dorsch, 'Two English Antiquaries: John Leland and John Stow', *Essays and Studies 1959* (London, 1959), pp. 18–29; T.D. Kendrick, *British Antiquity* (London, 1950), pp. 45–7; Leland, *Itinerary*, I, pp. vii–xx.
[9] Carley, 'Leland in Paris', pp. 1–50; Joseph M. Levine, *Humanism and History: Origins of Modern English Historiography* (Ithaca, 1987), pp. 79–82.
[10] Carley, 'Leland in Paris', pp. 24, 36–46.
[11] Carley, 'Leland in Paris', p. 28.
[12] Carley, 'Leland in Paris', pp. 15, 32.
[13] Carley, 'Leland in Paris', pp. 12, 18, 49; John Leland, *Cygnea Cantio* (STC 15444.5; London, 1545).
[14] Carley, 'Leland in Paris', pp. 12, 35, 48.
[15] Carley, 'Leland in Paris', p. 14.
[16] I.D. McFarlane, *A Literary History of France: Renaissance France 1470–1589* (London, 1974), pp. 46–7.
[17] McFarlane, *Literary History*, p. 49.

for its 'patriotic emphasis' and received favourable comment from More and Colet.[18] Such works contributed to a French 'absolutist conception of kingship, so popular in humanist circles in the near future', even if they also provided idealized accounts of kingship which fit within the mirror for princes genre and, later, the humanist emphasis on counsel.[19] Gaguin's only rival in popularity was Emilio's *De Rebus Gestis Francorum*, which chronicled the French monarchy in ten volumes, from its origins to 1488.[20] Back in England, Leland similarly studied to elevate the cultural majesty of Henry's kingdom and produce useful knowledge for its governance.[21]

There is no evidence that Leland picked up any of the buzz surrounding Giovanni da Verrazzano's voyages to North America or François I's on-off interest in an Atlantic empire. But Paris shaped Leland's travels into the monastic archives and his partisan attachment to 'hystoryographers' who nurtured the Trojan origins of the British peoples.[22] He fused the qualities of the poet-chronicler *rhétoriqueur* with the humanist scholar, thanks to his Parisian years – his choice of Einhard's account of Charlemagne and his great silver tablets is but one piece of evidence. Leland's poetry attests to the importance of Britannia and he thought explicitly in terms of a British past and a British present fused in the Tudor *imperium*. He noted the happy wanderings of one R. Crawford among 'the famous men of the British court ... and the serene face / Of Your prince and mine'.[23] His poem comparing Budé and Cuthbert Tunstall wondered 'with what praise will our Britain celebrate you? / Or how learned Gaul its Bude?' and called upon France to 'consider the British orator worthy to be / Compared with you, each one worthy of glowing praise'.[24] Leland repeatedly couched the present in turns of phrase that resonated with a classical British past. He noted how much Hyrde had been 'celebrated by the woaded British'. In an effort to secure a meeting with Du Bois, Leland flattered and promised Du Bois to bring 'the high praise of your erudition / From France to the flaxen Britons'. He looked forward to Chéradame's fame being demonstrated to the 'Watery Britons with a Homeric Bugle'.[25]

---

[18] Peter G. Bietenholz and Thomas B. Deutscher, eds, *Contemporaries of Erasmus* (three volumes; Toronto, 1985–87), II, p. 70; McFarlane, *Literary History*, p. 27.

[19] McFarlane, *Literary History*, p. 47; Anthony Grafton, 'Humanism and Political Theory', in *Cambridge History of Political Thought 1450–1700*, ed. J.H. Burns and Mark Goldie (Cambridge, 1991), pp. 9–29.

[20] *Contemporaries of Erasmus*, II, p. 429.

[21] R.J. Knecht, *Renaissance Warrior and Patron: the Reign of Francis I* (Cambridge, 1994), pp. 464–77.

[22] Knecht, *Renaissance Warrior*, pp. 371–4.

[23] Carley, 'Leland in Paris', p. 35.

[24] Carley, 'Leland in Paris', p. 36.

[25] Carley, 'Leland in Paris', pp. 28, 38, 43.

Leland fancied himself a 'British Muse' in his elegy to the Seine and expected that one day 'Britain will celebrate my Muses'.[26] By 1546 he aimed at an unassailable cultural pedigree for the king's *imperium*:

> I trust shortly to se the tyme, that like as Carolus Magnus had among his treasures thre large and notable tables of syluer, rychely enameled, one of the syte and descripcion of Constantynople, an other of the site and figure of the mangificent citie of Rome, and the third of the descripcion of the worlde. So shall your Maiestie haue thys your worlde and impery of Englande so sett forthe in a quadrate table of syluer ... that your grace shall haue ready knowledge at the fyrst sighte of many right delectable, fruteful, and necessary pleasures, by contemplacion therof, as often as occasyon shall moue yow to the syghte of.[27]

The association of Charlemagne and Henry creates a tantalizing image of a Tudor emperor in repose, surveying his *imperium* in silver relief. With the 'Civil History' as its companion, 'I trust so to open this wyndow', wrote Leland, 'that the lyght shal be seane, so long, that is to say, by the space of a whole thousand yeares, stopped vp, and the old glory of your renoued Britaine to reflorish through the worlde'.[28]

Leland appropriated Britain for a London-based regime, but what did it actually mean for Leland to use the expression 'impery of Englande'? By the 1540s the language of empire or *imperium* brought together three trends. First, by Henry VII's reign the imagery of the 'crown imperial' had become convenient shorthand for defining the power of the monarchy. Imperial monarchs wore closed crowns that signified complete and entire sovereign authority, recognizing only God as their superior. Subjects who fingered Henry VII's little groats or gold sovereigns would have seen his closed crown. The accompanying rhetoric became a favourite of Henry VIII's in closing off debate, including his dispute with Abbot Richard Kidderminster in 1515 over the reach of canon law and papal decrees against that of statute and common law in England. In the 1510s Henry acted on a territorial sense of *imperium*. Henry had an eye to reviving the Lancastrian empire in France. The successful siege of Tournai in 1513 prompted the most explicit and developed statement of Tudor imperial power to date. Finally, the great matter of the king's campaign to end his marriage to Queen Katherine and marry Anne Bolyen raised a crucial question. The only road to freedom lay in a papal annulment in Rome after the Legatine court set up in Blackfriars to hear Henry's case adjourned in 1529 without issuing a decree. There had to be a solution closer to home, within Henry's own grasp.[29]

---

[26] Carley, 'Leland in Paris', pp. 40, 49.

[27] Chandler, *Leland's Itinerary*, p. 10.

[28] Chandler, *Leland's Itinerary*, p. 11.

[29] John Guy, 'Tudor Monarchy and Its Critiques', *Tudor Monarchy*, ed. John Guy (London, 1996), p. 83; Thomas F. Mayer, 'On the Road to 1534: the Occupation of Tournai and Henry VIII's Theory of Sovereignty', in *Tudor Political Culture*, ed. Dale Hoak (Cambridge, 1995), pp. 11–30.

To declare that by 'divers sundry old authentic histories and chronicles ... this realm of England is an empire, and so hath been accepted in the world, governed by one supreme head and king having the dignity and royal estate of the imperial crown of the same' extended the king's well-rehearsed claims for his own unchallenged authority to that of the realm. As an empire, England sheltered from the jurisdiction of others, a 'body politic ... divided in terms and by names spirituality and temporality' that owed 'natural and humble obedience' to Henry next unto God. The Act in Restraint of Appeals to Rome (1533) was a declaration of jurisdictional independence from the authority of the bishop of Rome. As a practical matter it prevented an appeal by Queen Katherine against Archbishop Thomas Cranmer's divorce decree or the marriage of Anne and the king. Closing the borders to papal authority necessitated a statement about the Church in England. The Act of Supremacy formalized the king's long-standing claim to temporal and spiritual authority, recognizing Henry (and his successors) as 'the only supreme head in earth of the Church of England called *Anglicana Ecclesia*'.[30]

Leland's description of the Channel Islands included a marginal reference to the reduced size of the 'empire and wide dominion of the king of England' under the ill-fated King John. John 'Lackland' received the lordship of Ireland on the assumption that he would not inherit the Angevin dominions ahead of his brothers.[31] The Tudor *imperium* inherited and pursued similarly expansive territorial claims in Britain proper and beyond:

> [It] was intended not only to assert the independent ecclesiastical authority of the Crown but also England's overlordship of its neighbours in Wales, Ireland, and ultimately Scotland. Accordingly, it can be linked conceptually to the two Acts of Union that incorporated Wales to the English Crown between 1536 and 1543, to the Irish Parliament's declaration in 1541 that Henry VIII was 'King of Ireland', rather than merely its 'lord', and, finally, to English aggression against the Scots in the 1540s.[32]

Protector Somerset argued early in the reign of Edward VI that completing the old king's campaign to subjugate the Scots was not designed 'to create a new monarchy within Britain, but to restore the ancient one called "Great Britain", "which is no new name, but the old name to them both"'.[33] With delicious irony, the tables would be turned on Somerset's design when James VI discontinued 'the divided names of England and Scotland'. By proclamation in 1604 James assumed the style of king of Great Britain 'including therein according to the

30 Reprinted in G.R. Elton, *The Tudor Constitution* (Cambridge, 1960), pp. 344, 355.
31 Leland, *Itinerary*, IV, p. 187, n.
32 David Armitage, *The Ideological Origins of the British Empire* (Cambridge, 2000), p. 36.
33 Armitage, *Ideological Origins*, p. 37.

trueth, the whole Island'.[34] He did so as a Scottish king come south to London rather than as an English conqueror.

No one even modestly connected to the Henrician regime could misunderstand what the language of empire constituted, certainly not Leland. He had spent the 1530s inventorying those very histories, chronicles, and other works in the monastic libraries that Henry's humanist 'think-tank' used to substantiate their king's philosophy of *imperium*.[35] Empire and *imperium* were not simply shorthand for an authoritarian conception of royal power, jurisdictional autonomy, or supremacy over the Church.[36] Crucially, the crown imperial preceded the jurisdictional 'revolution' of the 1530s. The Tudor imperial project, focussed on that crown imperial, was not as Anglocentric and insular as the formulation of the 'empire of England' suggests. The Act of Appeals recognized the plurality of jurisdictions and territories simultaneously vested in the crown imperial and attached to the kingdom.[37] This was *imperium* as classical and medieval rulers and travellers understood it, 'the unitary claims of a superior power and the acknowledgment of a plurality of peoples' who acceded to its dominion.[38] A king of England could be an emperor, but that did not simply transform the empire, whatever its extent, into England or its subjects into the English.[39]

Leland appreciated the importance of Tudor imperialism for literary activity under Henry. His publications deliberately supported the king's ambitions. The *Antiphilarchia* (c.1541) defended Henry's spiritual *imperium* and justified the break from Rome, using the evidence of an early British church illegally subjugated and spiritually corrupted by the papacy. Leland simultaneously 'classicized' the British past and Tudor territorial *imperium* in his *Genethliacon Illustrissimi Eaduerdi Principis Cambriae*, a celebration of Prince Edward's birth begun in 1537 and printed in 1543. Heavily influenced by Virgil, Leland 'crams in allusion to the Latin poet, weaving the *Genethliacon* from a web of texts drawn from both the *Ecologues* and *Aeneid*'. The topographical elements highlight the marks of both the Roman imperial past and Arthur, the archetype British emperor. The Tudor *imperium*, its permanence secured by the birth of Edward, binds the peoples of England and Wales: Snowdonia hears the nymphs paying homage to Edward at Hampton Court while Cornish miners unite in song 'in spontaneous praise

---

[34] *Stuart Royal Proclamations Volume I: Royal Proclamations of James I 1603–1625*, ed. James F. Larkin and Paul L. Hughes (Oxford, 1973), p. 96.
[35] John Guy, 'Thomas Cromwell and the Intellectual Origins of the Tudor Revolution', *Tudor Monarchy*, pp. 213–30.
[36] Armitage, *Ideological Origins*, pp. 29–34.
[37] Elton, *Tudor Constitution*, p. 346.
[38] R.R. Davies, 'The Peoples of Britain and Ireland 1100–1400 I. Identities', *Royal Historical Society Transactions* 4 (1994), pp. 11–12.
[39] Philip Schwyzer, 'Archipelagic History', in *Oxford Handbook of Holinshed's Chronicles*, ed. Paulina Kewes, Ian W. Archer, and Felicity Heal (Oxford, 2013), p. 600; J.G.A. Pocock, *The Discovery of Islands: Essays in British History* (Cambridge, 2005), pp. 52–7, 294–300, 309.

of the new prince.'[40] Finally, Leland joined the defence of Brutus, Arthur, and British origin myths in 1544 when he presented the king with *Assertio Inclytissimi Arturii Regis Britanniae.*[41]

Leland's personal background and his unique, even eccentric qualities are only a starting point. All travellers share the stage with the artefacts they left behind: their notebooks, letters, and narratives, both those published and the others hidden in family attics and remote archives. Madness robbed Leland of the opportunity to leave much more than the notebooks of his travels. The great eighteenth-century antiquarian Thomas Hearne first printed *The Itinerary of John Leland the Antiquary* in nine volumes between 1710 and 1712, with subsequent editions in 1744-45 and 1768-70. In 1715 Hearne also produced *Joannis Lelandi Antiquarii de Rebus Britannicis Collectanea*, more commonly known as the *Collectanea*, a printed edition of Leland's quarto volumes of 'material garnered from the libraries of religious houses'.[42] In the early twentieth century, George Laurence Gomme undertook a 'new and popular' edition of the *Itinerary*, driven by the same fascination with folklore and the preservation of old customs and traditions that had led him to the inception of the Victoria County History.[43] Gomme's duties as the chief administrator for the London County Council consumed so much time that Lucy Toulmin Smith assumed control of the project. Her *Itinerary of John Leland in or about the Years 1535-1543* is now the standard edition.

By at least 1539 Leland was spending most of his summers on the road. After extended journeys in Wales, Kent, and the North-West before 1540, Leland probably spent 1540 and 1541 compiling data for now-lost itineraries of East Anglia and Sussex. It seems more certain that he spent 1542 traversing the West Country, 1543 in the West Midlands, 1544 in Yorkshire and the North-East, and 1545 in and around Bristol.[44] The *Itinerary* documents more or less continuous travel over a decade and records many of those 'single, connected' journeys.[45] However, the printed editions have inevitably given Leland's journeys an unreal coherence. Like Worcestre's, Leland's *Itinerary* is a dynamic hodgepodge of experiences and remembrances. The *Collectanea* incorporates some twelve notebooks, much closer to commonplace books of jottings and memorabilia. Neither of them is a travel narrative in any traditional sense.

---

[40] Shrank, *Writing the Nation*, pp. 82-3, 86-8.

[41] Carley, 'John Leland'.

[42] Oliver Harris, '"Motheaten, Mouldye, and Rotten": The Early Custodial History and Dissemination of John Leland's Manuscript Remains', *Bodleian Library Record* 18.5 (2005), p. 460.

[43] Robert Gomme, 'Sir George Laurence Gomme', *Oxford DNB* at www.oxforddnb.com.

[44] Chandler, *Leland's Itinerary*, pp. xvii-xx, xxviii-xxxi.

[45] Chandler, *Leland's Itinerary*, p. xxviii.

There are many layers of experience to recover. There are the notes Leland made during the journeys.[46] There are also his retrospective summaries and narratives drawn from that raw data. Then there are his revisions to both his original notes and narratives. Subsequent journeys, additional reading, or further consideration of his literary projects prompted these and other changes. Finally, Leland's several notebooks spoke to one another as he assembled and wrote.[47] However vaguely or imprecisely any particular project might be in his thoughts at the time of his actual journeys, the *Itinerary* is the work of a searching intellect. All of which helps us to look into Leland's ideas and intentions in the way a 'finished' book does not.

The imperial gaze that Leland turned on England and Wales during his travels came from several sources, then. He imbibed the waters of humanist scholarship and poetry at St Paul's and in Paris. Scholars committed to the intellectual and cultural advancement of Francis I's imperial kingship surrounded Leland in Paris.[48] He learned the techniques well and joined the court of Henry VIII set to emulate the bibliophilia of Lascaris and Budé or the scholarship of men like Lemaire de Belges and Gaguin. Much links Leland's travels to those of his medieval predecessors: the similar geographic ambition, recording of close topographical detail, fascination with the marks of the past on the landscape and built environment, and an ear for a good story.[49] He certainly shared much with John Rous, the Warwickshire traveller to whose itineraries and library Leland had access, or Worcestre, whose categories of data Leland unknowingly replicated, or John Kirkstede, who set out to 'index all of the religious works in the libraries of Britain'.[50] It is hard to pin down any direct interest Leland had in Atlantic exploration comparable to that of Rastell or More or Barlow, but his imperial geography did not stop at the water's edge. It did not escape Leland's attention that the town of Kingston was paved with stone slabs brought home as ballast by merchants selling salted and dried fish from Iceland.[51] Yet none of his predecessors or contemporaries quite so deliberately sought to advance an imperial project by their travels. His life and travels mark a departure, a new encounter with Britain in an age of European voyages of exploration and empire.

---

[46] Stan Mendyk, 'Early British Chorography', *Sixteenth Century Journal* 17.4 (1986), p. 467.

[47] Leland, *Itinerary*, III, pp. 42–3, 47, 114; Leland, *Itinerary*, IV, p. 11; Leland, *Itinerary*, V, pp. 31–50, 86–93.

[48] Conceptions of French *imperium* and the reign of Francis I are usefully surveyed (and compared with those of Henry VIII and the Emperor Charles V) in Glenn Richardson, *Renaissance Monarchy: The Reigns of Henry VIII, Francis I and Charles V* (London, 2002), pp. 22–35, 100–5, 109–16, 190–4.

[49] Antonia Gransden, *Historical Writing in England II: c. 1307 to the Early Sixteenth Century* (Ithaca, 1982), pp. 455–79; Gransden, *Legends, Traditions and History in Medieval England* (London, 1992), pp. 299–300; Daniel Woolf, *The Social Circulation of the Past: English Historical Culture 1500–1730* (Oxford, 2003), pp. 24–30.

[50] Kendrick, *British Antiquity*, p. 30, n. 4.

[51] Leland, *Itinerary*, I, pp. 48, 50.

Encountering the *Anglicana Ecclesia*

To begin, journeys through the Tudor heartlands in England carried special religious and political significance. Intent to document the unique 'native' history of Henry VIII's *Anglicana Ecclesia*, Leland chronicled the Church's long history of active spirituality through its bricks and mortar, seized opportunities to denounce papal corruption, and kept watch on the transfer of foundations, buildings, and attached lordships of the religious orders to their new secular owners. Leland's two accounts of Abingdon show his religious interests at work. Leland's first account is in his part II, made as part of his journey from London to the West Country begun on or around 5 May 1542. The second is in part X, which survives only in the form of John Stow's transcription of a lost original. The parts may record the same journey – there is a superficial similarity in the destinations – or it may document two separate journeys to the West during the second of which Leland retraced his steps. The account in II offers first-hand observation by Leland, while X reads more like the local information or hearsay that he later picked up.

According to II, the abbey was first located at Bagley Wood in Berkshire. Not prospering there, it moved at the instigation of a holy hermit (and kin to King Cissa) who lived in the woods and marshes some miles down river at Abingdon.[52] In X Leland corrects the locals who 'imagine right folishely' that a holy hermit, named Aben, contrived all this. Rather, the original abbey was located at Chilswell, north-north-east on the way to Oxford. A Saxon named Eanus founded it, by permission of Cissa.[53] This correction and other additions to the narrative in X may be a consequence of Leland's obtaining additional sources. At the end of his record in II, Leland wrote: 'Remembre to speke with Mr Bachelor in Abingdon, and the prior of Abingdon dwelling a mile from Abingdon, for the book *de Gestis abbatum de Abbingdune*.'[54]

The two narratives generally agree on the later history of the abbey. The royal patronage of Cissa played the crucial role in underwriting the abbey's early establishment. Soon after, a nunnery dedicated to St Helen was built. Both abbey and nunnery remained poor foundations, not least because of Danish assaults. Leland could not determine if the nunnery was ever subsequently rebuilt, but the abbey's fortunes turned when Abbot Æthelwold became bishop of Winchester. At his counsel, King Edgar 'dyd richely encrese it', including a diversion from the river Isis to 'serve and purge thoffices of thabbay'. Æthelwold's buildings were 'taken doune and new made by Norman abbates in the first Norman kinges tymes', including, as Leland added in X, Fabritius. He removed the old church

---

[52] Leland, *Itinerary*, I, p. 121.
[53] Leland, *Itinerary*, V, p. 75.
[54] Leland, *Itinerary*, I, p. 122; also Leland, *Itinerary*, V, p. 75.

that once stood in the orchard. Another abbot may actually have been responsi-ble for diverting the Isis to meet the abbey's water needs.[55]

Many surrounding villages once had only 'chapels of ease, and Abingdon Abbay was their mother chirch'. As the population grew, so additional buildings met their spiritual needs. Outside the west-end gate, one Abbot Nicolas built and lent his name to the chief parish church. A hospital staffed by twelve men was annexed to it. The church of St John also included a hospital and six almoners, apparently thanks to royal largess.[56] Edward the Martyr's 'reliques for the moste parte were kept in Abingdon, where sum sayethe he was in his tendre age brought up', while for some time after the Conquest the king's hawks and hounds were kept at nearby Culham. The town's most frequented parish church was St Helen's, built on the former site of the nunnery with an attached hospital staffed by six men and six women. Leland learned during his 1542 journey that there 'wer straunge thinges and tumbes found yn digging' around St Helen's during Æthelwold's time. Leland learned later that at 'such tyme as the olde course of the streme of Isis was changyd there were found dyvers straunge thyngs, and among them a crosse with an inscription'.[57]

Of the town proper, Leland reported that there 'is now an olde barne where the castelet or fortresse stoode' and the 'place of the common people is yet caullid the Castelle of the Rhae'. Abingdon itself 'stondith by clothing' and a fair market house with pillars and a lead roof protected the 'quik' business transacted there. Conflicts between the abbey and the surrounding townspeople attracted his interest. Leland reported that the abbey was 'spoyled' after a plea for a franchise provoked the men of Abingdon, Newbury, and Oxford, 'for the whiche great punishment was taken'. That most of the lands between Eynsham and Dorchester belonged to Abingdon and the abbey rents were once nearly £2000 per annum might explain something of the friction. The students at Oxford gave a new twist to the usual town–gown troubles when their zealous hunting ruined Radeley Park, belonging to the town.[58] Leland's additions in X included grim reference to the 'dyvers mischauncis' and drownings at the Isis ferry crossing. Recurrent tragedies finally drove the townspeople to petition for a bridge. Their successful plea diverted the traditional Gloucester–London traffic from Wallingford. According to local reports, Geffray Barbar gave money toward the bridge's construction and worked to obtain lands to support its main-tenance. It was also said that Barbar founded St Helen's hospital, while two childless daughters moved one 'Joannes de S. Helena' to pledge his lands to the hospital and bridge. Finally, Leland recorded two camps that reportedly played a role in battles between Saxons and Danes, the first at Serpenhil and the other at

[55] Leland, *Itinerary*, I, pp. 121–2; Leland, *Itinerary*, V, pp. 75–6.
[56] Leland, *Itinerary*, I, p. 122; Leland, *Itinerary*, V, p. 77.
[57] Leland, *Itinerary*, V, pp. 76–7.
[58] Leland, *Itinerary*, V, pp. 76–7.

Barow. A contingent of Saxons sent by the abbot apparently helped to vanquish the Danes, to the financial benefit of the abbey.[59]

The Abingdon accounts nicely capture how Leland recorded and interwove the temporal and spiritual features of the Tudor localities and dominions throughout the *Itinerary*. Leland's journey to the West in 1542 included a visit to the abbey church of Dorchester. 'Syns the suppression', Leland wrote, an unidentified 'great riche man, dwelling in the toun of Dorchestre, bought the este part of the church for 140. poundes, and gave it to augment the paroch church.'[60] When Leland reached the small village of Bossinny in Cornwall, he reported the vain efforts of a friar to have a proper fishing haven built.[61] On his return journey, Leland found in Winchester a 'hospitale for poore folkes a very litle without the Kinges Gate maynteinid by the monkes of St. Swithunes now supressid'. Leland recorded, on a now-damaged portion of the same manuscript, a curious episode in which Bishop Richard Fox (deceased 1528) apparently ordered the suppression of a parish church in Winchester and challenged the community to find a living for the incumbent.[62]

During Leland's journey to the West Midlands he encountered the tomb of a Brackley vicar 'buried quike by the tyranny of a lord of the towne for a displeasure' over a horse taken as mortuary payment. However, the locals reported that the lord afterward sought absolution in Rome and undertook great repentance.[63] In Coventry, Leland visited the abbey church, where there had once been a nunnery under the patronage of Cnut. In the days of Edward the Confessor, Leofric Earl of Mercia and his legendary wife Godgifu (Lady Godiva) – unnoted by Leland – converted it to a monastery and 'adornid it with gold and sylvar incredibly'. Leland reported 'It is now suppressyd.' In a kind of epilogue to this, Leland's return from Coventry took him by way of Southeham, a 'meane market towne of one streate' once within the lordship of the prior of Coventry, but since the suppression in the hands of one Knightley through exchange with Henry VIII himself.[64]

At Old Hampton (Hampshire) in 1542 Leland learned the story of the 'poore and smaul' chapel of St Nicolas and the 'great chirch of our Lady', St Mary's: 'one Matilde, Queene of England, askid what it ment that a great numbre of people walkyd about the chirch of S. Nicolas, and one answeryd: it is for lak of rome in the chirche. Then she *ex vota* promisid to make ther a new: and this was the originale of S. Marie Chirch.' The people's devotion to the Empress Maud's

[59] Leland, *Itinerary*, V, p. 78.
[60] Leland, *Itinerary*, I, p. 117.
[61] Leland, *Itinerary*, I, p. 177.
[62] Leland, *Itinerary*, I, p. 271.
[63] Leland, *Itinerary*, II, p. 37.
[64] Leland, *Itinerary*, II, pp. 107, 109.

patronage could be found to that day, not least by their fealty to the old church and the massive number of burials in and outwith the church itself.[65]

The work of Bishop John Veysey of Exeter – 'one of Henry's favourites' and 'an unreconstructed ... establishment conservative' – came in for extended treatment by Leland during his trip to the West Midlands.[66] Veysey hailed from Sutton Coldfield, a decayed town he determined to renew. According to Leland, Veysey obtained permission from the king to revive the market and 'deforest the chace' (where he built 'dyvars praty howsys of stone ... and planted his pore kynsemen in them'), repaired and built new houses generally, and instituted 'a gramer-schole and endewyd it with lands' at the former house or lodge of the Earl of Warwick; Veysey also built for himself 'a praty pile of brike, where he sometyme lyethe', known as More-Hall.[67] Leland recounted the pious works of Bishop William Smith, elevated to the sees of Coventry and Lincoln thanks to Margaret Beaufort's influence with Henry VII.[68] At St John's in Lichfield, Smith began a new foundation, setting up a master with two priests, ten poor men in a hospital, a schoolmaster and usher to teach grammar. But it was Henry VII who played a vital role as a 'great forderar' by endowing St John's with lands and impropriations of both an old hospital and a church in Wirral (Cheshire).[69]

Leland assembled the record of the *Anglicana Ecclesia* in these vignettes. Its spiritual meaning was recorded in the piety and patronage of the living and the dead – from schoolmasters, hospitalers, nuns, and the commons to monarchs, nobles, gentry, and clerics. Leland found exemplary virtues on either side of the religious revolution of the 1530s, yet his praise most often focussed on those who chose spirituality or pious action over private gain. Why? Even if Leland never completed his civil history or chronicle of Britain's rulers, this information was not merely the work of a topographical writer who recorded church buildings alongside castles and city walls or an obsessive 'antiquarian' madly scribbling epitaphs and tomb markings. For a scholar whose formative years were spent in the company of Parisian humanists devoted to adorning Francis I's *imperium*, the past served both descriptive and prescriptive purposes, whether that past was found in classical sources, written in medieval chronicles, or inscribed on the landscape itself. Leland described a Church under the authority not of the papacy or a 'bishop of Rome' but of an imperial crown. Leland made its fate inseparable from the moral virtues of kings, queens, nobles, and gentry, instead of the papacy.

The actions of the Empress Maud, bishops Veysey and Smith, and Henry VII all testify to a royal supremacy in deed if not in fact. This past could school

---

[65] Leland, *Itinerary*, I, p. 276.

[66] Eamon Duffy, *The Voices of Morebath: Reformation and Rebellion in an English Village* (New Haven, 2001), pp. 87, 95.

[67] Leland, *Itinerary*, II, p. 98.

[68] Margaret Bowker, 'William Smith', *Oxford DNB* at www.oxforddnb.com.

[69] Leland, *Itinerary*, II, p. 100.

Henry VIII in how to govern the Church with devotion and piety as its supreme head, how to act as – in the words of Britain's first genuine imperial king, James VI and I – 'a louing nourishing father to the Church'.[70] There could have been no more apt guide than Reading and Henry's own father. The town provided Leland with a rich tapestry of religious life, but what most interested him was the almshouse of poor sisters near St Laurence parish church. Abbott Thorne of Reading abbey suppressed the house during Henry VII's reign and gave the lands to the private use of the abbey's almoner. During the king's visit to Reading, Thorne answered Henry's curiosity about the house's current use. According to Leland, 'the king wyllid hym to convert the house [it]self and the landes *in pios usus*', to the cause of piety. Chastened, the abbot proposed turning it into a grammar school. The king agreed and 'one Wulliam Dene, a riche man and servant in thabbay of Reading, gave 200. markes in mony toward the avauncement of this schole' – as Leland learned from the epitaph on Dene's tomb in the abbey church.[71]

This episode, like dozens more recorded by Leland, offered cautionary, even critical, instruction. The impiety in this story and others came from acts of religious suppression, the abuse of authority for private gain, or both, charges against the Henrician regime all too easily levelled and substantiated. Nor do the examples of temporal abuse fit the stereotypical outlines of Tudor anti-clericalism or the lurid tales of Cromwell's investigators. Devoted, virtuous men and women religious animated the Church as readily as they moved into Leland's notebooks. Leland anticipated the later Protestant drive to purge 'Christianity in its primitive purity' of 'monastic fabrications'.[72] However, the later fixation on Protestantism and national identity is elusive if not invisible in Leland's descriptions. The generation that followed Leland, baptized in confessional rivalries and bloodshed, would be the ones to link a certain kind of confessional orthodoxy with an ancient British Church, national identity, and destiny.[73]

Not all, however. Tristram Risdon, one of Leland's readers, wrote about the religious houses in Devon between 1603 and the 1630s. He instructed fellow travellers: 'Now, for that ye shall meet with many Monasteries in the Itinerary of this County, Arguments of ancient Piety; therefore know the Manner of the Ceremonies used at the first Foundation of such Religious Houses.'[74] Leland's were discoveries and lessons fit for the complexities of the Henrician revolution

---

[70] James VI and I, *Political Writings*, ed. Johann P. Sommerville (Cambridge, 1994), p. 27 (from *Basilicon Doron*).

[71] Leland, *Itinerary*, I, p. 110.

[72] Alexandra Walsham, *The Reformation of the Landscape: Religion, Identity, and Memory in Early Modern Britain and Ireland* (Oxford, 2011), pp. 488–9.

[73] Colin Kidd, *British Identities Before Nationalism: Ethnicity and Nationhood in the Atlantic World 1600–1800* (Cambridge, 1999), pp. 99–115.

[74] Tristram Risdon, *The Chorographical Description, or, Survey of the County of Devon* (two volumes; London, 1714), II, pp. 37, 154.

and *imperium*: a king who governed the Church, policed the private gains of clerics, and nourished a form of piety appropriate to ambitious humanists if not godly reformers.

Cultural complexity in the North

Leland knew the past from the present, but both were equally alive to him in his journeys of discovery. If Christianity and the Tudor dynasty left their mark on England and Wales in Leland's notebooks, so too did the migration, invasion, and settlement of peoples from across the seas and within Britain itself. Leland discovered their remains woven into the fabric of history, the genealogies of the ruling elites, and the physical landscape. And, he found the evidence throughout his journeys: multicultural Britain did not simply appear in Leland's gaze or notebooks when he rubbed up against the 'usual' borders of regional or 'national' difference. The cultural complexity of Britain's people could be discovered almost anywhere.

When Caesar praised the particular 'humanite of the Kentisch men' and stated that the county was 'the key to al Englande', Leland took note.[75] He observed that the 'northern men in one of the iii firste Kinge Edwardes dayes dyd ille [rase]' the town of Stamford (Lincolnshire) and 'brennid [burned] many writinges of their [the town's] antiquites and privileges'.[76] Leland gave an account of the battle near Market Drayton between the forces of Edward IV and Henry VI: 'The Erle of Saresbyri and northern men on King Edwardes parte overcam the Lordes Audeley (slain) and Dudeley (woundid) with Quene Margaret, wife to Henry the 6, and Chestershir men lost the feld.'[77] Allegiance to a rival king was just one mark that distinguished these men. Being 'northern men' or 'Chestershir men' was also noteworthy. When Leland visited the West Midlands, the Liverpool of his time, to which 'Irisch marchauntes cum much thither', was quickly becoming the 'good haven' which would see it come alive in the Victorian Age, when Fenianism and Orange lodges called to seamstresses and cleaners, dockyard labourers, forcibly removed paupers, and onward migrants. Leland put down Liverpool's attractiveness as a port to its low customs duties, resulting in 'Good marchandis ... and moch Yrisch yarn that Manchester men do b[u]y ther.' In one of his more interesting natural history vignettes, Leland described the reedy chat moss which choked the ground and fresh-water fish about Morely Hall before spreading to Glazebrook and then, via Mersey Water, to the shores of Wales, the Isle of Man, and Ireland.[78] Not only did cultural complexity define Britain's past

---

[75] Leland, *Itinerary*, IV, p. 57.
[76] Leland, *Itinerary*, IV, p. 89.
[77] Leland, *Itinerary*, V, p. 12.
[78] Leland, *Itinerary*, V, pp. 40–3; Roger Swift, ed., *Irish Migrants in Britain, 1815–1914* (Cork, 2002).

and present, but its natural history and 'frutefulnes' transcended stereotypical boundaries among or between its peoples.

Leland promised Henry VIII a Tudor *Domesday Book*. He anticipated precisely the advice given to travellers going abroad to collect useful information of all kinds about foreign lands. Henry needed that useful information to govern this multicultural Tudor *imperium* and Leland's notebooks show how he grappled with cultural complexity in trying to obtain it. We can put ourselves in Leland's shoes as he encountered Britain's unique cultural zones by starting with his two journeys to the North, one pre-1540 and the other in 1544.[79]

Leland began his 1544 journey in Cambridge. He travelled to the ruined nunnery of Eltisley through the open-field champaign country of nucleated farming villages that first transformed Britain's rural landscape in the ninth century.[80] In the south choir at Eltisley he found the well devoted to Pandonia, the Scottish virgin buried within. From Fotheringhay, Leland backtracked to the south-west and called in at Northampton. He noted the Queen's Cross that marked the battle during Henry VI's reign at which many Welsh drowned in the Avon. Further west, at Weedon, Leland found the abandoned monastery of St Werburge, mentioned by Bede and destroyed by the Danes. From the vicar, Leland learned that the lordship of Weedon once belonged 'to Behkarwick, a monastrie yn Normandie' and after the 'priores alienes of the French ordre did lese their possessions yn England' Henry VI gave its lordship to Eton. Returning north, the lordship of Noseley, near Staunton, gave Leland pause to note its passage to the Hasilrig family, a name 'cam oute of Scotlande'.[81] The name may be familiar, for William Heselrig, the sheriff of Lanark reputedly killed by William Wallace for the murder of Wallace's beloved wife, as recorded in the English indictment and repeated by legend makers from Walter Bower in his *Scotichronicon* to the preposterous *Braveheart*.[82]

For Leland, the cultural complexity of Britain was built into the physical fabric of Lincoln. The city's topography was defined by the ethnic diversity of its builders:

> The first building was yn the very toppe of the hille, the oldest part wherof inhabited in the Britans tyme, was the northerest part of the hille, directly withoute Newport gate, the diches wherof yet remayne and great tokens of the old towne waulles buildid with stone taken oute of the [the] diche by it ... Sum say that this old Lincolen was destroyed

[79] Though William Burton penned 1538 at the head of Leland's manuscript, Chandler has dated this itinerary to 1544. On the medieval and early modern North, see Bruce M.S. Campbell, 'North–South Dichotomies, 1066-1550', in *Geographies of England; The North-South Divide, Material and Imagined*, ed. Alan R.H. Baker and Mark Billinge (Cambridge, 2004), pp. 145-74.
[80] Francis Pryor, *The Making of the British Landscape: How We Have Transformed the Land from Prehistory to Today* (London, 2010), pp. 251-8.
[81] Leland, *Itinerary*, I, pp. 8, 10, 14.
[82] Graeme Morton, *William Wallace: Man and Myth* (Stroud, 2004), pp. 23, 57-8, 64.

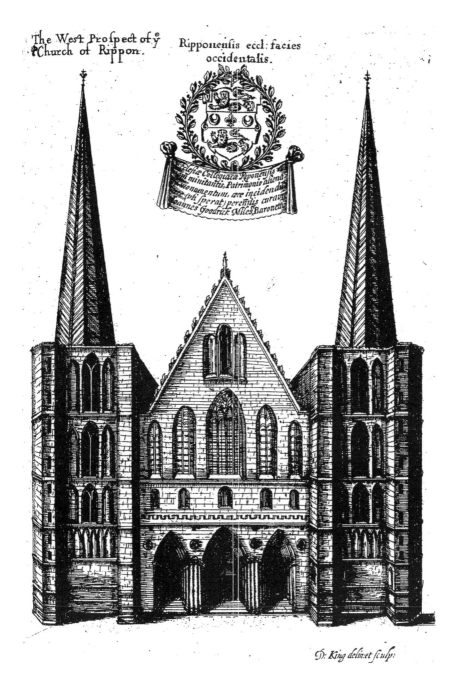

The West Prospect of y^e Church of Rippon.

Ripponensis eccl: facies occidentalis.

Ecclesia Collegiata Ripponensis
... ministris, Patrimonio aliena ...
... onumentum, ære incidendii ...
... (uti sperat) perennis curav ...
... oannes Goodrick Miles Baronett ...

D: King delin:et sculp:

3   Ripon Abbey from William Dugdale, *Monastici Anglicani* (London, 1862). RB 434114 Huntington Library, San Marino, CA, reproduced by permission. Image produced by ProQuest as part of *Early English Books Online*. www.proquest.com

by King Stephan, but I thinke rather by the Danes. Much Romanie [Roman] mony is found yn the northe [fieldes] beyond this old Lincoln. After the destruction of this old Lincoln men began to fortifie the souther parte of the hille, new diching, waulling and gating it, and so was new Lincoln made out of a pece of the old Lincoln by the Saxons.[83]

Lincoln's third period featured the building around Wikerford, 'for commoditie of water: and this parte is enwallid wher it is not defendid with the ryver and marisch ground'. Even here the interplay of peoples interested Leland. The south end of the new castle protecting Wikerford featured the inset image of the rich merchant Ranulphus de Kyme. Kyme's body lay in the chapel of the Whitefriars, whose foundation in Lincoln was the work of one 'Gaulterus, as I hard, caullid Dorotheus, Dene of Lincoln, a Scottish man'.[84]

A later excursion from York included a tour of the great port of Kingston, built on selling into England the fish caught in the waters of Iceland. The light-weight dried and salted stock fish required ships to take on additional ballast for the homeward journey and the 'great coble stone brought of Iseland' in the ships' holds 'pavid al the toun of Kingeston'.[85] Returning from Scarborough, Leland viewed the tombs of three Bruces in Pickering church and found Scottish footprints again at Myton village outside Tollerton, 'wherby the Scottes had victory of the Englisch host in Edward the 2. tyme'.[86] Durham offered evidence of the other great Normano-Scottish contender in the Scottish civil wars, the Balliols. Two notable marble tombs with French inscriptions in the chapel of Barnard Castle may have been Balliol tombs, but the lady chapel by Piercebridge was without doubt 'the fundation of John Bail[liol] King of [Sco]ttes.'[87]

The marks of another long-running dynastic conflict, the Anglo-Norse-Norman struggle for control of England, were found in old Ripon abbey.[88] Beyond the wall of the lady chapel and the three crosses standing at the east end of the chapel garth, Leland found 'no likely tokens left after the depopulation of the Danes in that place'. The 'commune opinion' was that only the pity of Archbishop Oda, 'cumming ynto the north partes' during the destructive campaign of King Eadred – whose name in the manuscript remains to be filled in by Leland – 'caussid a new work to be edified wher the minstre now is'.[89] The abbot of Fountains pulled down the east end of Oda's construction, 'a pece of exceeding ancient wark, and buildid a fair pece of new werk with squaird stones

[83] Leland, *Itinerary*, I, pp. 30–1.
[84] Leland, *Itinerary*, I, p. 31.
[85] Leland, *Itinerary*, I, pp. 48, 50.
[86] Leland, *Itinerary*, I, pp. 61, 66.
[87] Leland, *Itinerary*, I, p. 77.
[88] Angelo Forte, Richard Oram, and Frederik Pederson, *Viking Empires* (Cambridge 2005), pp. 170–216.
[89] Leland, *Itinerary*, I, p. 81; Catherine Cubit and Marios Costambeys, 'Oda', *Oxford DNB* at www.oxforddnb.com.

for it'.[90] The area around the stone bridge over the Ure at Boroughbridge and Aldborough offered antiquities of these contenders' Roman imperial predecessors, standing stones, sepulchres, and coins aplenty.[91] Leland's return journey to London in 1544 continued to offer much of the same: the entrance to the dungeon in Nottingham castle 'wher Davy Kinge of Scottes, as the castellanes say, was kept as a prisoner'; Belvoir castle, a product of the conquest, supposed Leland, first held by one Toterneius and later Albeney and Ros; and the sordid intrigues by which Lord Gray acquired Ampthill and the lands of Lord Fannope after bringing his Welsh bands to Edward IV's side at the battle of Northampton.[92]

Leland crossed the Thames at Staines and closed his notebook at Hampton Court. The pre-1540 journey supplies many more details about the peoples and places found during these northern travels.[93] They introduced Leland to topographies where Britons interacted with one another over the centuries, leaving their marks on the land while being shaped by it and their neighbours. No one achieved cultural mastery in the Anglo-Scottish Borders, places where cultures coexisted, competed, and blended for all travellers.[94] In Leland's time tension – diplomatic and dynastic, military, cultural, and religious – marked Henry VIII's relationship with his Renaissance rivals James IV and James V. It is hardly surprising that competition and conflict punctuate Leland's account of his journey to Cumberland and Northumberland. Yet Leland was attuned to the Borders as a more complex space of interaction that could not be reduced simply to the perennial conflict between Scotland and England.

Leland found a ruined land when he reached Carlisle. At Liddel Strength, Leland noted the moated keep of Walter Seleby. Seleby was killed and his keep destroyed by David II during the king's ill-fated march south to Durham and defeat at Neville's Cross in 1346. Burgh by Sands was notable for the 'ruines of a greate place, now clene desolated'. It was there that Edward I was buried before he could engage the Scots one last time and Robert Maxwell was 'sore wounded' during a major Scottish raid in 1524 that was accompanied by many slayings and drownings in the Eden. Maxwell could count himself lucky in 1542, surviving the disastrous Battle of Solway Moss and the subsequent death of James V to become one of Henry VIII's biddable men at the Scottish court.[95] At Netherby, astride the Eske north of Carlisle, there were once 'mervelus buyldinges, as appeare by ruinus walles ... and stayes or holdes for shyppes', stretching some

[90] Leland, *Itinerary*, I, p. 80.
[91] Leland, *Itinerary*, I, p. 85.
[92] Leland, *Itinerary*, I, pp. 96–7, 103.
[93] Leland, *Itinerary*, V, p. 1.
[94] William M. Aird, 'Northumbria and the Making of the Kingdom of the English', in *Nations in Medieval Britain*, ed. Hirokazu Tsurushima (Donington, 2010), pp. 45–70.
[95] C.A. McGladdery, 'Robert Maxwell', *Oxford DNB* at www.oxforddnb.com.

three miles along the 'Batable ground; so that it is as a limes [boundary] *Angliae et Scotiae*'.[96]

Earlier struggles, too, scarred this land. At Bowness, Leland found remains of the 'Pict wal' and reported that the stones further along the Roman wall were pulled down to build Drumburgh Castle. Conflict was not the whole story, though. According to Leland's rather tortured explanation, the city of Carlisle, derived from Lugulbalia, or 'Luele towne', because the 'Irisch men cawle [call a] bale a town, and so peradventure did the old Scottes'. And Carlisle's fields were more fertile than most in producing the remains of antiquity, including 'diverse cornelines and other stonys', seals, and 'brickes conteyninge the prints of antique workes'.[97]

Northumberland offered an equally complex history of encounter and inter-action. Leland initially seems to have relied upon the vicar of Corbridge, a life of St Oswin the martyr, perhaps the 'Antonine Itinerary', and Doctor Robert Davell (archdeacon of Northumberland).[98] Not surprisingly, Davell's ancestors earned extended coverage. They hailed from Normandy, specifically the lands around Alençon, and remained a great family until Loson and Hugh Davell found themselves on the wrong side of attainder for opposing Edward II and Piers Gaveston. The surviving four or five brethren held on to mean lands, while the Turwits took possession of prime properties in England and much of the family's Gascon lands.[99] Doctor Davell also supplemented Leland's informa-tion about the Roman wall in Northumberland, reporting that the church of St Nicholas in Newcastle was built atop remains of the 'Picth waulle'.[100]

Leland's ear for a good story served him well in tracing the foundation of Newcastle's city walls. In the reign of Edward I, the Scots made the mistake of openly abducting one of Newcastle's wealthiest citizens. Finally ransomed for a hefty sum, the shaken man returned home and 'began to make a waulle on the ripe of Tyne ryver from Sandehille to Pandon gate and beyond that to the towre agayne the Augustine Freres'. The rest of the town's merchants 'seying the towardnes of one man, sette to their helping handes' to protect themselves. By the reign of Edward III the 'strength and magnificens of the waulling of this towne far passith al the waulles of the cities of England and most of the townes of Europa'.[101] Leland picked up another good story in the doubtful honour of one of the 'Grays of Northumberland, a man of great brute in the tyme of Edwarde the 4'. Accused by a Scot of adultery with the Queen of Scotland, Gray 'cam with a band, as it is saide, of a 1000. men to Edingborow, and there caste down his

---

[96] Leland, *Itinerary*, V, pp. 50–3.
[97] Leland, *Itinerary*, V, pp. 50–3 (my insertion).
[98] Leland, *Itinerary*, V, pp. 56–7.
[99] Leland, *Itinerary*, V, pp. 58–9.
[100] Leland, *Itinerary*, V, pp. 60–1.
[101] Leland, *Itinerary*, V, pp. 59–60.

glove to fight in the lists with his accuser: but he departed withowte fighteing; yet was it supposid, that Gray was not accusid therof withoute a cawse'.[102]

Leland took pains to describe, sometimes in minute detail, the peoples and places immediately astride this altogether permeable border. The three parish churches of Riddesdale (Ellesdene, Holystone, Corsenside) along the 'Scottyshe marche' served 'the witriding [outriding] men othar wyse theues of that Englishe marche' who found themselves in need of spiritual sustenance – or cleansing reminiscent of the 3000 people reputedly 'christenyd in one day in primitiva ecclesia Sax' at Holystone.[103] Violence marked the Borders:

> Twede risythe in Twydedale in Scotland at a towne (as I here say) cawllyd Pybbell, and so comithe thrwghe the forest of Eterik in Scotland, and so thorwghe Tyndedale in Scotland, the people where of robbe sore and continually in Glyndale and Bamborowshire; and at a litle broke, cawlyd Ryden burne, the whiche partithe England and Scotland by este and west, and comithe into Twede, the great streame of Twede towchithe on the Englyshe grownde as a limes [boundary] betwene Scotland and it.[104]

Leland's account of the North does not capture the ancient peoples that battled for its possession and his inability to follow them into the heart of Strathclyde or 'Alt Clud' – the kingdom of the Rock as Norman Davies recently termed it – creates a false geographic break.[105] Yet his contemporaries who imagined Cumbria and Northumberland to be strange, undiscovered countries would have learned about the southern extension of one of Britain's great spaces of encounter and interaction.

Encounters with civility, barbarity, and otherness

When Leland left behind Shropshire for Wales, he entered the land of a people regarded as distinctly different. He knew Wales from the works of medieval Britain's most famous traveller and ethnographer, Gerald of Wales.[106] Leland's journeys through monastic libraries and compulsive reading introduced him to Gerald's ethnography. Ranulf Higden found them the same way for his fourteenth-century *Polychronicon*.[107] Along with Rous and Worcestre, Leland's journeys occurred in the intellectual footsteps of ethnographic writers like Gerald and Higden. His Welsh travels probably date from 1536–39 and only the

---

[102] Leland, *Itinerary*, V, p. 58.

[103] Leland, *Itinerary*, V, p. 62 (my insertion from Toulmin-Smith's explanatory notes).

[104] Leland, *Itinerary*, V, p. 67.

[105] Norman Davies, *Vanished Kingdoms: The Rise and Fall of States and Nations* (New York, 2012), pp. 35–80.

[106] Caroline Brett, 'John Leland, Wales, and Early British History', *Welsh Historical Review* 15 (1990–91), p. 178.

[107] Shrank, *Writing the Nation*, p. 85.

northern coastal fortresses, Anglesey, and Caernarvonshire seem to have escaped his wanderings.[108]

Leland took an interest in Welsh and etymology, but he struggled. Glamorgan required one of his frequent linguistic engagements:

> Glade is in the Walsch a countery or a land. And this province or cuntery is often caullid Morganhog. I take Moregan to have the name of More, that is to say the se[a], onto the shore wherof it lyith. The kefinnithes (confinia) of Glamorgan ly thus. Remny is the marche on the est side of it. Cremline a litle broke is the march of the west part of it. The Severne Se[a] boundith it from the mouth of Remny to the mouth of Cremlin. The rootes of the Blake Mountein marchith it by the northe.[109]

Toulmin Smith took Leland to task for his speculations. Morgan had nothing to do with the sea, but with the proper name.[110] The Morgan in question is generally taken to be Morgan ab Athrwys. In the eighth century he ruled Glywysing, which took in present-day Glamorganshire.[111]

The choice of 'march' and 'marchith' as a noun for boundary and as the verb for the act of drawing a boundary certainly suggests a heightened sense of Wales as a place of 'otherness'. The presence of the march shaped his treatment of Wales as he attempted to make sense of the jurisdictional muddle in Flintshire and Denbighshire:

> Al this Englisch Maylor [of Broughton] tho [it ly] not hard on Flyntshire, but h[ath Walshe] Mailor betwixte it and [Flynt,] yet it longith to Flynte[shire, and they] cum to sessions to Flynte. Yet they have liberte in t[oken of] the olde castle to kepe a p[risoner] 3. Dayes at Oureton, and so to [send hym to Flynt]. Walch Maylor caullid yn Englisch Bromefeld lying on the north side of De ... It lyith est apon Holt Bridge, the which devidith Chestershire from Bromefelde. Flintshir lyith north on it. Diffrin Cluit [Dyffryn Klwyd] lyith west on it. And Englisch Mailor, alias Mailor Sesneg, *id est Saxonica*, lyith south on it.[112]

Leland needed his linguistic sensitivity in the first years of the 1536 Act of Union. It aimed to root out the 'discrepant' laws, customs, and language (including both written and oral traditions) by making English the language of government, but had not done so.[113] The complexity of Welsh dialects and the language itself persisted for decades as a practical matter in the Court of Great Session and among justices of the peace and courts of Quarter Session, before

---

[108] Leland, *Itinerary*, III, pp. v–xi.

[109] Leland, *Itinerary*, III, p. 15. Cyffin would be the ordinary word for boundary in Welsh.

[110] Leland, *Itinerary*, III, p. 15, n.

[111] Hywel Wyn Owen and Richard Morgan, *Dictionary of the Place-Names of Wales* (Llandysul, 2008), p. 166.

[112] Leland, *Itinerary*, III, p. 69.

[113] Richard Suggett and Eryn White, 'Language, Literacy, and Aspects of Identity in Early Modern Wales', in *The Spoken Word: Oral Culture in Britain, 1500–1800*, ed. Adam Fox and Daniel Woolf (Manchester, 2002), pp. 62–3.

English triumphed.[114] Its long-term survival received an immeasurable boost when Welsh became the active medium in the contest for souls between Protestants and Catholics from the 1560s.[115] Unlike its Celtic cousins in Cornwall, the Gaedhealtacht, or the Isle of Man, Welsh in its many dialects competed and coexisted with English right through the Tudor and Stuart centuries into our own.[116] We might wonder why Leland worked so hard at Welsh, a language seemingly destined for destruction, if he was a little Englander who erased cultural distinctions for a homogenous Englishness.

Beyond differences written through the boundaries, the ethno-cultural mosaic of medieval Britain marked the land. So did the heavy print of Angevin imperialism. Leland wrote that the 'olde castel of Swineseye was builded or [re] pairid by the Normans and destroied by Lluelen prince of Wales that mayred King Johns dowghter. And it stoode by the bisshop of St. Dauids castle that now is there. A iii miles from Swinesey, communely cawillid in englisch Swansey ... there remained ruines of a castel destroied by prince Lluelin.'[117] Leland kept pace with Gerald and he extended the story beyond the twelfth century.

The Laceys received land around Denbigh from Edward I, once the king 'had extinctid the Prince of Wales, and had holely al Wales in his possession'. Longshanks 'much studied to the fortification especially of north Wales, and the marches of it' and Lacey was the person for the job. 'Lacy was a great lord marcher afore' and Leland had 'hard say that it was partely in consideration that he maried in the bloode of the Prince of North Wales' that he received Edward's trust.[118] A significant number of the medieval Normano-Scottish or Anglo-Scottish border nobility featured analogous mixing of bloodlines. However, extinction in the wars of independence, the need to 'choose sides' as the Anglo-Scottish boundary hardened, and the animosities of the Tudor–Stewart relationship seemingly pushed them into the background of Leland's treatment of the North.[119]

Like Gerald, Leland recounted Welsh conflicts that transcended a simplistic Anglo-Welsh opposition. Indeed, his account of 'Justine lord of Glamorganshir' – Iestyn ap Gwrgant – suggests that a homogenous Wales was no more a reality to him than a simple conflation of Britain with England. For Iestyn's great trouble was with 'Theodore Prince of Wales' - really Rhys ap Tewder, dominant

[114] Richard Suggett, 'The Welsh Language and the Court of Great Sessions', in *The Welsh Language before the Industrial Revolution*, ed. Geraint H. Jenkins (Cardiff, 1997), pp. 154–71; J. Gwynfor Jones, 'The Welsh Language in Local Government: Justices of the Peace and the Courts of Quarter Sessions c. 1536–1660', in *Welsh Language*, pp. 181–206.
[115] Glanmor Williams, 'Unity of Religion or Unity of Language? Protestants and Catholics and the Welsh Language 1536–1660', in *Welsh Language*, pp. 207–33.
[116] Brynley F. Roberts, 'The Celtic Languages of Britain', in *Welsh Language*, pp. 407–40.
[117] Leland, *Itinerary*, III, p. 127.
[118] Leland, *Itinerary*, III, p. 96.
[119] A.D.M. Barrell, *Medieval Scotland* (Cambridge, 2000), pp. 12–41, 92–136.

in southern Wales – during the years after the Conqueror was succeeded by his son William Rufus:

> Justine desired help of one Inon a Walsch man borderer onto hym, promising to hym his doughtter with greate landes. Inon got help of Haymo Erle of Glocestre, and had 12. or 13. knightes of his, and bette the Prince of Wales. Justine kept no promise with Inon. Wherefore Inon and the xii kinghtes drave Justine away and occupied his landes.[120]

Out of this 'dynastic' squabble, Einon 'had al the Walscherie for his parte, as up into the mountaines by north in Glamorganshire'.[121] The twelve knights became the storied figures who 'wan Glamorgane Cuntrey' and for whom were reserved places of honour in Cardiff Castle.[122] This great Welshry passed to Einon's heirs, but they divided their inheritance into pieces, with lasting consequences. The lands belonging to the knight Lounders passed to the dukes of Lancaster, those of the Flemings eventually passed to Gaspar, Duke of Bedford and Lord of Glamorgan and thence by escheat (lack of heirs) to the king himself.[123] More than once Leland remarked on the fragmentation and demise of landhold-ings, especially subdivision into petty units. Writers before and after Leland associated this sort of partible inheritance with the Welsh and Gaels – and, later, Amerindians. The practice put them beyond the bounds of the civility assumed to reside in primogeniture.[124]

Leland's journey through the marches included Montgomeryshire and Radnor, lands targeted by Owain Glyn Dŵr. Montgomeryshire was 'deflorichid' while the populace of Radnor paid a heavy price for Glyn Dŵr's purported bloodlust: 'the voice is there that after he wonne the castel he tooke a iii. score men that had the garde of the castel, and causid them to be [be]heddid on the brinke of the castel yarde, and that sins a certen bloodeworth groweith ther wher the bloode was shedde'.[125] Further south, at Hay on Wye, Leland visited the ruins of Walwyn. It once belonged to a gentleman by 'whose means Prince Lluelin was sodenli taken at Buelth Castel, and ther beheddid, and his hedde sent to the Kinge'.[126]

The journey to Hay is important for the close attention to unfamiliar detail more in evidence in Leland's Welsh notebooks than in his northern journeys. He wrote: 'When I approchid nere the Hay, and began to descend from thens I saw on the hither side of Wy a good mile from the Hay the castel of Clereho

---

[120] Leland, *Itinerary*, III, p. 38; John Davies, *A History of Wales* (Harmondsworth, 1993), pp. 105-6.

[121] Leland, *Itinerary*, III, p. 38.

[122] Leland, *Itinerary*, III, p. 34-5.

[123] Leland, *Itinerary*, III, p. 38.

[124] Leland, *Itinerary*, IV, pp. 43-4; Colin G. Calloway, *White People, Indians, and Highlanders: Tribal Peoples and Colonial Encounters in Scotland and America* (Oxford, 2008), pp. 43-87.

[125] Leland, *Itinerary*, III, p. 41.

[126] Leland, *Itinerary*, III, p. 111.

[Clyro]. After passing over Wy River, the which for lak of good knowleg yn me of the fourde did sore troble my horse, I cam *in crepusculo* [twilight] to the Hay.' The detailed account of this small border market town included its position along the Wye, the town walls with three gates, a castle 'which summtime hath bene right stately', its single 'poore paroche', and the chapel outside the walls where Leland heard mass on the Sunday.[127] The frequent descriptions like this signal his almost instinctive unfamiliarity with Welsh topography – topography that was nonetheless hardly unique in Britain. The contrast with Aberystwyth, for instance, is suggestive. In Leland's account, Aberystwyth was simply 'a market toun ons waullid' with greater privileges and a better market than its near-neighbour Cardigan.[128] Ironically, Leland spent more time recording the 'meri tale' told by the abbot of Whiteland of a Welshman who purchased river licences around Powysland for prices that sounded in English like 'a hogge of ii yeres, and the other a hogge of iii yeres'.[129]

The unique majesty of the Brecon Beacons awed Leland. 'Artures Hille', he wrote, 'of summe is countid the hiest hille of Wales, and in a veri cleere day a manne may se from hit a part of Malvern Hilles, and Glocestre, and Bristow, and part of Devnshir and Cornwale.' South-south-east of Brecon lay Llyn Savaoan, in 'bredth a mile, and a ii. miles of length and wher as it is depest a xiii. fathom. At great windes the water doth surge ther mervelusly. Lleueny cummith thorough this lake, no great river, and after great raine is parfightly seene of redde color in middest of the lake. After that it is frosen and with thaue beginnith to breeke it makth such a noise that a man wold think hit thunder.'[130] Asked to do so, Leland might have summed up the majestic vista in the same way as he did the uplands of Glamorganshire to the south: 'To go from est to west yn the highest part of Glamorganshir [is] miles of wild ground almost all.'[131]

Wales confronted Leland as an unfamiliar land, a place apart in many respects. But there is more to Leland's experiences there – and elsewhere – in Britain. Land and people's relationships with it possessed social and cultural meanings under the gaze of travellers.[132] Decades after Leland, John Norden's county mileage tables revealed associations of difference and topography. With Yorkshire, Norden added to the repetitive instructions that accompanied each mileage table a note that he had standardized the mileages across all the counties; 'I haue also oberued by trauaile in these parts, that these Northene miles, much exceed the miles in the South and Westerne parts of the Kingdome, which may something deceiue a Stranger.' Wales presented unique topographical challenges

---

[127] Leland, *Itinerary*, III, pp. 110–11.
[128] Leland, *Itinerary*, III, pp. 56, 123.
[129] Leland, *Itinerary*, III, p. 123.
[130] Leland, *Itinerary*, III, pp. 106–7.
[131] Leland, *Itinerary*, III, p. 16.
[132] R.R. Davies, *First English Empire: Power and Identities in the British Isles 1093–1343* (Oxford, 2000), pp. 103–6, 112–23.

that one would have assumed also affected Cumberland or the Lake District, Anglia, the Thames Estuary, or the coasts of Cornwall and Devon. Only for Wales did Norden pause to explain that, 'It is to be considered that by reason of the multitude of Hilles, Mountaines and Dales, and the bending of the Sea between St. Dauids and the point neere Bradsey Iland, causing passages and highways in many places so to curue and crooke, that the distances between Townes, may be something differing from this Table.'[133]

John Rastell lamented that the inhabitants of the New World had no buildings to speak of, just wood huts and caves, and thought how good a work it would be to instruct them in God and virtuous living. Thomas More betrayed his gentry values in describing the banishment of poverty and social misery in Utopia:

> The chief and almost the only function of the syphogrants is to manage and provide that no one sit idle, but that each apply himself industriously to his trade, and yet that he be wearied not like a beast of burden with constant toil from early morning till late at night. Such wretchedness is worse than the lot of slaves, and yet is almost everywhere the life of workingmen – except for the Utopians.[134]

Indeed, More's Utopians extended the attack on idleness into outright colonization. They put surplus hands to work on empty lands among natives willing to join them or, after wars of conquest, against peoples who resisted: 'They consider it a more just cause for war when a people which does not use its soil but keeps it idle and waste nevertheless forbids the use and possession of it by others who by the rule of nature ought to be maintained by it.'[135]

Within this lay two crucial prejudices. First, the Roman maxim of *res nullius* 'maintained that all "empty things", which included unoccupied lands, remained the common property of all mankind until they were put to some, generally agricultural, use'.[136] Second, and closer to home, More's attitude associated the 'deserving poor' with a commitment to hard work that would define poor relief from the time of Elizabeth I to the job-seeker's allowance of New Labour and Ian Duncan Smith's shambolic universal benefit. Roger Barlow's Irishmen embodied the prejudice against the 'undeserving poor'. They lived by theft rather than honest labour and left their rich land fallow. Andrew Boorde's descriptions of the Gaelic Scots and borderers, composed within a year of Barlow's 'Summarie of Geographie', mimicked these characterizations, and his view of Welsh industriousness was none too positive. These meanings were, then, the product of study, prejudice, and experience and Leland was not free of them.

---

[133] Tables for Yorkshire and Wales respectively in John Norden, *An Intended Guyde, for English Travailers* (STC 18605; London, 1625).

[134] Thomas More, *Utopia*, ed. Edward Surtz (New Haven, 1964), pp. 69–70.

[135] Quoted and analysed in Anthony Pagden, *Lords of All the World: Ideologies of Empire in Spain, Britain and France c. 1500–c.1800* (New Haven, 1995), pp. 76–7.

[136] Pagden, *Lords of All the World*, p. 76.

Welsh topography spoke to Leland about the awesome presence and power of nature, emptiness and solitude, struggles for subsistence, poor livelihoods, and untapped commercial opportunities. After attempting to delineate the commotes (traditional Welsh 'hundreds') of Denbighshire, Leland detailed a shire devoid of the nucleated villages and unbroken fields that defined normative, lowland society:

> There is no place yn al these commotes where the people dwelle *vicatim* [in villages], but al *sparsim* [scattered and spread out], saving Denbighe toun self. ... Lanvair Vade[len] is much baren, [but] for otes with [great] labor. No wood but turfe, Ful of hilles and bogges. ... In Hughe Aleth be many bogges, rokky hilles, and morisch ground: and the soil is to[o] cold to have good corne, yet yn diverse places it berith otes and some rye. It hath in sum places woodde. In these hilles be kept nete horse and shepe. This commote is the worst part of al Denbigh land and most baren.[137]

Nor was the institutional church's presence the equal of dioceses with hundreds of parishes and (still in the 1530s) religious houses: 'And yn al these commotes was no [howse] of prioriy or abbay, saving a place of White Freres at the very este ende of the toun of Denbigh.'[138]

There were such things as proper stewardship and optimal land use. Rouland Griffith reported to Leland that two commotes on Anglesey had for many years past been 'plentyful of corne and grasse', but that the sea 'hath clene devourid them up, and now it is totally a sandy warth' or meadow.[139] Leland's 'lost' itinerary of East Anglia and descriptions of the Fens surely would have told us much about his attitudes to land reclamation and preservation in similar circumstances. But his praise for the reclamation of meadows from the swampy pools around Sutton Coldfield and the work of a Mr Bouth at Dunham Masse in Cheshire – 'about that place by good culture is made veri good corne ground, where sumtime was very fernny and commune grounde' – suggests that Leland approved of the improvement of waste or marginal ground, let alone the preservation of fertile land.[140]

The lost forests of Ystrad Fflur are another case in point. Deforestation was hardly an isolated or Welsh phenomenon, but Leland's explanations emphasized the particular practices of the local inhabitants. First, the woods were never coppiced, whereby new shoots might have been nurtured to regenerate the woods. This failure was compounded by a second, allowing goats free roam through the new shoots; they 'hath so bytten the young spring that it never grew but lyke shrubbes'.[141] However, the central failure seems to have been a cultural one. The local men explicitly 'destroied the great woodis that thei shuld

[137] Leland, *Itinerary*, III, pp. 94-5.
[138] Leland, *Itinerary*, III, p. 95.
[139] Leland, *Itinerary*, III, p. 90.
[140] Leland, *Itinerary*, IV, p. 5.
[141] Leland, *Itinerary*, III, p. 118.

not harborow theves'.[142] Not only were these 'great woodis' deliberately wasted, but deforestation was the measure taken to combat thieves, presumably roving bands, given the severity of the response. By its end, Leland's description of wooded hills denuded by clear-cutting and hungry goats had turned to social commentary – one later shared by Donald Monro and George Buchanan when they contemplated the ruffians who sheltered in the forests on the islands around Lewis.[143] Leland penned a judgement not just about land use practices but about problems of law and order as well as the implicitly foolish, ignorant, or extreme response in the face of them. Neither the law-abiding, turf-digging local Welsh nor their outlaw brethren emerged from Leland's commentary in a positive light.

Law and order as well as people's socio-environmental relationships informed judgements about character and acted as markers of civility and barbarity.[144] Returning to the awe-inspiring Brecon Beacons reveals the dynamic. Gerald's *Journey* provided most of Leland's information about the mountain, but not his commentary on the people who lived in its shadows. Despite the mountains and woods, Brecknockshire was 'in the valles fruteful of corn, and especially of pastures, for the Walschmen yn tymes past, as they do almost yet, did study more to pasturage and tylling'. Pasturage of animals was a far cry from deforestation or tolerating waste ground, but it was not quite as normative as tillage and intensive cultivation undertaken from a desire to supply an agricultural marketplace. The same was true of commerce: the apparent failure of the people of Anglesey to exploit the 'good commoditie of fisching' was because they 'lakkith cunning and diligence'.[145] Leland either actively embraced or unthinkingly repeated normative assumptions in his explanation and the emphasis on pasturage over tillage: the people did so 'as favorers of their consuete [accustomed] idilness'.[146]

Far from being simply topographic or antiquarian, then, Leland imagined a rudimentary economic geography with cultural meaning. The cultural rituals, economics, and environmental dimensions of the salt industry in Worcestershire attracted scrutiny. Leland learned from the salters of Droitwich that a plentiful supply of wood was a regular concern. They consumed an estimated 6000 loads of young pole wood per annum, while the goal for each furnace was four full loads of salt per year.[147] Further along at Bremischam, Leland credited the smiths with most of the town's industry, especially the production of knives, bits, and all manner of cutting tools. Warwickshire and Staffordshire supplied the iron

---

[142] Leland, *Itinerary*, III, p. 118.

[143] George Buchanan, *The History of Scotland* (WING B5283A; London, 1689), pp. 28, 30; Monro's account is reprinted in Martin Martin, *A Description of the Western Islands of Scotland*, ed. Charles W.J. Withers and R.W. Munro (Edinburgh, 1999), pp. 226, 321.

[144] Michael Braddick, *State Formation in Early Modern England c. 1550–1700* (Cambridge, 2000), pp. 337–78.

[145] Leland, *Itinerary*, III, p. 134.

[146] Leland, *Itinerary*, III, p. 104.

[147] Leland, *Itinerary*, II, p. 94.

ore and sea-coals for the forges.[148] The pretty town of Northwich (Cheshire) on the Dane River was fouled by its salt works and made homely by the wood stacked outside the salt houses. Types of coal mined at Llan Elli and details of coalfields around Bolton found their way into accounts of Glamorganshire and Yorkshire, respectively.[149]

Salt, coal, wool, and textiles became his economic focus. Behind these commodities lay traditional assumptions about economic behaviour, and Leland's descriptive matter-of-factness gave over to judgement. The near kin of idleness in the Tudor lexicon of social attitudes included the likes of indolence, laziness, and ease loving. Those pejorative characterizations pointed eventually to vagrants, gypsies, masterless men, and sturdy beggars who subsisted by something other than settled, respectable employment.[150] These were the very people against whom the woods of Ystrad Fflur were cleared. Leland read the salt town of Droitwich in just this fashion.

Beauty in Droitwich, with its weekly market, was confined to a single lane. 'The towne of itselfe', Leland wrote, 'is somewhat foule and dirty when any reyne faullythe, with moche cariage thrwghe the streets, [being] over ill pavyd or not pavyd.'[151] The stench and muck of city lanes could not have been a unique experience. Why they troubled Leland in this case might be explained by his low opinion of the townspeople, though later writers felt similarly about the place.[152] Droitwich was built on the very profitable manufacture of salt, but for Leland there was something socially amiss about a situation in which 'the burgesses be poore for the moste parte; bycawse the gentlemen [have] for the moast parte the great gayne of it, and the burgesses have all the labowre'.[153] The inversion of the logical profit hierarchy coloured Leland's view, as did the revels associated with one of the salt springs.

According to local information, the most productive spring failed in the time of Richard de la Wiche, bishop of Winchester (d. 1253), who eventually restored its profitable course. The spring's recovery was the cause why the locals 'used of late tymes on his daye to hang about this sault spring or well once a yeere with tapestry, and to have drinking games and revels at it'. 'Such is the superstition of the people,' Leland concluded. Neither was he impressed that the 'Wichemen' defended their salt monopoly against the discovery and exploitation of new springs in the area. While admitting the probability that their works only operated from 'Midsomer to Christemes ... for the savynge of wod', Leland suspected that it might also reflect the desire 'to mayntayne the price of theyr salte'. He noted that salters who produced more than the annual target of four loads were left

---

[148] Leland, *Itinerary*, II, p. 97.
[149] Leland, *Itinerary*, IV, p. 4; Leland, *Itinerary*, V, p. 6.
[150] Christopher Hill, *Liberty Against the Law* (Harmondsworth, 1996), pp. 47–109.
[151] Leland, *Itinerary*, II, p. 92.
[152] Nikolaus Pevsner, *The Buildings of England: Worcestershire* (Harmondsworth, 1977), p. 134.
[153] Leland, *Itinerary*, II, pp. 92–3.

4   Wales, Devon, and Cornwall from the 'Kingdome of England' from John Speed, *Theatre of the Empire of Great Britain* (London, 1676). RB 204587 Huntington Library, San Marino, CA, reproduced by permission. Image produced by ProQuest as part of *Early English Books Online*. www.proquest.com

to the mercy of the open market. Before leaving Droitwich, Leland noted that the 'people that be about the fournacis be very ille colorid'.[154] The sort of socio-commercial features that disquieted Leland also troubled travellers who found them elsewhere in Britain and Ireland, as well as those who journeyed to Asia or the Americas, even in Thomas More's imaginative landscapes.[155]

Journeys among peoples apart

In 1542 and 1545, Leland embarked on two extended circuits to the West Country. He travelled through Devon and Cornwall on the earlier journey. A century later, Parliamentary soldiers would find Cornwall, much as Boorde had, to be strange, alien land inhabited by people who were both dangerously royalist and separatist, possessing a robust sense of their unique ethnic identity within Britain.[156] Once Leland crossed the Tamar into Cornwall, the great tin mines and the region's fisher towns loomed large in his experiences. He also found the peninsula jutting into the Atlantic to be a vibrant cultural crossroads. The French, Cornish, Britons, and Irish all left their marks and the Danes and Saxons made appearances. Axminster church was 'famose by the sepultures of many noble Danes slain in King Aethelstanes time at a batel on Brunesdoun therby: and by the sepultures likewise [of] sum Saxon lordes slain in the same feld'. Before reaching Axminster, Leland learned from the records in Axmouth priory that Mounteburgh abbey in Normandy had established the brother cells at Axmouth, Sidmouth, and Oterton.[157] He speculated that the old name for Barnstaple (Devonshire) was Abertaw, in 'the Britanne tunge', because of its location across the mouth of the Taw.[158] Leland found even more evidence of this ethno-cultural hodgepodge once he crossed the Tamar, which from the 'hed of it to the mouth devidith Devonshir and Cornewaule'.[159] Cornwall emerges as a place affected more than any other by recurrent conflict, migration, and exchange (cultural or commercial).

---

[154] Leland, *Itinerary*, II, pp. 92–4.

[155] John Langton, 'South, North, and Nation: Regional Differences and Consciousness in an Integrating Realm, 1550–1750', in *Geographies of England; The North-South Divide, Material and Imagined*, ed. Alan R.H. Baker and Mark Billinge (Cambridge, 2004), pp. 137–43; Andrew Hadfield, ed., *Amazons, Savages, and Machiavels: Travel and Colonial Writing in English, 1550–1630* (Oxford, 2001), pp. 117–285; Ania Loomba, *Shakespeare, Race, and Colonialism* (Oxford, 2009); Ania Loomba and Jonathan Burton, eds, *Race in Early Modern England* (Houndmills, 2007), pp.75–275.

[156] Mark Stoyle, *Soldiers and Strangers: An Ethnic History of the English Civil War* (New Haven, 2005), pp. 33–52 173–92 ; Stoyle, *West Britons: Cornish Identities and the Early Modern British State* (Exeter, 2002).

[157] Leland, *Itinerary*, I, p. 243.

[158] Leland, *Itinerary*, I, p. 169.

[159] Leland, *Itinerary*, I, p. 174.

Leland's route took him first along the north coast and included Padstow, an 'aucient [town] bering the name of Lodenek in Cornische, and yn Englisch after the trew and old writinges Adelstow. *Latine Athelstani locus.*' Not surprisingly, the town took Aethelstan 'for the chief gever of privileges onto it'. Its location on the north coast prompted 'many Britons [Welsh] with smaul shippes to resorte to Padestow with commoditees of their countrey and to by fische'. The town itself 'is ful of Irisch men', though Leland did not elaborate.[160] Bodmin too credited Aethelstan with its privileges, while Leland remarked on the connection to 'Base Normandy' of the 'Bovilles alias Beville', who held the manor of Gwarnick some miles away.[161] The ubiquitous Aethelstan – whom Carew in his *Survey of Cornwall* (1602) made the pre-eminent Anglo-Saxon aggressor – also founded St Burien's College, after Saint Buriana, a 'holy woman of Irelond [who] sumtyme dwellid in this place, and there made and oratory'.[162] A ride across rocky ground and moorland brought Leland 'to St. Budocus church. This Budocus was an Irisch man and cam into Cornewalle and ther dwellid.'[163]

Thanks to the war economy of the Channel community, Fowey or Fawey Haven 'was hauntid with shippes of diverse nations, and their shippes went to al nations'. Successful in battle, the merchant 'Gaullants of Fawey' sported their own arms entwined with those of their competitors at Rye and Winchelsea. Leland was particularly attracted to the exploits of Thomas Treury's wife. In the reign of Henry VI, she led her husband's men and repelled a French assault on the house. Her husband subsequently fortified the house with a tower and battlements, making it 'the glorie of the town'. So used were they to profiting from war, that the townsmen continued to assault French shipping during a truce in Edward IV's reign, leading to the confiscation of their ships. Carew later celebrated the aggressive warrior instincts of his fellow Cornish. Ironically, no conflicts had the same impact as the sand and tin tailings that silted Fawey Water. No more than four or five feet of clearance remained under the bridge's great stone arches at the time of Leland's visit.[164]

At Wadbridge, Leland heard an account of the construction of a bridge over the river Camel, meant to replace the long-serving and frequently dangerous ferry. Taking pity on the town, the vicar, one Lovebone, with 'great paine and studie' mobilized the people to construct a bridge with seventeen uniform stone arches. Leland seemed less certain about the report from one local man that the original foundations of the arches were set on sandy ground and Lovebone 'despairid to perform the bridg ontyl such tyme as he layed pakkes of wolle for fundation'.[165] More than a century later, John Aubrey studied a similar tradition,

---

[160] Leland, *Itinerary*, I, p. 179.
[161] Leland, *Itinerary*, I, p. 180–1.
[162] Leland, *Itinerary*, I, p. 189.
[163] Leland, *Itinerary*, I, p. 196.
[164] Leland, *Itinerary*, I, pp. 203–6.
[165] Leland, *Itinerary*, I, p. 178.

that Salisbury cathedral was 'built upon wooll-packs', alongside another that claimed as much for London Bridge. He thought the riddle lay in a figurative turn of phrase. He suggested that the cathedral and bridge were built with the proceeds of an impost on wool.[166]

The 'entertaining' quality of Leland's Cornish stories and descriptions is not without significance. Leland is notable for the instances in which he reminds himself (and informs us) that local sources provided many pieces of information. Thus attuned, Leland must have been proffered and have received his fair share of colourful stories and folklore. He did not approach sources uncritically and sought out 'articulate, literate' locals.[167] Cornwall provided him with a rich seam of local tradition, yet the West Country did not simply provide Leland with tidbits that gave his descriptions texture and richness. Colourful stories, legends, folklore, and bizarre happenings served to mark out peoples as different, deviant, and exotic in the minds of travellers. This was most often true when travellers encountered peoples in remote or isolated locations. Leland compiled local traditions and evaluated the people who held to them, past or present, in many parts of the Tudor *imperium*.

On his way through Oxfordshire to the West Country, Leland encountered the story of Edith Forne, the wife of one Robert of Oxford, grandson of Robertus de Oilleio who came into England with the Conqueror. Edith was instrumental in her husband's foundation of the order of Black Canons at Osney, as were some magpies:

> Edith usid to walk out [of] Oxford Castelle with her gentilwomen to solace and that often tymes, wher yn a certen place in a tre as often as she came a certen pies usid to gether to it, and ther to chattre, and as it wer to speke onto her. ... Wherapon she sent for one Radulph, a chanon of S. Frediswides, a man of vertuus life and her confessor, asking hym counsel: to whom he answerid, after that he had seene the fascion of the pies chattering only at her cumming, that she should builde a chirch or monasterie in that place.[168]

Robert obliged and Radulph was the happy beneficiary as Osney's first prior. A scene depicting the 'cumming of Edith to Oseney and Radulph waiting on her, and the tre with the chattering pies be paintid in the waulle of tharch over Edith tumbe in Oseney priorie'.[169]

During his journey through the Midlands in 1543, Leland made considerable notes about Brackley. He recorded that the town 'florishid in the Saxons tyme ontyll the Danes rasid it' – a feature he found again at Tamworth. Brackley returned to prosperity 'syns the Conquest' on account of its wool staple and

[166] John Aubrey, *The Natural History of Wiltshire*, ed. John Britton (London, 1847), p. 98.
[167] Woolf, *Social Circulation of the Past*, pp. 357–8.
[168] Leland, *Itinerary*, I, p. 123.
[169] Leland, *Itinerary*, I, p. 124.

privileges.[170] The town was also notable for its three stone crosses. Recently, thieves seeking treasure beneath one had toppled it – thievery was hardly something Leland associated only with certain peoples or locations. St Peter was the principal parish church, but he 'saw no tumbe or great antiquiti' within. The churchyard was another story, where Leland found 'two faire springs, or wells'. The account is a fascinating fusion of the fantastic and the routine:

> The one of theym is caullyd S. Rumoaldes Welle, wher they say, that with in a fewe dayes of his birth he prechid. The other is caullyd Welle. There issuithe a very litle streamlet out of eche of them ... one streamelet, not so abundaunt of watar as it hathe bene. For the sayenge is that it hath driven in tymes past a cutlers myll thereby.[171]

Portland presented Leland with, in his words, an 'isle very bleke', a place with 'very few or utterly no trees ... saving the elmes about the chirch'. Protected by its rocky shore, the isle was 'fruteful of corn and gresse', despite its somewhat stony soil, and abounded with sheep. Leland found eighty houses on the island, with the remains of nearly as many again. The island sported one main street, a 'castelet' nor far off it, and a lone parish church 'longe and sumwhat low, buildid in the hanging rootes of an hille by the shore'. Leland hints at a hard existence for the people, at least in part their own doing. They 'bring wood thither out of Wight and other places', though the island would produce more elms 'if they were their plantid'. 'They brenne [burn] also cowe dung dryed with the hete of the sunne', no doubt for fuel. 'The people of the isle lyve now by tillage,' Leland reported 'and sumwhat faulle from fisshing.' As for selling commodities (unspecified, but probably including wool, hides, and fish), Leland found them 'politique inough ... and sumwhat avaritiose'. The people appeared foolish in Leland's claim that they were good at slinging stones and defended the isle by that expertise – rather a far cry from the skilled warriors and mariners of Fowey Haven.[172] Images of a hard existence in bleak climes no doubt lay behind Leland's use of words like 'uplandisch towne' to describe Hanley in Gloucestershire or Bredon in Worcestershire.[173]

There is no evidence that Leland actually visited the Scilly Isles and he may have simply repeated what local informants told him. Regardless, lying some thirty miles south-west of Land's End, they offered for view an even more remote and challenging existence. Saint Mary Isle contained one poor town with rows of buildings 'sore defacid and woren'. As for livelihoods, Leland wrote that 'the ground of this isle berith exceding good corn', though this borders on irony when he continues that this was 'insomuch that if a man do but cast corn wher hogges have rotid it wyl cum up'. Within recent memory Saint Agnes was 'desolatid' when all five households inhabiting the isle 'cam to a mariage or a fest into S.

[170] Leland, *Itinerary*, II, pp. 36, 104.
[171] Leland, *Itinerary*, II, p. 37.
[172] Leland, *Itinerary*, I, pp. 251–2.
[173] Leland, *Itinerary*, IV, pp. 135–6.

Mary Isle, and going homewarde were al drownid'. Many islands showed signs of abandoned settlements, leaving them to the gulls, puffins, conys, and wild garlic. Not surprisingly, 'Few men be glad to inhabite these islettes … for [Spanish and French] robbers by sea that take their catail of force.'[174]

The peoples of Portland and the Scilly Isles lived an existence apart. They lived a hard life in remote locations without frequent contact with the king's subjects. Their customary way of life also set them apart. The people of Portland failed to exploit the possibilities for reforestation and apparently the full resources of fish at hand, despite being so adept at trade that their motives hinted at avarice. The Scilly islanders faced threats of piracy and looting, but the casting of seeds into pig dung suggests a people insufficiently industrious, despite prospects 'al the plenty'. The people of St Lides Isle crossed a boundary between ancient devotion and unwholesome rituals even for Leland, 'wher in tymes past at her sepulchre was gret superstition'.[175] Leland's notes about the Scilly Isles in the *Collectanea* included even more fantastic stories of the islands. The island of Innischawe (Trescow), or the Isle of Elder, was so called because 'yt bereth stynkkyng elders' at the same time it was overrun by wild boars. As for Rat Isle, its name came from having 'so many rattes that yf horse, or any other lyving best be browght thyther they devore hym'.[176]

Five centuries removed, all of this has a *Lord of the Flies* feel to it. Still, by comparison to the fantastic descriptions in medieval works like de Worde's edition of Anglicus' *De Proprietatibus Rerum* or Mandeville's *Travels*, stories like these make Leland's *Itinerary* rather mundane.[177] In both respects, the biases that affected travellers' encounters with cultural complexity found their way into the mental baggage that Leland carried on his journeys.

The multicultural Tudor *imperium*

The terrific hodgepodge that is the *Itinerary* reveals Leland to have been deeply attuned to cultural complexity among the peoples of Britain. This is not always how scholars read Leland through his printed works, including recently.[178] Leland's choice of Latin for the *Commentari de Scriptoribus*, his catalogue of British literary worthies, and his topographical poems the *Genethliacon* and *Cygnea Cantio* allowed him to both classicize and civilize the vernacular of his fellow Britons and make an 'additional assault on Cornish and Welsh identity' by converting 'vernacular place names into Latin'.[179] In the *Assertio*, Arthur offered

174 Leland, *Itinerary*, IV, pp. 190–1.
175 Leland, *Itinerary*, I, p. 190.
176 Leland, *Itinerary*, I, p. 318.
177 Loomba and Burton, *Race in Early Modern England*, pp. 62–5, 70–4.
178 Shrank, *Writing the Nation*, pp. 65–103.
179 Shrank, *Writing the Nation*, pp. 81–2, 89.

Henry the example of a ruler 'who united the kingdom and drove ungodliness from the land (in the form of the heathen Saxons, Danes, Picts, and Scots)'.[180] Cultural plurality and *imperium* were evidently not compatible. Leland's poetry, especially the *Genethliacon*, consciously promoted 'the image of a fully integrated island nation' that 'smothers any sense of a geographically, culturally, or politically divided realm'. Thus all signs of Cornish discontent under the Tudors – the 1497 rising – are wanting. Instead Tudor Cornwall is filled with loyal subjects whose 'local customs' are transformed by Leland into celebrations of the birth of Edward VI and the Tudor succession rather than markers of a unique ethno-cultural consciousness. Within 'the public forum of his poetry he suppresses any dissonant details that would jeopardize his image of a vibrant cohesive [English] nation'.[181]

Reading the *Itinerary* demands that we think more broadly about Leland. The Tudor *imperium* Leland intended to describe in his civil history emerges from his travels and notebooks as a multicultural British *imperium*. He met its subjects past and present, through the lives of ruling elites and commoners, over a landscape deeply inscribed with history and ethnography. The *Itinerary* was to have been the basis for his 'Civil History' and the notebooks reflect classical 'histories' like Caesar's writings on Gaul, Herodotus' *Histories* (especially the accounts of the Persian wars), or Xenophon's *Hellenica* and *Cyropaedia*. Leland himself specifically referenced Diodorus Siculus's *Bibliotheke* or 'Universal History' (including its geography and ethnography of the known world). Herodotus, Xenophon, and Diodorus combined history, topography, and ethnographic description.[182] All three offered Leland examples of civil history written within the context of imperial epics or from an imperial starting point. Theirs were histories of conquest and consolidation containing explanations of the governance of complex empires. They did not describe the Persian *imperium* as Persia writ large. Indeed, Xenophon would later prove formative with James VI and I, precisely because of its imperial framework and the portrait of a ruler who exercised temporal and spiritual authority over a composite, multi-ethnic *imperium*.[183]

Leland experienced the Tudor *imperium* in many forms. He recorded ethnographic markers and comfortably denoted people, places, and events with familiar labels such as Saxon, Norman, English, or the like as well as something more nuanced like 'northern men'. This cultural complexity crossed regional or national lines and cultural markers seldom applied only to one set of peoples. Foolish or credulous people lived in Worcester, Brecknockshire, Oxfordshire,

---

[180] Shrank, *Writing the Nation*, p. 95.
[181] Shrank, *Writing the Nation*, pp. 86–9.
[182] Donald R. Kelley, *Faces of History: Historical Inquiry from Herodotus to Herder* (New Haven, 1998), pp. 19–28, 35–8.
[183] John Cramsie, 'The Philosophy of Imperial Kingship and the Interpretation of James VI and I', in *James VI and I: Ideas, Authority, and Government*, ed. Ralph Houlbrooke (Aldershot, 2006), pp. 43–60.

Dorset, the Scilly Isles, and beyond: no one among the 'four nations' or 'three kingdoms' had a monopoly on those particular failings – or much else. A careful reading makes clear that Leland also carried with him assumptions about peoples connected to topography, livelihood, culture, and character that would have been familiar to Gerald of Wales or John of Fordun when they encountered the frontiers of cultural complexity in their travels.[184] Finally, the evidence of prejudicial, condescending, and exotic descriptions of peoples, customs, folkways, and the like put Leland in good company with fellow travellers past and future who wrote pejoratively about so-called Others.

In Leland's notebooks, in the raw material of his experiences, the peoples of Wales, Devon and Cornwall, the Midlands and the North, Yorkshire, Kent, and the like are not interchangeable subjects under a Tudor 'England' writ large. The troublesome adventurers in Fowey suggest a pattern of Cornish unrest when rubbing up against the demands of the crown that Leland recognized and understood. The Tudors' was also a claim to a British *imperium* that was not synonymous with England. Nor can we dismiss Leland's struggling efforts with Welsh (and Cornish) simply because he Latinized them in his poetical works. William Camden composed and published *Britannia* in Latin. Are we to suppose that he aimed to erase the Irish, Scots, Welsh, Cornish, a host of local particularities, and the English? What narrow presumption equates Latinity with Anglicization? The subjects of our next chapter, John Mair, Hector Boece, and John Lesley, composed and published culturally complex descriptions of Scotland in Latin before and after Leland. How do we reconcile them with such claims? It just will not do to assert that Leland erased cultural complexity in favour of a consciously homogenous Englishness; that Leland read Britain and England as one and the same.

The assumption defies insights from a different perspective, that of state formation in early modern Britain. Outside the political heartlands of the Tudor and Stuart regimes, state formation was partly a process by which 'influential local groups could consolidate, and legitimate, their social position' in 'the promotion of civility'; civility 'was not a matter of Anglicisation' and did not come 'at the expense of particularism, and it evidently did not depend on the homogenisation of the population below the level of the gentry'.[185] Additionally, Leland and many fellow English, Welsh, and Scottish travellers participated in what Daniel Woolf has described (for England) as the development and social circulation of a 'historical sense of a national past'.[186] Travellers also contributed to and exemplified the contested sense of a national past noted by Woolf: they encountered, recovered, and narrated cultural complexity.

---

[184] Davies, *First English Empire*, pp. 89–95.
[185] Braddick, *State Formation*, pp. 340, 355.
[186] Woolf, *Social Circulation of the Past*, pp. 12–13.

Only the narrowest reading of the *Itinerary* or the Tudor mental world of travel and discovery for which Leland planned his *Civilis Historia* could find building blocks of a homogenous English nationhood. However, when death released Leland from his madness, his notebooks passed to a generation of writers who dramatically narrowed his horizons, turning him into the father of English history. It is to that transformation that we now turn, and the story begins in Stewart Scotland.

3

The Peoples of Stewart Scotland

When Robert Sibbald became the king's Geographer in Scotland in 1682, Charles II charged him to publish the 'Description of the *Scotia Antiqua* & *Scotia Moderna*, and the Natural History of the Products of His Ancient Kingdom'. From his digs in Edinburgh, Sibbald collected maps and manuscripts and assembled the reports of local informants who responded to the detailed questionnaires he circulated for this 'Scottish Atlas'. He was the natural choice for Bishop Edmund Gibson's commission to revise the Scottish chapters for a new edition of Camden's *Britannia* (1695). Gibson required Sibbald to identify additional books and manuscripts for interested readers. He listed a clutch of local descriptions, some tracts on specialized topics like minerals or the seats of the nobility, but just three descriptions of Scotland as a whole. Sibbald's own *Scotia Illustrata* joined Petruccio Ubaldini's description of Scotland lifted from Hector Boece's *Scotorum Historia* and John Lesley's description of the Scots from his *De Origine, Moribus & Rebus Gestis Scotorum*.[1]

The list does not look impressive after almost two centuries of travel and discovery across Britain. There are several explanations, including Sibbald's own eccentricities and a vibrant manuscript culture among 'local' travellers. For, now, two matters shaped the sixteenth-century encounter with Scotland. Quite simply, no one Scottish traveller compiled a mass of first-hand observations comparable to Leland's in England. Perhaps Scottish topography and language communities (with a multitude of local dialects) presented unique challenges, especially for a traveller who journeyed into the Gaedhealtacht or an uplander who sought to traverse the cultural boundaries and prejudices of lowland Scotland.[2] Intellectual

---

[1] Robert Sibbald, *Advertisement ... to Publish the Description of the Scotia Antiqua & Scotia Moderna* (WING S3721A; Edinburgh, 1682); William Camden, *Britannia: Or a Chorographical Description of Great Britain and Ireland* (London, 1695); Charles W.J. Withers, *Geography, Science and National Identity: Scotland since 1520* (Cambridge, 2001), pp. 69–84.

[2] Adam Fox and Daniel Woolf, eds, *The Spoken Word: Oral Culture in Britain, 1500–1800* (Manchester, 2002), p. 25. See the detailed examination of these prejudices in Ulrike Morét, 'Gaelic History and Culture in Mediaeval and Sixteenth-Century Lowland Scottish Historiography' (Ph.D. thesis; University of Aberdeen, 1993), pp. 14–22 and generally. I came to the thesis after I had completed the manuscript for this book. I have incorporated some

traditions played an equally important role. The examples of John of Fordun and Walter Bower cemented the connection between descriptions of Scotland's peoples and writing the country's history. Admiration for classical historians and geographers – Herodotus, Livy, Tacitus, Ptolemy, Xenophon – who wrote with an ethnographic eye further encouraged John Mair and Hector Boece when they began new histories of Scotland.

Two kingdoms shared Britain, despite the best efforts of first Norman, and then English, conquerors. They waged what James Goldstein termed a 'war of historiography', with Scots determined to control the history and ethnographic identity of their country.[3] Like its island neighbours, Scotland too owed its foundation to multiple migrations and long, complex cultural interactions. Ancient Britons, Picts, Scots, Norse, and Anglo-Normans (or Franci) all claimed it.[4] Medieval and Renaissance Scottish writers constantly grappled with this history in accounting for the ancient settlement of the kingdom and the origins of the Scots.[5] To write the history of Scotland, especially one that established its ancient independence, meant writing a multicultural history. Topographic and ethnographic descriptions that recognized and exploited this past became essential introductions to a realm brought together – at times retrospectively – through a common history and the ambitions of its Stewart kings.[6]

John Mair (1521), Hector Boece (1527), Boece's translator John Bellenden (1533), and John Lesley (1578) dealt with Scotland's founding ethnic groups and contemporary cultural–topographic divides in their histories.[7] They

of the salient points that elaborate on my own and referenced other portions that add to the analysis. Readers interested in a thorough, close reading of sixteenth-century histories can obtain Dr Morét's thesis at no cost via the British Library EThOS service at http://ethos.bl.uk/Home.do.

[3] R. James Goldstein, *The Matter of Scotland: Historical Narratives in Medieval Scotland* (Lincoln, NE, 1993), pp. 23–103; Roger Mason, 'From Chronicle to History: Recovering the Past in Renaissance Scotland', in *Building the Past = Konstruktion der eigenen Vergangeheit*, ed. Rudolf Suntrup and Jan Veenstra (Frankfurt/New York, 2006), pp. 53–63.

[4] Matthew H. Hammond, 'Ethnicity and the Writing of Medieval Scottish History', *Scottish Historical Review* 85.1 (2006), p. 19.

[5] John Leslie, *The Historie of Scotland*, ed. E.G. Cody (two volumes; Edinburgh, 1885–95), I, pp. 75–81; Dauvit Broun, 'The Picts' Place in the Kingship's Past before John of Fordun', in *Scottish History: The Power of the Past*, ed. Edward J. Cowan and Richard J. Finlay (Edinburgh, 2002), pp. 11–28; Steve Boardman, 'Late Medieval Scotland and the Matter of Britain', *Scottish History*, pp. 47–72. Roger A. Mason, 'Civil Society and the Celts: Hector Boece, George Buchanan and the Ancient Scottish Past', *Scottish History*, pp. 95–119; Colin Kidd, *British Identities before Nationalism: Ethnicity and Nationhood in the Atlantic World 1600–1800* (Cambridge, 1999), pp. 123–45.

[6] Nicola Royan, 'The *Scotorum Historia* of Hector Boece: A Study' (D.Phil. thesis; Oxford University, 1996), pp. 282–4. I am grateful to Dr Royan for kindly sharing a copy of her thesis.

[7] William Ferguson, *The Identity of the Scottish Nation: An Historic Quest* (Edinburgh, 1998), pp. 1–143; Hugh Trevor-Roper, *The Invention of Scotland: Myth and History* (New Haven, 2008), pp. 1–72; Colin Kidd, *Subverting Scotland's Past: Scottish Whig Historians and the Creation of an*

encountered Scotland both as armchair travellers and as travellers in deed. As armchair travellers they called on Fordun's *Chronica Gentis Scotorum* or *Chronicle of the Scottish Nation* and its continuation by Bower in the *Scotichronicon*. Fordun and Bower were the essential foundations for any description of Scotland and its peoples, whether built on first-hand experience or archival journeys. Mair and Boece too fulfilled this role for Lesley, writing in the 1560s and 1570s. None of the three undertook a systematic tour of Scotland, but Mair and Lesley certainly knew Scotland well from journeys occasioned by life and work, while Boece undertook fieldwork that even took in Pictish Ogham stones.[8] Each of them crafted his descriptions as a 'circuit' round the kingdom, echoing an imaginative journey. They thus expressed the passion for travel and discovery and offered sixteenth-century Scots ethnographic descriptions of their kingdom.

Foundations

John of Fordun's modest background makes even his birthplace difficult to pin down. Well travelled and perhaps with some fluency in Gaelic, Fordun compiled his *Chronica* sometime before his reputed death c. 1363.[9] He carried the history of Scotland through the reign of David I (1153) and collected more than two hundred tidbits of Scottish history.[10] Separating Fordun and his travels from his sources is a complicated business. He successfully wove a continuous narrative out of a rich body of material, from Gaelic legends to English chronicles.[11] Important ethnographic characterizations came from sources that predated the *Chronicle* or constituted an earlier 'proto-Fordun' c. 1285.[12] Further, medieval writers showed a good deal more sensitivity in handling the shifting cultural complexities that eventually became a superficial conflation of highland and lowland with ethnographic markers and classical concepts of civility and barbarity.[13] What finally emerged as Gaelic or highland barbarity was built on existing debates and developed first by 'those promoting a new social order, particularly cloistered

Anglo-British Identity, 1689–c.1830 (Cambridge, 1993), pp. 1–29; Roger Mason, *Kingship and the Commonweal: Political Thought in Renaissance Scotland* (East Linton, 1998), pp. 8–103, 165–86.

[8] Morét, 'Gaelic History', pp. 66, 88–91; Royan, '*Scotorum Historia*', pp. 3, 225–34.

[9] Goldstein, *Matter of Scotland*, pp. 106–7.

[10] Ferguson, *Scottish Nation*, pp. 43–50; D.E.R. Watt, 'John of Fordun', *Oxford DNB* at www.oxforddnb.com; Trevor-Roper, *Invention of Scotland*, pp. 15–17.

[11] Martin MacGregor, 'Gaelic Barbarity and Scottish Identity in the Later Middle Ages', in *Mìorun Mòr nan Gall, 'The Great Ill-Will of the Lowlander'?: Lowland Perceptions of the Highlands, Medieval and Modern*, ed. Dauvit Broun and Martin MacGregor (Glasgow, 2009), p. 11.

[12] Dauvit Broun, 'Attitudes of Gall to Gaedhel in Scotland before John of Fordun', in *Mìorun Mòr nan Gall*, pp. 52–3, 73–6; MacGregor, 'Gaelic Barbarity and Scottish Identity', pp. 9–17; Dauvit Broun, *Scottish Independence and the Idea of Britain: From the Picts to Alexander III* (Edinburgh, 2013), pp. 215–68.

[13] Broun, 'Attitudes of Gall to Gaedhel', pp. 55–63.

communities staffed by English monks and nuns' in the twelfth century and later by the 'self-conscious projections of a "civilized" ideal, such as the vision of peace and stability under a strong king'.[14]

Fordun's *Chronicle*, then, cannot simplistically be attributed to one person's travels, or studied as though it recorded a fixed understanding of peoples and place in Scotland. He evidently determined to make good the destruction of the Scottish archives after Edward I had carried them off:

> So, after searching his own devastated country for what remained of its records, he set out on a journey of research abroad. He is said to have spent some years travelling, always on foot, through the neighbour kingdoms. From one of his continuators we have a description of him, wandering 'like a curious bee, through the meadows of England and the oracles of Ireland, carrying his manuscript in his bosom'. Pausing in towns and colleges, churches and abbeys, he conversed with historians and chronologers, listened to their gossip, and stored it away 'like sweet honey in the hive of his folded notebook'.[15]

The journeys equipped Fordun to convey a vivid sense of the Scottish landscape:

> It is a country strong by nature, and difficult and toilsome of access. In some parts it towers into mountains; in others it sinks down into plains. For lofty mountains stretch through the midst of it, from end to end, as do the tall Alps through Europe ... Impassable as they are on horseback save in very few places, they can hardly be crossed even on foot, both on account of the snow always lying on them, except in summer-time only; and by reason of the boulders torn off the beetling crags and the deep hollows in their midst.[16]

The Scottish peaks impressed Fordun's eye, along with the forests that hugged the foothills, teaming with animals, and the crystal-clear springs that begat streams and rivers. By contrast, the Scottish seaboard consisted of lowland terrain, 'pretty level and rich, with green meadows'.[17]

The Scottish people left their unique marks on the land. Seaboard dwellers created 'fertile and productive fields of corn and barley', beans, peas, and most other produce including honey (and wax), though not grapes (wine) or olives (oil). Upland and highland fields yielded far less, chiefly oats and barley. Fordun found them, as productive lands went, 'very hideous, interspersed with moors and marshy fields, muddy and dirty'. Their saving grace was pasturage fit for cattle and sheep and, in turn, milk products and wool. Fish, fowl, marble, iron, and lead could all to be found in abundance and Fordun trotted out Herodotus, Isidore of Seville, and Solinus to sing the praises of Scotland's great fertility and wholesome climate.[18]

[14] Broun, 'Attitudes of Gall to Gaedhel', p. 82.
[15] Trevor-Roper, *Invention of Scotland*, p. 16.
[16] *John of Fordun's Chronicle of the Scottish Nation*, ed. William F. Skene (two volumes; Burnham-on-Sea, 1993), p. 36, hereafter cited as *Fordun's Chronicle*.
[17] *Fordun's Chronicle*, I, p. 37.
[18] *Fordun's Chronicle*, I, p. 37.

These lands marked Scotland's peoples, and divided them. The pattern was set early when Fordun's wild, inspiring peaks 'separated the Scots from the Picts, and the kingdoms from each other'. Influenced by his travels, the design of Ranulf Higden's *Polychronicon* with its attention to topography and ethnography, and following the lead of the 'proto-Fordun' chronicle, Fordun agreed that topography produced 'de divisione gencium Scociae & linguarum' or the 'nations of Scotia and their Languages'. This meant that the 'manners and customs of the Scots varied with the diversity of their speech'.[19] The 'Teutonic' speakers – Saxons – 'of the coast are of domestic and civilized habits, trusty, patient, and urbane, decent in their attire, affable, and peaceful, devout in Divine worship, yet always prone to resist a wrong at the hand of their enemies'. By contrast, the Scottish-speaking 'highlanders and people of the islands ... are a savage and untamed nation, rude and independent, given to rapine, ease-loving, and of a docile and warm disposition, comely in person, but unsightly in dress, hostile to the English people and language, and owing to the diversity of speech, even to their own nation, and exceedingly cruel [but] faithful and obedient to their king and country, and easily made to submit to law, if properly governed'.[20]

An account of the 'manners and customs of the Scottish nation of the olden time' followed this contradictory blend of highland qualities and '"the emergence of the Lowlander"' who 'had changed their language, and thereby moved on and "got civility"'.[21] Here Fordun or, more likely, his predecessor combined a description from Solinus with one attributed to Isidore of Seville's *Chronica Majora* (universal history). The Scots of old were 'a rugged and warlike people' and the nation's young lads were fed their first solid food from the tip of their fathers' swords. These grown Scots, victors in battle, drank the blood of their slain foes and smeared their faces with the remains. Old Scots were high spirited, sparing of diet, fierce, wild, and stern in countenance, rugged yet affable among their own kind, and great lovers of sports and hunting. Isidore's contribution actually came from Bartholomaeus Anglicus' *De Proprietatibus Rerum* (c. 1245) and made it possible to expand on these heroic qualities.[22] As well, the Scots' 'peculiar dress much disfigures' their 'graceful figure and goodly face' and they could be connected with those who were 'once in Ireland' and resembled 'the Irish in all things – in language, manners, and characters'.[23]

The 'real' Fordun's travels did not inspire him to compose simply a narrative of the journeys. The *Chronicle* began with the marriage of the Greek prince

---

[19] *Johannis de Fordun Scotichronicon* (five volumes; Oxford, 1722), I, p. 79; Goldstein, *Matter of Scotland*, pp. 107–8; *Fordun's Chronicle*, I, p. 38; Dauvit Broun, 'Becoming a Nation: Scotland in the 12th and 13th Centuries', in *Nations in Medieval Britain*, ed. Hirokazu Tsurushima (Donington, 2010), pp. 101–2.

[20] *Fordun's Chronicle*, I, p. 38.

[21] MacGregor, 'Gaelic Barbarity and Scottish Identity', p. 14.

[22] MacGregor, 'Gaelic Barbarity and Scottish Identity', pp. 14–15.

[23] *Fordun's Chronicle*, I, p. 38.

Gathelus to Scota, daughter of the ill-fated Ramses II. Exiled from Egypt in time to escape locusts, burning hail, and a blood-red Nile, Scota and her husband settled in Spain. From thence their descendants migrated to Ireland, before Fergus MacFerquhard led them into Scotland. Fordun also worked to establish that the island was properly called Albion, whose two parts were rightly labelled Scotia and Britannia. He determined to up-end those 'transcribers of a rival nation' (Geoffrey of Monmouth) who 'entirely perverted, corrupted, violated, and very often indiscreetly changed' histories to produce 'the common opinion of modern times ... that the whole of Albion was called Britannia, from Brutus, who only colonized its southern regions'.[24]

Fordun's *Chronicle* reached a wider audience when Sir David Stewart of Rosyth commissioned Walter Bower, abbot of Inchcolm, to transcribe and bring the narrative up to date. Working between 1441 and 1445, Bower expanded Fordun's original five books to sixteen, by which point Bower had written an account of his own times that ended with the violent murder of James I in 1437.[25] The work proved enormously popular. Copies of this *Scotichronicon* 'were made, and commented on, in every Scottish monastery or church to replace the records carried away', so that by 'the end of the fifteenth century it was the orthodoxy of Scotland, not to be doubted or disputed'.[26] The story told by Fordun and Bower dominated the historical imagination in Scotland well beyond their lifetimes, especially the foundation myth of Gathelus and Scota, the topographical–cultural divide between highland and lowland, and interest in the manners and customs of the earliest Scots. Here, then, were fourteenth- and fifteenth-century descriptions of Scotland in which travel played a role, even an uncertain one. Mair and Boece built on these medieval foundations.

The Greater Britain of John Mair

John Mair achieved three things that most academics covet: a respected presence in the classroom, publications that became standard texts for students (across Europe), and leadership of a talented team of junior scholars. Mair achieved all of this between taking his M.A. at the Collège de Ste Barbe in 1494 and departing the Sorbonne for Scotland in 1518. Mair's next eight years were productive ones. His time as principal of Glasgow University – followed by a stint at St Andrews – included the composition of the *History of Greater Britain, England and Scotland* (*Historia Majoris Britanniae tam Angliae quam Scotiae*), published in 1521 and dedicated to James V. Mair wrapped the story of Scotland around political

[24] *Fordun's Chronicle*, I, p. 34.
[25] D.E.R. Watt, 'Walter Bower', *Oxford DNB* at www.oxforddnb.com; Walter Bower, *Scotichronicon*, ed. D.E.R. Watt (nine volumes; Aberdeen/Edinburgh, 1996–2000).
[26] Trevor-Roper, *Invention of Tradition*, p. 20.

commentary. It circulated widely and proved popular.[27] Still, it seemed ready made to provoke and alienate. His robust defence of Scotland's independence underpinned a call for Anglo-Scottish unity. On top of which Mair demolished both nations' origins myths, disposing of Geoffrey of Monmouth and the sweet romance of Scota and Gathelus.[28]

By 1526 Mair had returned to Paris, where he almost certainly lectured to John Calvin, Ignatius of Loyola, François Rabelais, and George Buchanan.[29] His fellow Parisian Scot, Hector Boece, admired his theological insights and 'it is probable that Mair was on Boece's reading lists when the latter lectured at Aberdeen'.[30] Mair continued to write and he dedicated his commentary on the *Nicomachean Ethics* to the disgraced Cardinal Wolsey in 1530 because of the 'shared love of "our common country", for Scotland and England are "enclosed in one Britain"'.[31] When Mair returned to Scotland for good in 1531 he may have been driven by the same affection that compelled him to describe his native land and its peoples and record their history: 'Our native soil attracts us with a secret and inexpressible sweetness and does not permit us to forget it.'[32]

Mair's *History* has a wonderfully idiosyncratic character in its respect for the peoples and divisions of Britain:

> So that the whole part of the island which is held by the king of the southern island is called the kingdom of England, and the rest is the kingdom of Scotland. Yet all the inhabitants are Britons ... Either the original inhabitants of the island alone are Britons, and therefore the dwellers in Wales at this present will be the only Britons, against all common use of language; or the English, who are descended from the Saxons, and others of foreign origin, but are native of the island, are Britons: and in this way it will behove us to speak of the Scots born in the island as Britons also ... I say, therefore, that all men born in Britain are Britons ... [33]

This sense of place and people informs the whole description. Thus Britons of all stripes could celebrate their 'proud temper' against foreign foes even if the Scots excelled their neighbours in their readiness to take up arms in defence of their homeland. Bloodshed 'within the island in civil war' was a dangerous consequence, however, and the 'Scottish and English robbers and inveterate thieves' who plagued the disputed Borders were only the latest pests.[34]

---

[27] Royan, '*Scotorum Historia*', pp. 28–9.

[28] Kidd, *Subverting Scotland's Past*, pp. 18–19; Alexander Broadie, 'John Mair', *Oxford DNB* at www.oxforddnb.com.

[29] Broadie, 'John Mair'.

[30] Alexander Broadie, *The Shadow of Scotus: Philosophy and Faith in Pre-Reformation Scotland* (Edinburgh, 1995), p. 6.

[31] Broadie, 'John Mair'.

[32] Quoted in Broadie, 'John Mair'.

[33] John Major, *A History of Greater Britain as Well England as Scotland*, trans. Archibald Constable (Edinburgh, 1892), pp. 17–18.

[34] Major, *History of Greater Britain*, pp. 7, 19–20, 29–30.

God provided no place with everything its people needed, forcing neighbours to embrace one another if for no other reason than self-interest. Britain was no different. Coal, wood, fertile soil, good pastures, fine wool, barley, variable seasons, and excellent rivers and harbours made it a prosperous land. Mair lamented the absence of viticulture in Britain, but God gave the British trade goods worth their tonnage in wine. And, God gave them barley. Mair lovingly described the production of barley ale, from the youths who trod underfoot the water-softened barley, to the meticulous care taken by the alewives, and the double brewing it received in Scotland. Mair testified that no Briton would prefer the ale brewed in Paris: 'it keeps the bowels open, it is nourishing, and it quenches thirst'. No wine could produce 'a stronger race of men' than the people who lived on this stomach-churning brew.[35]

The French would not suffer one British speciality: a Frenchman returned from Britain with the traditional flatbread made from oats 'and showed it about as a monstrosity'. Mair defended bread made from barley – just 'such bread were Christ and his apostles want to eat' – but for his part he preferred oat bread, especially since 'I nowhere remember to have seen on the other side of the water such good oats as in Britain'. Two ingenious baking methods could be found in Scotland. In the first, the dough was spread on an iron plate supported above a fire by three legs – a method that Edward I encountered in Scotland, according to Jean Froissart's chronicle. The second method, the baking of hearth cakes, brought derision from townsfolk toward their country brethren. But these hearth cakes too were mentioned frequently in the Bible, though not under the vulgar name of bannock.[36] With a grand turn and a keen eye to cultural complexity, Mair declared:

> It is the food of almost all the inhabitants of Wales, of the northern English (as I learned some seven years back), and of the Scottish peasantry; and yet the main strength of the Scottish and English armies is in men who have been tillers of the soil – a proof that oaten bread is not a thing to be laughed at.[37]

His appetite for stories of ale, bannocks, and oatcakes satisfied, Mair took a more traditional topographic turn. His attention to rivers, cities, universities, and churches included fulsome praise for English musicians and a second-place finish for his first alma mater, Cambridge, against Oxford. Equally proud of Scotland's universities, Mair could not bring himself to find the Scottish Church anything but a poor second. Its distant parishes and unskilled priests were 'not worthy of comparison'. This discussion evolved into a critique of rural society. Mair laid rural poverty at the feet of the gentry and nobility: leases of just four or five years positively discouraged the kind of sturdy communities Mair found in England or France. The effects could be observed in the impermanent hovels of

---

[35] Major, *History of Greater Britain*, pp. 13–14.
[36] Major, *History of Greater Britain*, pp. 7–12.
[37] Major, *History of Greater Britain*, p. 9.

the peasants (despite an abundance of stone), the absence of trees, hedges, and orchards, or the failure to dung and improve the land. All of this was 'no small loss and damage to the whole realm' and fuelled endemic poverty and violence.[38]

Fond memories once more pushed in when Mair recalled early summer mornings when people from his own village of Gleghornie (near Haddington) made a rich harvest of polypods and crabs at low tide. The impregnable stronghold of Bass Rock loomed in the Forth, but Mair's mind was on the fat, succulent solan geese that nested there through the summer. From Bass Rock, Mair's attention moved to harbours, rich mountain pastures, and the Orkneys, Shetlands, and Western Isles. The Irish-speaking inhabitants of the Western Isles lived on oats, barley, and cattle – far more savoury than the beef to be had in France, though the same could not be said for British mutton. Robert the Bruce first understood that the Isles' importance lay in these cattle and the 'stout warriors' who raised them, a reserve of flesh and fierce soldiers kept on side through the king's 'slender title of [lordship of] the Isles'. No wise king of Scots would part with the Isles – nor would their descendants who pulled the men of the Gaedhealtacht into the imperial forces that seized global dominion in the eighteenth and nineteenth centuries.[39]

In his first chapter concerning the manners and customs of the Scots, the enmity of Scotland and England quickly side-tracked Mair. Mutual hatred proved that 'two neighbouring kingdoms, striving for the mastery, never cherish a sincere desire for peace'. Not for the first time did Mair propose a union through intermarriage, going so far as to suggest that Scotland's best kings had been born of English mothers. He clearly had in mind James II, borne by Joan of Beaufort, a second cousin to Henry VI, and his own sovereign, Margaret Tudor's son James V. Perhaps, as Sabellicus (Marcantonio Coccio) claimed, the Scots could be accused of having a jealous temper or tending to haughtiness. But whether the Scots' faults were greater than those of other nations or their neighbours in England was not a judgement Mair was ready to make. He agreed more readily with those who claimed that Scots routinely pretended to noble blood and chastized them for forgetting that virtue was the only real nobility; that 'which is commonly called nobility is naught but a windy thing of human devising'.[40] On this, at least, Mair and Boece would agree.

Of Scottish society, Mair was far from praiseworthy. British nobles – by which Mair meant the Scottish and English nobility – were as civilized as their Continental counterparts, though they seldom went about unarmed. However, Scottish nobles had two significant faults. First, they were quarrelsome among themselves, ensuring that 'their very retainers cannot meet without strife'. Second, the lesser nobility or landholding gentry did not educate their children

---

[38] Major, *History of Greater Britain*, pp. 19–31; Broadie, 'John Major'.

[39] Major, *History of Greater Britain*, pp. 33–8.

[40] Major, *History of Greater Britain*, pp. 40–6.

in morals or letters, 'no small calamity to the state'. They 'ought to search out men learned in history, upright in character, and to them intrust the education of their children, so that even in tender age these may begin to form right habits, and act when they are mature in years like men endowed with reason.'[41] As one who made a living teaching and training future servants of the crown, the emergent *noblesse de pen*, Mair spoke for the humanist ideal and the political culture that his king sought to create.

Mair praised the common people and the peasantry as keepers of the warlike spirit in both nations, yet Scottish farmers (comparable to English yeomen) had their faults. They looked upon skilled artisans – shoemakers, tailors, and the like – with contempt and encouraged their children to aim no higher than to become troublesome retainers of some noble. That said, farmers were made 'of a harder fibre' through temperance and daily labour than were townsfolk, 'accustomed to luxurious eating and drinking'.[42] Strength, then, ultimately lay with Scotland's quarrelsome nobility and hardy farmers, but Mair anticipated the social-political clampdown on which James VI embarked a half-century later – perhaps, like the future king, with one eye on a seemingly more ordered society across the Tweed.

There 'are in the island three different tongues, and the speaker of no one of these understand another'.[43] Scottish society was fundamentally divided between two of them:

> Further, just as among the Scots we find two distinct tongues, so we likewise find two different ways of life and conduct. For some are born in the forests and mountains of the north, and these we call men of the Highland, but the others men of the Lowland. By foreigners the former are called Wild Scots, the latter [domestic] Scots. The Irish tongue is in use among the former, the English tongue among the latter. One-half of Scotland speaks Irish, and all these as well as the Islanders we reckon to belong to the Wild Scots.[44]

A pejorative account of a highland–lowland divide inevitably followed.

The 'Wild Scots' took up arms more rapidly, in part because of their more northerly disposition and because 'born as they are in the mountains, and dwellers in forest, their very nature is more combative'. In contrast, the domesticated Scots were entrusted with the governance of the kingdom, 'inasmuch as they understand better, or at least less ill than the others, the nature of civil polity' – an essential qualification, given Mair's assessment of lowland nobility and peasantry. Wild Scots with something to lose – cattle, sheep, and other possessions – more readily bowed before the 'courts and law of the king'. Others chose a life following 'their own worthless and savage chief in all evil

[41] Major, *History of Greater Britain*, pp. 48–9.
[42] Major, *History of Greater Britain*, p. 47.
[43] Major, *History of Greater Britain*, p. 18.
[44] Major, *History of Greater Britain*, pp. 48–9. For the choice of 'domestic' over 'householding', see Morét, 'Gaelic History', pp. 34–7.

6   Ethnographic engravings bordering the 'Kingdome of Scotland' from John Speed, *Theatre of the Empire of Great Britain* (London, 1676). RB 204587 Huntington Library, San Marino, CA, reproduced by permission. Image produced by ProQuest as part of *Early English Books Online*. www.proquest.com

courses sooner than they will pursue an honest industry'. The plaid mantle, saffron-coloured shirt, broadsword, small halberd, and single-edged dagger all visually distinguished the wild Scots. Only the pleasing melodies of their harps redeemed them. The highland–lowland divide mirrored the bitter enmity between Britain's two kingdoms: 'our householding Scots, or quiet and civil-living people – that is, all who lead a decent and reasonable life – these men hate, on account of their differing speech, as much as they do the English'.[45]

Mair's *History* expressed his love of Scotland within a British perspective. It supported his call for Anglo-Scottish union. He also brought to it the interest in ethnography first found in his discourse on Amerindians from *In Secundum Librum Sententiarum*. His Paris contemporary, Hector Boece, offered a very different account, one that would become caught up in the religious upheavals in Britain after both men had left the scene.

The *Scotorum Historia, Croniklis of Scotland,* and religious revolution in Britain

The kingdom of Fife may have separated the birthplace of Mair from the Dundee of Hector Boece, but both men captured the voice of lowland Scottish travellers. Also widely read, Boece's *Scotorum Historia* earned literary kudos that eluded Mair.[46] Returning from his studies at the University of Paris, having become fast friends with the great humanist Erasmus, Boece became one of Bishop William Elphinstone's first teachers in the newly founded King's College of Aberdeen. Firmly settled as the college's principal by 1505, Boece set to work on his history of Scotland. Published in 1527 in Paris, Boece's history recast the familiar narrative in the style of Livy, firmly anchored in the 'mirror for princes' genre, with Fordun and Bower's foundation myths dressed in 'Sunday-best Latin'.[47] It evidently delighted James V. He commissioned a Scots-language edition from John Bellenden (probably presented to the king in 1533) and made Boece's original the centrepiece of a French account of Scotland for his short-lived queen, Madeleine de Valois. Enthusiasm for the work at James's court even led to an edition by William Stewart in pentameter couplets.[48]

Boece's history became the starting point for numerous readers in the coming decades. In the 1540s Leland and John Bale railed against Boece's attack on the mythic pasts of Brutus, Arthur, and claims to English suzerainty. The Italian Petruccio Ubaldini composed a 'free' translation of Boece's history in 1550 and

[45] Major, *History of Greater Britain*, p. 50.
[46] Royan, 'Scotorum Historia', pp. 305–6.
[47] Nicola Royan, 'Hector Boece', *Oxford DNB* at www.oxforddnb.com; Morét, 'Gaelic History', pp. 51–78.
[48] William Stewart, *The Buik of the Croniclis of Scotland*, ed. William B. Turnbull (three volumes; London, 1858).

dedicated the manuscript to the earl of Arundel, before seeing it through the press in 1588.[49] William Harrison carefully read and studied Boece's *Historia* and John Bellenden's Scots translation, *The Hystory and Croniklis of Scotland* (1540). Having done so, he contributed an English translation, 'the Description of Scotlande', to the 1577 edition of Raphael Holinshed's *Chronicle*; for which Harrison also contributed a description of England, based in good part on Leland's travel notebooks. Finally, Lesley and George Buchanan followed in Boece's topographical and literary footsteps with their very different histories of Scotland in 1578 and 1582, respectively.

The decades separating Harrison, Lesley, and Buchanan from Boece's original might have been centuries, after religious changes in Britain. In England and Wales, the 1530s ushered in Henry VIII's break from Rome. The reigns of Edward VI and Elizabeth I laid the groundwork for a Protestant Church, despite Mary I's restoration of Catholicism in the years separating them. In 1559–60, Scottish lords fired by religious passion and nationalist zeal deposed the regent, Marie of Guise. She governed Scotland on behalf of Queen Mary, James V's only legitimate heir, and her husband, the French King François II. Mary's mother died in April 1560 and François followed her to the grave in December. Shunted aside by her mother-in-law, Catherine de Medici, Mary returned to Scotland. The Scotland she returned to rule in 1561 was governed by her half-brother James Stewart and the Lords of the Congregation, the beneficiaries of English military intervention that tipped the scales against the regent's French-backed forces in 1560. The triumphant Lords had summoned a parliament in the name of their absent queen and renounced the authority of the pope, prohibited Catholic worship, and instituted a Calvinist confession of faith. The religious revolution was confirmed by the deposition and exile of Mary herself in 1567, and left the country in the hands of the one-year-old James VI and his 'regents'. James would eventually become both the 'nursing father' and antagonist of the Calvinist Kirk that grew alongside him. Boece's descriptions of the Scots became bound up with these religious changes, and we want to focus on the interaction of Bellenden's Scots edition and William Harrison's 'Description of Scotlande'.

Harrison penned his autobiography in a copy of the *Scriptorum Illustrium Majoris Brytannie*, John Bale's catalogue of British literary worthies. St Paul's School, Christ Church, and Merton led Harrison to a chaplaincy in the household of William Brooke, Lord Cobham, and two parish livings in London. All of these became congenial positions for a committed, evangelical Protestant.[50] God's plan for humanity was written into the history of the world. Eager to uncover the divine design, Harrison accepted Holinshed's commission to write 'three

---

[49] Alessandra Petrina, 'A View from Afar: Petruccio Ubaldini's *Descrittione del Regno di Scotia*', unpublished paper presented to the 'Thirteenth International Conference on Medieval and Renaissance Scottish Language and Literature' (Padua, 2011).
[50] Glyn Parry, 'William Harrison', *Oxford DNB* at www.oxforddnb.com.

engrossing books on the history and physical and social geography of Britain'.[51] This is how Harrison came to contribute an English translation of Bellenden's *Croniklis*.

Harrison explained his editorial method: 'I translated Hectors description of Scotland out of the Scottish into the English toung, being not alitle ayded therein by the Latine, fro[m] whence sometime the translator [Bellenden] swarueth not a litle, as I haue done also fro[m] him [Bellenden], now and then, following the Latine, and now and then gathering such sence out of both as most did stande with my purposed breuity.'[52] Over the course of three or four days Harrison worked between both editions to compose his 'Description'.[53] Doing so, he recognized that translators and readers of the *Scotorum Historia* shaped their editions for their own purposes. Bellenden did so more than once. He presented James V with a handsome Scots version in manuscript, but worked and reworked it into the *Croniklis* between 1536 and 1540.[54] He intervened in the text beyond mere translation: Bellenden considered the 'text open to paraphrase as well as translation. There are, however, occasions when the word used gives a false interpretation, when the translation is incorrect, when the omission of phrases distorts the passage or when material is added which changes the outlook of its context. ... it is important that Bellenden should not be taken as the sole witness for what Boece has to say.'[55]

What might readers take away from contrasting Bellenden's and Harrison's editions of Boece? The *Croniklis* is the product of Boece and Bellenden's times. The Scots speaks to us fairly well across the centuries, but I will provide English equivalents to certain words or turns of phrase as needed. We need to exercise caution in reconciling the substance of Boece's *Historia* within Bellenden's *Croniklis*. Bellenden demonstrated an identifiable lowland sensibility, by comparison to Boece in addressing Scotland's cultural complexity. Bellenden had little time for the Gaelic heritage of the Scots and he muted Boece's interest in linguistic exchange and integration.[56] Chronologically, however, they stood on the same side of the religious–political divide that opened up in 1559-60. Comparisons with Harrison's religious attitudes still hold, even as we juggle

---

[51] Parry, 'William Harrison'

[52] William Harrison, 'Description of Scotlande' (1577), *The firste volume of the Chronicles of England, Scotlande, and Irelande ... Faithfully Gathered and Set Forth, by Raphaell Holinshed* (STC 13568; two volumes; London, 1577), p. 21, hereafter cited as 'Description of Scotlande'.

[53] 'Description of Scotlande', sig. *b.ii*r.

[54] *Heir Beginnis the Hystory and Croniklis of Scotland* (STC 3203; London, 1540), hereafter cited as *Croniklis*. Nicola Royan, 'The Relationship between the *Scotorum Historia* of Hector Boece and John Bellenden's *Chronicles of Scotland*', in *The Rose and the Thistle: Essays on the Culture of Late Medieval and Renaissance Scotland*, ed. Sally Mapstone and Juliette Wood (East Linton, 1998), pp. 136-7, 140.

[55] Royan, 'Boece and Bellenden', pp. 140, 148.

[56] Royan, 'Boece and Bellenden', pp. 140-8.

Boece's and Bellenden's imprint in the *Croniklis*. We will still uncover revealing moments when Harrison translated and characterized Scotland through the lens of Holinshed's England, his own quest to fashion a universal 'Chronology' that reconciled the island's religious convulsions with the divine ordering of history, and increasingly angry assumptions about English supremacy.[57]

For Boece, the Scots' origins were Gaelic 'and the Picts, the Saxons, and the Normans who settled in the Scottish sphere of influence [in Britain] become subsumed in the Scottish identity and antiquity'.[58] Bellenden's 'nationalist' account gave coherence to the Scots that belied this complex mingling of peoples or the shifting borders and fortunes of the kingdom, including the triumph of Scots from a range of linguistic exchanges. In deliberate contrast to Mair's use of Britain and his unionist sympathies, Boece reverted to Fordun's usage and named 'the land-mass of Scotland, England and Wales as "Albion", not "Britannia"'. He confined Brutus and claims for Britannia to the southern part of the island. Bellenden found the distinction a less pressing matter.[59] Harrison followed the pattern, but omitted Bellenden's opening chapters that included the etymology of Albion, the peopling of the island, and the ethnic divisions of its peoples. Out of diversity – Scots, Picts, Britons, and the many tribal names handed out by the Romans – Bellenden promised to show how 'two peple Inglishmen and Scottis' came to dominate the island 'vnto the tyme of king Hary ye uiii regnand now with gret felicite aboue Inglishmen'.[60]

Whatever their ethnic complexity, Albion sometimes affected all its peoples equally. The island's easy abundance 'makis the peple the les industrius and crafty delyting ay [always] mair in sleuth [slouth/sloth] than ony exerctioun'. The riches taken by foreign nations from Britain's fishing grounds proved the point. Abundance led to other abuses. Both Bellenden and Harrison agreed with the local people who blamed greed for the decay of the herring fishery in Inverness, 'quehn ony auaricious and unhappy men fechtis for the fische that god sendis be [by] his infinit gudnes to the sustentatioun of the peple and dissoulis the see be thair blude'.[61] There were other problems with Albion's people, despite their courage, hardiness, and aptitude for crafts. For Boece/Bellenden, as well, 'gif the Albianis had sic grace, that yai [they] mycht leif with concord amang thaym self, or gif thair realmes be ony honest way mycht cum vnder the empire and senzorie of ane kyng', they might better live without need of trading partners – and more readily fend off the designs of foreign powers on the island. Strife was not the only obstacle to Albion's people achieving their full potential: 'For thay ar gevin

[57] G.J.R. Parry, *A Protestant Vision: William Harrison and the Reformation of Elizabethan England* (Cambridge, 1987), pp. 141–97; Roger Mason, 'Scotland', in *Oxford Handbook of Holinshed's Chronicles*, ed. Paulina Kewes, Ian W. Archer, and Felicity Heal (Oxford, 2013), pp. 656–60.

[58] Royan, 'Boece and Bellenden', pp. 138.

[59] Royan, 'Boece and Bellenden', pp. 144–5.

[60] *Croniklis*, sig. B.i–B.ii.

[61] *Croniklis*, sig. B.vb; 'Description of Scotlande', p. 6.

to sic vnnaturall uoracitie and desire of uncouth metis and drinkis, that thay can nocht restrene thaym self fra immoderate excesse.' God – in a neat reply to Mair – deprived Albion of vineyards so as to encourage temperance and moderate living, but to no avail. Gluttony, dissipation, and – for Harrison – the loss of 'generatiue force' plagued its people. Finally, in the person of the Druids, the people of Albion were once renowned for their religiosity, 'rycth expert baith in naturally and morall Philosphie'.[62] No more, for Harrison.

What, then, of Albion's people in Scotland? By 'diuyne beneuolence' the Scots emerged triumphant in their bloody struggle with the Picts. With spectacular indifference, Boece/Bellenden and Harrison ignored the Welsh and wrote that these Scots most resembled the qualities of Albion's people. This was true 'speciallie among the Scottis in the hieland', who become not just a people apart, but a people almost lost in time:

> For the peple thairof hes no repaire with marchandis of vncouth realmes. And because thay ar nocht corruppit nor myngit with vncouth blude, thay ar ye more strang and rude, and may suffre mare hungir, walking and distres, than ony vthir peple of Albion ... [63]

Scotland was thus internally divided between highland and lowland, ancient and present, virile and timorous. It had once been divided geographically between Picts and Scots as well, along the Mers, but this internal march had been relocated and turned into the contemporary Anglo-Scottish Borders by the kingdom's expansion to the Tweed. It still shared the essential quality of violence found when two hostile rivals collided. Both texts agreed that many 'riche and plentuus boundis [districts] of Scotland lyis waist for feir of thair inuasion'.[64]

Bellenden and Harrison journeyed with Boece through the medieval regions of Scotland, from Galloway and Kyle to the Orkneys and Shetlands, and back again to Ross, Lothian, Clydeside, and the rest. Boece's description marked a significant increase in information from Fordun or Mair, including topographic details and basic information about livelihoods and resources. Not unlike Mair, Boece could not resist digressing to points of unique interest. Robert the Bruce was once menaced by wild bulls in the Caledonian forest around Stirling. The country around Buchan was especially 'plentuus'; no surprise, then, that the rivers Don and Dee produced more salmon than any others in Albion. Moray ran Buchan a close second on both counts, although salmon were caught in Moray using an ingenious wicker basket that trapped the great fish at high tide and kept them penned until they could be collected. Like many rustic or local ways recorded by Boece, Bellenden termed this practice 'vncouth' – for Harrison

---

[62] *Croniklis*, sig. B.iia–B.iiia; also 'Description of Scotlande', p. 2.
[63] *Croniklis*, sig. B.iiia; Morét, 'Gaelic History', pp. 61–2 on Boece's view of the Gaels as the '"living replicas" ... the ancestors of all living Scots both in the Highlands and Lowlands'.
[64] *Croniklis*, sig. B.iiib; 'Description of Scotlande', p. 3.

the fishing method was simply 'strange'.[65] Besides salt, Fife included many noble towns and abbeys, though it was Harrison who mentioned the 'famous vniuersitie' of St Andrews.[66] The principal of King's College may have been more interested in passing on to Bass Rock, where 'Euery thi[n]g yt [that] is in yt [that] crag, is ful of admiration & wounder', including the solan geese.[67]

There are instances when we can tell that Bellenden translated Boece's original almost verbatim: he retains Boece's voice as a traveller. One is of particular interest as we attempt to understand how Bellenden and Harrison engaged the text:

> In Murray land is the kirk of Pette, quhare the banis [bones] of lytill Iohne remanis to gret admiratioun of pepill. He hes bene fourtene fut of hycht ... we saw his hanche [pelvis] bane als mekill [muckle or great/large] as the haill [whole] bane of ane man. For we schot our arme in the mouth thairof. Be quhilk apperis how strang [strong] and square pepill grew in our regioun afore they wer effeminat with lust & intemperance of mouth.[68]

Boece's Little John, with a pelvis the size of a large thigh, testified to the great race of men in Albion from whom the Scots had descended, and degenerated. Harrison happily accepted that 'gluttony and excesse' had wasted the people of Boece's 'region', yet Little John 'was no Scot, but an Englishman that fled into Irela[n]d and then into Scotland' according to a marginal note.[69]

Little John's bones were not the only ones that caught Boece's attention. In the town of Thane in Ross the 'blissit banis of sanct Dutho restis in great ueneratioun of peple'.[70] Not far away lay a valley with two round houses shaped like bells. Harrison seems to have inserted himself into the text alongside Boece/Bellenden, writing:

> In this region moreover is ye towne called Thane, where the bones of Dutho an holy man (as they say) do reste, & are had in greater estimation among the superstitious sorte (*as sometime over the whole Iland, than the holy Gospel of God and merites of his Sonne, wherby we are onely saued.* Two ancient houses are likewise maintained in one vale of Ross, whose formes resemble so many, but to what ende as yet I do not find.[71]

Harrison recast the imprint of faith and devotion on the Scottish landscape in terms of superstition, juxtaposed with his own justification by faith. He laboured at it, though. Boece's account of the 'faithfulness of the Scots is directed towards the orthodoxy of Christian belief' and seems animated by 'a disquiet about heresy and other threats to the fundamental theology of Christianity'. According to Boece,

---

[65] 'Description of Scotlande', p. 6.
[66] 'Description of Scotlande', p. 7.
[67] *Croniklis*, sig. B.iva– B.vb.
[68] *Croniklis*, sig. B.vb.
[69] 'Description of Scotlande', p. 6.
[70] *Croniklis*, sig. B.va.
[71] 'Description of Scotlande', p. 5 (emphasis mine).

these heresies arose outwith Scotland and arrived from other realms like England.[72] Indeed, proximity to the Saxons caused the Scottish borderers to give 'up all the ancient customs' now preserved in the countries uplands.[73] John Lesley would be receptive to this story of faithful highland Scots who resisted foreign heresy and manners, but not Harrison.

Bellenden's translation reported that in Fordun 'the blissit banis of sa[n]ct Paladie restis in gret ueneratioun of peple'. Harrison restored Boece's own voice on the matter (albeit in English) when he wrote that in Fordun 'the bones of Palladius do rest, who is taken generally for the Apostle of our nation'. Gone were the venerable bones and the people's idolatry, replaced by a proper recognition of the man who led the Scots out of their heathenism to Christ. Harrison was not above simply removing the evidence of the pre-Reformation Church from the landscape. Out went the religious orders and houses in Angus, the great abbey at Dunfermline, the abbot and monks of Iona, and the island abbey of the Augustinians in the Forth.[74]

Not far from Holyrood was 'a certayne oyly spring ... and the people are perswaded hereof, that it is uery medicinable agaynst all Cankers and skalles'.[75] Harrison apparently could not bring himself to relate the full story of the self-replenishing oily spring:

> This fountaine rais throw ane drop of sanct Katrynis oulle [oil], quhilk wes brocht out of mont Synay fra hir sepulture to sanct Margaret the blisit quene of Scotland. Als sone as sanct Margaret saw the oulie [oil] spring Ithandlie [continuously] be [by] diuine miracle in the said place, sche gart [caused or gave instructions for] big ane [a big] chapell thair in the honour of sanct Katherine.[76]

Neither the humble canons in Angus nor Queen Margaret, the great patron saint of Scotland, were fit material for an evangelical edition of Boece's travels. Some surprising and impressive topographic discoveries awaited a traveller who prepared by reading only Harrison.

The establishment of a Calvinist Kirk in Scotland after the ouster of the French did not intrude on the evangelicalism that coloured Harrison's reading of the Scots. In the Forth, 'uncouth and wounderfull fische' often appeared and were thought to portend the 'mortalitie of men and beistis quhare yai ar sene'. Harrison's prejudices turned this local omen into a national character trait: 'wherefore their onely sight doth breede great terrour vnto the Scottishe nation, who are very great obseruers of vncouth signes and tokens'.[77] Worse could be found in Buchan:

---

[72] Royan, *Scotorum Historia*, pp. 83–5.
[73] Morét, 'Gaelic History', p. 62.
[74] 'Description of Scotlande', pp. 7, 12.
[75] 'Description of Scotlande', p. 8.
[76] *Croniklis*, sig. C.ia.
[77] *Croniklis*, sig. B.vib; 'Description of Scotlande', p. 8.

In this regioun is ane carnell [cairn] of stanis [stones] liand togiddir in maner of ane croun. And ryngis (quhen thay ar doung [struck]) as ane bell. Ane temple wes biggit [constructed] (as sum men belieuis) in the said place, quhare mony auld ritis [rites] and superstitionis wer mad to euill spretis [spirits].[78]

This reading of the landscape was not scathing enough for Harrison: 'Some are of the opinion, that one Idoll Temple or other stoode heretofore in that place whylest the Scottishe nation was addicted to the worshyppyng of Divels.'[79]

Here both Bellenden and Harrison closed the topographical description. Bellenden admitted that many other regions in Scotland might be described but 'thay ar nocht sa notable', while Harrison capped his antipathy: 'they are not so notable as those which we haue already touched, therefore I thinke it but folly to deale any farther with them'.[80] Boece's *Scotorum Historia* did not end on that note, however. Judging by the chapters that followed, we ought to sympathize with Bellenden's task of breaking Boece's description into sensible pieces. A description of the wildlife of Scotland included stories of dogs that tracked border thieves and rievers into their native countries by the scent of the stolen goods and the 'uncouth and strange' procreation of salmon. Mussels, cockles, sundry strange fish, and tales of pearls filled out another chapter. A chapter describing Barnacle or Claik geese and the Isle of Thule was sandwiched in between one that described the major Western Isles (plus Man and Arran) and another that tackled Orkney and Shetland. A long comparison of the old and new manners of the Scots and a genealogy of English kings back to Brutus closed Bellenden's edition. Harrison felt it necessary to add his own account of the Picts, lifted verbatim from Herodian.

The description of the Western Isles and the ethnography demand a closer look. Bellenden wasted no time in turning a familiar prejudice against the islanders into Scots: Islay was 'rycht plentuus of corne and full of metallis, gif thair were ony crafty and industrious peple to wyn the samyn'.[81] Perhaps Harrison was less troubled in duplicating Bellenden's account of the Lewis islanders as a people apart who sent the most innocent among them to lay a taper on the altar, 'whereof fire commeth downe from heave[n] and kindleth or setteth the same on fire' during their prayers.[82] Descriptions of rough seas, dangerous currents, and great sucking whirlpools would one day be captured by Romantic writers and the cinema lens of Michael Powell and Emeric Pressburger's Corryvreckan in *I Know Where I'm Going!* (1945).

Passing on from a people apart in the Western Isles, Boece/Bellenden and Harrison found in the Orkneys, Shetland, and the islands beyond a people more

---

[78] *Croniklis*, sig. C.ib.
[79] 'Description of Scotlande', p. 9.
[80] *Croniklis*, sig. C.ib; 'Description of Scotlande', p. 9.
[81] *Croniklis*, sig. C.iiib.
[82] 'Description of Scotlande', p. 13.

and more akin to the prelapsarian humans who populated European discovery narratives of the Atlantic world.[83] On Orkney, Harrison reported, 'there is great abundance of Barley wherof they make the strongest Ale that is to be founded in Albion, and thereof knowen, that they are the greatest drynkers of any men in the worlde'. Yet no Orkney islanders had ever lost their wits or fallen into madness from this early Skullsplitter ale. Indeed, in the Orkneys there was little use of physic and other purgatives since 'mankinde liueth there most commonly unto extreme age in sound & perfite health, whose bodies also are of strong constitution & very white of colour'. The inhabitants' hardiness and good health matched the fertility of the island itself and its animal species. The Shetland islanders were much the same, though 'in steede of stronge Ale, content themselues with water, and uery slender diet'.[84]

Beyond Shetland lay other islands even farther removed from the faults of humanity:

> And youcht ye peple of yis Ilis be pure, Zit thay leif langer and ar better content of thair lyuis than thay that hes mair welth and riches of the warld. No contentioun is amang thaym for singulare proffet. ... Thir peple ar nakit of all ambitoun and uice, and neuer truble with uncouth weris [wars]. Amang all pleseiris [pleasures] ... thay think na thyng so gud as to leif in concord and peace ... And followis be the samyn futsteppis of crist [Christ].[85]

Harrison's translation polished the islanders' noble glow:

> This finally is to be added vnto their comendation, that they are simple, playne, uoyde of crafte, and all maner of Serpentine suttlety, whiche endeth commonly with mischiefe, and reigneth in the Maine. ... If any giftes of nature are to be numbred as parcelles of worldly riches and renowne, they are not without these also: for the people of these Iles are lusty, fayre, strong of body, and highe of stature. ... What should I say of their helth, whiche is and may be preferred aboue all treasure ... for here among these men, you shall uery seldome heare of sicknesse to attache any, untill extreame age come that killeth them altogether ... As for their quietnesse of minde, it is always such as is constant, unchangeable, and therefore incomparable unto any riches or huge masse of worldly treasure.[86]

These islanders, without covetous hearts, may have been dramatically outside humanity's failings, but they were also outside the first-hand experiences of Boece, Bellenden, or Harrison. Bellenden and Harrison both preserved verbatim Boece's admission that he had never met these peoples. Like many travellers,

[83] David Abulafia, *The Discovery of Mankind: Atlantic Encounters in the Age of Columbus* (New Haven, 2008), pp. 114, 116, 177–8.
[84] 'Description of Scotlande', pp. 14–15; also *Croniklis*, sig. C.va–vb.
[85] *Croniklis*, sig. C.vb.
[86] 'Description of Scotlande', p. 15.

Boece hoped that his candour and the credentials of his chief informant, in his case the bishop of Orkney, would reassure skeptical readers.[87]

Boece apparently intended to plunge into his history of Scotland at that point. But 'sindry [sundry] nobill men hes desyrit me to schaw ye auld maneris of Scottis (quhilkis ar skatterit in sindry partis of yis buke) under ane co[m]pendius [tract], that it may be knawin how far we in this present dayis ar different'. Boece composed a summary of Scottish manners with clear intent. He held up the older Scots as a distinctly unflattering mirror to their fallen descendants, hoping that those Scots not wholly corrupted would lead the rest to renewal.[88] They bore a striking resemblance to the Scots of Fordun's *Chronicle*.

The older Scots were a temperate people, in both conversation and behaviour. They ate simple food and bread. They hunted for meat – which promoted fitness and martial vigour – and lived off tame cattle, but most often consumed fish because conflict so frequently left their lands (and animals) wasted. These Scots broke their fast simply, then refrained until dinner, 'throw quhilk thair stomok was nevir surfetly chargit to empesche [hinder] thaym of vthir besines' or, as Harrison put it somewhat more directly, 'whereby it came to passe, yt [that] their stomackes were neuer overcharged, nor their bones desirous of rest thorow the fulnesse of their bellies'.[89] Merrymaking was a time for ale or aqua vitae made from local 'herbis as grew in thair awin yardis', but only water was fit for wartime. Indeed, the Scottish army marched on stomachs filled with those famous hearth cakes, eating meat only if it was captured from the enemy, and then half raw. Their reserve rations came in the form of 'ane gret vessell brocht full of butter, cheis, mele [meal], milk, & vinacre [vinegar] temperit togidder'.[90]

Continual exercise, including hill running and wrestling, made these Scots ever fit for war. Scottish parents toughened their children by dipping them into chill water and exposing them to the extremity of the elements, especially by making them go barefooted. Like their ancient Spanish cousins, the Scots sported shaved heads, save for one little tuft on the forehead, and went about uncovered except when sick. Their hose were made of finer linen or wool and they alternated between winter and summer mantles. They slept on bunks of straw, teaching their children from their earliest years to, in Harrison's words, 'eschew ease & practice the like hardnesse'.[91] To preserve the hardy nature of the Scottish nation, mothers nursed their children and rejected milk from any other sources as dangerous and 'vncouth'.[92]

Defeated in battle, the army melted into the countryside and hills to take the field another day. When battle was joined, the best of the nobility sought the front

---

[87] *Croniklis*, sig. C.vb. and 'Description of Scotlande', p. 16.
[88] *Croniklis*, sig. C.via–vib. 'Description of Scotlande', pp. 16–17.
[89] *Croniklis*, sig. D.ia. 'Description of Scotlande', p. 18.
[90] *Croniklis*, sig. D.ia.
[91] 'Description of Scotlande', p. 18.
[92] *Croniklis*, sig. D.ia.

ranks. 'The wemen war of lytle les vassalage and strenth,' wrote Bellenden, 'than was the men. For al rank madynnis [maidens] and wyfis (gif thay war nocht with child) gein [go] als weill to battall, as the men.' With great solemnity and ritual, soldiers dipped their swords in to taste the blood of the first living creature slain in battle.[93] This was no environment for the faint-hearted. Scots apprehended and killed cowards and deserters on the spot. In an early example of eugenics, the Scots gelded (castrated) any man who manifested weaknesses that might be passed to his offspring. Women with comparable afflictions were banished from the company of men, threatened with their own and their child's death if they subsequently became pregnant. Gluttons, drunkards, and other great consumers of victuals were likewise killed. For his part, Harrison embellished Bellenden's account with tales of the women and children being run through with lances, and our friends the gluttons being allowed to have one final smorgasbord before being executed by drowning in the nearest stream or river. These Scots, then, were people resolute and brutal in war, not above feuding among themselves.[94]

The Scots were not simply a warrior race, though. God had provided this region, so barren and unfruitful by distance from the sun, with 'all maner of necessaryis to ye sustenatioun of man', 'gif thair war sic pepyll that cuid laubour it effering [appropriate] to the nature thairof'. This backhanded compliment was offered in the context of praising Scottish excellence in the science of medicine, especially the expert use of medicinal herbs. Language among the early Scots was ethnically determined: 'Thay usit the rytis and maneris of Egiptianis fra quhome thay tuk thair first begynnyng', using a hieroglyphic language in their secret correspondence. The hieroglyphic form of the ancient language perished, but the fine cadences of the spoken original and its ordinary written counterpart were preserved among the highlanders and their poets and bards. Sounding a note of almost Romantic attachment to the highlanders who preserved the nation's ancient culture, both texts remarked on the traditional carroch still used in salmon fishing. By contrast, the Saxon tongue was the most lasting legacy when Scots met their English neighbours for trade and warfare in the lowland marches and borders.[95]

'Bot we wyl [now leave] the maneris of our ancient frendis', wrote Bellenden as he turned Boece's mirror on his fellow Scots.[96] The rot in the Scottish character began with Malcolm Canmore (c. 1058). At first sight we might assume that the vengeful feud between Macbeth, who took the throne in 1040 by murdering Duncan I, and Malcolm, the dead king's eldest son, provoked Boece's anger. Rather, the problem for Boece probably lay with Malcolm's exile in England and the army of Englishmen and Northumbrians that brought him back to Scotland

[93] *Croniklis*, sig. D.ib. 'Description of Scotlande', pp. 18–19.
[94] *Croniklis*, sig. D.ib. 'Description of Scotlande', pp. 18–19.
[95] *Croniklis*, sig. D.iia. 'Description of Scotlande', pp. 19–20.
[96] *Croniklis*, sig. D.iia.

and the throne. After the deaths of Macbeth (1057) and his heir Lulach (1058), Malcolm's ties with England corrupted the Scots:

> For quhen oure nychtburis [neighbours] the Brytonis war maid effeminate be lang sloth, and boun[d] out of Britane be the Saconis [Saxons] in Walis, we began to haue Alliance ... with Inglysmen, specially efter the ecterminioun [extermation] of Pichtis and be frequent and dayly company of thaym [Englishmen] we began to rute [root] thair langage, and superflew maneris in oure brestis. Throw quhilk the virtew & temprance of our eldaris began to be of lytl estimation amang ws [us]. tha[n] we war geuyn efter the arrogance and pride of Inglishmen to vane glore & ambution of honouris.[97]

Malcolm's later taste for cross-border raids into England did nothing to deter Boece/Bellenden from identifying this as the moment when valorous Scots embraced riches and titles as the (false) marks of virtue.[98]

Scottish decline mimicked the corruption of the Roman republic, a staple topic for humanist readers like Boece steeped in Livy and Tacitus.[99] Neither Boece nor Bellenden was lost for vivid descriptions of their fallen countrymen: 'dronkyness', 'schamefull and immoderyt voracitie', 'the hungry appetit of glutonis', 'all maner of droggis [drugs] ... (that may nuris [nourish] the lust and insolence of pepyl) ar brocht into Scotland with maist sumptuus price to na les dammage than perdition of the pepyll', and 'auarice'. The effects were clear for all to see, a strong, hardy people wasted and sickened by 'uoluptuus leuying and intemperance', incapable of repeating the martial exploits of their ancestors and guilty of producing one enfeebled generation after another.[100] Harrison expanded the details of Bellenden's version, with something of an evangelical zeal, calling the Scots to account 'as men not walking in ye right pathe', while offering his fellow Englishmen, with their own problems of indolence and high living, a stern warning.[101]

As we might expect, Boece/Bellenden held out hope for the restoration of virtue, for 'in syndry partis of this realme, remanis zet ye futsteppis of mony auld virtewis usit sum tyme amang our eldaris. Bot als risis euery day new feruent deuotioun to the ornament of chrisin faith.'[102] The rebirth of the Scots depended upon the recovery of old values and new devotions to Christianity. There 'was neuir pepyl mair sicker [secure] inye cristin faith, nor zit mair constant in thair faithful promis, than the scottis hes bene ay sen thair first beginning' and the Scots could be led to their ancient virtue by understanding 'want yai na maner of uirtew yt yair eldaris had, except the temperance of thair bodyis'.[103] From

---

[97] *Croniklis*, sig. D.iia–iib.
[98] See Morét, 'Gaelic History', pp. 74–8
[99] Royan, '*Scotorum Historia*', pp. 3, 98, 297.
[100] *Croniklis*, sig. D.iib–D.iiia.
[101] 'Description of Scotlande', pp. 20–1.
[102] *Croniklis*, sig. D.iiia.
[103] *Croniklis*, sig. D.iiia.

Harrison's standpoint in the 1570s, the Scots still waited for their redemption.[104] He rewrote Bellenden's closing and prayed 'God graunt them also to returne to their former frugality, and that with speede. Amen.'[105] John Lesley revived the redemptive power of Scottish nobility and devotion to God, but in a radically different context. The final disintegration of Christendom in Britain, with the abrupt severing of Scotland from the Catholic Church in 1559-61, dramatically altered Lesley's engagement with the cultural complexity of the Scots.

The Catholic Scots of John Lesley's *Historie*

William Harrison would have found an appalling example of the unredeemed Scots in the Catholic bishop of Ross, John Lesley. Lesley spent 1568 and 1569 in York, intriguing with Queen Mary's supporters in their scheme to marry the exiled queen of Scots to the English duke of Norfolk. Lesley occupied his Christmas and New Year in penning a treatise that countered allegations that Mary had played the role of femme fatale in the murder of her husband, Henry Darnley. The treatise also defended Mary's claim to the English throne as the great granddaughter of Henry VII. Lesley might have done better to accommodate himself to the new regime in Scotland and his hosts in England. A spell of imprisonment between February and April 1569 did not deter his intrigues. The imprisonment of Norfolk and the failed rising of the Catholic Northern earls of Northumberland and Westmorland led once more to Lesley's own confinement, this time in the bishop of London's house. He was released in May 1570, but worse was to come in 1571, thanks in to his involvement in the Ridolfi Plot, a second abortive attempt to bring together Mary and Norfolk. Two days caged in the Tower, under the watchful eyes of William Cecil's agents, brought the songbird in Lesley to a pretty tune, providing Burghley with full details of the plot. Norfolk went to the scaffold and Lesley spent another eighteen months in confinement before finally sailing into exile in France in January 1574.[106]

Lesley did not occupy his time in England entirely with intrigue. He spent part of 1568 in reading the histories of Polydore Vergil and Bede, the chronicles of Froissart, Fabyan, and Edward Hall, and summaries by John Stow. Lesley found – apparently to his surprise – 'mony and sundry thingis sett forth ... far contrar to our annales, registeris, and trew proceedingis collected in Scotland'. While Lesley felt that 'the trew histories of our country be largely, truly, and eloquently treated and wreattin be that cuning and eloquente historiographe

---

[104] 'Description of Scotlande', p. 21.

[105] 'Description of Scotlande', p. 21.

[106] Rosalind K. Marshall, 'John Lesley', *Oxford DNB* at www.oxforddnb.com. Stephen Alford, *Burghley: William Cecil at the Court of Elizabeth I* (New Haven, 2008), pp. 168–81; Margaret J. Beckett, 'Counsellor, Conspirator, Polemicist, Historian: John Lesley, Bishop of Ross 1527–96, *Records of the Scottish Church History Society* 39 (2009), pp. 5–10.

Hector Boecius', he decided to bring that story up to date, filling in the period between James I's death in 1436 and Mary's reign.[107] House arrest in London allowed Lesley the opportunity to do just that. The history he finished in 1570 remained in Scots and in manuscript until its publication in 1830 for the Bannatyne Club.[108]

Continental exile prompted a second look at the manuscript.[109] What had begun as a continuation of Boece evolved into a new, distinct work: Lesley created a full-blown account 'Of the origin, manners, and history of the Scots'.[110] In the address to 'the nobility and people of Scotland', Lesley explained that

> many persons, both in our own and foreign countries, pressed me not only to publish this in the Latin language, but also to add a compendium of the previous history already written, correctly, though inelegantly, by John Major, and elegantly enough, by Hector Boece, but, as many complained, with too much diffuseness and prolixity. I proceeded therefore to compress and epitomise this portion; while to the former, which in its Scottish dress could interest Scotsmen only, I have, with some trouble, given the power to speak to all through the medium of Latin. In writing this work, I have not only confronted previous histories with the annals kept in our public archives, and with the oldest codices religiously preserved at Paisley, Scone, and our other monasteries, but I have consulted Tacitus, Suetonious, Ammianus, Marcellinus, Eutropius, Herodianus, and other writers of neighbouring nations.[111]

Lesley completed this *Historie of Scotland* when he moved to the papal court as Mary's representative. The edition published in Rome in 1578 boasted a dedication to Pope Gregory XIII. Lesley explained that when 'I realised that the same benefit which I received from these studies (of Scottish history) might be enjoyed by my fellow-countrymen, I set myself to arrange, or rather rewrite, the history of the Scots, which I had roughly put together when in prison, and brought with me to Italy as my plank of safety from shipwreck.'[112]

Lesley's feeling for Scottish Catholicism seems to have become more heartfelt in exile and accordingly influenced how he responded to Boece (and Mair). Boece provided him with a good deal of the raw material needed to write an idealized Catholic history of Scotland and the Scots.[113] Learning of the *Schottenklöster* – the once vibrant Scottish (actually, Irish) monasteries and abbeys in Germany – Lesley proposed transforming these into the training colleges for

---

[107] Leslie, *Historie*, I, p. xviii.
[108] Leslie, *Historie*, I, pp. xi–xxii.
[109] Leslie, *Historie*, I, pp. xviii–xix; published in 1830 for the Bannatyne Club.
[110] A Latin manuscript in the Vatican archives that breaks off in midsentence continues the history down to 1571, but may well not be Lesley's work. Leslie, *Historie*, I, pp. xxi–xxii; Margaret Beckett, 'The Political Works of John Lesley, Bishop of Ross (1527-96)' (Ph.D. thesis; University of St Andrews, 2009), p. 200.
[111] Leslie, *Historie*, I, pp. xx–xxi.
[112] Leslie, *Historie*, I, p. xx.
[113] Beckett, 'Political Works of John Lesley', pp. 217–20.

a new generation of Scottish missionaries.[114] Lesley persuaded Pope Gregory to install the Linlithgow priest Ninian Winzet at Ratisbon abbey so he could spearhead the *Schottenklöster* project.[115] Encouraged by Winzet, Lesley's *Historie* and his plans for the *Schottenklöster* opened a new front in his battle against the Protestant regime in Scotland and his queen's captors.[116] As if to confirm the relationship, Father James Dalrymple of Ratisbon turned the Latin *Historie* back into Scots in 1596, forming the basis for the 'modern' edition published by the Scottish Text Society.[117] Lesley hoped that just as the Catholic Scots would go forth from the *Schottenklöster* and nurse their brethren, the Scots of his *Historie* would leap from its pages and embolden their modern counterparts to summon the virtues of their forebears, return to the ancient faith, and embrace a Counter-Reformation destiny.

Lesley's encounters with the peoples of Scotland owed their beginnings to his birth in Kingussie, nestled alongside the Spey as it followed its course to the Moray Firth. Here Lesley probably crossed paths with highlanders and lowlanders before his travels into Aberdeenshire as a student and, later, as a cleric in the diocese.[118] In the aftermath of the revolution of 1559-60, he accompanied a delegation of Catholics summoned to Edinburgh to defend the mass against the likes of John Knox. Lesley and his Aberdeen colleagues were detained for a time and subjected to sermons by the reformers. Mary's return from France in 1560 improved his fortunes. He was appointed professor of canon law at King's College Aberdeen, made a judge in the Court of Session and privy councillor, and promoted to the abbey of Lindores and bishopric of Ross. Lesley finally made his way north to Ross just as Mary's rule collapsed. He backtracked too late to rejoin her after the escape from Lochleven, but travelled through the Borders to reach York and, eventually, Burton-on-Trent and London.[119] Only the most remote parts of Scotland would have been wholly undiscovered country for Lesley.

On reading Lesley's description of Scotland, it is clear why Robert Sibbald referred his readers to it: Lesley's was the most thorough topographical description of Scotland available. He aligned his *Historie* with Mair and Boece, but his ethnography had a distinct purpose:

---

[114] Marshall, 'John Lesley'.

[115] Marshall, 'John Lesley'; J.H. Burns, 'George Buchanan and the Anti-monarchomachs', in *Scots and Britons: Scottish Political Thought and the Union of 1603*, ed. Roger Mason (Cambridge, 1994), pp. 139-40; also Mark Dilworth, 'Ninian Winzet', *Oxford DNB* at www.oxforddnb.com.

[116] Beckett, 'Political Works of John Lesley', p. 221.

[117] The Scottish Text Society edition derives from Dalrymple's Scots manuscript version of the 1578 edition, edited alongside a 1675 reprint of the Latin edition and incorporating a Latin manuscript of Lesley's in the Vatican archives. Leslie, *Historie*, I, pp. xi-xxii.

[118] Morét, 'Gaelic History', pp. 88-91.

[119] Marshall, 'John Lesley'; Beckett, 'Political Works of John Lesley', p. 25.

> That I, afore the eyne [eye] baith of our Nobilitie, and of the lai people, in quhatsae-
> uir state or degrie, mycht sett doun as in ane bredd or table, a certaine ernist or hett
> affectione of the catholik religione, and a vehement constance in defending thairof.

Like Boece, Lesley described 'mony vthiris worthie and notable vertues, in
quhilkes our Elderis, sumtyme florisched, and war mekle [greatly] renoued'.
However, the qualities of these ancient Scots would now call to their modern
brethren who had fallen from the true faith: 'the radier walde thay ryse frome
thair darke errouris in quhilkes thay ar incloset, and returneng sinceirlie to the
catholik concorde, now at last mychte begin to follow the sway of true vertue
sa deip imprented with the fustepis of thair foirbears'.[120] Here was a Counter-
Reformation history set to confront the Scottish revolution and a Presbyterian
Kirk with a very different claim on Scotland, its past, and its peoples.

Lesley's topography wrote the religious orders back into the spiritual life of
the nation and rebuilt the church's foundations on its monasteries and abbeys.
Through them, Lesley celebrated Catholic spirituality and the perseverance of
his co-religionists. He attacked the violence directed toward them by his heretical
opponents and their self-serving political allies. The Borders contained the 'riche
monasteries' of Melrose, Jedburgh, Kelso, and Coldingham, with the houses 'of
haly nunis' in Coldstream and Eccles. Lesley made special mention of these
monasteries because their yearly revenues had not been 'violated by any law of
the kingdom' until the 'the furie of thir wod [mad] men through the hail Realme
haue castne doune'.[121] Galloway 'lykewyse afor the haeresie began, [was] decored
with a famous and fair monasterie' (St Ninians) and Lesley praised the 'wisdome
and authoritie of certane illustir and nobill men' through whose intervention
another Galloway monastery 'stadis yit haill [undamaged].'[122] Not far away,
Glasgow 'Afor the haeresie' boasted an academy well respected for philosophy,
grammar, and political instruction. Of even more note was the monastery at
Paisley: the 'bewtie of the biging [building] and ecclesiastical vestments, an decore
of the yardes, may esilie contend with mony kirkes, quhilkes this day ar halden
maist ornat in vthir cuntreyes'.[123] The 'beautiful and excellent' foundations at
Arbroath, St Andrews, Dunfermline, Holyrood, and Melrose stood as Catholic
monuments. So did Lindores, Culross, Pittenweem, and Balmerino and the
nunnery at Aberdour.[124] Perth offered an instructive contrast. In all things it was
fair, beautiful, and well-disposed 'excepte the destructione of religious places',
among which was once 'a noble clostre and large of the Cartusianis, quhilke the
heides of the toune Caluinists ouirthrew first of al in thir furie, first, I say afor
ony vthir'.[125] As British Catholics worked to revitalize 'spaces and sites that had

---

[120] Leslie, *Historie*, I, p. 1.
[121] Leslie, *Historie*, I, p. 11, n. ‡.
[122] Leslie, *Historie*, I, pp. 11–13.
[123] Leslie, *Historie*, I, p. 16.
[124] Leslie, *Historie*, I, pp. 16, 37.
[125] Leslie, *Historie*, I, pp. 33–4.

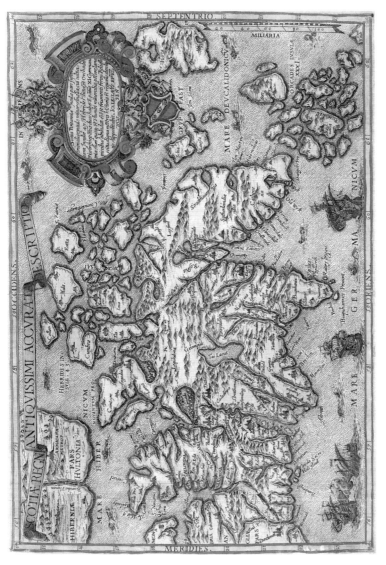

7 'Scotiae Regni Antiqvissimi Accvrata Descriptio' from John Leslie, *De Origine Moribus, et Rebus Gestis Scotorum Libri Decem* (Rome, 1578). Reproduced by permission of the National Library of Scotland.

been venerated by their medieval predecessors', Lesley's *Historie* pointed them to the 'hallowed places that had been vandalized or abandoned' which could become the scenes of 'covert devotion.'[126]

Lesley rediscovered the world of pious devotion in the shadow of Holyrood, at the oily spring in Liberton: 'Is said that quhen it first sprang to have beine spilte out of S. Catharines oyle, quhen thair the pig [earthen pitcher] quhairin it was, negligentlie was brokne, quhen frome the Mounte Sinay it was brocht to S. Margaret: Bot it is gude (as we vnderstand) to kure and to remeid diuers dolouris [blemishes] of the skin.'[127] This was a fair reworking of Boece/Bellenden's account, but how the spring fared in later descriptions gives us some sense of what Lesley was up against in attempting a Catholic topography. For Harrison, it still belonged to a time when the Scots worshipped devils and diligently observed uncouth signs and tokens. George Buchanan had nothing to say on the matter, but his relative David Buchanan wrote a new account for the Scottish volume of Joan Blaeu's great *Atlas Novus* in 1654. He described a 'spring from whose outflow oil bubbles up along with water or a fatty, dense balsam, floating on the water. The local people collect this on fixed days and preserve it for several months, and they use it as an excellent remedy against distortions and pains in the limbs and against *agria*, a type of scabies.'[128] Blaeu printed Buchanan's account four years after Cromwell and the New Model Army soldiers had defaced the shrine.[129] Decades later, Robert Sibbald obtained a report of the well – reading very much like Buchanan's – as he gathered first-hand accounts by local informants for his 'Scottish Atlas': 'To the south of Libertoun Kirk there is a Wellspring which sends up with the Water an Oyl or rather a Balsam reasonable thick and fat. ... a sovraign cure for wrests, Akings, &c.'[130] Sibbald simply dropped the matter when he revised the Scottish chapters of *Britannia* for Gibson in 1695. The mystical passed from the superstitious to the medicinal to the forgettable.[131]

Lesley carried over much of what Boece recorded. Greedy fishermen in the Cromarty Firth were once again punished with the diversion of herring to less bountiful waters, though their wicker nets still produced an excellent yield of salmon. At the other end of Loch Ness, the 'rude peple' of Lochaber proved positively xenophobic toward strangers who might ply the waters for salmon.[132] This contrasted with Ayr, at whose 'prettie sey porte ... strange natiouns oft

---

[126] Alexandra Walsham, *The Reformation of the Landscape: Religion, Identity, and Memory in Early Modern Britain and Ireland* (Oxford, 2011), pp. 155, 166, although Walsham does not address Lesley in her study.

[127] Leslie, *Historie*, I, pp. 23–4.

[128] *The Blaeu Atlas of Scotland* (Edinburgh, 2006), p. 62.

[129] Walsham, *Reformation of the Landscape*, p. 422.

[130] *Geographical Collections Relating to Scotland made by Walter Macfarlane*, ed. Arthur Mitchell and James Toshach Clark (three volumes; Edinburgh, 1906–8), III, pp. 122–3.

[131] Leslie, *Historie*, I, pp. 55–7.

[132] Leslie, *Historie*, I, pp. 38–42.

arryues' to trade.[133] The pious of Ross, 'for the religiounis cause, was wonte to make a frequent and gret pilgrimage' to the relics of St Duthak in Tain, while the two round, bell-like towers in the Vale of Ross had two fine monasteries to keep them company.[134] And, Little John's remains still haunted the Scottish past:

> In Moray land in the kirk of a certane village or clachan named Petty are keipit the banes of a certane persone quhome thay cal litle Johne, departed bot the space of thrie hundir yeirs, as the commone brute amang thame is, quhome the Antiphrastiks, that is, thay quha quhat they speik meines contrare, callis litle: quhais Wydnes [width] of his banes and gretnes teiches that he was xiiii. fute lang. In his thie bane, or as we speik, his hanche bane, is nocht ane of his age quha may nocht esilie hand and arme put in togither.[135]

Lesley proved an adept parrot in his story of the islands. Man and Iona were notable for their contributions to Scotland's ancient devotions. Man 'was the first sait of thame called druides, and ... the fontane of al halynes and doctrine maist singular', while Scots of Iona 'saved civilization', 'quhair lykewyse was keipit in custodie mony buikes of antiquitie, quhilkes out of Rome, quhen be the Gothis it was ouircum'.[136] As in Boece's telling, the islanders of Orkney and Shetland were exceptionally healthy and long lived, although Lesley omitted many of the fabulous and entertaining details of their hardiness as a people apart.[137]

The topography of Catholic Scotland came alive in Lesley's hands. For the travelling scholar-writers in early modern Britain, topography inevitably shaded into ethnography. It was difficult to separate the qualities of a country's peoples from the features of its landscapes. In Scotland people left unique marks on the country, while the land in turn defined their lives. The land also divided them. Highland, lowland, and complex regional dynamics defined the land as much as the people. Civility gave way to barbarity, depending upon whom one travelled among. We see all of this at work in Lesley's description.[138] Among their customs, manners, and cultural markers, steadfast devotion to Catholicism defined the Scots, who framed the history to follow.

Lesley began with the peopling of Britain:

> In alde tyme thrie peples onlie war in Britannie, the Britanis, the Scots, and the Peychtis [Picts]. ... [The Isle] be violence, force, and compulsione occupied be strangeris, hes oft bene changet, as the Inglishe historiographouris beiris at large, for to the Britanis gyueng place succeidet the Romanes; quhen the Romanis war expelit, the peychtis and the Scottis tuke possessione: The Britanis now callis the Saxonis to dryue out the Scottis and peychtis, quha neist succeidet to thay roumes [domains]; quhen the

---

[133] Leslie, *Historie*, I, p. 15.
[134] Leslie, *Historie*, I, p. 43.
[135] Leslie, *Historie*, I, p. 46.
[136] Leslie, *Historie*, I, pp. 55–7.
[137] Leslie, *Historie*, I, pp. 64–5.
[138] See Beckett, 'John Lesley', p. 14 for Lesley's attention to ethnic identity in other works.

Saxounis war dantouned [subdued] succeidet the Danes of Denmark: quhen the Danes ar dung [forced] out, the Nortmans establishes that forme of ane Impire, in quhilke we this day sie the dignitie of the Inglishe name perseueiring ... [139]

This history of migration, encounter, and settlement played a crucial role in a Catholic reading of Scotland and its people.

The 'Britains of Cambrie or Wallis', besieged by Caesar and now 'vnder the kingdome and Impire of Ingland', kept 'incorrupte baith thair language and maneris'. The Welsh welcomed the benevolent union wrought by Henry VII's accession and the acts of union that followed under his son, especially becoming 'ane people vndir ane law, aequal maneris and conditiones [with] the Inglesmen'.[140] Lesley may have imbibed too much Tudor propaganda. More importantly, the Welsh offered a fine example of a people 'in the Catholik religione verie constant', despite the break from Rome and the re-establishment of a Protestant Church under Elizabeth. Perhaps Lesley had in mind St Winifrede's well at Holywell in Flintshire. The support of powerful Catholic families like the Mostyns and Pennants made it a Counter-Reformation hotspot, despite the regime's disapproval.[141] Seventy years later the godly warriors of the New Model Army would scarcely credit the Welsh with being Christian, let alone good Protestants.[142]

These descendants of the ancient Britons who held fast to their culture and faith had something to teach their Scottish cousins. God favoured Scotland too: it 'hes ben maist ancient, and to God and man hes bene bathe grate and acceptable, testifies thair daylye habitatione in the land quhilke presentlie thay inhabite, thair sure and constante libertie from age til age, thair lawfull successione of kingis sa mony hundir yeirs; thair quick receiueng of the christne religione, and evin vnto this age sa constantlie in it perseueiring ... in this mirk and mistie tyme, this warlde now sa neir ane end, and weirand [worn] sa fast away'. If they were not descended from some mythic or godly founder, they were certainly the children of 'sum stout and excellent persounis baith in virtue and nobilitie'.[143]

The imprint of virtue and nobility could be found, naturally, in the Scots' manners and customs. Lesley shamelessly cribbed Boece. The Scots did not spend their lives in curious cheer or eating dainty and delicate dishes. They preferred water, whole-wheat hearth cakes, stewed meat, and a nutritious, fatty meat broth, consumed on a schedule that included only breakfast and a late supper. Illness naturally passed them by. Men and women kept to plain, decent

---

[139] Leslie, *Historie*, I, p. 82.
[140] Leslie, *Historie*, I, p. 84.
[141] Alexandra Walsham, 'Holywell: Contesting Sacred Space in Post-Reformation Wales', in *Sacred Space in Early Modern Europe*, ed. Will Coster and Andrew Spicer (Cambridge, 2005), pp. 211–32.
[142] See below, Chapter 8.
[143] Leslie, *Historie*, I, p. 70.

clothing without jewellery: a short wool coat, simple breeches for men 'mair to hyd thair memberis than for ony pompe or pryd', linen shirts coloured with saffron, and mantles (cloaks), though the nobility preferred larger and more colourful ones than the commoners.[144] They slept rough, wrapped in their mantles. As a warrior people the Scots were swift in pursuit and clever in retreat, their nobility sought the front ranks, and they went into battle provisioned with their great crocks of butter, milk, and cheese and armed with the short, long, and broad swords, wearing leather coats. They exercised their bodies in peacetime and brought 'vp thair bairnes first to exercise thame in schoteng arrowis, neist in casting dartes, thaireftir in feiding [feeding] horses, and prouoking thame to rinn; and last in handling of waiponis'.[145] All this martial vigour naturally led to feuds.[146] Yet no people 'war les diligate [delicate] than thay, les leicherous, and mair abhorred voluptuous plesour'.[147]

The Scots who most closely resembled their noble ancestors were the Gaels who lived in the Gaedhealtacht.[148] This was certainly Boece's contention, and Lesley made the connection the centrepiece of his description: 'for quha this day ar, haue hithrito keipet the institutiounis of thair elderis sa constantlie, that nocht onlie mair than 2 thowsand yeiris thay haue keipet the toung vncorrupte: bot lykwyse the maner of cleithing and leiueng, that ald forme thay vnchanget aluterlie haue keipet'.[149] Like their Welsh cousins, the highland Scots preserved their faith along with their culture and tongue: 'Thair constancie quhilke this day thay haue keipet is not worthie of sobir [mean] and slicht prais, chieflie that in the catholik religione far les thay defecte, and far fewar than vthiris of the mair politick sorte amang vs.'[150] Not quite a covenanted people, but Lesley deliberately tied the ancient nobility and virtue of the Scots to their fidelity to God and Catholicism.

Lesley was attuned to the cultural complexity among Scotland's peoples, especially in a century increasingly dominated by religious prejudice and a highland–lowland division between civility and barbarity.[151] Lesley had little time for crude xenophobia and he defended his focus on cultural complexity. 'I have spent rather much time to describe these things exactly', he explained, 'because great is the insolence of certain people to disparage maliciously what is to our praise. Because when they read that the ancient Scots (whose image is still retained by those from the most remote part of Scotland) were not endowed with

---

[144] Leslie, *Historie*, I, p. 93.

[145] Leslie, *Historie*, I, p. 92.

[146] Leslie, *Historie*, I, pp. 89–95.

[147] Leslie, *Historie*, I, p. 94.

[148] Roger Mason, 'Civil Society and the Celts: Hector Boece, George Buchanan and the Ancient Scottish Past', *Scottish History*, pp. 100–3.

[149] Leslie, *Historie*, I, p. 95.

[150] Leslie, *Historie*, I, p. 96.

[151] Mason, 'Civil Society', pp. 95–106; Kidd, *British Identities*, pp. 123–7.

the same elegance of customs which they mostly applaud in themselves, these polished and delicate men immediately try to brand all Scots with some mark of barbarity; they do not realise that even in these, there is much that ought to be praised to an extraordinary degree.'[152] Lesley was right. Finlaggan, the capital of the MacDonald Lords of the Isles, razed in 1493 with the destruction of the lordship, tells the story for us now. The MacDonalds consciously built a traditional Hebridean settlement on two islands in Loch Finlaggan on Islay. But the 'proto-urban' community on the main island included 'substantial structures, with clear Norse ancestry', paved streets, metallurgy, and commercial contacts that brought Bordeaux to the inhabitants' tables. The man-made second island included the Council Hall, reached by a wooden causeway.[153]

Finlaggan did not tell its story until the 1990s, but Lesley understood the significance of cultural exchanges and middle grounds where peoples and cultures met and interacted. He challenged critics to recognize the inevitability of cultural sharing even within differences, noting linguistic sharing between Scots and English as well as dress and eating habits that looked at least a little like those in France or Flanders.[154] Hailing from Kingussie and with time spent in Aberdeen, he naturally counted the Grampian foothills as one of the 'midcuntries' between highland and lowland.[155] There was another such cultural 'middle ground' in Scotland: 'as sum of thame quha inhabites the borders of Scotland toward Ingland, haue maneris from the rest far different, sa in this place sum of thame I purpose to reherse'.[156] The religious foundations in the Borders escaped the mad zeal of evangelicals, but they still existed in a region of 'baulde men of Weir [war]', especially among those 'quha ar not diuydet frome the Inglesmen be sum kynd of way, be a wattir or hill'. Very different Scots populated this march, stretching from Berwick along the North Sea to Lothian. Though some cultivated justice and studied politics, 'verie unlyke ar thay to all the rest of the bordirmen round about, quha nathir in peace or weire can be stainchet [checked] from takeng the pray'.[157]

Lesley's was not a flattering rehearsal of the borderers' customs and manners. These Scots flouted the authority of the king and his agents, rejoiced in taking the 'grettest libertie and licence' without consequence, and would sooner steal than live from the fruits of their own labour. No wonder they subsisted on meat and dairy products from herds with a bit of barley beer – having 'verie lytle vse of breid', good beer, or wine. They treated their 'scheiphouses and luges [lodge]' like 'castelis and palices'. Among the king's subjects, the borderers pursued the

---

[152] Quoted in Morét, 'Gaelic History', p. 92.
[153] Francis Pryor, *The Making of the British Landscape: How We have Transformed the Land from Prehistory to Today* (London, 2010), pp. 358–60.
[154] Leslie, *Historie*, I, p. 97.
[155] Leslie, *Historie*, I, p. 52.
[156] Leslie, *Historie*, I, p. 97.
[157] Leslie, *Historie*, I, pp. 10–11.

most deadly, unrelenting blood feuds. Yet, once pledged, the borderers kept faith and they delighted in music and singing. What most redeemed them for Lesley was that they had not 'vanelie fallin frome the faith of the Catholik Kirk, as mony vthiris haue done'.[158]

Here, then, were Scots who must be understood for the full scope of their virtues and vices, and in all their cultural complexity. But this was not the age of Walter Scott or Romantic travellers who set off for the Highlands intent upon recovering Scotland's heroic past or catching sight of Britannia's noble savages. Lesley did not write uncritically of highlanders, ancient or modern, but he sought to complicate a simplistic reading of them. Indeed, so intent was Lesley on this point that he digressed to refute other canards toward the Scots of old. Some writers – Mair and Boece among them – claimed that the ancient Scots 'war wonte to eit the fleshe of the captiues' and others that their 'women war wonte to slay their men with thair awne handes quhen from the field thay war cum hame ouircum be thair enemies'. For Lesley, 'the alde crueltie of fewe sulde noch be ascriuet to the hail Scottis natione', while necessity might explain many unusual actions and events in a people's past. Lesley admitted that their masters too easily led them to sedition and strife, but he laid the blame squarely on those chiefs and warned against stereotyping an entire people by such features: 'quhen as thay write sik wordes, thay accuese the hail scottis men, not considering that gif ane thing was not praisworthie in thame, or in ane sorte; many things that thay haue by worthie of singular prais'.[159] Still, Lesley's was a difficult argument to make, even to his translator. In a marginal note for readers, Dalrymple understood Lesley's point that the 'wyldnes of Scottis bot sum, sulde not be ascriuet to al the natioune', but then entirely lost it with a thoroughly reductive marginal note that highlighted the 'deidlie feides in Scotland betuene clan and clan'.[160]

The linguistic contests in Britain provided an opening to further challenge stereotypes. The Saxons' tongue, English, had come to dominate Britain, pushing to the margins or seeing off entirely the languages of the Britons, Picts, Danes, and Irish. This was true among the so-called 'politick Scottis' who now spoke a form of English.[161] 'Bot the rest of the Scottish quhome we halde as outlawis and wylde peple', Lesley explained, '(Because the institutions of thair elderis, and that alde and simple manr of cleithing and leiueng thay hald yit, and wil not forsaik thair opinione); we, I say, because the mair horrible places of the Realme thay occupie, cal thame quha dwel in the mountanis or the mountane people, thay vse thair alde Irishe toung.'[162] The turn into Scots makes this a bit tortured, but the meaning comes through. Lowland-dwelling Scots constructed their mountain-dwelling highland brethren as outlaws and wild people on the

[158] Leslie, *Historie*, I, pp. 97–102.
[159] Leslie, *Historie*, I, p. 96.
[160] Leslie, *Historie*, I, pp. 99, 101.
[161] Leslie, *Historie*, I, pp. 106–9.
[162] Leslie, *Historie*, I, p. 86.

basis of their cultural differences, because they held to the customs, manners, and folkways of their ancestors.[163] But Lesley challenged – and recanted – this by confessing to be among those lowland Scots.

Outsiders created the wild highland Scots, chiefs fundamentally bore the blame for real instances of outlaw behaviour, and no group or people should be defined by singular practices or customs. Above all, Scotland and the Scots were a good deal more complicated than highland and lowland allowed.[164] Lesley seemingly anticipated the vituperative associations of Gaeldom, Catholicism, disloyalty, and backwardness to come. At least two purposes are at work in Lesley's decision to frame his *Historie* by re-narrating Scottish topography and ethnography. He confronted an ethno-cultural history that no one could hide and used it to marginalize his Calvinist opponents. When Lesley wrote that 'haeresie occupies al baith in lenth and bredthe' he rejected stirring up 'the displeisour and auld rancour of the furious haeretiks against the Catholiks, for it lyes not in the prayer of man bot in the power of God is put a certane secreit and sure maner of medicine to be applied to this Ill, quhilke we hope he sal adhibite [seal] or it be lang [before long], cheiflie quhen this day ar verie mony of Scotland decored [with] al vertues and inflamed [with] the pure and sincere luue of the rycht Religione, quha throuch thair exile, quhilke for the luue of Christe thay willinglie haue accepted'.[165] Rather, Lesley called his brethren back to the true faith and their true nature as first presented by Mair and Boece, and now renewed by the description and *Historie*.

Lesley wrote of his fellow religious exiles here, but his topography and ethnography made them the visible representatives of the many unseen Scots who still kept faith with their ancestors' nobility and Catholicism, and those who might be called back to them. Spiritual devotion animated mystical sites and folk ways. The religious orders and dedicated parish clergy peopled the spiritual landscape. Monasteries and abbeys celebrated religious fidelity, while their destruction indicted Protestant fanaticism. Scotland's least 'civilized' people in the Highlands and Borders would call their modern brethren back from religious schism. They preserved the ancient nobility and constancy in religion (Catholicism) needed. Indeed, Lesley argued that the barbarity attributed to those peoples revealed less about reality than it did about the constructs fashioned by lowland politicians and writers. If a barbaric madness or violence afflicted anyone, it afflicted the Calvinist zealots and their political allies – the 'wod' (mad or forest) men who constituted a rupture with the Scottish past and Scottishness.

Lesley wanted his *Historie* to lead the Scottish people to an understanding of themselves within the Catholic tradition. He confronted them with their ancestors' fidelity as a spur to rejecting the Kirk. Lesley's was a vision of unity

---

[163] Leslie, *Historie*, I, p. 96.
[164] Leslie, *Historie*, I, p. 103.
[165] Leslie, *Historie*, I, pp. 110–11.

directed to all but the most stubborn and self-serving of his opponents. Further, his vision extended to the cultural mosaic of Britain itself. The 1584 edition of Lesley's treatise defending the claims of Mary and James VI to the English throne included a subtle challenge to the rhetoric of a Protestant British *imperium*. He called for a Catholic Britain realized by renewed devotion to the universal Church, symbolized by the English and Scottish soldiers who joined hands 'in peace and faith' in the title-page woodcut.[166] If Lesley could imagine unity that crossed the Tweed, it may be because he already overcame the mental boundary between highland and lowland in finding – or at least imagining – the Catholic Scots. Perhaps most illuminating is that Lesley's descriptions show an intellect at work grappling with and seeking to understand the complexity of the Scottish peoples, and doing so within an equally complicated sense of the peoples of Britain. Lesley understood that there was real human complexity beneath the surface of the four nations – perhaps better than any number of writers who followed him.

A nation of Catholic Scots keeping their heads down in the country's uplands and Anglo-Scottish Borders (and elsewhere) was a more attractive international cause than a country lost to a Presbyterian Kirk. Lesley hoped his Catholic Scots would encourage European support for Mary's cause in the 1570s, when there still seemed – and perhaps was – so much to play for religiously and dynastically in Britain. And, they almost seemed designed to answer the Protestant spin given to Boece's history in Harrison's translation for Holinshed. Instead, George Buchanan seized the Scottish past for the Protestant cause.[167] Lesley and Buchanan transformed the Scots of Mair's and Boece's travels into the ethno-cultural foot soldiers of confessional warfare, pitting loyal Catholics against the reformed Kirk's Presbyterian ancestors. Buchanan and his followers, alongside their English counterparts, did a better job in setting the terms of debate for the future. They crafted visions of godly nations that clashed with the cultural complexity of Boece or Leland, who encountered multicultural Britain before the religious revolutions. We now turn to that question.

---

[166] Christopher Highley, *Catholics Writing the Nation in Early Modern Britain and Ireland* (Oxford, 2008), pp.105–6; Beckett, 'Political Works of John Lesley', pp. 237–43, 252 on Lesley's view of Anglo-Scottish amity, union, and finding a common ground culturally between the Scots and English.

[167] Mason, 'Civil Society', pp. 104–19.

4

Cultural Complexity and Godly Nations

The ghost of John Leland fairly leaps out from the descriptions written by the travellers and authors who took up the encounter with multicultural Britain after his death. So commonplace did Leland's notebooks become that James Matthew Thompson, a fellow and tutor of Magdalen College Oxford, sought out Leland, Gerald of Wales, and Thomas Pennant for extracts concerning Wales in 1902.[1] Thompson's family holidayed in Penmaen-mawr, Caernarvonshire and Thompson later married the local vicar's daughter. He found the *Itinerary* 'an unpleasant book of mere hints'.[2] Thompson was an avid traveller 'who believed in the exemplary character and early formation of Britain's representative political institutions ... [and] the existence of clear-cut national characteristics'.[3] The incomplete, unformed character of Leland's notes left him cold. Thompson became a deacon in 1903 and made his name as a historian with a series of books on the French Revolution, writing 'clearly and compellingly' as 'a whig with a social conscience'. Yet Thompson nearly destroyed his career in its earliest years with *Miracles in the New Testament* (1911), denouncing the invention of the virgin birth and resurrection. Pressured to resign, Thompson preserved his tenure, if not his ecclesiastical duties, in the name of academic freedom and rational inquiry.

Leland's *Itinerary* did not inspire Thompson's scrutiny of religious nonsense, but he had one thing very much in common with the generation of travel-ler-writers who followed Leland, Mair, and Boece. They studied the narratives for useful information, passed judgement on descriptions, and reassembled the raw material for their own purposes. Either as travellers directly or as armchair travellers, they did so with a variety of interests and motives. This chapter focuses on two related questions. First, how did they respond to the cultural complexity of the original accounts, their own experiences, or both? Second, in what ways might the religious revolutions in Britain affect the encounter with cultural complexity, especially from the 1560s and 1570s?

---

[1] L.W.B. Brockliss, 'James Matthew Thompson', *Oxford DNB* at www.oxforddnb.com.
[2] Aberystwyth, National Library of Wales, Ms 22880B, p. 1.
[3] Brockliss, 'James Matthew Thompson'.

Political and national rivalries, religious plurality, and undertones of Anglo-Protestant imperialism encouraged travellers (among others) to filter the cultural complexity of Britain through confessional rivalries and prejudices. History, topography, and ethnography were all fields of engagement in the battle for the nation's soul. We observed this in William Harrison's treatment of Boece/Bellenden as well as John Lesley's Catholic Scots. Lesley did not overwrite the essential cultural complexity of Scotland (or Britain), but the same could not be said of Harrison's reductive approach to Scottish godliness – or ungodliness. Lesley's rival, George Buchanan, set out to update Boece's *Scotorum Historia* with his own *Rerum Scoticarum Historia*. He did so with distinct polemical intent, focussed on the origins of the Scottish kingdom, lawful resistance to tyrannical (and ungodly) rulers, and Presbyterian origins. In England, Harrison, John Stow, William Burton, and William Lambarde struggled with or ignored Leland's multicultural perspective on the Tudor *imperium* and ultimately pushed him toward the Anglocentric pigeonhole in which he remains stuck.

George Buchanan and the Protestant writing of Scotland

The two men at work on histories of Scotland in the 1570s could not have nursed more disparate views of the country's religion or the exiled queen at the centre of the conflicts. No ideologue or propagandist was more implicated in the destruction of Mary's reputation than her former court poet, George Buchanan, the man with whom she once read Livy and shared a deep love of French poetry and the word-smith who contributed to the masques that celebrated the queen's marriage to Henry Darnley and the baptism of Prince James.[4] When he broke with a queen whose regime offended his religious, political, and moral sensibilities, Buchanan penned words designed to destroy both Mary's standing as God's anointed and her reputation as a queen and woman. First came *De Iure Regni apud Scotos Dialogus* or a *Dialogue on the Law of Kingship Among the Scots* (1567). Buchanan drew heavily on classical writers and the examples of Scottish kings chosen and held accountable by their subjects to fashion a case for resistance to ungodly rulers.[5] He followed this in 1568 with a 'Detection' of the queen's activities, a potted history of the final tumultuous months of Mary's reign that explained the death of Darnley as the fruit of an adulterous murder pact between the queen and her purported lover, the earl of Bothwell.[6] Buchanan and Mary's

---

[4] John Guy, *My Heart is My Own: The Life of Mary Queen of Scots* (London, 2004), pp. 147, 152; Roger A. Mason and Martin S. Smith, eds, *A Dialogue on the Law of Kingship among the Scots: A Critical Edition and Translation of George Buchanan's* De Iure Regni apud Scotos Dialogus (Farnham, 2004), pp. xxiii–xv, hereafter cited as *Buchanan's De Iure Regni*.

[5] *Buchanan's De Iure Regni*, p. xxvii.

[6] *Buchanan's De Iure Regni*, p. xxx; George Buchanan, *Ane Detectioun of the Doingis of Marie Quene of Scottis* (STC 3982; London, 1572).

self-serving half-brother Moray hoped that these, combined with the lurid fabrications of the Casket Letters, would cement Mary's guilt and force her abdication.[7]

Ideological and political concerns did not originally inspire Buchanan's
devotion to the history of Scotland and its peoples. Buchanan spent roughly
a decade in Paris between 1525 and 1535, studying under Mair and perhaps
rubbing shoulders with Boece and Leland. By 1555, a former acquaintance
of Buchanan's, Giovanni Ferrerio, who later published an updated edition
of Boece's *Scotorum Historia*, expected Buchanan to follow in the footsteps of
Mair and Boece.[8] History was central to the *studia humanitatis*. When Buchanan
was sent to Paris for diplomatic reasons a decade later, it seems his friends
among French humanists persuaded him finally to crown his literary career by
completing the *Historia*.[9] Politics, humanism, and love of country undoubtedly
lay behind the great portion of the *Historia* that chronicles the Scottish past,
but we may ultimately owe the opening books of Buchanan's work to the Welsh
scholar Humphrey Llwyd.

Published posthumously in 1572, Llwyd's *Comentarioli Descriptionis Britannicae
Fragmentum* demolished Boece's account of Scotland's early kings 'whose
reigns Buchanan had made much use of to support his theory of "democratic"
monarchy'.[10] Llwyd had no time for the romantic exile of Scota and Gathelus or
anything that might constitute an authentic or real history of the Scots before
the Romans. Buchanan's determination to destroy Llwyd's account is etched into
the first three books of the *Historia*. They probably began as a separate treatise on
the Welsh and Scots, 'de origine gentium Britannicarum'.[11] Buchanan hinted at
the piecemeal nature of the *Historia* and his motives: 'When I first determined to
Write the Famous Atchievement of our Ancestors, and, after I had purged them
from the mixture of vain Fables, to vindicate them from oblivion; I thought
it conducive to my purpose, to repeat from the very beginning ... What the
situation of the Countrys were; What was the nature of the Soil and Air; What
were the ancient Names and Manners, and Who were the first Inhabitants, of
the Islands, called of old, Britany.'[12]

By this circuitous approach Buchanan produced an account of Scotland
very much in the mould of his sixteenth-century predecessors, but he knew he
was 'assurit to content few, and to displease mony tharthrow'.[13] It would not

---

[7] Guy, *Queen of Scots*, pp. 373–423.
[8] I.D. McFarlane, *Buchanan* (London, 1981), p. 417; Roger A. Mason, 'From Buchanan to
Blaeu: The Politics of Scottish Chorography, 1582–1654', *George Buchanan: Political Thought in
Early Modern Britain and Europe*, ed. Caroline Erskine and Roger A. Mason (Farnham, 2012),
pp. 16–18.
[9] Hugh Trevor-Roper, *The Invention of Scotland: Myth and History* (New Haven, 2008), pp. 43–4.
[10] McFarlane, *Buchanan*, p. 419.
[11] McFarlane, *Buchanan*, p. 426; Mason, 'Buchanan to Blaeu', pp. 15–18.
[12] George Buchanan, *The History of Scotland* (WING B5283A; London, 1689), p. 1.
[13] Buchanan to Daniel Rogers in August 1577, quoted in McFarlane, *Buchanan*, p. 423.

only annoy those who preferred Llwyd's account of British History. Buchanan depicted 'a remarkably austere political world in which virtuous kings live soberly according to the law, while vicious tyrants, enslaved by their passions, are held to account by noblemen selflessly devoted to the commonweal of the realm'.[14] Less obviously than the firebrand John Knox in his *First Blast of the Trumpet Against the Monstrous Regiment of Women*, who made Catholic female monarchs (Mary Tudor, Marie of Guise, later Mary Queen of Scots) an abomination before God fit to be deposed, Buchanan implicitly questioned the virtue and authority of rulers who thwarted godly religion. Buchanan spent his last years completing his great history partly to supply Mary's son with these '"faithful monitors from history, whose counsel may be useful in your deliberations, and their virtues patterns of imitation in active life"'.[15] He did not live to see it emerge from the Edinburgh printing house of Alexander Arbuthnet in 1582.

James had no interest in a history that made him accountable to his subjects and the *Historia* was examined and banned in 1584. James further advised his son in his own advice manual, *Basilikon Doron*, to punish anyone found in possession of Buchanan's infamous libel or professing its ideas.[16] The prospect of Buchanan's *Historia* troubled the exiled queen's supporters and fellow Catholics. One Scottish observer wrote that 'Our Papists, of whom there are a great number here, when they learned that Buchanan's *Historia* was shortly to be printed ... were mightily exercised by fear that their actions, painted in their proper colours, would be exposed to the light of day.' For hope and solace, they turned 'to the books by Lesley, bishop of Ross, which were printed in Rome'.[17]

It was not until after the quasi-republican revolutions in England and Scotland in 1688–89 drove the Catholic James VII and II from both thrones that an acknowledged English translation became timely. The bookseller and history writer Nathaniel Crouch offered copies for sale, fittingly, at the corner of Popes-Head Alley, Cornhill in 1690. Buchanan's Protestant zeal did him no harm during the great age of antiquarian scholarship in the eighteenth century. Between 1722 and the end of the century, five English editions came off the presses in London, Edinburgh, and Glasgow. At least five people had a hand in first bringing Buchanan's *History* to market: the printer E. Jones, the Whig bookseller Awnsham Churchill (who brought out Edmund Gibson's 1695 and 1722 editions of Camden's *Britannia*), Crouch, James Fraser, and an unidentified translator or translators. One among them notably intervened in the text: a detailed set of marginal notes and headings, based on careful and engaged reading, that guided the reader and corrected Buchanan.[18]

---

[14] *Buchanan's De Iure Regni*, pp. xxxi and lxvii.

[15] *Buchanan's De Iure Regni*, p. xlv.

[16] James VI and I, *Political Writings*, ed. Johann P. Sommerville (Cambridge, 1994), p. 46.

[17] John Lyndsay to Peter Young c. 1577–82, quoted in McFarlane, *Buchanan*, pp. 423–4.

[18] Brian Moffat, 'James Fraser', *Oxford DNB* at www.oxforddnb.com. See the marginal note marked (h) in Buchanan, *History*, p. 21 for an example of such careful reading.

From the start, Buchanan's pleasing Latinity made itself known and one soon encountered the debate with the dead Llwyd that proved just as lively and spiteful in translation. Where Scotland's ancient past was concerned, 'the consent of so many Nations, almost from the very beginning, both among themselves, and with the Ancients, both Greeks and Latins, shall be of greater accompt with me, than all the Hodgepodge Trash of Lud [Llwyd], raked by him out of the Dunghill, on purpose to be ridicul'd, and preserved only for ignominy'.[19] Buchanan's bitter struggle occupied most of his second book and our marginalia writer revealed both a strong sense of its explicitly ethnic dimensions and a desire to supplement the original information wherever possible. Thus he guided readers with the most up-to-date identity of the peoples Buchanan discussed, from the Arverni or 'Burgundians' to the 'Ancient Scots ... Or Highlanders' and the 'Caledonians a mixt People of Picts and Scots' about whom Buchanan avowed ''tis plain, they were Picts'.[20] The annotator supplied readers with a handy definition for Caesar's use of 'Indigenae' to refer to the peoples of Britain: 'Indigenous, i.e. born in the same Country.'[21] But migration was crucial to Buchanan's discussion both for the right account of the peopling of Britain and for understanding that those first peoples sought out Britain and Ireland for the cause of liberty: 'He that weighs these causes of Transmigration, will not wonder, if many of them did prefer a mean condition abroad, conjoyned with Liberty, before a Domestick and bitter Servitude.'[22]

Buchanan found religion, language, and place-names to be critical connections among migrant peoples and settled nations.[23] Lothian, 'so named from Lothus, King of the Picts ... far excel all the rest, in the Civility of its Inhabitants, and in plenty of all things for the use of Life'. Fife remained a special place to the Principal and would-be curricular reformer of St Andrews University, a country self-sufficient with a notable collection of fishing villages like Crail and Leven lining the shore.[24] Topography bred a kind of gentle civility in Lothian and Fife as well as Abertay and Buchan. By contrast, in some parts of Ayrshire, 'the Country abounds more with valiant Men, than with Corn or Cattle; for the Soyle is poor and sandy, and that sharpens the Industry of the Inhabitants; and their Parsimony confirms the Strength both of their Bodies and Minds'.[25] The inhabitants of Sutherland, 'according to the Nature of the Soil, are more given to Pasturage than Tillage', while mountains of white marble 'are of little or no

[19] Buchanan, *History*, p. 5.
[20] Buchanan, *History*, pp. 41, 47, 56.
[21] Buchanan, *History*, p. 50.
[22] Buchanan, *History*, p. 51.
[23] Buchanan, *History*, p. 56.
[24] Buchanan, *History*, p. 18.
[25] Buchanan, *History*, pp. 13–14.

use to the Inhabitants, because That luxuriant Humour, which affects Curiosity, hath not yet reached to this Place'.[26]

Boece's bell-shaped towers that inflamed Harrison's religious feelings and another near Carron Water puzzled more than irritated Buchanan. While the 'common People have several Fancies, according to their divers Humours, concerning the Use and Author of this Structure', Buchanan thought he knew better. The tower along the banks of the Carron was a temple to the god Terminus because of its round, open-top design and because it marked the terminus of the Roman *imperium*. However, the presence of similar towers among the islands and the pair in Ross forced Buchanan to reconsider: 'These things made me suspend my Opinion, and to judge that these were Monuments or Trophies of some famous Deeds, placed, as it were, at the fag-end of the World, that they might be preserved from the Injury and Fury of Enemies.' Just what needed the protection of the fag-end of the world eluded Buchanan, but he concluded that the structures were either monuments or, 'as some think', sepulchres 'built by rude and unskilful Workmen, after the similitude of the Temple erected at Carron'.[27]

Thus did civil arts like construction decline as one journeyed beyond the lowlands. Language too changed, as Buchanan keenly observed with his felicity for tongues, including Gaelic.[28] Every language originated among 'Men rude and impolite [and] came forth harsh rugged, and uncouth', but use over time 'puts off its natural Horror and Unpleasantness, becoming more gentle and sweeter to the Ear, and more easily insinuating into the minds of Man'.[29] The 'Language of the Highlanders', as the annotator labelled it, was an exception:

> And there is no cause, why I take it less in disdain, that the old Scotish Language doth by degrees decay, than that, thereby, I joyfully perceive those barbarous Sounds, by little and little, to vanish away, and, in their place, the swetness of Latin words to succeed: And in this Transmigration of Languages, if one must needs yield to another, Good-now, of the Two, let us pass from Rusticity and Barbarism, to Culture and Humanity; and, by our Choice and Judgment, let us put off that uncouthness which accrued to us by the Infelicity of our Birth.[30]

The great Latinist positively rejoiced at the (fanciful) extinction of Gaelic, but he did not expunge it entirely from his text. Strathearn, as it was 'called in Highland, or old Scots, Language', took its name from strath, a land lying astride the banks of a river. Likewise, 'the Vulgar, following the Propriety of their Country Speech' turned Navern into Strath-Navern. Buchanan also Latinized

---

[26] Buchanan, *History*, p. 21.
[27] Buchanan, *History*, p. 15.
[28] Mason, 'Buchanan to Blaeu', p. 15.
[29] Buchanan, *History*, p. 6.
[30] Buchanan, *History*, p. 6.

much of the language, so that St Andrews was known to highlanders as 'Fanum Reguli' and Angus by 'Aeneia'.[31]

Dunkeld brought these ethno-linguistic divisions into stark relief. Buchanan rejected the vulgar name of this pleasant ecclesiastical seat in the foothills of the Grampians, preferring the ancient name Caledonia: 'For those [hazel] Trees, growing thick in such unmanured places, and shadowing the Country, like a Wood, gave Name both to the Town, and also to the People thereabouts. For the Caledons or Caledonians, heretofore one of the famousest Nations amongst the Britains, made up one part of the Kingdom of Picts.'[32] Caledonia had an important double significance that Buchanan would not allow the vulgar tongue of its people to obscure. Our marginalia writer followed Buchanan's lead, noting that Sutherland was 'A name given it by the Picts, as some think.'[33]

Buchanan composed a path-breaking, detailed account of the Western Isles, the Orkneys, and Shetland that took up fully 60 per cent of his topographic description.[34] The uniqueness of these islands fascinated lowland travellers and they played a vital role in explaining – or not – the ancient peopling of Scotland. Those far-flung possessions also represented the maritime *imperium* of Lindsay's *Rutter* and James V's circumnavigation. They demanded recognition in an age of first Spanish and Portuguese and then English expansion in the Atlantic world, even if Buchanan promoted civic republicanism in opposition to the loathsome tyranny of emperors and empires.[35] By its late seventeenth-century publication, we can just detect in Buchanan's *History* the first signs of renewed interest in the islands that would explode in the next century, especially with the narratives of James Wallace and Martin Martin. Buchanan forsook classical authors, 'who have delivered nothing certain on this Subject'. After challenging the familiar name Hebrides as a 'new Name' unknown to the Ancient writers, Buchanan recorded his debt to Donald Monro, 'a Pious and Diligent Person, who himself Travelled over all those Islands, and viewed them Ocularly'. Monro negotiated the transition from Catholic archdeacon of the Isles in the 1550s to being a good minister of the Presbyterian kirk in Kiltearn, Cromarty.[36] His first-hand view of the islands and their peoples would make up for the absence of Buchanan's own, should anyone read with a sceptical eye.

Buchanan launched without pause into a description of the islanders, one given an obvious ethnographic heading in the margin: 'The Disposition, customs, &c. of their Inhabitants'. The description may have come from Monro's account, but everything about their ordinary lives spoke to the 'Ancient

---

[31] Buchanan, *History*, pp. 17–18, 21.
[32] Buchanan, *History*, p. 18.
[33] Buchanan, *History*, p. 21.
[34] Buchanan, *History*, pp. 22–3.
[35] Arthur Williamson, 'An Empire to End Empire: The Dynamic of Early Modern British Expansion', *Huntington Library Quarterly* 68 (2005), pp. 233–5.
[36] Mason, 'Buchanan to Blaeu', pp. 26–8.

8   The Highlands and Western Isles from 'Scotiae Regni Antiqvissimi Accvrata Descriptio' from John Leslie, *De Origine Moribus, et Rebus Gestis Scotorum Libri Decem* (Rome, 1578). Reproduced by permission of the National Library of Scotland.

Parsimony' of Boece's temperance. Flesh was usually cooked in water in skins or stomachs, but sometimes eaten raw. Nothing went to waste among the parsimonious islanders, including the boiled meat broth, a favourite along with a long-lived drink of whey and, most temperately, water. Buchanan remarked on their fine oat and barley cakes or bread as though sampling them himself: they were 'not unpleasant to the Taste, and, by frequent use, they are very expert at making and moulding it'.[37]

Buchanan must have found the fine points of their attire and sleeping habits genuinely interesting: 'Of all Colours they love the Purple and Blew, most. Their Ancestors wear Party-coloured Plads, variously striped; which custom some of them do still retain. But, now-a-days, many of them wear their Apparel of a dark brown colour, almost like Heath, that so lying in the Heath-bushes, they might not, in the day-time, be discovered by their Cloaths.'[38] Forsaking colourful plaid was not simply designed to camouflage them in the heath, when defying even the 'fiercest weather' by sleeping rough. The heath bewitched the islanders. They covered their floors with it and slept on its aromatic boughs by choice. Heath 'being endued with a Natural power of exiccation, doth exhaust superfluous Humors, and restored vigor to the Nerves ... so that they, who lye down in the Evening weary and fain, in the Morning rise up nimble and spritely'.[39] All was not quite as idyllic as it appeared, though. Given the chance to sleep in a proper bed, 'they throw the Bed and Blankets of their Hosts on the ground, and wrap themselves up in their own Garments'. They feared 'such barbarous effeminatenes (for so they call it) should taint and corrupt their Native and inbred hardiness'.[40]

Buchanan relayed this critique without comment, but it offered a natural segue to warfare. Among their weapons, the islanders used hooked arrows that ripped apart a wounded man's flesh when pulled out. That Buchanan described these weapons so matter-of-factly sets him apart from later English writers raised on accounts of Gaelic barbarity, especially virulent after the Nine Years' War in Ireland (1595–1603) and the racist denunciations of Fynes Moryson, Edmund Spenser, and Sir John Davies.[41] The English trader Richard Jobson accordingly framed his encounters with peoples of the Gambian Delta in *The Golden Trade*, published in 1623 to defend the Guinea Company's African monopoly and spur investors. Jobson described a pike thrown 'like Irishmens darts, with heads

---

[37] Buchanan, *History*, p. 23.
[38] Buchanan, *History*, p. 23.
[39] Buchanan, *History*, p. 23.
[40] Buchanan, *History*, pp. 23–4.
[41] Graham Kew, *The Irish Sections of Fynes Moryson's Unpublished Itinerary* (Dublin, 1998); Edmund Spenser, *A View of the State of Ireland*, ed. Andrew Hadfield and Willy Maley (Oxford, 1997); John Davies, *A Discouerie of the True Causes Why Ireland Was Neuer Entirely Subdued* (STC 6348; London, 1612).

all barbed, full of crueltie to the receiuer'.[42] A half-century after Buchanan's *Historia*, this cruel weapon helped to define the savagery of the Gambians by associating them with the Irish – the ethnic brethren of the Western islanders. Buchanan continued by noting that the sound of bagpipes led the islanders into battle, while their leisure hours were likewise typically punctuated by the sound of music, often produced by 'Instruments, of a peculiar kind, called Clarshachs; of which some have strings made of Brass-wire'. As well, they 'sing Songs, not unelegant, containing commonly the Elogies of Valiant Men'. Bards too fulfilled their accustomed purpose while their 'Language is some what like the old Gawlish'.[43]

Buchanan's account recreated Monro's circuit. One might have expected Iona to produce some fiery invective against popery, but Buchanan's reformist instincts were drawn to the apparent piety of an early Church in Britain untainted by papal corruption:

> [Iona is] famed for as many ancient Monuments, as could be well expected in such a Country; but it was yet made more famous by the severe Discipline and Holiness of St Columbus. It was beautified with two Monasteries, one of Monks the other of Nuns; with one Curia, or (as they call it,) a Parish Church, and with many Chapels, some of them built by the Magnificence of the Kings of Scotland; and others by the Petty Kings of the Islands ... [44]

Hirta or St Kilda troubled Buchanan, though. For Monro, the 'inhabitants thairof are simple creatures, scant learnit in ony Religion', but Buchanan's words produced a more hostile translation: 'The Inhabitants are ignorant of all Arts, and especially of Religion.' For Buchanan the problem seems to have been the practice of sending a priest to baptize any children born in the previous year, made worse by the custom that 'every Man baptizeth his own Children' if the priest does not come.[45]

Where the islanders made a good living, Buchanan followed Monro in singing their praises. Skye's greatness lay in its size, rich woodland, salmon-filled rivers, pastures that nourished cattle and mares, and fields of corn. The fields of Lewis demanded more care, and seaweed to replenish the soil for barley every other year. The island's waters offered an abundance of whales to compensate, while one shoreline cave left a deep pool at low tide that 'Multitudes of People, of both Sexes, and of all Ages' fished with spectacular results. The people of Rona were ignorant of religion, but perhaps it was the absence of a priest that allowed Buchanan to admit they lived well, indeed 'are the only Persons in the whole

---

[42] Richard Jobson, *The Golden Trade* (STC 14623; London, 1623), p. 45.

[43] Buchanan, *History*, p. 24.

[44] Buchanan, *History*, p. 26.

[45] Monro's account is reprinted in Martin Martin, *A Description of the Western Islands of Scotland*, ed. Charles W.J. Withers and R.W. Munro (Edinburgh, 1999), p. 329; Buchanan, *History*, p. 30.

World, who want nothing but have all things to Saiety'. Further, 'besides, being ignorant of Luxury and Covetousness, they enjoy that Innocency and Tranquility of Mind, which others take great pains to obtain'. These islanders shared with their noble New World cousins everything needed for real happiness, but with an innocent failure to 'understand the excellency of their Condition'.[46]

Some islands had less-innocent inhabitants and features. Two islands near Lewis belonging to the Mackenzies were covered with woods 'good for nothing but to harbour Thieves in, to rob Passengers' or 'Pyrates'. For Monro, the islands sheltered 'rebells', but both men agreed that thieves lurked in the woods of Pabay near Skye to 'way-lay Travellers as they pass'.[47] Near Garvellan, or Craggy Island, lay the Isle of Pgymies, with, according to Monro, 'ane little kirk in it of thair awn handie wark'. Many strangers 'digging deep into the Earth [of its chapel] have found, and yet do find, little and round Heads, and the small Bones of other parts of human Bodies, nothing derogating from the ancient Reports concerning Pygmies'.[48] Wild sheep had the run of the so-called Sanctuary Islands (Flannan islands), and only extreme hunger could tempt hunters to consume their foul-tasting flesh. A strange spring in the hills of Barra fed a great, sandy bay with small, shapeless animals that supposedly matured into the great wealth of cockles harvested at low tide. Monro directed readers to Boece for confirmation of the connection between the spring and the cockles, while Buchanan's seven-teenth-century reader identified them as periwinkles.[49]

Buchanan moved to, in the words of the margin heading, the 'Inhabitants of the Orcades, Parsimonious and long-liv'd'. However, Buchanan turned his back on the long-lived prelapsarian humans of Boece or Lesley. The islanders certainly did not endanger their longevity with overwork. If trees and shrubs were absent from the island, the blame lay not with the soil or climate but the 'Laziness of the Inhabitants'. The islanders' prodigious drinking marked the degeneration of the people's 'Ancient Discipline' in favour of pleasure and luxury. This 'pollution of Manners did infect the Great ones mostly, and the Priests', according to Buchanan, but 'Among the Vulgar, many footsteps of their former moderation do yet remain.'[50] Buchanan followed with a more tempered survey of the individual islands, noting the important influence of long-term Danish contacts.

The Shetlands did not provoke criticism. The inhabitants of great Shetland stuck to the shoreline, especially after a failed attempt to form 'Plantations' in the interior. On the lesser isle of Yell, 'no Creature can live therein, unless he be born there', but this did not stop a Bremen merchant setting up shop on the island to supply the needs of its few inhabitants. They lived much like the

---

[46] Buchanan, *History*, pp. 28, 30, 32.
[47] Buchanan, *History*, pp. 28, 30; Martin, *Description*, pp. 226, 321.
[48] Martin, *Description*, p. 333; Buchanan, *History*, p. 30.
[49] Buchanan, *History*, pp. 29–30; Martin, *Description*, p. 325.
[50] Buchanan, *History*, p. 34.

Orcadians, although more heavily influenced by outside contacts. Their clothing, weights and measures, and speech all betrayed a strong 'German' influence, sharpened by trade with the Norwegians in oil, butter, fish, and cloth. Unlike the Orcadians, Buchanan avowed 'They know not what 'tis to be Drunk', instead spending time once a month 'innocently Merry and Jocund ... for the maintaining of Mutual Friendship'. One Shetlander named Lawrence testified to their clean hardiness. Married at 100, he fished the roughest waters in his skiff until the age of 140 before passing quietly of old age.[51]

Buchanan found among the Gaels of the Highlands and Islands vital qualities that advanced his polemical interests. Like Lesley, Buchanan found essential nobility and virtue in the ancient past and its descendants. Second, an ancient contractual, quasi-republican Scottish constitution was alive and well in the Gaedhealtacht, where 'the clan chiefs – or phylarchi as he liked to call them – were still unquestionably elected by their clansmen and bound on pain of resistance to follow the advice of their councils'.[52] This was not mere fancy: 'Buchanan might be said to have highlighted and idealised the conciliar dimension of the exercise of aristocratic power (whether in the Lowland or the Highlands).'[53] Finally, Buchanan numbered among those Protestants who 'set about rewriting the early history of Christianity in Scotland in order to prove precisely what medieval chroniclers had consistently sought to deny: namely, that Celtic Christianity, the faith of St Columba and the Culdees, was indeed different, distinctive and unique ... a primitive Presbyterian discipline from which it had subsequently and disastrously declined.'[54] The Scottish Kirk, like the *Anglicana Ecclesia*, suffered from subjugation by a corrupting papacy. However, the Presbyterians' kirk freed itself in a 'popular' revolution that aimed to restore the self-governing congregations or communities of the culdees, not to install a popish royal supremacy. For Buchanan, then, Scotland's cultural complexity (and distinctiveness vis-à-vis its neighbours) constituted an essential feature of a godly Scotland. Its survival and flourishing depended on the recognition and appropriation of that complexity for the Presbyterian cause even as it left behind the language of the Gaels.

Buchanan's *Historia* did not pass quietly into old age. Arbuthnet published two Latin editions in 1582, but it was regularly proscribed for more than a century. Latin readers turned to a number of Continental editions between 1583 and the end of the seventeenth century, usually finding the *Historia* conveniently paired with *De Iure Regni*. The press of G. Mosman in Edinburgh finally produced a new domestic edition in 1700. But Buchanan's description had a 'hidden' life in the century that separated it from the editions of Mosman and Churchill. Some

---

[51] Buchanan, *History*, pp. 36–7.
[52] Roger Mason, 'Civil Society and the Celts: Hector Boece, George Buchanan and the Ancient Scottish Past', *Scottish History: The Power of the Past*, ed. Edward J. Cowan and Richard J. Finlay (Edinburgh, 2002), p. 111.
[53] Mason, 'Civil Society', p. 112.
[54] Mason, 'Civil Society', pp. 117–18.

few pieces augmented Camden's 1607 edition of *Britannia*. John Monipennie translated Buchanan's description without acknowledgement for his *Abridgement or Summarie of the Scots Chronicle* in 1612. Monipennie's additions, 'a catalogue of the nobility and lairds' and their seats, petered out the further north and west he went and eventually Buchanan's descriptions alone remained when Monipennie had exhausted his own first-hand knowledge and information. Timothy Pont gathered a storehouse of cartographic and topographical data during his painstaking travels in the 1580s and 1590s that might have made up for such deficiencies, had he not died prematurely. James Balfour of Denmilne assembled his remarkable 'Topographic Notes' and passed on Pont's field notes and maps to John Scot of Scotstarvit. Their labours and those of Robert Gordon of Straloch and his son James combined with Buchanan's legacy to define the Scottish volume of Joan Blaeu's *Atlas Novus* in 1654 and its wondrous set of forty-nine maps, many of them based on Pont's original drafts.[55] Buchanan's description provided 'textual material that accompanied the regional maps', but something truly remarkable greeted readers right from the start: Andrew Melville's *Scotiae Topographia*, 'a faithful rendition into Latin verse of the entire text of Buchanan's description of Scotland as found in Book I of the *Historia*'.[56]

Buchanan believed his description had something to offer, and his successors agreed. Buchanan felt pressed to renew the travels and discoveries of Mair and Boece for two reasons. He explained that 'Hector Boetius, in his Description of Scotland; hath delivered some things not so true, and he hath drawn others into Mistakes, whilst he was over-credulous of those, to whom he committed the Inquiry after Matters, and so Published their Opinions, rather than the Truth.'[57] Countless travellers pleaded the same case in justifying their journeys and new accounts. Buchanan duly purged his description of Boece's folklore. Indeed Buchanan's powerful focus on descriptive topography threatened to empty Scotland of the colourful people who populated it.[58]

Buchanan also kept an eye on what Leland's successors were up to in England. 'English Writers,' he wrote 'have plainly and clearly enough described their own several Counties.' Among those writers was Harrison, the translator of Boece/ Bellenden – and an intense, avid reader of Leland's *Itinerary*. Buchanan saw no reason to cede the discovery, history, and ethnography of Scotland to Scottish Catholics, Welsh antiquarians, or English chroniclers. Scottish traveller-writers determined to define their nation while also explaining the cultural complexity of its peoples through time. In the second half of the sixteenth century, the long-nursed national rivalry between island cousins influenced the discovery of

---

55 Mason, 'Buchanan to Blaeu', pp. 36–8, 40–6.
56 Mason, 'Buchanan to Blaeu', pp. 14, 43.
57 Buchanan, *History*, pp. 12–13.
58 Mason, 'Buchanan to Blaeu', pp. 25–6.

multicultural Britain in an age of confessional conflict. To fully understand how, we must return to the dominions of Elizabeth Tudor.

William Harrison and Leland's Tudor *imperium*

John Leland kept a working library dedicated 'to the study of British affairs' and made dozens of manuscripts available to scholars like John Bale and Thomas Elyot. Either during Leland's last years of madness or upon his death, John Cheke took possession of the library, apparently at Edward VI's command. Queen Mary's accession in 1553 displaced the Edwardians, drove Cheke into exile, and scattered Leland's library. Printed books passed to William Cecil, William Paget, John Dee, and – later – Archbishop Matthew Parker, humanist intellectuals at the centre of the Elizabethan regime.[59] Leland's manuscripts 'were inaccessible and probably unknown even to the most astute and well-connected of researchers' until John Stow borrowed and transcribed fifteen of them in 1576.[60] William Harrison made the earliest and most extensive use of the *Itinerary* when he composed the 'Description of Britaine' for Holinshed's *Chronicles* in 1577.[61] Harrison's engagement with Leland reveals tensions between national identities and local realities, between the purportedly 'Protestant England' of Gloriana and the polyglot Tudor *imperium* of Leland's time.

The *Chronicles* began with the Dutch printer Reyner Wolfe. Wolfe arrived in England in 1533 and became a mainstay in the market for evangelical works under Edward. Wolfe survived the Marian restoration and returned to form under Elizabeth. As early as 1552, Wolfe began assembling information for no less than a 'vniversall Cosmographie of the whole world, and therewith also certaine perticular Histories of euery knowen nation'.[62] Wolfe's financial resources as a successful printer made it possible to conceive of such an ambitious project. When Wolfe died in 1573/74, his son-in-law and others financed the project, while his former partner, Raphael Holinshed, took the lead in producing the text and seeing it through the press.[63]

---

[59] Oliver Harris, '"Motheaten, Mouldye, and Rotten": The Early Custodial History and Dissemination of John Leland's Manuscript Remains', *Bodleian Library Record* 18.5 (2005), pp. 461–3.

[60] Harris, 'Leland's Manuscript Remains', pp. 464–5, 479.

[61] Paulina Kewes, Ian W. Archer, and Felicity Heal, eds, *Oxford Handbook of Holinshed's Chronicles* (Oxford, 2013) appeared after I had completed this chapter. I have not revised my original analysis of Harrison, although I have noted relevant essays in the footnotes that follow.

[62] *The Firste Volume of the Chronicles of England, Scotlande, and Irelande* (STC 13568; two volumes; London, 1577), I, dedication to William Cecil, hereafter cited as Holinshed, *Chronicles* (1577); Andrew Pettegree, 'Reyner Wolfe', *Oxford DNB* at www.oxforddnb.com; G.J.R. Parry, 'William Harrison and Holinshed's *Chronicles*', *Historical Journal* 27.4 (1984), p. 791.

[63] Annabel Patterson, *Reading Holinshed's Chronicles* (Chicago, 1994), pp. 8–9.

Holinshed published chronicles of England (to the Conquest), Scotland (to 1571), and Ireland up to the Kingship Act of 1541.[64] A good deal of the world was missing, but certain commitments by the project team made this inevitable, irrespective of investment concerns. Holinshed's team joined Leland in their desire 'to discover, salvage, and preserve in print ephemeral, manuscript, or otherwise endangered records [in a] "documentary history"'.[65] Their methods included marginal references to sources, eyewitness accounts, the use of 'verbatim reporting' from diverse and competing sources, and the treatment of cultural history, especially 'literature' as 'an indispensable part of the [historical] record'.[66] No universal history could possibly meet these standards of scholarship, thoroughness, and first-hand investigation. An army of Leland's travelling the world, studying its peoples, and beavering away in local archives for a lifetime just might do it. The gulf between the descriptions of Boorde or Enciso-Barlow and the thoroughness aimed at by Wolfe and Holinshed's collaborators could not have been starker or less capable of being bridged.[67] Financial constraints and practical limitations on travel and research made Holinshed's historical and cultural boundaries those of the three kingdoms.

Holinshed and his team struggled to find the ideal structure for their 'New British History' – a struggle shared since by many historians – with few precedents to hand.[68] The massive English history published in a second volume was the work of Holinshed, drawing on a wide range of sources. By contrast, Harrison used Mair's *Historia* as the basis for the Scottish chronicle-history. The account of Scottish history told from the standpoint of sympathy for Anglo-Scottish union made it a better fit. The task fell to the Dubliner Richard Stanyhurst to produce a topographical description of Ireland. Stanyhurst drew on Edmund Campion's unfinished two-volume history of the island for his chronicle.[69] Abraham Fleming and the individuals responsible for the 1587 edition after Holinshed's death expanded the range of sources, especially in the sections concerning Scotland and Ireland; Francis Thynne covered 1571 to 1586 with extracts from the histories of Lesley and Buchanan.[70]

Holinshed's *Chronicle* seemingly respected the unique histories of the three kingdoms and the interactions among them. His team did not simply set three chronicle-histories of England (and Wales), Scotland, and Ireland side by side.

---

[64] Parry, 'Harrison', pp. 791–2. Holinshed, *Chronicles* (1577), I, dedication to Cecil.

[65] Patterson, *Reading Holinshed's Chronicle*, p. 7.

[66] Patterson, *Reading Holinshed's Chronicle*, pp. 35–55.

[67] Felicity Heal and Henry Summerson, 'The Genesis of the Two Editions', in *Holinshed's Chronicles*, pp. 3–12.

[68] Philip Schwyzer, 'Archipelagic History', in *Holinshed's Chronicles*, pp. 599–600, 606–7.

[69] Patterson, *Reading Holinshed's Chronicle*, p. 9; Colm Lennon, 'Richard Stanihurst', *Oxford DNB* at www.oxforddnb.com.

[70] Patterson, *Reading Holinshed's Chronicle*, pp. 56–70; Henry Summerson, 'Sources: 1587', in *Holinshed's Chronicles*, pp. 77–92; Roger Mason, 'Scotland', in *Holinshed's Chronicles*, p. 648.

Deeply attuned to the breaks from Rome and the dramatic disintegration of religious 'unity', the team felt that these changes 'should be expressed as multivocality' that captured the religious complexity and fault lines of the kingdoms and peoples through time.[71] This is one important reason why the 'production of parallel histories of England, Ireland, and Scotland [implied] that the three countries should be considered as historically separate yet interdependent, a union of not quite equal partners'.[72] Philip Schwyzer points to the formative effects of the 'British nationalism' of the 1540s (the heyday of Tudor claims to a British *imperium* expressed in a spate of texts printed by Reyner Wolfe) and Humphrey Llwyd's *Breviary of Britaine* (1572), an archipelagic text used extensively by Holinshed's team in 1577 and his successors in 1587.[73] Roger Mason suspects that this was not a real interest, and certainly not realized in the project's execution with the editorial interventions that tended to privilege an Anglocentric history.[74]

For the 1577 edition Harrison wrote an opening topographical description of England and Wales. Thanks to its many editors, Harrison's work is typically known as a 'Description of England', but this belies the hybrid character identified by its actual title: 'An Historical Description of the Islande of Brytane, with a brief rehearsall of the nature and qualities of the people of Englande, and of all such commodities as are to be found in the same.'[75] The material was broken into three chapters, only the first of which could be said to focus on Britain; books two and three distinctly focussed on England. Nonetheless, the running head for all three books applied during production was 'The description of Britaine'.[76]

Harrison conceived and crafted the description out of a discordant mass of 'letters and pamphlettes from sundrie places and shires of Englande', meetings with divers 'talkers' whose accounts had to be sifted for contradictions and rivalries, and the works of other authors drawn in part from his reading for his own 'English Chronology'.[77] Yet, wrote Harrison, 'One helpe, and none of the smallest that I obtayned herein was by such commentaries as Leland had

[71] Patterson, *Reading Holinshed's Chronicle*, p. 7.
[72] Patterson, *Reading Holinshed's Chronicle*, p. 33.
[73] Schwyzer, 'Archipelagic History', p. 597–606.
[74] Mason, 'Scotland', pp. 652–60.
[75] G.J.R. Parry, *A Protestant Vision: William Harrison and the Reformation of Elizabethan England* (Cambridge, 1987); Parry, 'Harrison and Holinshed's *Chronicles*', pp. 789–810; Parry, 'Trinity College Dublin MS 165: The Study of Time in the Sixteenth Century', *Historical Research* 62 (1989), pp. 15–33.
[76] Parry, 'Harrison and Holinshed's *Chronicles*', pp. 793, 798 on Harrison's 'British' ambitions.
[77] William Harrison, 'Description of Britaine', *Holinshed's Chronicles* (1577), epistle dedicatory; also Glyn Parry, 'Harrison's "Chronology" and Descriptions of Britain', in *Holinshed's Chronicles*, pp. 93–110.

collected sometime of the state of Britaine, bookes vtterly mangled, defaced with
wet, and weather, and finally imperfite through want of sundrie volumes.'[78]

Harrison aimed to be comprehensive. The first book of the 'Description'
detailed the topography of Britain, including the air and soil, the ancient names
of the island, the sundry nations which had dwelled in it and 'the generall constitution of the bodies of the Brytons', languages in use, early political divisions
into kingdoms, the ancient pre-Christian religions, rivers and surrounding
islands, the four great Roman highways, the Roman Wall dividing England from
the Picts, and, of course, the division of the island into three parts by Brutus and
the imperial rights of Locrine's children. The two books focussed on England
covered everything from topography, wildlife, the built environment, agriculture,
trade, and natural resources to shires, universities, dioceses, antiquities, law and
society, coins, even marvels and saffron. Leland's travels and descriptions offered
ready data.[79] Harrison expanded the scope of the material by drawing on other
sources, at times challenging Leland. Finally, Harrison packaged Leland's information to serve his own purposes and interpreted it to particular effect.[80]

Leland's notebooks and published works provided Harrison with material to
produce something more than an insular description of England. Holinshed's
Chronicles and Harrison's 'Description' followed contemporary practice in
which Wales was 'perceived in the sixteenth century as a distinct country with
a distinctive history, yet also as part of the wider realm' of England. For Wales,
Harrison drew on Leland and, even more substantially, 'his contemporary and
fellow Oxford graduate, the humanist chorographer and historian Humphrey
Llwyd (or Lhuyd) of Denbigh'. Holinshed's history of England interpreted the
'porous nature of the borderland that allowed the gradual fusion of England and
Welsh peoples'.[81] Errant footsteps aside, Leland never travelled to Scotland but
Harrison shared with him an intimate knowledge of the country through the
works of Mair, Boece, and Bellenden.

In his preface to the Chronicles, Holinshed lamented the 'lacke of meane[s] to
obtayne sufficient instructions by reportes of the time present' from 'moderne
eyewitnesses' for its hastily assembled contents. Harrison worried that his patron,
William Cecil's relative and close friend William Brooke, Lord Cobham, might
take a dislike to his 'Description' on this account:

> I haue not by myne owne trauaile and eyesight viewed such thinges, as I doe here
> intreate of. Indeede I must needes confesse that except it were from the parish where
> I dwell, vnto your Honour in Kent, or out of London where I was borne, vnto Oxford
> and Cambridge where I haue beene brought up, I never trauailed 40. miles in all

---

[78] Harrison, 'Description of Britaine', epistle dedicatory.
[79] William Harrison, The Description of England, ed. George Edelen (Ithaca, 1968) cross-refer-
enced and identified many of Harrison's references to Leland.
[80] James P. Carley, 'Harrison and Leland', in Holinshed's Chronicles, pp. 187–201 provides a
succinct overview with some close reading of Harrison's use of Leland.
[81] Ralph Griffiths, 'Wales', in Holinshed's Chronicles, pp. 679, 683, 691.

my lyfe, neuerthelesse in my report of these thinges, I use their authorites who haue performed in their persons whatsoeuer was wanting in mine.[82]

Harrison hoped that Leland's work would tap Brooke's affection for those who 'trauaile to set forth such thing as lye hidden in their countries' and shield him from the learned, godly, curious, or mean-spirited who stood ready to carp as well as correct 'the first that ... hath taken vpon him[self] so particularly to describe this Isle of Britaine'.[83]

When Harrison voiced these concerns, he demonstrated that the passion for attentive and expansive travel, self-conscious journeys of discovery, and the study of human complexity, of ethnography had become fully embedded in the mentalité of the period.[84] Harrison shaped the *Itinerary* and *Collectanea* in a manner that reveals how the multicultural Britain of Leland's experiences existed uneasily with the 'writing of England' after mid-century.[85] Even once removed, though, Leland's culturally complex Tudor dominions coloured Harrison's 'Description'. Just as had Leland – or Higden, for that matter – Harrison found Britain alive with the encounters and interactions of diverse peoples. Such encounters were the foundation of human history. For Harrison, 'fewe or no Nations can iustly boaste themselves to haue continued sithence their countrie was first replenished [since the Flood], wythout any myxture, more or lesse, wyth other people'. This certainly applied to Britain. Lured by 'manifolde commodi-ties', many peoples and princes 'therefore haue comen hither and settled the[m] selues here in thys Isle', beginning with Samotheans and the posterity of Japheth and followed by the giant Albion and Brutus.[86]

Legendary peoples gave way to the Romans. The chapter 'What sundry Nations haue inhabited in this Islande' and others suggest how focussing on 'nations' could block attention to the cultural complexity within.[87] The Romans proved to be 'wofull guestes to this our Islande', in part because of ethno-cul-tural differences. They remained a people apart from the Britons whom they encountered and lived amongst. Worse, the unique customs and manners of the different ethnic groups that made up the Roman presence proved especially undesirable, 'sith that wyth them came in all manner of vice and vicious liuing, all ryot and excesse of behvaior, which their Legions brought hyther from eche corner of their dominions, for there was no prouince under them from whence they had not seruitours'. 'For as they planted their forworne Legions in the most fertile places of the Realme,' Harrison wrote, 'and where they might best lye

[82] Harrison, 'Description of Britaine', epistle dedicatory.
[83] Harrison, 'Description of Britaine', epistle dedicatory.
[84] Andrew Hadfield, *Literature, Travel, and Colonial Writing in the English Renaissance 1545–1625* (Oxford, 1998), pp. 17–133.
[85] For example, Richard Helgerson, *Forms of Nationhood: The Elizabethan Writing of England* (Chicago, 1992), pp. 107–1, 249–83.
[86] Harrison, 'Description of Britaine', fol. 2r–v.
[87] Harrison, 'Description of Britaine', fol. 2v.

for the safegarde of their conquestes: so their armies did commonly consist of many sorts of people, and were as I may call them, a confused mixture of other countries.' It was possible for the legions to be both polyglot and Roman, but Harrison chose 'to retayne onley that name for tham all' when he decried their presence.[88] It was simply easier and neater to think and write in terms of defined peoples or nations.

Tudor claims to the British *imperium* influenced descriptions of a polyglot Britain and highlighted tensions among peoples. Against the claims of Scottish 'historiographers' like Boece, Harrison called on Leland to defend the Tudor claim to a British *imperium* that included Scotland. As had Nicholas Adams for Edward I and John Hardyng for Henry V, Leland purportedly made the case in writing for Henry VIII:

> The tytle also that Lelande giveth his booke, which I haue had written with his own hands, beginneth in this manner. 'These remembraunces following are found in Chronicles authorized remaining in diuers monasteries both in Englande and Scotlande, by which it is euidently knowen & shewed, that the kinges of England haue had, and nowe ought to haue the sovereignetie ouer Scotlande; with the homage and fealtie of the kings their reigning time to time.'[89]

Harrison charted the long struggle for political superiority over 'the whole Empire of all Britaine' among a string of successor kings through to the Tudor claims of Henry VIII and Edward VI. For Leland and Harrison, there existed a culturally complex British *imperium* contested between the ancestors of the present-day Scots and English, though with the undoubted right to it vested in the Tudor monarchy as the ultimate descendants of Brutus's son Locrine.[90] Mair's unionist sympathies may have been the velvet covering this iron fist, when Harrison used it for the history of Scotland proper.

For Harrison, 'How and when the Scottes should arriue here out of Irelande, and from whence the Pictes shoulde come unto us, as yet it is uncertaine.' Traveller-historians like Mair or Boece might make claims for their ancient presence in Britain, but Harrison rejected the claims with élan:

> (to say freely what I thinke) I iudge them rather to haue stolle[n] in hither, not much before Saxens ... neither doe our hystories make any report, neyther their owne agree among the[m]selues by manye hundreth yeares. Wherefore as the tyme of their arriuall here is not to be founde out, so it shall suffice to gyue notice that they are but strangers, and such as by obscure inuasion haue nestled in thys Islande.[91]

The language of stealth, invasion, and strangers, especially strangers with its well-established meaning over matters of migration and difference, would

---

[88] Harrison, 'Description of Britaine', fol. 2v.
[89] Harrison, 'Description of Britaine', fol. 40r.
[90] Harrison, 'Description of Britaine', fols 40r, 74r–v (Harrison's chapter concerning the shires of England and Wales).
[91] Harrison, 'Description of Britaine', fol. 2v.

have resonated with Harrison's readers.[92] His chapter devoted to charting the traditional tripartite division of the island described Shropshire with the long-standing adjective for pure and unmixed ethnicity, 'mere': once the seat of the Welsh kings of Powys, Shropshire 'nowe is inhabited with meere English'.[93] The contest for Britain embraced ethnography – labels, origins, migration and settlement – duelling historical traditions, and genealogical claims. Recognition of cultural complexity did not preclude xenophobia either. Here were precursors to the racist fears of an invasion of post-colonial migrants, 'asylum seekers', or Polish carpenters.

Harrison had little good to say for any people who migrated to Britain in the distant past. The Saxons first became acquainted with Britain as pirates. They had already spoiled their neighbours 'in most lamentable and barbarous manner' and needed fresh plunder. The 'negligent behauiour of ye Brytons and fertilitie of our soyle' tempted the invaders to full conquest. It paved the way for a demographic revolution, the inward migration 'by little and little' of 'their wyves and children'. Harrison's description has a clear theme of migration, settlement, encounter, and displacement:

> within a whyle they began to molest the homelings (for so I finde ye word Indigena to be englished in an old booke that I haue, wherin Aduena is translated also as homeling) and ceased not from time to time to co[n]tinue their purpose, vntill they had gotten possession of the whole, or at the leastwise the greatest part of our cou[n]try, the Britons in the meane season being driuen eyther into Wales & Cornewall, or altogither out of the Islande to seeke newe inhabitations.[94]

'In like maner the Danes (the next nation that succeeded)' came to pillage 'the frontier of our Island' until they too settled in Britain, 'let in by the Welchmen or Brytons to reuenge them vpon the Saxons'. The Danes surpassed everyone in barbarity. So 'great was their lordlinesses, their crueltie, and insatiable desire for riches,' Harrison thundered, 'beside their detestable abusing of chast matrones & young virgines (whose husbandes and parentes were daily inforced to become their drudges and slaues whylest they sate at home and fed like Drone bees of the sweet of their trauayle & labours) that God I say would not suffer the[m] to continue any while ouer vs'. With marvellous irony, Harrison's god sent the Normans as liberators, but, when Britain's peoples were not moved to 'repentaunce and amendement', divine anger turned the Normans into 'a people of

---

[92] The experience of 'stranger communities' facing both resistance and acceptance can be studied in Randolph Vigne and Charles Littleton, eds, *From Strangers to Citizens: The Integration of Immigrant Communities in Britain, Ireland, and Colonial America, 1550–1750* (Brighton, 2001); Nigel Goose and Lien Luu, eds, *Immigrants in Tudor and Early Stuart England* (Brighton, 2005); Scott Oldenburg, *Alien Albion: Literature and Immigration in Early Modern England* (Toronto, 2014).

[93] Harrison, 'Description of Britaine', fol. 6r.

[94] Harrison, 'Description of Britaine', fol. 3r.

whom it is worthily doubted, whether they were more harde and cruell to our countrymen then the Danes, or more heauye and intollerable to our Islande then the Saxons or Romaynes'.[95]

Harrison's account of the Norman yoke neatly integrated two intellectual strands, an interest in a description of Britain with his increasingly apocalyptic view of human history.[96] Harrison's godly, providential outlook and search for the 'True Church' dramatically expanded in his unpublished 'Chronology' and the 1587 revision of the 'Description'.[97] Less dramatically, Harrison closed the chapter in 1577 with the observation that 'Thus we see howe from time to time this Islande hath not onely bene a praye, but as it were a common receptacle for straungers', the consequence of which was the destruction of the island's 'naturall homelinges', its original Britons.[98] When Camden came to write his account of the peopling of Britain in a few years' time – an altogether more detailed account – he too would echo these providential punishments by outsiders. Both men drew on Gildas's *De Excidio et Conquestu Britanniae* or 'On the ruin and conquest of Britain'. The spectre of providence powered increasingly neurotic, violent fears for restored Protestantism from 1559 right through the troubles of the early Stuarts.[99] Ethno-religious diversity signalled the failure to bring the true reformed Church to all the nations of Britain: God troubled covenanted peoples for backsliding.

Beyond the history of migration, invasion, conquest, or the struggle for *imperium*, Harrison found Britain's cultural complexity in its peoples' languages, just as Boorde had. Harrison took particular interest in tracking the apparent change and improvement of English.[100] He also wrote, 'in mine opinion the Brittish of Cornewall is thus corrupted, sith the Welch tong that is spoken in the north and south part of Wales, doth differ so much in it selfe, as the English vsed in Scotlande, doth from that which is spoken among vs here in this side of the Islande'.[101] His enmity toward the Scots took an ethnographic turn, even while accepting the hybrid culture of the Anglo-Scottish Borders and North of England: 'The Scottish englishe is much broader and lesse pleasaunt in vtterance, then ours, because that nation hath not hitherto indevoured to bring the same to any perfit order; and yet it is such in maner, as Englishmen theymselues doe

[95] Harrison, 'Description of Britaine', fol. 3r.

[96] Alexandra Walsham, 'Providentialism', in *Holinshed's Chronicles*, pp. 427–42 examines the complex strands of providentialism in the *Chronicles* generally.

[97] Parry, *Protestant Vision*, pp. 128–9, 267–70; also Ralph Houlbrooke, 'England', in *Holinshed's Chronicles*, pp. 632–4.

[98] Harrison, 'Description of Britaine', fol. 3r.

[99] Alexandra Walsham, *Providence in Early Modern England* (Oxford, 1999), pp. 243–325; the characterization is mine.

[100] Harrison, 'Description of Britaine', fols 4v–5v.

[101] Harrison, 'Description of Britaine', fol. 4v.

speake, for the most part beyonde the Trent.'[102] The Scots' status as 'strangers' in Britain also found linguistic validation:

> For in the North part of the Region, where the wilde Scottes, otherwyse called the Redshankes, or Rough footed Scottes (bycause they go bare footed & clad in mantels ouer their saffron shirtes after the Irishe maner) doe inhabite, they speake good Irishe, whereby they shew their originall to haue in times past bene fetched out of Irelande.[103]

Harrison's interest in the linguistic and literary legacy of Britain put him in good company with Leland and Bale.[104]

According to Harrison, Leland's consciousness of cultural complexity owed something to Aristotle's theories of racial difference:

> Leland, noting somewhat of the constitution of our bodies saith these words ... the Britons are white in color, strong of body, and full of blood, as people inhabiting near the North and far from the equinoctial line, where the soil is not so fruitful and therefore the people not so feeble; whereas contrariwise, such as dwell toward the course of the sun are less of stature, weaker of body, more nice, delicate, fearful by nature, blacker in color, and some so black indeed as any crow or raven. Thus saith he.[105]

Harrison was not persuaded by climactic theory, preferring like William Worcestre or Jean Bodin to evaluate ethnic or national character through a broader range of influences, including environmental imperatives and cultural transmission.[106] Consequently, good and bad qualities marked Harrison's English: the hardiness of English men and their 'comeliness' into middle age, the beauty and proportion of English women or the fact that they aged better than the 'wretched and hard-favored' French women, the failure of poor English men and women to educate their children to obedience and godliness.[107] Harrison's focus on the complexity of Britain's people went only so far, however. 'I could make report likewise of the natural vices and virtues of all those that are born within this island,' he closed, 'but as the full traction hereof craveth a better head than mine to set forth the same, so will I give place to other men that list to take it in hand.'[108] Only those who could actually undertake the journeys of discovery and encounter would fully illuminate these matters for future readers or armchair travellers like Harrison. Fynes Moryson aimed to be such a person, as we learn in the next chapter.

---

102 Harrison, 'Description of Britaine', fol. 5v.
103 Harrison, 'Description of Britaine', fol. 5v.
104 Harrison, Description, p. 391.
105 Harrison, Description, pp. 445–6.
106 Jean Bodin, Method for the Easy Comprehension of History, trans. Beatrice Reynolds (Columbia, 1945), pp. 85–152.
107 Harrison, Description, pp. 445–9.
108 Harrison, Description, p. 450.

Cultural prejudices at work in Harrison's 'Description' shaded into a sort of socio-economic nationalism.[109] Leland's evidence for cultural complexity in the form of artefacts like varieties of Norman stone found no favour. Harrison challenged readers to deny that 'we have quarries enow and good enough in England, sufficient for us to build withal, if the peevish contempt of our commodities, and delectations to enrich other countries, did not catch such foolish hold upon us'.[110] He indicted the English entrepreneurial character on this basis:

> But such, alas, is our nature that ... for desire of novelty we oft exchange our finest cloth, corn, tin, and wools for halfpenny cockhorses for children, dogs of wax or cheese, twopenny tabors, leaden swords, painted feather, gewgaws for fools, dogtricks for dizzards, hawkshoods, and such like trumpery, whereby we reap just mockage and reproach in other countries.[111]

English failure frustrated Harrison and he savaged Leland's account of the fishermen of Hull who paved the city streets with their ballast of grey stones from Iceland. The 'Hullanders or Hull men will say how that stockfish is light loading, and therefore they did ballast their vessels with these Iceland stone to keep them from turning over in their so tedious a voyage.' But Harrison wanted his readers to appreciate that a self-destructive love of foreign commodities lay behind what the fishermen 'will say'.[112] There was more amiss than simply an addiction to foreign supplies or neglect of domestic resources. Harrison noted that iron was actually cheaper when imported because 'it is our quality when we got any commodity to use it with extremity towards our own nation, after we have once found the means to shut out foreigners'.[113] Had he lived to see the 1601 parliamentary attack on price-fixing monopolists or the heyday of projectors in the seventeenth century, Harrison would undoubtedly have been confirmed in his opinion that this was an English pathology.

Livelihoods in agriculture, husbandry, manufactures, and trades took on ethno-cultural significance. For Harrison, the balance of husbandry to intensive agriculture among the peoples and nations of Britain supported a value-laden, topographic hierarchy. In their pastoralism, the early Britons resembled Irish graziers who 'dwelled in movable villages by companies, whose custom was to divide the ground amongst them ... till by eating up the country about him he was enforced to remove further and seek for better pasture'.[114] England's ground yielded the most bountiful crops of cereal grains, as did 'some parts of Wales', but 'the best of Scotland be scarcely comparable to the mean of either or both'.

---

[109] Keith Wrightson, *Earthly Necessities: Economic Lives in Early Modern Britain* (New Haven, 2000), pp. 98–104, 132–58.
[110] Harrison, *Description*, pp. 357–9.
[111] Harrison, *Description*, p. 359.
[112] Harrison, *Description*, p. 360.
[113] Harrison, *Description*, p. 369.
[114] Harrison, *Description*, p. 429.

Scotland made up for this with plenty of quarries and rich mines.[115] Harrison reported the English north–south divide of declining fertility and crop yields as one travelled north.[116] Overall, English fields had come to yield substantially more and the 'cause is for that our countrymen are grown to be more painful, skillful, and careful through recompense of gain'. This stood in marked contrast to the experience of their ancestors, when 'a great compass hath yielded but small profit, and this only through the idle and negligent occupation of such as daily manured and had the same in occupying'.[117]

Idleness and the want of initiative once plagued all peoples of Britain, but its effects followed a cultural hierarchy:

> I might set down examples of these things out of all the parts of this island, that is to say, many of England, more out of Scotland, but most of all out of Wales, in which two last rehearsed very little other food and livelihood was wont to be looked for (beside flesh) more than the soil of itself and the cow gave; the people in the meantime living idly, dissolutely, and by picking [robbing] and stealing one from another. All which vices are now (for the most part) relinquished, so that each nation manureth her own, with triple commodity to that it was beforetime.[118]

Harrison's estimation of the Welsh may have been encouraged by frequent reference to the *Itinerary*. This applied to the almost fantastically fruitful pastures of Cardigan, where, in Harrison's reading, 'all the cattle in the country are not able to eat it down', leaving it to rot and form bogs and quagmires. What was certainly Harrison's own was an unusual Anglocentric slip. Coming several decades after the Tudor acts of union, he wrote that the 'best pasture ground of all England is in Wales'.[119] This economic partisanship combined with evangelical zeal took a xenophobic turn when Harrison admitted that Italy – like Cardigan – was extraordinarily 'fruitful' and fit to be 'called the paradise of the world, although by reason of the wickedness of such as dwell therein it may be called the sink and drain of hell'.[120]

Descriptions of cities and towns turned into attacks on urban decay, the burdensome relationship of the peasantry and landholders, and rural poverty. For this Harrison could thank Leland for having journeyed to so many towns, villages, and parishes. Thus, 'Leland in sundry places complaineth likewise of the decay of parishes in great cities and towns, missing in some six or eight or

---

[115] Harrison, *Description*, p. 432.
[116] Harrison, *Description*, p. 434; also John Langton, 'South, North, and Nation: Regional Differences and Consciousness in an Integrating Realm, 1550–1750', *Geographies of England; The North–South Divide, Material and Imagined*, ed. Alan R.H. Baker and Mark Billinge (Cambridge, 2004), pp. 135–43.
[117] Harrison, *Description*, p. 432.
[118] Harrison, *Description*, p. 432.
[119] Harrison, *Description*, p. 432.
[120] Harrison, *Description*, p. 433.

twelves churches and more, of all which he giveth particular note.'[121] Decay did not just plague 'our isle and nation, but unto most of the famous countries of the world heretofore, and all by the greedy desire of such as would live alone and only to themselves'. Like expanding cancers on the landscapes, these solitary, greedy persons included 'lords of the soil' who defrauded people of their right to the commons or allowed local engrossers to pull down empty houses that might be used by the poor.[122] Harrison, ironically, welcomed the destruction of the religious orders that helped to create a new class of 'lords of the soil' when monastic properties were sold. He skipped over this transformation and focussed directly on the landlords. It was obvious to him that in a decayed town, 'a gentleman having three parts of the town in his own hands, four households do bear all the aforesaid payment' where once the crown's taxes were shared among 'fifty wealthy householders'. The lesson came directly from Leland 'in his *Commentaries* [*Itinerary*] (*lib.* 13), lately come to my hands, which thing he especially noted in his travel over this isle'.[123]

Harrison discovered much about England and Wales in Leland's notebooks. He found the complex imprints of humans on the land and the past, from parishes, political economy, and the built environment to laws, local notables, and, of course, antiquities.[124] He cribbed and repeated, but this too helped to bring Leland's journeys and encounters to light.[125] Indeed, as an armchair traveller, Harrison had to exploit Leland's notebooks if Holinshed's *Chronicle* hoped to offer a credible description of the peoples of Britain. But Harrison pushed his material to satisfy expectations and serve his own purposes, including nationalist chauvinism and a compulsion to reproach the English for not becoming an even greater commercial nation. As Harrison demonstrates, Leland's *Itinerary* and *Collectanea* could be highly mutable texts for the study of multicultural Britain or the nations that called it home, past and present. They would be given new meaning in the hands of those who witnessed the religious turmoil of the Elizabethan years.

Leland's remains and godly nations

Traveller-writers driven by religious and political conviction or evangelical zeal interpreted and manipulated the descriptions of Mair, Boece, and Leland. Leland's manuscripts could be made to serve the interests and prejudices of those with a stake in the religious changes only just unfolding in Britain when he made his journeys. Harrison owed much to Leland in crafting his account

---

[121] Harrison, *Description*, p. 215.
[122] Harrison, *Description*, pp. 217, 440.
[123] Harrison, *Description*, p. 218.
[124] Harrison, *Description*, pp. 42, 47, 163-6, 198, 205, 254, 294, 300, 443, 456.
[125] Harrison, *Description*, pp. 209-14, 287-91.

of Britain and the failings of the English, but that did not make him any more faithful to Leland's descriptions of the Church than he had been to Boece/ Bellenden's. Leland joined descriptions of topography and natural history with details of the Church, its bricks and mortar as well as its clergy and spiritual practices.[126] Harrison openly reworked the material even when godly piety was not directly at stake.

We can begin with Leland's account of the salt works at Droitwich:

> Leland hath written abundantly in his Commentaries of Britain and whose words only I will set down in English as he wrote them, because he seemeth to have had diligent consideration of the same, without adding anything of mine own to him, except it be where necessity doth enforce me for the mere aid of the reader in the understanding of his mind.[127]

Yet even subtle and apparently insignificant additions aimed for a particular reading. Where Leland remarked on the socio-economic inversion of the town, in which the hard-working burgesses made only the poorest gain from the salt works by comparison to the 'gentlemen', Harrison added a marginal comment that made this an axiomatic problem of the market: 'A common plague in all things of any great commodity, for one beateth the bush but another catcheth the birds, as we may see in batfowling.'[128] Leland had been unimpressed with the 'superstition of the people' that celebrated the restoration of the mines by the bishop of Chichester. Harrison shared the judgement and aimed to impress it upon readers. Leland's account of 'drinking games and revels' at the mine became 'sundry games, drinkings, and foolish revels at it'.[129]

Leland's description of Cwm Ystwyth included the account of a crow that stole a miner's purse and led him on a merry chase while his comrades perished in a cave-in. Harrison embellished this credulous story into a tale of providential deliverance: 'I am persuaded that the crow was God's instrument herein, whereby the life of this poor laborer was preserved.'[130] Harrison compared this favourably to a German shoemaker's crow who, 'or else the devil within him', once answered a question with a quote from Psalm 76. Harrison rather disingenuously asked his reader but 'wither am I digressed from lead unto crows and from crows unto devils?' before numbering several iron mines detailed in Leland's *Itinerary*.[131]

The founding of Osney Priory near Oxford found a home in Harrison's account of the universities of England. In Leland's matter-of-fact retelling, Edith

---

[126] Harrison, *Description*, pp. 67, 294, 328, 330, 364, 431, 439 (topography); Harrison, *Description*, pp. 43, 50–1, 56, 280 (Church).
[127] Harrison, *Description*, p. 375.
[128] Harrison, *Description*, p. 376, n.
[129] Harrison, *Description*, p. 376.
[130] Harrison, *Description*, p. 368.
[131] Harrison, *Description*, p. 369.

Forne was instructed by her 'vertuus' confessor, the canon of St Frideswide's, to found a church on the site of the tree with the chattering magpies. As with Boece's descriptions of Scottish religiosity, Harrison looked with evangelical disapproval on lady Oxford's piety:

> Edith, a woman given to no less superstition than credulity, began also the Abbey of Osney ... upon a fond (but yet a rare) occasion, which we will here remember, though it be beside my purpose, to the end that the reader may see how ready the simple people of that time were to be abused by the practice of the clergy.[132]

Harrison marvellously embroidered the account. Asked why the magpies 'molest and vex her', the canon responded:

> 'Oh, madam,' saith he, the wiliest pie of all, 'these are no piece but souls in purgatory that crave relief.' 'And is it so, indeed?' quoth she. 'Now, depardieu [in God's name], if old Robert will give me leave, I will do what I can to bring these souls to rest.' Hereupon she consulted, craved, wept, and became so importunate with her husband that he joined with her, and they both began that synagogue, 1120, which afterward proved to be a notable den.[133]

Harrison corrupted Leland's story of piety and virtue. Under the malign influence of the priest, the superstitious and credulous Edith and her stereotypically irrational female nature served the unholy ends of the Romish clergy. It may have been beside the immediate purpose of describing Oxford and Cambridge, but it was certainly part of Harrison's providential bent to retell the story. Working with Leland's notebooks rather than a 'finished' text made it easier to express religious prejudice in fictitious dialogue and pure embellishment.

Religious upheaval, changing orthodoxies, and prejudice presented challenges to the generation of writers like Harrison, Stow, and Camden whose work touched on past events, present regimes, or both. Leland played a vital role for these authors. Indeed, Leland's treatment of the Church fairly demanded deliberate manipulation. Despite Leland's undoubted support for the royal supremacy and his view of a corrupt and corrupting papacy, so much of his description of the Church's rich spiritual and institutional past stood at odds with the views of evangelicals like Harrison.[134] By contrast, Leland's treatment of the Church would not have presented a problem for John Stow, another avid reader.

Stow copied some fifteen of Leland's eighteen folio and quarto volumes before he lent them to Harrison.[135] Stow's devotion undoubtedly reflected plans for his own 'Historie of this Iland', intended to tap a range of antiquarian manuscripts,

---

[132] Harrison, *Description*, p. 68.

[133] Harrison, *Description*, p. 68.

[134] Peter Marshall, 'Religious Ideology', in *Holinshed's Chronicles*, pp. 411–26 examines the religious politics at work.

[135] Harris, 'Leland's Manuscript Remains', pp. 471–3.

Prospectus Ruinarum Abbatiæ de OSNEY, juxta Oxon:

9 Osney Abbey engraved by Wenceslas Hollar from William Dugdale, *Monastici Anglicani* (London, 1682). RB 434114 Huntington Library, San Marino, CA, reproduced by permission. Image produced by ProQuest as part of *Early English Books Online*. www.proquest.com

narrative histories, and 'chorographical descriptions of English provincial cities'.[136] His attachment to Leland's manuscripts probably reflected a shared respect for that religious past. The strong resemblance to Holinshed's *Chronicles* and Harrison's 'Description' frustrated Stow's ability to attract a publisher. No printer spent precious capital competing against venerable works.[137] This poisoned the relationship between Harrison and Stow, fuelling accusations in the 1603 edition of the *Survey* that Leland's 'Commentaries' had been 'presented "as the labours of another (who was forced to confesse he never travelled further, then from London to the University of Oxford)"'.[138]

Stow still produced some justly familiar works that ran to many editions: *A Summarie of Englyshe Chronicles* (1565) and several abridged editions, *The Chronicles of England* (1580), the abridged *Annales of England* (1592), and *A Survey of London* (1598).[139] Leland's notebooks provided only occasional references for the *Chronicles* and *Annals*. As a topographical record of Stow's itinerary of London, the *Survey* 'owed much to Leland in terms of approach', but issues of actual content are less clear cut. Stow's contemporaries assumed that Leland was a valuable source. In the eighteenth century Thomas Hearne believed that 'Leland compiled a detailed account of London which was used by Stow but subsequently lost', something Hearne's contemporaries accepted. On the face of it, Leland's main presence in Stow's *Survey* was his own monument in the parish church of St Michael ad Bladum, reports of the lost books of St Peter's Library, Cornhill, and Stow's attack on Harrison's account of Gerrard the Giant's staff and his comment that the 'Description' was 'drawne out of Iohn Leyland his comentaries (borrowed of myselfe)'.[140]

Nostalgia played a crucial role in Stow's *Survey* of London, especially 'his anxieties about the changes he had witnessed within his lifetime'.[141] Those anxieties included changing 'sociable boundaries', the decay of hospitality during the economically troubled 1590s, and the corruption and self-interest associated with the age of the projector – not unlike Harrison's social commentary of

---

[136] G.J.R. Parry, 'John Stow's Unpublished "Historie of this Iland": Amity and Enmity amongst Sixteenth Century Scholars', *English Historical Review* 102.404 (1987), p. 636.

[137] Parry, 'Stow's Unpublished "Historie"', pp. 637–42.

[138] Parry, 'Stow's Unpublished "Historie"', pp. 642–4.

[139] For Stow's works, see Parry, 'Stow's Unpublished "Historie"', pp. 633–47; Barrett L. Beer, *Tudor England Observed: The World of John Stow* (Stroud, 1998); M.J. Power, 'John Stow and His London', in *The Changing Face of English Local History*, ed. R.C. Richardson (Aldershot, 2000), pp. 30–51; Ian Gadd and Alexandra Gillespie, eds, *John Stow (1525–1605) and the Making of the English Past; Studies in Early Modern Culture and the History of the Book* (London, 2004).

[140] John Stow, *A Survey of London*, ed. Charles Lethbridge Kingsford (two volumes; Oxford, 1908), I, pp. 194, 342, 348–9.

[141] Ian Archer, 'The Nostalgia of John Stow', *The Theatrical City: Culture, Theatre and Politics in London 1576–1649*, ed. David L. Smith, Richard Strier, and David Bevington (Cambridge, 1995), p. 19.

the 1570s.[142] Demographic change drove some of these anxieties, but religious upheaval also played a significant role in the disintegration of 'the "catholic" interpretation of the medieval past as a time of "charity, hospitality, and plenty"'. As well, 'the damage done to the physical fabric of the City over the course of his lifetime', not least conversion of monastic establishments to house the city's ever-booming population and the 'collapse of Londoners' support for their churches', especially 'the church fabric', fuelled Stow's disquiet.[143]

Stow was no Catholic recusant and he prospered under the Elizabethan settlement, even gaining the patronage of the bibliophile Archbishop Matthew Parker. He also found common ground with William Lambarde and John Bale, the 'hot Protestant' promoter of Leland, in decrying the destruction of monastic libraries – if not the monasteries themselves.[144] Yet Stow's sympathies seem to have been decidedly traditional.[145] Even where Stow recorded positive changes, for instance when noting that a church was 'recently rebuilt or refurbished', he harked back to the pre-Reformation past: 'it appears that the improvements to which he refers were not at all recent, and had been carried out before the Reformation, a watershed which he probably never ceased to regret'.[146] Self-censorship for reprints of the *Summary* and *Survey* bear this out, including removal of his 'upbeat' account of the Marian restoration of Catholicism and lines enjoining prayers for the dead from transcriptions of epitaphs. Stow, in the words of Patrick Collinson, underwent 'a process of conversion by conformity' to the Protestant establishment even if the *Survey*'s topographical details demonstrated a 'continuing commitment to the fabric and the social and mystical community of London's parishes'.[147]

These two readers of Leland's manuscripts, Harrison and Stow, stand in marked contrast to one another. Stow venerated a religious past very much in keeping with Leland's notebooks. According to Ian Archer, 'Stow's avowed purpose recording the good works of preceding generations was the display of a "godly example by posterity to be embraced and imitated".'[148] There was much in Leland's *Itinerary* that accomplished the same goal of highlighting exemplary virtue and located it on either side of the policies of the 1530s. Nonetheless, Stow's response was decidedly his own:

> There could be no more eloquent testimony to his lack of sympathy for evangelical Protestantism than his failure to mention the endowment by leading London

---

[142] Archer, 'Nostalgia of John Stow', pp. 20–1.

[143] Archer, 'Nostalgia of John Stow', pp. 21–8.

[144] Patrick Collinson, 'John Stow and Nostalgic Antiquarianism', *Imagining Early Modern London: Perceptions and Portrayals of the City from Stow to Strype, 1598–1720*, ed. J.F. Merritt (Cambridge, 2001), pp. 40, 46; Archer, 'Nostalgia of John Stow', pp. 30–1.

[145] Collinson, 'John Stow', pp. 42–5.

[146] Collinson, 'John Stow', pp. 46–7.

[147] Collinson, 'John Stow', p. 46.

[148] Archer, 'Nostalgia of John Stow', p. 31.

merchants of parochial lectureships and the support of others by means of subscription among parishioners: by the time of the publication of his Survey thirty-five parishes supported lectureships. The remarkable progress made in the creation of an effective preaching ministry went unpraised by Stow.[149]

Wilful ignorance of this kind was not something Stow shared with Leland, who was ready to note lay piety so as to encourage more.

The deliberate recasting of Leland's manuscripts by Harrison suggests how problematic they could be for evangelicals who sought to 'reform' the (English) past. The 'Catholic antiquarian' William Burton made conspicuous use of Leland's manuscripts in his attention to the 'pious reputations of various monasteries' and their historical connections to Christendom in his *Description of Leicestershire* (1622).[150] Burton took an interest in the story – 'as it goeth currant by tradition' – of the holy nun at a small monastery in Langley, whose virginity and purity were so great that her face was animated 'by a shining radyancy and brightnesse'. This led Burton to remark on the similarities with the qualities of St Frideswide and her foundation of the monastery in Oxford, as related in William of Malmesbury's chronicle. This in turn led him to Leland, who 'reporteth in his first Tome, out of an old Manuscript [*Flores Historiarum*], that her face was of that bright shining lustre, that Algarus Prince of Mercia viewing the same with an amorous passion, was in an instant (for a time) stroken blinde'.[151] This was the world of piety and virtue foretold by chattering magpies, not the corruption of Edith Forne's devotion by her confessor.

The Kentish traveller and antiquary William Lambarde had his own religious interest in Leland's manuscripts.[152] Lambarde achieved fame in his own lifetime for the *Perambulation of Kent*, published in 1576, when Stow and Harrison set to work with Leland's notebooks. Lambarde's *Perambulation* sprang from his researches into histories of England for what was intended to be a grand 'historical dictionary or "store house", out of which he intended to draw suitable information for histories of all the shires in England'. By now this sort of project sounds all too familiar, and Lambarde fared no better than most of his contemporaries. He abandoned it 'after Camden sent him a manuscript copy of the *Britannia* to review and criticise'.[153] Lambarde would not be the last traveller

---

[149] Archer, 'Nostalgia of John Stow', p. 29.
[150] William Burton, *The Description of Leicestershire* (STC 4179; London, 1622), pp. 43, 53–4, 63–4, 113, 156–7, 162–4, 308.
[151] Burton, *Description of Leicestershire*, p. 156; see *The Itinerary of John Leland*, ed. Lucy Toulmin Smith (five volumes; Carbondale, IL, 1964), II, p. 153, hereafter cited as Leland, *Itinerary*.
[152] William Lambarde, *A Perambulation of Kent* (STC 15715.5; London, 1576), pp. 62–9, 129–37, 148–57, 181–9, 192–4, 217–26, 254–7, 290–2, 374–81; Collinson, 'John Stow', pp. 38–40.
[153] Lambarde's 'Description' is described in Retha M. Warnicke, *William Lambarde: Elizabethan Antiquary 1536–1601* (Chichester, 1973), p. 26.

whose projects Camden pushed into the dustbin – as Fynes Moryson found out in the next century.

Lambarde read Leland's *Assertio* in defence of Arthur, referenced the *Cygnea* and *Genethliacon* – by 'a man generally acquainted with the antiquities of this Realme' – and had access to topographical manuscripts concerning Kent, perhaps some now lost.[154] Like Leland's, Lambarde's was an outspoken and aggressively Anglocentric reading of Geoffrey of Monmouth's British History.[155] Lambarde included a short chapter in the *Perambulation* attacking William Petyt and Polydore Vergil for their scepticism and referred 'suche as desire more aboundant testimonies, to the reading of Iohn Leland, and Syr Iohn ap Rese [John Prise], two learned men, that haue plentifully written therein'.[156] Prise authored the *Historiae Brytannicae Defensio* against Vergil and a famous collection of Welsh devotional tracts, *Yny Lhyvyr Hwm* or *In This Book*.[157] Leland's primary value for both the *Perambulation* and the *Dictionarium Angliæ* was as an authority in defence of the Galfridian legends – 'the greatest Friend that every Geffrey found', according to Lambarde in the *Dictionarium Angliæ* – and in topographical matters, especially questions of place-names.[158]

The *Perambulation* also included robust attacks on the authority of the papacy as well as the religious orders. The religious house at Montidene came in for abuse and occasioned an attack on religious institutions throughout Kent: 'I finde, that the yerely extent of the clere value of the Religious liuings within this Shyre, amounted to fiue thousande poundes' not including 'Bishoprickes, Benefices, Friaries, Chauntries, and Saintes offerings ... which thing also I doe the rather note, to the end that you may see, howe iuste cause is giuen us, bothe to wonder at the hoate zeale of our auncestours in their spirituall fornication, and to lament the coldenesse of our owne charitie, towardes the maintenaunce of the true spouse of Iesus Christ'.[159] Leland offered Lambarde little support in grinding his religious axes, however.

Lambarde noted the existence of a Carmelite or White Friar house in Sandwich, 'whereof I read none other good thing, saue that it brought foorth the one learned man, called William Becly, in the reigne of Henry the first'. To Lambarde's approval, a learned townsman, Roger Manwood, 'hathe for the increase of Godliness and good letters, erected and endowed a faire Free Schoole there, from whence there is hope, that the common wealth shall reape more

---

[154] Lambarde, *Perambulation*, pp. 90, 173, 349, 384.
[155] Lambarde, *Perambulation*, preface, pp. 1–3,12–14, 117, 209, 278–85.
[156] Lambarde, *Perambulation*, p. 59.
[157] Huw Pryce, 'Sir John Prise', *Oxford DNB* at www.oxforddnb.com.
[158] Lambarde, *Perambulation*, pp. 105, 117, 173, 349; William Lambarde, *Dictionarium Angliæ Topographicum & Historicum. An Alphabetical Description of the Chief Places in England and Wales* (London, 1730), pp. 21, 28, 63, 78, 93–4, 155, 190, 191, 218, 231, 262, 285, 314, 318, 371, 385, 446.
[159] Lambarde, *Perambulation*, p. 230.

profite after a fewe yeares: then it receaued commoditie by the Carmelites, since the time of their first foundation'.[160] Evidently Leland's report that there was in Sandwich 'a place of Whit freres, and an hospital withowt the town fyrst ordened for maryners desesid and hurt' was not evidence of any good 'commoditie' arising from the Carmelite foundation.[161]

Lambarde's primary interest in Dover's religious houses was their worth at the dissolution, including a valuation at £98 per annum for St Radigund's, whose foundation, 'large and fayr' choir, and continued operation Leland noted.[162] As for Leland's bare report of three members of the Crevicure family buried at Leeds Priory, Lambarde remarked that 'in auncient time, even the greatest personages, held Monkes, Friars, and Noones, in such veneration and liking, that they thought no citie in case to flourish, no house likely to haue long continuaunce, no Castle sufficiently defended, where was not an Abbay, Pryorie, or Nonnerie, eyther placed within the walles, or situate at hande and near adioyning'.[163] Lambarde and Harrison welcomed the end of a religious world that had none of the redeeming virtue found in it by Leland and Stow. There was no room for that religious world in the descriptions of England that adopted the hallmarks of a Protestant topography or ethnography.[164] Only in the ensuing decades would English Catholics serve up Catholic counterparts to these descriptions, especially in local studies, and join the kind of battle that Lesley fought over Scotland and its people.[165]

The localism of traveller-writers like Lambarde, Stow, Burton, even Harrison emphasized national religious identity alongside a robust antiquarianism and good doses of gentry self-satisfaction and promotion. In England county historians followed in the footsteps of Leland at the local level, while Welsh gentry and Scottish nobles promoted the study of important families and their intimate connections to the countryside in manuscript histories and descriptions. Counties bounded local studies that frequently constructed 'images of settled, unchanging local societies' dominated by gentry, lairdly, or noble families whose lives and fortunes shaped attention to topography, 'learning, religion and custom, as well as building and physical artefacts'.[166] Elites who wrote local

---

[160] Lambarde, *Perambulation*, p. 107.

[161] Leland, *Itinerary*, IV, p. 48.

[162] Lambarde, *Perambulation*, p. 132.

[163] Leland, *Itinerary*, IV, p. 43; Lambarde, *Perambulation*, p. 264.

[164] Alexandra Walsham, *The Reformation of the Landscape: Religion, Identity, and Memory in Early Modern Britain and Ireland* (Oxford, 2011), p. 480.

[165] Christopher Highley, *Catholics Writing the Nation in Early Modern Britain and Ireland* (Oxford, 2008), pp. 80-117. On Catholic antiquarians in the Midlands, including Burton, see Richard Cust, 'Catholicism, Antiquarianism and Gentry Honour: The Writings of Sir Thomas Shirley', *Midland History* 23 (1998), pp. 60-2 and generally.

[166] Cust, 'Catholicism, Antiquarianism and Gentry Honour', p. 61.

studies or patronized others that did were embedded simultaneously in their localities and political, cultural, and religious life at the national level.[167]

None of this precluded sensitivity to cultural complexity as a lived reality in communities throughout Britain, as we will learn from Richard Carew (Cornwall), George Owen (Pembrokeshire), Robert Gordon of Straloch (Aberdeenshire), and others in the chapters that follow. Yet it seemingly discouraged thinking of county or municipal bounds as porous or engaging with cultural complexity beyond antiquarian or genealogical esoterica. We can consider Solicitor-General John Dodderidge. The intelligent, respected judge maintained his Devonian connections throughout his life, joined the Society of Antiquaries, and composed a celebrated common law tract, *The English Lawyer* (1631).[168] Dodderidge's *History of the Ancient and Moderne Estate of the Principality of Wales, Dutchy of Cornewall, and Earldome of Chester* had precious little to say about cultural complexity in its political-legal history other than to explain how these three appendages became part of the English crown or, in the Welsh case, the existence of competing legal traditions in the Law of Hywel Dda, marcher lordship, and English common law.[169] Interestingly, John Hooker bequeathed his chorographic notes about Devon to Dodderidge, mistakenly hoping that he would see them into print.[170] In Dodderidge's case, national interests and affairs created a very English framing of the past and a practical detachment from local cultures. The cultural complexity that Leland so often found in the localities, but which he understood within the frame of a multicultural Britain, receded into an antiquarian past that infrequently informed narrow national identities.

Lambarde's work epitomizes the evolution in reading Leland's *Itinerary* and *Collectanea* that carried right through to the twentieth century. Lambarde abandoned hopes of publishing his topographical dictionary of England, but he completed it all the same. The *Dictionarium Angliæ Topographicum & Historicum. An Alphabetical Description of the Chief Places in England and Wales* was finally published from Lambarde's original manuscript in 1730.[171] Both Lambarde and Harrison burned with an evangelical piety that encouraged visions of a Protestant 'England' as a chosen, covenanted nation whose preaching ministry, especially, could restore the primitive Church and a lost Christianity.[172] Lambarde possessed that form of Anglocentrism that translated into 'vivid contempt for

---

[167] Jan Broadway, *'No Historie So Meete': Gentry Culture and the Development of Local History in Elizabethan and Early Stuart England* (Manchester, 2006), pp. 14–79; Daniel Woolf, *The Social Circulation of the Past: English Historical Culture 1500–1730* (Oxford, 2003), pp. 73–137.

[168] David Ibbetson, 'John Dodderidge', *Oxford DNB* at www.oxforddnb.com.

[169] John Doddridge, *The History of the Ancient and Moderne Estate of the Principality of Wales, Dutchy of Cornewall, and Earldome of Chester* (STC 6982; London, 1630), pp. 1–80.

[170] Broadway, *'No Historie So Meete'*, p. 34.

[171] Warnecke, *William Lambarde*, pp. 26–9.

[172] Parry, 'Harrison's "Chronology"', pp. 108–10; Christopher Hill, *The English Bible and the Seventeenth Century Revolution* (London, 1993), pp. 264–74.

other national groups'.[173] It also featured sloppiness in his choice of words, a real handicap for someone writing a dictionary. His entry for Albion in the *Dictionarium Angliæ* defined it as 'the most auncient Name of this Island; for longe was it called *Britannia*, and but latelye *Anglia*.'[174] The entry for Brytannia took a very different position, though. Significantly, Lambarde associated the definition with Leland:

> Others destribute the Name *Brytanniae* into *Primam, Secundum, Flaviam, Maximiam, & Valentiam*, wherof this last Opinion liketh *Leland* nothinge at all. And not without Cause, for it semeth more reasonable, that the two distinct Kingdomes of *Ingland* and *Scotland* should be eche called by the Name of the hole Ile, then [than] that every Part or Province of one Kingdome should be so termed. The comon Opinion (excludinge al Division and Pluralitye in the Name) called the hole Ile, conteyning *England, Wales*, and *Scotland*, by the Name of *Brytannia* only.

No one kingdom or province's name had claim to being applied to the whole island, not when Britannia or Britain was the proper term.

The last formulation is striking both for being described as the 'common opinion' in 1570 and for its association with Leland. *The Lives of Those Eminent Antiquaries John Leland, Thomas Hearne, and Anthony à Wood* published in 1772 helps us to understand what became of that common opinion. This biography of Leland owed a good deal to Thomas Hearne's publication of the *Itinerary* and *Collectanea* and Anthony Wood's edition of *De Viris Illustribus*, Leland's account of British literary worthies. *Those Eminent Antiquaries* presented a heroic portrait of Leland recovering the past from medieval barbarism:

> [He] pursued the natural bent of his genius [and] not content with this general description of the kingdom, he inspected the libraries, the windows, and other monuments of Antiquity ... wherever he heard there were any footsteps of Roman, Saxon, or Danish buildings, he went in search of them ... In his travel his labour was prodigious [and] he made diligent search into the very bowels of Antiquity ... In the continued removal of Leland from one part of the kingdom to another, the recommendation of friends and gentlemen of interest in the several counties was both profitable and necessary, for his better instruction and accommodation.[175]

Despite the good use 'made of Leland's papers in their imperfect state' by Burton, Camden, Holinshed, Drayton, Dugdale, Stow, Lambarde, and Wood himself, the biographer lamented that Leland 'lived not to have carried his great undertakings into execution himself'.[176] He felt the absence of Leland's own description of Britain. Yet it was 'evident, that great benefit accrued to the history of this kingdom' and Leland was, in the author's view, 'justy stiled the Father of

[173] Warnecke, *William Lambarde*, p. 25.
[174] Lambarde, *Dictionarium Angliæ*, p. 1.
[175] *The Lives of Those Eminent Antiquaries John Leland, Thomas Hearne, and Anthony à Wood* (two volumes; Oxford, 1772) I, pp. 10–14.
[176] *Lives of Those Eminent Antiquaries*, I, pp. 28–32.

English History'.[177] The biographer simply followed Hearne's lead in his preface to the *Itinerary* (1710), which singled out Leland as England's pioneering antiquarian whose 'Authority is look'd upon and cited as equal if not superior to any in Points that concern the Subject of Antiquity.'[178]

Here Leland's travels and his notebooks that recorded Britain's complex cultural identity made him the father of English history and an antiquarian in the narrowest sense. He and Camden too deserved to 'be held in honour for their respective labours in the service of their country'.[179] Not only that, for his biographer, Leland saw past 'the superstitious parade, and the more pernicious errors of that [Catholic] Church' to lament the lost libraries of the monasteries, a fine feature of one who 'renounced Popery' and possessed 'a well disposed zeal for the reformation of religion'. Leland's opposition to the papacy forced him into the clothes of a Protestant zealot and he supposedly earned 'many enemies, in that age of bigoted sentiment'.[180] By 1772, then, Leland and his works had been safely incorporated within an anti-Catholic Protestant England living out its Tory-Anglican prejudices. An Anglocentric cataloguer confirmed Leland's capture in 1812 when he claimed *The Laboryouse Journey of Johan Leylande* for books of 'English History – Topography, Antiquities' during the sale of the duke of Roxburghe's great library.[181] This might have made sense to an imaginary 'father of English History', but it would have been an undiscovered country for the real John Leland.

Summa: Book One

The Stewarts and Tudors divided Britain between them and governed multi-ethnic realms where the cultural complexity of their subjects was recognized, studied, and comprehended – however imperfectly. The new discovery of humanity in the Atlantic community helped to transform medieval precedents for travel and encounter within Britain. Beginning about 1520, Britons set out to explore the island they shared. They determined to study the place and its people in all their detail and complexity, much after the fashion of travellers to the Americas and beyond. History, topography, and ethnography received renewed, sustained attention, oftentimes together in the same journeys and under the covers of the same narratives. Travellers deliberately studied and sought to explain the cultural complexity that confronted them on their travels or in their reading of others'

---

[177] *Lives of Those Eminent Antiquaries*, I, p. 32.

[178] *The Itinerary of John Leland the Antiquarian* (nine volumes; Oxford, 1710–1712), I, pp. v–vii, xvi.

[179] *Lives of Those Eminent Antiquaries*, I, p. 65.

[180] *Lives of Those Eminent Antiquaries*, I, pp. 11–12, 40.

[181] Robert H. Evans, *A Catalogue of the Library of the Late John Duke of Roxburghe* (London, 1812), p. 255.

journeys. Ethnographic perspectives and descriptions of varying sophistication shaped, in some cases defined, travel narratives and other works incorporating such material.

John Leland, John Mair, and Hector Boece, travellers of one sort of another between the 1520s and 1540s, paved the way for this new discovery of multi-cultural Britain. For practical and ideological reasons Mair, Boece, and Leland aligned their travels and descriptions with the bounds of their respective ruler's *imperium*. Mair and Boece wrote multicultural histories of Stewart Scotland in two obvious respects. First, they wrote, however imperfectly, of the ethnic groups and peoples who had built the realm that would eventually belong to the king of Scots and finally take the name Scotland after just one of the peoples that contended for control of North Britain. Second, they continued a long and complicated 'writing' of the Scots that concerned the qualities of the people(s) who bore that name; grappling with what combination of ethno-cultural, topographic, or political qualities made one Scottish. We typically spot this process via convenient – and misleading – shorthand categories like highlander, lowlander, and borderer.[182] Even as they wrote during the reign of James V, perhaps the most thrusting of Stewart dynasts intent upon the unity and mastery of his *imperium*, both Mair and Boece presented cultural complexity as one of the essential qualities of Scotland and its history.

On a grandiose scale John Leland set out to do much of what Mair and Boece kept within the covers of a single history. Leland travelled through the Tudor dominions to collect the first-hand information for a grand 'Civil History' that would describe Henry VIII's 'empyre of England'. Henry's *imperium* emerges from Leland's travels and notebooks as a polyglot one. The long history of migration, encounter, and settlement marked its landscape, Church, and the historical memory of Leland and his local contacts. And ethno-cultural uniqueness defined many peoples and regions of the Tudor *imperium* through which Leland travelled. Leland never wrote his 'Civil History' and we do not know if he would have subsumed this cultural complexity under a chauvinist Englishness or accommodated it, like Mair and Boece, within the borders of a multicultural realm ruled by the king of 'England'. What is clear, though, is that no 'father of English History' composed what survived to become the *Itinerary* and *Collectanea*.

Mair, Boece, and Leland represent new encounters with multicultural Britain that emerged in the decades immediately following the Atlantic voyages of discovery. They found at first-hand the cultural complexity within places that we conventionally think of as Scotland or England or Wales, but which they understood to be polyglot realms under monarchs who claimed temporal

---

[182] The essays in Matthew Hammond, ed., *New Perspectives on Medieval Scotland 1093–1286* (Woodbridge, 2013) address the rich cultural complexity that undermines the utility of such labels or concepts.

(and, eventually, spiritual) *imperium* over their diverse subjects. The upheavals that separated the Tudor and Stewart realms from Rome between the 1530s and 1560s created new kinds of cultural complexity in religious life and politicized ethno-cultural diversity for rulers and local communities.[183] The project by which Renaissance imperial monarchs asserted unitary dynastic supremacy and royal authority in the fifteenth (Stewarts) and early sixteenth (Tudors) centuries turned into a quickening pace of governance by which complexity and diversity, especially in religious practices, became dangerously different – deviant – by definition. Monarchs and their closest counsellors focussed on religious conformity or uniformity might imagine the realm in terms of religious identities that became surrogate and reductive national identities. And horizons narrowed, despite evolving conceptions of civility and barbarity that emerged from contact with Amerindians, other 'lesser peoples', and the Ottoman empire. Elizabeth I intervened to help establish a 'friendly' Protestant regime in Scotland in 1559–60, at the desperate urging of William Cecil, one of those ministers who had served her brother's regime during the Rough Wooing of Scotland in the 1540s. Cecil thought in terms of a Protestant British *imperium* under the sovereignty of a Tudor emperor who dominated Scotland by historic right and dynastic incorporation. His vision represented a broader if particularly Anglocentric version of 'Anglo-Scottish protestant culture' or 'sectarian inclusivity'.[184] Only fitfully did or could Elizabeth's horizons extend beyond England and self-preservation, despite the urgings of Protestant internationalists or ambitious maritime projectors like John Dee and the Hakluyts.[185]

Multicultural Britain existed in tension with a narrower focus on religious-political or national identities.[186] As Daniel Woolf argues in his study of historical culture, 'the English developed a more or less coherent – which does not mean "uncontested" – historical sense of a national past' in which 'the particular history of England itself and its relations with its British and Continental neighbours/enemies' was contested. He notes the 'slow and uneven' processes by which 'the local past was often submerged into a "national" past contained in history-writing and civilized discourse'.[187] Travellers aided this process in crucial respects. Travellers contributed to creating 'a hierarchy of knowledge

---

[183] Walsham, *Reformation of the Landscape*, pp. 12–13, 97–113, 120–5, 478–9.

[184] Jane A.E. Dawson, 'Anglo-Scottish Protestant Culture and Integration in Sixteenth-century Britain', in *Conquest and Union: Fashioning a British State 1485–1725*, ed. Steven G. Ellis and Sarah Barber (Harlow, 1995), pp. 87–114; Scott Oldenburg, *Alien Albion: Literature and Immigration in Early Modern England* (Toronto, 2014), pp. 9–11, 23–71.

[185] Peter C. Mancall, *Hakluyt's Promise: An Elizabethan's Obsession for an English America* (New Haven, 2007), pp. 3–5, 128–55.

[186] Anna Suranyi, *The Genius of the English Nation: Travel Writing and National Identity in Early Modern England* (Newark, DE, 2008), pp. 38–53 argues for a dominant (and reductive) English nationalism among English travellers, especially those journeying abroad.

[187] Woolf, *Social Circulation of the Past*, pp. 12–13, 273–4.

that privileged the written over the oral so far as the authority of accounts of the past were concerned', a dynamic compounded by 'access to the means of (re-)production, the printing press'.[188] Written travel narratives, too, privileged certain encounters with cultural complexity and certain local sources over oral tradition and memory. Printed and manuscript narratives could not help but be removed from the immediacy of a rough journal, let alone the original experience. An analysis of John Leland that finds the writer of the English nation in his published output and minimizes the importance of the manuscript 'Itinerary' and 'Collectanea' implicitly and unthinkingly perpetuates the distortion.[189]

John Lesley, George Buchanan, William Harrison, and a handful of Leland's readers in England travelled, wrote, and engaged with their predecessors in similarly contested contexts. For Lesley and Buchanan, highland, lowland, and borderer constituted the main ethno-topographical categories, and the interplay of ethnic groups and cultural complexity had less of a role for its own sake. Building from Boece's account, Lesley's ethnography sought to appropriate the ancient Scots for the cause of Scottish Catholics and he sparred with the religious and political ambitions of 'Protestant England'. In his efforts to improve Boece's story, Buchanan sought the origins of proto-republicans and -Presbyterians among Scotland's founding peoples. His history also wrote back against English, Welsh, and Catholic writers of Scotland.

William Harrison's engagement with Boece/Bellenden and the Scottish past had a cruder, Anglocentric quality in the hostile stereotyping of the Scots for their unreformed religious life. Harrison, Lambarde, and Stow had priorities that focussed on Protestant England. These avid readers of Leland's notebooks ignored the cultural complexity and multi-ethnic footprints that he found in so many guises in favour of a reductive religious and ethnographic reading of his journeys. Welsh Catholics and Protestants, who waged their battle for souls in Welsh, engaged – indeed, crucially preserved – one marker of Britain's cultural complexity that originally focussed Leland's journeys; they did so against the prejudices of fellow Protestants in England.[190] What we see at work in early modern Britain is a similar process of abstraction that would in the eighteenth century allow '"Negro" or "Hottentot" ... to stand as an image of all "Africans", and to stand comparison with an abstracted and idealized European' thanks to 'the reduction of human experience and variation' well-known and well-documented to travellers in Africa and the Americas.[191]

---

[188] Woolf, *Social Circulation of the Past*, p. 274.

[189] Woolf, *Social Circulation of the Past*, pp. 370–1.

[190] Glanmor Williams, 'Unity of Religion or Unity of Language? Protestants and Catholics and the Welsh Language 1536–1660', in *The Welsh Language before the Industrial Revolution*, ed. Geraint H. Jenkins (Cardiff, 1997), pp. 207–33.

[191] Nancy Stepan, *The Idea of Race in Science: Great Britain 1800–1960* (Basingstoke, 1982), p. xviii.

Despite the best efforts of rulers, clerics, writers, and some local actors after mid-century to align confessional stances with national or ethnic identities, cultural complexity on the ground could not be so easily suppressed or configured along normative lines. Britons lived out their cultural complexity in much more than just their confessional identities, among the minority who could even be bothered to adopt one or define themselves as religious.[192] Despite attempts to promote religious conformity, even uniformity, plurality, and cultural particularism more often characterized local reality.[193] This is the story travellers tell us in Book One. Lesley, Harrison, Lambarde, and the like represent just one strand of engagement with the discovery of a multicultural Britain, an island defined by centuries of migrations, encounters, and exchanges among a host of distinct ethno-cultural groups or peoples. In Book Two, we leave behind this broad perspective and pursue a different point of view. Rather than recover the polyglot character of the Tudor *imperium* or Scotland, we will encounter seventeenth-century Britain through the journeys and experiences of travellers who deliberately sought out the ethno-cultural complexity of the island's peoples. Fynes Moryson is the focal point. Moryson developed the century's most systematic ethnographic framework for examining, describing, and interpreting cultural complexity when he composed the account of his storied travels through Europe and the Middle East. No Briton travelled with so much innate cultural curiosity or potential to reveal the complexity of Britain and its peoples. We now take up the accomplishments and failures of Moryson and his seventeenth-century counterparts.

---

[192] Penry Williams, *The Later Tudors: England 1547–1603* (Oxford, 1995), p. 494.
[193] Lloyd Bowen, 'Fashioning Communities: The County in Early Modern Wales', in *The County Community in Seventeenth-Century England and Wales*, ed. Jacqueline Eales and Andrew Hopper (Hatfield, 2012), pp. 78–99; Michael Braddick, *State Formation in Early Modern England c. 1550–1700* (Cambridge, 2000), pp. 287–313, 340–78.

BOOK 2

The Undiscovered Britain
of Fynes Moryson

5

The Travels and Projects of Fynes Moryson

The high summer sun blasted the route between Aleppo and Antioch and all who journeyed along it. Fynes and Henry Moryson followed the custom of their two-hundred-strong camel caravan and rode between late afternoon and the dawn's first light, pitching their tents and eating a weary breakfast before a fitful midday rest. Fynes compared it to cosying up before a coal fire on a summer's day in England. He literally feared for his sanity, but the conditions took a fatal toll on Henry Moryson. As they reached Antioch, the flux that Henry battled flared up and he made the fatal mistake of 'stopping this naturall purge, by taking Red wine and Marmelat'. A desperate camel journey over the hills toward the English factory at Iskenderun racked Henry's constitution. So did the repeated refusals by the 'faitheless Muccaro' attending him to pause and let the younger Moryson purge himself. In Fynes' regretful words, 'mischiefe lighted upon mischief' to end his brother's life on 4 July 1596. In his grief –'from the remembrance whereof my mind abhorreth' – Fynes watched as the Turks seized all of Henry's belongings for the sultan and refused him a decent burial at Iskenderun without further extortions. These were the final insult, added to the Turks' taunts and laughter when the two brothers took their last embraces.[1]

Despite the emotional blow of his brother's death in a hostile, alien land, Fynes Moryson remained an open, curious, inveterate traveller throughout his life. Most of Moryson's journeys connected him with continental Europe and the Ottoman Empire, though he made a short foray to Scotland and spent almost three years in Ireland as a secretary to Lord Mountjoy during the Elizabethan reconquest. Moryson encountered a remarkable variety of peoples. His travels exposed him to customs and cultural traditions that surpassed the experiences of all but a handful of his contemporaries. Moryson decided to record his experiences and insights and took up his pen in earnest in 1609. John Beale of Aldersgate published a partial account of Moryson's travels as *An Itinerary*

---

[1] *The Itinerary of Fynes Moryson in Four Volumes* (four volumes; Glasgow, 1907), II, pp. 63–8, hereafter cited as Moryson, *Itinerary*.

Written by Fynes Moryson in 1617.[2] Moryson readied the second volume for publication some time around 1626. Beale passed on it and Moryson never found
another interested printer.[3]

Moryson's complete 'Itinerary' consists of the published volume and
its second half that we might call the 'Manuscript'. Any reader tackling this
sprawling 'Itinerary' finds a terrific hodgepodge of parts and pieces. The First
Part, as Moryson labelled it, narrated his travels between 1591 and 1598. The
Second Part consisted of his Irish journal (a semi-official account of Mountjoy's
campaigns). The Third Part discussed travel itself, before describing in several
Books and many Chapters the geography and apparel of the 'twelve dominions'
Moryson visited. A Fourth Part took readers through separate and detailed
descriptions of the polities, religious practices and churches, and peoples who
inhabited those dominions. Moryson crafted a massive cross-cultural comparison
of peoples and nations right across early modern Europe, from war-torn Ulster,
the counties of England and Wales, and the court of James VI at Falkland Palace
to the polyglot dominions of the Habsburgs and the Ottoman Empire.

Even a cursory reading reveals that first-hand encounters fired Moryson's
interest and imagination. This explains why his *Itinerary* is still studied today.
Yet he too has been pigeonholed, as an example of the West's engagement with
Islam and the East. Moryson himself did not create this artificial distinction
between Britain and 'the Continent' or the Near East as spaces for travel and
encounter. Moryson covered the same ground as Boorde's pithy verses or Pierre
d'Avity's monumental *Estates, Empires, and Principalities of the World*. But Moryson
did so in incomparable detail, built not just on accounts to hand but his own
experiences. His 'Itinerary' marked out cultural complexity among British, Irish,
European, and Asian peoples in comparison and contrast to one another, using
a standard ethnography. This alone makes Moryson significant for the encounter
with early modern Britain.

Moryson's career as a troubled author is equally important. He felt that
the *Itinerary* met a hostile, even malicious reception – even if Samuel Purchas
thought it presented a feast for readers interested in '"the rarities and varietys of
many Kingdomes"'.[4] Readers of the *Itinerary* did not greet it with the enthusiasm
or respect that Moryson craved. From his standpoint and Beale's, the *Itinerary*

---

[2] *An Itinerary Written by Fynes Moryson ... Containing His Ten Yeeres Travell Throvgh the Twelve
Dominions of Germany, Bohmerland, Sweitzerland, Netherland, Denmarke, Poland, Italy, Turky,
France, England, Scotland, and Ireland* (STC 18205; London, 1617).

[3] The unpublished itinerary has been transcribed and edited in its entirety in Graham Kew,
'Shakespeare's Europe Revisited: The Unpublished *Itinerary* of Fynes Moryson (1566–1630)'
(Ph.D. thesis; Birmingham University, 1995), pp. 1–1742, hereafter cited as 'Unpublished
Itinerary'. This edition replaces the incomplete transcription by Charles Hughes, *Shakespeare's
Europe*, 2nd edn (New York, 1967). See also Graham Kew, *The Irish Sections of Fynes Moryson's
Unpublished Itinerary* (Dublin, 1998).

[4] 'Unpublished *Itinerary*', p. xcix.

failed. Its poor reception offers important insights as to how readers approached the cultural complexity of Britain in the seventeenth century as opposed to the sixteenth. Reception of the *Itinerary* and financial difficulties that accompanied its failure kept Moryson from publishing the 'Manuscript'.

Another literary ambition also collapsed. Moryson promised in the 'Manuscript' to write a detailed, stand-alone description of England and Scotland.[5] Had Moryson published his 'Itinerary', had he completed and seen through the press this other treatise, we would now be studying the first systematic ethnography of the peoples in Britain and Ireland alongside their European and Middle Eastern neighbours, one that used common categories for analysis and comparison and based descriptions on first-hand experience. The rest of this chapter and those which follow recover and imaginatively reconstruct Britain's peoples as seen through the journeys and encounters of those like Moryson who travelled with an ethnographic eye (imperfectly) attuned to the cultural complexity around them.

Fynes Moryson's life and 'Itinerary'

Moryson was born into a family that prospered from its service to the Elizabethan regime in Lincolnshire.[6] Little is known of Fynes's mother, Elizabeth, but his father, Thomas, established himself as a clerk of the Pipe and mayor of Great Grimsby (1576), representing the town in Parliament through 1588-9. It was Moryson's misfortune to be a middle son among minor gentry: the bulk of his father's estate went to his elder brother Edward in 1592 and Fynes's inheritance of the advowson of Louth seemed to signal his father's intention that he should take up a clerical career.[7] Fynes bitterly resented the financial effects of primogeniture, prompting his harsh comments against prodigal men of wealth and power in England – 'so niggardly towards their kinsmen, yea, children and wives, as they provide not necessaries for them'.[8] The resentment later turned into an apology for the disorderly conduct of English soldiers in the Netherlands. They were, Moryson explained, typically younger brothers forced to become soldiers, driven by a life of penury and hazardous combat to 'doe unfit things'.[9]

Moryson did not become a soldier or fall from the privileged class. Alongside his brothers, he very likely received a humanist education at the 'hands of a resident schoolmaster who looked after the large Moryson brood', learning his

---

[5] 'Unpublished *Itinerary*', p. 649.
[6] For Moryson's background, 'Unpublished *Itinerary*', pp. lvii–lxxxix; Edward H. Thompson, 'Fynes Moryson', *Oxford DNB* at www.oxforddnb.com.
[7] 'Unpublished *Itinerary*', p. lix.
[8] Moryson, *Itinerary*, IV, pp. 94–5.
[9] Moryson, *Itinerary*, IV, p. 61.

Latin via primers and fixtures in the humanist canon like Aesop and Cicero.[10] He was the first among his younger brothers to matriculate at Peterhouse, Cambridge in 1580. The great scholar and bibliophile Andrew Perne held the mastership.[11] Perhaps Perne fired Moryson's geographic imagination. One could easily track Moryson's later travels using Perne's spectacular library. Alongside several 'world' maps Perne owned maps of the Tartar dominions, Greece, Germany, Palestine, France, Bohemia, Jerusalem, Egypt, Spain, as well as England and Drake's voyages. During the composition of his 'Itinerary', Moryson demonstrated a familiarity with works owned by Perne in one form or another, including Jean Bodin's *Six Bookes of a Common-weale* (French, 1576; English, 1606), Camden's *Britannia* (Latin, 1586), *The Traueiler of Ierome Turler* (1576), Francesco Guicciardini's history of Italy, and the works of Tacitus, Caesar, Polybius, Livy, Agricola, and Sebastian Münster. Perne's other books of history, cosmography, geography, and the like numbered many hundreds. Among them were seminal works concerned with Britain by Ptolemy, Bede, Geoffrey of Monmouth, Gerald of Wales, William of Newburgh, Higden's *Polychronicon*, Buchanan's *Rerum Scoticarum Historia* and *De Iure Regni*, Knox's history of the Church in Scotland, and the chronicles of Grafton, Hardyng, and Holinshed. Moryson's student days and 'Itinerary' readily overlapped with Perne's bibliophilism and intellectual interests.[12]

Moryson took his B.A. in 1584 and M.A. in 1587, receiving a fellowship of £20 to support the study of civil law.[13] He obtained permission in late summer 1590 to leave Peterhouse to study on the Continent. Moryson left Leigh for Stade and the Elbe on 1 May 1591, with pirates in hot pursuit. Four years passed before Moryson returned to England, landing at Dover in May 1595. He embarked on a second itinerary in November with Henry. Nearly two years passed before Moryson landed alone at Gravesend in July 1597. At home for the rest of 1597, Moryson began his intended 'British' travels in April 1598, with Scotland the first destination. At Falkland he caught a glimpse of his future king, James VI, before urgent business back in England cut short the journey. Two years later Moryson found himself in Ireland, thanks to Richard Moryson's connections, a rising star in the queen's army of conquest. Moryson's travels ended in May 1603 when he accompanied Mountjoy and the vanquished Earl of Tyrone to London for James VI and I's coronation.

A short summary hardly does justice to the scope of Moryson's travels. He spent 1591 in Germany, finally settling in Leipzig to carry on the study of German begun that summer in Wittenberg. Moryson passed the winter of 1592

---

[10] 'Unpublished *Itinerary*', p. lxviii.

[11] Patrick Collinson, 'Andrew Perne', *Oxford DNB* at www.oxforddnb.com.

[12] E.S. Leedham-Green, *Books in Cambridge Inventories* (two volumes; Cambridge, 1986), I, pp. 458–71; 'Unpublished *Itinerary*', pp. xc–cxxviii.

[13] The chronology and itinerary of Moryson's travels that follows is drawn from the 'Unpublished *Itinerary*', pp. 1743–59.

in his studies and left Leipzig in March for Prague and Bohemia. His time in Prague was punctuated by a precognitive dream of his father's death, which word from home confirmed during his journey to Nuremberg. Not wanting to return to England proper, Moryson travelled to the Netherlands long enough to settle his small inheritance. By the end of April Moryson was well into Austria and Switzerland, before revisiting his travels in Germany and the Netherlands for the rest of the year. He occupied the winter of 1593 as a student at Leiden and restarted his travels with a circuit of the Low Countries that included a rapid escape from Dokkum ahead of the Spanish sack of Groningen. Moryson traversed Hamburg, Denmark, and the Baltic coast by boat before landing at Danzig in early September for his journey through Poland, Austria, and Italy. He spent 1594 and early 1595 making his way through the Italian city-states and finessing the dangers of being a Protestant among Catholics. Moryson departed from Italy in March 1595 and met with Theodore Beza in Geneva, before failing to heed advice to avoid war-torn France. He continued his celebrity spotting, adding a sight of the French court and Henry IV to Christian of Denmark, Tycho Brahe's observatory, the king and queen of Poland, cardinals Allen and Bellarmaine in Italy, and later the Ottoman sultan. He was briefly held as a suspected Catholic priest upon landing in Dover in May 1595. Beginning in November, the Moryson brothers made their way from Flushing through the Low Countries, Germany, and Austria to Italy and Venice. In April 1596, the brothers set sail for the vast Ottoman dominions in Greece, the eastern Mediterranean, Turkey, and the Holy Land, including calls in Cyprus, Crete Constantinople, and Jerusalem. Fynes returned to England via Venice and the overland route through Germany to Stade and Gravesend in 1597.

Moryson's only journey in 1598 was the short excursion to lowland Scotland and Fife taking in Berwick, Dunbar, Prestonpans, Musselburgh, Edinburgh, and Kinghorn. He crossed a stormy Irish Sea to Dublin to join Mountjoy's establishment in the fall of 1600. Moryson hoped that Mountjoy's return to England in 1603 and elevation to Earl of Devonshire would finally launch him on a 'public' career. Devonshire's disgrace and death in 1606 left Moryson without a patron or employment. Hoping to improve his fortunes as an author, Moryson set to work on a history of the dominions visited during the 1590s.[14] Evidently deeply dissatisfied with the work, Moryson destroyed the manuscript some time in 1609, although its contents no doubt furnished the 'Itinerary' that he next began.[15] The failure of the 'Manuscript' to find a publisher capped off what was for Moryson a life of disappointed hopes and aspirations. He died on 12 February 1630.

Moryson's career captures the gritty reality of joining first-hand travel to ethnography over a daunting cultural canvas. He felt driven to encounter peoples

---

[14] 'Unpublished Itinerary', pp. lxxx–lxxxiii.
[15] 'Unpublished Itinerary', pp. lxxv–lxxxvii.

and study complex cultures. He shared what he took to be a common desire of all travellers, to see as many new countries as possible, never repeating an itinerary, and nurturing the interests of a 'willing minde' even if it meant detours and enduring trouble along the way.[16] Once he returned to England and began work, Moryson penned a discourse on travel. In it he defended travellers against objections that they spread 'vices, ill customes, and very heresies' like plague carriers. He demanded to know 'how should we have discovered new Worlds (or rather unknowne Regions of the old) had not this industry of Travellers been?'[17] Rather, as Moryson continued, 'A man shall hardly learne at home the divers natures of hearbes, and other things, or the divers dispositions of one and the same body, according to the difference of the clyme, aire, and diet.'[18] Experiencing, describing, and, ultimately, understanding cultural complexity was a worthy goal: 'I thincke variety to be the most pleasing thing in the World ... Such is the delight of visiting foraigne Countreys, charming all our sences with the most sweet variety.' 'We are Citizens of the whole World,' Moryson concluded. Indeed, the nature of existence demanded exploration of the world in all its complexity, and without unthinking prejudice, for 'We betray our ignorance or our selfe love, when wee dispraise forraigne things without true judgment, or preferre our owne Countrey before other, without shewing good reason thereof.'[19] This philosophy explains the most significant feature of the 'Itinerary'. Moryson finally and fully united the discovery of the new and the old – of foreign lands and home – only fleetingly captured by Worcestre's *Itineraries*, Boorde's pithy verses, or Barlow-Enciso's *Geographie*. For Moryson, multicultural Britain was as much an undiscovered country as the farthest reaches of the Ottoman Empire and part of a common project of cultural analysis.

Perseverance and cultural openness expressed themselves in Moryson's disguises and the dissembling he affected on the road.[20] Sometimes he sought to pass unnoticed as a native, scholar, servant, or other commoner. On other occasions he sought access to places not allowed to foreigners, such as Kronborg Castle, where he viewed the chambers once used by James VI and Anna of Denmark.[21] At other times Moryson sought protection on account of his faith or nationality.[22] Inevitably, the motives and disguises blurred, as they did when he cloaked his Protestantism but not his English identity in order to meet Cardinal Allen in Rome.[23] Moryson admitted that the poorer the apparel he

[16] Moryson, *Itinerary*, I, p. 112.
[17] Moryson, *Itinerary*, III, p. 361.
[18] Moryson, *Itinerary*, III, p. 366.
[19] Moryson, *Itinerary*, II, p. 1.
[20] Moryson, *Itinerary*, I, pp. 79–80, 333–4, 347; also Peter C. Mancall, 'Introduction: What Fynes Moryson Knew', *Journal of Early Modern History* 10.1&2 (2006), pp. 1–9.
[21] Moryson, *Itinerary*, I, pp. 124–5.
[22] Moryson, *Itinerary*, I, pp. 85–7, 219, 223, 232, 301–2, 361–2, 395.
[23] Moryson, *Itinerary*, I, pp. 259–60.

wore in disguise, the more assertive he became toward his nominal 'betters', so much so that he was initially suspected of being a Catholic priest upon arriving in Dover in 1595.[24] In 1597 it was his Italian dress that landed him in the same trouble before another friend vouched for him.[25] Having in Italy developed the custom of entering a church and touching the font of holy water so as to disguise his Protestantism, he was corrected by none other than Theodore Beza for continuing the habit in a Geneva church.[26] Moryson showed an instinctive understanding for other peoples in the 'roles' he assumed, an understanding that he brought to bear in writing the 'Itinerary'.

Despite Moryson's cultural curiosity, he developed his share of negative, even hostile thoughts during these encounters. As a committed Protestant, Moryson 'experienced' sinful superstition in Catholic dominions. Friars, monks, and priests peddled nonsense far and wide, including those who related wondrous tales in Palestine.[27] Lodging, conditions, high prices, and sharp dealing typically invoked his most bitter comments – as they did among most travellers. A filthy inn in Prague made him happy to be bedded furthest from the stove, 'delighting more in sweet aire, then the smoke of a dunghill'. He found Prague so filthy that he expected that 'the stinch of the streetes drive backe the Turkes'.[28] To Moryson's eye, Hesse to Brunswick was a journey to be made quickly, the better to avoid 'grosse meat, sower wine, stinking drinke, and filthy beds'.[29] The violent majesty of nature, which sometimes elicited an almost Romantic sensibility in Moryson, could become positively deadly, thanks to the stupidity of others. Drunken and negligent mariners made navigating the many bridge piers of the Danube at Ulm only more perilous – one wonders if Moryson ever navigated London Bridge with similar fears.[30] No one was spared Moryson's interest or comment, including his fellow countrymen and their island neighbours. Lodging in an Englishman's house in Harlingen in the United Provinces, Moryson wrote of his host 'who either dispising England and the Englishmen, or too much respecting his masters of Friesland, gave me such entertainment, as I tooke him one of the old Picts'.[31]

Moryson travelled with a curious eye and wrote with a sharp pen. The travel narrative and first-hand experiences almost certainly came from diaries and notes that Moryson kept during his travels. He advised would-be travellers to let 'nothing worth the knowledge passe his eyes or eares, which he draweth not to his owne possession' by committing to memory or recording 'rare observations'

---

[24] Moryson, *Itinerary*, I, p. 422.
[25] Moryson, *Itinerary*, II, p. 115.
[26] Moryson, *Itinerary*, I, p. 390.
[27] Moryson, *Itinerary*, II, p. 17.
[28] Moryson, *Itinerary*, I, pp. 27–9; Moryson, *Itinerary*, II, pp. 57, 100–1.
[29] Moryson, *Itinerary*, I, p. 76.
[30] Moryson, *Itinerary*, I, pp. 43–4.
[31] Moryson, *Itinerary*, I, p. 91.

at the time. Moryson kept to his advice in tending to oral traditions, identifying Arthur's Seat as just one among many topographic monuments made famous by balladeers.[32] Worthwhile knowledge embraced a bewildering variety of topics:

> [The] fruitfulnes of each Countrey, and the things wherewith it aboundeth, as the Mines of mettals and precious stones, the chiefe lawes and customes of the workers in those Mines, also Bathes and the qualitie of the water, with the diseases for the curing whereof it is most proper, the names[,] springs and courses of Reivers, the peasant Fountaines, the abundance or rarity of Pastures, Groves, Wood, Corne, and Fruits, the rare and precious Plants, the rare and proper Beasts, the prices of necessary things, and what he daily spends in his diet and horsemeat, and in hiring Horses or Coaches, the soyle of every dayes journey, the plenty of Fishes or Flesh, the kinds of meat or drinke, with the sauces and the rarer manners of dressing meates, the Countreys expence in apparell, with the constancy and ficklenesse in wearing it, the races of Horses ... the scituation of Cities and Provinces, the healthfulnes of the Aire, the Chorography, the buildings, the ritches, the magnificence of Citizens ... Statues, Colosses, Sepulchres with the Inscriptions, Lybraries, with the most rare Bookes, Theaters, Arches, Bridges, Forts, Armories, Treasures, Monasteries, Churches, publike houses, Universities, with their Founders, revenewes, and disputations.[33]

Moryson added the imperatives to visit the 'most learned men' who excel in military arts or unique virtues. Travellers must record

> the policy of each State, and therein the Courts of each King or Prince ... their revenewes, the forme of the Common-wealth, whether the Prince be a Tyrant or beloved of the people, what Forces he hath by Sea or land ... the manners of the people, their vices, vertues, industry in manuall Arts, the constitution of their bodies, the History of the Kingdome ... the disposition of the people, whether it be religious, superstitious, or prophane, and the opinions of Religion differing from his, and the most rare Ceremonies thereof ... the trafficke of Merchants ... the commodities they carry out and most want, the Havens and roades for Ships, their skill in navigation, and whether they use subjects or strangers for their Marriners ... the value of the Coynes in each Countrey ... [34]

These details were to be recorded 'each day, at morne and even at his Inne, within writing Tables carried about him, and after at leasure into a paper booke, that many yeers after he may looke over them at his pleasure'. In the meantime, travellers should guard their jottings, lest they should prove 'offensive and perhaps dangerous' in certain situations; the best safeguard was to either send the notebooks away on a half-yearly basis with other acquisitions or write in cipher, always standing ready to offer a bogus and innocuous translation.[35] Leisure afforded the opportunity to fashion the notebooks into a 'polished' travel

---

[32] Adam Fox and Daniel Woolf, eds, *The Spoken Word: Oral Culture in Britain, 1500–1800* (Manchester, 2002), p. 29.
[33] Moryson, *Itinerary*, III, p. 372.
[34] Moryson, *Itinerary*, III, p. 373.
[35] Moryson, *Itinerary*, III, p. 374.

narrative alongside available sources.[36] As Moryson explained, 'At my retourne from Scotland ... I retyred my selfe to Healing [his sister's house in Lincolnshire] ... In which place ... whilest I passed the idle yeere, I had a pleasing opportunitie to gather into some order out of confused and torne writings, the particular observations of my former Travels, to bee after more deliberately digested at leasure.'[37] In manuscript, such a narrative provided for one's own enjoyment, for circulation among other readers, or as a working copy for actual publication. Each stage potentially removed Moryson and his readers from the immediacy of his travels, but the concern to safeguard sensitive notebooks confirms Moryson's efforts to record and preserve the 'rawness' of the actual experiences. Moryson built his 'Itinerary' out of just these passions, experiences, and techniques.

All of this should have set up Moryson for success, yet the *Itinerary* faced a critical response and the 'Manuscript' failed. After destroying his 'History' in 1609, Moryson wrote and expanded the 'Itinerary' into an ugly, unwieldy mosaic. He disastrously yoked his travel narrative to the lengthy account of Mountjoy's reconquest of Ireland and his explanation did little to reconcile these two parts: 'hope of preferment drew me into Ireland. Of which journey being to write in another manner, then I have formerly done of other Countries, namely, rather as a Souldier, then as a Traveler, as one abiding in Campes, more then in Cities, as one lodging in Tents, more then in Innes'.[38]

Moryson returned to travel in the Third Part and began to develop the ethnography. Its first book contains Moryson's travel essay, followed by more than two dozen precepts for would-be travellers, an assortment of opinions about cultural complexity from 'old writers', and stereotypes picked up by Moryson during both his reading and travels. The second book describes the options for conveyance (horses, coaches, and the like) and offers a chapter on sepulchres, monuments, and buildings before radically changing tack to describe the topography, economic geography, and diet of each dominion. This carried over into a third book. The fourth book similarly took up the subject of national apparel before launching into an analysis of the polities visited. Having saddled the *Itinerary* with his Irish journal, Moryson tacked on descriptions of Ireland and its peoples 'for travellers instruction'.[39]

Moryson's 'Manuscript' resumed his description of the polities in its Fourth Part. Three books followed that examined religious practices and the characteristics of the peoples themselves. A final book included an add-on discourse about

---

[36] 'Unpublished *Itinerary*', pp. cxxviii–cxxix.

[37] Moryson, *Itinerary*, II, pp. 165–6.

[38] Moryson, *Itinerary*, II, pp. 165–6.

[39] Moryson, *Itinerary*, II, p. 166. The only major portion of the *Itinerary* subsequently reprinted before the twentieth century was the Irish journal, reprinted in two volumes in Dublin in 1735 with some of the Irish descriptions from the unpublished itinerary added at the end of the second volume. Fynes Moryson, *An History of Ireland, From the Year 1599, to 1603* (Dublin, 1735).

the Jews and Greeks, Ottoman subjects without 'national homes' under their own control. While he laboured on the 'Manuscript', Moryson made a fundamental alteration. He included accounts of topography, economic geography, diet, and apparel for Scotland and England (and Ireland) in the *Itinerary*, but he abandoned any effort to produce the corresponding political and religious chapters for England and Scotland in the resumed 'Manuscript'. He composed only some few folios about the nature of the English people. Precious little material attended to the cultural complexity beneath the label 'English' and he wrote nothing about the Scots and Welsh. Instead, Moryson promised would-be readers that England and Scotland would be the subject of a separate treatise.

Where, then, do we find the peoples of Britain within this complex history of travels and troubled projects? First, we have the actual descriptions of the English and Scots that Moryson included in his Third and Fourth Parts. Those in the *Itinerary* are chiefly derived from Camden's *Britannia*, but intermingled with Moryson's own travel experiences and what he assumed would be common knowledge. Experience and 'conventional wisdom' are most pronounced in his description of the English in the 'Manuscript'. Moryson embedded cross-cultural comparisons between the peoples of Britain and Ireland and those of Europe and Asia throughout the 'Itinerary'. However, these are most common in the unpublished 'Manuscript' and have therefore eluded attention. We will never know for certain what Moryson would have written in his lost treatise, but the *Itinerary* and 'Manuscript' together allow us to rescue Moryson from his 'clash of civilizations' pigeon-hole and explore how this most ubiquitous and experienced traveller attempted to master – or not – the peoples of multicultural Britain. Here we begin with the *Itinerary*. The next chapter takes up the 'Manuscript'.

The peoples of Britain in Moryson's *Itinerary*

For avid readers of his accounts of continental Europe and the Middle East, Moryson's descriptions of Britain in the *Itinerary* come across as sparse, derivative, and superficial. For the accounts of the geography, situation, fertility, traffic, and diet of Scotland and England, he cribbed the organization and much of the detail from Camden's *Britannia* – 'whom I gladly follow in this description'.[40] He cast Britain as a bipolar world divided between England and Scotland. He echoed Leland's sense of a lost British *imperium* when he wrote that 'London, the seate of the Brittans Empire, and the Chamber of the Kings of England, is so famous, as it needes not bee praysed.'[41] Writing in the first decade of James's reign, it might have been politic to make such distinctions and avoid the typical England–Britain conflation, though Moryson slipped in praising the greatness of the physical Church of 'our Northerne Iland England' in comparison to

---

[40] Moryson, *Itinerary*, IV, p. 142.
[41] Moryson, *Itinerary*, IV, pp. 142–3.

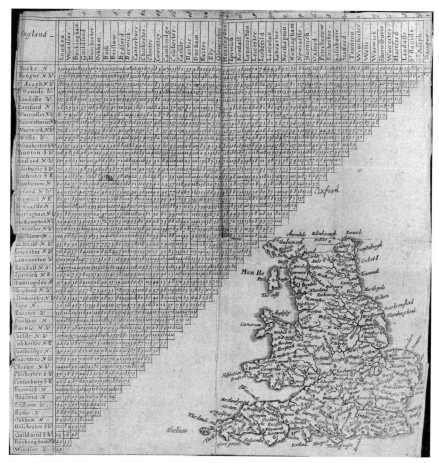

10 'England' engraved by Jacob Langeren, from *A Direction for the English Traviller* (London, 1643). Reproduced by permission of the Llyfrgell Genedlaethol Cymru/ The National Library of Wales.

southern climes.[42] Still, he followed Camden in using the Roman tribal names (Regni, Atrebatti, Dobuni etc.), adopted the same county-by-county organization, and recorded the ethnic groups who had left their mark in Britain (Romans, Britons, Picts, Scots, 'English-Saxons', Danes, and Normans).

Within what was essentially an abstract of *Britannia*, we occasionally find glimpses of Moryson's own interests and attitudes. The park at Woodstock (Oxfordshire) was credited as the first park in England, 'but our Progenitors were so delighted with hunting, as the Parkes are now growne infinite in number'.[43]

---

[42] Moryson, *Itinerary*, III, p. 438.
[43] Moryson, *Itinerary*, IV, pp. 148–9.

This was essential information to borrow from *Britannia*, since Moryson detailed the customary hunting practices in all the dominions visited. Yet we already glimpse how a national focus closes out more complex readings of peoples and places even for the ethnographic Moryson. For Moryson parks, chases, and hunting marked the English nation and its topography, yet, while private hunting had been practised among the Saxons, the Normans made these ubiquitous features of the English landscape by introducing royal hunting forests, forest laws, and extending the right of nobles to keep their own chases.[44] As for Woodstock town itself, it 'hath nothing to boast, but that Jeffry Chaucer the English Homer was borne there'.[45] Pride in English ale, especially against 'German' beer, was a notable feature of Moryson's writing – a fascination Celia Fiennes shared a century later in her journeys through England. Thus, Derbyshire boasted a 'proverbially' good ale to go with a fabulous landscape, including caves in the Peak District: 'this hole (with reverence be it spoken) is vulgarly called, the Divels ars[e] at Peuke, of which many fables are told, and the place is accounted among the miracles of England'.[46] He remarked on the fame and consumption of English ale in the Netherlands and Germany, despite German laws prohibiting its public sale – the Germans 'yet privately swallow it like Nectar'.[47]

England's temperate climes made possible year-round cultivation of laurel and rosemary, the profitable harvest of apricots, musk melons, figs that equalled the taste of those in Italy, and an abundance of apples, pears, cherries, and plums 'for which the Italians would gladly exchange their Citrons and Oranges'. Moryson composed a weak echo of Leland in describing the salt pits of Worcestershire and Cheshire (Nantwich). Chester, once garrisoned by the 'twentieth Legion called victrix' and from where Moryson sailed for Ireland, boasted cheese comparable to the best that Holland had to offer.[48] The influence of Harrison seems apparent throughout this section. Moryson even rehearsed Harrison's complaint that the English neglected the possibilities for viticulture because they 'are so naturally inclined to pleasure'. Being so well served with French wine and exploiting the best hillsides for grazing sheep and cattle echoed another of Harrison's charges, the love of foreign commodities at the expense of domestic industry.

The abundance of corn occasioned another familiar complaint against the English. Shortages resulted from exporting or hoarding while 'private men finding greater commoditie in feeding of Sheepe and Cattell, then in the Plough, requiring the hands of many servants, can by no Law be restrained from turning corne fields into inclosed Pastures'. Moryson also blamed the status competition of 'this prodigall age' for creating incentives to dispark forests in favour of

[44] Francis Pryor, *The Making of the British Landscape: How We have Transformed the Land from Prehistory to Today* (London, 2010), pp. 289–90.
[45] Moryson, *Itinerary*, IV, pp. 148–9.
[46] Moryson, *Itinerary*, IV, p. 152.
[47] Moryson, *Itinerary*, IV, p. 166.
[48] Moryson, *Itinerary*, IV, p. 154.

grazing and pasturage. England was also rich in fowls and fish, and maritime resources generally. All of which led Moryson to proclaim 'that this Iland (or part of an Iland) abounds with all things necessary for honest clothing, large and dainty feeding, and for warre by land and sea'. England's natural plenty included cattle, sheep, dogs, horses, and pigs (none more savoury than the bacon of Westphalia, though).[49] The French and Scots coveted swift English hunting horses. The stamina of work horses drew an interesting ethnic proverb: 'the English, especially the Northene men, ride from day breake to the evening without drawing bit, neither sparing their horses nor themselves, whence is the Proverb, that England is the Hell of Horses, the Purgatory of Servants, and the Paradise of Women; because they ride Horses without measure, and use their Servants imperiously, and their Women obsequiously'.[50]

Experiences abroad clearly sharpened Moryson's pen toward England and the English. He denounced the prejudice that led English 'Gentlemen [to] disdaine trafficke, thinking it to abase Gentry'. He even contrasted them with the usual whipping boy for dangerous and undesirable qualities: in Italy 'the very Princes disdaine not to be Merchants', thereby preserving 'the dignity and patrimony of their progenitors, suffering not the sinew of the Commonwealth upon any pretence to be wrested out of their hands'. Both English and French elites seemed to operate from the opposite assumption: 'Gentlemen should live of their revenews, Citizens by trafficke, and the common sort by the Plough and manuall Artes'. Consequently, landed gentry of both nations were forced to sell their patrimonies to 'Citizens and vulgar men', not least lawyers. Moryson put this down to some combination of misguided sentiment, rashness, sloth, or prodigality – 'greater then in any other Nation or age'. He pointed up the scale of the gentry's loss by remarking on the scope of English trade – from Iceland to Muscovy to the East and West Indies – and trumpeting both the greatness of English maritime power and the unmatched daring of its mariners – a far cry, at least rhetorically, from the days of Worcestre and Rastell. Signalling his embedded comparisons, Moryson also referred readers to his analyses of Germany and Poland for fuller details of English trade in the Baltic.[51]

Moryson's description of the English diet began with Caesar's observation that the ancient Britons were devoted to flesh and milk to the exclusion of planting wheat. Caesar thus found the ancient Britons in the same near-pastoral state that English writers commonly associated with Irish (or Gaelic) barbarity. The present-day English feasted on hens, geese, hares, venison, and great abundance of conies with their fat, tender flesh. This occasioned another cross-cultural comparison. Moryson reminded his readers that ordinary Germans were socially excluded from venison and hares – the preserve of princes and gentlemen

[49] Moryson, *Itinerary*, IV, pp. 165–9.
[50] Moryson, *Itinerary*, IV, p. 169; also Moryson, *Itinerary*, III, p. 462.
[51] Moryson, *Itinerary*, IV, pp. 169–71.

– which left them marvelling that the English would choose conies over hares, the Germans finding their own conies tasted 'more like roasted Cats'.

The English diet had its own social markers. Husbandmen astutely chose brown bread of barley and rye for 'abiding longer in the stomack, and not so soone digested with their labour' over the 'pure white bread' eaten by citizens and gentlemen. Out of abundance came a number of English delicacies: oysters so plentiful and savoury they were once sought as far away as Ancient Rome, godwits (marsh birds) and other sea fowls, fallow deer baked into pasties ('a dainty rarely found in any other Kingdome'), brawn of boar (possibly the boiled and pickled variety), a variety of white-meats and preserves that only the French could match, and many more 'in greater abundance then other Nations' that would 'bee tedious' to repeat. Moryson assumed that readers would recognize familiar ground in this and much else.[52]

Moryson escaped three of the four worst harvests in England in the 1590s but he returned long enough to witness the massive price rise and plunging wages that would usher in the new century. He turned a critical pen on his social equals and betters whose actions drove higher prices: gluttonous appetites, prodigality in having the money to indifferently pay more than things were worth, and the refusal to coin small monies of brass or other metals as had other countries. As we will learn later, Thomas Hamilton, Earl of Haddington and a key figure in the government of Scotland under James VI, would later find much in the *Itinerary* to nurture his interest in currency and national dispositions toward political economy. English practices pushed up prices, but so too did the vulgar plenty of the English table, with food prepared far in excess of real hunger for the sake of demonstrating wealth and hospitality. Nor were eating customs a benefit, with gross meats served first, followed by dainties 'which invite to eate without hunger, as likewise the longe sitting and discoursing at tables, which makes men unawares eate more'.[53]

Moryson naturally reported on inns and hospitality, but those experiences also deepened his ethnography. One oddly placed chapter in his Third Part described the best means of travel in the different dominions, including Britain and Ireland. Horses were best, though few gentlemen of means were without coaches any longer and their presence in London had left the streets 'stopped up with them'. A traveller was unlikely to find a coach for hire outside the capital, 'howsoever England is for the most part plaine, or consisting of little pleasant hilles, yet the waies farre from London are so durty' and inhospitable for journeys longer than one or two days.[54] Moryson countered the complaints by Germans travellers that English innkeepers overcharged them for inferior meals and otherwise ill-used them. Had 'these strangers' known English or employed an honest guide they

---

[52] Moryson, *Itinerary*, IV, pp. 171–2; also Moryson, *Itinerary*, IV, pp. 138–40.
[53] Moryson, *Itinerary*, IV, pp. 172–4.
[54] Moryson, *Itinerary*, III, pp. 480–1.

would have found accommodation besides that run by 'knaves' who flocked to places like Gravesend 'onely to deceive strangers, and use Englishmen no better'. The rest of England, even many of its smallest villages, offered inns with good and cheap 'entertainment' for guests and 'humble attendance' upon them not to be found in any other nation.[55]

Strangers would find that the English celebrated three great 'publike Feasts of great expense and pompous solemnity': the king's coronation, the feast of St George and the annual instalments of the Knights of the Garter, and calling to law of the sergeants; the Lord Mayor's installation added a periodic fourth.[56] The English record on drinking was mixed. At these feasts the English typically drank two or three healths and 'in generall the greater and better part of the English, hold all excesse blameworthy, and drunkenesse a reprochfull vice'. Aside from a brief period when commanders and soldiers who fought in the Netherlands returned with the 'custome of the Germans large garaussing', only clowns and vulgar men drank beer and ale excessively. Most gentlemen imbibed sweetened wine, and the English taste for sweetness led to the prodigious consumption of currants, much to the bemusement of the Greeks, who produced and exported them.[57]

When Moryson turned to Scotland, he clearly relied upon the significantly greater detail about Scotland in Camden's last Latin edition of 1607 or Philemon Holland's 1610 English translation, some of adapted it from Buchanan's *Rerum Scoticarum Historia* with echoes of Lesley's *Historie*.[58] The interplay of tribes and peoples across the lands of the 'ancient' British *imperium* figured prominently in Moryson's crib. Lothian – 'of old called Pictland' – included the towns of Dunbar, Haddington, and Musselburgh, 'places wherein hath beene seen the warlike vertue of the English and Scots'. Edinburgh was a town 'long under the English Saxons and about the yeere 960 (England being invaded by the Danes) it became subject to the Scots'.[59] North of Stirling lay the Grampians and the land of the Caledoni, 'somewhat more barbarous then the rest (as commonly they are more rude towards the North) where not onely the aire is cold, but the Country wast and mountanous'. The triumphs of Edward I were somewhat more lasting in Moryson's account. Longshanks reached Cromarty Firth after he had 'subdued all with his victorious Army, having beaten the Scots on all sides'.[60]

Peoples crisscrossed the Western Isles, and Iona housed the cell and monastery of 'Columbus, the Apostle of the Picts'. Yet Moryson wondered why the Scots

---

[55] Moryson, *Itinerary*, IV, pp. 174–5; also Moryson, *Itinerary*, III, pp. 479–82.

[56] Moryson, *Itinerary*, IV, pp. 175–6; also 'Unpublished *Itinerary*', p. 1668.

[57] Moryson, *Itinerary*, IV, p. 176.

[58] Roger A. Mason, 'From Buchanan to Blaeu: The Politics of Scottish Chorography, 1582–1654', in *George Buchanan: Political Thought in Early Modern Britain and Europe*, ed. Caroline Erskine and Roger A. Mason (Farnham, 2012), pp. 47–9.

[59] Moryson, *Itinerary*, IV, p. 178.

[60] Moryson, *Itinerary*, IV, pp. 177–80.

Cambridge shire, wth some confiniy Townes.	Cambridge	Elye	Lynton	Reche	Littleport	Wisbiche	Soham	Long Stanten	Carton	Barrington	Castle Comps	Cronland Linc	Peterborow Linc	Yaxley Hunt	Huntingdon	St Iues Hunt	St Neots Hunt	Potton Bedf	Bigglesworth Bed	Royston Herts	Hauerell Suf	New Market Suf	Childersley	Thetforde	Gamlingay	Sutton
Myldnall Suf N E	15	8	15	8	7	15	5	16	21	19	15	25	24	24	20	18	25	26	27	23	14	7	18	9	25	13
Sutton N W	8	6	14	13	8	16	8	5	10	12	17	17	13	12	8	6	13	14	17	16	18	12	8	5	14	50
Gamblingay S E	11	18	16	17	21	20	20	9	3	7	19	25	20	17	3	9	4	2	4	9	21	20	7	17	39	
Thetferde N E	8	2	12	4	5	15	4	8	13	13	14	19	17	16	14	10	17	18	20	17	15	8	10	37		
Childerfley W	5	12	11	10	15	24	13	3	4	5	15	23	18	16	7	5	8	7	9	9	16	14	43			
Newmarket Su N E	10	8	8	5	10	20	5	12	17	14	9	26	24	23	16	15	21	20	22	17	8	46				
Hauerell Suf S E	12	16	6	11	18	25	13	16	19	14	2	3	4	31	30	22	19	23	21	22	15	38				
Royfton Herf S	9	18	10	15	22	31	19	11	9	5	13	30	26	24	14	13	12	8	9	31						
Bigglefw Bedf S	14	21	17	19	24	32	23	12	7	9	20	28	23	20	11	12	7	3	34							
Potton Bedf S	11	19	16	17	22	30	20	10	4	7	19	25	20	18	9	10	5	32								
St Neots Hunt	13	18	18	18	20	27	20	9	5	10	21	22	17	14	6	7	43									
St Iues Hunt	8	11	15	11	13	20	14	4	6	9	18	17	13	11	3	47										
Huntingdon N W	11	14	17	14	16	22	16	6	6	10	20	17	12	10												
Yaxley Hunt N	19	17	26	19	17	18	20	14	15	20	28	8	3													
Peterborow Li N	20	17	27	20	17	16	20	16	18	22	30	6														
Crowland Linc N	24	19	30	23	18	14	22	20	23	26	33															
Caftle Comps S E	10	13	4	10	18	28	15	13	13																	
Barrington S W	5	14	8	11	18	27	15	7																		
Caxton S W	8	15	14	14	18	26	17																			
Long Stanton N W	5	10	12	8	13	20																				
Soham N E	10	3	13	4	5																					
Wisbiche N	23	13	27	17																						
Littleport N	13	4	17																							
Reche N E	7	5	9																							
Lynton S E	7	14																								
Elye N E	10																									

11 'Cambridgeshire' engraved by Jacob Langeren, from *A Direction for the English Traviller* (London, 1643). Reproduced by permission of the Llyfrgell Genedlaethol Cymru/The National Library of Wales.

thought islands 'yeelding very little profit' were 'a great strength to the kingdom' and worth the Norwegians' asking price. By implication, the current inhabitants mirrored 'the old inhabitants (whether Scots, or Irish) being of desperate daring, and impatient of being subject to any lawes' – a view that Moryson and his sovereign shared. The right to the Orkneys, inhabited by islanders speaking 'the Gothes language', had been obtained from Denmark.[61]

The climate and situation of Scotland compared unfavourably to England's. If the 'Northerne parts of England have small pleasantness, goodnesse or abundance of Fruites and Flowers, so in Scotland they must have lesse, or none

[61] Moryson, *Itinerary*, IV, pp. 180–1.

at all'. Leaving the Home Counties and Camden behind, Moryson drew on his own experiences. 'And I remember, that coming to Barwick in the moneth of May,' he reminisced, 'wee had great stormes, and felt great cold, when for two moneths before, the pleasant Spring had smiled on us at London.' He attested to a west–east divide in topography, juxtaposing the 'pleasant little Territory of open fields, without inclosures, fruitfull in Corne' that was Fife with the woods, mountains, and lakes in the generic, unvisited land to the west and north. Barley and oats dominated cereal production, while there were fish and cattle aplenty. Both the cattle and horses were smaller than English breeds, leaving the Scots more than willing to 'give any price for one of our English Gueldings'.[62]

Moryson did not hold Scottish merchants in much regard. He emphasized 'the small strength' of their navy and poor experience of their mariners. Light customs encouraged traffic, but the Scots benefited the most by the English war with Spain: 'the Scots as neutrals by carrying of English commodities into Spaine, and by having their ships for more security laden'. The opportunistic Scots 'grew somewhat richer and more experienced in Navigation', yet, despite their daring, Moryson could not understand 'why their Marriners should not bee bold and couragious, howsoever they have not hitherto made any long voyages, rather for want of riches, then for slothfulness or want of courage'. Ironically, Moryson's judgement echoed Hakluyt's complaint against English maritime and imperial timidity in those same years. Moryson noticed that the trade to France and the Baltic provided the infrastructure for notable Scottish out-migration. In France, Denmark, and Poland 'they lived at this time in great multitudes, rather for the poverty of their owne Kingdome, then for any great trafficke they exercised there'.[63]

The Scottish diet supported Moryson's connection between poverty and diaspora. Red colewort and cabbage were staples, as were barley, oats, and root vegetables. There was little fresh or salted meat. Moryson recounted his experiences at a knight's house:

> [The servants] brought in his meate with their heads covered in blew caps, the Table being more then halfe furnished with great platters of porredge, each having a little peece of sodden meate; And when the table was served, the servants did sit downe with us ...

Scottish gentlemen might reckon their wealth by the capacity for such hospitality, but Moryson was unimpressed with the fluid social boundaries at table.

He recorded the complete absence of any 'Art of Cookery, or furniture of Household stuffe, but rude neglect of both.' And this despite the fact that 'my selfe and my companion, sent from the Governour of Barwicke about bordering affaires, were entertained after their best manner'. Only the best sort of urban dwellers could afford wheat bread in place of the vulgar 'harth Cakes of Oates',

[62] Moryson, *Itinerary*, IV, pp. 181–2.
[63] Moryson, *Itinerary*, IV, pp. 182–3.

and that only thanks to the transportation of wheat from England by Scottish merchants. Indeed, Berwick marked a distinct cultural boundary between the Scots and English in this respect. 'When I lived at Barwicke,' Moryson wrote, 'the Scots weekly upon the market day, obtained leave to in writing of the Governour, to buy Pease and Beanes', a dearth finally remedied by English sales into Scotland.[64] Moryson was even more explicit in his travel narrative proper, describing Berwick as a town 'abounding with all things necessary for food, yea with many dainties, as Salmons and all kindes of shell-fish, so plentifully, as they were sold for very small prices'.[65]

Horses provided the chief means of travel in Scotland. There were few coaches in Edinburgh, despite James's promotion of English fashions. The age-old use of horse-litters continued.[66] Drink and inns left something to be desired.[67] The Scots liked their wines pure (and sour), without sugar after the English fashion. Taverns as such were hard to come by. Moryson wrote that the typical 'bedsteads were then like Cubbards in the wall' (calling to mind Richard Hannay's fugitive night at the crofter's cottage in Hitchcock's *Thirty-Nine Steps*). They could be had from many citizens by simple entreaty or introduction. The better sort of citizens offered their own ale, 'their usual drinke (which will distemper a strangers bodie)', and it was more common to find excessive drinking among the Scots than the English. Indeed, Moryson agreed to accept an invitation to drink at Court only after his Scottish host had promised to shield him from pressure to keep pace. 'Remembering this,' Moryson reflected later, 'and having since observed in my conversation at the English Court with the Scots of the better sort, that they spend great part of the night in drinking, not onely wine, but even beere ... I cannot altogether free them from the imputation of excesse, wherewith the popular voice chargeth them.'[68]

It is easy to detect the interplay here between Moryson's own travels and comments. He found himself in Berwick on business of an undisclosed sort and his initial motive to travel into Scotland proper was a desire to see the court of James VI. He passed through the Humes' homestead at Aton before reaching impoverished Dunbar. From there it was a short distance to Haddington, notable for being taken and kept against the French, who had garrisoned Dunbar 'in the time of faction' during the Scottish revolution of 1559–60. Other towns led to Musselburgh, also 'famous for a great Victorie of the English against the Scots', and Queen Anna's court at Dalkeith.

Edinburgh proper was the seat of the kingdom, the courts of justice, and Holyrood. He found there the 'chaire of Arthur (of Arthur the Prince of the Britanes, whose monuments famous among all Ballad-makers, are for the most

---

[64] Moryson, *Itinerary*, IV, pp. 183–4.
[65] Moryson, *Itinerary*, II, pp. 116–17.
[66] Moryson, *Itinerary*, III, pp. 482–3.
[67] Moryson, *Itinerary*, III, pp. 482–3.
[68] Moryson, *Itinerary*, IV, pp. 184–5.

part to be found on these borders of England and Scotland.)'. The city boasted just one broad and fair street, the High Street or Royal Mile, all 'the rest of the side streetes and allies being of poore building and inhabited with very poore people'. The 'unexpungable' castle stood at the opposite end, while St Giles dominated its midpoint. Moryson found St Giles 'large and lightsome, but little stately for the building, and nothing at all for the beauty and ornament', a curious reaction to a cathedral whose unique closed, crown-shaped spire was a bold claim to *imperium* on the part of James VI's grandfather.[69]

Moving to the port city of Leith, Moryson again thought of French imperial ambitions and the battles among nations defined by distinct confessional identities. Its fortification and development were a direct consequence of Valois designs upon Scotland and England. Marie of Guise had arranged for the marriage of her daughter Mary to the future François II, 'who now had in hope devoured the possession of that Kingdome, and in the yeere 1560. began to aime at the conquest of England'. Across the Forth to Kinghorn, Moryson found the fruitful region of Fife and the many homes of nobles and gentlemen. Arriving at Falkland, Moryson caught a gratifying sight of James and his hunting party, even if the palace was remarkable only for its decrepit condition. His journeys to St Andrews and Stirling were abortive, although he offered some brief snippets about each, including the jurisdictional dispute between the archbishops of St Andrews and York, and the king's childhood spent at Stirling Castle. Moryson returned by way of Berwick, but not before giving would-be travellers an itinerary by which to transit the west side of Britain and cross to eastern Ireland.[70]

Apparel was a typical marker of cultural complexity. For instance, Moryson found a distinct similarity between Turkish breeches and Irish trousers, save for the revealing tightness of the Irish garments. The sight of an old Irish woman covered with just a loose mantle and rag of linen at the groin turned his stomach. A Bohemian baron travelled into northern Ireland from Scotland and was met at a lord's house by sixteen scantily clad Irish women who crossed their legs unchastely and attempted (with the encouragement of their lord) to get him to sit naked by the fire.[71] Moryson's experiences encouraged him to critique the fashions of his fellow countrymen.

Caesar may have reported that the Britons sported skins and long hair, but that was hardly to be compared to contemporary fashion among the English: 'Now the English in their apparell are become more light then the lightest French, and more sumptuous then the proudest Persians. More light I say then the French, because with singular inconstancy they have in this one age worne out all the fashion of France and all the Nations of Europe ... The English I say are more sumptuous then the Persians, because despising the golden meane, they

[69] Moryson, *Itinerary*, II, pp. 116–19.
[70] Moryson, *Itinerary*, II, pp. 119–21.
[71] Moryson, *Itinerary*, IV, p. 236.

affect all extreameties.'[72] The English proved themselves fools among their own countrymen. Not only did the demand for ever more fashionable garments send English merchants to the farthest corners of Asia, but the merchants 'to their owne gaine, daily in forraigne parts cause such new colours and stuffe to be made, as their Masters send painted out of England to them'. The insatiable English desire for fashion taught 'strangers to serve our lightnesse with such inventions as themselves never knew before', making them party to the corrupting influence of vulgar and extravagant tastes.[73] Perhaps because of his own uncertain social standing, Moryson argued that there were real consequences of such corruption. Fools mocked wiser heads for 'wearing apparell of old and good fashion ... till at last they are forced to be foolish with the fooles of their time'.[74] To make his point, Moryson recounted the fable of the rain shower sent by Jupiter to turn those who forsook shelter into fools. One lone 'Philosopher' kept dry by remaining in his study, only to pray that he too be rained on and turned into a fool after emerging to the ridicule of the crowd, 'and so live quietly among fooles, rather then beare the envy of his wisedome'.[75]

Cultural contacts with France and Germany, as well as the general 'poverty' of their country, worked to the advantage of lowland Scots. Virtually every man or woman outside the elite wore clothes of coarse, homemade cloth, with sky-blue caps. City merchants generally sported pale-coloured garments made of French or English cloth, while courtly gentlemen tended toward English cloth, silk, or light fabrics with little or no lace in the French fashion. Married gentlewomen wore 'close upper bodies, after the German manner, with large whalebone sleeves after the French manner, short cloakes like the Germans, French hoods, and large falling bands about their necks'. Unmarried women followed the sober example of their Continental cousins in Germany rather than the unmarried Englishwomen, who kept their 'brests naked' to show off cleavage. The poorest Scotswomen typically wore 'cloakes made of a course stuffe, of two or three colours in Checker worke, vulgarly called Plodan' (plaid). No Scots followed the English fashion, better men and those at court followed the French fashion, and their female counterparts followed the fashions of Germany.[76] For Moryson, cultural proximity to England had nothing to recommend it with respect to dress and fashion. The Scots and English shared a king and rugged borders, but they remained distinct peoples.

For Leland and Camden there were many permeable borders in Britain: Devon and Cornwall, Wales, the Scottish Borders, the highland–lowland line in Scotland proper, the North of England, the Irish Sea community, and perhaps a sense that London, Kent, and Yorkshire each had particularly unique flavours to

---

[72] Moryson, *Itinerary*, IV, pp. 231–2.
[73] Moryson, *Itinerary*, IV, p. 231.
[74] Moryson, *Itinerary*, IV, pp. 233–5.
[75] Moryson, *Itinerary*, IV, p. 232.
[76] Moryson, *Itinerary*, IV, pp. 235–6.

Lancaſhire wth ſome confi ning Townes	Lancaſter	Preſton	Kirkham	Ormeskirke	Leuerpoole	Warrington	Wygan	Bolton	Burie	Rochdale	Mancheſter	Blackborne	Gisborne Yor	Colne	Garſtrange	Clethero Caſtle	Wierdale	Hornby Caſt	Thurland Caſtle	Bolton paſſage	Cartlone paſſage	Cunyſide paſſ	Vluerſtone	Glayſtone Caſt	Dalton Caſtle	Kirkby Langſdale W
Kendale Weſtm N	15	30	30	40	49	50	40	40	40	40	46	32	24	30	23	27	19	13	12	12	10	14	14	17	17	9
Kirkby Lansd N E	10	22	33	33	42	40	33	31	31	31	37	23	15	21	16	18	11	5	3	9	11	17	17	19	21	204
Dalton Caſt N W	15	29	26	6	45	47	39	40	43	45	49	35	33	30	22	32	21	20	21	14	10	4	3	3	202	
Glayſton Caſt N W	11	27	24	14	41	40	36	38	41	42	47	32	31	37	20	31	19	19	19	12	9	2	5	199		
Vluerſton N W	13	29	26	36	45	48	40	40	42	44	48	33	31	37	22	31	20	18	18	12	7	2	207			
Cunyſide paſſ N W	13	27	25	35	42	46	38	19	20	42	46	32	29	35	20	30	18	16	17	10	6	198				
Cartlone paſſ N W	9	25	23	34	44	44	36	36	37	38	44	28	25	31	17	25	14	11	11	6	194					
Bolto paſſage N	3	10	18	28	37	38	29	30	30	31	36	22	18	24	11	18	6	3	6	3	190					
Thurland Caſt N E	8	14	20	31	40	38	30	28	29	29	35	20	13	19	14	15	8	3	9	186						
Horneby Caſt N E	6	18	19	29	37	36	28	27	28	28	33	19	13	19	12	14	7	186								
Wyerdale S E	5	12	12	23	30	30	22	22	23	24	29	14	12	17	5	12	185									
Clethero Caſt S E	17	12	16	22	31	25	18	14	13	13	10	7	5	6	1167											
Garſtrange S	8	8	7	17	25	26	19	21	21	27	13	15	20	163												
Colne S E	23	17	22	27	34	27	21	16	14	12	9	11	6	165												
Gisborne Yor S E	17	16	20	28	35	30	23	19	18	17	23	12	140													
Blackeborne S E	19	7	12	16	23	18	11	8	9	10	15	165														
Mancheſter S E	14	10	24	21	24	12	13	3	6	7	146															
Rochedale S E	29	17	22	22	27	17	14	8	4	154																
Bury S E	28	14	19	18	23	14	10	4	160																	
Bolton S E	26	12	16	14	20	11	7	170																		
Wygan S E	26	11	11	8	13	3	150																			
Warrington S E	35	19	13	13	13	160																				
Leuerpoole S	34	20	20	9	166																					
Ormeskirck S	26	12	11	176																						
Kirkham S	15	6	167																							
Preſton S E	16	169																								

12 'Lancashire' engraved by Jacob Langeren, from *A Direction for the English Traviller* (London, 1643). Reproduced by permission of the Llyfrgell Genedlaethol Cymru/ The National Library of Wales.

them. Moryson certainly had first-hand experiences of these cultural 'borders'. Within England, Moryson completed journeys between London and Gravesend, Dover, Berwick, and Lincolnshire. He studied the cultural frontiers in England as they were drawn in the proverbs and opinions of old writers:

> The Kentish men of old were said to have tayles, because trafficking in the Low-Countries they never paid full payments of what they did owe, but still left some part unpaid. Essex men are called calves (because they abound there), Lankashire egge-pies ... Norfolk wyles (for crafty litigiousnes): Essex stiles (so many as make walking tedious) ... Cornish men best Horse-riders and Wrastlers, and most active men. Lincolnshire

Belles and Bag-pipes, Devonshire White-pots, Tewksbery Mustard, Banberry Cakes, Kings-Norten Cheese, Sheffeld knives, Darby Ale, are proverbially spoken of.[77]

Some of these found their way into the topographical descriptions cribbed from Camden's *Britannia*.

The posting to Ireland took Moryson from London to Chester, where he waited for passage to Dublin in 1600. He later returned to London by way of Beaumaris in Wales. He was certainly attuned to the Welsh 'frontier' and lifted details from Camden. In the *Itinerary*, he wrote that Shropshire 'was a fortified and manned frontyer against the Welsh, then divided from the English and their enemies, and thereupon was named the Marches'. Ludlow boasted the palace of the prince of Wales and the 'Court of Justice erected for Wales & the borders, not unlike to the French [regional] Parliaments, and instituted by Henry the eight'. The decay of Wroxeter benefited the border town of Shrewsbury, 'now the chiefe Cities, fortified by art and nature, rich by making wollen cloth, and trading with the neighbouring Welchmen'.[78]

Moryson shared with Leland a sense that the North of England was a place apart. Yorkshire was notable on many counts, including the alleged birth of the future Emperor Constantine in York, but Moryson devoted particular attention to the one-time jurisdiction of the archbishop over 'twelve Bishops in England, and al[l] the Bishops of Scotland' and the establishment by Henry VIII of 'a Councell (as he did also in Wales) not unlike the Parliaments of France, to give arbitrary justice to the Northerne inhabitants'.[79] As he reached Cumbria and Northumbria an interesting set of attitudes went to work. Like Leland, he noted 'the ruines of a wall, which the Romans built to keepe out the Pictes from making incursions'. But Moryson explained the wall by virtue of the Picts' 'being so poore as they cared not to subdue them'.[80] Moryson crossed the Roman wall and made a brief turn through Lothian and Fife. Here again he borrowed from Camden, particularly the interplay of tribes and peoples over the lands of the 'ancient' British *imperium* in Scotland.[81] Conflict chiefly defined the Borders. Unlike his sovereign, Moryson complimented the English borderers who became 'warlike and excellent horsemen' from 'exercising themselves in warre against the Scots, now resisting their incursions upon these borders'.[82] The fortification of Newcastle 'against the incursions of the bordering Scots' was noted before he paid tribute to the 'happy Raigne of James King of England and Scotland' – not king of Great Britain, as James styled himself – which rendered Berwick the 'last and best fortified Towne of all Britany'.[83]

---

[77] Moryson, *Itinerary*, III, p. 463.
[78] Moryson, *Itinerary*, IV, p. 154.
[79] Moryson, *Itinerary*, IV, pp. 158–9.
[80] Moryson, *Itinerary*, IV, p. 160.
[81] Moryson, *Itinerary*, IV, pp. 177–81.
[82] Moryson, *Itinerary*, IV, p. 160; also Moryson, *Itinerary*, III, p. 463.
[83] Moryson, *Itinerary*, IV, pp. 160–1.

If Moryson's parroted topography of England, Wales, and Scotland made some room for cultural complexity and interaction, any account of the islands off shore necessitated treating them explicitly as crossroads of peoples, especially the Isle of Man. Indeed the Manx practically disappeared under references to other peoples: 'the Inhabitants whereof are like the Irish in language and manners, but have something of the Norway men ... the people in the Northerne part speake like Scots, and in the Southerne part like Irish'. The island was notable for being fruitful in barley, wheat, and particularly oats and cattle, while the inhabitants burned peat, in the absence of wood or coals. 'In generall the Inhabitants have their proper Tongue and Lawes,' wrote Moryson, while he praised them as people who 'abhorre stealing, and from begging, and are wonderfully religious generally' and, unlike their Irish-speaking cousins, 'most readily conforming themselves at this day to the Church of England'. Cultural encounter and conflict dominated Man's history: 'Edwin King of Northumberland, subdued the Northerne people, and subjected them to the Crowne of England, yet with many changes of Fortune, this Iland long had their owne Kings even since the Normans conquered England, and since the time that John King of England passing into Ireland, by the way subdued this Iland about the yeere 1210, till the Kingdome came to the Scots in the yeere 1266.'[84]

We gain some sense from the *Itinerary* of how Moryson would have approached cultural complexity within Britain in his promised ethnography. Yet Moryson betrayed the tensions between the scale of his 'Itinerary', cultural complexity, and 'nations'. In the *Itinerary* Moryson was untroubled by submerging the Welsh under the heading of England when he divided 'Britany' between Scotland and England. Indeed, the borders and counties of Wales were treated very much like imperial dominions in his selections from Camden. The chief approval comes for counties and towns of value to England and its history. Thus Monmouth could in no way approach the glory of its most famous son, 'Henry the fifth Conquerer of France', while the great Welsh saint Winifred, 'defloured by force' and 'killed by the Tyrant', became simply a 'Christian Virgin' who gave her name to the famous fountain in Holywell. The matter-of-factness with which the 'most faire Castle' of Caernarvon was built by Edward I wrote out the conquest, let alone its brutality. By contrast, 'the Flemming having their Townes drowned by the Sea, had a Territorie of this County [of Caermarthen] given them to inhabit by Henry the first, before Wales was subdued, and they ever remained most faithfull to the Kings of England'. The 'Mountenous people' of Merionethsire could graze their sheep without danger of wolves, thanks to the wolf-tribute imposed on the Welsh prince Luduall by King Edgar, by which 'the wolves were destroied through all England'.[85] Romantic reference to Snowden as the 'Alps of Britany' did not conceal an underlying antipathy toward England's former

[84] Moryson, *Itinerary*, IV, p. 162.
[85] Moryson, *Itinerary*, IV, pp. 154–7.

enemy. The fate of the Welsh led to only one outcome, English supremacy and jurisdiction. Moryson's sense of Britain as a geography in which peoples encountered one another, interacted, and thereby became something else again seems to have been limited to the ancient tribal divisions and successive ethnic migrations described in Camden's *Britannia*. This was not the complexity Mair, Boece, and Leland engaged. How do we explain it?

The failure of Moryson and travel in Britain

Moryson sometimes betrayed a prickly side, and he complained that the *Itinerary* had faced unfair criticism and carping. Toward the end of his life, perhaps having conceded that the manuscript 'Itinerary' would never find a publisher, he bemoaned his misfortune:

> I shall give no reply at all to any critic, because I am now old and am devoting the remainder of my life to theological studies; the labour involved, most troublesome at this time of life, should persuade them, as it is equally free to me, and for any one else whose feelings are in harmony with truth, to consider that it would be for posterity, whom neither will be able to drag over to his own side, to judge whose error smacks of frailty, and whose of malice.[86]

Moryson did not retire to his theological speculations any more willingly than Arthur Conan Doyle's Sherlock Holmes took up the contemplation of Nature and beekeeping on the Sussex Downs. This was enforced retirement poisoned by a long-nursed grudge over literary disappointment.

The first tastes of disappointment no doubt lay behind Moryson's original decision to evade the planned treatment of England and Scotland in the Fourth Part of the 'Itinerary' and instead promise a separate treatise. How did he explain the decision? He informed would-be readers of the 'Manuscript' who had expected to find a description of the English polity that

> Being to write more exactly of the Common wealth of England, then of others, lest while I seem to affect knowledge of other kingdomes, I should bewray [reveal] my ignorance in the State of my owne Country, I haue thought good to referr the same to a Treatise to be written of purpose ... which Treatise I haue begunn, but it will require tyme and leysure to perfect it, And so for this tyme I passe it ouer vntouched.[87]

The imputation of ignorance is the key and Moryson repeated this explanation in his chapter on English customs in the 'Manuscript'.[88] What frightened Moryson into these defensive comments? The complex descriptions of dominions like

---

[86] 'Unpublished *Itinerary*', p. c, n. 24, translation of Moryson's Latin original by Frank Beetham, Department of Classical Studies at Birmingham University, received and reproduced by Kew.

[87] 'Unpublished *Itinerary*', p. 649.

[88] 'Unpublished *Itinerary*', p. 1657.

Germany or the Ottoman Empire point to how much knowledge of Britain Moryson needed if he was to avoid the imputation of ignorance.[89] As he set out to complete the 'Itinerary', he must have realized that he did not know 'home' sufficiently well to complete chapters for England and Scotland in the 'Manuscript' or a stand-alone ethnography of the two realms.

Where did that leave Moryson?[90] One avenue he did not take may be the most telling. He did not opt to cobble together English and Scottish chapters or his British ethnography by cribbing the work of others, as he had with Camden's *Britannia* in the *Itinerary* – or as Speed had so masterfully done with his borrowings in *Theatre of the Empire of Great Britain*.[91] There were sufficient works to hand: Camden, Speed, Holinshed, Boece/Bellenden, Lesley, Buchanan, even Leland's notebooks, had he been able to lay his hand on them. He could have completed descriptions of the Scottish and English polities, even if they would have remained unleavened with his typical first-hand experiences. As for religious practices, Moryson included England and Scotland in one chapter with France and Ireland in the 'Itinerary'. Here Moryson did crib from Camden. He offered a potted history of the papal usurpation of the early Church in Britain and its corrupting influences, despite which the English still managed to build a magnificent church of bricks and mortar to which they offered deep devotion and piety.[92] Out of his own experiences, Moryson might just have supplied for England the sort of rich discussions of devotional practices that he had for other dominions like Germany. However, Moryson had little, if any, first-hand experience of the Scottish Kirk, leaving him with the politically problematic works of John Knox or David Calderwood. James listed Buchanan and Knox among those 'infamous libels' that should remain supressed at all costs.[93] As for the chapter describing the people of England, Moryson recorded but a few 'singularities remembred in a shorte meditation'.[94] He explained that 'in the meane tyme till that treatise be compiled I desyre leaue to for strangers sakes breefly to note some singularities of England in these poyntes'.[95] Moryson's defensiveness betrayed the concern that his brevity would be taken for ignorance of 'home' and the practical inability to offer anything more substantive.

---

[89] 'Unpublished *Itinerary*', pp. 3–145 (the Ottoman polity), pp. 796–897 (German religious practices and churches).

[90] My reading of the market for Moryson's 'Itinerary' departs from Kew's, which seems to me overly schematic and anachronistic concerning genres and potential readers; for example, 'professional as well as amateur travellers'. 'Unpublished *Itinerary*', pp. xciv–ciii.

[91] Stan A.E. Mendyk, '*Speculum Britanniae*': *Regional Study, Antiquarianism, and Science in Britain to 1700* (Toronto, 1989), p. 79.

[92] 'Unpublished *Itinerary*', pp. 1172–5.

[93] King James VI and I, *Political Writings*, ed. Johann P. Sommerville (Cambridge, 1994), p. 46.

[94] 'Unpublished *Itinerary*', p. 1671.

[95] 'Unpublished *Itinerary*', p. 1657.

Moryson did not simply realize that he needed more time with his books, and I disagree with Graham Kew's easy speculation that Moryson would have resorted again to *Britannia* in his British ethnography.[96] Moryson confronted a significant problem. At some point in completing the 'Manuscript', he surely recognized that his 'home' travels had been inadequate and – perhaps excepting the journey from Berwick to Scotland – qualitatively different from journeys elsewhere in Europe and the Middle East. He simply did not have the first-hand experiences of encounter and interaction among the peoples of Britain suitable for finishing his great project if the English and Scottish chapters were to be part of it. He had not traversed Britain with a deliberate eye for ethno-cultural complexity.

A diary kept by an anonymous Scottish traveller c. 1655–56 exemplifies the degree to which familiarity or geographic proximity to home could work against depth and detail of ethno-cultural observation.[97] The description of the journey to London began at Haddington and the traveller crossed into England at Berwick, 'strongly fortyfyed upon the Scots syd'.[98] The traveller recounted the journey with descriptions of Newcastle, Durham, and York, the colleges of Oxford and exotic artefacts in the anatomy school, and various sites about London (including Drury Lane, Westminster, and Hampton Court's scores of chimneys).[99] Travellers' diaries 'created an opportunity for personal reflection on the world around them' and this traveller's journey certainly 'commenced when he left his home in Scotland, and so he described the sights of England on his way to London'.[100] Yet England was a good deal closer to home than this Scotsman's destination, and the character of the descriptions reflected that. His ethnographic gaze is inert until he moves through France and embarks for Alexandria at Marseille. Like modern travellers through Provence, he took in the Roman presence in Durance, the great traffic and conjunction of peoples in Marseille, a hermit's chapel back of Cassis, and a multiplicity of *terroir* spiced by local wines and aromas of lavender, juniper, and thyme.[101] Missing from the short descriptions through England is something as simple as this: 'the peopell in Marseilles and throwgh all provenc ar more sullen ~~and less~~ & rugged then the French in the wast part[e]s of franc'.[102] Almost 350 tightly written pages filled this diary, but Britain took up a scant eighteen of them.

One traveller who did not fail in his home travels was William Lithgow. Lithgow hailed from Lanark, the third child of a prosperous town burgess,

---

[96] 'Unpublished *Itinerary*', p. cxxxiii.
[97] British Library, Sloane MS 3228, 'Journey to the Holy Land'.
[98] BL, Sloane MS 3228, fol. 1v.
[99] BL, Sloane MS 3228, fols 1v–10v.
[100] Alison Games, *The Web of Empire: English Cosmopolitans in an Age of Expansion 1560–1660* (Oxford, 2008), 27.
[101] BL, Sloane MS 3228, fols 50r–54v.
[102] BL, Sloane MS 3228 fol. 54r–v.

and attended Lanark Grammar School, receiving 'a solid classical education plus a knowledge of the Bible and catechisms'.[103] Lithgow completed extended journeys across the Middle East, Central Europe, and North Africa, spanning 1612 to 1621. Brutally tortured in Spain, he convalesced over several years in England after 1621 before returning home to Scotland in 1627. He spent 1627 and 1628 travelling across Scotland and the Western Isles. He proudly celebrated the affableness of Scots far and wide, the productivity of the country (real and potential), and decried, much like a latter-day Mair or Boece, the indolence and degeneration of the country's elites. This abbreviated account appeared in the 1632 edition of his *Totall Discourse of the Rare Adventures, and Painefull Peregrinations of Long Nineteene Yeares Trauayles*.[104] Lithgow did not cast a consistent or systematic ethnographic eye on the lands he traversed, and his religious attitudes towards Muslims, Jews, Catholics, and Orthodox Christians were those of a bigot. Nonetheless, Lithgow's Scottish travels would have been an opportunity to explore the interaction of journeys home and away that we do not have with Moryson. Unfortunately, Lithgow never published his completed 'Surueigh of Scotland', and the manuscript was lost.[105] The encounter with cultural complexity in Britain required deliberateness, even from cosmopolitan travellers like Moryson, Lithgow, and the anonymous diarist.

Moryson's ethnographic framework would have been a real departure, but he did not have the substantive encounters or observations to make good on it with Britain. When Moryson attempted to include Scotland in the chapters about proverbial wisdom in the *Itinerary*, he confessed: 'I hastily passed through part of Scotland bordering upon England, and had no skill in the Irish tongue, so as I observed no such Proverbs in those Kingdomes.'[106] Moryson never returned to Scotland, never passed through its unique ethno-cultural topography, and he knew only those parts of England and Wales through which he had travelled on the way to somewhere else. Neither his limited travels in Britain nor their seemingly inattentive character was up to the task. A wandering nature and passion for rubbing shoulders with new people might not have been enough for Moryson as he approached sixty and nursed his financial and literary disappointments in the 1620s.

Moryson was not in a position to offer readers in the market descriptions of Scotland, England (and Wales) with the comparable depth and complexity he had for the other dominions in the 'Itinerary'. Evidently he dared not, either. Moryson apparently described or even circulated portions of the manuscript of the *Itinerary* before its publication in 1617. In the published edition he addressed

[103] Clifford Edmund Bosworth, *An Intrepid Scot: William Lithgow of Lanark's Travels in the Ottoman Lands, North Africa and Central Europe, 1609–1621* (Aldershot, 2006), pp. 16–17.
[104] William Lithgow, *Totall Discourse of the Rare Adventures, and Painefull Peregrinations of Long Nineteene Yeares Trauayles* (STC 15713; London, 1632), pp. 495–501.
[105] Lithgow, *Totall Discourse*, p. 493; Bosworth, *An Intrepid Scot*, p. 173, n. 59.
[106] Moryson, *Itinerary*, III, p. 463.

the response: 'But behold, when I thought to have finished my taske, carpers consumed with envie, who barke at travellers as dogs at the Moone, and thinking to gaine reputation by other mens disgrace, they are not ashamed to say, that vagabond Caine was the first Traveller.' Evidently these unnamed carpers attacked Moryson for having claimed too much for his travels, perhaps their novelty or the value and quality of the information.[107]

Moryson painted himself as one 'despised or neglected' – certainly he did not find his travels to be the pass to serving 'the Counsellors of States, and Peeres of Realmes'. Instead he claimed to find comfort in virtue for its own sake, in this case 'the fruit of travell is travell it selfe'.[108] The criticism still stung. When he took up his pen to complete the 'Itinerary', Moryson would neither parrot the work of others and risk charges of false originality or offer a work whose information could be deemed superficial or insubstantial. Either within the bounds of the 'Itinerary' – quite literally and physically – or in a separate treatise, what could Moryson have offered readers interested in a traveller's account of Britain? How could he outdo or go beyond the remarkable fusion of topographical detail and geographical breadth in Camden's *Britannia* or Speed's *Theatre of the Empire of Great Britain*? Those great folio volumes appeared in successive editions that cemented their dominance in the market. Faced with the realities of the trade, 'high, up-front, and one-off investment, coupled with potentially very slow returns', no printer took a risk on Moryson and his 'Manuscript'.[109]

Moryson was not alone. The *Britannia*-like projects of William Lambarde, John Norden, and less-ambitious chorographers all failed to overcome some combination of the absence of a strong patron and investment capital, reluctance on the part of printers and booksellers to compete with Camden or Speed, criticism in the marketplace, or the limits of one individual's travels (qualitatively or in sheer miles covered).[110] At least some of John Norden's ire at 'ouer-curious inspectators' and 'common reprouers' came from criticism of his careful effort to provide accurate mileages, parish boundaries, and place-names.[111] Neither originality nor innovation promised forgiving, let alone enthusiastic, readership.

Two later descriptions of Britain, heavily indebted to the likes of Camden, Speed, John Ogilby, and English county historians, suggest what Moryson was up against. In 1660, the Kent schoolmaster and antiquary Joshua Childrey published his *Britannia Baconica: Or The Natural Rarities of England, Scotland, & Wales*. Eager to 'expell the poison of superstition', Childrey offered up a careful county-by-county description of Britain, with empirical details related 'according

---

[107] Moryson, *Itinerary*, III, p. 363.

[108] Moryson, *Itinerary*, III, p. 364.

[109] 'Unpublished *Itinerary*', pp. xliii–xlv, clxix; James Raven, *The Business of Books: Booksellers and the English Book Trade 1450–1850* (New Haven, 2007), p. 41.

[110] Mendyk, '*Speculum Britanniae*', pp. 58, 64–7, 82–3.

[111] John Norden, *Nordens Preparatiue to His Speculum Britanniae* (STC 18638; London, 1596), pp. 17–31.

to the Precepts of the Lord Bacon; Methodically digested'. He wrote with three sorts of people in mind. 'Vulgar' readers needed to be reassured that not all strange phenomena came to light, because travellers made 'use of their Authority to lye' about their experiences. 'Here are no stories told you of what is to be seen at the other end of the world,' Childrey promised, 'but of things at home, in your Native Countrey, at your own doors, easily examined with little travel, less cost, and very little hazard.' In short, there were genuine peculiarities to be discovered 'at home' that could put unthinking scepticism in its proper frame.[112]

Childrey also appealed to scholars, especially ones who wanted 'such Histories as this to be written' – natural histories. To that end, Childrey did not meddle with 'Antiquity, Pedigrees, or the like, those being copiously handled by several of our Countrymen already; as the learned Cambden in his *Britannia*, Mr. Dugdale in his Description of Warwickshire, Mr. King in his Vale Royal, Mr. Lambert in his Perambulation, Mr. Philpot in his Villare Cantianum, and others'.[113] Childrey did not intend to duplicate their work, but his *Britannia Baconica* would have been a thin book indeed without them. Journeys in Kent, Wiltshire, and Gloucester may have given him some few first-hand observations, but Childrey overwhelmingly excerpted and repackaged others' material.[114] From his armchair, Childrey asked readers 'that if his native Country afford any other Rarity ... he will be pleased to communicate it for the sake of Learning'. Readers in Dorset were begged to 'bestow upon us a punctuall account of that raining of blood at Pool with all its circumstances'.[115]

Childrey ultimately wrote the book for gentry travellers. They could 'know by this Portable-book' – that they should take with them – 'that they may see England is not void of those things which they admire in their travels' abroad. He must have had in mind gentry for whom the development of the Continental Grand Tour, exotic overseas voyages, and the mid-century conflicts had discouraged travel in Britain:

> As Italy hath Virgils Grott, and the Sybills Cave by Puteoli; so England hath Okeyhole by Wells. We have ... the Alpes in North-Wales; Mount Baldus under the Picts Wall ... the Pyramides at Burrowbriggs, the Pearls of Persia on the shores of Westmorland; the Diamonds of India on St. Vincents Rock.[116]

'And what is ther worth wonder abroad in the world,' Childrey fairly demanded to know, 'whereof Nature hath not written a Copy in our I-land? I would have those that know other Countreys so well, not to be strangers to their own,

[112] J. Childrey, *Britannia Baconica: Or The Natural Rarities of England, Scotland, & Wales* (WING C3870; London, 1660), sig. A8a–b.
[113] Childrey, *Britannia Baconica*, sigs B1b–B2a.
[114] W.P. Courtney, 'Joshua Childrey', *Dictionary of National Biography* (Oxford, 1887) archived at *www.oxforddnb.com*.
[115] Childrey, *Britannia Baconica*, sig. B6b.
[116] Childrey, *Britannia Baconica*, sig. B1a–b.

which is a compendium of all others.'[117] What Childrey expected of others was something he could not accomplish by his own, first-hand expertise. Ignorance of home worried Moryson enough to make him postpone and ultimately abandon his British ethnography. Childrey's *Britannia Baconica* tapped the burgeoning fascination with natural history approached with a 'scientific spirit', and reprints quickly followed in 1661 and 1662.[118]

As the century ended, James Brome looked to pull off much the same trick. He published the first of his purported journeys through Britain in 1694 as *Mr Rogers's Three Years Travels*, reprinted in 1697. The 1694 volume made two fundamental claims. While there were 'indeed voluminous Treatises of this Nature already extant, which claim a just Praise in their kind ... none, in my judgment, so well handled, so compleat, and truly recommendable as this'. This was a true and complete account, presented by an author who had travelled for three years and offered 'nothing but his own Ocular Observations, whereas others, confining themselves to their Studies, have obtruded upon the World what they have taken upon the bare Credit of those, who were, perhaps more slothful than themselves'.[119] Here, then, almost seventy years after Moryson had finished the 'Manuscript', was a description of Britain that promised to outdo its competitors and contain nothing that its author had not witnessed in person. Something was gravely amiss, though.

An edition followed under Brome's own name in 1700, but no prior connection was admitted. Brome explained that he had not yet discovered who had obtained 'false Copies' of the descriptions and published them in 1694, but he felt compelled to correct the wretched patchwork, 'so horribly Imperfect, and abominably Erroneous', and 'expose the Plagiarism and Dishonesty of such vile Pultroons, and scandalous Undertakers'.[120] Brome's chutzpah was of a piece with his prose. He might have started the search for the 'mysterious Cheat' with his own publisher Abel Roper, who was responsible for both the 1697 edition of Mr Rogers's travels and Brome's own in 1700. Brome's real problems were that he had never travelled to the places he claimed first-hand knowledge of, had plagiarized the works of others, and still managed to get the details wrong.[121] At least, those were the charges he levelled against Mr Rogers's travels.[122] By 1700 Brome's disguise must have evaporated amidst a hostile response from

---

[117] Childrey, *Britannia Baconica*, sig. B1b.

[118] Mendyk, '*Speculum Britanniae*', p. 169.

[119] *An Historical Account of Mr. Rogers's Three Years Travels over England and Wales* (B4857; London, 1694), sigs A2b–A4b.

[120] James Brome, *An Historical Account of Mr. Brome's Three Years Travels over England, Scotland, and Wales* (B4858; London, 1700), sig. A2a–b.

[121] Brome's description of his college, Christ's College, Cambridge, is considered authentic. Anita McConnell and Vivienne Larminie, 'James Brome', *Oxford DNB* at www.oxforddnb. com.

[122] Brome, *Travels*, sig. A2b–A3a.

readers who indeed expected something more than a rehash of Camden, Speed, or the like. In other words, Brome faced just the sort of response Moryson had feared when contemplating the British chapters of the 'Itinerary' or a British ethnography.

Having cautioned readers against his plagiarizing antagonists, Brome explained that his would be a comprehensive – and correct – description, including many 'Observations, which were yet never taken notice of by any English Topographer'. Brome proceeded to plagiarize *Britannia Baconica*, using Childrey's challenge to his readers to admit that 'there is not any thing worth our Wonder Abroad, whereof Nature hath not written a Copy in our own Island'. Just as disreputable was Brome's Anglocentricity when compared to Leland or Moryson or Camden. Dedicating the book to Basil Dixwell, Constable of Dover Castle, Brome described his travels as 'a short Account of our Own British Island' and lamented the fascination for 'new and unheard-of Rarities from abroad, as if our English Soil was so barren in its Productions, that it could not divert the Curious'.[123]

With something like a literary wink, Brome challenged the 'snarling Criticks, and carping Momus's of the Age, who can sooner find a Fault than mend it'. He confidently armed himself with an apt moral:

> Attempt brave things, then set your Heart at rest,
> Let not the senseless Mob disturb your Breast:
> If some speak ill on purpose for to teaze you,
> Others will speak the best, and let that please you.[124]

Fault-finders did not stop Brome from publishing another edition of his travels in 1707, but there is an appropriate end to his story. A Mediterranean travelogue once attributed to Brome in the *Dictionary of National Biography* no longer is.[125]

Reading Moryson's *Itinerary*: the Earl of Haddington's busy pen

In the preface to his new edition of *Britannia* in 1695, Edmund Gibson directed readers interested in general descriptions of England to Leland's *Itinerary* ('Transcripts whereof have been taken by Gentlemen of Curiosity'), Harrison's account from Holinshed's *Chronicle*, Drayton's *Poly-Olbion*, Fuller's *Worthies*, and Aubrey's collections. As for 'Blome's Britannia, Wright's three years Travels; and other Surveys of England printed since 1607', they were dismissed as 'little more than Extracts out of Mr Camden'.[126] Perhaps, then, Moryson correctly judged his predicament, yet the story does not have to end on a note of failure.

---

[123] Brome, *Travels*, sig. A1a–b.
[124] Brome, *Travels*, sig. A2b.
[125] McConnell and Larminie, 'James Brome'.
[126] William Camden, *Britannia: Or a Chorographical Description of Great Britain and Ireland* (London, 1695), preface.

One family acquired Moryson's *Itinerary* soon after its publication in 1617. The National Library of Scotland now owns the copy that once belonged to Thomas Hamilton, the first Earl of Haddington.[127] Someone in the Hamilton household read Moryson's *Itinerary* actively and intently. Indeed, few readers in the period could have underlined so much, added so many marginal headings, or used plus marks with such abandon in such a hefty folio. The best candidate must be the earl himself – 'very learned, but of a choleric constitution' by one account.[128] Yet Hamilton's son would have found no cause to part with the volume. Young Thomas Hamilton, at barely fifteen, 'obtained a licence to travel abroad in July 1615 "as he shall thinke moste fitte for his instruction in literature, language, and custome of diuers nations"'. The lad became a Scottish Moryson for the next few years.[129] Hamilton studied in Paris from 1581 to 1587, otherwise the younger Thomas may well have lived out some of the armchair travelling his father did in the text and margins of Moryson's *Itinerary*.

Hamilton came to play an integral part in James VI's government of Scotland.[130] He became a regular judge in the Court of Session in 1592, but his financial expertise opened bigger doors. Moving on from Queen Anna's household, Hamilton played a leading role in the treasury commission known as the Octavians. When the commission was wound up, Hamilton became the principal crown prosecutor as Lord Advocate and moved to the secretaryship in 1612. He used his position as Advocate to advance James's claims to supremacy over the Presbyterian Kirk. He brought witchcraft and heresy firmly under the criminal courts and dutifully forced the king's Anglican-style Articles of Perth – including the 'idolatrous' command to take communion kneeling – through the 1618 General Assembly of the Kirk and the Scottish Parliament in 1621. Hamilton himself kneeled at communion during James's return to Scotland in 1617. He died in 1637, just as the imposition of Anglican religious ceremonies imported by Charles I began to come to deadly fruition.

Hamilton did not relinquish his long-standing interest in finance and political economy during these years. In the Scottish parliamentary session of 1621, he may well have proposed a tax on annual rents in the commercial sector. The younger Hamilton's mother had been Margaret Foulis, sister to the notorious 'goldsmith and financier' Thomas Foulis. Hamilton became the king's Master of the Metals, charged to handle the crown's interest in silver, gold, and specie. This came hard on the heels of turning over the mining rights to the silver veins found on his estate at Hilderstone near Linlithgow in 1607. Hamilton's lucrative

---

[127] *An Itinerary Written by Fynes Moryson ... Containing His Ten Yeeres Travell Throvgh the Twelve Dominions of Germany, Bohmerland, Sweitzerland, Netherland, Denmarke, Poland, Italy, Turky, France, England, Scotland, and Ireland* (London, 1617). The National Library of Scotland shelf mark for this copy is NLS Tyn.316, hereafter cited as *Itinerary Written by Fynes Moryson* (Tyn.316).

[128] Julian Goodare, 'Thomas Hamilton', *Oxford DNB* at www.oxforddnb.com.

[129] David Stevenson, 'Thomas Hamilton', *Oxford DNB* at www.oxforddnb.com.

[130] Goodare, 'Thomas Hamilton'.

investments complemented his political rise from Lord Binning in 1613 to the earldoms of Melrose (1619) and Haddington (1627).

Right from the start of Moryson's travelogue (Part I), Hamilton took an interest in mining, minerals and metals, specie, coinage, and political economy. Cribs, marginal headings, heavy underlining, and a plentiful number of plusses and 'nota' testify to his reading. For example, the silver mines of Freiburg set a high standard of expertise, and may have offered hope that deeper veins lay under the disappointing ground of Hilderstone.[131] Perhaps Hamilton's dealings with Robert Cecil in the silver mines included an exchange about the English Lord Treasurer's interest in projects to plant mulberry trees, raise silkworms, and create a British silk industry. Hamilton later noted Moryson's journey among the mulberry trees of the Arno valley. There Moryson broke a bough from a tree to shade himself and was gently warned by a Florentine that a steep fine and prison awaited those who damaged the duke's silkworms and nesting places.[132]

Hamilton very nearly underlined and cribbed the whole of Moryson's chapter on foreign coinage, especially the descriptions of James dealing with the coinage in England, Scotland, and Ireland. Interest in base moneys, so-called farthing tokens of brass and copper, is usually assumed to have been as cynical and self-serving as most projectors' schemes in the period.[133] Hamilton's attention may have included genuine concern for public good. Moryson disputed the conventional wisdom that cheap goods were the surest sign of a poor country, with Poland and Ireland in mind. Rather, 'riches make vs not able to want any thing to serue our appetite, at what price soeuer it is set'.[134] His description of Italy included the analysis of small monies, inflation, and the wasteful rich together with one of his many embedded comparisons:

> The Italians haue small moneys of brasse, and for the least of them a man may buy bread, little pieces of spice, or any such thing that is to be sold. ... This benefit may the English well know by want of like moneys, whereby the hire of Porters, all rewards and each almes being giuen in siluer, and the small pieces thereof being rare, all expences are much increased.[135]

Hamilton wrote in the margin that this was the 'harme by want of small moneyes.'[136]

[131] The pagination in Moryson's original *Itinerary* is not continuous, but restarts with each of the three Parts. References will therefore include the Roman numeral for the Part number and relevant page number. Thus *Itinerary Written by Fynes Moryson* (Tyn.316), I, pp. 11–12 is the correct reference for the Freiburg mines.

[132] *Itinerary Written by Fynes Moryson* (Tyn.316), I, p. 147.

[133] John Cramsie, *Kingship and Crown Finance under James VI and I 1603–1625* (Woodbridge, 2002), pp. 130–4.

[134] *Itinerary Written by Fynes Moryson* (Tyn.316), III, pp. 102–3.

[135] *Itinerary Written by Fynes Moryson* (Tyn.316), III, pp. 113–14.

[136] *Itinerary Written by Fynes Moryson* (Tyn.316), III, p. 150.

Hamilton might well have been an eager reader, but what did he glean about the English and Scots in reading the *Itinerary*? One thing that did not interest Hamilton was Moryson's abbreviated turn through the eastern lowlands, other than the 'good and cheap diet' found in Berwick.[137] Hamilton owned the 1600 edition of *Britannia*, the penultimate Latin edition before the English translation by Philemon Holland in 1610. Hamilton spotted a good number of points in the topographical descriptions of England and Wales that Moryson had borrowed from Camden. Understandably, Hamilton commented on the archbishop of York's disputed jurisdiction over the Scottish Church with underlining, 'Nota', and an unusually large plus. He also noted the Roman wall used to keep out the Picts and the 'Emperike Surgeons (that is, of experience without learning)' of Scotland who regularly passed through Cumberland in search of healing herbs. As he finished reading this chapter, Hamilton betrayed an abiding interest in drunkenness by underlining Moryson's account of the temporary infection of the English with German 'garaussing'. The descriptions of the Germans proper first raised Hamilton's hackles and he penned several fulsome 'nota', including their vomiting and pissing at table. He did not spare the descriptions of his own countrymen, underlining their drinking habits as well.[138]

Hamilton was an intense reader, and that included Moryson's descriptions of Scotland. He underlined virtually the entire description, with one revealing exception. Stirling, Menteith, and Clydesdale took in the former lands of the Damonii. Hamilton underlined only the portion of what Moryson wrote as follows: '<u>Here the Riuer Cluyde runnes by Hamelton (the seate of the Hameltons</u> Family of English race'.[139] 'A now lost account of the family, supposedly written c.1450' reported that the Hamiltons were descended from the earls of Southampton and had fled England during the turmoil of Edward II's reign, while another account suggested the earls of Leicester as their likely progenitors. The English origin 'seems most likely' to modern scholars, but Thomas Hamilton would have none of it in his own time.[140] He also wanted nothing of English dress, noting approvingly Moryson's ensuing critique of their attire, while passing over Scottish habits except for the coarse cloth worn by the wives of inferior citizens and rural folk.[141] There were limits to Hamilton's willingness to support his king's embrace of England and the English, even if kneeling at communion and an English-style royal supremacy over the Presbyterian Kirk were not among them.

It must have been with a thought to his son, either afoot in Europe or about to set out, that Hamilton scrutinized Moryson's instructions and precepts for travellers. Hamilton shared contemporary fears that his son would return home

---

[137] *Itinerary Written by Fynes Moryson* (Tyn.316), I, pp. 272–4.
[138] *Itinerary Written by Fynes Moryson* (Tyn.316), III, pp. 86–90, 144, 152, 156.
[139] *Itinerary Written by Fynes Moryson* (Tyn.316), III, p. 153.
[140] Alan R. Borthwick, 'Hamilton Family', *Oxford DNB* at www.oxforddnb.com.
[141] *Itinerary Written by Fynes Moryson* (Tyn.316), III, pp. 178–80.

changed, corrupted by foreign vices or customs. He recorded with 'nota' an account of a son who had returned from France and refused any longer to ask his father's blessing.[142] However, Moryson was an enthusiastic traveller whose instructions concerned making the most of a journey, and Hamilton read them approvingly. 'For as the Wiseman said,' Moryson wrote and Hamilton cribbed in the margin, 'that he was a Citizen of the World'. 'For my part,' Moryson continued, 'I thinke variety to be the most pleasing thing in the World, and the best life to be, 'neither contemplatiue alone, nor actiue altogether, but mixed of both.' As Moryson warmed to this theme, Hamilton followed through the lines with his pen and summed up how the delight in variety could be exemplified in many ways.[143] Indeed, this precept could well have served as an epitaph for Hamilton. As his original *Dictionary of National Biography* biographer observed: 'Haddington was a student and a man of varied culture. Men of letters were numbered among his friends, and, as is evident from the notes and observations he left behind him, and the marginal references on his books, he was widely read not only in civil law but in history, especially the history of his country.'[144] Hamilton cultivated his intellect while living an active public life. He penned many a law report, memoranda of proceedings, or notes that aided his duties while preserving the collective memory of Scottish governance. His armchair travels with Fynes Moryson served those same ends. Had he known Hamilton or learned what this avid reader had done with his copy of the *Itinerary*, Moryson might have carried on with a little less disappointment.

* * * * *

Moryson called on his books and his travels to create these descriptions of the English and the Scots. It is not hard to spot an important process at work here, though. The ethnography – the descriptions of character, customs, practices, livelihoods, diet, fashion – came alive when he drew on personal experience that he took to be common knowledge. Books played second fiddle, including, for all its descriptive value, Camden's *Britannia*. For Moryson, travel and first-hand experience with cultural complexity were the keys to understanding and describing peoples in contemporary Britain as well as in Ireland, continental Europe, and the Middle East. The failure of Moryson's literary projects deprived readers from his time to our own of a detailed, systematic comparative ethnography written from first-hand travel and direct experience. The descriptions from the *Itinerary* give some sense of what that ethnography would have read like. One caveat becomes obvious. Moryson found it practical and congenial to write

---

[142] *Itinerary Written by Fynes Moryson* (Tyn.316), III, pp. 3–6.
[143] *Itinerary Written by Fynes Moryson* (Tyn.316), III, p. 10.
[144] T.F. Henderson, 'Thomas Hamilton', *Dictionary of National Biography* (Oxford, 1890) archived at *www.oxforddnb.com*.

in terms of distinct nations: English, Scots, French, and the like. How well he accommodated the experience with complexity from locale to locale, beneath these handy and homogenizing labels, remains an important question. We now turn to the 'Manuscript' to gauge the extent of what was lost.

6

English Between the Lines

Fynes Moryson began his account of Germany in the *Itinerary* with the observation that it experienced 'farre greater cold then England lying more Northerly'. It does not say much for Moryson's sense of latitude, but the cultural implications were notable.[1] Moryson described the 'hot stoves' or saunas used by Germans to counter their cold clime:

> And as well to keepe out cold as to retaine the heate, they keepe the dores and windowes closely shut; so as they using not only to receive Gentlemen into these stoves, but even to permitt rammish clownes to stand by the oven till their wet clothes be dried, and themselves sweat, yea, to indure their little children to sit upon their close stooles, and ease themselves within this close and hot stove (let the Reader pardon my rude speech, as I bore with the bad smell), it must needes be, that these ill smelles, never purged by the admitting of any fresh ayre, should dull the braine, and almost choke the spirits of those who frequent the stoves.[2]

Moryson did not at first enjoy the experience, but 'after I had used them, custome became another nature, for I never injoyed my health in any place better then there'.[3]

The importance of dried and stored fruit in the German diet followed, as did comments about clothing and climate that neatly segued into commodities:

> The Italians have a Proverb ... God gives cloathes according to the colds, as to the cold Muscovites hee hath given furres, to the English wooll for cloth, to the French divers light stuffes, and to Southerlie people stoore of silkes, that all Nations abounding in some things, and wanting others, might be taught, that they have neede of one anothers helpe ...[4]

Men of inferior rank tended to wear coarse German cloth. Gentlemen and the better sort enjoyed colourful clothing – they explained to Moryson that 'the variety of colours shewed the variety of God's workes'. They liked English cloth

---

[1] *The Itinerary of Fynes Moryson in Four Volumes* (four volumes; Glasgow, 1907), IV, p. 14, hereafter cited as Moryson, *Itinerary*.
[2] Moryson, *Itinerary*, IV, p. 15.
[3] Moryson, *Itinerary*, IV, p. 15.
[4] Moryson, *Itinerary*, IV, p. 17.

of green or yellow rather than Italian silks and velvets. It was in the context of
sober German apparel that Moryson would have expected his attack on English
fashion and general approval of Scottish habits – women who dressed after the
German fashion – to be read.[5]

Of German traffic, Moryson reported:

> I never observed them to have any common prayers morning or evening as our English
> ships have while they bee at Sea, but the Marriners of their own accord use continually
> to sing Psalmes, and they are punished by the purse who sweare, or so much as once
> name the divell, from which they abhore. And herein they deserve to be praysed above
> the Hollanders, in whose ships a man shall heare no mention of God or his worship.[6]

Whatever their tastes in fashion, the English stood first in piety at sea, followed
closely by the Germans, with their great rivals the Dutch in near proximity to
the atheists, despite their Calvinist credentials. Bringing these and other topics
together, Moryson wrote that the Germans prospered from not playing 'at Dice,
seldom at Cardes, and that for small wagers. They seldome feaste, and sparingly ...
They are apparelled with homely stuffes, and weare their clothes to the uttermost
of their lasting, their household stuffe is poore, in gifts they are most sparing.'[7]
The contrast with the English in attire – and a love of dice and cards he would
later explain – could not be more marked.[8]

Moryson littered the chapters of the 'Itinerary' with just such cross-cultural
comparisons. He expected his readers to study the individual chapters with
reference to one another, and stick to his topical organization. Readers should
study all of the dominions through their polities before moving on to religious
practices and descriptions of their peoples. If we defy Moryson's design, we miss
many explicit and implicit comparisons between the English and their European
and Ottoman neighbours. Moryson encountered people who had much to teach
him about his fellow English and the English about themselves. His Britain was
a geographical space for travel, encounters with cultural complexity, and experiences of civility, barbarity, and the 'Other' just as much as the Continent,
the East, the Orient, or the Empire. His ethnographic framework and practice
of cross-cultural comparison and interrogation thus defied the too-often
parochial gaze of his contemporaries. Reading between the lines challenges us
not to separate Moryson's travels in and outwith Britain from each other and
perpetuate assumptions of island distinctiveness or alien 'otherness'. Almost
inevitably, given the canvas over which he travelled, Moryson's descriptions tend
to focus on the qualities of nations and patterns of migration, settlement, and

[5] Moryson, *Itinerary*, IV, pp. 204–11.
[6] Moryson, *Itinerary*, IV, pp. 19–20.
[7] Moryson, *Itinerary*, IV, p. 17.
[8] Graham Kew, 'Shakespeare's Europe Revisited: The Unpublished *Itinerary* of Fynes
Moryson (1566–1630)' (Ph.D. thesis; Birmingham University, 1995), p. 1665, hereafter cited
as 'Unpublished *Itinerary*'.

cultural exchange that shaped them. There was simply less scope or space for the complexity he encountered locally to find its way into the narrative. Ultimately, this analysis helps us to appreciate the kind of ethnography that Britons lost when Moryson abandoned his work in the 1620s.

Men and women of many natures

Moryson tackled three massive topics in the 'Itinerary': polities or 'common-wealths' as he called them, religion, and the character of peoples.[9] No analysis can examine the cultural complexity across all of these. This chapter focuses on ethnography through Moryson's chapters on the characters of peoples. He studied them through the same set of categories: nature, manners, strength of body, and wits; manual arts and sciences; universities and schools; language; ceremonies associated with marriage, childbearing, christenings, and funerals; diverse customs; sports and exercises, especially hunting, hawking, fowling, birding, and fishing. He chose categories that reflected his own interests and those to be found in well-established authors from Sebastian Münster to Ranulf Higden and William Harrison.[10] In these chapters Moryson repeated material from others about situation, apparel, polities, and religion; matters that he thought captured the essential character of these peoples.[11] But the most direct comparisons drew on his own experiences, especially in Germany and the Ottoman empire, where Moryson spent the most time.[12] Still, virtually every dominion acted as a mirror for Moryson in evaluating his fellow countrymen and women.

Moryson first concerned himself with peoples' essential nature and manners (typical behaviours). Moryson praised the Germans for integrity, trustworthi-ness, constancy, equity, gravity though tending toward dullness, simplicity that made them suspicious of being deceived, coolness in argument and debate, and modesty, especially in women. But they inclined to 'one Nationall vice of drunckennes in such excesse (espetially the Saxons), as it staynes all theire Nationall vertues'.[13] The warrior Swiss might share with their German cousins the estimable quality of quietly returning to 'civilian' pursuits after fighting in the wars, but those 'rude inhabiters of mountaynes' covered for much of the year with snow 'haue no smalle invitation to spend the tyme in drincking'. That said, the Swiss were apt to avoid sharp quarrels when drunk, while the vigilance of magistrates and 'cheefe men' worked to deter some measure of excess.[14]

---

[9] Recall that the commonwealths in Germany, Switzerland, and the Netherlands were included in the 1617 *Itinerary*.

[10] 'Unpublished *Itinerary*', pp. xc–xcii, cxii–cxxvii.

[11] Compare Moryson, *Itinerary*, IV, p. 15 with 'Unpublished *Itinerary*', pp. 1212–13.

[12] 'Unpublished *Itinerary*', pp. 1209–13.

[13] 'Unpublished *Itinerary*', p. 1201.

[14] 'Unpublished *Itinerary*', pp. 1320–2; also Moryson, *Itinerary*, IV, p. 415.

Excessive drinking likewise plagued the Danes, but Moryson put this down to their ethnic origins. The southern provinces like Schleswig were 'still inhabited by the Saxons of Germany' and shared the Saxons' nature and manners, while the Danish islands adopted many of the same 'vertues, vices, and Customes' by virtue of contact and cultural exchange.[15] Heavy drinking and some measure of related disorders plagued the Bohemians and Poles.[16] Islamic prohibitions on drink did not quite work as planned, in Moryson's experience: 'to this day they plant no vines themselues, but when they come where Christians haue it, they take it in this age, freely giuen, or by force, and drincke it with great excesse'. He continued, 'in the houses I haue seene some drincke Harac a kynde of Aquauity (allowed by their lawe) in such measure, as I thought would [not] only take away theire sences but burne their entralls'.[17] The French and English distinguished themselves by reproaching drunkenness. Moryson's stand on the Scots' reputation for drunkenness was one of polite qualification.[18]

Drunkenness explained social ills – quarrelling and violence – or incapacity in marks of civility like manual arts, hard work, or enterprise. Such vices became especially potent forms of ethnographic commentary when integrated with gender, a category of interest to Moryson. The Bohemians suffered from just this combination (plus Catholicism):

> Agayne the wemen of Bohemia, Contrary to the Custome of the women in Germany drincke with as large intemperance as the men, and goe alone by themselues without the company of men to Taverns and Schenckhausen (or houses where beare is solde) And so come shorte of that Modesty and chastitie for which the wemen of Germany are renowned. Nether are they indeede generally reputed so chast as the wemen of Germany. Besides that according to the generall liberty giuen by the Roman Church (not only in Italy but also in Polonia), the Citty Prage hath a publike Stewes allowed by the Magistrate where the Harlotts dwell[ing] in streetes appointed for their habitation.[19]

Germany provided the standard for female modesty, not least because German women 'hold it obscenity once to name their Duggs [breasts], much lesse will they expose them to sight, and least of all permitt them to be touched'.[20] They thus invited a cool contrast with those Englishwomen whose tastes in fashion included exposed cleavage, but a favourable comparison for Scotswomen. The women of both Scotland and England presumably compared favourably for sobriety.

Moryson wrote that the women of the Netherlands (and their male counterparts) adhered to customs that 'seemed very strange to me'. Landing at Dokkum

---

[15] 'Unpublished *Itinerary*', pp. 1380–2.
[16] 'Unpublished *Itinerary*', pp. 1399, 1413–14.
[17] 'Unpublished *Itinerary*', p. 1479.
[18] Moryson, *Itinerary*, IV, pp. 142, 176, 184–5.
[19] 'Unpublished *Itinerary*', p. 1399.
[20] 'Unpublished *Itinerary*', p. 1202.

in Friesland, Moryson found a group of gentlewomen of special worth and beauty. At the inn they 'supped not priuately in theire Chambers, according to the Custome of England, but at the publike table for all passengers, and after supper retyred to the fyre, where formes were sett round about it, and Flagons of Beare sett to warme at the fyer'.[21] Stranger things were to come:

> If a man drincke to a woman, he carryed her the Cupp, and kissed her, and a woman drincking to a man carryed the Cupp to him, and kissed him not so much as bending his head to meete her ... This is the generall Custome in all Fresland, so as some husbandes haue quarrelled with men, for not kissing their wyues and daughters at the deliuery of the Cupp to them, as if they thought them not worthy of that Curtesy, or dispised them, as poore, foule, or reputed infamous.[22]

'But nothing is more strang,' according to Moryson's English sense of propriety and gender roles, 'then that this Custome, though performed in much mirth and cheerefullnes yet is free from the least suspition of vnchastity.'[23]

The Dutch persistently reversed gender roles. Demographics favoured women, and they made good on their numbers:

> In the morning they giue theire husbandes drincking mony in their pursses, who goe abroad to be merry when they list, leaving theire wyues to keepe the shop and sell all thinges. And nothing is more frequent, then to see the girles to insult and domineere (with reproofes and nicknames) ouer theire brothers. ... Yea many woemen go to Sea to traffique at Hamburg for marchantdize, whyle theire husbands stay at home.[24]

The 'young wenches' of Leiden showed no shame at ordinarily doing 'those necessityes of nature in the open and fayre streetes, which our wemen will not be seene to doe in private houses'. Their menfolk milked cows and carried pails fastened to a 'wooden yoke ... which they wore about their neckes' in a manner that must have been equally different from English practice. Seeing the Dutch women sport linen trousers against the cold, biting wind must have seemed positively mundane by comparison, even if 'the Virgins in winter tyme are most braue in apparell, and haue most Iollity of meeting with young men' on the frozen canals.[25]

Moryson hoped that these 'old customes of particular places, are no certaine signes of unchastity', but he struggled to account for them nonetheless.[26] Was it something to do with wartime losses, a phlegmatic humour bred by the watery provinces that disabled men from begetting males, or women putting off marriage until their thirties, 'which must needs make the Women more powerfull in generation'? Moryson would almost certainly have lighted on social

---

[21] 'Unpublished *Itinerary*', p. 1367.
[22] 'Unpublished *Itinerary*', p. 1367.
[23] 'Unpublished *Itinerary*', p. 1367.
[24] 'Unpublished *Itinerary*', p. 1368.
[25] 'Unpublished *Itinerary*', pp. 1369–70.
[26] Moryson, *Itinerary*, III, p. 420.

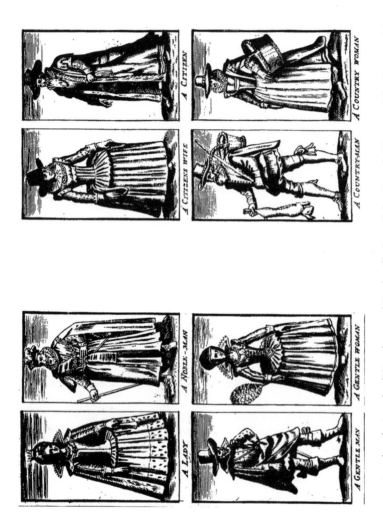

13 Ethnographic engravings bordering the 'Kingdome of England', from John Speed, *Theatre of the Empire of Great Britain* (London, 1676). Huntington Library, San Marino, CA (RB 204587), reproduced by permission. Image published with permission by ProQuest. Further reproduction is prohibited without permission.

practices as an explanation. As he reflected elsewhere, 'Barbarous people as beasts are easily provoked, and by art soone appeased, and hauing not the sterne of reason to governe them, are caryed to and fro in a moment of blynde force of nature, as also ignorant Chilldren and wemen easily change all affections.'[27] Indeed, Moryson devoted a good deal of attention to family relationships and gender practices in his analysis of the legal regimes in different dominions, clearly seeing in them the codification of both social customs and some measure of civility against barbarous practices. For this reason Moryson took the time to explain laws concerning adultery, protection of virginal reputations, bastardy, and the rights of wives, widows, and female children and relatives.[28] Not surprisingly, then, he ultimately put little or no weight on climactic or biological explanations: 'I should be too credulous, if I should thinke All Families to be sicke of this disease; and I must confesse, that in few other Nations all Families are altogether free from like accidents: but I may boldy say, that the Women of these parts, are above all other truly taxed with this unnatural dominering over their Husbands.'[29]

Moryson found plenty of women and gender practices in other lands that challenged his sensibilities and to which English women might be favourably compared. Some Danish (and German) mothers brought 'young Harlotts' into their houses to nurse their children, though no mother sent her children out of doors to be nursed. Polish and French women, by contrast, took 'nurses' into their homes, but otherwise followed the same practices.[30] English women (and men) compared unfavourably in attire, but two customs among French women cast their English counterparts in a better light: carrying 'the badge of pryde at their girdles, namely litle looking glasses, therein to beholde their faces and attyre' and using masks to cover their faces and walk 'with great liberty ... euen alone without any man to attend them in the streetes of Paris ... the husband meeting his wife in the streete can hardly know her'.[31]

Their enviable mastery of global trade brought the Dutch into contact with all manner of peoples. Yet neither those encounters nor the wealth that came from them changed the fundamental Dutch character. They remained a just and unpretentious people, frugal in diet and appearance.[32] They might be free of the Germans' morose nature, but the Dutch gave in to drinking quarrels (like the English) spurred by 'base ignominious raylings, and horrible oathes' and settled too frequently by knife fights (according to well-agreed rules). Even so, temperance virtually ruled by comparison to Germany, and Dutchmen were

---

[27] 'Unpublished *Itinerary*', p. 1633.
[28] See the attention Moryson devoted to women under German law, especially Moryson, *Itinerary*, IV, pp. 298–324.
[29] Moryson, *Itinerary*, IV, pp. 468–9.
[30] 'Unpublished *Itinerary*', pp. 1392, 1423, 1649.
[31] 'Unpublished *Itinerary*', p. 1651.
[32] Moryson, *Itinerary*, I, p. 48.

more physically robust, thanks to exercise and avoiding the Germans' hot-stoves. The women of Brabant and Flanders were very fair and attired in simple linen that set off their beauty, but Moryson could not say the same of the women of Holland. Simplicity could never be attributed to the English, thanks to their fashion sense: the Dutch made the point when they greeted Moryson and his English bretheren with strange gazes and fingers curious to feel their apparel 'as if they had neuer seene a stranger'. Nonetheless, Moryson had no doubt that they excelled any people, including his own, as 'most witting in all meanes to grow rich, as the experience of our age hath taught vs'.[33]

The Dutch gained refinement from their French neighbours but they did not borrow their defining quality of levity. Moryson, drawing directly from Jean Bodin, described 'a quicke nimblenes in motions and actions ... all wayes laughing and skipping ... so nimble in gestures, as they seeme to talke with head and hand aswell as with the toung; and when they goe the Spaniards say they runne, and in all Counsells they haue dispatched the buisines before the Spaniards can enter into consultation of it'.[34] Moryson may have enjoyed Bodin's jibe at the Spaniards' expense, but he also thought that French levity produced inconstancy. He noted the tendency to civil war, not least the religious wars of the 1570s. Irresolution also caused the fickle love for changing fashion, to which Moryson traced English fashion sense. The French were to that day 'reputed great dissemblers', though if the influence of the Jesuits might be beaten back they could be saved from the disingenuousness of the Italians. They also had some natural inclination to quarrels, suffered from a 'venerious' disposition with 'the spirite of Clarett wyne in their agilitie of their bodyes', and did not run to fat, despite their frequent daily meals, thanks to their quickness of body and spirit, 'keeping them continually in mirth and motion, being euer leaping and singing'.[35]

Comparisons of the Danes, Bohemians, and Poles with the English worked across a fairly narrow range of qualities. Not so when Moryson turned his pen to describing the Ottoman Turks or their many subject peoples: 'The Turkes Empire is so vast, and consists of so many Provinces, and nations no lesse differing in nature and all conditions one from the other, then distant in remote Clymes, as whatsoeuer may be sayd of their nature, manners and the like cannot possibly agree to all persons and seuerall partes of them.'[36] When writing in general terms, then, Moryson described the metropolitan Turks, those who ruled the empire and occupied its most populous territories, especially the Mediterranean coasts.

Sensitive to the cultural complexity of the empire Moryson may have been, but he was in no doubt about its peoples' essential 'beastly nature':

---

[33] 'Unpublished *Itinerary*', pp. 1338–44; Moryson, *Itinerary*, IV, p. 467.
[34] 'Unpublished *Itinerary*', pp. 1630–1.
[35] 'Unpublished *Itinerary*', pp. 1633–42.
[36] 'Unpublished *Itinerary*', p. 1427; Moryson, *Itinerary*, IV, p. 119.

I will say generally in a word, that they are inhabited with Mores and Arabians, and the scumme of many nations, as barbarous, theevish, base, ignorant, Cruell, and wicked people, as can be imagined, likely to crucifye out [sic] lord agayne and agayne ... as they cease not daily to persecute him in his members. ... Generally the Turkes are a people most proude, disdaynefull, inhospitall, cruell, boasting & thincking no nation like them selues either for wisdome or Valor ... [37]

The Turk who grabbed Moryson's hat for a 'Close stoole' offered just one of many insults that he tasted as a stranger from those who thought 'destroying Christians, the most rea[d]y way to paradise'. Not surprisingly, the Turks kept no inns and the only lodging available was from 'poore Christians liuing miserably vnder them'. However, ordinary Turks fought among themselves too, brawling with and chiding one another 'like Oyster wyues', but never with weapons, given the cruel severity of justice for those found to have drawn blood in a quarrel. [38]

Ottoman practices offered the most exotic comparison with English women. The jealous nature of Turkish men kept 'theire wemen most strictly from the sight of all men'. Husbands, fathers, and eunuchs alone were permitted sight of Turkish women and seclusion was the rule, except for those few times a week when women were allowed to visit the public baths or their friends, travelling together and fully covered. For Moryson this was not reverence or piety but tyranny. He linked the practice to the tyrannical castration of eunuchs, offering a graphic account of how 'they cutt off all the Preuities flatt to the belly, leauing them a litle hole to voyde vrine, for which purpose they vse a quill'. [39] Jealousy, tyranny, cowardice, and disordered nature found sexual expressions: 'The Turkes are generally more giuen to fleshly lust, towardes wemen and males, espetially faire boyes, then any Italians, Greekes, or any other nation whatsoeuer, yea the very wemen vse no lesse vnnaturall lusts among themselues.' Moryson described the sexual practices before praising one Turkish manner, the reverence shown toward parents and elders. Turkish women came in for some qualified praise, especially their large, dark eyes and fair skin, but Ottoman society valued them only physically and sexually, with no regard for 'learning or qualities of mynde'. [40] In contrast, Moryson would have had before him the life of his own queen or the examples of learned Englishwomen like Margaret Roper, Catherine Parr, or the scholarly and well-connected Cooke sisters Mildred, Ann, Katherine, and Elizabeth (partners of William Cecil, Nicholas Bacon, Henry Killigrew, and John Russell, respectively).

The Turks affected 'singular gravity in behauior and dispise[d] merye Iesting persons' and were extremely covetous by nature. They typically sated their greed in sexual indulgence, rich clothes, and gormandizing, even while being among the most idle, slothful, and base people in the world. Not surprisingly, the

---

[37] 'Unpublished *Itinerary*', pp. 1427–8.
[38] 'Unpublished *Itinerary*', pp. 1429–30.
[39] 'Unpublished *Itinerary*', pp. 1432–4.
[40] 'Unpublished *Itinerary*', pp. 1432–41, 1477, 1487.

Turks ran to fat and were a people of little spirit and a 'dull grosse wit'. With heads shaven but for one lock, hairy eyebrows, and full massive beards, Turkish men had no need of England's superior barbers. As for the rest of their body hair, 'they alltogether take [it] away when they bathe, with a Redd powder that makes it fall off by the rootes'. The seclusion of the women contributed to fair complexions, but overzealous cleanliness from religious devotion left them prematurely wrinkled. While some men were valued as sailors or smiths or saddlers, Moryson concluded that there was little regard for learning or qualities of mind – something of a change from early Renaissance attitudes about the Ottoman court or active cultural engagement with it.[41]

Arts, sciences, and learning

If civility and barbarity could be assessed by a people's nature and gender norms, Moryson believed their arts, sciences, and learning equally instructive. Fresh from Peterhouse with a passport to study civil law, and a fascination for languages, Moryson naturally placed great store in institutions of learning. Indeed, he seems to have left Peterhouse with an obsessive interest in the minutiae of academia, everything from gowns and attire, famous faculty, ranks and appointments, pedagogy, lectures and disputations, courses and degrees, examinations, university officers and regulations to lodging and diet, parents, and academic life generally. He scrutinized Wittenberg, Leiden, and Padua at first hand as a student. German universities mirrored the empire's political decentralization and it 'were infinite to describe them all', so Moryson chose Wittenberg as the example 'where by the quallity of the rest may be gathered'.[42]

In Oxford and Cambridge England possessed universities 'wherein no kingdome can compayre with it by many degrees' and they excelled 'all other in the worlde ... in the magnificall foundation of them' and in many subjects and degrees.[43] Even so, the Germans had one thing to teach their English counterparts, who in Moryson's telling found the German devotion to academic learning just a bit impractical and idle.[44] The 'richer sort' of German parents sent their children's private tutors on to university with them. If English parents copied the practice, it would ensure 'Children would not leese so much tyme as they doe, espetially in the vniversities, where our English parents seldome enquire after the diligence of Tutors to whome they committ their Children'.[45]

[41] Lisa Jardine, *Worldly Goods: A New History of the Renaissance* (London, 1996), pp. 130, 137–9, 231–2, 251–2; Lisa Jardine and Jerry Brotton, *Global Interests: Renaissance Art between East and West* (Ithaca, NY, 2000).

[42] 'Unpublished *Itinerary*', pp. 1229–54.

[43] 'Unpublished *Itinerary*', pp. 1643–4, 1667.

[44] Moryson, *Itinerary*, IV, p. 326.

[45] 'Unpublished *Itinerary*', pp. 1241–2.

Whether Moryson had his father or his own tutors in mind is hard to say, but the 'helicopter parents' of his modern counterparts need no encouragement.

Student life at German universities bothered Moryson. Unlike their English counterparts, German universities lacked proctors to 'keepe the night watches', so nothing was more frequent at Wittenberg than for students to frequent prostitutes and parade through the streets drunk and rowdy.[46] German universities retained ridiculous traditions and ceremonies. For example, German freshmen were admitted or 'salted' in a ceremony called the deposition of horns, which, it was claimed, was first used at the 'Vniversity of Athens'. This hazing began with students lying within a magic circle. The depositor made to remove their horns with a pair of pinchers before stretching shorter students and mock cutting-down to size the taller ones. The students rose up when water was cast on them and then faced a long barrage of 'Captious and sophisticall questions' to test their wits and constancy before being led to a bath. Then the students were bidden to take off their filthy garments and pronounced civil in apparel and manners after receiving a bit of salt in the mouth and having wine poured on them.[47] Evidently this interested Moryson because there were no peculiar ceremonies or hazing at English colleges!

For a committed Protestant, Switzerland offered fine schools and Moryson singled out Basel and Zurich – though 'no vniversity' – for particular praise. Switzerland produced many scholars of divinity and they supported the well-furnished bookshops, despite the utilitarian and martial quality of Swiss learning. Religious divides plagued Dutch universities, and Moryson approved of the foundation of Leiden to keep young minds from Jesuit-dominated Douai. The Dutch could be justly proud of having produced Agricola and Erasmus, even if their players and comedians were the poorest 'that can be imagined'.[48] In contrast to English students, only the poorest Danish students at Copenhagen University lived in college. The most privileged Dutch students quickly left Copenhagen for the universities of Germany; a pattern that was repeated in Poland, save for those students who studied at Cracow.[49]

Of all the European universities, Paris earned the most respect from Moryson because it so nearly captured the structure and magnificence of Cambridge and Oxford. Academic freedom of a sort mattered to Moryson, and he praised François I, 'bred in that vniversity', for restoring Paris's liberties after the armed oppression of Louis XII. François expanded its privileges and added professors in Languages and Mathematics to their colleagues in Divinity, Law, Medicine, and Arts.[50] Not surprisingly, then, Moryson praised the skill and maturity with which the French wrote about science, as well as the fame that attached to their

---

[46] 'Unpublished *Itinerary*', p. 1247.
[47] 'Unpublished *Itinerary*', pp. 1249–51.
[48] 'Unpublished *Itinerary*', p. 1347.
[49] 'Unpublished *Itinerary*', pp. 1325–30, 1348–50, 1417.
[50] 'Unpublished *Itinerary*', pp. 1644–7.

doctors of civil and canon law, learned physicians, and reformed divines 'for their sound doctrynes in the Pulpitt, and in their printed bookes'.[51]

If Moryson saw in Paris and the English universities a kind of academic freedom that was unique or particularly praiseworthy, he could not say the same for the Ottoman empire. By Moryson's account, the Turks believed that learning among Christians only made them factious and opened the way to Ottoman advances in the Balkans. Their 'cheefe learning being in the skill of Mahometts lawe, and their Priests being reputed great Clarkes who can reade it, being written in the Arabian toung, and can make, a dull and verball exposition of the Text'.[52] Antoine Geuffroy's description of the court of the Great Turk (Paris, 1546) supplied Moryson with information about the Arabic editions of Aristotle – at which he fairly sniffed – stories of paper painted with weapons of war carried into battle like lucky charms, and the segregated schools in which men and women respectively learned 'Philosophy, Astronomy, and Poetry'.[53] Moryson seemed willing to accept 'some skill in Philosophy', 'Phisicke [learned] by experience rather than art', astronomy for purposes of fortune telling, and a 'good guift for Poetry' among the Turks, thanks to George Sandys' account (c. 1615).[54]

Moryson called up his first-hand experience to trump any possibility that the English could learn from the Ottomans:

> For my parte I holde the Turkes to be generally a most Ignorant nation, blessing themselues in this ignorance, as giving them much ease, for howsoeuer the Priests haue skill to reade, and in akynde to expounde theire lawe in the Arabian tongue, yet they [sic] lay Turkes are so Ignorant … it is dangerous for any man, to vse foule paper [toilet roll] to such base vses as Christians Commonly doe. For the Turkes are so ignorant, and superstitious, as seeing any peece of written paper lye on the grounde, they take it and lay it vp with reverence, suppising [sic] some wordes of the [warrior] Alcoron may be written therein.[55]

Moryson still found the Ottomans deviant, simply by definition. His analytical categories could not accommodate them, for, as he wrote, 'Nether did I euer fynde any of the foresayd publike schooles much lesse vniversityes among them, except those schooles which are to trayne vp young Ianisaryes in military exercises.' Nor could they be accommodated within his own experience or powerfully English cultural assumptions: printing was unknown, lawyers were wholly absent in an 'expidite [i.e. arbitrary] course of Iustice' which allowed for 'litle or no

---

51 'Unpublished *Itinerary*', p. 1643.
52 'Unpublished *Itinerary*', pp. 1444–5.
53 'Unpublished *Itinerary*', p. 1445.
54 'Unpublished *Itinerary*', p. 1446.
55 'Unpublished *Itinerary*', pp. 1447, 1486. The latter is a more pejorative account of a very similar description in the earlier section; 'if they see a paper lye on the grounde, they take it vp and with a kisse lay it vp, saying that parhapps some wordes of the [warrior] Ancoron are written in it'.

pleading', and histories were despised 'because men dare not write truly of tymes present, nor well knowe tymes past'.[56] For 'those that write otherwise', Moryson reiterated, 'the Turkes generally to be very Ignorant'.[57]

Moryson was not simply an esoteric intellectual in all this. Skills in 'practical' arts, professions, and the sciences mattered. The dullness and intemperance of the Germans did not prevent Moryson from commending their excellence in manual arts. For this he credited their industry and plodding diligence in chosen 'professions'. He implicitly contrasted the English (and others) who 'affect to haue some superficiall knowledg in all thinges, for discourse and ostentation of learning'. The English had their love of foreign commodities and willingness to import foreign expertise, but the Germans were 'famous … among all nations' for their manufactures 'by which also they bring from them much mony into Germany'.[58] He naturally mentioned Gutenberg, along with watermills, self-rocking cradles, wheeled ploughs, and the precision of German clocks, fit for expanding their knowledge of astronomy.[59]

German respect for manual labour made for a very different experience of apprenticeship compared with its English counterpart: artisanal skill was celebrated in yearly feasts, artisans worked in closed chambers with stoves rather than braving the cold in open shops, and German masters treated their apprentices 'with much lesse severity then our Artizans doe in England'. In Germany, journeymen lived up to the term, travelling widely and perfecting their skills in 'the houses of the best workmen of their trade' as a right. Such mobility sat uneasy with English prejudices about masterless men, flogging so-called sturdy beggars, praising hunger as a powerful inducement to industriousness among artisans, and, later, driving feckless, idle Gaels and Amerindians off their lands.[60] Plodding diligence was in part a practical reaction among Germans to their love of drink: 'distrusting theire memoryes, weakned with Continuall drincking', they relied upon mere memory.[61] Perhaps for this reason German (and Dutch) professors 'dictate theire Lectures, and the Students write them worde for worde'.[62]

German physicians could teach their English counterparts and others something, as Moryson learned at first hand when he fell ill at Leipzig. He deemed them very honest, learned, and practitioners of an admirable standard of care: 'they visitt the sicke twise each day, with much diligence and compassionate Curtesye, not scorning to handle any sore parte, or to looke vpon any Ordure, to discouer the disease'. Further, they broke all convention by refusing payment

---

[56] Moryson, *Itinerary*, II, pp. 58–9.
[57] 'Unpublished *Itinerary*', pp. 1447–8.
[58] 'Unpublished *Itinerary*', p. 1215.
[59] 'Unpublished *Itinerary*', pp. 1216–17; Moryson, *Itinerary*, I, pp. 35–6.
[60] 'Unpublished *Itinerary*', pp. 1218–19, 1662; Moryson, *Itinerary*, IV, p. 32.
[61] 'Unpublished *Itinerary*', p. 1244.
[62] 'Unpublished *Itinerary*', p. 1350.

unless their ministrations worked and taking no more than their scheduled fees, no matter the severity of the illness. Apothecaries met similar standards of professionalism. Perhaps, for this reason, fewer empirics or mountebanks worked to sooth the sick with their potions and ointments.[63] Moryson found charlatans at home in the Anglo-Scottish Borders: 'the Emperike Surgeons (that is, of experience without learning), of Scotland come yeerely to those fields of the borders, to gather hearbs, good to heale wounds, and planted there by the bordering souldiers of the Romans, the vertue of which herbs they wonderfully extoll.'[64]

Just one nation could best the Germans for industriousness: Britain's great commercial rivals in the Low Countries.[65] Neither the *Itinerary* nor the 'Manuscript' could have added to what was commonly attributed to Dutch industriousness and commercial prowess.[66] Trade and value-added industries underpinned Dutch prosperity: raw silk bought in from Turkey, woven in Italy, and transported into England; linen, wool, and cotton turned into cloth and Arras tapestries; Danzig hemp made into ropes and cables; English herring caught, salted, and sold far and wide.[67] As one anonymous contemporary bluntly put it:

> what wee [English] doe; what they [Dutch] doe:
> wee make clothes, they dresse itt.
> wee raise wooles, they dresse them.
> wee make tynne, they worke itt.
> wee have ffishing, they the fishe.
> wee have coales, they transporte them ...
> in course of m[er]chandise exceed us & all ye world.[68]

For Moryson, cloth and Arras hangings were only the most obvious instances in which the Dutch excelled even the Germans, let alone his fellow English.

More than skill and aptitude were at work. Even 'the richest amongst them cause theire Children to be taught some arte or trade, whereby they may gayne theire bread in the tymes of warr, of banishment, or of like adversityes', while Dutch journeymen, like their German neighbours, travelled widely to work alongside the finest masters. Indeed, Dutch orphanages were charged to send the best wits to university and put the others to trade.[69] And, in implicit rebuke of their competitors, Moryson praised the Dutch willingness to live sparingly in far-flung cities so as to gain local knowledge and advantage in sourcing cheap

[63] 'Unpublished *Itinerary*', pp. 1222–3.
[64] Moryson, *Itinerary*, IV, p. 160.
[65] 'Unpublished *Itinerary*', p. 1642; regarding the French, Moryson, *Itinerary*, IV, pp. 136–7.
[66] Moryson, *Itinerary*, IV, pp. 474–7; John Cramsie, 'Commercial Projects and the Fiscal Policy of James VI and I', *The Historical Journal* 43.2 (2000), pp. 345–64.
[67] Moryson, *Itinerary*, IV, pp. 55–6.
[68] Quoted in Cramsie, 'Commercial Projects', p. 349.
[69] 'Unpublished *Itinerary*', p. 1354.

goods for finishing or re-export.[70] By this means, Moryson wrote, 'they draw the commodities of all Nations to them, and fetch them from the very Indies, and in like sort they transport them to the remotest parts, where they yeeld most gain'.[71] Despite its own landed and commercial wealth, England could still learn from the industrious Germans and the adroit trading of the Dutch. The inferiority of Dutch barbers or German players must have been small consolation.

Linguistic contrasts

Moryson's longest periods of settled living occurred when he set his mind to learning German in Wittenberg and Leipzig. Linguistics mattered to him intellectually, practically, and as a marker of civility or barbarity. He was more at ease praising English, its native speakers, and the English facility for languages than any features of his countrymen and women, other than their commitment to the reformed religion. Here the English compared more favourably with their industrious Protestant co-religionists in Germany. For Moryson, Latin, Slavonic, and Germanic were the 'fountaynes of all the most parts of the languages of Europe' and the Germans were ready conversationalists in Latin, 'hauing practised the same from their Childhood' (along with music and mathematics). Indeed they bettered the English in conversational fluency to start – 'wee never vsing it but in disputations' – but 'after small practise, we speake it more readily and eligantly'.[72] In Moryson's mind this was a clear benefit of the academic study of Latin at university, especially 'long vse of Grammer and reading of Authors' rather than conversational learning.[73] German itself contained many words from Latin and Greek – 'from whome also they tooke the Custome of larg drincking and long feasts' – and Moryson adopted an accusatory tone in describing the Germans' 'ill dissembling and borowing of them, not otherwise disguising the worde then by adding some leter to the end'.[74]

Despite classical borrowing, Moryson considered German 'more fitt rudely to commande' than to woo a heart's desire or offer a pleasing sound of civility, 'it being an Imperious short and rude kynde of speech, and such as would make our Children affrayd to heare it'. This carried over into the German preference for loud music, and even in 'still musicke of Lutes and like Instruments' they like those 'who strike hard vpon the strings'.[75] Many 'abuses in pronounciation' led to tragi-comic results: the mispronunciation of 'v' by a German in Italy produced not the statement 'I have seen the Pope with all the Cardinals'

---

[70] Moryson, *Itinerary*, IV, p. 55.
[71] Moryson, *Itinerary*, IV, p. 56.
[72] 'Unpublished *Itinerary*', pp. 1254–5.
[73] 'Unpublished *Itinerary*', p. 1255.
[74] 'Unpublished *Itinerary*', p. 1257.
[75] 'Unpublished *Itinerary*', p. 1221.

but 'I have buggered the Pope, with all the Cardinals'. Further mistakes led to Pythonesque moments involving courtesans and bordellos. The passage of time had changed the meaning of English words with Anglo-Saxon-Germanic origins on top of other odd usages: 'master' for those acquiring an M.A. at university as against Die Herrn or 'lord'.[76] Competing English and Dutch use of 'master' produced its own social comedy at the expense of the English social order: when Queen Elizabeth's English officers were saluted by their soldiers as masters, the Dutch wondered why tradesmen 'should be so brave in apparell'.[77]

Bohemia provided Moryson with an early example of the sort of polyglot language communities that would bedevil the Habsburgs right through to the empire's demise in 1918:

> [When] the late Emperor, at his admittance to be king of Bohemia, prommiced his Oath in the Garman [sic] toung, the Moravians refuse to take or giue Oath otherwise then in their owne toung, which the Emperor not vnderstanding, was notwithstanding forced to learne ... the Province Silesia, incorporated also to that kingdome vseth theire owne German language ... The Bohemians & Moravins (and also the Inhabitants of Polonia the lesse being all discended of bordering nations) speake the old Sclavonian tounge (vnder which name I sayd Dalmatia to be Contayned) but they vse diuers Dialects, lesse or more differing one from the other ... [78]

When Moryson came to the Poles proper, he remarked on the near-absence of vowels in the written language, 'and howsoeuer so many Consonants cause asperity and distortion of the mouth in speaking: yet the gentlemen at this day pronovnce theire wordes gently vsing the consonants rather in theire penns then in theire speech'.[79] Would Moryson have been as thoughtful about Welsh, had he completed his British ethnography? Perhaps Moryson believed in a connection between these linguistic features and his experience of the Poles speaking the most corrupt Latin he encountered, or having few if any famous writers of their own.[80]

The Ottomans presented Moryson with another polyglot dominion. The 'subiects of this Empyre spake as many languages as be the nations of which it consists, being so many as I will not vndertake to knowe or nomber them'. Yet it surprised Moryson that 'howsoeuer they had the power to Conquer all these nations, yet they haue not made theire language vniversall' – perhaps the Ottomans had a greater appreciation for the challenges of linguistic conquest than did Moryson and other proponents of extinguishing Gaelic in Ireland. As for Turkish, 'the language of it selfe is rude, and written (as the Polonian) with many Consonants', but without the Poles' practice of smoothing the rough

---

[76] 'Unpublished Itinerary', pp.1258–60; Moryson, Itinerary, I, 145.

[77] 'Unpublished Itinerary', pp. 1360–61.

[78] 'Unpublished Itinerary', p. 1403.

[79] 'Unpublished Itinerary', p. 1419.

[80] 'Unpublished Itinerary', p. 1419–20.

asperity in speech. The language had been 'refyned in time' by characters and words borrowed from Persian and Arabic concerning religion, and others from Greek and Italian merchants about navigation. Various terms, phrases, and usages attracted Moryson's interest, including the Turkish equivalent for 'God saue the king' in the salute for their emperor.[81]

Moryson sometimes rose above linguistic chauvinism. The Danes might sport bowl haircuts and engage in barbarous clamours, but their linguistic impact on English was undeniable:

> The Danes of old invaded England, and for a shorte tyme ruled there as Kings, and left there many wordes of their language, as namely Mate with the Danes, signifyes Meate with the English, hatt, and Agayne, and Sparrow, and many other wordes are the same in Danish as in English. The worde koyne is danish ... of which worde litle altered comes the English worde Queen, which is the title of wemen raigning absolutely or of the kings Crowned wife in England.[82]

Few peoples surpassed the English for language(s), proven by a natural amorousness expressed in 'the pleasant Study of Poetry' in which English had 'attayned excellency'.[83] Yet, according to Moryson, it was thanks to a diverse range of cultural and linguistic contacts that the 'English language is very copious of wordes and expressions of any thinge to be spoken, and being mixed is therefore more and not lesse to be esteemed'.[84]

Customs and manners

An eye for even the most arcane and esoteric cultural complexity marked Moryson's interest in practices associated with ceremonies (marriage, funerals, childbirth, and the like), pastimes, hunting, and fishing, but Moryson reserved a separate section in each chapter for 'customes' proper.[85] It is hard not to read these portions as a grab bag, yet they tend to highlight features thought to be essential to a people's nature. Not surprisingly, then, a good deal about German drinking, inns, and feasts set them apart from the English. In winter, the Germans drank in their stoves, sitting bareheaded and sometimes with their doublets open to 'the naked breast', while the better sort employed pages to fan them against summer heat and flies. They expressed the comradeship of drinking by joining hands 'with such force as if they would splitt one anothers thumbs from the fingers'. Gentlemen 'often whispered together (which wee repute ill manners), and asked the other guests many strang questions'. One quizzed Moryson about

[81] 'Unpublished *Itinerary*', pp. 1448–51.
[82] 'Unpublished *Itinerary*', pp. 1388–9.
[83] 'Unpublished *Itinerary*', p. 1665.
[84] 'Unpublished *Itinerary*', p. 1668; also his discussion of language in Italy, 'Unpublished *Itinerary*', pp. 1565–9.
[85] 'Unpublished *Itinerary*', p. 1331.

the succession, 'where of the English were then [in the late 1590s] by Statute forbidden to speake', and he could not but marvel at how openly the Germans discussed matters of state.[86] The decentralization of the empire clearly worked to their advantage. Indeed, they thought of the empire as a commonwealth, and their folklore apparently proved the point. The Germans cherished storks and positively encouraged them to nest above 'their Senate houses' and other buildings for luck and as a sign of justice, saying (to Moryson) 'that they neuer build in any kingdome, but only in Common wealths, which they repute the most Iust governments'.[87]

Conditioned under the authoritarian ambitions of the Tudor *imperium* and the febrile politics of Elizabeth's last years, Moryson clearly found German political liberty puzzling and uncomfortable. Despite his condemnation of Ottoman tyranny, he welcomed the extension of the Tudor state following on the from Henrician revolution of the 1530s, citing with approval the utility of parish registers, presumably for determining one's parish of residence and settling disputes over parentage and inheritance.[88] Moryson also lamented that the English – in part conditioned by the long, baleful history of idle monks, finally put to an end under Henry and Cromwell – had a natural addiction to pleasure (idleness) and a 'boldeness lesse to feare death then want'. For these reasons, 'more people are executed in England for stealing and Roberyes by the high way, then in many vast kingdomes, abroad'. But the brutality of the justice system had a salutary effect. Offences declined and the severity of justice taught industriousness to the English 'natives', for whom an honest keep became a matter of life and death.[89] The hue and cry against malefactors was one of England's 'three very olde and very laudable Customes'; along with children asking their parents' blessing, and tolling a bell to enjoin prayer for the sick.[90] Moryson even speculated that Elizabeth had rejected the incorporation of the United Provinces within the Tudor *imperium* in 1585 because the queen thought 'it probable, that the Netherlanders, being a people which had often taken Armes against their Prince, of all other things least bearing new taxes and impositions (which they professed, next the persecution of Religion, to be the chiefe cause of this warre), would alwaies be apt to stir up sedition'.[91]

Moryson recorded many a peculiar custom in the German lands. The Germans thought it bad manners to reach with their knives for bread and instead asked for it to be passed or brought to them. Moryson found this nicety misplaced, considering that they took an entire shoulder of meat into their own trenchers instead of having portions carved for them. Civility and courtesy were

---

[86] 'Unpublished *Itinerary*', p. 1287.
[87] 'Unpublished *Itinerary*', p. 1304.
[88] 'Unpublished *Itinerary*', p. 1669–70.
[89] 'Unpublished *Itinerary*', p. 1662.
[90] 'Unpublished *Itinerary*', p. 1670; Moryson, *Itinerary*, IV, pp. 94–5.
[91] Moryson, *Itinerary*, IV, p. 459.

clearly not found in the drunken custom of kissing neighbours at the next table, 'sometymes' with foming mouthes'. They were liable to promise anything when 'in theire potts', and no bargains were considered made until confirmed by a sober wife. From the North Sea to Nuremberg, there was no shame among the Germans for drinking to the point of sickness or pissing under the table. Inns, private houses, and public drinking stoves all stocked at least one 'faule bett', a long, narrow bed covered in leather, for Germans who 'drincke healths till they leese their owne'.[92]

No people as industrious and learned as the Germans could be totally consumed by drunkenness, and Moryson described a few customs not tainted by drink. Regular Saturday bathing must have been a virtue among the Germans, with most citizens 'of any account' having a private stove for the purpose. The fair, golden hair of so many German women impressed itself on Moryson, thanks to their practice of spreading their hair to dry in the sun upon the brims of straw hats. That said, women used their Saturday baths primarily for cleanliness' sake, but men used the hot stoves to sweat the alcohol out of their systems. Neither were above using the stoves and public baths more 'for wantonnes and loue, then for Corporall diseaces', especially since the sexes were often separated by a mere blanket. If proximity in the bath failed to do the trick, women in lower Germany were known to use love potions or other kinds of 'witch crafts' on unsuspecting men – Moryson claimed to have seen three virgins use charmed apples which in turn killed one man and sickened another before the third was warned off the poisoned fruit. Perhaps that was why no Englishman would 'lay vp theire cleane linnen (as it were to be perfumed)' with either apples or quinces, which they held to be unpleasant, unwholesome, and generally infectious.[93]

Even so, the Germans and English shared clocks which struck twenty-four times a day on the hour and games of chance, though German cards were painted on the inside and sported faggots and circles in place of clubs and diamonds. The love of dice and cards was something the Germans and English shared with their neighbours in France, but it was left to the French and English to turn those pastimes into vices.[94] In turn, the Germans and French shared something that was somewhat less interesting to Moryson's idea of Englishness: music and song, even if German musicality had a bit more to do with the Church and French 'men and wemen delight more in singing and haue more skill in that Art, then any nation I knowe'.[95] More than anything, these three peoples found common ground in their devotion to all sorts of hunting and fishing, even if Moryson never saw hunting with hawks and hounds during his travels in Germany or

[92] 'Unpublished *Itinerary*', pp. 1288–92.
[93] 'Unpublished *Itinerary*', pp. 1300–2.
[94] 'Unpublished *Itinerary*', p. 1653.
[95] 'Unpublished *Itinerary*', pp. 1653–4.

235

France and his description of wolf hunting positively leapt from the Germans' barbarian, forest-dwelling past in Tacitus and Caesar.[96]

Even the most cursory journeys fitted Moryson with customs that defined Britons, typically the English, by comparison. He admitted that his 'cursory iorny' through Bohemia provided little except one of only two instances in all his travels of a gentleman hawking; the other was in Poland. 'I thincke', he reflected, 'these exercises are much more vsed by the English and Scotts, then in any other part of all other partes of the worlde.'[97] The Netherlands, Poland, and the Ottoman empire presented Moryson with particular contrasts. 'Among theire Customes, some seemed very strange to me,' Moryson wrote of the Netherlands after his arrival at Dokkum.[98] Moryson ridiculed the substitution of sand for rushes on Dutch floors: 'they seeme to foule their howses themselues, for feare other should foule them'.[99] Much of what Moryson reported of Dutch customs seemed, like German drinking, to come back to questions of gender, though. Thus the famous Dutch drainage systems – which made the country unfit for hunting with hounds – became a tale of frozen canals, skating, and ice hockey that lent themselves too readily to immodest movements by women, over-familiar meetings with men, and a general condemnation of Dutch mothers for giving 'great liberty to theire daughters'.[100] Less shocking but equally unfamiliar were the drains and gutters not in the middle of the street, 'as Commonly with vs' but at the curbside. Not surprisingly, in the Dutch republic Moryson found again that bothersome devotion to the stork and justice.[101]

Travel in the Ottoman empire opened Moryson's eyes to customs both mundane and extraordinary. England had more bells than 'all the Contenent of Europe and that part of Asia which I haue seene', but the Turks summoned the people to prayers by 'hallowing as loude as our falcornes' from the 'steeples of the moschees'; neither had they any clocks and they told time by the sun, moon, and stars.[102] Appearance was another matter. Judges wore azure coats and the great commanders wore violet, but black was avoided as the Devil's colour. The most holy colour was green, reserved for the descendants of Muhammad, and unwary Christians who wore so much as a shoestring of green could expect a cudgelling at the first offence and death for the second – Moryson exercised due caution in hiding the green taffeta lining of his doublet. All Turks wore white turbans, except for Muhammad's descendants (green) and the janissaries (caps), and the greatest Turks adorned them with splashes of coloured fabric, jewels, feathers, or the like. Cleanliness before God prompted bathing even more

---

[96] 'Unpublished *Itinerary*', pp. 1306–18.
[97] 'Unpublished *Itinerary*', p. 1410.
[98] 'Unpublished *Itinerary*', p. 1367.
[99] 'Unpublished *Itinerary*', pp. 1369–70.
[100] 'Unpublished *Itinerary*', pp. 1370–3, 1375–6.
[101] 'Unpublished *Itinerary*', p. 1373.
[102] 'Unpublished *Itinerary*', p. 1472.

frequent than the Germans', often twice a day and to such an extent that harlots would not give 'the second vse of their bodyes if they haue not bathed after the first'. Men ordinarily wore arms, with the by-now infamous cudgels the weapon of choice – especially for beating 'Multitudes of Christians or Common Turkes'. Turbans were not doffed in reverence, but people put off their shoes in mosques and before magistrates.[103]

Under a tyrannical emperor who made slaves of all people, and their property his own, bribes and obsequiousness were required in every walk of life. The janissaries paid to escort and protect Christians embodied these evils, willing for a 'fewe Aspers or pennce to beate a Common Turke' at the asking.[104] Very little of what Moryson wrote about customs in the Ottoman empire was not shaped by assuming the Turks to be cruel and barbarous. For Moryson, the history of slavery in human societies was in part a history of the progress of civility and barbarity, from the time 'when might was right, and the weaker and poorer were made subject to the stronger and richer' to a time when slavery 'was more cruelly or more gently exercised, as the nations were or became more barbarous or Ciuill'.[105] Moryson used this odd definition of progress to make one of his most explicit rankings of peoples and societies:

> And howsoeuer Christian Charity and humility hath in many kingdomes abolished this cruell Custome, and in all Christian kingdomes abated the taranny [tyranny] therof, yet this day the husbandmen of the Country, in Denmarke, in Poland, and many partes of Germany are meere slaues ... And to this day, the kingdome of Spayne, the State of Venice, and some fewe Cittyes and Provences of Italy, vsing Gallyes at Sea, haue slaues bound in Iron Chaynes to rowe in them ... [106]

No doubt the poor and distressed who, to Moryson's approval, swung from English gibbets for property crimes had time to reflect on their good fortune in being born in a Christian kingdom.[107] The Ottoman empire was nonetheless unique, for none of these European slaves was born as such, as they were in the empire, and 'Turky is the only Empire knowne to mee, where slaues governe the State.'[108]

Pastimes forced Moryson to leave behind homogenous stereotypes and acknowledge the empire's cultural complexity:

> In Palestine I haue seene the mores (which are tawney not blacke, and together with the Arabians inhabite those Countryes) ... in the fieldes represent playes or Commedies, but barbarously in respect of ours, and I haue seene the wemen mores vse publike

[103] 'Unpublished *Itinerary*', pp. 1474–8; Moryson, *Itinerary*, I, p. 451.
[104] 'Unpublished *Itinerary*', p. 1473.
[105] 'Unpublished *Itinerary*', p. 1481.
[106] 'Unpublished *Itinerary*', pp. 1481–2.
[107] For a very different reading drawn from the sources of the period, Christopher Hill, *Liberty Against the Law: Some Seventeenth Century Controversies* (London, 1996), pp. 3–70.
[108] 'Unpublished *Itinerary*', p. 1482.

dauncing in the fieldes, as allso the Turkish wemen daunce alone, and with other wemen after the Moresco and very wanton fashion.[109]

Moryson judged the women immodest because of their 'laciuious gestures and motions of the body' and ridiculous for their 'skippings and leapes'. Yet, curiously, he found them 'delightful for many comely motions of the body' and their dexterity in accompanying the rhythm of the music with small stones or shells clicked between their fingers. The money 'they bege from the beholders' was shared out with the musicians. The Turks generally loved musical instruments, including the lute – 'hauing not so many stringes as ours' – and 'a kynde of Bagpipe', but 'fewe haue any great skill to vse them, and for my parte I neuer heard nor sawe any of them excelent in the Art of Musicke'.[110]

The peoples of Syria and parts of Egypt – 'as I thincke especially in Affricke' – were cunning wrestlers. For Moryson this was an exotic pastime, performed 'with great earnestness, as if honor and life lay vpon the victory' by well-oiled men, naked except for a tight loincloth. Tightrope walking and other gymnastics performed to music were a wonder that Englishmen would think impossible, except that 'in our tyme wee haue seene one example in England by a Turke who shewed strange Actiuity vpon Roapes, as many yet liuing may remember'. Only in their great love of chess and respect for hunting with falcons did Moryson describe pastimes among the empire's peoples that were not barbarous, childlike, or strangely exotic.[111]

There was a space for travel and encounter closer to home that called to mind the Ottoman empire for Moryson: Ireland. No one familiar with the early modern English writing of Ireland should be surprised to find Moryson's most pejorative, hostile ethnography in his Irish chapters, perhaps partly thanks to reading Edmund Spenser's *View of the State of Ireland* in manuscript.[112] The Irish and degenerate Anglo-Irish, Gaelicized descendants of the island's Anglo-Norman conquerors and colonists, were beyond the pale of civility, more so for Moryson than even the Ottomans. For Moryson, the barbarity and tyranny of Irish society and Gaelic lordship paralleled the barbarous customs and tyrannical subjugation perpetrated by the sultan's regime. Men's trousers and the turban-like headscarves of Irish women neatly tied together these two most barbaric peoples

---

[109] 'Unpublished *Itinerary*', p. 1487.

[110] 'Unpublished *Itinerary*', pp. 1487–92.

[111] 'Unpublished *Itinerary*', pp. 1487–92.

[112] 'Unpublished *Itinerary*', pp. clxxxviii–clxxxix; Anna Suranyi, *The Genius of the English Nation: Travel Writing and National Identity in Early Modern England* (Newark, DE, 2008), pp. 59–69, 75–82; Brendan Bradshaw, Andrew Hadfield, and Willy Maley, eds, *Representing Ireland: Literature and the Origins of Conflict 1534–1660* (Cambridge, 1993); Andrew Hadfield, *Spenser's Irish Experience: Wilde Fruite and Salvage Soyl* (Oxford, 1997); descriptions in Andrew Hadfield and John McVeagh, eds, *Strangers to that Land: British Perceptions of Ireland from the Reformation to the Famine* (Gerrards Cross, 1994).

and nations. But this was a gross comparison, and Moryson knew it. The real parallel lay with one of the subject peoples under the Ottomans: the Arabs.

On the road to Jerusalem, where Moryson would find what he called the 'scumme of divers Nations', he was warned by his guide to travel quietly lest their party rouse the Arabs, Turks, or other thieves, 'like if they awaked to offer us violence, or at least to extort some money from us'.[113] Once safely in Jerusalem, he wrote 'that the Arabians, howsoever subject to the Turk, yet exercise continuall robberies with all libertie and impunitie, the Turkes being not able to restraine them, because they [the Arabs] are barbarous and live farre from their chiefe power, where they can easily flye into desart places'.[114] It would not be a stretch to substitute mere Irish for Arabs or forests and bogs for desert and come up with the same result. But we do not have to rely on our own reading, for Moryson too saw in the Arabs a direct parallel with the Irish: 'The Arabians are not unlike the wild Irish, for they are subject to the great Turke, yet being poore and farre distant from his imperiall seat, they cannot be brought to due obedience, much lesse to abstain from robberies.'[115] One wonders if Moryson quite grasped that he had associated the young Stuart *imperium* of James VI and I with the tyrannical Ottomans. Or that no one reading this would find reference to what must have been, rhetorically at least, the key difference between the regimes: the imperial project in Ireland aimed to bring order and 'due obedience' as the prelude to creating civility out of barbarity, while the Ottoman instinct was for despotism alone.[116]

Exploring undiscovered Britain

What, then, should we make of Moryson's cultural comparisons between the English and the peoples he encountered during his travels? Moryson awkwardly inserted a telling statement while describing his encounters with the Ottomans:

> The desyre of Travelors to see newe Cittyes, people, and manners of men, is so del[i]ghtful, as Commonly it growes to a disease of endlesse perigrinnation, but I thincke nothinge so powerfull to cure the itch of this hunor [sic], and make them loue theire one [sic] Country, as to liue sometyme among the miscreants, and suffer their scornes.[117]

Moryson called on his readers – chiefly English readers – to understand themselves through open and unstated comparisons to this complex collection of peoples in Europe, the Middle East, even Ireland. During his journeys,

---

[113] Moryson, *Itinerary*, I, p. 466; Moryson, *Itinerary*, II, p. 5.
[114] Moryson, *Itinerary*, II, p. 18.
[115] Moryson, *Itinerary*, I, p. 466.
[116] The Tudor–Stuart project in Ireland is surveyed in Michael Braddick, *State Formation in Early Modern England c. 1550–1700* (Cambridge, 2000), pp. 379–97.
[117] 'Unpublished *Itinerary*', p. 1431.

Moryson satisfied an abiding itch to travel, but rubbing up against complex cultures enabled self-discovery for both Moryson and his readers.

Travel equipped him to discover the peoples of Britain because it typically nurtured an acute awareness to cultural complexity, especially the interactions and exchanges among peoples. The descriptions of languages are instructive, whether in comments about the 'sweetening' influence of French on the Dutch dialect or the extensive borrowings found in any 'national' language, be it German, Turkish, or English. Moryson repeatedly described natures and customs shared among and between peoples. The Bohemians and Poles descended from the same race and both were valiant and courageous by nature, yet he found the Bohemians placid, humble, and courteous in contrast to the Poles' vanity, excessive pride, and quickness to avenge any perceived slight or wrong.[118] Moryson aptly described the polyglot Ottoman empire as so many 'nations no lesse differing in nature and all conditions one from the other, then distant in remote Clymes, as whatsoeuer may be sayd of their nature, manners and the like cannot possibly agree to all persons and seuerall partes of them'.[119] In the Isle of Man, Moryson found a similarly complex ethnic geography much closer to home.[120] Here commonwealths and nations worked as handy and sensible organizational tools for the 'Itinerary', but they did not crowd out cultural complexity or necessitate crude, reductive ethnographies.

Moryson had an almost-instinctive focus on the unique spaces for encounter and cultural exchange along the 'borders' – to use his term – that nominally divided peoples. In some instances, borders were places where 'naturall goodnes is somewhat infected and altered by the vices of bordering nations'. This particularly affected the Germans, leaving those along the French border more deceptive and those neighbouring Italy more given to fornication. On that basis Moryson wrote that 'generally the borderers of all nations are Commonly the worst people, and vse more then others to apply themselues to the manners of their neighbours'.[121] Permeable borders, especially those between peoples of the same 'race', gave Moryson the confidence to describe one people in keeping with the character of their better-known brethren. He had no experience of child-bearing, christenings, or funerals in Switzerland and assumed that his readers would be satisfied with a comment like this: 'Only I will say that as in language and manners they differ litle from the inhibitants of vpper Germany, so I thincke they are not vnlike them in these particular Customes.'[122] Here of course Moryson's positions proved contradictory: presumably the Swiss neither were infected with the vices of their neighbours nor had declined from the practice of their German brethren over the centuries. That said, Moryson recognized

---

[118] 'Unpublished *Itinerary*', pp. 1398–9, 1412–15.
[119] 'Unpublished *Itinerary*', p. 1427.
[120] Moryson, *Itinerary*, IV, p. 162.
[121] 'Unpublished *Itinerary*', p. 1209.
[122] 'Unpublished *Itinerary*', p. 1331.

the limits of his travels and kept such presumptions in check, admitting, for instance, that 'my cursory iorny yealded me small or no experience' of Danish pastimes and hunting.[123]

To what extent, then, did such cultural sensitivity frame Moryson's account of multicultural Britain? It is telling that reading between the lines uncovers the Scots and Welsh only once. In the first case, hawking was a pastime 'much more vsed by the English and the Scotts, then in any other part or all other partes of the worlde'.[124] In the other, Moryson marvellously conflated the Welsh and English at the same time that he relegated them to cultural irrelevance and used them to make sport of the Turks: 'Neither is the Art of Cookery greater in Turkey then with us in Wales, for toasting of Cheese in Wales, and seething of Rice in Turkey, will enable a man freely to professe the Art of Cookery.'[125] The English palate and elaborate feasting could not have made the cheese-toasting Welsh 'one of us' in anything but the most superficial and superior terms. Were hawking and toasted cheese really the only non-English points of reference that came to mind in hundreds of pages of cross-cultural comparisons? Did the Welsh Marches and Scottish Borders offer no parallels to their European counterparts as Moryson crossed them in his literary journeys?

Here the decision to drop the peoples of Britain from the 'Itinerary' and the absence of the promised ethnography of Britain are particularly acute. England and Scotland dominated the landscape, while between them England seemed to exercise supremacy over the narrative itself. Ironically, the best evidence for English dominance comes from reading between the lines of Moryson's cross-cultural comparisons. It is evident that the English top the cultural league table, even if they compare unfavourably in some individual respects – German industriousness, Dutch trading acumen, English obsessions with fashionable attire. In drawing comparisons, cultural complexity existed chiefly between England and its European and Middle East neighbours. This despite how frequently Moryson described the complexity within the dominions he visited, not least the Ottoman empire. Descriptions of Syrian and Egyptian sports did not invite comparison to Cornish prowess in wrestling. Nations loomed large once Moryson left behind the ancient tribes and ethnic groups of *Britannia* for the Isles in which he lived and travelled.

Moryson nonetheless conceived of something remarkable: an itinerary that aimed to describe the peoples of Britain on equal terms with their European and Asian neighbours, using a common ethnographic framework, grounded in the first-hand experience of travel and encounter. His work blurred, if it did not obliterate, the mental barriers that bounded nature's fortress. This was revolutionary stuff in the 1610s. However, there could be no substitute for first-hand

---

[123] 'Unpublished *Itinerary*', p. 1409.
[124] 'Unpublished *Itinerary*', p. 1410.
[125] Moryson, *Itinerary*, IV, p .131.

experiences, especially for a traveller who envied those better travelled and whose perseverance included travelling in disguise. Moryson travelled 'to enable my understanding, which I thought could not be done so well by contemplation as by experience; not by the eare or any sence so well as the eies'.[126] Too late, he recognized that his travels through Britain lacked the scale and attentiveness of those in Europe and the Middle East. Failure did not only leave Moryson discouraged, it left most readers in Britain without a more complex and relative understanding of themselves.

The same cannot be said for other British travellers during Moryson's lifetime or the rest of the seventeenth century. In England, Camden's *Britannia* encouraged a veritable flood of travellers to emulate local historians like Lambarde or Carew in writing the histories of the counties. As well, the Tudor incorporation of Wales and the Union of Scotland and England in 1603 prompted much greater travel between the 'nations' of Britain. Those travellers all did what Moryson had failed to. What some of those travellers found in Wales and Scotland – what Moryson himself might have found – is the question we explore in the next two chapters. The rich experiences to be had in those lands emphasize what Moryson would have been up against if he had aimed to duplicate the focus on cultural complexity found elsewhere in the 'Itinerary' in a description of Britain. Cursory and armchair travels would not do. Moryson and the travellers who found their way into his undiscovered Britain set a standard by which the complexity of the British peoples was eventually presented to readers. Now we join Moryson's contemporaries in Scotland.

---

[126] Moryson, *Itinerary*, I, p. 424.

7

Arthur's Seat

In the high summer of 1618, two strangers stopped along an Edinburgh street. Both men were weary and dirty from their day's journey. One thought it had left his 'minde attyred with moody, muddy, Moore-ditch melancholy'. They caught the attention of one of Edinburgh's denizens. The melancholy one fixed John Maxwell with a disconcerting stare, drawing him across the street to demand of the man's companion why 'he lookes so wistly on me?' Foiled in his first effort to make an acquaintance in the unfamiliar town, the English poet John Taylor had impishly resolved that 'the next gentleman that I met withall, should be acquaintance whether hee would or no'. Taylor made a good choice in staring down Maxwell:

> [The gentleman], with unexpected and undeserved courtesie, brought me to a lodging, and caused my horse to bee put into his own stable, whilest we discoursing over a pinte of Spanish ... having rested two houres and refreshed myselfe, the gentleman and I walked to see the city and the castle, which as my poore unable and unworthy pen can, I will truly describe.[1]

John Taylor took the title 'water-poet' as a play on his trade as a Thames boatman, or waterman. More than fifteen years' plying the Thames to the Tower and the South Bank theatres paid off in 1614 when Taylor became a 'King's waterman'. Success in his literary ventures, inspired by contacts with Bankside players and playwrights, at first proved more elusive. A pamphlet exchange with the travel writer Thomas Coryate brought some notoriety, but 'promoting his image as a "personality" and turning it to financial account' in the nascent genre of exotic travel narratives finally brought him lasting fame. A journey down the Thames in a boat made from brown paper and kept buoyant with inflated animal bladders, two dangerous passages by sea to the Humber and Avon rivers, and an odyssey to Prague and back provided fruitful material. It was the journey to Scotland recorded in *The Pennyless Pilgrimage* that was Taylor's first and most successful effort.[2]

---

[1] P. Hume Brown, ed., *Early Travellers in Scotland* (Edinburgh, 1973), p. 109.
[2] Bernard Capp, 'John Taylor', *Oxford DNB* at www.oxforddnb.com.

After a fortnight in the Borders and lowlands of Scotland in 1598, Fynes Moryson abruptly turned for home. He never returned to the land of his future king, but there were many others like Taylor who were interested to discover the land and its people. Two events after 1600 drew travellers to Scotland: the accession of James VI in 1603 and the wars of the three kingdoms in the 1640s and 1650s, triggered by the meddling of Charles I and Archbishop William Laud with the Presbyterian Kirk in 1637. Indeed, according to Ben Jonson, William Warner 'since the Kings comming to England [ha]d marrd [revised] all his Albions England' with new editions in 1606 and 1612.[3] For English or Welsh travellers to Scotland in the seventeenth century these events sparked interest in ethnic and religious differences, and fired prejudices on one or both accounts.

Jonson, the celebrated playwright and friend of Robert Cotton and William Camden, proposed to write an account of 'his foot pilgrimage hither & to call it a discoverie'. He nursed the 'jntention to writt a fisher or Pastorall play & sett the stage of it jn the Lowmond Lake'.[4] Jonson's grandfather hailed from the Borders around Carlisle and Annandale. He made the journey in the summer of 1618, perhaps still haunted by the imputation of anti-Scottishness produced by an unflattering portrait of Scots in *Eastward Ho.*[5] Taylor followed four weeks later and recounted his experiences in the *Penniless Pilgrimage*. Jonson's original account was consumed in the fire that swept through his lodgings in 1623.[6]

Both men quite literally followed James, who returned to the land of his birth to do a bit of meddling himself in the practices of the Kirk in 1617. James's entourage included one writer whose hateful account of Scotland was later laid at the door of Anthony Weldon. William Brereton pursued his interests into Scotland in 1636, the year before the fateful ruckus broke out over the new prayer book and liturgy introduced by Charles and Laud. The Welshman James Howell reported on the aftermath of these changes in 1639. Thomas Tucker surveyed Scotland's major commercial centres when he was sent north in 1655 to help settle the customs and excise for the new Protectorate government that ruled the short-lived Republic of Great Britain and Ireland. In significant numbers, the English and Welsh finally joined continental Europeans like Jean Froissart, Aeneas Sylvius, Peder Swave, and Henri Duc de Rohan who journeyed to Scotland. These visitors from the South allow us to see Scotland from within and without. For many of them, Scotland was an undiscovered country on the island of Britain. They sought out the Scottish nation, but sometimes came

---

[3] 'Conversations with William Drummond of Hawthornden', in *Ben Jonson*, ed. C.H. Herford and Percy Simpson (eleven volumes; Oxford, 1952–1961), I.2, pp. 133, 154, hereafter cited as Jonson, 'Conversations'.

[4] Jonson, 'Conversations', p. 143. James Loxley has edited a surviving manuscript account of the journey for the new Oxford edition of Jonson's complete works; see his 'My Gossip's Foot Voyage', *Times Literary Supplement* 5554 (11 September 2009), pp. 13–15.

[5] Jonson, 'Conversations', pp. 139–40, 164–5.

[6] Hume Brown, *Early Travellers*, p. xxii.

face to face with the cultural complexity of the Scots. They – and the travellers through Wales examined in the next chapter – stand in for Moryson and the encounters with cultural complexity that could have been the foundation for his lost ethnography of Britain.

Noble Scots and stinking people

John Taylor began his good-humoured journey to Edinburgh content to rely upon the kindness of local hosts for lodging and provisions. Our 'penniless pilgrim' succeeded admirably. He especially benefited from acquaintances among the Scots whom James had left behind to govern the country. The upland journey from Carlisle and crossing both the Annan and Eske on foot left Taylor bone weary. Unlike Jonson, famous in Scotland and soon to become a burgess of Edinburgh, Taylor did not merit a bagpipe serenade or dance by the local sheep shearers.[7] The differences between English and Scottish miles tricked Taylor, a difference he recounted in playful fashion: 'indeed the Scots doe allow almost as large measure of their miles, as they doe of their drinke, for an English gallon, either of ale or wine, is but their quart'.[8] He positively relished the simple lodging and fare to be had in Moffat. While Taylor's companion travelled mounted 'like the George without the dragon', he continued on foot the next day to Blythe Bridge, a sorry village where he chose between lodging out of doors or 'in a poore house where the good-wife lay in child-bed, her husband being from home, her own servant mayde being her nurse'. Necessity made Taylor lodge with this woman of 'incomparable homeliness ... where we gat egges and ale by measure and by tale'. The pigeons that cooed in his sleeping companion's face helped to pass the night before the next day's journey to Edinburgh.[9]

Words did not fail Taylor in describing the magnificent, impregnable castle and James II's great siege cannon Mons Meg, forged in Belgium and taken into battle at Roxburgh Castle alongside another that exploded and killed the king. The Royal Mile charmed Taylor, especially the tall stone buildings occupied by merchants and traders that fronted the street and between which ran narrow lanes leading to the fair houses of the Edinburgh nobility. At the far end, Taylor found Holyrood to be a 'stately and princely seate'. The sumptuous chapel and royal arms carved into the stone of the inner court left a lasting impression. Taylor thought its Latin inscription, translated as '106 fore-fathers have left this to us unconquered', a worthy motto for a dynasty protected by both God and their 'peacefull king'. The city's entertainment exceeded Taylor's expectations, as did the variety of food, fish, bread, and fruit. Taylor played on the Scots' reputation for drinking, first avowing that ale and wine were scarce and the Scots miserly

[7] Loxley, 'Gossip's Foot Voyage', pp. 13–15.
[8] Hume Brown, *Early Travellers*, p. 107.
[9] Hume Brown, *Early Travellers*, pp. 107–8.

with both before twisting the tale to report 'that every night before I went to bed, if any man had asked me a civill question, all the wit in my head could not have made him a sober answer'. Taylor faulted Edinburgh in just one respect. Had the city been founded a mile nearer the Forth, trade and traffic would have made it one of Europe's greatest city's. James's bedchamber groom, Bernard Lindsay, satisfied Taylor that nearby Leith made up the difference.[10]

Taylor crossed the Forth to Kinghorn to see its 'wondrous well' or healing spring:

> I did heare that it had done much good, and that it hath a rare operation to expell or kill divers maladies; as to provoke appetite, to helpe much for the avoyding of the gravell in the bladder, to cure sore eyes, and old ulcers ... for novelty I dranke of it, and I found the taste to be more pleasant than any other water, sweet almost as milke, yet as cleare as cristall.[11]

From Burntisland, Taylor travelled to Stirling and visited his friends the Earl of Mar and William Murray. He promised to return in two days, but it was not until over a month later and a much more extensive tour of Scotland that Taylor rejoined his travelling companion, Robert Hay. His tour would reveal the complexity of people and place encountered by too few travellers who hugged the lowlands.

Taylor passed the weeks in making a circuit of notable places and the houses of other 'establishment' figures like George Bruce at Culross. The spectacular ruined abbey caught Taylor's eye in Dunfermline, but Bruce's sea-coal mine in Culross really seized his imagination and pen. The mine must have been something to behold. Workmen had dug the shaft into the sands along the Forth, built a circular stone frame around the opening to protect it from high tide and heavy seas, excavated forty feet through sand and rock to reach the coal seam, and then pushed the mine forward more than a mile under the Forth itself. As Taylor evocatively described it, 'when men are at worke below, an hundred of the greatest shippes in Britaine may saile over their heads'. Taylor himself went down the mine, and returned impressed that so many people had been put to work and that miners could work upright, thanks to the design – no calloused scabs or 'buttons' running down the spines of these miners, in contrast to those immortalized by George Orwell in *The Road to Wigan Pier*.[12] The Scottish miners confronted dangerous leakages of water, for which Bruce had invented a pump powered by a horse team. Bruce's entrepreneurship also included making sea salt. Taylor's wry nature led to two odd reflections upon his visit to the works. He could become a wealthy tapster in London if he had a cellar comparable to Bruce's mine in which to store beer and bottled ale. More bizarrely, Taylor jested about the Gunpowder plotters, who in 1605 had aimed to blow up the English

---

[10] Hume Brown, *Early Travellers*, pp. 109–12.
[11] Hume Brown, *Early Travellers*, p. 113.
[12] George Orwell, *The Road to Wigan Pier* (London, 1937), pp. 26–8.

Parliament, kill the king and the Protestant establishment, and replace both with a Catholic regime, using James's young daughter Elizabeth as a figurehead. Taylor suggested that they might have instead dug under the Thames to blow up the royal barge and those of the MPs, had they witnessed the example of Bruce's mine.[13]

From Stirling and Perth, Taylor passed into the Grampians and a very different world. Travelling up the rocky, 'fearfull and horrid' valley of the Eske, Taylor came to an 'Irish house, the folkes not being able to speake scarce any English', where he lodged. His night's sleep was not a peaceful one:

> I had not laine long, but I was enforced to rise; I was so stung with Irish musketaes [mosquitoes], a creature that hath sixe legs, and lives like a monster altogether upon mans flesh; they doe inhabite and breed most upon sluttish houses, and this house was none of the cleanest ... [yet] had not this Highland Irish house helped me at a pinch, I should have sworn that all Scotland had not been so kind as to have bestowed a louse upon me; but with a shift that I had, I shifted off my canibals, and was never more troubled with them.[14]

Taylor reached the summit of Mount Keene the next day, leaving behind a warm summer's day in the valley for an icy, impenetrable mist on the mountaintop. He wrote: 'my teeth beganne to dance in my head with cold'. Soaked through, Taylor made a descent through rocks, bogs, and heath that left him convinced a three-legged dog would outrun a horse, let alone a person, to the valley below.

Braemar offered Taylor something altogether more complicated, a curious middle ground mixing highland and lowland cultures. Once a year, 'many of the nobility and gentry of the kingdome (for their pleasure) doe come into these high-land countries to hunt, where they doe conforme themselves to the habite of the High-land men, who for the most part, speake nothing but Irish; and in former time were those people which were called the Red-shankes'. Taylor saw this cultural tourism at first hand and composed a vivid description of the highland garb these lowland chameleons affected once a year:

> Their habite is shooes with but one sole apiece; stocking (which they call short hose) made of a warme stuffe of divers colors which they call Tartan; as for breeches, many of them, nor their forefathers, never wore any, but a jerkin of the same stuffe that their hose is of, their garters being bands or wreathes of hay or straw, which a plead [plaid] about their shoulders, which is a mantle of divers colours, much finer and lighter stuffe than their hose, with blue flat caps on their heads, a handkerchiefe knit with two knots about their necke ...

This was not just playing a part. The local residents refused to hunt with men who kept to their ordinary attire.[15] Highland garb apparently admitted lowlanders to

---

[13] Hume Brown, *Early Travellers*, pp. 116–17.
[14] Hume Brown, *Early Travellers*, p. 119.
[15] Hume Brown, *Early Travellers*, pp. 120–1.

this cultural world and broke down the stark duality usually associated with the terms.

Taylor hunted and lodged with the earl of Mar, with whom he supped on a fantastic variety of roasted meats and fish as well as 'good ale, sacke, white, and claret ... with most potent Aquavitae'. Mar's cook was so zealous that Taylor believed the roasting, baking, boiling, and stewing could 'have scalded the Devill in his feathers'. Failing that, the evening campfire – a pyre stacked higher than a maypole – would surely have seen off any malign spirits. Mar's generosity impressed Taylor, who avowed that the earl willingly thanked his friends with stands of fir larger than the greatest earldoms in Scotland or England. If the earl's great forests did not stand in remote rocky mountains, so far removed from commercial trade, they could provide masts for all the ships in all the world for decades to come.[16]

Taylor took in Badenoch, Castle Grant, Darnaway, Elgin, Spynie, and Huntly, enjoying the hospitality of one noble family or another. As his predecessors had, Taylor remarked on the pleasant and plentiful prospect of Moray. Taylor's month-long diversion in the Grampians ended on a fantastic note. Crossing back into the Mearns at Breckin, Taylor was disturbed in his sleep by 'a wench that was borne deafe and dumb' who offered to share his bed for the night. Taylor recounted:

> I thinke that either the great travell over the mountaines had tamed me: or if not, her beautie could never haved moved me. The best parts of her were, that the breath was as sweet as sugar-carrion, being very well shouldered beneath the waest [waist] ... But howsoever, shee made such a hideous noyse, that I started out of my sleepe, and thought that the Devill had beene there.[17]

Taylor pushed 'the dumb beast' from his chamber and 'for want of a locke or a latch, I staked up my doore with a great chaire'.[18]

'Thus having escaped one of the seven deadly sinnes', Taylor returned to Edinburgh by way of Forfar, Dundee, Kinghorn, Burntisland, and Leith. He had an amiable reunion with Ben Jonson, who gave him 22s. to drink his health back home in England. Taylor spent eight days in good company 'to recover myself of falls and bruises which I received in my travell in the High-land mountainous hunting'. In the lost Haddington village of Adam, Taylor partook of the solan geese, eaten at a sideboard like oysters and of necessity 'well liquored with two or three good rowses of sherrie or Canarie sacke'. He said farewell to the Auchmuchtys over ten pints of ale in Dunbar and returned to his penniless travels, having already left his money at the Netherbow in Edinburgh.[19]

---

[16] Hume Brown, *Early Travellers*, p. 123.
[17] Hume Brown, *Early Travellers*, p. 125.
[18] Hume Brown, *Early Travellers*, p. 125.
[19] Hume Brown, *Early Travellers*, pp. 125–7.

This was Taylor's cue to sing the praises of his Scottish hosts. Ten, fifteen, even twenty men and horses might appear at the home of Scots like these and be received with flesh, fowl, fish, lodging, good cheer, and a hearty welcome. 'This is this worthy gentleman's use,' wrote Taylor, 'his chiefe delight being only to give strangers entertainment gratis.' Beyond Edinburgh, Taylor met and lodged with honest hosts who wore their blue bonnets like other men wore beaver hats. Indeed these men proudly wore 'no other shirts but of flaxe that grows on his grounde, and of his wives, daughters, or servants spinning' and 'stockings, hose, and jerkin of wooll of his owne sheepes backes'.[20]

Taylor found in these Scots a mirror to hold up to his fellow English men and women. Like an echo of Moryson, he explained that no mercer, draper, embroiderer, or haberdasher was driven to bankruptcy to meet the demands of an extravagant clientele desperate for ever-fancier clothing to flaunt their proud nature. Instead of squandering such money, Scotland's 'plaine, home-spune fellow keepes and maintaines thirty, forty, fifty servants ... every day releeving three or foure score people at his gate'. Taylor read the Scottish reputation for meanness very differently from other writers:

> This is a man that desires to know nothing so much as his duty to God and his King, whose greatest cares are to practise the workes of piety, charity, and hospitality: he never studies the consuming art of fashionless fashions ... his legs are alwayes at liberty, not being fettered with golden garters, and manacled with artificial roses, whose weight (sometime) is the reliques of some decayed lordship. Many of these worthy housekeepers there are in Scotland, amongst some of them I was entertained; from whence I did truly gather these aforesaid observations.[21]

Here was a noble, socially responsible frugality that said much about the Scottish character. Such an account of the Scottish nobility would morph into a Romantic fiction when the redefinition of noble society in favour of acquisition and commercial gain turned elites into improvers and, eventually, perpetrators of clearance.[22]

Taylor continued his journey to Berwick, where he almost seems to have given a new twist to one of Boece's tales. Salmon ran the Tweed in abundance, but the Sabbath and local ordnance left them to run free of Berwick's fishers one day of the week. When one group of fishermen defied the Lord and the law, taking three hundred salmon one Sunday, the great fish disappeared from the Tweed, which the people of Berwick affirmed 'to be Gods judgement upon them for the

---

[20] Hume Brown, *Early Travellers*, pp. 127–8.
[21] Hume Brown, *Early Travellers*, p. 128.
[22] Colin G. Calloway, *White Peoples, Indians, and Highlanders: Tribal Peoples and Colonial Encounters in Scotland and America* (Oxford, 2008), pp. 60–87; T.M. Devine, *Clanship to Crofters' War: The Social Transformation of the Scottish Highlands* (Edinburgh, 1994), pp. 1–83.

prophanation of the Sabbath'.[23] As in Ross, greedy fishermen tempted God and found divine punishment.

As with so many English travellers, once Taylor had crossed the Tweed his narrative became a cursory itinerary of the long journey home, peopled with unremarkable acquaintances and marked by changes of horse. Perhaps with Moryson familiarity bred indifference until a conscious determination to travel and discover retuned the senses, as it did when Taylor made his way to the West Country, Wales, and Sussex late in life. Yet Taylor was no ordinary traveller and he took to verse for his epilogue:

> I vow to God, I have done Scotland wrong,
> And, justly, 'gainst me it may bring an action,
> I have not given't that right which doth belong,
> For which I am halfe guilty of detraction:
>
> Yet had I wrote all things that there I saw,
> Misjudging censures would suppose I flatter,
> And so my name I would in question draw,
> Where asses bray, and prattling pies doe chatter:
>
> Yet (arm'd with truth) I publish with my pen,
> That there th'Almightly doth his blessings heape,
> In such aboundant food for beasts and men,
> That I ne'er saw more plenty or more cheape.
>
> Thus what mine eyes did see, I doe beleeve,
> And what I soe beleeve, I know is true:
> And what is true unto your hand I give,
> That what I give, may be beleev'd of you.[24]

Taylor's loving rejection of English xenophobia might well have made even his king blush. One of his contemporaries made James turn an angry red. Someone in the king's retinue that returned to Scotland in 1617 spent time in Leith composing a scathing description of the Scots. The letter or the sentiments expressed in it apparently reached the king. It was first published in the Netherlands as a *Discription of Scotland* in 1626 and attributed to a Doctor Corbett. Another edition appeared in 1649, this time attributed to James Howell. The name of Anthony Weldon, a clerk of the kitchen and the Greencloth – the board responsible for provisioning the king's entourage – was eventually tied to the tract, probably because of Weldon's attack on the king in his *Court and Character of King James*, published in 1650.[25] Such uncertainty perhaps served the interests of the actual author.

The king's ire would have been easy to understand. Bile spilled across the pages:

---

[23] Hume Brown, *Early Travellers*, pp. 128–9.
[24] Hume Brown, *Early Travellers*, p. 131.
[25] Joseph Marshall and Sean Kelsey, 'Anthony Weldon', *Oxford DNB* at www.oxforddnb.com.

First, for the country, I must confess it is good for those that possess it, and too bad for others, to be at the charge to conquer it. The air might be wholesome but for the stinking people that inhabit it; the ground might be fruitful had they the wit to manure it. Their beast be generally small, women only excepted, of which sort there are none greater in the whole world. There is great store of fowl too, as foul houses, foul sheets, foul linen, foul dishes and pots, foul trenchers and napkins ... for their butter and cheese, I will not meddle withal at this time, nor no man else at any time that loves his life.

Weak puns continued. The country had deer aplenty but the only thing dear the traveller met with was lodging, food, tobacco, and English beer. This traveller did not find ingenuity in the sea-coal mines, but a failure of industry because there were not more. Their pottage was mainly grass, and the prickly thistle was a fit national flower.[26]

The author described something of the king's progress to Scotland before turning to the country's 'wonders'. Among the wonders were that the Lord Chancellor's word was believed, the Master of the Rolls spoke well, and the privy councillors were free from corruption. The traveller had no love for the Scots on any account. Scotsmen treated their wives as slaves and were in turn slaves to their horses and their swords for justice. Scotswomen were a favourite target for this angry, misogynist writer (even by early modern standards):

The country, although it be mountainous, affords no monsters but women ... The ladies are of opinion, that Susanna could not be chaste, because she bathed so often. Pride is a thing bred in their bones, and their flesh naturally abhors cleanliness; their body smells of sweat, and their splay feet never offend in socks. To be chained in marriage with one of them, were to be tied to a dead carcass, and cast into a stinking ditch, formosity and a dainty face are things they dream not of.[27]

There was no sophistication in the Scottish polity: 'their parliaments hold but three days, their statutes are three lines, and their suits are determined in a manner in three words, or very few more'.[28] The austerity of the Presbyterian Kirk offended the traveller far more:

They christen without the cross, marry without the ring, receive the sacrament without reverence, die without repentance, and bury without divine service ... They use no prayer at all, for they say it is needless; God knows their minds without pratling ... Their Sabbath exercise is a preaching in the forenoon, and a persecuting in the afternoon ...

The traveller ridiculed the absence of holidays and the Scots' reverence for St Andrew, 'who they said got that honour by presenting Christ with an oaten cake after his forty days fast'. As for so many English travellers, Scottish oatcakes proved an offence to the palate and cultural sensibilities. The Scots did themselves no

26 Hume Brown, *Early Travellers*, pp. 97–8.
27 Hume Brown, *Early Travellers*, pp. 102–3.
28 Hume Brown, *Early Travellers*, p. 102.

favours with this traveller by swearing that Christ fed the ten thousand with oatcakes, since 'no other bread of that quantity could have sufficed so many'.[29] Mair and his readers would have understood, though.

'And therefore, to conclude,' wrote our traveller, 'the men of old did no more wonder that the great Messias should be born in so poor a town as Bethlem in Judea, than I do wonder that so brave a prince as king James should be borne in so stinking a town as Edinburgh in lousy Scotland.'[30] It seems doubtful that this backhand praise could have wiped away the hate and ridicule for the king. Taylor and 'Weldon' neatly bookend the responses by the first Englishmen to cross the 'middle shires' of James's new-born Stuart *imperium*. They demonstrate how English travellers encountered the Scots and discovered the country on its own terms as well as through their own assumptions and attitudes. The ethno-religious complexion of the Stuart *imperium* became unstable in the 1630s as Charles I tried to guide his father's inheritance through the tense politics of the Thirty Years War.

Scotland and the wars of three kingdoms

George Buchanan's *Historie* made the deposition of Mary Queen of Scots an ordinary function of the Scottish 'constitution'; the Presbyterian Kirk expressed the natural religious disposition of the Scots, originating with the self-governing religious communities or culdees among the Gaels of the islands and highlands. Mary's son, James, could not have disagreed more: Buchanan and his ilk were the enemies of monarchy itself and nothing was more important than rebuilding the power and majesty of the Scottish Crown. The relationship of Crown and Kirk loomed large in James's project. A Kirk born in defiance of royal authority, shorn of bishops, empowered by its own 'grass-roots' organization of synods, presbyteries, and pseudo-parliament (the General Assembly) looked dangerously like a republican-inspired rival for power. James began the process of establishing a meaningful royal supremacy over the Kirk when he came of age. Legislation declaring the king's supremacy over the Church – Henry VIII would have approved – the neutralization of the General Assembly, and the progressive restoration of bishops with supervisory and disciplinary powers all worked to rebalance religious-political authority in the crown's favour. This might have stood as one of James's successes had not he – by timid and tentative steps – and Charles attempted to remodel the liturgy and order of the Kirk in a fashion much closer to its Anglican neighbour. The introduction of new canons and a prayer book in 1636 and 1637, respectively, triggered a national uprising in defence of the Kirk and Scotland's equal standing against the indifference and insensitivity of the Caroline regime. Thousands of Scots signed the National

---

[29] Hume Brown, *Early Travellers*, p. 101.
[30] Hume Brown, *Early Travellers*, p. 103.

Covenant in 1638. They defied their king's religious policies in Parliament and, finally, as soldiers in the field in the army of the Covenant.[31]

Confessional distinctions united and divided Protestants across ethnic and national boundaries in Britain. Episcopacy and the 'beauty of the holy' – the emphasis on ceremony and liturgy – found adherents in Scotland as well as in England or Wales. Evangelicals hoped to make good a common British Reformation by focussing on prayer and preaching, congregationalism, and a lived faith that infused communities. Catholicism, folk beliefs, and indifference added to these religious textures. They joined with ethno-cultural complexity to create the unique peoples encountered by travellers and, in some cases, anticipate the conflicted interactions and responses. The Puritan and future parliamentary general William Brereton journeyed to Scotland on the eve of the Caroline religious revolution. Scotland was one destination for a summer-long journey in 1635 that began in Handford, passed through the North of England, and returned home by way of the east coast of Ireland, Bristol, and the Welsh Borders. Brereton apparently wrote his narrative from notes kept during his travels. The itinerary remained in manuscript throughout his life. It was not finally rediscovered, and published by the Chetham Society, until 1844.[32]

Brereton's travels through England read like a narrative version of Leland's *Itinerary*; regular attention to local notables with whom he lodged, climate, livelihood, topography and the built environment, local colour, even the number of arches in the great bridges at Newcastle, London, Berwick, and Bristol. Brereton developed a deep affection for Newcastle. Its hilltop location along the salmon-filled Tyne, the great collieries that employed and warmed the city's commons, the quay and impregnable city walls – built 'against the incursions of the Picts' – made Newcastle 'beyond all compare the fairest and richest town in England' behind only London and Bristol.[33] On his way north, Brereton took in the salt works at Tynemouth and Shields, visited the earl of Northumberland's (re)building works at Alnwick Castle, listened to the supernatural explanations for the tides that controlled passage across the causeway to Holy Island, and lodged on the island at the 'dainty little fort' of Captain Rugg, 'famous for his generous and free entertainment of strangers, as for his great bottle nose'.[34]

Brereton took the east gateway into Scotland and found a Berwick very different from Moryson's, a poor town beset by 'many indigent persons and beggars' and a shallow, narrow haven. Leaving the town's stout walls behind the

[31] Tim Harris, *Rebellion: Britain's First Stuart Kings, 1567–1642* (Oxford, 2014), pp. 168–204, 360–72.
[32] William Brereton, 'Travels in Holland, the United Provinces, England, Scotland and Ireland', *Remains Historical and Literary Connected with the Palatine Counties of Lancaster and Chester*, Chetham Society reprinted (New York, 1968).
[33] Brereton, 'Travels', p. 85.
[34] Brereton, 'Travels', pp. 86–8, 90, 93–4.

Prospectus Civitatis TAODUNI ab Oriente. The Prospect of ye Town of DUNDEE from ye East.

14 'Prospect of ye Town of Dundee from ye East' engraved by John Slezer from Slezer, *Theatrium Scotiae* (Edinburgh, 1693). Reproduced by permission of the National Library of Scotland.

next day, Brereton grappled with just where the political and cultural boundaries lay between Scotland and England in this cultural middle ground:

> Friday we departed from Berwicke, which, though it be seated in Scotland, yet it is England and is annexed to the crown of England ... and here the country is not reputed Scottish, until you come to a town, four miles distant from Barwick, called Aten ... hence you pass (after you leave a few corn-fields near the town) over the largest and vastest moors that I have ever seen ...[35]

Scotland truly began here, in the vast, barren moorland of Tweeddale, devoid of sheep and coal, wood, and turf for fires. Here too Brereton and his companions found the Scots. Near Dunbar they found Scots fertilizing the ground with a thick blanket of 'grass, weeds, and wreck brought by the sea'. In the village of Roxburgh, 'we observed the sluttish women washing their clothes in a great tub with their feet, their coats, smocks, and all tucked up their breech'.[36]

Shepherds, farmers, fishermen, and travellers populate John Slezer's prospects of Scotland drawn in the 1670s. Washerwomen figured prominently in the foreground of Dundee from the east. Lewdness did not enter into the depiction. By contrast, Brereton's slovenly washerwomen would be turned into immoral

---

[35] Brereton, 'Travels', p. 96.
[36] Brereton, 'Travels', p. 96–7.

and immortal sluts when an anonymous traveller to Scotland claimed to have had the same experience outside Dunbar in 1704:

> At first I wondered at the sight, and thought they would have been ashamed, as I was, and have lett down their cloaths till I were by; but tho' some would lett them down halfe way their thights, others went round and round ... particularly a couple of young wenches that were washing together, at my coming by, pulled vp their cloaths the higher, and, when I was by, stood still and fell a-laughing.[37]

Our eighteenth-century traveller was determined to confront the next lewd washerwoman about her lack of modesty. The traveller met his match in a 'sturdy old woman' who resented his comment that she would ruin her breeches by not pulling them up in her stomping. She challenged him first to buy her a new pair when he was again in England. Being 'out of reache of her thumb and nails', the traveller dared to look back, only to find the washerwoman holding up one leg and calling after him to 'Spoile my breeches, brother!' The traveller learned his lesson and 'never durst to say anything to any of them afterwards'. He thus quietly passed by the lewdest scene of all, a young washerwoman ogled by the local boys with an old man sitting 'with his nose at the very taile of her', smoking his pipe.[38] If our anonymous traveller had read Brereton's manuscript and lifted the tale, he certainly gave it a lewd embellishment in the last years before the union of 1707.[39]

Brereton could not make the turn west to Edinburgh without noting Bass Rock, forever famous for the solan geese, and the Isle of May with its freshwater spring. The sands around Haddington offered Brereton and his companion only saltpans, while a 'foot-boy's negligence' left them in mean and nasty lodging for their first night in Edinburgh. Brereton took in the political scene. He found 'the greatest rudeness, disorder, and confusion, that I ever saw in any court of justice' in his visit to the Court of Session. More ominously, Brereton noted the importance of Archbishop John Spottiswoode in Charles I's administration. Spottiswoode exemplified how the 'clergy of late extend their authority and revenues' so that 'it is here thought and conceived that they will recover so much of that land and revenues belonging formerly to the Abbeys, as that they will in short time possess themselves of the third part of the kingdom'. Brereton astutely read the king's purpose in this clerical rehabilitation: 'to sit and carry voices in parliament; which, if it can be effected, then there will be always in the parliament-house so strong a party for the king ... as they will be able to sway

---

[37] *The North of England and Scotland in MDCCIV* (Edinburgh, 1818), p. 39. The manuscript version used by the printers, Oliver and Boyd, for William Blackwood is preserved in the National Library of Scotland as NLS MS 2506.

[38] *The North of England and Scotland*, p. 40.

[39] Martin Rackwitz, *Travels to Terra Incognita: The Scottish Highlands and Hebrides in Early Modern Travellers' Accounts c. 1600 to 1800* (Münster, 2007), pp. 454–61 for a summary of travellers' impressions of women's habit and 'Caledonia washing'.

the whole house. Divers of the clergy incline this way, and many also are mighty opposite and averse hereunto.'[40]

Our Puritan traveller provided a thorough description of the reformed Kirk: the governance of the Kirk and local community by pastors, elders, and deacons; provision for the poor and punishment of drunkards, fornicators, blasphemers, and a host of other scandalous actors with the stool of repentance, penance, censure, and admonishment; the order of service, including commemoration of the Lord's Supper at a narrow table placed in the middle of the kirk aisle. But Brereton witnessed the Kirk under threat from liturgical change stemming from the articles James had rammed through between 1617 and 1621, before the new Caroline canons and prayer book. The 'ceremonies of the Church of England are introduced and conformity is much pressed, and the gesture of kneeling is also much pressed'. The de facto abolition of the General Assembly of the Kirk made resistance more difficult, but resistance there was: 'The discipline of the Church of England is much pressed and much opposed by many pastors and many of the people,' the greatest part of whom were 'very honest and religiously zealous'.[41] Liturgical innovation and the nature of the Scottish polity were both at stake when the godly women of Edinburgh brought the first new service to a halt in St Giles Cathedral in 1637.

In five years Scottish Covenanters would be Brereton's comrades in arms against the king, but he departed from Scotland unimpressed with its people in almost every respect. The 'sluttish, nasty, and slothful' people left Brereton 'constrained to hold my nose' against the oppressive atmosphere of Edinburgh, some few well-mannered and 'reformed' denizens aside. In particular, the people fetched fresh water only every other day, making it particularly noxious to drink, considering that 'when it is at best is bad enough.' Even worse, their 'houses of office are tubs or firkins placed upon the end, which they never empty until they be full, so as the scent thereof annoyeth and offendeth the whole house'. No doubt the earl of Gowrie's head, still affixed atop the Tollbooth, added to the city's gruesome sights, though Brereton did not miss a beat by mentioning in the next breath that he ate a dinner of Tollbooth pies, sold twelve for a penny.[42]

Ordinary Scots' dress caught Brereton's attention. Common Scotswomen wore the plaid, 'a garment of the same woollen stuff whereof saddle cloths in England are made, which is cast over their heads, and covers their faces on both sides, and would reach almost to the ground, but that they pluck them up, and wear them cast under their arms'. They were not the only ones. In Edinburgh Brereton saw many highlanders in their plaid, 'a kind of loose flap garment hanging loose about their breech, their knees bare'. In contrast to most Scots, Brereton approved of the unspoilt hardiness of the highlanders, 'proper,

---

[40] Brereton, 'Travels', pp. 97–101.
[41] Brereton, 'Travels', pp. 106–10.
[42] Brereton, 'Travels', pp. 102–4.

personable, well-complectioned men, and able men; the very gentlemen in their blue caps and plaids'.[43]

A second day in Edinburgh provoked Brereton to repeat his complaints. 'The sluttishness and nastiness of the people is such,' he confessed, 'that I cannot omit the particularizing thereof, though I have more than sufficiently often touched upon the same'. The stench in their houses, halls, and kitchens was so strong that it could be positively tasted in the air. Brereton was sure that the Scots never cleaned their pewter for fear 'it should too much wear and consume thereby'. Filthy feet yielded filthy washing when entrusted to Scottish washerwomen, after which 'it looks as nastily as ours doth when it is put unto and designed to the washing'. Brereton could only hold his nose against such foul linen when he turned in. Were that not enough, to 'come into their kitchen, and to see them dress their meat, and to behold the sink (which is more offensive than any jakes [privy]) will be sufficient supper, and will take off the edge of your stomach'.[44]

Before leaving Edinburgh, Brereton armed himself with two pistols and a pair of knives and called in at a bookseller's to purchase an unknown 'Itinerary of Scotland and Ireland'. Brereton's narrative took a turn to the perfunctory once he left Edinburgh for Linlithgow, Falkland, Dunfermline, Loch Lomond, Stirling, Glasgow, and Ayrshire. The approach to Glasgow carried him through land devoid of forests and populated by the poorest people and dwellings he had ever observed. At Glasgow, Brereton took in the university, the tollbooth, and the archbishop's palace and inserted in this narrative odd lists of the country's fairest cities and bridges. Carrick in Ayrshire brought him into contact with the ringing rock – a rock that tingled like a bell when struck with a knife – and strange footprints in a cave, human and animal, that reappeared every day even when the ground was disturbed.[45]

The journey south to Irvine passed through country fallen on hard times, barren and poor due to drought, abandoned by its tenants, and left to the fruitless efforts of its one-time landlords. James Blair hosted Brereton in Irvine and informed him that more than ten thousand Scots had migrated in the past two years, many of them passing through Irvine on their way to northern Ireland, sometimes hundreds at a time. When asked, 'none of them can give a reason why they leave the country, only some of them thow make a better use of God's hand upon [them], have acknowledged to mine host in these words, "that it was a just judgment of God to spew them out of the land for their unthankfulness"'.[46]

The cryptic prose suggests the zeal of evangelical Presbyterians, vexed by the religious innovations that Brereton had spotted earlier, and determined to find safe haven among their co-religionists in the Ulster plantations. For instance,

---

[43] Brereton, 'Travels', pp. 103, 105, 117.
[44] Brereton, 'Travels', pp. 105–6.
[45] Brereton, 'Travels', pp. 111–18.
[46] Brereton, 'Travels', p. 119.

when Brereton later reached Ayr, his hostess denounced the local minister for pressing the changes on the congregation, especially kneeling at communion. One man who was certain about the migrants' intentions was the king's lord deputy in Ireland, Thomas Strafford, earl of Wentworth. Wentworth determined to choke off the movement of any migrants without warrants and worked to return others to Scotland. Brereton was unsure what to make of those whom he met in Irvine, but finally concluded that 'there may be observed much matter of admiration' about them and 'doubtless, *digitus Dei* is to be discerned in it'.[47] On 4 July, Brereton boarded a crowded ship crewed by 'good expert mariners' at Portpatrick, landing the next day on the Irish coast near Carrickfergus after a rain-soaked night spent aboard ship waiting out the 'most cruel, violent, and tempestuous storms'.[48]

Ireland affected Brereton's views of Scotland – and one wonders what impact Moryson's own bitter turn there would have done to his sensibilities on a return visit to Scotland. When Brereton arrived in Ireland, he 'saw' a country of British planters and missed opportunities for social and economic improvement. Almost without fail he noted the origins of those whom he met and lodged with. At the 'brave plantation' of Arthur Hill near Belfast, Brereton found many 'Lanckashire and Cheshire men are here planted; with some of them I conversed.' Leaving Hill's Belfast plantation, Brereton journeyed to Linsley Garven. He travelled through 'a paradise in comparison of any part of Scotland', struck by the natural beauty and the labours of Lord Conway, the proprietor, to enrich the unimproved land.[49]

Civility and barbarity were more starkly drawn in Ireland than in Scotland, let alone England. Poverty never caught Brereton's attention in Scotland the way it did in Ireland, a 'wild country, not inhabited, planted, nor enclosed', dotted with 'the poorest cabins I have seen'.[50] Brereton also encountered something in Ireland without parallel in his experiences of Presbyterian Scotland: Old English (Anglo-Irish) Catholic recusants who worshipped openly and held civil rights. These included mayors, aldermen, and sheriffs selected in Drogheda, in the Protestant heartland of the Dublin Pale.[51] Somewhat fickle, Brereton wrote that Dublin itself 'is beyond all exception the fairest, richest, best built city I have met with in this journey (except Yorke and Newcastle). It is far beyond Edenborough; only, one street in Edenborough (the great long street) surpasseth any street here.' St Patrick's Cathedral in Dublin also put the Scots to shame, 'in best repair, and most neatly whited and kept of any church I have seen in Scotland or Ireland'.[52]

---

[47] Brereton, 'Travels', pp. 119–20.
[48] Brereton, 'Travels', p. 125.
[49] Brereton, 'Travels', pp. 128–9.
[50] Brereton, 'Travels', pp. 132, 135, 149.
[51] Brereton, 'Travels', pp. 134, 148.
[52] Brereton, 'Travels', pp. 137–8.

Gender marked differences in Ireland as they had in Scotland. In Wexford, Brereton described the fine attire of the townswomen – more attractive than their Edinburgh counterparts. However, their Catholicism imparted an immoral sensual quality: 'The most of the women are bare-necked, and clean-skinned, and wear a crucifix, tied in a black necklace, hanging betwixt their breasts. It seems they are not ashamed of their religion, nor desire to conceal themselves; and indeed in this town are many papists.'[53] In Waterford, Brereton found another town dominated by the Old English, although, in his mind, they had already become one with the 'Irish' by their Catholicism. 'Most of the inhabitants Irish,' he wrote, 'not above forty English, and not one of these Irish goes to church,' which explained the decayed condition of the town's seven churches. Waterford brought back a vivid memory from Scotland: 'Here we saw women in a most impudent manner treading cloathes with their feet; these were naked to the middle almost, for so high were their clothes tucked up about them.'[54] Considering the instances of repetition in Brereton's narrative, one wonders if he had transposed this tale from memory or his notes. Either way, it shows how his travels in Ireland put Brereton in mind of his experiences in Scotland, a feature not to be found in his English travels except when he marked the wall of Glastonbury Abbey as higher than any to be found in Glasgow or Winchester.[55]

Brereton concluded his 'Summer's Progress' at Chester, but finished his narrative with several additional items: a summary of copper and silver coins in circulation in Scotland; a barebones itinerary with dates, stops, and distances; and another account of his subsequent recovery from a flux or bout of dysentery – a fit companion to the vivid descriptions of his loose bowels in Ireland. Brereton also took the time to write a short pronunciation guide to 'Speech in Scotland'. Unlocking accents in Scotland required more than a 'few general prescripts ... only experience and use acquired by cohabitation' among them would do. He found Scots both puzzling and promising: 'if all the properties of languages were concurrent there, as well as significancy in pathetic speeches and innumerable proverbs and by-words, they might compare with any people in the world'.[56]

When James Howell, the great Welsh letter writer and gossip, arrived in Edinburgh in late summer 1639, he saw the revolutionary effects of the religious meddling Brereton had first spotted. That June, English militiamen met a Covenanter army at the border town of Duns Law for a battle of words and show, ending with the Treaty of Berwick. Alexander Leslie led the Covenanters across the Tweed in August to a battle worth the name at Newburn, defeating a 10,000-strong English army and occupying the north of England as far as Newcastle.[57] Writing to Lord Clifford, who had prepared the defences swept aside by the

---

[53] Brereton, 'Travels', p. 156.
[54] Brereton, 'Travels', p. 160.
[55] Brereton, 'Travels', p. 173.
[56] Brereton, 'Travels', p. 188–9.
[57] Michael Lynch, *Scotland: A New History* (London, 1991), pp. 270–1.

Covenanters, Howell explained that 'I have now seen all the King of Great Britain's dominions; and he is a good traveller that hath seen all his dominions. I was born in Wales, I have been in all the four corners of England ... and now I am come through Ireland into this kingdom of Scotland.'[58]

Howell arrived at a propitious moment. Edinburgh's Royal Mile was 'one of the fairest streets that ever I saw', even after travels to France and continental Europe. Midway between Edinburgh castle and Holyrood stood the unfinished parliament house commissioned by the king. Here, at the end of August, the Scottish Parliament met, with the fate of Charles's rule at stake:

> I am come hither in a very convenient time, for here is a national assembly and a parliament, my Lord Traquair being his Majesty's Commissioner. The bishops are all gone to wreck, and they have had but a sorry funeral: the very name is grown so contemptible that a black dog if he hath any white marks about him, is called Bishop. Our Lord of Canterbury [Archbishop Laud] is grown here so odious, that they call him commonly in the pulpit, the Priest of Baal, and the son of Belial.

Besides Charles and Laud's attacks on the Kirk, the Scots smarted at the king's failure to be an active personal ruler in Scotland. The Scots with whom Howell spoke had hoped to see the 'maiden head' of the new Parliament taken by the king, to 'come hither to sit in person'. For Howell, 'they did ill who advised him otherwise'.[59]

The conflict found its way into every corner of Edinburgh, even Howell's lodgings at a local tavern. Howell summoned a bootmaker, and the tavern owner used the occasion to share a chopin (quart) of wine with the artisan. Looking on, Howell saw the men fall into a heated debate about bishops. The cobbler knew his mind, calling bishops 'the firebrands of hell, the panders of the whore of Babylon, and the instruments of the devil; and that they were of his institution, not of God's'. The tavern owner accepted none of this, reminding the shoemaker that Titus and Timothy were both bishops and that 'our Saviour is entitled the Bishop of our Souls'. That might be, but the shoemaker knew that the abuses of their own bishops had degraded the office. 'Well then,' the tavern owner retorted, 'imagine that you, or a hundred, or a thousand, or a hundred thousand of your trade should play the knaves, and sell calf-skin leather boots for neats-leather, or do other cheats, must we therefore go barefoot?' The cobbler was at a loss how to defeat this clever turn and Howell approved that 'my vintner got the day'.[60] By 1647, heated by five years of war, Howell began identifying Charles I's opponents with 'wild Arabs'.[61]

---

[58] Hume Brown, *Early Travellers*, p. 159.
[59] Hume Brown, *Early Travellers*, pp. 159–60.
[60] Hume Brown, *Early Travellers*, p. 160.
[61] Quoted in Anna Suranyi, *The Genius of the English Nation: Travel Writing and National Identity in Early Modern England* (Newark, DE, 2008), p. 79.

The cobbler, however, lived to see his position triumph, and the ensuing conflicts of the 1640s and 1650s brought the Scots into intimate and regular contact with their British (and Irish) neighbours. They occupied the north of England after the battle of Newburn and Treaty of Ripon. The Solemn League and Covenant, agreed in 1643 between the Scots and the king's enemies in the English Parliament and pledged to establish Presbyterianism throughout Britain and Ireland, made the English and Scots temporary allies. While the alliance lasted, Scottish soldiers were present in most of the theatres of war in England and the army was headquartered at Newark. When the alliance collapsed and Charles made an Engagement with his more moderate opponents in Scotland, the Engager army took to the field and was defeated at the Battle of Preston.[62] The Scottish presence presented problems for both parliamentarians and the king. Race-baiting propaganda, first-hand encounters with Scottishness, and the typical depredations of soldiers in wartime positively antagonized the prejudices of local communities in England, with lasting effects.[63] Few of those English men and women must have shed a tear as centuries of independence finally ended when the New Model Army subjugated Scotland in 1651 and 1652.

Thomas Tucker was one Englishman who found himself in Scotland after the parliamentary conquest. The Commonwealth government sent Tucker and others north to investigate the state of the country, in his case to examine customs, excise, and Scottish trade. Tucker's account is fundamentally an economic assessment, and an invaluable one at that. But even this early technocrat could not help but compare Scotland with its southern neighbour or escape by now familiar cultural assumptions. The comparisons did not flatter:

> the barrenesse of the countrey, poverty of the people, generally affected with slothe, and a lazy vagrancy of attending and followeing theyr heards up and downe in theyr pastorage, rather than any dextrous improvement of theyr time, hath quite banished all trade from the inland parts ... with all the islands up toward the most northerne headland, being inhabited by the old Scotts, or wilde Irish, and speaking theyr language, which live by feeding cattle up and downe the hills, or else fishing and fowleing, and formerly (till that they have of late been restrayned,) by plaine downeright robbing and stealeing.[64]

Fish, salt, and coal dominated Scottish exports as Tucker made his circuit of the country's ports. Tucker had a parliamentarian and commercial view of the relationship between Leith and Edinburgh, and 'did not that citty [Edinburgh] (jealous of her own safety,) obstruct and impede the groweing of this place, it would, from her slave, in a few yeares become her rivall'. There are evangelical hints too. Where once the castle of Edinburgh invited 'people in the time

[62] Lynch, *Scotland*, pp. 271–9.
[63] Mark Stoyle, *Soldiers and Strangers: An Ethnic History of the English Civil War* (New Haven, 2005), pp. 73–90, 198–208.
[64] Hume Brown, *Early Travellers*, p. 163.

of theyr intestine troubles to plant and setle there', so the peace and union created under the new Republic would now invite Edinburgh's inhabitants 'to discend from theyr proude hill into the more fruitfull plaine, to be filled with the fulnesse and fattenesse thereof'.[65]

Tucker also betrayed a certain social antagonism in describing the weak trade of Fife and the Tay Valley, Scotland's 'best and richest' region. Its richness sprang 'more from the goodnesse and fertility of the soyle and lands than any traffique' because the 'gentry of that nation' who planted themselves there 'have wholly driven out all but theyr tenants and peasants even to the shore side'. The only profitable trade was to be found in the 'pittifull small townes' of East Neuk, inhabited by 'seamen, colliers, saltmakers and such like people'. St Andrews 'continued still proud in the ruines of her former magnificence, and in being yett a seate for the Muses'. Dundee next came into view but it too had had a happier, wealthier past before General George Monck's cannons – justifiably, for Tucker – changed all that: 'the many rencontres [encounters] it hath mett with all in the time of domestick comotions, and her obstinacy and pride of late yeares rendring her a prety to the soldier, have much shaken and abated her former grandeur; and notwithstanding all, shee remaynes still, though not glorious, yett not contemptible'.[66]

Tucker showed some appreciation for the trade of the highlanders. Their wools, skins, and hides brought in 'great plenty' to Perth and were 'bought up and engrossed by the Lowlandmen' there. Inverness was the trading hub for the north-west and a dynamic cultural meeting place: 'The inhabitants beyond Murray land (except in the Orkneys) speake generally Ober garlickh [Gaelic], or Highlands, and the mixture of both in the towne of Invernesse is such that one halfe of the people understand not one another.' Thurso and Wick trafficked in beef, hides, and tallow down the coast, while Kirkwall added some grain and fish to the same traffic with the Dutch. Passing to the west, Tucker found the west coast 'planted with ancient Scotts or wilde Irish', stored with cattle, craggy hills, and supposedly 'destitute of all trade'. It was at Glasgow that Tucker found real hope for Scottish commerce. The Glaswegians' unsuccessful attempts to crack the Caribbean trade with Barbados did not detract from 'the mercantile genius of the people'. Only the shallowness of the Clyde 'chequed and kept under' the 'stronge signes of her increase and groweth'. None of the other ports and towns Tucker surveyed in completing his circuit at Dumfries held such promise, with the possible exception of Ayr, thanks to the construction of an English citadel there in 1652. The citadel outlived the British Republic that ended in 1660.

---

[65] Hume Brown, *Early Travellers*, p. 164.
[66] Hume Brown, *Early Travellers*, pp. 169–71.

The Restoration prejudices of John Ray and Thomas Kirke

Nine years after the Scots had crowned him king at Scone, Charles Stuart landed in Dover to accept the three kingdoms as Charles II. The Stuart monarchy in its first decade of revival was nothing if not an exercise in religious bigotry. The Republic's imperfect experiments with liberty of conscience and the abolition of the coercive powers of the state Church came to an end. Anglicans and Scottish Episcopalians determinedly persecuted religious Dissenters or radical Covenanters who might still nurse the spirit of tyrannicide and republicanism. The great naturalist John Ray was one of the many harmless figures snared by the so-called Clarendon Code, the body of legislation that restored the Church of England and empowered the regime to prosecute those who dissented from it. Ray, a smith's son from Black Notley, Essex, took his degree at Trinity College, Cambridge but lost his fellowship in 1662 when he refused to swear to the Act of Uniformity. Before this, Ray's naturalist instincts had carried him into the far corners of Britain. He and Francis Willoughby of Middleton, Warwickshire, spent the better part of 1660 exploring Britannia's natural history, arriving in Scotland in mid-August.[67]

Like others before them, Ray and Willoughby crossed the Tweed at Berwick. As it had done for Brereton, the journey to Dunbar brought the two men face to face with the Scots. The familiarity of the descriptions leaves no doubt as to how fixed certain images of the Scots had become in the minds of English travellers. Common Scotsmen wore 'blue bonnets' and the 'women only white linen, which hangs down their backs as if a napkin were pinned about them'. Out of doors, men and women wore a 'coloured blanket which they call a plad, over their heads and shoulders'. Once again, Scottish women fared badly in the traveller's notebook: 'The women generally to us seemed none of the handsomest. They are not very cleanly in their houses, and but sluttish in dressing their meat. Their way of washing linnen is to tuck up their coats, and tread them with the feet in a tub.'[68] With the reappearance of the washerwomen near Dunbar, we might suspect that travellers' eyes opened only for images that stories at home had primed them to see.

Food and housing did nothing to win Ray's affection. Glazed windows were absent from even the best houses in Scotland, the king's palaces included. Rather, the Scots could often be found poking their heads through rounds holes in the fir boards that served as the windows and outside walls of their houses, even in 'their principal towns'. The cottages of crofters and cottars were even worse, 'pitiful cots, built of stone, and covered with turves [turf], having in them but one room, many of them no chimneys, the windows very small holes, and not glazed'. Warming pans made every Scottish house, humble or ostentatious, a chilly resort. For staples like bread, cheese, and drink, the Scots 'cannot make

[67] Scott Mandelbrote, 'John Ray', *Oxford DNB* at www.oxforddnb.com.
[68] Hume Brown, *Early Travellers*, p. 231.

them, nor will they learn', while butter left Ray thinking 'one would wonder how they could contrive to make it so bad.' Pottage of colewort or kale and husked barley left much to be desired. Even the famed solan geese, which Ray sampled at Dunbar, left him unconvinced: 'It feeds upon mackerel and herring, and the flesh of the young one smells and tastes strong of these.' Despite the intense farming of oats and rye, Ray decided that the Scots were 'very lazy, at least the men, and may be frequently observed to plow in their cloaks'.[69]

Ray left Dunbar and his descriptions of the Scots behind after visiting the monument to George Home, the Jacobean earl of Dunbar, in the town's church. Castles and fortifications, civic buildings, churches and cathedrals, and universities occupied his attention in Leith, Edinburgh, Perth, Stirling, and Glasgow. He attended to two features often associated with early modern Scotland. According to local informants, Ray claimed that during their fortnight in Scotland 'divers women were burnt for witches ... to the number of 120'. Returning to England by way of Dumfries, Ray encountered a young Presbyterian minister named Campbell who 'prayed for the preservation of their church government and discipline, and spake openly against prelacy and its adjuncts and consequences'. Ray described the typical kirk service and came away convinced that the Scots 'frequent their churches much better than in England, and have their ministers in more esteem and veneration ... [and] seem to perform their devotions with much alacrity'. He found 'few or no sectaries and opinionists among them' but a people devoted to their Kirk, with one crucial exception: 'the gentry, who love liberty, and care not to be so strictly tied down' by the Kirk's moral community.[70] It would be these gentry who allied with the restored Stuart regime to establish an Episcopal polity that drove men like Campbell from their pulpits and executed his more zealous brethren who refused to conform.[71] Yet any fellow feeling that Ray may have felt for Scots in danger of persecution went only so far. Scotland was a proud country whose people 'cannot endure to hear their country or countrymen spoken against', but it nonetheless 'abounds with poor people and beggars'.[72]

One Restoration traveller devoid of any fellow feeling for the Scots was Thomas Kirke of Crookwige, Yorkshire. Kirke travelled through Scotland for more than three months in 1677. He anonymously published *A Modern Account of Scotland* in 1679. Seventeenth-century Scotophobes need look no further than the opening description. Why visit Italy for antique vistas when the topography of Scotland 'derives its original from the chaos?' No noble descendants of antiquity here, the 'first inhabitants were some stragglers of fallen angels, who rested themselves in the confines, till their Captain Lucifer provided places for

[69] Hume Brown, *Early Travellers*, pp. 231–3.
[70] Hume Brown, *Early Travellers*, pp. 235, 239.
[71] Clare Jackson, *Restoration Scotland 1660–1690: Royalist Politics, Religion, and Ideas* (Woodbridge, 2003), pp. 104–30.
[72] Hume Brown, *Early Travellers*, p. 231, 239–40.

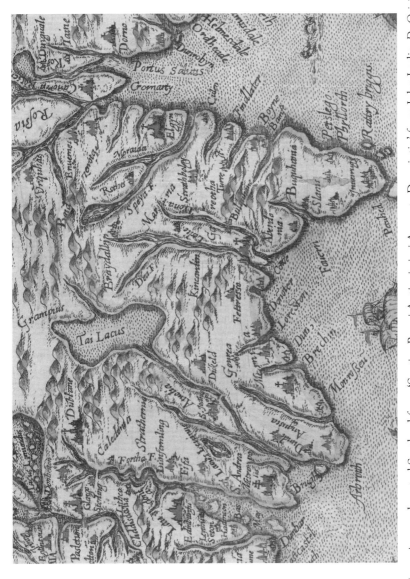

15 The Grampians and central Scotland from 'Scotiae Regni Antiqvissimi Accvrata Descriptio' from John Leslie, *De Origine Moribus, et Rebus Gestis Scotorum Libri Decem* (Rome, 1578). Reproduced by permission of the National Library of Scotland.

them in his own country'.[73] Then followed Scota and her descendants, a story from Scottish chronicles not to be doubted:

> [The] plagues of Egypt being entailed upon them, that of lice (being a judgment unrepealed) is an ample testimony, those loving animals accompanied them from Egypt, and remains with them to this day, never forsaking them (but as rats leave a house) till they tumble in their graves. The plague of biles and blains is hereditary to them, as a distinguishing marke from the rest of the world, which (like the devil's cloven hoof) warns all men to beware of them. The judgment of hail and snow is naturalized ... The plague of the darkness ... being applicable to their gross and blockish understandings (as I had from a scholar of their own nation).[74]

Resentment at the union of crowns – indeed, having to share Britain at all with the Scots – seemed to fuel Kirke's prejudice. Where Italy was compared to a leg, Scotland should be compared to a louse, 'whose proboscis joyns too close to England has suckt away the nutriment from Northumberland'. The thistle was the perfect emblem for these British neighbours, 'having some colour of a flower, but the bulk and substance of it, is only sharp and poysonous pricks'.[75]

Wood was scarce except for the upland stands of fir, like those Taylor had marvelled at in the Grampians. But the Scots who frequented these woods in 'the Highlands' shared something with the Welsh who once dwelled in hilltop coppices: they were 'dens for those ravenous wolves with two legs' that 'prey upon their neighbourhood'. Enclosures were unheard of in Scotland, 'the whole being one large waste, surrounded with the sea'. 'If the air was not pure and well refined by its agitation,' continued Kirke, 'it would be so infected with the stinks of their towns, and the steams of their nasty inhabitants, that it would be pestilential and destructive.' No breeze could blow away the cobwebs of Kirke's prejudiced mind, and he added that the Scots' 'nostrils (like a Jew's) chiefly delight in the perceptible effluviums'.[76]

Flora, fauna, fish, birds, and animals all provided opportunities for hate-filled commentary. Not content to actually report on the birdlife, Kirke wrote of one ravenous fowl with one webbed foot, one foot suited for land, and a third for water, 'but whether or no this fowl ... be not the lively picture of the inhabitants, I shall leave to wiser conjectures'. The ordinariness of cows, horses, sheep, and hogs ('more like porcupines') was itself worthy of contempt. The many lakes, lochs, and islands on a map looked 'like a pillory coat bespattered all over with dirt and rotten eggs, some pieces of the shells floating here and there, representing the islands'.[77]

---

[73] Hume Brown, *Early Travellers*, pp. 251–2.
[74] Hume Brown, *Early Travellers*, p. 252.
[75] Hume Brown, *Early Travellers*, p. 253.
[76] Hume Brown, *Early Travellers*, p. 254.
[77] Hume Brown, *Early Travellers*, pp. 254–6.

Amidst these descriptions, Kirke inserted a pompously overwritten variation on the now-familiar account of washerwomen:

> The exercise of their arms, I shou'd say feet, is much about linen; sheets are sufferers, a fit receiver is provided (not unlike a shallow pulpit to mind them of their idol sermons) wherein foul linen is laid to suffer persecution, so they turn up all, and tuck them about their wastes, and bounce into buck-tub, then go their stock, and belabour poor lint till there be not a dry thread on't.[78]

Kirke betrayed his religious and ideological prejudices. Scottish cities were 'poor and populous' and Edinburgh, 'high and dirty', matched its inhabitants, but the universities stood out for particular ridicule. The students in the four universities (Edinburgh, St Andrews, Aberdeen, Glasgow) lived among the townspeople and met in college only to 'consult their oracle Buchanan', the great enemy of divine-right monarchy. Preferment to the Kirk drove them, seeking 'to prate out four or five glasses with as much ease as drink them' 'commencing Master of Arts ... before one wou'd judge them fit for the college'.[79]

Kirke's ignorance and prejudice produced a wonderful jumble of contradictory impulses that defined the Tory Anglican approach to the Kirk and Presbyterianism. The Restoration Kirk may have been Episcopalian in structure and under the king's supremacy, but its liturgy and worship was overwhelmingly Presbyterian. Like the Catholic Lesley, Kirke deplored the destructiveness of the Scottish Reformation: 'goodly structures being either wholly destroyed (as at St Andrews and Elgin, where by the remaining ruines you may see what it was in perfection) or very much defaced'. He condemned the Kirk not just for destructiveness but for its own use of religious space, no doubt with St Giles cathedral in mind, 'for it is common here three, four, or five kirks under one roof, which being preserved entire, would have made one good church, but they could not then have had preaching enough in it; out of one pulpit now they have thirty sermons per week'. Kirke could not help but contradict his own judgment, though. He wrote that zealous preaching was needed by the Scots, considering 'their stools of repentance in every kirk, well furnished with whore-mongers and adulterers of both sexes'. In Kirke's telling, the stool of repentance became a 'high place' to shame whores that worked to 'the benefit of strangers, who (some think) need not this direction' to seek them out to pass the time while in town.[80]

The ghost of Mr Presbyter – the stock figure for those English who feared or rejected the zeal of their Presbyterian allies in the 1640s – was alive and well in the Scotland that Kirke visited:

> They use no service-book, no whore of Babylon's smock (as they term a surplice) nor decency, nor order in their divine or rather contumelious service. Wou'd a king think himself honoured by subjects, that petitioned him without bonet vailed ... while

---

[78] Hume Brown, *Early Travellers*, p. 255.
[79] Hume Brown, *Early Travellers*, pp. 255–7.
[80] Hume Brown, *Early Travellers*, pp. 257–8.

precious Mr Presbyter grimaces, prays or houls, the monster-rabble vails; but as soon as the text is taken, blew-bonnet takes place again, and this pulpit-prater is esteemed more than God's ambassadour, having the Holy Spirit at his beck, to prompt him every word he speaks, yet not three sentences of sense together, such blasphemy, as I blush to mention.[81]

Kirke gave no ground to these fellow Protestants when it came to baptism. In baptism, 'only water is poured on the infant, and such words used as) Sir John's Mephistophilus supplies him with, and so the child commences Christian' without the holy oil used by Anglicans – and Catholics – to anoint the bairn.[82]

Marriage seemed to define everything that was wrong with the Scots living under the heavy hand of Mr Presbyter. A Scottish marriage was not sufficiently ritualized or ceremonial for the High Anglican Kirke. Instead, the 'young couple, being attended with tagrag and bobtail, gang to the kirk, where Mr Scruple (like a good Casuist) controverts the point in hand to them [marriage], and schools Mr Bridegroom in his lesson, then directs his discourse to Mrs Bride'. Faithfully instructed, the marriage is performed and 'Home they go with loud ravishing bag-pipes, and dance about the green till they part ... and, perhaps, Sir Roger follows Mrs Bride to her apartment, to satisfie her doubts, where he uses such pungent and pressing arguments as she never forgets as long as she lives.'[83]

Having disposed of birth and marriage, Kirke ridiculed the Scots' way of death and mocked the Scottish tongue in which the passing of a loved one was announced to the congregation. He rudely observed that 'All agree that a woman's tongue is the last member she moves' at the moment of death, before launching into a prolonged attack on the Scots' pride. According to Kirke, 'the meanest man must have a grave-stone full fraught with his own praises (though he be the vilest miscreant on earth) and miserable'. Epitaphs were etched 'in English and Latin, nay Greek too, if the can find a Greek word for cordinger', although given 'such miserable Scotch orthography ... 'tis hard to distinguish one language from another'.[84]

Kirke added nothing new to existing descriptions of Scottish housing, clothing, food and drink, music, roads, and hospitality except unalloyed contempt and a self-satisfied wit. Kirke's misogynist comment on a woman's tongue was no one-off comment. To 'put one's head into their kitchen doors ... you enter Hell alive, where the black furies are busied in mangling dead carcasses and the fire and brimstone, or rather stew and stink, is ready to suffocate you, and yet (which is strange) these things are agreeable the humours of the people'. Perhaps moved by the sting of personal rejection, Kirke's account of Scottish women made them something very much less than human, let alone feminine:

[81] Hume Brown, *Early Travellers*, p. 258.
[82] Hume Brown, *Early Travellers*, p. 258.
[83] Hume Brown, *Early Travellers*, p. 258.
[84] Hume Brown, *Early Travellers*, pp. 258–9.

The women are commonly two-handed tools, strong-posted timber, they dislike English men because they have no legs, or (like themselves) posts to walk on; the meaner go bare-foot and bare-head, with two black elf-locks on either side their faces; some of them have scarce any cloaths at all, save part of their bed-cloaths … those women that can purchase plads, need not bestow much upon other cloaths, these cover-sluts being sufficient. Those of the best sort that are very well habited in the modish silk, yet must wear a plad over all for the credit of their country.[85]

As for the Scots as a people, they were 'proud, arrogant, vain-glorious boasters, bloody barbarous, and inhuman butchers. … theft is in perfection among them, and they are perfect English haters'. Naturally, cattle thieves roamed the Highlands, while everywhere the nobility and gentry, oppressive by nature, treated their tenants, to the lowest man, woman, and child, as 'gally-slaves'. Out of fearful devotion, they made their lord's quarrel their own, so that 'if you offend the laird, his durk shall be soon sheathed in your belly, and, after this, every one of his followers'. Lest anyone doubt Kirke's word, they had only to turn to the innumerable cruelties and 'strange butcheries' chronicled in Scotland's histories, including forty kings 'barbarously murthered', half as many again who had fled in deadly fear, and numerous bloody feuds among the nobility themselves – not quite how Buchanan expected people to read the Scots' republican pedigree. Rudeness was no stranger, while the Scots' cruelty descended even to eating a live cow. 'The Lowland language may be well enough understood by an English man,' Kirke wrote, 'but the Highlanders … are so currish, that if a stranger enquire the way in English, they will certainly answer in Erst [Erse], and find no other language than what is inforc'd from them in a cudgel.'[86]

Here was a 'Weldon' for Restoration prejudices, but there is more at work in Kirke's travels than meets the eye.[87] Kirke kept a detailed journal of his travels in Scotland. He covered a lot of ground from May to August 1677. He entered Scotland via Berwick and made his way along the east coast (Dunbar, Edinburgh, Kinghorn, St Andrews, Dundee, Arbroath, Aberdeen, and points in between), turned west to Elgin, Inverness, and the Orkneys, returned by a similar route until breaking toward Perth, Glasgow, and Ayrshire, finally sailing for Ireland from Portpatrick. Kirke betrayed something of his prejudice against Mr Presbyter and his low opinion of Scottish women, otherwise his 'Journal' and *Modern Account* might have been written by different travellers.[88] He and his various travelling companions were well received throughout their journeys. Orkney irritated with its poor lodging and dear rates and there were ordinary nuisances in the absence of lodging – including a memorable ride to Inverness through a high summer's

---

[85] Hume Brown, *Early Travellers*, p. 260.
[86] Hume Brown, *Early Travellers*, pp. 260–2.
[87] *Tours in Scotland 1677 and 1681 by Thomas Kirk and Ralph Thoresby*, ed. P. Hume Brown (Edinburgh, 1892), p. vi.
[88] *Tours in Scotland*, pp. 8, 10, 27–8.

night with its weak hour or two of semi-darkness.[89] Otherwise, Kirke found much to comment on favourably across the lowlands, including 'many fine seats' set in groves of trees on the journey to Edinburgh.[90] The same could be said of Burntisland, the earl of Rothes' Leslie House, Aberdeen, Dornoch, Linlithgow ('one of the prettiest towns I have yet seen in Scotland'), and Glasgow, bestride 'the river Clyde, a most pleasant stream'.[91] Even his encounter with the Kirk elicited bemusement or, at worst, restrained disapproval.[92]

The worst experiences involved encounters with drink, Scottish women, and highlanders. Kirke's eye for drunkenness followed from his own fondness for ale and wine. Kirke and his companions called in at Lady Huntly's in Banff for a glass of wine, only to be accosted by the arrival of a Captain Ogilby. Ogilby insisted on playing the host and forced so much wine on the guests that they finally fled. The following day, the sheriff entertained them at the Bonny Wife inn; 'in half an hour's time we drank more wine than some of us could carry away'.[93] At Dunbar, a woman at the inn removed her shoes and stockings when Kirke arrived. Perhaps, he thought, women 'esteem it an honour to go bare-foot and bare-leg'.[94] Arriving in Montrose, Kirke noted that women did not change their names when they married, as evinced by his landlady. Near Inverness, Kirke came upon a rotten bridge, beneath which he found an 'abundance of nasty women possing clothes with their feet, their clothes tucked up to the middle'.[95] In the 'Journal', these women perplexed Kirke. In the *Modern Account* they joined a nation of women who profoundly offended his sensibilities, and were savaged by his pen in retaliation.

The gallows gave substance to the oppressive nobility whom Kirke later denounced. At the Laird of Meldrum's house near Aberdeen, he learned that most lords kept gallows 'to condemn and hang any offenders in their liberties' not turned over to the sheriff.[96] Looking for a good vantage point for a view of Loch Ness, Kirke found a 'gibbet, whereon hung two Highlanders' right arms'. One belonged to a horse thief later hanged for his mischiefs, the other to a man who had nearly beaten to death a pedlar. Brutal justice united Scots, but the 'wild Irish' and complicated kit of the Highlanders made Inverness unique.[97] Kirke also found in use the stool of repentance and the branks, an iron mask with a mouthpiece designed to painfully stop the tongue.[98] Kirke's account of

---

[89] *Tours in Scotland*, pp. 27, 30–7.
[90] *Tours in Scotland*, pp. 12.
[91] *Tours in Scotland*, pp. 16–17, 23, 34–5, 43, 47.
[92] *Tours in Scotland*, pp. 7, 8, 19–20, 21.
[93] *Tours in Scotland*, pp. 24–5.
[94] *Tours in Scotland*, p. 10.
[95] *Tours in Scotland*, pp. 21, 27–8.
[96] *Tours in Scotland*, p. 24.
[97] *Tours in Scotland*, pp. 28–9.
[98] *Tours in Scotland*, pp. 10, 28.

Liberton came without judgement. The well 'has an oil swimming upon it, and they often dry it, and find much bituminous oil at the bottom of it, which they make use of for anointing little children's joints for the rickets, &c. They say that St Catherine travelling this way with her cruise of oil, fell here and broke it, and ever since it has run with oil.'[99]

A close reading of the 'Journal' yields nothing worse than this and Kirke's tone lacked his later viciousness. However, this journey of discovery and its encounter with the Scots disappeared. The 'Journal' nestled into Kirke's library and papers, leaving us no clue as to whether it was read or by whom. His great friend Ralph Thoresby added it to 'the other manuscripts in his Museum at Leeds' after Kirke's death in 1706. Thoresby, who would later collaborate on the new *Britannia* of Edmund Gibson, made something of an odd couple with Kirke. The celebrated *Diary of Ralph Thoresby* (c. 1666–1724) 'gives us a delightful picture of a simple, upright, and genial character' committed to a life lived with integrity and spiritual understanding.[100] Thoresby recorded his brief tour of the Borders and Lothian (1681) in keeping with his character, rugged terrain and penetrating mists borne with grace and resolution. By contrast, readers followed Kirke's travels through the Weldonesque *Modern Account*. Kirke made a lie of his actual experiences, pandering to prejudice. This traveller's encounter with Scotland became the foundation for literary deception and xenophobia.

Moryson's undiscovered Scotland

These English and Welsh travellers have been stand-ins for Fynes Moryson and the kind of ethnographic eye he might plausibly have cast on the peoples of Scotland. Taylor and 'Weldon' were Moryson's real contemporaries. Each in his fashion produced both a narrative of his journey through Scotland and an ethnographic account of the Scots from an Englishman's perspective. Taylor's curiosity and determination to discover Scotland and its peoples opened up a broader canvas than the crabbed 'Weldon', whose geographic foray was as brief and limited as James's had been in 1617. Taylor's travels did not take in large parts of Scotland and he only briefly crossed the Grampian line, but he entered a highland–lowland middle ground long enough to document and appreciate a more complex cultural interaction than those simple labels typically allowed. Both kinds of description had ready precedents in Moryson's *Itinerary* and 'Manuscript' and we can well imagine his British ethnography covering the same ground, perhaps without the hate-filled ridicule. Still, given Moryson's identification of the Arabs and the Irish within the Ottoman empire and Stuart *imperium*, his reaction to the Gaels remains the hardest to anticipate.

[99] *Tours in Scotland*, p. 42.
[100] *Tours in Scotland*, pp. vi–vii, viii.

Howell, Brereton, and those who travelled after Moryson's death in 1630 encountered Scotland throughout decades of tumultuous religious and political change. Brereton's journey through Britain and Ireland has a *fin de siècle* quality, travelling through Charles I's kingdoms at the moment when the deceptive, artificial calm of the 'personal rule' would disintegrate. From the standpoint of Howell and English travellers, the prolonged disintegration and destruction of the Caroline regimes accentuated ethno-religious differences. The fault-lines that opened between England and Scotland in the later 1640s and the oppressive Restoration monarchy encouraged broader cultural hostilities. Thomas Kirke must be the poster child for a certain kind of English encounter with Scotland, where every ethnographic category provided an opportunity to record and spin the most negative observations. Kirke even indicted Scotland with its flora and fauna.

Kirke's porcupine hogs and ravenous fowls note important changes taking place among the interests of British travellers. Fifteen years earlier, John Ray had carried with him into Scotland the explosive mid-century interest in natural history, part of what we know more familiarly as the 'scientific revolution'. The rich topography and the close association of the Scots with their environmental relationships would have made Scotland an incomparable destination for those determined to discover and understand anew the natural world in Britain. Ray's interests represented a real departure from Morsyon's. Thomas Tucker arrived in the vanguard of the only successful English conquest of Scotland to that moment. He scrutinized the economic potential of a subject country and its people with the kind of attention to political economy that earned Haddington's close and interested reading of Moryson's *Itinerary*. By the next century, travellers like Tucker would drive the cause of 'improvement', the socio-economic re-engineering of 'primitive' societies and peoples, and make it a defining basis for the encounters among Britons, imperial policy, and stadial theories of social evolution pioneered by Scottish Enlightenment thinkers from Henry Home, Lord Kames to Adam Smith.[101]

All of these travellers encountered a Scotland that eluded Moryson in his brief foray, a Scotland to which Boece and his fellow sixteenth-century discoverers did not attend to as much as their battles over the British past, Catholic Scotland or ancient republicanism. Some of them reveal Scotland much as Moryson might have found it within his ethnographic interests. Later travellers highlight the evolution of travel itself beyond Moryson's interests and lifetime. From them we discover something of the Scotland that Moryson himself had needed to engage with if he hoped to write a rich ethnography based on first-hand experiences. Otherwise, Moryson could not hope to write with the same interest and insight about Scotland's cultural complexity that he had of the astounding confusion

---

[101] For example, Calloway, *White People, Indians, and Highlanders*, pp. 20–91; Jennifer Pitts, *A Turn to Empire: The Rise of Imperial Liberalism in Britain and France* (Princeton, 2005), pp. 23–58.

of peoples in Jerusalem or the pounding camel journey to Iskendren that killed his brother.

Moryson's travelling contemporaries point up a final important feature of the seventeenth-century encounter with multicultural Britain. They did not wait around for him or Camden or anyone else to describe its cultural complexity for them. Moryson's 'Itinerary' could not compete against the likes of Camden and Speed. But the rapidly growing number of travellers crisscrossing Britain on journeys of discovery would turn such grand accounts into antiquarian remains all their own. For now, though, we need to consider another part of Britain that Moryson knew little of, and showed even less interest in: the lands of the ancient Britons in Cornwall and Wales.

8

Among the Ancient Britons

The soldier-writer Thomas Churchyard composed an unusual verse description of Wales in 1587. *The Worthines of Wales* promised 'wonders and right strange matter'. Churchyard's Wales nearly outshone Scotland as Britain's salmon fishery:

> A thing to note, when Sammon failes in Wye,
> (And season there: goes out as order is)
> Than still of course, in Oske [Usk] doth Sammons lye,
> And of good fish, in Oske you shall not mis.
> And this seemes straunge, as doth through Wales appeere,
> In some one place, are Sammons all the yeere;
> So fresh, so sweete, so red, so crimp withall,
> As man might say, loe, Sammon here at call.[1]

Churchyard may have heard the story during his travels, but can we pin down where and with whom it originated?

We might begin with the Welsh antiquary Humphrey Llwyd. Llwyd included a brief topographical description of Wales in his *Cronica Walliae*.[2] Llwyd did not live to see it through the press after its completion in 1559.[3] Instead, with the support of William Cecil and Henry Sidney (Lord President of the Council in the Marches of Wales), David Powel published an expanded and corrected version of Llwyd's *Cronica* in 1584 as *The Historie of Cambria, Now Called Wales*. A repackaged version of Llwyd–Powel's *Cronica* was published in 1663 as *A Description of Wales*, attributed to Sir John Prise. Powel took over the original project from a fellow scholar interested in the history and geography of Britain, the famed John Dee. He followed up in 1585 with an omnibus collection that included the *Historia Britannica* of Ponticus Virunnius (an abridgement of Geoffrey of Monmouth) and the works of Gerald of Wales.[4]

---

[1] Thomas Churchyard, *The Worthines of Wales* (STC 5261; London, 1587), sig. C4.
[2] Humphrey Llwyd, *Cronica Walliae*, ed. Ieuan M. Williams (Cardiff, 2002), pp. 12–14; see John Price, *Historiae Brytannicae Defensio* (STC 20309; London, 1573).
[3] R. Brinley Jones, 'Humphrey Llwyd', *Oxford DNB* at www.oxforddnb.com.
[4] Ronald H. Fritze, 'David Powel', *Oxford DNB* at www.oxforddnb.com.

Among these possibilities the source is not actually hard to find. The original account, translated into English, runs something like this: 'There is no lack of freshwater fish, both in the Usk and the Wye. Salmon and trout are fished from these rivers, but the Wye has more salmon and the Usk more trout. In winter salmon are in season in the Wye, but in summer they abound in the Usk.'[5] As Leland had, Churchyard read Gerald's *Journey Through Wales*. With Leland's notebooks 'lost', the authoritative Gerald was the natural starting point for Churchyard. Before 1585, travellers would have known Gerald's *Wales* only through manuscripts.[6] Powel compiled them for publication, but made his own 'arbitrary' combination of different versions and left out entirely Book II of the *Description* because it cast the Welsh in an unflattering light.[7] When, at the height of his literary career, the sometime soldier Churchyard returned from Wales to write his *Worthines* in 1587, he was among the first people in England to read Powel's edition.[8]

Churchyard and travellers like him would renew the encounter with Wales for their own times. They joined fellow travellers who journeyed through that other refuge of the ancient Britons, Cornwall. They met their modern descendants and locales with real attention to ethnography and cultural complexity. Like their Scottish counterparts in the previous chapter, these travellers open a window into the undiscovered Britain of Fynes Moryson. The encounters with Scotland, Wales, and Cornwall have similarities: the exploration (for the English) of the unknown, the heightening of ethnic and religious prejudices in the 1640s and 1650s, Restoration bigotry, and, in the case of John Taylor, the same traveller. By contrast, in George Owen of Henllys and Richard Carew, we have travellers whose respective accounts analyse the cultural complexity of Pembrokeshire and Cornwall at a minute, local level typically lacking among Moryson's stand-ins who journeyed to Scotland. Journeys through Wales reveal two competing, sometimes complementary, ethnographic perspectives at work, the character of nations and the complex reality of the *pays*. We begin with Churchyard.

Thomas Churchyard's poetic encounter

A Shrewsbury native, Churchyard began his journey through the Welsh Borders at Monmouth in 1586.[9] He skirted Brecknockshire, moved through Shropshire from Ludlow to Shrewsbury, and completed brief forays into Denbigh and Flintshire. Churchyard sensed an opening in the market for a popular account

---

[5] Gerald of Wales, *The Journey Through Wales* and *The Description of Wales*, trans. Lewis Thorpe (London, 1978/2004), p. 93.
[6] Robert Bartlett, *Gerald of Wales 1146–1223* (Oxford, 1982), pp. 216–17.
[7] Gerald, *Journey*, pp. 44, 52.
[8] Churchyard, *Worthines of Wales*, sigs A2b, B2b.
[9] Raphael Lyne, 'Thomas Churchyard', *Oxford DNB* at www.oxforddnb.com.

of Wales, perhaps encouraged by Powel's publication of the *Cronica Walliae*. He also sensed an opportunity for preferment by dedicating the *Worthines of Wales* to Queen Elizabeth and playing to the Tudors' distant Welsh roots.[10] Others had written about Wales, but a new account was needed to bring the 'sweet Soyle and good Subiects thereof' into a favourable light. Churchyard would 'deliuer but what I haue seene and read: alledging for defence both ancient Authors, and good tryall of that is written'.[11] Like many travellers, he proposed to test received wisdom against first-hand experience and market his own account for its veracity and novelty.

Taking a page from Rastell and Boorde, Churchyard relayed his discoveries in verse and black letter type, with marginal comments to help the content along. Anglo-Welsh union was the point when the Welsh 'yeelded vnto Lawe' and proved themselves to be loyal, law-abiding subjects, enabling their innate civility to flourish: hospitable, industrious, intelligent, and gentle. As Churchyard explained,

> For meeke as Doves, in lookes and speech they are,
> Not rough and rude (as spiteful tongues declare) ...
> no sooner out of shell ...
> they knowe good maners well.
> How can this be, that weaklings nurst so harde,
> (Who barely goes, both barefoote and uncled)
> To gifts of mynd, should haue so greate regarde,
> Except within, from birth some grace were bred. ...
> Which shewe they rise, from auncient race and line.[12]

Churchyard wielded a critical pen against the treatment of Wales in the histories of contemporary writers:

> As learned men, hath wrote graue works of yore,
> So great regard, to natiue Soule they had:
> For such respect, I blame now Polydore:
> Because of Wales, his iudgement was but bad.
> If Buckanan, the Scottish Poet late
> Were here in sprite, of Brittons to debate:
> He should finde men, that would with him dispute,
> And many a pen, which would his works confute.[13]

What made Vergil and Buchanan writers of 'fables' was their want of first-hand experience:

---

[10] Churchyard, *Worthines of Wales*, sig. *2v.
[11] Churchyard, *Worthines of Wales*, sigs A1r–A2v.
[12] Churchyard, *Worthines of Wales*, sig. B2r–v.
[13] Churchyard, *Worthines of Wales*, sig. C2r.

> Yet writer sees, not how all matters goeth
> In field: when he, at home is at his pen.
> This Pollidore, sawe neuer much of Wales,
> Though he haue told, of Britons many tales ...
> And men may write, of things they heare by eare:
> So Pollidore, oft tymes might overweene,
> And speake of Soyles, yet he came neuer there. ...

When they 'say they knowe that thing / They never sawe ... And by their bookes, the world in error bring'. Admittedly, they could not bear witness to a past they did not experience, but Gerald, Bede, Gildas, and Geoffrey had and should not be gainsaid.[14] Churchyard's travels set him apart:

> The eye is iudge, as Lanterne cleere of light,
> That searcheth through, the dim and darkest places ...
> But where no face, nor iudging eye doth come,
> The sence is blynd, the spirit is deaffe and dome:
> For wit can not, conceive till sight send in
> Some skill to head, whereby we knowledge we win.[15]

It is a nice irony that Churchyard closed these admonishing verses, then recycled Gerald's story of the salmon in the Wye and Usk rivers before launching his own topographic description.

Having travelled through Wales, explored the landscape on which the Britons' history was written, and encountered their descendants, Churchyard set out to interrogate and re-narrate the works of older writers, supply a modern topographical description, reclaim for Wales its greatness, and give its people their due alongside other great nations.[16] Topography served this purpose, for instance in Monmouthshire. Churchyard blamed feuds among the Welsh princes for the destruction of the 'publicke state'. Had Wales been a settled polity, Greenfield, north of Newport, offered the perfect seat for her would-be king:

> A fine sweete Soyle, most pleasant unto sight,
> That for delight, and wholesome ayre so pure,
> It may be praisde, a plot sought out so well,
> As though a King, should say here will I dwell ... [17]

The fine soils of Greenfield encouraged one of Churchyard's only moments of critical ethnography, attacking the relative predominance of pastoralism in the Welsh lowlands:

> And in this place, and many parts about,
> In grasse and Corne, and fertile ground enough:

---

14 Churchyard, *Worthines of Wales*, sigs C2r–v, C3v.
15 Churchyard, *Worthines of Wales*, sig. C3r–v.
16 Churchyard, *Worthines of Wales*, sig. A2r.
17 Churchyard, *Worthines of Wales*, sig. F2v.

And now a while, to speake of Wales throughout,
Where if men would, take paynes to ply the Plough:
Digges out of drosse, the treasure of the earth,
And fall to toyle, and labour from their birth:
They should as soone, to store of wealth attaine,
As other Soyles, whose people takes great paine.
The most of Wales, likes better ease and rest,
(Loues meate and mirth, and harmlesse quiet daies)
Than for to toyle, and trouble brayne and brest,
To vere the mynd, with worldly wearis waies.
Some stand content, with that which God shall send,
And on their lands, their stock and store doth spend ... [18]

The picture was not as grim as it sounded, though. The Welsh lowlanders had lately begun the hard labour of clearing the land. They uprooted sturdy oaks, cleared out rocks, and enriched the soil with lime, with good results:

Wales is this day (behold throughout the Shieres,
In better state, than twas these hundred yeeres ...
I meane where weedes, and thistles long hath growne,
(Wild drosse and docks, and stinking nettles vile)
There Barley sweete, and goodly Wheate is sowne,
Which makes me rich, that liu'd in lacke long while.[19]

Churchyard would return to this discussion when he took up the differences between highland and lowland dwellers.

Monmouth boasted a site critically important for Churchyard's theme of a land fit for a king:

Carleon now, step in with stately style,
No feeble phrase, may serue to set thee forth:
Thy famous Towne, was spoke of many a myle,
Thou hast been great, though now but little worth.
Thy noble bounds, hath reacht beyond them all,
In thee hath been King Arthurs golden Hall:
In thee the wise, and worthies did repose,
And through thy Towne, the water ebs and flowes.[20]

Caerleon might be a shadowy ruin, but it did not deserve neglect:

Both Athens, Theabes, and Carthage too
We hold of great renowne:
What then I pray you shall we doe,
To poore Carleon Towne.[21]

[18] Churchyard, *Worthines of Wales*, sig. F2v.
[19] Churchyard, *Worthines of Wales*, sig. F3r.
[20] Churchyard, *Worthines of Wales*, sig. D1r.
[21] Churchyard, *Worthines of Wales*, sig. D1v.

Churchyard restored it to Wales and its history with his many verses. In just a few of them he celebrated Caerleon's fame as a place where not just kings and peers but 'learned men full many yeares, Receiu'd therein their grace', entirely fitting for a people among whom 'gifts of mynde, should haue so great regarde'.[22] He could but wish – perhaps a bit dangerously if his queen read it as implied criticism – that God would send them Arthur's sort again 'to daunt the pride of the Romish practices'.[23]

For a child of the Welsh Borders who embraced the Union, Shropshire may have constituted the ideal fusion of the British past and Anglo-Welsh present.[24] Churchyard began with Ludlow in his native Shropshire, a county long ago part of Powys. Churchyard penned verses to some of the dead in the church before describing Ludlow castle, seat of the Lord President of the Marches. The castle contained many finely wrought arms, fit for so stately a place and testimony to Welsh workmanship. One carving captured Churchyard's imagination: the cross of St Andrew joined to the arms of Prince Arthur, the dead brother of Henry VIII. Churchyard, a veteran of the Anglo-Scottish wars of the 1540s, had discovered a perfect symbol for the Tudor claim to *imperium* in Britain.

In his native Shrewsbury, Churchyard saw a teeming commercial town, where hard work was prized and houses built with new-found wealth put poor neighbours to shame. People from as far away as Bristol 'for Welsh ware, exchaungeth English pence'.[25] He also found a 'Welsh' town, regardless of political boundaries:

> Now come to poynts, and rules of ciuill men,
> Good maner calde, that shewes good nature still:
> And so with Wales, ye may compare them then,
> The meanest sort, I meane of slendrest skill.
> For as some whelpes, that are of gentle kinde,
> Exceedes curre dogges, that beares a doggish minde:
> So these meeke folke, that meetes you in the streete,
> Will curchie [curtsy] make, or shewe an humble spreete.
> This argue sure, they haue in Wales bin bred,
> Or well brought vp, and taught where now they dwells. ...
> My theame is Wales, and to that theame I goe,
> Perhaps some seede, of that same Soyle is here ... [26]

Shrewsbury might lie on the other side of the border, but it had been founded on Welsh soil. Among its denizens one knew the Welsh by their civility, and that civility, like the soil itself, confirmed Shrewsbury as truly Welsh.

---

22 Churchyard, *Worthines of Wales*, sig. D3r.
23 Churchyard, *Worthines of Wales*, sig. F1r.
24 Churchyard, *Worthines of Wales*, sig. K1r.
25 Churchyard, *Worthines of Wales*, sigs K1v, K3v.
26 Churchyard, *Worthines of Wales*, sig. K2r.

Churchyard was not finished, almost literally singing the praises of Welsh commoners in Shropshire. They showed an admirable reticence to haggle over prices in the market, content to sell their wares and 'trudge they home, both barelegge and unshod, / With song in Welsh or els in praysing God'. This touched off Churchyard's most uncompromising depiction of the Welsh character, one he challenged readers, especially English ones, to deny:

> O plaine good folke, that haue no craftie braines,
> O Conscience cleare, thou knowst no cunning knacks:
> O harmlesse hearts, where feare of God remaines,
> O simple Soules, as sweete as Virgin ware.
> O happie heads, and labouring bodies blest,
> O sillie Doues, of holy Abrahams brest:
> You sleepe in peace and rise in ioye and blisse,
> For heauen hence, for you prepared is.
>
> Where shall we finde, such now dealing now adaies;
> Where is such cheere, so cheape and chaunge of fare:
> Ride North and South, and search all beaten waies,
> From Barwick bounds, to Venice if you dare,
> And finde the like, that I in Wales haue found,
> And I shall be, your slaue and bondman bound.
> Takes Wales goodwill, and giue them neighbours loue.[27]

Here was an image of common Welsh nobility that would be tapped for centuries, from the miners of *The Proud Valley* who welcomed Paul Robeson's baritone 'David Goliath' into their choral society to the affectionate mayhem of Ealing's *A Run for Your Money*. It was also one that, like its modern cinematic counterparts, cast a critical light on supposedly sophisticated urban counterparts. When Churchyard followed up by commending the gentility of the Welsh gentry, the keepers of 'all ciuil manners myld' without whom the 'Countrey would grow wyld', he added yet another dimension to a favourable ethnography.[28]

The journey to Denbighshire carried Churchyard through the valley of the Dee and brought him to the foothills of the mountains. He composed a 'discourse of Mountaynes' that reflected on the Welsh who inhabited the country's uplands. Churchyard departed from the tone and prejudice of so many highland accounts. Rather, Churchyard praised the highland topography:

> These ragged Rocks, bring playnest people forth,
> On Mountaine wyld, the hardest horse is bred:
> Though grasse thereon, be grosse and little worth,
> Sweete is the foode, where hunger so is fed.
> On rootes and hearbs, our fathers long did feede,
> And neere the Skye, growes sweetest fruit in deede:

---

[27] Churchyard, *Worthines of Wales*, sig. K4v.
[28] Churchyard, *Worthines of Wales*, sig. L4r–v.

On marrish meares, and watrie mossie ground,
Are rotten weedes, and rubbish drosse unfound. ...
In foulest daies, fayre weather may be gest.
As bitter blasts, on Mountaynes bigge doth blowe,
So noysome smels, and fauours breede belowe:
The hill stands cleere, and cleane from filthie smell,
They finde not so, that doth in Valley dwell.[29]

The hills brought forth people who matched the rugged topography and delighted in their highland life:

The Mountayne men, liue longer many a yeere,
Then those in Vale, in playne, or marrish soyles
A lustie hart , a cleane complexion cleere
They haue on hill, that for hard liuing coyle,
With Ewe and Lambe, with Goates and Kids they play,
In greatest toyles, to rub our weare day:
And when to house, and home good fellowes drawe,
The lads can laugh, at turning of a strawe.[30]

Churchyard turned on its head the usual relationship of highland and lowland in the narratives of travellers – as John Lesley had in his history of Scotland. The people of the valleys owed much to the hills that flanked them, and they owed their thanks to God:

The maker first, of Mountaynes and of Vale,
Made Hill a wall, to clip the Dale:
A strong defense, for needful fruit and Corne,
That els by blast, might quickly be forlorne. ...
So Mountaynes made, to saue the lower soyle,
For feare the earth, should suffer shamefull spoyle. ...
How could poore soules, in Cottage quiet bee,
If higher grounds did not defend their seate.[31]

This would not have been the most provocative of Churchyard's comments, however. He rejected the familiar stereotype of degenerate, wild, and violent highland peoples and blamed society's ills and corruptions on its lowlands:

Wealth fosters pride, and heaues up haughty hart,
Makes wit oreweene, and man beleeue to farre:
Enfects the mynde, with uice in euery part,
That quickly sets, the sences all at warre.
In Valley ritch, these mischiefes nourisht are,
God planted peace, on Mountayne poore and bare:
By sweat of browes, the people liues on hill,

[29] Churchyard, *Worthines of Wales*, sig. M1v.
[30] Churchyard, *Worthines of Wales*, sigs M1v–2r.
[31] Churchyard, *Worthines of Wales*, sig. M2r–v.

Not sleight of brayne, ne craft nor cunning skill. ...
The losse of wealth, grypes long a greedie mynd.
Poore Mountayne folke, possesse not such great store,
But when its gon, they care not much therefore.[32]

Here and in Monmouth we find a complex reading of topography and eth-nography. The idle and ease-loving Welsh of the lowlands had lately forsaken their indolence for industrious labour to bring agricultural wealth from the ground. Yet there were some among them who gave in to a greater vice of lowland society, an all-consuming love of material gain that drove away contentment with a decent, stable life of subsistence. All of them sheltered in the shadow of the uplands, home to a highland people who embodied real civility in their plain dealing, simple contentment, and gentleness. There is an approving scent of the noble savage in all of this, despite Churchyard's service in England's imperial–colonial wars in Scotland (1547) and Ireland (1550–51).[33]

Churchyard carried on to Flintshire, where he fell ill. For the second time, the rigours of the journey apparently got the better of the sixty-three-year-old former soldier.[34] When the next spring dawned,

My muse I hope, shall be reuiu'd againe,
That now lyes dead, or rockt a sleepe with paine.
For labour long, hath wearied for the wit,
That studious head, a while in rest must sit ... [35]

'Here endeth my first booke of the worthines of Wales,' Churchyard concluded, 'which being wel taken, wil encourage me to set forth another.'[36] Churchyard lived to a ripe age, dying in 1602 at something around eighty-two, and produced many works in his final years. He promised readers of his anthology, *Churchyards Challenge*, in 1593 that they would soon see the completion of the *Worthines of Wales*, but it never happened. His first description of Wales, then, may not have been a smashing success. Perhaps different projects distracted Churchyard or readers preferred his other literary efforts, from martial poetry to topical pamphlets to his own take on *Shores Wife*.[37] Or, perhaps his ethnography and topography of Wales faded into obscurity when confronted by the literary might of Camden's *Britannia*.

---

[32] Churchyard, *Worthines of Wales*, sigs M2v, M3r.

[33] Lyne, 'Thomas Churchyard'.

[34] Churchyard, *Worthines of Wales*, sig. H2r.

[35] Churchyard, *Worthines of Wales*, sig. N4r.

[36] Churchyard, *Worthines of Wales*, sig. N4r.

[37] Lyne, 'Thomas Churchyard'.

George Owen of Henllys and Pembrokeshire

A traveller who found positive encouragement from Camden was George Owen of Henllys in Pembrokeshire. Camden called Owen 'an exquisite Antiquary' and the two collaborated in their respective projects, the history of Owen's family in Pembroke and the Welsh portions of *Britannia*.[38] Owen's interest in Pembroke had much to do with receiving the barony of Cemais and Newport Castle from his father when he turned twenty. With an annoying officiousness, Owen took too serious an interest in the vestiges of heritable authority that still attached to his barony despite the abolition of the marcher lordships with the 1536 Act of Union. Owen's efforts to make the most of his right to hold manorial courts, impose rents and customary services on the burghers of Newport, and collect feudal duties from his tenants sent him on an 'unceasing quest for material relating to the lordship' in whatever archives might prove useful.[39]

Owen's interests in genealogy and antiquarianism expanded beyond these self-serving ends. He assembled a 'coterie of antiquarians' that included George Owen Harry, George William Griffith, and Thomas Jones and made Cemais into '"a centre of great activity in genealogy, heraldry and history, and a favourite gathering place for the Welsh bards"'. This network became a crucial link with '"the flourishing antiquarian and historical studies of the Elizabethan and Jacobean period"'.[40] Owen also set out to correct what he believed to be a poorly proportioned map of Pembroke in Christopher Saxton's *Atlas of the Counties of England and Wales* (c. 1579–80). He sent his own map and a description of Milford Haven to the earl of Pembroke in 1595 for the Lord Deputy's evaluation of the coastal defences against Spanish attack. This map was lost but Owen produced another in 1602, which Camden used in the 1607 edition of *Britannia*. Finally, Owen was a projector, determined to improve agriculture and husbandry on his estates and in Pembrokeshire generally; he completed a treatise on the value of marl as a fertilizer in 1599.[41]

These complex interests came together in the *Description of Pembrokeshire*. Owen envisioned two volumes. He designed the first to be a general description. Reminiscent of Harrison's 'Description of England' in Holinshed's *Chronicles* – a book he had read – Owen covered Pembroke's situation and topography, its settlement, the nature of the people who inhabited it past and present, political divisions and governance, natural resources, economic activity, the built environment from castles to bridges, wants and defects, and wonders, pastimes, customs,

---

[38] William Camden, *Britannia: Or a Chorographical Description of Great Britain and Ireland* (London, 1695), p, 633; George Owen, *The Description of Pembrokeshire*, ed. Dillwyn Miles (Llandysul, 1994), pp. xxx, xxxvi.
[39] Owen, *Description*, pp. xxvii–xxx.
[40] Owen, *Description*, pp. xxxiii–xxxvi.
[41] Owen, *Description*, pp. xxxvii–xli.

and famous men.[42] Owen completed this volume between December 1602 and May 1603.[43] The second volume would detail antiquities and places of note in each of Pembroke's hundreds and parishes, a kind of proto-Pevsner guide. Whatever Owen completed of the second volume disappeared, except for a fragment in the National Library of Wales.[44] There are two manuscript copies of the first volume, both in the hands of scribes, with the second checked by Owen himself. The contents of neither volume appeared in print until George Fenton published the first extracts in 1795. You would be hard pressed to improve on Pembroke's *Description* as just the sort of ethnographic detail toward which Fynes Moryson gravitated.

Pembroke had a culturally complex history in keeping with Wales and James VI and I's soon-to-be Stuart *imperium*.[45] Owen explored the reasons why the county was 'usually called Little England beyond Wales and that not unworthily'. He explained:

[The] reasons why it took that name may well be conjectured, for that the most part of the county speaks English, and in it no use of the Welsh. The names of the people are mere English, each family following the English fashion in surnames. Their buildings are English-like, in townreds and villages, and not in several and lone houses. Their diet is as the English people use, as the common food is beef, mutton, pig, goose, lamb, veal and kid, which usually the poorest husbandman does daily feed on. The names of the county places are altogether English ... These reasons, and also for that most of the ancient gentlemen come thither out of England ... [46]

In their language, personal names, diet, and settlement in nucleated villages, the people of Pembroke resembled the English. The settlers who migrated to Pembroke carried these markers of Englishness with them and left another mark on the land in its place-names. Owen added another regular ethnic marker, the law, for that 'it is manifest that the king's writ in ancient time did run in Pembrokeshire'.[47]

Owen asked readers to join him for a journey of discovery:

So that a stranger travelling from England and having ridden four score miles and more in Wales, having heard no English, nor English names of people, or of places, and coming hither to Pembrokeshire, where he shall hear nothing but English, and seeing the rest before agreeable to England, would think that Wales were environed with England, and would imagine he travelled through Wales and come into England again.[48]

[42] Owen, *Description*, pp. 89, 98, 186.
[43] Dillwyn Miles, 'George Owen', *Oxford DNB* at www.oxforddnb.com.
[44] Owen, *Description*, pp. xli–xlii.
[45] Owen, *Description*, pp. 3, 8.
[46] Owen, *Description*, pp. 36–7.
[47] Owen, *Description*, p. 37.
[48] Owen, *Description*, p. 36.

This was a powerful instance of defining the boundaries of ethnicity, but Owen knew the picture was more complicated in two crucial respects. First, there were no easy labels for the hodgepodge of peoples who had settled Pembroke and from whom the current inhabitants were descended. Second, whether or not the county was a little England planted in the south-western corner of Wales, Owen recognized the shire's division between 'the Englishry and the Welshry'. This division typified the marcher lordships and 'plantations' of Anglo-Norman Wales, an explicit process of ethnic resettlement, but one whose boundaries proved culturally porous when studied closely at the local level.[49] Welsh travellers and scholars throughout the seventeenth century likewise recognized and reported on the cultural complexity of Wales and its locales.[50]

If teachers could set their students one gobbet as an antidote to monocultural British History, a thoughtful critique of Owen's chapter on the peopling of Pembroke might open their eyes. According to Owen, 'before the coming of William the Conqueror into England the same [Pembroke] was quietly possessed and enjoyed by the Ancient Britons, the Welshmen, so now called, who were the first inhabiters that any notice is heard of, of whom there are to this day many ancient gentlemen'. Owen imagined that these ancient Britons lived under their native Prince of Wales, recast in a very Tudor imperial mould as the ruler 'to whom they yielded their whole obedience, not knowing any superior on earth'. Invading England, the Normans 'subdued and supplanted the Saxon kings and nobles' and cast a covetous eye on the Prince of Wales' dominions. The Normans 'daily intruded their borders' and parcelled out what land they seized to the Norman 'lords of England ... whereby divers English lords won from the Princes of Wales and their subjects whole counties in Wales and built castles, towns and strongholds, and peopled the same with English garrisons to keep the same'.[51]

In the course of a few sentences the Norman invaders of England had become conquering 'English lords', but only by virtue of serving under the Norman and Angevin kings of England and holding titles to land there. Owen could say with confidence that 'the most part of the gentlemen of the shire now living are rather Norman than any other nation' in ethnicity. The same could not be said for most settlers and commoners:

> For otherwise the English tongue had not been their common and mother speech, as it was ... and by this their English speech here in Pembrokeshire, I gather that the greatest part of those people that came into Pembrokeshire with these earls were Saxons and Englishmen, and it is very like that the Conqueror, having purpose to supplant the English nation out of England would rather employ them and the Flemings in the wars

---

[49] Robert Bartlett, *The Hanged Man: A Story of Miracle, Memory, and Colonialism in the Middle Ages* (Princeton, 2004), pp. 1–96.

[50] Lloyd Bowen, 'Fashioning Communities: The County in Early Modern Wales', in *The County Community in Seventeenth-Century England and Wales*, ed. Jacqueline Eales and Andrew Hopper (Hatfield, 2012), pp. 78–98.

[51] Owen, *Description*, pp. 38–9.

against the Welshmen than the Frenchmen he brought with him, saving such as were of account and which he meant to prefer by his service.[52]

As for a Flemish presence, Owen consigned it to the past. The Flemish might be the ancestors of 'divers of the common people, swains and labourers', but 'if any of their progeny be remaining yet is the memory thereof, with their language, quite forgotten'. The Flemish colonizers were as unwelcome in the past as in Owen's present. The so-called Flemings' Way, the path taken into Pembrokeshire, crossed the highest hill that 'they might the better decry the privy ambushes of the country people which might in straits and woods annoy them'.[53] One could almost transpose derring-do against ambushes in the Appalachian Mountains or Northwest frontier. This, then, was no homogenous past that Owen wrestled with but a complex interaction of history, first-hand experience, and the persistence of memory around questions of ethnicity, language, conquest, and migration.[54]

The unconquered Welsh, 'the first owners of the country', inhabited upper Pembrokeshire in the hundreds of Cemais, Cilgerran, Dewisland, and part of Narberth. The inhabitants of Owen's own barony stood out:

> [They] do much vaunt of their ancient antiquity, much before any other of the shires, accounting themselves more ancient gentlemen in the county ... by good proof of ancient writings and record that their ancestors have been owners of those lands they now enjoy many years before the coming of Strongbow into this country, which was in the time of King Henry I.

No wonder Owen had such difficulty with the commons and gentry in Cemais when he attempted to enforce the vestigial privileges of marcher lordship. He attacked a powerful memory of resistance and difference among his Welsh-speaking neighbours. By contrast with the Welshry, Roose, Castlemartin, most of Daugleddau, and the rest of Narberth 'were wholly put to fire and sword by the Normans, Flemings and Englishmen, and utterly expelled the inhabitants thereof and people the country themselves, whose posterity remain there to this day, as may appear by their names, manners and language, speaking altogether the English, and differing in manners, diet, buildings, and tilling of the land from the Welshmen'.[55]

For Owen, an antiquarian at home in the intellectual world of Camden's *Britannia* and the late Tudor *imperium*, the idea of Pembroke as 'Anglia Transwallia' may have been as much wishful thinking as topographic reality. The *pays* in Pembroke hummed with ethnic tensions and prejudice. First, the Welshry and Englishry divided the county culturally, politically, and physically:

---

[52] Owen, *Description*, pp. 39–40.
[53] Owen, *Description*, p. 107.
[54] Owen, *Description*, p. 39.
[55] Owen, *Description*, p. 42.

And although this be now well near 500 years past, yet do these two nations keep each from dealing with the other, as mere strangers, so that the meaner sort of people will not, or do not usually, join together in marriage ... you shall find in one parish a pathway parting the Welsh and England, and the one side speak all English, the other all Welsh, and differing in tilling and in measuring of their land, and divers other matters.[56]

As a sheriff and justice of the peace, Owen could attest to one difference at first hand. The 'diversity of speech breeds some inconveniences, so that often times it is found at the assizes that in a jury of twelve men there will be one half that cannot understand the other's words'. Owen described an instance when a Welsh and an English trier took three days to settle the challenge against a jury's ruling.[57]

Owen constructed a third ethnography: he divided the county between the Welshry in its upper part, the Englishry in lower Pembrokeshire, and recent Irish migrants. The Elizabethan reconquest that Moryson described in his *Itinerary* engulfed Ireland at the moment Owen wrote the *Description*. Moryson wrote about the Gaelic Irish or 'mere-Irish'; the Protestant English administrators and colonists typically called the 'New English'; and the Anglo-Irish who lived between both worlds as Catholic descendants of Ireland's first Anglo-Norman conquerors and dominant landholders 'loyal' to the distant English crown. Pembroke's own Gerald of Wales carried the same blood as the Geraldines who dominated Anglo-Irish interests on and off for centuries until the 1540s. The Irish Sea traffic was not one way either, and Pembroke had an established Irish presence. Conscription for the Tudor armies disproportionately impacted on 'nearby' counties in the west of England and Wales like Pembroke, especially those with major embarkation ports such as Milford Haven (or Chester and Bristol in England).[58] The sacrifices of local boys inflamed existing prejudices and those 'Irish' who fled the conflict faced a hostile reception in Britain.[59]

The turn of the seventeenth century was, then, another unenviable time to be Irish in Britain. Owen's hostility to his neighbours calls to mind contemporary politicians used to stoking prejudice against 'bogus asylum seekers' or peddling the unthinking bigotry of a 'Whites Only' Britain. The Irish were 'so powdered [sprinkled] among the inhabitants of Roose and Castlemartin that in every village you shall find the third, fourth, or fifth householder an Irishman, and now of late they swarm more than in times past by reason of these late wars in Ireland'. 'And if it so continue for the time to come,' Owen added, 'in a short

---

[56] Owen, *Description*, p. 43.
[57] Owen, *Description*, p. 43.
[58] John McGurk, *The Elizabethan Conquest of Ireland: The 1590s Crisis* (Manchester, 1997), pp. 51–80.
[59] Glanmor Williams, *Recovery, Reorientation and Reformation: Wales c. 1415–1642* (Oxford, 1987), pp. 367–72.

time they are likely to match the other inhabitants in number.'[60] Who were these refugees that settled alongside the established Irish? According to Owen, they 'for the most part speak and use here the English tongue', while a steady chain of migrants from Wexford 'say they understand no Irish'. These English-speaking 'Irishmen' were almost certainly yeomen farmers, minor gentry, and artisans from Anglo-Irish communities with just enough means to make the passage to Milford or another one of Pembroke's havens. We can surmise that they were Catholic Anglo-Irish migrants from Owen's claim that the only English or Welsh inhabitant left in some towns was the Anglican parson, perhaps the only position in the parish closed in practice to these particular Irish migrants.

These Anglo-Irish might as well have been the mere Irish or Gaels. Owen refused to acknowledge anything but the cultural markers that made them 'Irish'. Of a Wexford Irishman who purported to not understand Irish or Gaelic, Owen complained 'neither do any well understand his English'. Those Irish whom Owen credited with speaking English did so 'in such sort as that all men may discern them to be that country's people'. Further, they revealed their true Irishness 'as also by the rudeness of their manners, for the servant will usually "thou" his master and think it no offence'. If more proof was needed, 'these Irish people here do use their country trade in making of aquavitie in great abundance which they carry to be sold abroad the country ... by means thereof it is grown to be a usual drink in most men's houses instead of wine'. That said, Owen matter-of-factly reported the high quality of aqua-vitae sold 'better cheap than ever I could buy the like in any part of England'.[61] Perhaps this captures the ambivalent position of the Irish in South Wales. Unthinking and long-lived prejudice accompanied a more practical accommodation with a migrant community that neither local officials nor inhabitants were prepared to drive out. With that, the Irish in Pembroke disappeared from Owen's *Description* more readily than they evidently could from his own experiences.

All the people of Pembroke embraced 'peace, quietness, and neighbourly love', but class and ethnicity produced differences. Whether their ancestors had been Anglo-Saxon, Welsh, or Flemish, the 'general and common sort of people' of Pembrokeshire shared qualities distinct from their gentry and urban neighbours. Owen found this 'kind of people ... to be very mean and simple, short of growth, broad and shrubby, unacceptable in sight for the their personal service ... so that of all the counties of Wales I find and speak by experience Pembrokeshire to be the worst manred and hardest to find personable and servicable men'. What made the Pembrokeshire commons the worst in Wales? Blasted by wind and hail from off shore, the champaign ground forced the people to keep herds 'in greater number than other counties in England do'.[62]

---

[60] Owen, *Description*, p. 43.

[61] Owen, *Description*, pp. 43–4.

[62] Owen, *Description*, p. 45.

Owen stereotypically attributed idleness to people who lived more by husbandry than intensive agriculture, but nature played its part in stunting them. From ages ten or twelve, they were forced into the open fields to tend their flocks against the sun's power 'to parch and burn their faces, hands, legs, feet and breasts in such sort as they seem more like tawny Moors than people of this land'. In winter the 'cold, frost, snow, hail, rain and wind' tormented and chapped the flesh from their bones. Tilling, burning lime, and digging coal awaited them in their mature years, so 'while they live they never come in shape, favour or comeliness to be accounted among the number of personable men'. Yet a good number of 'these meaner sort' thrived as seamen and mariners, leaving Owen to think that this, and their tendency for plain dealing, marked them as descendants of Henry I's Flemish colonists. Only Churchyard's mountain Welsh escaped the bruising life of their lowland counterparts.[63]

The Pembroke commons might be much alike in these terms but deviated along ethno-cultural lines. Farming practices stood out as a major difference between the Englishry and Welshry. The English sowed wheat, rye, barley, beans, and peas with careful attention to the best growing seasons and improving the fertility of the land. The Welsh, 'being the worse husbands, apply more the tilling of oats' and relied on summer wheat, a larger-grained wheat that was longer in the field and came to grief without enough sun or a timely harvest in the fall. Why did the Welsh persist in these practices on land that could support proper wheat and rye? Ancient practice played a significant part, the Welsh 'being brought up therein are hardly drawn to alter their custom although it be the better'. 'Such force has custom in man's nature', wrote Owen. An even more ancient practice worked against the Welsh, though. The practice of gavelkind, whereby all the sons divided a father's patrimony, left the land in 'small pieces of ground and intermingled up and down one with another ... to remain champion and without enclosures or hedging, and winter corn'. Left unprotected, winter wheat would be consumed by the elements and nearby livestock; the preference for husbanding these animals was itself another cause. However, cultural assimilation was at work.[64] Though Owen complained that 'yet are not the common laws of England practised in so frank and free a course' as he might like, the Union had abolished partible inheritance (gavelkind) and the Welsh were learning the English practice of consolidating scattered plots and enclosing them.[65] Owen made his own contribution to agricultural improvement by shining the light on the rich, heavy marl supposedly deposited by the biblical flood – 'And how the common people came to this opinion I know not, but it is very like to be true.'[66]

---

[63] Owen, *Description*, pp. 46–8.
[64] Owen, *Description*, pp. 62–5.
[65] Owen, *Description*, p. 153.
[66] Owen, *Description*, pp. 72–6.

Owen cast an improver's eye on his county in recording its wants, defects, and natural inconveniences. He blamed the people for many of the deficiencies and did so with a bias against the Welsh. The county lacked fruit trees of all sorts, from apples and pears to plums, apricots, and walnuts. The soil might have something to do with their absence, 'yet certain it is as much by negligence of the inhabitants in planting, preserving and cherishing of fruit trees'. This left the country bereft of trees generally. The people also carried the blame for the lack of fishponds, a wool trade, and superior horse breeds. The absence of enclosures gave Owen another opportunity to blame parents for putting their children to work in herding, 'spoiling, in that idle trade, both outwardly their shape of body and inwardly the gifts of the mind'.[67]

Owen further decried the absence of trained schoolmasters and schools to educate the 'youth in the knowledge of God and good arts'. He suggested that perhaps his Welsh ancestors' zeal to found abbeys caused them to neglect schools, but he put the primary blame once again on parents for forcing their children into husbandry. Here again Englishness offered the way forward, by continuing the trend toward intensive agriculture: 'if every village would maintain one or two common herds for the townreds as in most places in England is used, and not every householder in the town to employ two or three young people herein … and so by consequence to bring them up all among beasts to be beastly people, but this will be remedied when it pleases God'.[68] Schooling in the true knowledge of God might remedy a great inefficiency among the Welsh coalminers. 'The workmen of this black labour observe all abolished holy days and cannot be weaned from that folly.' We might appreciate the miners' zeal, considering that 'the dangers in digging this coal is the falling of the earth and killing of the poor people, or stopping of the way forth, and so die by famine, or else by the sudden irruption of standing waters in old works'.[69]

Owen reported on the natural wonders in Pembroke and those who hailed from the county and made their mark. Taking a page from John Bale, literally, he also celebrated Pembrokeshire worthies like St David, Merlin, Gerald, Richard II's lord chancellor Adam Houghton, Thomas Elyot, Owen's own father, William, and Richard Davies, who translated the New Testament into Welsh. The natural wonders usual took the form of great stones, springs, rock formations, pits, strange findings on hilltops, a plague of caterpillars feasted upon by the local pigs, or the like. The literary and the natural came together for Owen in his lordship. Within two miles of his own manor, stood the parish of Whitechurch. He accepted the reports of old and young alike that no adder had ever been seen alive in the parish, despite their presence in adjoining parishes. Owen wondered about what 'affinity this parish only, and none other, should

---

[67] Owen, *Description*, pp. 146–7.
[68] Owen, *Description*, pp. 147–9.
[69] Owen, *Description*, p. 94.

have with the land of Ireland, or with the county of Buchan in Scotland, which, as Boetius [Boece] writes, breeds no rats, neither will they live being brought thither from elsewhere'.[70] Owen possessed a fine library at Henllys and read the works of Gerald, Camden, Powel, Saxton, Vergil, Bale, and Holinshed, and also had access to Leland's notebooks. However, we do not know if Bellenden's edition of Boece or Harrison's English translation in Holinshed's *Chronicle* was the edition he turned to in his library. When Owen connected the adders of south-western Wales, the snakes driven from Ireland, and rats terrified by the soils of northern Scotland, he captured perfectly the mind of someone who travelled and wrote within the intellectual world of Camden's *Britannia*, but with Moryson's interest in comparative ethnography.

In his penultimate chapter Owen rejoiced in Pembroke's reputation as a second England beyond Wales. One had only to read Gerald's *Journey* to learn that Pembroke stood with the English crown even when other parts of Wales again fell to the Welsh princes. They became the loyal servants of the English kings in their wars of conquest in Wales and Ireland.[71] With an almost craven zeal, Owen wrote:

> If Pembrokeshire people then were the means of subduing Ireland and Wales to the kings of England ... what glory can be greater and what praise more worthy, and what other counties in this land may vaunt themselves of such valiant attempts and happy success, and therefore no marvel that this county was magnified above all the rest of Wales to be a County Palatine. And well might the king of England call this his Little England Beyond Wales.[72]

Owen wrapped Pembroke and himself in a cloak of Tudor patriotism: 'What shall I say of the people, seeing the land and soil itself and the actions attempted therein have fatally from age to age prognosticated joy, peace, love and tranquility to the whole realm, as namely that here was born the Prince of Peace, King Henry VII.'[73] Christ dethroned, Owen brought Henry Tudor's story full circle in Pembroke, for it was in the county of his birth that Henry 'made his first landing and first footing when he came to enjoy the Crown and confound the parricide and bloody tyrant Richard III'.[74] As Owen completed his *Description*, a new prince of peace had come:

> And, lastly more than all before, is yet said how of the body of Henry VII is sprung our most gracious and sovereign King James by whose happy and blessed coming to the imperial crown of this realm is joined together the whole Isle of Britain, never heard, or read of, since the death of Brutus, first king of the whole, being now 2170 years since.[75]

---

[70] Owen, *Description*, pp. 190–7.
[71] Owen, *Description*, pp. 198–200.
[72] Owen, *Description*, p. 200.
[73] Owen, *Description*, p. 201.
[74] Owen, *Description*, p. 202.
[75] Owen, *Description*, p. 203.

Pembroke and its native son George Owen both became loyal subjects of
the Stuart *imperium* literally and figuratively by the close of the *Description of
Pembrokeshire*.

Wales in the Stuart *imperium*

The creation of the Stuart *imperium* in 1603 did not have the same constitutional
complications for Wales that it had for Scotland. Formal union between Wales
and the English crown was more than sixty years old, while English jurisdiction,
as Owen noted with delight, stretched back centuries. Welsh gentry like Owen,
who dominated governance in Wales, 'interpreted Tudor policy as the Crown's
handing back of local authority over Wales to the Welsh – "self-government" ...
confirming, in the most public and indisputable fashion, the rights of the native
families to bear authority in their own localities'.[76] Reformed Protestantism took
hold in Elizabeth's reign and acceptance was helped along by two important
initiatives. Religious change was packaged as a restoration of 'the Church as it
had existed in pristine purity in the days of the ancient Britons'. It was communicated to the Welsh in their own language through translations of the Bible and
Book of Common Prayer enmeshed with the rich oral cultures that grew up around
Welsh Protestantism – later Nonconformity – despite a pronounced 'north-
south linguistic divide'.[77] The Welsh self-consciously patronized, promoted,
and protected their language and literature as unique marks of identity even
as English became 'the language of law, government, administration, politics,
education, and polite society'. Welsh and English coexisted easily for most,
especially for those like Leland, Bale, Llwyd, Dee, and Sidney who found ancient
Britain's literary greatness in the Britons and their language.[78] Finally, a Welsh
dynasty ruled the country while James VI's unique dynastic position and descent
from Henry VII made him the best candidate to be Brutus or Arthur that the
likes of Owen had ever seen.

More practical Anglo-Welsh connections accompanied these. Travellers were
just a subset of all the peoples on the move in early modern Britain and Ireland.[79]
Owen was one of the many Welsh whose movement into England (and back)

---

[76] Williams, *Recovery, Reorientation and Reformation*, p. 441; Michael Braddick, *State Formation
in Early Modern England c. 1550–1700* (Cambridge, 2000), pp. 344–55.
[77] Richard Suggett and Eryn White, 'Language, Literacy, and Aspects of Identity in Early
Modern Wales', in *The Spoken Word: Oral Culture in Britain, 1500–1800*, ed. Adam Fox and
Daniel Woolf (Manchester, 2002), pp. 67, 75.
[78] Williams, *Recovery, Reorientation and Reformation*, pp. 441, 452–62.
[79] Mark Brayshay, 'Royal Post-Horse Routes in England and Wales: the Evolution of the
Network in the Later-Sixteenth and Early-Seventeenth Century', *Journal of Historical Geography*
17.4 (1991), pp. 373–89; Brayshay, 'Waits, Musicians, Bearwards and Players: the Inter-Urban
Road Travel and Performances of Itinerant Entertainers in Sixteenth and Seventeenth
Century England', *Journal of Historical Geography* 31.3 (2005), pp. 430–58.

picked up speed after 1485, drawn 'to take the path to the centre of political and economic gravity'. Economic conditions at home pushed many migrants, from the Montgomeryshire girls who became maids in Chester to the weavers who settled in Berkshire, 'clothiers to Somerset, tanners to Shropshire, coopers to Suffolk, and some shopkeepers to Kent'. The Irish were not the only ones who sought out Wales. Between 1550 and 1670, English families were drawn to the border shires of North Wales, including Flintshire (700 families), Denbighshire (680), and Montgomeryshire (570). Whether as labourers, lawyers, scholars, students and tutors, merchants, clerics, or stock figures of fun on the stage like Taffy, the Welsh made a significant mark in England.[80] By contrast, long-distance movements across the Scottish Borders in either direction 'are likely to have been small before the seventeenth century'.[81] 'Sawney Scot' and his travelling companions after 1603, real or imagined, were less amiable figures south of the Tweed.[82]

Individuals like Leland or Llwyd travelled ahead, alongside, and in the vanguard of such people. Taylor the Water-Poet published the *Carriers Cosmographie* in 1637, a guide to the lodgings near London where one might find 'Carriers, Waggons, Foote-posts and Higglers' able to carry letters or whatnot into the hinterland, including Taylor's own books and those of other travellers sold by their London-based printers and booksellers.[83] He provided the same information for those seeking sea-borne passage for themselves or their goods to England, Scotland, and Ireland. Taylor's guide details practical connections for travel and cultural exchange in the first decades of the Stuart *imperium*. Options for reaching Wales by post were well established. Denbigh (on Thursdays) and Monmouth (on Fridays) had direct service. Chester was served by multiple carriers on Thursdays, Fridays, and Saturdays, Shrewsbury by two carriers on Thursdays, and both Hereford and Worcester on Fridays and Saturdays. As Taylor informed his readers, some 'may obiect that I have not named all the townes and places that Carriers doe goe unto in England and Wales', but 'what a man sends to Hereford may thence be passed to Saint Davids in Wales, the Worcester carriers can convey any thing as farre as Carmarethen, and those that goe to Chester may send to Carnarvon'. By contrast, there was still only one option for Scotland,

---

[80] Williams, *Recovery, Reorientation and Reformation*, pp. 462–9; Katharine W. Swett, '"Born on My Land": Identity, Community, and Faith Among the Welsh in Early Modern London', in *Protestant Identities: Religion, Society, and Self-Fashioning in Post-Reformation England*, ed. Muriel C. McClendon, Joseph P. Ward, and Michael MacDonald (Stanford, 1999), 249–63; Margaret Spufford, *Small Books and Pleasant Histories: Popular Fiction and its Readership in Seventeenth-Century England* (Cambridge, 1981), pp. 55–6, 182–4.

[81] Ian D. Whyte, *Migration and Society in Britain 1550–1830* (Houndmills, 2000), pp. 107–8.

[82] Whyte, *Migration*, p, 108; also Linda Colley, *Britons: Forging the Nation 1707–1837* (New Haven, 1992), pp. 105–25.

[83] James Raven, *The Business of Books: Booksellers and the English Book Trade 1450–1850* (New Haven, 2007), p. 61.

the future East Coast Main Line to Edinburgh by way of Berwick. Interested parties were advised to find the foot post at the King's Arms in Cheapside. They could post from there on Monday 'any letter to Edenborough ... so they may be conveyed to and from to any parts of the Kingdome of Scotland'.[84]

The contacts that accompanied Angevin imperialism and Anglo-Welsh political union defined the geography of travel differently for Wales than for Scotland. Well before 1603, England and Wales (and Ireland) constituted a single geographic space for Welsh travellers like Gerald, Llwyd, Powel, or Owen and their English counterparts Leland, Camden, and Moryson. Thus, at the end of his travel narrative, Moryson offered readers possible itineraries through Britain and Ireland. One itinerary started at Edinburgh, crossed through the debatable land to Carlisle and then down the west of England to Chester, 'whence they shall have commodity to passe the Sea to Dublin in Ireland'. While Moryson's would-be travellers waited for their passage, 'they may make a cursory journey into Flintshire, and Caernarvenshire in Northwales, to see the antiquities thereof, or otherwise may goe directly to Holy Head, and thence make a shorter cut to Dublyn'. From Munster, 'they may commodiously passe to the South parts of Wales, and there especially see the antiquities of Merlyn, and so taking their journey to the West parts of England'.[85]

Neither route betrays much interest in Wales except for antiquities, which we would expect from someone whose only first-hand experience was his own passage to Ireland or came at second hand from *Britannia*. Indeed, Moryson professed 'onely to prescribe this course, to such as are curious to search all the famous monuments and antiquities of England, mentioned in Camdens compleate description thereof'.[86] Moryson assumed that he and Camden shared readers. Yet he intended to write something different that he hoped – wrongly – others would also find of interest. However, Moryson followed Camden assiduously and his chapters covering topography, diet, apparel, and the like certainly did not offer a unique description of Wales. Moryson's course through the counties of Wales precisely followed Camden's order, no better proof than that he penned the *Itinerary* with a copy of *Britannia* open beside him. Henry V still hailed from Monmouth, Merlin was 'begotten by an Incubus Devill', the Flemings of Pembroke 'ever remained most faithfull' to the crown that settled them there when their own lands flooded, and St Winifred's well watered a sweet-smelling moss.[87] All this smacks of an Anglocentric familiarity resulting from the long-standing ties between Wales and England and a lazy acceptance of what Camden's *Britannia* had to say about the peoples of the Tudor *imperium*.

---

[84] John Taylor, *The Carriers Cosmographie* (STC 23740; London, 1637), sigs A2v, B1v–2r, B4r, C1r–v, C3r.

[85] *The Itinerary of Fynes Moryson* (four volumes; Glasgow, 1907), II, p. 121, hereafter cited as Moryson, *Itinerary*.

[86] Moryson, *Itinerary*, II, p. 121.

[87] Moryson, *Itinerary*, IV, pp. 155–7.

Considering the relative dearth of travel narratives like Churchyard's, perhaps this makes Moryson a typical figure among early seventeenth-century travellers.

The English, Welsh, Cornish, Irish, and Scottish soldiers who marched and fought in the wars of the 1640s crossed and re-crossed cultural boundaries in Britain. Indifference did not characterize their encounters with multicultural Britain. Leaders, propagandists, and news writers among all parties were acutely conscious that theirs was a multi-ethnic struggle as much as a religious one and responded accordingly: this 'dimension of the conflict encouraged the appropriation and propagation of competing images of the Welsh in the newsbooks and pamphlets of the mid seventeenth century'.[88] Importantly, it marked a change that suggests Moryson may not have been atypical. For Lloyd Bowen, it 'was not a common component of the political discourse in the early seventeenth century for the simple reason there were few issues of a distinctively Welsh nature which excited comment in England', while during the wars 'English commentaries upon their Celtic neighbours become something of a commonplace, with Welsh stereotypes being disseminated in the popular sphere with a frequency previously unknown'.[89]

One fundamental reality conditioned descriptions of Wales and the Welsh in the 1640s and 1650s. The Welsh overwhelmingly supported the Royalist cause and Charles I. They did so for many of the reasons that the Anglo-Welsh Union and Elizabethan reformation successfully put down roots: dynastic loyalty, a vested interest in restored self-government, and affection for a Reformation – in the language of Wales – that purported to restore the Britons' ancient Christianity.[90] The once 'indulgent and satirical quality' of English descriptions changed dramatically. Henry V's loyal Fluellen, Leland's noble Britons, and the strange-spoken bumpkin gave way to more hostile stereotypes. Godly Parliamentarians looked upon the Welsh Reformation as half-done at best, 'so deeply traditional as to be scarcely Protestant at all'. It was a short distance from this view to fears of a 'Welsh popish Army' ready, like its Irish counterpart, for use against Charles's opponents.[91] Dynastic loyalty transformed a comment about inveterate Welsh poverty, thievery, or the plain, loyal Welshman into 'gullible and simple-minded' folks 'seduced' by the king.[92] Indeed, the presence of Welsh soldiers and their womenfolk in England did nothing but inspire pamphleteers to even more hostile description, 'typically bare-footed and ragged, if

---

[88] Lloyd Bowen, 'Representations of Wales and the Welsh during the Civil Wars and Interregnum', *Historical Research* 77 (2004), p. 359. Mark Stoyle, *Soldiers and Strangers: An Ethnic History of the English Civil War* (New Haven, 2005) makes the strongest case for the ethnic dimension of the conflict in the English and Welsh theatres of war.

[89] Bowen, 'Representations of Wales', p. 362; Peter Lord, *Words With Pictures: Welsh Images and Images of Wales in the Popular Press, 1640–1860* (Aberystwyth, 1995), pp. 9–51.

[90] Stoyle, *Soldiers and Strangers*, pp. 12–27.

[91] Stoyle, *Soldiers and Strangers*, pp. 18–20.

[92] Stoyle, *Soldiers and Strangers*, pp. 20–1, 29, 158–63.

one is to believe contemporary accounts, equipped with strange weapons and speaking a strange tongue'.[93]

Two ominous trends emerged. Writers associated the Irish and the Welsh and, as Charles's fortunes waned in the English theatre of war against the New Model Army, on-going loyalty to the crown was firmly identified with ethnic difference: "'That barbarous country [of Cornwall] and heathen Wales is all the helpe that our king and prince have to keepe them from their Parliament ... except some Irish rebels [and] Lorraine French.'"[94] Just as many Protestants found it hard to accept that Catholics in Ireland could be loyal subjects, so zealous Protestants in England began to associate Welsh loyalty to Charles I with the state of the reformed church in Wales: 'what will you expect from Wales when the gospell hath scarce twinkled ... for they scarce had any more reformation then the common prayer book, a masse booke junior'.[95] English and Welsh reformers like Vavasour Powell deliberately aimed to define Wales as a 'spiritual fastness' in desperate need of reforming missions. They laid the foundation for Roger Williams' home natives. The Welsh minister Alexander Griffith retorted that, far from being Powell's infidels, the Welsh '"were neither Jewes, Turkes, nor Pagans before your holiness came thither but were as good Christians (every whit) as they are now"'.[96]

The image of a 'benighted country' that must be taught loyalty to the Commonwealth and the godly path to salvation easily pushed aside Leland's once 'noble Britons' among English pamphlet readers and policy makers. The ethnic dimensions of the conflicts of the 1640s – and efforts to remake Wales in a godly image during the 1650s – were a world removed from the indifference of Moryson's *Itinerary*. Cornwall's Britons found themselves in a parallel conflict, and it is to the encounter with the Cornish that we now turn.

The Britons of Cornwall

The publication of Richard Carew's *Survey of Cornwall* in 1602 owed much to William Camden's encouragement. Carew befriended Camden and Philip Sidney at Christ Church, Oxford before three years at the Middle Temple and a return to the family estates made him one of Cornwall's leading gentry.[97] Settled at Antony House, Carew set out to describe the territory of the ancient Britons and their modern descendants that once took in a good deal of Devon and the South-West before the successful onslaughts of the Saxon kings. A lively, curious

[93] Stoyle, *Soldiers and Strangers*, pp. 20–1, 29.
[94] Quoted in Stoyle, *Soldiers and Strangers*, p. 150.
[95] Quoted in Bowen, 'Representations of Wales', p. 368.
[96] Bowen, 'Representations of Wales', pp. 372–6.
[97] Stan Mendyk, 'William Carew', *Oxford DNB* at www.oxforddnb.com.

intellect, deep interest in his native county, and a talent for nicely turned phrases all pushed Carew to pen this survey.

Only after it had circulated in manuscript for some years did friends like Camden persuade Carew to revise and publish it. It was no easy task. Carew understood that even a handful of years brought noticeable changes among a people and place: 'a wonder it were, that in the ceaselesse reuolution of the Vniuerse, any parcell should retaine a stedfast contribution'. 'Reckon therefore (I pray you),' he continued' that this treatise plotteth downe Cornwall, as it now standeth.'[98] Carew composed his *Survey* as two books, the first a topical account of Cornwall and its peoples and the second a pseudo-journey around the county's hundreds, liberally dosed with travel narrative. Could the identical design of Carew and Owen's surveys be entirely coincidental? Carew revealed a cultural sensitivity and acuity that certainly rivalled Moryson's or Owen's.

Carew began with the condition of the Cornish. This included unique attitudes and practices concerning tenures and landholding, a logical topic for someone immersed in estate matters. They created a built environment fit for the county's natural rigours: 'The ancient man[n]er of Cornish building, was to plant their houses lowe, to lay the stone with morter of lyme and sand, to make the walles thick, their windowes arched and little, and their lights inwards to the court, to set hearths in the midst of the roome, for chimneyes, which vented the smoake at a louer in the toppe, to couer their planchings with earth, to frame the roomes not to exceede two stories.' The gentry now defied the elements as 'they seat their dwellings high, build their walles thinne, lay them with earthen morter, raise them to three or foure stoaries, mould their lights large, and outward, and their roofes square and slight, coueting chiefly prospect and pleasure'. Glass and plaster were late additions. For poor cottagers, cob walls and thatch roofs prevailed, despite ill-fated attempts to 'brooke the Cornish weather' with brick or lath.[99]

Carew betrayed his knack for linguistics in discussing naming practices. Where 'the Saxons haue not intruded their newer vsances, they partake in some sort with their kinsmen the Welsh: for the Welshmen catalogize ap Rice, ap Griffin, ap Owen, ap Tuder, ap Lewellin, &c ... So the westerne Cornish ... intitle one another with his owne & his fathers christen name, and conclude with the place of his dwelling'.[100] Among the names one would find were John Thomas Pendaruis. 'Most of them begin with Tre, Pol, or Pen,' Carew explained, 'which signifie a Towne, a Top, and a head: whence grew the common by-word. By Tre, Pol, and Pen, / You Shall know the Cornishmen.' Carew's sensitive ear proved too sensitive to some linguistic differences. Cornish might 'hold an affinity with the Welsh ... But the Cornish is more easie to bee pronounced, and

---

[98]   Richard Carew, *A Survey of Cornwall* (STC 4615; London, 1602), sig. 4a.
[99]   Carew, *Survey of Cornwall*, sigs 36a–38a, 53a.
[100] Carew, *Survey of Cornwall*, sig. 54b.

not so vnpleasing in sound, with throat letters, as the Welsh.'[101] As if anticipating assumptions about the primitive simplicity of native languages, Carew wrote that Cornish 'is stored with sufficient plenty to express the conceits of a good wit, both in prose and rime'. For essential proof, Carew reported that 'the Lords Prayer, the Apostles Creed, and the ten Commaundements, haue bene vsed in Cornish beyond all remembrance'.[102]

Still, the language gave ground before the advance of English, even if some would greet a stranger in Cornish with 'I can speake no Saxonage.' The Cornish who spoke English did so well, 'receyuing it from the best hands of their gentry, and the Easterne Marchants: but they disgrace it in part, with a broad and rude accent ... somewhat like the Somersetshire men' and created their own oddities of English usage.[103] 'The other rude termes, wherewith Devon and Cornish men are often twyted [reproached]' could be defended by their antiquity, propriety, and significance, 'for most of them take their source from the Saxon, our naturall langauge'.[104] Carew would develop this theme in 'The excellencie of the English tongue' when it appeared in Camden's *Remaines of a Greater Worke Concerning Britain* in 1614, championing English while accepting the 'contributions of foreign tongues and cultures' that others rejected.[105]

Qualities of mind and body made the Cornish their own people. Thanks to verses and particulars received from Camden, Carew could affirm that the Cornish once resembled the 'first Inhabitants, or Aborigenes' found by Brutus to be 'huge of body, rough of liuing, & sauage of conditions'. Carew accepted the testimony of Diodorus Siculus that the Cornish 'grew to a larger measure of ciuility, then other their fellow, but more remote Ilanders' by contacts with foreign merchants and the coming of Christianity, a 'fruitful age of Canonizatio[n]' to which the Cornish contributed many worthy saints.[106] Like Leland and Bale before him – and his near neighbour across the Bristol Channel in Pembrokeshire, Owen – Carew marked the progress of civility through notable Cornishmen and the advance of learning in theology, medicine, statecraft, and war.[107] The 'old Veale of Bodmyn' brought a Ciceronian flourish from Carew when he asserted that, like Gorgia of Leontium's command of the liberal arts, no mechanical art escaped this fellow's knowledge or expertise: carpenter, joiner, millwright, mason, clockmaker, carver, metal founder, architect. 'The Cornish mind thus qualified,' concluded Carew, 'are the better enabled to express the same by the strong, actiue, & healthfull constitution of their bodies.' Indeed, Cornishmen, like their hardy counterparts in other remote regions such as the

---

[101] Carew, *Survey of Cornwall*, sig. 55a.
[102] Carew, *Survey of Cornwall*, sigs 55b–56a.
[103] Carew, *Survey of Cornwall*, sig. 56a.
[104] Carew, *Survey of Cornwall*, sig. 56b.
[105] Mendyk, 'Richard Carew'.
[106] Carew, *Survey of Cornwall*, sigs 57b–58a.
[107] Carew, *Survey of Cornwall*, sigs 58b–62b.

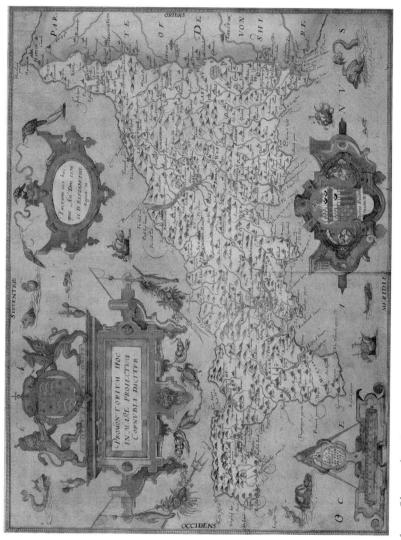

17 Cornwall from Christopher Saxton, *An Atlas of England and Wales* (London, 1579). Reproduced by permission of the Llyfrgell Genedlaethol Cymru/The National Library of Wales.

Hebrides, lived to old age and some achieved a fantastic number of years. They included the four old souls who died within a few months of each other in Carew's parish and reckoned 340 years in total among them.[108]

Carew laboured to explain why the evident learning in civil and common law never yielded a bounty of Cornish jurists. Perhaps the county's poverty, distance from the 'supremer Courts' in London, or the 'multiplicity of petty ones neere at hand, appertaining to the Duchy, Stannary, and Franchises' worked against a Cornish presence at the centre of judicial power in Westminster.[109] The 'Cornish bench' had its own flavour:

> [E]quity bearest more sway, then grauity ... and in confusion they mayntayne equality: for though they speake more then one at once, yet no one mans speech, or countenance, can carry a matter against the truth. Neither doe assertions, but proofes in hearings; nor vouchings, but shewing of law cases, in deciding, order the controuersies: and as diuersitie in opinions breedeth no enmity, so ouer-ruling by most voyces, is taken for no disgrace.[110]

Turns as a justice of the peace, sheriff, and bailiff might have endeared the upright and honest judges 'God hath blessed this Westerne circuit with' to Carew. They excelled at tempering a quick conceit with steady judgment, severity in punishing with mild mercy in remitting sentences, and gravity joined to kind conversation.[111] The Cornish bench and jurists might have unique, admirable qualities, but too many mayors, recorders, and town clerks used their offices to settle petty scores and impoverish neighbours, rivals, and strangers.[112]

Hierarchy trumped ethnicity as Carew worked his way through the social orders from the nobility to the husbandmen and the poor.[113] There were some yet living who could remember the worst qualities of Cornish husbandmen: poor wretches holding land in common; living by meat products (sour milk, cheese, and butter) with hardly a grain of wheat or rye to mill; coarse garments leaving legs and feet to the mercy of the elements; women who rode astride their horses; straw beds and wool blankets with not a piece of linen in sight; low, earthen-walled houses with only a hole in the wall for a chimney. But 'now most of these fashions are vniuersally banished, and the Cornish husbandman conformeth himself with a better supplied ciuilitie to the Easterne patterne'. That eastern pattern included the English side-saddle, but the westerly progress of civility – or cultural imperialism – had not reached all parts of Cornwall. Some 'Westerne people ... together with the Welsh, their auncient countrimen'

---

[108] Carew, *Survey of Cornwall*, sigs 62b–63a.
[109] Carew, *Survey of Cornwall*, sigs 59b–60a.
[110] Carew, *Survey of Cornwall*, sig. 89b.
[111] Carew, *Survey of Cornwall*, sig. 89b.
[112] Carew, *Survey of Cornwall*, sigs 86b–87a.
[113] Carew, *Survey of Cornwall*, sigs 65b–66a.

nursed a 'fresh memorie of their expulsion long agoe by the English' into 'a bitter repining at their fellowship'.[114]

Bitter Cornish (and Welsh) husbandmen were nothing compared to the poor. Few counties could count so many poor, but the problem lay not in Cornwall: 'Ireland prescribeth to be the nurserie, which sendeth ouer yeerely, yea and dayly whole Ship-loades of these crooked slips, and the dishabited townes afford them rooting', despite statutes designed to ward them off. In the most vicious terms Carew denounced the failure of constables and magistrates to rid the county of these Irish vagabonds because of which 'those vermine swarme again in euerie corner' bringing 'idlenes, drunkenensse, theft, lecherie, blasphemie, Atheisme, and in a word, all impietie'.[115] As with Owen and Moryson, the Anglo-Irish wars exacerbated established ethnic hostility toward the Irish, especially among peoples in the counties most pressed for taxes, soldiers, and supplies and most susceptible to the flow of refugees. Here Carew's ethnic animosity dulled his cultural sensitivity.

Carew's hostility to the Irish reads ironically when he takes up pastimes and certain religious practices. The Cornish played a game Carew called hurling, though his detailed description reads more like rugby or Gaelic football. They played two kinds. Hurling to goals involved laying out some kind of pitch with goals marked by bushes eight or ten feet apart. The best hurlers guarded these goals while teams advanced the ball. Hurling to goals was a rule-bound game and players repaid infractions with their fists. According to Carew, these 'hurling matches are mostly vsed at weddings, where commonly the ghests [sic] vndertake to encounter all commers'. By contrast, hurling to the country matched several parishes against each other with either the neighbouring town itself or a gentleman's seat acting as the goal. Understandably, Carew described this as a more diffuse and confused game, with ragged and bloodied teams battling through hedgerows, watercourses, and fields to reach the goal and – usually – a well-earned barrel of beer. In all this, 'the ball may bee compared to an infernall spirit; for whosoever catcheth it, fareth straightwayes like a madde man, strugling and fighting with those that goe about to holde him'.[116]

One senses that Carew saw his share of hurling and came to think of the game with a mix of dismay and admiration, captured in one of his most vivid and lively passages:

> I cannot well resolue, whether I should more commend this game, for the manhood and exercise, or condemne it for the boysterousnes and harmes which it begetteth; for as on the one side it makes their bodies strong, hard, and nimble, and puts a courage into their hearts, to meete an enemie in the face: so on the other ... when the hurling is ended, you shall see them retyring home, as from a pitched battaile, with bloody pates,

[114] Carew, *Survey of Cornwall*, sigs 66b–67a.
[115] Carew, *Survey of Cornwall*, sigs 67a–68a.
[116] Carew, *Survey of Cornwall*, sigs 73b–75a.

bones broken, and out of ioynt, and such bruses as shorte[n] their daies; yet al is good play & neuer Attourney nor Crowner troubled for the matter.[117]

Wrestling accomplished much the same ends without the brutality. The Cornish boasted that neither Greeks nor Turks nor, indeed, their 'once countrymen and stil neighbours, the Bretons, can bereaue them of this Laruell' for wrestling. This was understandable when 'you shall hardly find an assembly of boyes, in Deuon or Cornwall' unwilling to 'giue you a muster of this exercise'.[118] Carew valued the physical training useful in war that these games, along with Sunday archery, provided, especially for the inhabitants of a coastal county on the 'front line' of maritime conflict.[119]

In his description of the spiritual estate Carew went on to praise the first religious foundations in Cornwall, including the monasteries and churches that nursed those who 'labor the Lords vineyard'. He praised too the Cornish clergy, churchwardens, and the like who saw the 'buildings & ornaments appertaining to Gods seruice, decently maintayned, & good order there reuere[n]tly obserued'.[120] For Carew, feasts, harvest days, church ales, the broad humour of the Guarney miracle play, and three-men songs enriched Cornish life.[121] However, 'many Ministers haue by their ernest inuectiues both condemned these Saints feasts as superstitious, and suppressed the Church-ales, as licencious'. Carew approved these festivities to the extent that they had been originally instituted and might yet be reformed to achieve the 'entertaining of Christian loue, conforming mens behauiour to a ciuill conuersation, compounding of controuersies, appeasing of quarrels, raising a store, which might be conuerted, partly to good and godly vses'.[122] He found piety and Christian fellowship in all this despite his coldness for 'distinctively Catholic' traditions.[123] For zealots, however, it testified to the remnants of popery and the corruption of guileless souls. A lieutenant from Norwich in 1635, with a journey to the North behind him, refused to cross the Tamar into 'ye horned-nock-hole Land's-end, nor her horned wayes to the rough, hard-bred, and brawny strong limb'd wrestling Inhabitants thereof'.[124] The ethnic identity that encouraged Parliament's soldiers to demonize the Cornish had much to do with pastimes and religious activities.

---

[117] Carew, *Survey of Cornwall*, sig. 75b.
[118] Carew, *Survey of Cornwall*, sig. 75b.
[119] Carew, *Survey of Cornwall*, sigs 72a, 75b.
[120] Carew, *Survey of Cornwall*, sigs 80b–82b.
[121] Carew, *Survey of Cornwall*, sigs 68a–72b.
[122] Carew, *Survey of Cornwall*, sig. 69a–b.
[123] Nicholas Orme, 'Popular Religion and the Reformation in England: A View from Cornwall', in *Religion and the Early Modern State: Views from China, Russia, and the West*, ed. James D. Tracy and Marguerite Ragnow (Cambridge, 2004), pp. 368–9.
[124] R. Pearse Chope and Alan Gibson, eds, *Early Tours in Devon and Cornwall* (Newton Abbot, 1967), pp. 83, 91; quoted in M.J. Stoyle, '"Pagans or Paragons?": Images of the Cornish during the English Civil War', *English Historical Review* 111.441 (1996), p. 299.

Land's End might have been *terra incognita* as far as Anna Trapnel was concerned in the 1650s. Trapnel's mother raised her to be a literate and independent thinker imbued with a special calling. She found it in an 'intense quest for salvation and truth, involving phases of suicidal Calvinist despair, fasting, trances, visions, and associations with various puritan congregations'. Uncanny prophetic visions earned Trapnel a place among the Fifth Monarchists – who awaited the fifth and final world empire, that of Christ – and the suspicion of the Cromwellian regime in the early 1650s. God called her to confer with the Fifth Monarchists in Cornwall and she recounted her journey, meetings, imprisonment, and removal back to London in a *Report and Plea or A Narrative of Her Journey from London into Cornwall* (1654).[125]

Despite the call from her comrades, Trapnel's mind was 'so strongly bent against that journey' that she refused until God ordered her to go, assuring her that the Lord would be her companion all the while and chastising her for cavilling as 'Moses did when he was to go to Pharaoh'.[126] Trapnel's sisters and brothers in London objected to her absence from them, but God held her steadfast with a vision:

> I beheld high rocky-hills, and variety of places and towns, and how I should be as I rode in the Coach, much melody I should have; this I saw, and heard this saying, That as sure as Paul in Act.16.9 had a vision appeared in the night: There stood a man of Macedonia and prayed Paul, saying, Come over into Macedonia and help su [sic]; & the Lord said, as truely do I thy Lord call thee to Cornwall by this vision ... [127]

Trapnel recorded precious little of her actual journey, save to note that the rocky terrain repeatedly reminded her that Christ was her rock.[128]

The Cromwellian regime, suspicious of social unrest and radical dissent despite the godly credentials of the New Model Army and its leaders, found common cause with Cornish traditionalists when Trapnel arrived. Local ministers met her witnessing to Christ with, in Trapnel's words, 'all their might, run their jangling bells against me, and called to the Ruler to take me up'. The ministers did their jobs well and many locals apparently wondered 'what an impostor, and a dangerous deceiver was come into Cornwal ... and thus they spit venome against me'.[129] Trapnel wrote that 'it did me no hurt', but the treatment coloured her views of Cornwall and its people. Arrested at Truro and interrogated, Trapnel met with her fellow Fifth Monarchist Captain Langden while she waited for removal to London: 'when I come there, I will write of Cornwell, Cornhell in the West. He said you might have suffered at London, but not as here said I; for here

---

[125] Stevie Davies, 'Anna Trapnel', *Oxford DNB* at www.oxforddnb.com.

[126] Anna Trapnel, *Report and Plea or A Narrative of Her Journey from London into Cornwall* (STC T2033; London 1654), pp. 1–2.

[127] Trapnel, *Report and Plea*, p. 3.

[128] Trapnel, *Report and Plea*, p. 10.

[129] Trapnel, *Report and Plea*, p. 18.

they deal very uncivilly, and unchristian like by me.'[130] Trapnel later returned to Cornwall and ventured into Wales to witness among her brothers and sisters, but neither of these conservative religious and royalist strongholds must have been conducive to her visions, even as she settled into a peaceful millenarianism awaiting the monarchy of Christ.[131]

The Cornish who rose in defence of their unique way of life and their special place as keepers of an ancient British Christianity would have found themselves in the pages of Carew's ethnography. Their Parliamentary enemies plundered the cultural complexity described by Carew to create a grotesque stereotype of 'ragged lowsie varlets' and 'popish ignorants, who periodically issued forth from their "lurking holes" in the tin-mines in order to pillage and plunder'.[132] By contrast, the Devonians of Tristram Risdon's Survey of the County of Devon, begun upon the publication of Carew's account and finally completed in the 1630s, suffered no such descriptive fate. In his brief overview, Risdon emphasized the fellowship and affinity of the two counties and made regular comparisons, from situation and British origins (when 'they were anciently one Province, one Nation, and one Kingdom') to tin mining, hurling, and rebelliousness.[133] Like Carew, Risdon described a barren county made fruitful, populated with martial 'Inhabitants very laborious, rough, and unpleasant to Strangers travelling these Ways'.[134] But Devonians numbered among the ranks of those soldiers who had failed to prevent Cornish Royalists from mobilizing their county for the king in October 1642.[135]

The military prowess that Carew wrote of helped to deliver most of the South-West into Cornish hands by summer 1643, including Devon. Cornish success thus ensured that treachery and identification with the hated Irish became commonplace before Parliamentary soldiers forced the king's supporters to surrender in spring 1647. By then, English Parliamentarians had turned Carew's Cornish from culturally unique yet, finally, loyal subjects of the crown into a treacherous Other within Britain, prey to Parliamentary soldiers and righteous prophets like Anna Trapnel alike.

[130] Trapnel, Report and Plea, p. 29.
[131] Davies, 'Anna Trapnel'; B.S. Capp, The Fifth Monarchy Men: A Study in Seventeenth-century English Millenarianism (Totowa, NJ, 1972), pp. 101–2, 109–13.
[132] Stoyle, 'Pagans or Paragons?', pp. 305–6, 308.
[133] Tristram Risdon, The Chorographical Description, or, Survey of the County of Devon (two volumes; London, 1714), I, pp. 3, 2–9 and II, pp. 2–10.
[134] Risdon, Survey of the County of Devon, I, p. 2.
[135] Stoyle, Soldiers and Strangers, pp. 42–3.

The final pilgrimage of John Taylor

> Now in the seventy fourth yeare of mine Age,
> I take an English and Welsh Pilgrimage ...
> Twelve Voyages and Journies I have past,
> And now my Age sayes this may be my last,
> My Travels Story shall most pleasant be
> To you that read, though painfull unto me.[136]

John Taylor's *Short Relation of a Long Iourney* came off the presses in the spring of 1653, following a July-to-September circuit into Wales. Taylor hoped that his fans – he numbered them near three thousand – would now make good their subscriptions with actual purchases. As with his Scottish journey, Taylor relied upon the hospitality of the local gentry and canvassed the country with an open countenance. The war etched itself into the Welsh landscape, but not the Water-Poet's sensibilities.

This was no easy journey for Taylor, aged seventy-four and with a gammy leg, but his pithy opening verse challenged even a 'Scottish Jock or Jackey; Or any light-heel'd nimble footed Lackey / To travel such a jaunt as I have done'. Arriving in Chester he met an aged Italian doctor whom the locals considered a 'Mountebank'. Taylor admired this man who 'cured the Rich, for as much as hee could get', healed the meaner sort for what they could afford, and gave alms to the poorest. Travelling to Flint, Taylor found a town devastated by war, and the onward journey to Holywell brought him to 'Saint Winifrids Chapell, which is now much defaced by the injury of these late Wars'. Taylor accepted the well's healing properties to a point, that 'none made the worse' by taking the 'Christalline, sweet, and medicinable' waters. Many beggars of all ages 'richly embroidered all over with such Hexameter poudred Ermins (or Vermin) as are called Lice in England' resorted there.[137]

Taylor's coastal circuit from north to south introduced him to the cultural contact zones along the coastal plains. Here migration, trade, war, or simply travel brought Welsh, English, Irish, and others into short-term contact or permanent communion. For the onward journey from Holywell, Taylor 'hired a little Boy (to direct me in the way) that could speak no English, and for lack of an Interpreter, we travelled speachless eight miles'. At Aberconwy, Taylor found hospitable lodging with a 'Mr Spencer (an English man) he is Post Master there'. The next day 'I mounted Dun, Dun mounted Penmen Mawre', and Taylor praised Snowdon and the hills of Merioneth and Cardigan in verse. Reaching Caernarvon after a short visit to Bangor, Taylor gained a new guide and provisions from the garrison commander Thomas Mason and the local justice of the peace, a Mr Lloyd. He found in Harlech a town 'all spoild, and almost inhabitable

---

[136] John Taylor, *A Short Relation of a Long Iourney Made Round ... Wales* (STC T512; London, 1653), p. 3.

[137] Taylor, *Short Relation*, pp. 5, 9–12.

by the late lamentable troubles'. Onward to Bermouth, devoid of provisions, Taylor took coarse lodging with 'John Thomson, a Lancashire English man'. Aberystwyth offered none of its modern pleasantries, for which Taylor resorted to the house of Richard Price and the company of Thomas Evans.[138]

His journey half over, Taylor stopped to reflect on his contacts with this eclectic mix of people in an unfamiliar and bloodied land. Welsh guides could be interesting sorts. 'I that knew neither the intricate wayes,' Taylor explained, 'nor could speake any of the Language, was necessitated to have Guides from place to place.' Hiring guides at harvest time was a dear proposition. This had something to do with the commoners Taylor associated with on his journey, 'for it is to bee understood that those kind of labouring people had rather reap hard all day for six pence, then to go ten or twelve miles easily on foot for two shillings'. He was matter of fact in accepting the price of pulling labourers away from a harvest that would sustain them through the year. Arriving at the house of 'the ancient worthy and hospitable' Walter Lloyd, Taylor found bountiful housekeeping and good company on the journey to Conway before setting off to Carmarthen on his own. Miles over stony hillocks left him longing for travel in England. With four miles to go, Taylor spotted a 'field-chamber' of oats for the night, but a turn 'out of the stony way' found 'a softer bed, for we were both in a Bog or Quagmire, and at that time I had much a do to draw myselfe out of the dirt, or my poore weary Dun out if [sic] the Mire'.[139] Taylor memorably recounted the resolution of this errant leg:

> [With] Owl-light to guide me, no tongue to ask a question, the way unknown, or uneven; I held it my best course to grope in the hard stony way againe, which having found (after a quarter of an houres melancholy paces) a Horsman of Wales, that could speak English, overtook me and brought me to Caermarden, where I found good and free entertainment at the house of one Mistris Oakley.[140]

Carmarthen offered him a town of plenty after his journey through North Wales. So did English-speaking Pembrokeshire; inevitably Taylor repeated the stock description, 'therefore they call it little England beyond Wales'. Through Tenby and Milford Haven, Taylor arrived in St Davids, where the war confronted him again: 'The goodly Church of s. Davids hath beene forced lately to put off the dull and heavy coat of peacefull Lead, which was metamorphosed into warlike bullets.' Further comment sharpened this turn of phrase. Henry VII's father lay interred in the cathedral, 'for whose sake ... (K. Henry the eight) did spare it from defacing, when hee spared not much that belonged to the Church'.[141] The Royalist earl of Carbery, Richard Vaughan, welcomed Taylor to his house at Golden Grove, a place 'justly stiled the Cambrian Paradise, and

---

[138] Taylor, *Short Relation*, pp. 12–16.
[139] Taylor, *Short Relation*, pp. 16–17.
[140] Taylor, *Short Relation*, pp. 17–18.
[141] Taylor, *Short Relation*, pp. 18–20.

Elizium of Wales' where others would also find the earl's literary tastes pleasant company.[142] A deadly shadow fell over this idyll when a gentleman arrived at Golden Grove to share a miserable story of the heavens opening up over the mountains of Radnorshire. A father and son had scrambled up a great oak to escape the sudden explosion of floodwaters over their farm, but the 'merciless waters' had seized the farmer's daughter and carried her down the mountain-side, smashing her against the stony riverbed until her long hair caught on a stump. Barely alive, the poor wretch had watched as the torrent uprooted the great oak and drowned her kin.[143]

Unlike the godly warriors who had demonized and killed the Welsh, Taylor lamented leaving Wales. Religious life played an important role in those feelings. Arriving in Barnsley, having passed unrecognized through the town of his birth (Gloucester), Taylor found the strictest observance of the Sabbath of all the places in England or Wales that he visited. Little children were not suffered to walk or play and two women faced either sixpence fines or an hour in the stocks after 'prophane walking' in the fields. Peeved with the authorities, these 'willfull women' saved their money and made a 'jest out of the matter' with an hour in the stocks. 'There is no such zeale in many places and Parishes of Wales', Taylor contrasted; 'for they have neither Service, Prayer, Sermon, Minister, or Preacher, nor any Church door opened at all, so that people do exercise and edifie in the Church-Yard at the lawfull and laudable Games of Trap, Catt, Stool-ball, Racket, &c. on Sundayes.'[144]

The journey evidently summoned a lasting affection for Wales and the Welsh. For readers now desirous to learn more, Taylor first encouraged them to 'travell for it as I have done'. He next offered armchair travellers Camden's *Britannia* or 'Mr Speeds laborious History, and their Geographicall Maps and Descriptions'. Yet as Taylor prepared his tract, he side-lined both Camden and Speed in favour of the *Cronica Walliae*. He directed readers to Powell's 1584 edition, but then thought better of asking an interested reader to pick up Camden, plough through Speed's 'laborious' account, or tackle the black letter *Cronica*. Instead, Taylor composed his own abstract from the *Cronica* for the *Short Relation*. He did so after the subscription notices had gone out advertising just his 'Journey and Entertainment'.[145]

Taylor gave the *Cronica* the kind of political reading that encouraged the Commonwealth authorities to arrest him for espionage upon his return from the West Country in 1649.[146] He omitted entirely the opening description of Wales by John Prise, perhaps thinking that *The Short Relation* offered a sufficient primer.

---

[142] Taylor, *Short Relation*, p. 20; Ronald Hutton, 'Richard Vaughan', *Oxford DNB* at www.oxforddnb.com.

[143] Taylor, *Short Relation*, p. 21.

[144] Taylor, *Short Relation*, pp. 26–7.

[145] Taylor, *Short Relation*, p. 5–6.

[146] Bernard Capp, 'John Taylor', *Oxford DNB* at www.oxforddnb.com.

Instead Taylor framed his chronicle with two remarkable rhetorical questions: 'what reason the English had to make warr against the Welsh' and 'What cause did the Welsh give to the English to make Warre upon them, to invade, plunder, spoile, and kill?' Taylor answered the second question first, writing of a people with their own language, laws, and customs who owed homage or allegiance to no crown and 'never went forth of their owne bounds to rob the English, or to spoile and invade England, or any other Nation'. In short, the Welsh gave the English no cause. Instead, the answer to the first question 'is, or may be, Because the English were ambitious and covetous, and also stronger then their Neighbours, and being able and willing to do injury, and oppress the Welsh, they many times attempted to subject and conquer them'. But this was not a simplistic Anglo-Welsh conflict. Taylor's excerpts emphasized the long history of resistance by the people of North Wales, South Wales and Powys to their eastern neighbours, when 'the Saxons, Danes, English, Irish, and Flemmings, all severally, and sometimes joyned together, to conquer, and make prey and purchase of poor Wales, they all striving to have the Goods and Lands that belonged not to them'.[147] Taylor ended his crib with the defeat of Llywelyn in 1282, even though the *Cronica* carried on for a few years more. After his journey through Wales, perhaps Taylor found it disagreeable to finish his account as the *Cronica* ended: 'After this there was nothinge done in Wales worthy memory, but that is to bee redde in the Englishe Chronicle.'[148]

The racist ethnography of William Richards' *Wallography*

If John Taylor's readers found Wales far removed from the lurid, hostile accounts of Parliamentary propagandists, William Richards' journeys would seem to confirm the lasting virulence of anti-Welsh stereotypes. Richards left his native Northamptonshire to begin his studies at Trinity College, Oxford in the waning days of the Protectorate. He earned his B.A. in 1663 and M.A. in 1666 and became an Oxford fellow in the summer before the Great Fire engulfed London. In 1675 Richards left his living at Marston in Oxfordshire to take up the rectorship of Helmdon, the place of his birth. Two years before, Richards made his only journey to Wales. It was not until October 1681 that he completed the narrative that Obadiah Balgrave published in 1682 as *Wallography; or The Britton Describ'd.*[149] *Wallography* promised a pleasant relation of the journey into

---

[147] Taylor, *Short Relation*, pp. 29–31.

[148] Llwyd, *Cronica Walliae*, p. 224.

[149] An analysis of *Wallography* as satire can be found in Michael Roberts, '"A Witty Book, but mostly Feigned": William Richards' *Wallography* and Perceptions of Later Seventeenth-century England', in *Archipelagic Identities: Literature and Identity in the Atlantic Archipelago, 1550–1800*, ed. Philip Schwyzer and Simon Mealor (Aldershot, 2004), pp. 153–65.

Wales and many 'choice' observations of the 'Nature and Humour, Actions, Manners, Customs &c. of that Countrey and People'.[150]

In his dedication to Richard Wenman of Casswell, Oxfordshire, Richards explained his intentions.[151] He made 'bold to imitate one Alexander of Greece, who still as he went dragooning about the World, describ'd the wandrings', but did so with a difference:

> Whereas he gave only a bare Image and Portraicture of the Country, I shall draw the Character of the Inhabitants, and shall not only express in a Map or Table the meer Picture of the Place, and tell you that here stands one Town and twenty Miles off stands another, but my Design is to give you a Narrative of what I observ'd concerning the Nature of the (1) Soil, and of the (2) Inhabitants, their Original, Persons, Diet, Apparel, Language, Laws, Customs, Policy, &c.[152]

Richards' Alexander must have been the relatively obscure Alexander 'Polyhistor', the Greek ethnographer whose 'vast literary output included compilations of geographical material and wonder-stories of various lands and peoples'.[153] This reference opened a critique of travel writing that helps us to appreciate how important voyages of discovery and ethnography had become in the intellectual environment for Restoration travel narratives.[154] It applied to encounters with exotic others and multicultural Britain.

First, Richards dismissed travel narratives that neglected the ethnographic data he promised in preference for itineraries, maps, and mileage tables. He obviously had in mind John Ogilby's *Britannia* (1675), which 'drew out 2519 miles of road in the form of 100 strip maps' using a waywiser, a 'great wheel' for measuring distance that was well known to the traveller John Evelyn and Ogilby's friend Robert Hooke.[155] Ogilby's description of the road from London to Aberystwyth would have disappointed Richards: 'at 192'5. you touch upon the river Ridal, at 196'7. and 2 Furlongs farther entering Llanbadern-Vaur of 6 Furlongs Extent on the Road; a well built Town with a fair Church, formerly an Episcopal See, and now the Parish Church to Aberistwith which you enter

[150] Charlotte Fell-Smith, 'Richard Williams', *Dictionary of National Biography* (archive) at www.oxforddnb.com.

[151] W.R., *Wallography: or The Britton Describ'd* (WING R101; London, 1682), sig. A3r-v.

[152] W.R., *Wallography*, sig. A4r.

[153] Alexander 'Polyhistor' is even more obscure for modern readers whose first language is English. See Simon Hornblower and Anthony Spawforth, eds, *The Oxford Classical Dictionary* (Oxford, 1996), p. 60.

[154] R.W. Frantz, *The English Traveller and the Movement of Ideas* (Lincoln, NE, 1934/1967), pp. 15–29.

[155] Charles Withers, 'John Ogilby', *Oxford DNB* at www.oxforddnb.com.

at 198'7. of 4 Furlongs Extent'.[156] Such precision made Ogilby's *Britannia* a remarkable achievement.[157] Richards shunned it.

One thing Richards disliked about Alexander Polyhistor's narrative was what he termed its 'TomCoriantism'. Richards explained the reference to the well-known Thomas Coryate, 'a silly travellor, who in King James his time beat upon the hoof about two or three thousand miles, and return'd home as very a Cox-combe as he went out'. Evidently, then, Alexander's 'wonder-stories' of far-off lands had a bit too much of the exotic and fantastic about them, putting them in the same category as Coryate's *Crudities*.[158] Richards also had in mind his countrymen who undertook the Grand Tour or sought out exotic locales around the world: 'For one tells us in Octavo that he hath been at Constantinople; another that he hath been at Vienna; a third that he hath been in Spain ... He tells what Wonderments have surpriz'd him, what Fragments of Antiquity have amaz'd him, what Structures have ravish'd him.'[159] He especially disliked those who joined the increasing ranks of travellers who composed accounts of their travels upon their return home.[160] For 'in a word,' Richards charged, 'he is big with Descriptions, and obliges you with the Narrative of all his Observations and Notices; seeing every one almost that hath but untruss'd in a Foreign Country, will have his Voyage recorded, and every Letter-Carrier beyond the Sea would be thought a Drake or a Candish [Cavendish]'.[161]

Richards ridiculed the pretensions and trivialities of the growing number of travel narratives. A particular type of traveller provoked his strongest ire:

> When a Fellow ... hath entitled himself by some misdemeanours either to the Pillory or Gibbet, to disinherit himself of his deserved Right, he flirts into Holland, or is transported into some Forreign Countrey; where conversing a little while, he thrusts into th' World the History of his Adventures, he varnisheth over his Banishment with the Name of Travel, stiles that his Recreation which was indeed his Punishment, and so dignifies a Ramble by the name of Journey.[162]

As a cleric preferred to a living in the newly restored Church of England, Richards might have had in mind the handful of his thousand or so colleagues who refused to subscribe to the so-called Clarendon Code and were driven from the Church

---

[156] John Ogilby, *Britannia, Volume the First, or, An Illustration of the Kingdom of England and Dominion of Wales by a Geographical and Historical Description of the Principal Roads Thereof* (WING 0168; London, 1675), p. 6.

[157] Withers, 'John Ogilby'.

[158] W.R., *Wallography*, sig. A3v.

[159] W.R., *Wallography*, sigs A4v–A5r.

[160] See Michael G. Brennan, *English Civil War Travellers and the Origins of the Western European Grand Tour* (London, 2002), pp. 7–11; also Jeremy Black, 'The Grand Tour', *Journeys Through the Market: Travel, Travellers and the Book Trade*, ed. Robin Myers and Michael Harris (Folkstone, 1999), pp. 65–91.

[161] W.R., *Wallography*, sig. A5v.

[162] W.R., *Wallography*, sig. A4v–A5r.

into exile. We cannot say what authors and works offended Richards, or be more specific about just what miscreants turned banishment into travel in his eyes. Yet Richards' are contemporary comments that seem to confirm the importance of exile as a motive for and motif of travel among travellers like John Evelyn who fled Britain's troubles beginning in the 1630s.[163]

There is emotion in Richard's preface: hostility toward superficial travel by silly or miscreant travellers; antipathy for certain types of narratives including those that stopped at repetitive itineraries and mileage tables or omitted substantial ethnographic details; and disapproval for page-turning stories of exotic, foreign countries rather than the discovery of Britain itself. He put his own journey into the context of these criticisms. 'I thought with my self why may not I have the liberty of relating my Journey,' he wrote, 'and of communicating my Observations to Mankind.' Richards continued in a defensive tone, 'I must confess my Pilgrimage was not far, but perhaps it was chequer'd with as great variety both of Pleasure and Peril as a longer Progress; neither are my Remarques very solemn and stately, but yet they were such as gratify'd my curiosity, and pleas'd my humor as well as the Observations of longer Journals.'[164]

What kind of response was *Wallography* to all of this? Frankly, Richard's answer was an angry and bizarre one. To start, he gave every impression of setting out to write a serious ethnography that joined the company of Moryson, Owen, Carew, and Taylor, but the tone abruptly changed. He hoped that in its uncommon, rare, and unusual details Wenman might 'find so much Comoedy in this Walk, as may dispose you to smile away an hour in the perusal of it'.[165] Richards' sober beginnings disappeared: 'my Remarques are spick and span new, and if they are ridiculous, they are not unlike the Person upon whom they are written. For the Welch People are a pretty odd sort of Mortals, and I hope I have given you a pretty odd Character of them, and so I think I am pretty even with them for Oddness. A Taphy is observ'd to be a Trickish Animal.'[166]

Richards defined the markers of civility the moment he left London:

> We travelled all that day with much pleasure, being treated as we went, with the Delicacies of Nature: the Air was kind and soft; the Fields were trim and neat; the Sun benign and cherishing; the whole Creation was obliging, and from every thing we met we receiv'd a Civility so that this day pass'd over with much satisfaction.[167]

The bucolic setting soon disappeared. Playing on the most stark urban–rural prejudice, Richards described the falling-away of civility almost from the end of that first day. Rural bumpkins soon populated the landscape through England. In one hamlet Richard stumbled 'upon an House, or a Dunghill modell'd into

---

[163] Michael G. Brennan, ed., *The Origins of the Grand Tour* (London, 2004), pp. 19–36.

[164] W.R., *Wallography*, sigs A5v–A6r.

[165] W.R., *Wallography*, sigs A6v–A7r.

[166] W.R., *Wallography*, sig. A7r–v.

[167] W.R., *Wallography*, p. 2.

the shape of a Cottage, whose outward surface was so all to-be-negro'd with such swarthy plaister, that it appear'd not unlike a great blot of Cow-turd'. Having associated dung and black skin, Richards forced his frame through 'a dwarfish size' door to take in a one-room house with its poor belongings. He found a 'whole Litter of Children was strew'd upon the Floor' while the 'Good-Housewife of this little Tenement' presented quite an image, 'Mouth mumping [mumbling], and her Hands knitting', with a lamb following and a cat in the van leading the way home.[168]

Along with skin colour, Richards attended to another favourite topic of travellers: women and gender norms. With echoes of the washerwomen of Dunbar or Inverness, Richards wrote of 'a woodden kind of Anvil', where the 'She-Vulcans were hammering out with Battle-Door the Filth of Linnen, whose unctuous Distillations were the Nile that water'd the little Egypt of the adjacent garden'.[169] One individual seized Richards' attention, 'an eminent Cot-quean, a meere Woman in the habit of a Man, a kind of Mal-cut-purs'd Creature, an Epicaene Animal of a twisted Gender, who hath a Petticoat Soul in a Trunk-Breech'd Body, and scandalizeth Virility by skill in Housewifery'. Richards then produced an elaborate play on the language of craftsmanship to describe the person's culinary skills. He speculated that a local gentleman kept this 'Hen-Hous-wife-Mortal ... to be a Bull-beggar to the Rats; and also to terrifie a worse kind of Vermin which we call Theeves'. With wonderful hypocrisy, Richards then reported that they sampled the hospitality of 'this soemasculine wight' and gave an overblown description of the simple meat and pottage meal they 'enjoyed'.[170] This individual offended Richards' sensibilities as much as his words offend our own, but gender could prompt 'monstrous' descriptions just as readily as colour and customs in a travel narrative.

Richards' encounter with a 'Bag-piper' and his juggling companion gave him a great store of material for fun and ridicule: 'The Piper appear'd of a tawny Complexion, his Nose bending with an Arch upward; his Eyes being somewhat hollow, seem'd to increase the promontory of his jetting Forehead. In a word, there was charm enough in his Aspect; He was well built, his whole Frame and contexture was sweet and regular; I must needs say, I have seldom met with any handsomer Model, or Platform of a Man.'[171] The piper's attire inspired him to smirking ridicule: 'He wore a Miscellany of Apparel, a Gallimassry of Cloaths, as I humbly conceive, twas a Tyth suit, compos'd of various and several sorts; such as a Club of Raggs, and Randezvous of Fragments, must needs be a Collection (like the Jerkin of the Jay) of several Feathers from divers Birds.'[172] He seemed to approve of the 'ravishing Ditties' the piper produced, even if the pipes were like a

---

[168] W.R., *Wallography*, pp. 16–22.
[169] W.R., *Wallography*, pp. 52, 63.
[170] W.R., *Wallography*, pp. 62–6.
[171] W.R., *Wallography*, p. 29.
[172] W.R., *Wallography*, pp. 28–31.

gizzard tucked under his arm. He was less approving of the juggler. The annoying clang of the juggler's various implements antagonized a swarm of bees that made 'a Pin-cushion of his Body', causing him to swell and burst from his clothes. A bath of honey counteracted the allergic reaction, but this home remedy put the juggler in a worse predicament. Like some tragic, inverted Pooh story, a bear caught a whiff of the honey and took off in hot pursuit of the juggler.[173]

Ridicule was not long in coming after Richards arrived in Wales proper, its location 'ditcht in from England' by Offa.'[174] He supposed the Welsh were descended from the Gauls, 'from whom they seemd to be but a few Aps remov'd; Ap Galloys Ap Gauls, Ap Wallois Ap Wales'. They inspired not a loving embrace, but the desire to strike them with 'the Fist of Indignation' being 'a rude People'. They urgently needed greater efforts at instruction in 'cultivating and manuring, in disciplining and taming them', just as it was 'harder for a Bearward to teach civility to the Beasts of Africa, than to those that come from a more mannerly Country'. Richards denied that he meant to call them beasts, but agreed with the geographers who wrote that the Welsh inhabited a wilderness and writers that compared them to a hard people dragged from a stony land.[175]

Richards proceeded to pen the crudest, hateful account of any people in Britain:

[If] we compare this Kingdom to a Man (as some do Italy to a Man's Leg) they inhabit the very Testicles of the Nation. And I pray what are those but the vilest of Creatures that breed well in the Privities of the greater Brittish World, as those that are hatcht in the Pudenda of the lesser? But whether Welch-men are the Aborigines of their Countrey, as Crab-lice are the Autocthones of theirs, and proceed only (like them) from the excrements of their Soil, we shall not here dispute.[176]

Richards pulled back just a bit in defining Welshness:

They are of a Boorish behaviour, of a Savage Physiognomy; the shabbiness of their Bodies and the Baoticalness of their Souls, and that, which cannot any otherwise be exprest, the Welchness of both, will fright a Man as fast from them, as the odness of their Persons invites one to behold them.[177]

The repulsive attraction of the Welsh lay in their inhumanity: 'Some of them are such rude and indigested Lumps, so far from being Men, that they can scarce be advanc'd into Living Creatures.'[178]

From this starting point, Richard offered an ethnography with categories familiar to us from Moryson and other seventeenth-century travellers. Clothes gave 'excellent harbour to the Vermin of his Body' and usually consisted of

---

[173] W.R., *Wallography*, pp. 32–4.
[174] W.R., *Wallography*, p. 79.
[175] W.R., *Wallography*, pp. 80–1.
[176] W.R., *Wallography*, pp. 81–2.
[177] W.R., *Wallography*, p. 82.
[178] W.R., *Wallography*, p. 82.

trousers – 'a Brace of Cloak-bags ... tacked together are a perfect Emblen of his orural [rural] Attire' – and a Monmouth cap with a button. Cuffs and 'clean Linnen are an upstart Invention ... whereas Primitive Brittishness was never acquainted with habiliment of a Shirt.' Their feet must have been 'of a hot Complexion' since bare toes were so common and the only hose they knew were the torn and ragged offspring of their trousers. Adopting pidgin English and female pronouns that replicated the hostile anti-Welsh pamphlets of the 1640s, Richards reported that the 'Perfection of a Welch-mans Equipage' was 'an old Sword of hur nown breeding, which hur hath brought up from a Tagger'. They used this weapon with great valour against bees, 'a kind of Enemy which the Taphy is much afraid of, in regard he is armed with a Pike in's Rere'.[179]

The people and topography were as one. Mountainous terrain ideally suited to clambering goats presented a 'variety of Precipice to break ones neck; which a Man may sooner do than fill his belly, the Soil being barren, and an excellent place to breed a Famine'.[180] 'As for the Diet of the Britton', Richards rehashed stereotypes dusted off in the 1640s:

> You may see him pictur'd sometimes with that crevis in his head call'd a Mouth, charg'd at both corners with a crescent of Cheese ... and his Hat adorn'd with a Plume of Leeks: Good edible Equipage! which when hunger pinches, he makes bold to nibble; he first eats his Chease and his Leeks together, and for second course he devours his Horse.[181]

The people themselves were 'of the lowest size'. The Welsh face 'usually bubbles into Tumors and Pustles' while their bodies stank of brimstone from the sulphurous ash applied to drive away the pests that caused 'Scrubado' or the 'itch' as it was known.[182]

The heroic subjects of Welsh bards were fit for mockery and their expressions of love were anything but, often descending into senseless 'Anticks' or worse. One Welshman in love, 'having a glympse through the Key-hole of her Saffron Body, burst out into a Panegyrick of the Beeswaxness (as he phras'd it) of her Tawny Complexion'. Another 'We heard of ... went a wooing with a Gun upon his shoulder, being resolv'd (it seems) if Love be a warfare, not to enter unarm'd into the Camp of Venus.'[183] Richards' account of how this encounter resolved itself seems designed to be read in the worst tradition of public school humour:

> [In] the brisk Encounter of a close Embrace, this warlike Instrument took an occasion somewhat unmannerly to go off, and Blunderbuss'd the Mistress on her Breech on one side of the house and poor Taphy on his Nose on the other; for that being much

[179] W.R., *Wallography*, pp. 86–9.
[180] W.R., *Wallography*, pp. 89–90.
[181] W.R., *Wallography*, p. 91.
[182] W.R., *Wallography*, p. 92.
[183] W.R., *Wallography*, pp. 97–102.

dismay'd at this unhappy Accident, one scrabled one way, and the other another, to the total separation of a pair of Lovers, and to the utter spilling of a Mess of Love.[184]

Recreation too encouraged Richards' prurient humour. The Welsh and English shared many ordinary sorts of recreation – football, for instance – but 'In-door Divertisements' in rainy weather were another matter. The indoor diversions included 'Rump pressing, Hot-cockles, Chap-smutting, Snap-apple, and the like', while Richards could not resist an incomprehensible story of playing 'Cockall'. This led into a discussion of Welsh laziness and thievery. These accomplished drovers 'are apt to drive sometimes more than their own'. The 'sin of Nastiness' plagued them too, 'wallowing in filthiness like so many Swine; so that the whole Province seems to be but a general Sty'. Poorer women were especially foul. 'The Tenements they live in are sutable to the Guests that possess them', continued Richards predictably, 'for as these seem to be Dirt moulded into Men, so those are the same matter kneaded into Houses ... every Edifice being a Noahs Ark, where a Promiscuous Family, a Miscellaneous Heap of all kind of Creatures did converse together in one Room.'[185]

What Richard claimed to admire most about the Welsh was 'the Virginity of their Language, not deflowr'd by the mixture of any other Dialect'. This was a relative affection: the 'sincerity of the Brittish remains inviolable' but it was 'a Tongue (it seems) not made for every Mouth; as appears by an Instance of one in our Company, who having got a Welch Polysyllable into his Throat, was almost choak'd with Consonants, had we not by clapping him on the back made him disgorge a Guttural or two, and so sav'd him'. Those among us who recall their first encounter with bilingual signage in Wales might just find Richards' anecdote humorous, but his amusements served his nasty reading of the Welsh. According to Richards, the people nursed a hostility to the English that had its roots in this attachment to their language.[186] His retort turned Welsh into a 'Native Gibberish ... prattled throughout the whole Taphydome, except in their Market Townes, whose Inhabitants being a little rais'd, and (as it were) pufft up into Bubbles above the ordinary Scum do being to despise it.' Even the better sort of Welsh townspeople, those who had 'refin'd into the Quality of having two Suits', accepted English as one more exercise in pretension. They fancied 'themselves above their Tongue', banished Welsh from their houses, instructed their children 'in the Anglican Ideom', and sent them to schools 'with Professors of the same'. This gave Richards 'some glimmering hopes that the Brittish Lingua may be quite extinct, as may be English'd out of Wales, as Latin was barbarously Goth'd out of Italy'.[187] When Richards and his party were suddenly forced to

---

[184] W.R., *Wallography*, pp. 102–3.
[185] W.R., *Wallography*, pp. 105–10.
[186] W.R., *Wallography*, pp. 122–3.
[187] W.R., *Wallography*, pp. 123–4.

return home he reflected on the 'pity such a rare sight as Wales should want a trumpet, nay and a Fool too to proclaim and expose it to the World'.[188]

Richards' *Wallography* outdid Weldon and Kirke; no mean feat. It makes for grim reading, perhaps as much for its feeble humour and would-be comic tone as for the prejudices and stereotypes to be found in it. Richards' Welsh were certainly not the noble Britons described in sixteenth-century accounts. Perhaps Richards found some inspiration in the pre-war 'stage Welshman' or the pamphlets of the 1640s, given his use of Taffy, pidgin English, and the female pronoun.[189] The descriptions of the journey through England to the Welsh Borders also lampooned rural England. He may have been a Northamptonshire rector, but Richards' affinity was for the supposed urban sophistication and civility of London. Richards' second section resembles hardly at all the narrative of a journey or itinerary, but he used the popularity and literary standing of the travel narrative to peddle what was certainly a racist ethnography. His descriptions of the Welsh are transposable with descriptions of the Irish and the peoples of Africa or accounts of Arabs, Tartars, and Jews.[190] Allusions to beasts, skin colour, noses, and cranial formation make it difficult not to think that Richards read or otherwise imbibed such travel narratives and other ethnographies. Richards repeatedly stereotyped the Welsh, writing 'The whole Nation (like a German family) is of one Quality ... the whole Nation indeed being but one grand Remark.'[191]

Richards' *Wallography* anticipates eighteenth-century travellers, colonists, and writers who employed 'racialized notions of nation' in which 'a line of descent or group was identified and signified through religion, custom, language, climate, aesthetics and historical time as much as physiognomy and skin colour'.[192] They did so to pernicious and essentialist effect. The travel narrative proved to be a handy genre in many respects for Richards. His *Wallography* would shortly share space with the equally nasty *Trip to North-Wales* (1701) penned (perhaps) by Edward Ward, a writer who found the 'trip format' a handy one for his satires.[193] In their hateful way, Richards' and Ward's accounts highlight an important evolution in the travel narrative genre and the encounter with multicultural

[188] W.R., *Wallography*, pp. 126-7.
[189] J.O. Bartley, *Teague, Shenkin and Sawney: Being an Historical Study of the Earliest Irish, Welsh and Scottish Characters in English Plays* (Cork, 1954), pp. 63-74.
[190] See Ania Loomba and Jonathan Burton, eds, *Race in Early Modern England* (Houndmills, 2007), pp. 12-28, 183-272.
[191] W.R., *Wallography*, pp. 84, 126.
[192] Kathleen Wilson, *The Island Race: Englishness, Empire and Gender in the Eighteenth Century* (Abingdon, 2003), pp. 11-12; also Roxann Wheeler, *The Complexion of Race: Categories of Difference in Eighteenth-Century British Culture* (Philadelphia, 2000), pp. 2-175.
[193] The supposition is based on the work's sometime attribution to Edward Ward (and Edward Bysshe) and Ward's literary style. James Sambrook, 'Edward Ward' at www.oxforddnb.com; also full citation of E.B., *A Trip to North-Wales Being a Description of the Country and People* (London, 1701) at *Eighteenth Century Collections Online*.

Britain. Seventeenth-century readers did not divorce journeys of discovery – imaginative, authentic, or somewhere in between – at home from those abroad. The shadowy connections between travels in Britain and elsewhere – Worcestre, Rastell, Boorde – had resolved into direct relationships.

Summa: Book Two

Even before the advent of the Welsh Tudors, the lands of the ancient Britons, Wales and Cornwall, had been the most accessible to travellers. In Churchyard, Carew, Owen, and Taylor we find entirely plausible stand-ins for Moryson. A deep interest in ethnography drove them. They crossed cultural boundaries and journeyed through contact zones in multicultural Britain. Churchyard and Taylor represent a less systematic encounter with cultural complexity, whereas Carew and Owen scrutinized their respective counties and their peoples across an impressive range of ethnographic categories as scholar-travellers. Both men had the learning to import the conventions of classical ethnographic writers and connections to antiquarian networks, including those devoted to local histories. Like their mid-century and Restoration counterparts who journeyed to Scotland, war affected travellers' encounters with Wales and Cornwall. Ray and Richards signal that the 'scientific revolution' also affected travel and the study of Britain – a subject we will consider further in Book Three. Finally, the increasingly expansive and sophisticated travel narrative genre simultaneously embraced journeys of discovery at home and abroad.

What, then, of Fynes Moryson's undiscovered Britain? Undiscovered is obviously a tease. Moryson's Britain was never really there to be discovered except by reading between the lines of his surviving works or as an imagined account. From them we can identify what it would have dealt with – ethnography and cultural comparison – and cautiously suggest that Moryson would have rendered the descriptions with significant depth and cultural sensitivity. We learn a good deal more by joining Moryson's ambitions to the actual journeys of other seventeenth-century travellers in Britain. They too manifested a passion for travel and intended to write ethnographic descriptions of the peoples they encountered, or included rudimentary details of that kind in their narratives. In short, the travellers examined here centred their descriptions on deliberate journeys of discovery and ethnographic analysis.

Moryson's emphasis on the English – even if inadvertent or unintentional – opens a new dimension of what John Pocock calls the 'English problem' at the heart of 'British history'. A good part of the latter involves 'a history of the encounter of peoples not (or no longer) English with an expanding English state and (in more senses than one) empire'.[194] Moryson and his stand-ins reveal an

---

[194] J.G.A. Pocock, *The Discovery of Islands: Essays in British History* (Cambridge, 2005), pp. 53–4, 296–300.

overwhelmingly English encounter of this kind with the peoples of Britain, but at an ethno-cultural level. If, as Pocock suggests, 'the "new British history" of the English' will have to be the 'old British history [of English state and empire] retold', the ethnographic traveller may well open genuinely new avenues from which to do so.[195] Still, that is not primarily how we should read Moryson. He aimed to encounter and master Britain in its entirety in his 'Itinerary' and, eventually, his British ethnography. Travel, discovery, and comparative ethnography taking in Britain, continental Europe, and the Middle East were the foundation for much broader ambitions. There is a good deal more to Moryson than the sympathetic Orientalist in the making or a champion of English national genius.

Moryson and his various stand-ins trained two complementary yet competing and sometimes incompatible ethnographic gazes on Britain. One gaze, for which Moryson himself must be the exemplar, focussed on nations and worked to determine their essential features and characteristics. The second, operating on both a much smaller geographic scale or by traversing a country more extensively, opened itself to complexity and diversity within a particular nation or people. John Taylor would have been hard-pressed to assign a single set of ethnographic features to either the Scots or Welsh in his separate journeys among them. George Owen and Richard Carew stand out as travellers who communicated the rich complexity of Pembrokeshire and Cornwall, respectively.

Of course Moryson painted on a much larger canvas, as did William Camden and John Speed. Among them only Camden could claim to have accomplished something remotely like a single account of multicultural Britain built on first-hand experience: Moryson could not hope to compete against *Britannia*. Yet by the end of the seventeenth century *Britannia* could not compete against the incessant demands for up-to-date descriptions of Britain (and the rest of the world) based on travel and encounter. The Britain gazed on by Moryson resembles Graham Robb's France and the French, reduced to 'Paris and a few powerful individuals'. Imagining Wales on a 'national' level, Humphrey Llwyd's 'virtual tour' of Wales in the *Cronica Walliae* 'took the old cantrefs and commotes as the basic building blocks of this territory ... a historical and linguistic community tied together by blood, language, and common memory'. Llwyd and others (like Owen) simultaneously 'presented themselves to the public as "Cambro-Britons", individuals who enjoyed a dual allegiance to Wales and its broader (and more ancient) political incarnation under a British monarch', later James VI and I.[196] Still, travellers like Owen, Carew, Taylor, even Kirke and Richards, bring us much closer to Robb's 'distant figures' and the locality and particularity of the *pays* – or the cantref and commote.[197] Moryson's stand-ins in Scotland, Wales, and

---

[195] Pocock, *Discovery of Islands*, p. 299.
[196] Bowen, 'Fashioning Communities', pp. 95, 97–8.
[197] The Scottish counterparts to Owen and Carew, who engaged Scotland at the level of the *pays*, are examined in detail in Chapter 11. So too are their English counterparts, in Chapter 12.

Cornwall, then, accomplish something even more significant than recreating an undiscovered Britain. They signal the explosion of personal journeys and encounters with multicultural Britain. The future ultimately belonged to those travellers and writers.

Camden, writing with his gaze fixed firmly on the nations of Britain, did not think the work of those with a finer view of cultural complexity was mutually exclusive of his own. He knew and worked with Owen (and Carew), even if we cannot say if Camden ever actually read the *Description of Pembrokeshire*. The person who definitely made use of Owen's account a century later was Edward Lhuyd. Sometime in 1692, Erasmus Saunders, a Pembrokeshire native and graduate of Jesus College, Oxford – nicknamed the 'Welsh college' for its many Welsh students – met the Welsh antiquarian John Lewis. Saunders informed Lhuyd, whom he was assisting in the revision of *Britannia*, that 'Mr. Lewis had loaned him "a MS. compil'd by Mr. Cambden's correspond't in Pembrocksh."'.[198] In precisely the partnership of local travel and scholarly labour that Camden envisioned, Saunders passed on Owen's *Pembrokeshire* to Lhuyd.[199] The relationship of Camden, Owen, and Lhuyd over a century raises a key question: could the different ethnographic gazes be made to accommodate and inform one another in the encounter with multicultural Britain? The answer starts with the story of Camden's *Britannia* at both ends of the seventeenth century and the evolution of travel and discovery in the intervening decades.

---

[198] Owen, *Description*, pp. xlii–xliv; also Camden, *Britannia* (1695), p. 636.
[199] Camden, *Britannia* (1695), p. 633.

BOOK 3

Multicultural *Britannia*

9

William Camden and the Settlement of Britain

Sometime in 1600, two men set out for the stark moors and uplands of Cumbria. Part of their long journey followed the coastline where the river Derwent emptied into the sea, an area famous for salmon fishing. Taking in the stately seat of the Curwens at Workington, the elder traveller hoped to be excused of vanity in noting his descent from the family on his mother's side. Crossing the Derwent, the two men followed the broken remains of a Roman wall for some six or seven miles to the mouth of the river Ellen. There they found the Roman fort of Alvana 'situated on a pretty high hill, from whence is a large prospect into the Irish Sea'. Alvana was once garrisoned against sea-borne invaders, by command of the great Roman general Stilicho.[1] Through the pen of the Alexandrian propagandist and court poet Claudian, Britannia herself thanked Stilicho for his watchfulness:

> And I shall ever own his happy care,
> Who sav'd me sinking in unequal war:
> When the Scots came thundring from the Irish shores,
> And th'Ocean trembled, struck with hostile oars.[2]

Sheltered from nature's fury and the Irish-Scots, the fort's Dalmatian defenders and the small town that grew up around them left a lasting impression on the landscape. Their Cumbrian descendants had long since reclaimed the town for corn, but under a zealous plough those same fields yielded the remains of altars, inscribed stones, and statues. These artefacts seized the interest of our travellers, thanks to the diligent efforts of one local gentleman, John Senhouse, to protect and preserve them.[3] The younger traveller took up his pencil to make a drawing of a very old and beautiful red stone altar in the middle of Senhouse's yard, capturing its inscriptions and figures. His older companion praised Senhouse, 'not only because he entertain'd us with the utmost civility, but also because he

---

[1] Peter Salway, *Roman Britain* (Oxford, 1984), pp. 415–26.
[2] The translation is from William Camden, *Britannia: Or a Chorographical Description of Great Britain and Ireland* (London, 1695), 824, hereafter cited as Camden, *Britannia* (1695).
[3] For Senhouse's identity, Daniel Woolf, *The Social Circulation of the Past: English Historical Culture 1500–1730* (Oxford, 2003), p. 224.

has a great veneration of Antiquities'. Their host preserved a past that 'by other ignorant people in those parts are broke to pieces, and turn'd to other uses, to the great damage of these studies'.[4] For both travellers, Senhouse and his little Cumbrian trove stood out as an island of civility in a landscape of barren moors, howling winds, and harsh manners. These men depended on Senhouse and others like him in their 'design to illustrate our Native Country'.[5]

Robert Cotton was twenty-eight when he embarked on this Cumbrian journey with his one-time headmaster from Westminster School. A decade before his travels in the North, Cotton had honed his field skills in his native Huntingdon. Cotton never completed his history of the county, but the materials for it became part of the great library or 'Collection' to which both his name and fame were forever attached. In the words of John Selden, the great legal scholar and fellow bibliophile, who knew him well, Cotton 'deservedly won immortal fame both abroad and at home not only for his collection of books and manuscripts ... but also through his kindness and willingness to make them available to students of good literature and affairs of state'.[6] Cotton ultimately illustrated his native country through his Collection and the generations who have since studied the British past through it.[7] Cotton's former head, the then fifty-year-old William Camden, left his mark on his native country in an even more storied fashion.

The creation of *Britannia*

Within a year of Camden's birth in May 1551, John Leland's body finally gave out against the madness that tortured his mind. There is something almost fateful in the timing. More than anyone, Camden went on to realize Leland's plan for a great civil history or 'De Antiquitate Britannica'.[8] The antique past of Britain fascinated both men, and the movements of Britons, Romans, Anglo-Saxons, Picts, Scots, Danes, and Normans marked the landscape deeply. The marks left by great noble families and personages are likewise recorded with some zeal. Both works have the unmistakable qualities of itineraries. We move between towns and villages, cross rivers and mountains, and encounter people's differences in the footsteps of two tireless and adept travellers. In perhaps no other respect did Camden duplicate Leland's intention more obviously than by producing a county-by-county topographic survey. One can understand how Camden's nemesis, Ralph Brooke, lighted on plagiarism as one way to attack his

---

[4] Camden, *Britannia* (1695), p. 824.
[5] Camden, *Britannia* (1695), p. 824.
[6] Quoted in Stuart Handley, 'Sir Robert Bruce Cotton', *Oxford DNB* at www.oxforddnb.com.
[7] Kevin Sharpe, *Sir Robert Cotton 1586–1631: History and Politics in Early Modern England* (Oxford, 1979), pp. 23–50.
[8] F.J. Levy, *Tudor Historical Thought* (San Marino, CA, 1967), p. 158; A.L. Rowse, *The England of Elizabeth* (London, 1950), p. 32.

rival. Brooke reproduced Leland's 'New Year's Gift' so that it would 'appeare vnto the indifferent Reader, who was the first author and contriuer of this late borne Britannia', accusing Camden of having taken 'the tytle and whole credite thereof to yourself'.[9] Brooke's charge amuses by the standards of an age very much laxer than our own while Camden did not hide his debts to Leland and his notebooks.

Camden's roots tied him to the Curwens of Cumberland and Lancashire on this mother's side and the London Camdens, late of Lichfield, through his father, Sampson. Camden's education began at Christ's Hospital for 'orphaned and poor children'. It continued at the renowned St Paul's School, then in the hands of Alexander Nowell and its head John Cooke. Camden entered Oxford as a chorister and moved on to Christ Church with the support of Dr Thomas Thornton. Thornton's household brought Camden into contact with Philip Sidney, George and Richard Carew, and the younger Richard Hakluyt, all of whom nurtured Camden's interests. Camden's days at Oxford were troubled by religious controversies, which cost him two fellowships and delayed the grant of his B.A. The lively mix of alienation and affection in Camden's feelings for Oxford can be seen in his refusal of the M.A., finally offered in 1613 – twenty-five years late – alongside the appointment of Degory Wheare to the new Camden professorship in History in 1622. Camden found the platform for academic and literary success at Westminster School, though there should be no doubt – and cannot be for anyone who reads the consciously instructive *Britannia* – that Camden took to his responsibilities as a teacher.[10] Both school and schoolmaster thrived together for more than twenty years, beginning in 1575. Camden's tenure at Westminster brought him into a 'close, homogenous community of scholars and political and religious thinkers and officers' that grew to include William Cecil, Gabriel Goodman, John Stow, John Dee, Daniel Rogers, William Lambarde, Robert Cotton, Henry Spelman, and Ben Jonson.[11] From beginning as a poor student, Camden became someone who 'seems to have known everyone in London in a position to help him in his task'.[12]

---

[9] Ralph Brooke, *A Discoverie of Certaine Errovrs Pvblished in Print in much Commended Britannia 1594* (STC 3834; London, 1599), p. 80. For the controversy see G.J.R. Parry, 'John Stow's Unpublished "Historie of this Iland": Amity and Enmity amongst Sixteenth Century Scholars', *English Historical Review* 102.404 (1987), pp. 633–47.

[10] Wyman Herendeen, *William Camden: A Life in Context* (Woodbridge, 2007), pp. 96, 130–53.

[11] For this summary of Camden's life, see Wyman H. Herendeen, 'William Camden', *Oxford DNB* at www.oxforddnb.com; Thomas Smith's life of Camden that opened Gibson's 1695 edition of *Britannia*. Also F.J. Levy, 'The Making of Camden's *Britannia*', *Bibliothèque d'humanisme et Renaissance* 26.1 (1964), pp. 70–97; Levy, *Tudor Historical Thought*, pp. 148–61; Graham Parry, *The Trophies of Time: English Antiquarians of the Seventeenth Century* (Oxford, 1995), pp. 22–48; Angus Vine, *In Defiance of Time: Antiquarian Writing in Early Modern England* (Oxford, 2010), pp. 80–99; Rowse, *England of Elizabeth*, pp. 41–2.

[12] Levy, 'Making *Britannia*', p. 84.

Learned colleagues from London, Oxford, and continental Europe inspired Camden and nurtured *Britannia*.[13] No one was more important than the Flemish cartographer Abraham Ortelius. The Roman world fascinated Ortelius and he searched for a scholar capable of filling one of its great voids, the history of Roman Britain. Ortelius's *Synonymia Geographica* brought together work by Humphrey Llwyd and Leland, Robert Talbot's study of the 'Antonine Itineraries' – the only surviving guides to the Roman settlements and roads in Britain – and further investigations by Daniel Rogers. Neither Llwyd nor Rogers proved up to the task. Perhaps thanks to John Dee, Ortelius and Camden met in London in 1577. Ortelius pressed the young, rising scholar to resume his travels and investigations. As Camden reported in the preface to the 1607 edition of *Britannia*, the 'great Restorer of old Geography, Abraham Ortelius, thirty years ago, did very earnestly solicit me to acquaint the World with the ancient State of Britain, that is, to restore Britain to Antiquity, and Antiquity to Britain; to renew what was old, illustrate what was obscure, and settle what was doubtful'. The 'honour of my native Country encourag'd me', Camden explained, but Ortelius ultimately persuaded him to accept the hard slog which lay ahead. Camden made quick headway, despite juggling travel, research, and teaching. In three years he completed a 'preparatory draft' that focussed his energies for completing the first printed edition in 1586.[14]

By the time of its publication, *Britannia* had become something more than a history of Roman Britain, let alone the province of Britannia within the empire.[15] Camden began with an overview of Britain, the Britons, British etymology, and the names of the island drawn from the earliest extant sources. Camden described the origins and character of the peoples who marked Britain – Romans, Picts, Scots, Anglo-Saxons, Danes, and Normans – before briefly tracing the dominant political divisions and institutions. Something very like Leland's county-by-county survey occupied most of the book. 'I settl'd the bounds of each County (tho' not to an inch)', Camden wrote in his 1607 preface, though his counties rather neatly fit the Romans' identification of Celtic tribal lands. The provincial divisions of Munster, Leinster, Meath, Connaught, and Ulster organized the very brief overview of Ireland. Camden rounded out the topographic text with *Britannia*'s islands. Finally, he returned to etymology in the page indices to towns and counties, including the identification of ancient locations with their modern counterparts. For Stuart Piggott, then, '*Britannia* was originally planned to elucidate the topography of Roman Britain, and to present a picture of the Province, with reference to its development through Saxon and medieval times, which would enable Britain to take her rightful place at once within the world

[13] Levy, 'Making *Britannia*', p. 89.
[14] Levy, *Tudor Historical Thought*, pp. 146–53; Levy, 'Making *Britannia*', pp. 86–90; William Camden, *Britannia* (STC 4508; London, 1607), 'Mr Camden's Preface'.
[15] Levy, *Tudor Historical Thought*, pp. 152–5. For general analyses of *Britannia*, Herendeen, *William Camden*, pp. 180–333; Parry, *Trophies of Time*, pp. 26–42.

of antiquity and that of international Renaissance scholarship.'[16] Yet Piggott's reading may be still too narrow when we dig into Camden's engagement with cultural complexity.

The 1586 edition of *Britannia* 'won the plaudits of Ortelius and a whole array of northern humanists'.[17] If Camden's original goal had been to reconnect Britain to Europe through its Roman past, later editions of *Britannia* owed as much to its popularity at home as to Camden's scholarly desire for perfection. The inclusion of rare documents and sources increased and more history was included, but the book's growing size had much to do with the inclusion of genealogical information and expanded ethno-topographical descriptions: 'From the 1590s onward its readers were presumed to be English, interested in the antiquities of Britain but concerned as well with its topography and with the histories of its noble families.' Growing readership led to new Latin editions in 1587, 1590, 1594, 1600, and 1607. The pull of an ever-expanding English audience encouraged a first English edition in 1610, translated by Philemon Holland with Camden's assistance. After Camden's death, this edition in turn was expanded and reprinted in 1637.[18] *Britannia*'s format grew with its prestige, from a 'small and rather ugly octavo of around 550 pages, unillustrated, and with the type closely packed on the pages' to the lavishly illustrated version of 1607 and the great folios, starting with Edmund Gibson's edition of 1695.[19]

Travel and archival research were the twin foundations of *Britannia*. Camden's library and those of his colleagues were instrumental for the latter.[20] For John Selden, it ranked among the greatest libraries in the land, and friends and acquaintances cast covetous eyes at the collection.[21] Over six hundred of Camden's original books have now been traced, including more than twenty in which Camden made notes as he read. Among those are Camden's own works, including the 1615 edition of the *Annals* and the 1607 edition of *Britannia* that later belonged to Cotton and Thomas Hearne. Not surprisingly, Camden owned the model Italian histories of Guicciardiani, the 1593 edition of Norden's *Speculum Britanniae*, Robert Dallington's *View of France* (1604), and other histories and topographical studies of France and the Netherlands, some with Camden's annotations. He studied the assessment of England's colonial failures in Ireland by the Irish Attorney General John Davies (1612) and Barnaby Rich's deeply hateful *New Description of Ireland* (1610). Camden owned two editions of John Monipennie's handy *Certain Matters* (1594 and 1603), which included

---

[16] Stuart Piggott, 'William Camden and the *Britannia*', in *The Changing Face of English Local History*, ed. R.C. Richardson (Aldershot, 2000), p. 21.

[17] Levy, *Tudor Historical Thought*, p. 154.

[18] Levy, *Tudor Historical Thought*, pp. 154–5.

[19] Levy, 'Making *Britannia*', p. 70.

[20] Richard L. DeMolen, 'The Library of William Camden', *Proceedings of the American Philosophical Society* 128.4 (1984), pp. 326–409.

[21] Sharpe, *Robert Cotton*, pp. 55–8; DeMolen, 'Library of William Camden', p. 333.

brief topographic surveys of Scotland indebted to borrowings from Buchanan's history. He also owned his new king's *Basilicon Doron* and the Union tracts by Robert Pont and John Thornborough. The British *imperium* in its different forms and guises also interested Camden, including Humphrey Gilbert's account of his voyages in search of a North-West Passage, the fishing-fleet projects of Tobias Gentleman and others, *England's Heroicall Epistles* (1598) by Michael Drayton, Polydore Vergil's edition of Gildas along with Leland's *Assertio* in defence of Arthur, and Richard White's *Historarium Britanniae* (1600).[22] Camden's great advance on Leland occurred thanks to the antiquarian work of men like Lambarde, Rogers, and Llwyd, especially linguistic studies.[23] It is not surprising, then, to find the 1572 Cologne edition of *Commentarioli Britannicae Descripionis Fragmentum* heavily annotated by Camden and a portion of Gerald of Wales' *Journey* excerpted in the volume.[24] All of Camden's works demonstrate the love of scholarship signalled by these and other books.

There was nothing particularly mysterious about Camden's methods as a traveller: 'I have travell'd almost all over England, and have consulted in each County, the Persons of best skill and knowledge in these matters. ... I have examin'd the publick Records of the Kingdom, Ecclesiastical Registers, Libraries, and the Acts, Monuments, and Memorials of Churches and Cities.'[25] Still, his journeys are surprisingly hard to pin down.[26] It is tempting to imagine Camden taking a double 'gap year' before assuming his post at Westminster School, softening the bitterness of his Oxford days by searching byways and fields for the remains of ancient Britain. Certainly, after his encouraging meeting with Ortelius in 1577, Camden took to the roads regularly until old age confined him to his study. He took in Suffolk, Norfolk, and East Anglia in 1578 and journeyed to Yorkshire and Lancashire in 1582, with another turn round Suffolk. The first two editions of *Britannia* were printed before Camden toured Oxfordshire in 1588 and undertook the long journey through the West Country to Ilfracombe in Devon. Francis Godwin joined Camden for the most ambitious journey to date in 1590: Wales. Routes that led to Salisbury, Wells, and Oxfordshire kept Camden on the road in 1596, two further editions of *Britannia* having appeared in the meantime in 1590 and 1594. At fifty, Camden set off with Cotton for his ancestral homeland in Cumberland. The two men took in the North and Carlisle in a journey that lasted from midsummer to December 1600. Usually assumed to be the last of his great journeys, Camden referred to a second journey through Lancashire in 1603, fittingly the year of James VI's accession and the

[22] DeMolen, 'Library of William Camden', pp. 347–407.
[23] Levy, 'Making *Britannia*', pp. 92–3.
[24] DeMolen, 'Library of William Camden', p. 382.
[25] Camden, *Britannia* (1695), 'Preface'.
[26] This summary of Camden's journeys is drawn from Herendeen, 'William Camden'; DeMolen, 'Library of William Camden', p. 328; Levy, *Tudor Historical Thought*, pp. 148–50.

creation of a British *imperium* ruled by an Arthur of flesh and blood rather than fanciful legends.[27]

Camden wrote his great work from journeys into the archives, travels across England and Wales, and collaboration with an impressive number of local experts and other factotums.[28] For more than a century between 1586 and Gibson's edition of 1695, Camden's readers would have found the peoples of multicultural Britain in several guises. The separate nations of England (and Wales), Scotland, and Ireland each occupied their own sections of the text. Beneath the national labels, readers found county denizens and local inhabitants of former Celtic tribal lands. Prefacing the entire work were the histories of the great ethnic groups of Britannia's past. A modern editor might have titled this first section of Britannia 'the settlement of Britain' or suggested a catchier title that captured the dramatic encounters and violent clashes among the Britons, Scots, Picts, Anglo-Saxons, Danes, and Normans, with supremacy in Britain at stake. Camden certainly told the story with breadth and dash.

More than entertainment compels us to revisit Camden's settlement story, though. There is more to *Britannia* when read in its entirety, when restoring the settlement of Britain to its intended place as the starting point for the rest, and when revisiting the details with something more than antiquarian or classical concerns in mind. Camden wrote with more diverse interests and audiences in mind. He would have been perplexed by Geoffrey Elton's characterization of *Britannia* as a general survey of England, the traditionally narrow focus on its antiquarian or genealogical content, and the general indifference to his two hundred-some-page account of the island's settlement.[29] Our recovery of multicultural *Britannia* begins there.

The settlement of Britain

Camden followed his humanist training to the texts of classical antiquity in writing his history of the original peoples of Britain, part foundation epic, part morality tale. The island was a prize worth having: fertile soil, temperate air, and the moderating influence of the surrounding seas made it into the 'granary and magazine of the Western Empire' under the Romans. Camden apologized in advance if he seemed 'too fond and lavish in the praises of my own Country', but he could not resist the verses of the ancient poet who celebrated Britain:

> In thee, my darling Isle, shall never cease
> The constant joys of happiness and peace.

---

[27] Camden, *Britannia* (1695), p. 792.
[28] Herendeen, *William Camden*, pp. 204–8, 304–20; Vine, *In Defiance of Time*, pp. 85–99; Stan Mendyk, 'Early British Chorography', *Sixteenth Century Journal* 17.4 (1986), pp. 473–9; Woolf, *Social Circulation of the Past*, pp. 359–60.
[29] G.R. Elton, *England Under the Tudors*, 3rd edn (London, 1991), p. 434.

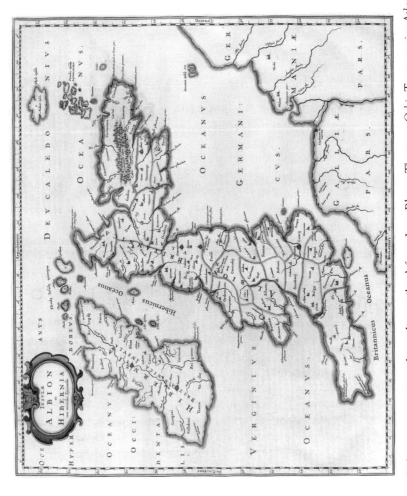

18 'Insulae Albion et Hibernia cum minoribus adjacentibus' from Jean Blaeu, *Theatrum Orbis Terrarum sive Atlas Novus* (Amsterdam, 1654). Reproduced by permission of the National Library of Scotland.

What e're can furnish luxury or use
Thy sea shall bring thee, or thy land produce.

No one who considered 'the Fortunate state and happy circumstances of this our British Island' could argue with the poet that it 'is certainly the master-piece of Nature'. Camden and his fellow Britons were of a piece with Nature's masterwork. 'I need not enlarge upon its Inhabitants,' he wrote, 'nor extol the vigour and firmeness of their constitution, the inoffensiveness of their humour, their civility to all men, and their courage and bravery, so often tried both at home and abroad; and not unknown to the remotest corner of the earth.'[30]

But from where had these people originated and to whom did they owe their stellar qualities? This was no easy matter to pin down. Camden explained that Britain's first inhabitants 'had other cares and thoughts to trouble their heads withal, than that of transmitting their originals to posterity'. They lacked the peace and leisure to fashion a 'civiliz'd life' of learning. Besides which, the Druids and bards who might have preserved and recorded that history 'thought it unlawful to commit any thing to books or writing'. Camden lamented the loss of the stones, pyramids, obelisks, and other monuments that might have preserved the memory of such things. They had 'long since yeilded [sic] to, and perished by the injuries of time' and could not provide anything but a fragmentary record. These circumstances opened the door 'in many nations' for 'a sort of men, who very studious to supply these defects out of their own invention'. Unable to offer the truth, 'they might at least delight and please some mens Wanton fancy', which 'some men quickly embrac'd, without a more curious search into the truth ... [and] swallow'd them without more adoe'. Camden clearly had Geoffrey of Monmouth in mind, but he refused to be drawn into another debate over the British History, leaving 'the controversie intirely to the whole body of learned Antiquaries; and leaving every man freely to the liberty of his own judgment'. After summarizing the competing origin stories attached to Brutus and Scota, Camden judged that in a matter of 'so great antiquity, it is easier to proceed by conjecture, than to offer at any positive determination'.[31] For Camden, the most substantial conjecture was that the original Britons had descended from Gomer (grandson of Noah and son of Japheth) and come by way of Gaul.

What is of interest here is not the well-tilled ground of the British History debate or the Mosaic origins of the Earth's peoples for those living in the sixteenth century.[32] This chapter is not an analysis of Camden's truth claims. Rather, it is the method by which Camden intended to establish the kinship of Britons and Gauls that makes his account of Britain's peopling important. Camden would do so 'by arguments taken from the name, situation, religion,

---

[30] Camden, *Britannia* (1695), p. iv.
[31] Camden, *Britannia* (1695), pp. iv–vi, xi.
[32] Colin Kidd, *British Identities Before Nationalism: Ethnicity and Nationhood in the Atlantic World 1600–1800* (Cambridge, 1999), pp. 9–72.

customs, and language of both nations'.[33] More simply put, Camden scoured the classical sources as an ethnographer, following the lead of classical authors with the same interests like Herodotus or Tacitus. We do not normally associate Camden the careful and conscientious ethnographer with *Britannia*. Camden also searched for comparable markers that would tie together peoples rather than simply seeking out marks of distinction and difference to separate them. Cultural complexity and continuity mattered. Further, Camden's foundation history enabled him to decode the ethno-cultural markers that he found across Britain in his travels, and vice versa. History and precedent guided fieldwork, while first-hand experience made it possible to debate or rewrite received history. Camden did all of this in characteristically spirited fashion, playfully poking sticks in a few eyes of conventional wisdom, despite his pose of humble conjecture.

Camden satisfied himself that Britons and Gauls agreed in their most ancient name, derived from Gomer. Camden gave the geographic connection (situation) a common-sense twist: 'why should we not think that our Britain was first of all peopled by the Gauls, which were our next Neighbours; rather than that the Trojans, Italians, Albans, or Brutians, who live at such a vast distance from it, were its first Inhabitants'. Camden imagined the straits of Dover to be positively inviting by comparison to those long sea voyages. What interest the Gauls may have had in Britain prompted an almost timeless explanation where human migration is concerned. 'We may therefore reasonably imagine,' suggested Camden, 'that the antient Gomeri were either pusht on by such as press'd forward for room, or sent abroad, to ease an overpeopled country, or carry'd from home by the natural itch which mankind hath to see foreign countries.' On the authority of Tacitus, Caesar, and Dio Cassius, Camden concluded that the Gauls had carried with them their native religion. The practices of Druids and bards in Britain and Gaul copied one another down to the importance of oak groves as settings for religious rites. Both peoples lived in the same sort of 'commonwealth', a federation of petty kings who decided matters of extraordinary urgency in a 'Council of the whole nation' and chose from among themselves one 'general Commander' to lead them into battle.[34]

'Nor were these nations unlike in their manners, customs, and ways of living', according to Camden. He found several areas of comparison in reading Strabo, Tacitus, and Caesar. Both peoples, 'stout and given to war', loved bloodshed and could not be turned from engaging the enemy, no matter the danger. Britons and Gauls fought with the same arms and weapons, including war chariots. Both peoples were quick witted, though Camden reported that Tacitus gave the Britons an edge for having 'grown ambitious of eloquence' after first rejecting the Romans' Latin. Bloodthirsty warriors they may have been, but the Gauls and Britons were both accounted 'well-meaning and a downright honest sort of

---

[33] Camden, *Britannia* (1695), p. xii.
[34] Camden, *Britannia* (1695), pp. xii–xvi.

people' by Strabo and Tacitus. Political factions and infighting that belied the idealized commonwealths of kings were put down to 'natural inconstancy and levity'. Out of this grew the Gauls' reputation for credulity, but the Britons had not left them behind in that respect, 'for they have an ear still open to every idle story; and out of superstitious fear or hope, give credit to any of the siliest Predictions'. Both peoples lived in the same sorts of houses and sited them in the midst of forests, wore chains of gold around their necks and rings on their middle fingers, and sported long hair and sleeveless cloaks or 'Brachæ'. Camden's contemporaries among the English inherited from these early ancestors a love for great retinues that 'far outwent all other Europeans'.[35]

Language was of critical importance to Camden's researches and travels, whether identifying the stations of the 'Antonine Itineraries' and decoding modern place-names, recording the inscriptions of tombs and reading ancient coins, or exploring the languages of Britain's peoples from the Britons to Saxons and Normans. Its ethnographic importance could not be disputed. Language was the 'surest evidence of the original of a nation. For there is no man, I suppose, but will readily allow, that those people which speak the same Language, must necessarily be derived from one common original.'[36]

For disputants on all sides of these early modern culture wars in Britain, the implications were profound and Camden seemed to positively enjoy confronting his readers with them:

As for instance, suppose all our Histories that ever were written had chanced to be lost, or suppose no Author had ever told us, that we English are descended from the Germans, the natural Scots from the Irish, the Britains of Bretagne in France, from our Britains of this Island; yet the great affinity of language, would alone manifestly prove it: nay would be of so much more weight than the authority of the best Historians. If therefore I can here make it out, that the ancient Gauls and our Britains speak the same language; the consequence is so clear, that all men will be forced to allow, that they must have certainly had one and the self same original.[37]

Camden then declared:

But that the language of the ancient Gauls, was the same with that of the Britains (making an allowance for some small variety in the Dialect) we may reasonably infer from that place in Cæsar, where he writes, that it was usual for the Gauls, who would be thoroughly instructed in the Discipline of the Druids, to go over into Britain to our Druids to learn it. Now seeing the Druids had no Books, of necessity we must conclude, that their instructions were given in the same language which was used by the Gauls.[38]

---

[35] Camden, *Britannia* (1695), pp. xvi–xviii.
[36] Camden, *Britannia* (1695), p. xviii.
[37] Camden, *Britannia* (1695), p. xviii.
[38] Camden, *Britannia* (1695), p. xviii.

Tacitus put it more simply, that the Britons and Gauls 'differ not much in their speech'. Camden examined a host of words shared among the two peoples, from gods and religious terminology to the everyday language of material things, the natural world, and place-names.

For support Camden finally called upon his contemporaries. George Buc, 'a man eminent both for his extraction and learning', recorded that the Germans called a Frenchman 'Wallon' and that when the 'German Saxons first came over hither, and heard the Britains speak the Gaulish tongue, they call'd them Walli, i.e. Gauls'. Camden even resorted to the work of his rival, Buchanan. Buchanan reported that 'Walch doth not among the Germans barely signifie a Stranger, but most properly a Gaul.' Indeed, the homeland of the Britons' descendants in Wales was at the present day called Galles by the French. Finally, Camden used Buchanan's *Rerum Scoticarum Historia* to inform readers that 'the antient Scots divided all the British Nations into Gaol and Galle', or foreigners and non-Gaels.[39]

Having made his case, Camden had hoped to be able to call on Daniel Rogers' projected treatise for details of the government, law, and customs of the Britons. However, Rogers was 'snatch'd away by an untimely death, before he had done any thing upon this subject' and Camden pressed his classical sources into service. Inevitably, Camden repeated himself by revisiting these sources and in making a Cook's tour through the Britons' appearances in each of them. For Caesar, the most civilized Britons lived in Kent because its location allowed them access to the more refined customs and manners of the Gauls. All Britons dyed themselves with woad, fought with chariots, and lived incestuously, but the inland Britons lived on milk and flesh and dressed in skins. Solinus and Tertullian provided details of the process by which the skin was cut and dye rubbed in to produce permanent raised tattoos. Diodorus Siculus wrote nostalgically in his universal history that the Britons lived as the ancients did, plain and upright in their dealings, without the craft and subtlety of 'our countrymen', and subsisting on food that had 'nothing of the dainties of rich men'. Written at the time of Claudius's invasion of Britain, Pomponius Mela's *de Chorographia* drew parallels between the Britons and other barbarian peoples: painted bodies, war made for pleasure, and ambitious kings who aimed to expand their territories at the expense of their rivals and the empire. Tacitus found the unconquered Britons fiercer than either their British brethren or cousins in Gaul. Peace had rendered the latter peoples effeminate, bringing in idleness among them, to the ruin of their natural bravery and thirst for liberty.[40]

At the end of this section, Camden denied that the great Carthaginian general, Hannibal, had ever crossed into Britain. Unskilled students of Polybius had

[39] Camden, Britannia (1695), p. xxv; Wilson McLeod, *Divided Gaels: Gaelic Cultural Identities in Scotland and Ireland c. 200–1650* (Oxford, 2004), p. 24.
[40] Camden, *Britannia* (1695), pp. xxxiii–xxxvi.

misread the corrupted Greek text, but they were like other readers who looked for the 'discovery' of Britain by the Ancients in credulous and fabulous tales. This prompted Camden to explain the proper periodization of human history. The period from the Creation to the biblical flood was simply unknown, 'by reason we known nothing of it'. History from the flood to the first Olympiad was known by nothing that was not 'false and fabulous'. What made the period from the Olympiad to the present proper human history was that 'the transactions of that space are related by good Historians'. For Camden, 'no learned Nations, except the Jews, had any true or historical relations before that age'. Therefore, in contrast to Geoffrey of Monmouth, whose 'British history ... begins three hundred and thirty years before the first Olympiad, which was then such a rude and ignorant age in these parts', Camden intended to begin his history with the Romans. That history would be built not upon 'fables, which would argue the Author's vanity in writing, as well as his folly in believing; but from the uncorrupted monuments of Antiquity', its historical texts and artefacts.[41]

Britain and the Roman *imperium*

One theme dominates Camden's account of Roman Britain: the charge that he received from Ortelius to 'restore Britain to Antiquity, and Antiquity to Britain'. More simply put, Camden made the case that Britain mattered in the classical world. The problem, of course, was that the Roman presence did not appear to be very robust, in contrast to the Anglo-Saxons or Normans. Camden noted first that the Britons had the qualities needed for a dogged, even heroic, resistance. Had they put aside the fatal habit of squabbling among themselves, they might have fended off the Romans entirely. But was Britain worth the effort in the first place? Camden let the Romans answer that question:

> It was esteemed so great an action to conquer but a small part of Britain, that anniversary games, triumphal arches both at Rome and at Bullogne in France, and lastly a glorious triumph, was decreed by the Senate in honour of Claudius; and to see it, the governers of provinces and some outlaws were permitted to be present. Upon the top of the Emperor's palace was fixed a naval crown, to imply his conquest and sovereignty of the British sea.[42]

According to Camden, the empire had treated its victories in Britain as the 'most famous monuments and instances of the Roman Bravery'. Britain and its hitherto unknown peoples were 'now surrounded by a Roman stream'. An unknown poet rescued from obscurity by Joseph Scaliger - whose *Catalecta* Camden had among his books - recorded the achievement:

---

[41] Camden, *Britannia* (1695), pp. xxxvi–xxxviii.
[42] Camden, *Britannia* (1695), p. xlv.

> A land now conquer'd, and untouch'd till now,
> Crown with new lawrels thy triumphant brow.
> Nations unseen, and scare believ'd as yet,
> To thy victorious yoke their neck submit.
> Euphrates th'East, Rhine clos'd the North before,
> The Ocean now's the middle of thy power.[43]

Conquest ultimately defined the complex encounters between Romans and Britons. The 'stations and garrisons of the Legions and Roman soldiers, prov'd very often the foundations of Towns and Cities' throughout the empire. Britain was no different, but from these towns 'the yoke of subjection was first laid upon the Britains by troops and garrisons, which were constantly kept here to the great terror of the Inhabitants; and then by tribute and imposts ... suck the blood out of them, to confiscate their goods, and exact tribute'. This was, in Camden's words, the 'Roman yoke', held in place by a Roman administration whose lectors bore 'rods and axes for the awe and punishment of the people'.[44]

The Roman yoke nonetheless brought Britain more fully into the empire's massive network of cultural, political, and commercial exchanges. The four great Roman roads that Camden – and Leland – took such pains to discover and traverse were but one tie to the greater *imperium*. Camden saw them in both respects, as instruments of *imperium* and vital avenues for travellers:

> Augustus at first had certain young men set at some small distance from one another; but after that, wagons instead of them, that he might have quick and speedy intelligence from all parts of the Empire. And near upon these roads were the cities built, as also inns or mansions for the accommodation of travellers with all necessaries ... where travellers could change their post-horses, draught-beasts, or wagons.

Roman buildings, 'so very stately, that we cannot look upon the remains of them at this very day, without great admiration', likewise marked the British landscape, as did 'the Picts wall' and the low valleys raised high by fen drainage.[45]

A cultural transformation crossed the Channel and passed up the Roman roads. 'Yet, however grievous this yoke was,' Camden wrote, 'it prov'd of very good consequence to us. For together with it came the blessed Doctrine of Christ Jesus ... and upon the light of his glorious Empire, barbarism soon vanish'd from among the Britains, as it had done in all other placed upon the approach of it.' Civility travelled with the Romans themselves, not just with the missionaries who piggybacked on the empire's conquests. The Romans 'by planting their Colonies here, and reducing the natives under the forms of Civil Government and Society, by instructing them in the liberal Arts, and sending them into Gaul, to learn the laws of the Roman Empire ... did at last so transform and

---

[43] Camden, *Britannia* (1695), pp. xlviii–l.
[44] Camden, *Britannia* (1695), p. lxv.
[45] Camden, *Britannia* (1695), pp. lxv–lxvii.

civilize them … they were not inferiour to those of any other Provinces.'[46] Britons who submitted to the Roman yoke traded barbarity for civility – a lesson from Britain's Roman past that, for Camden, Moryson, and so many English, the Irish stubbornly refused to learn in its updated Tudor–Stuart form.

This expansion of the Roman *imperium* merited the best prose and verses of Tacitus, Seneca, and Scaliger's unknown poet, yet not every part of Britain was worth the effort after all. Unlike the province of Britannia, 'the farther part of the Island was left to the Barbarians, as neither pleasant nor fruitful', at least to start.[47] In Camden's mental world, the empire fell to its barbarian invaders. Barbarian invasions of Britannia also connected Britain to its proper place within the narrative of Rome's decline and fall. British barbarians posted themselves in the fens and thick woods, where they sallied against the Romans. Camden's preferred account by Herodian recorded a temporary armistice under Severus and the emperor's construction of 'a wall from sea to sea quite across the Island'. Having taken the title *Britannicus Maximus*, Severus died at York, distraught over the designs against him by his wicked son Antoninus. Ineffectual leadership forced Antoninus to return many of his father's fortifications and territories to the Britons. It fell to Britannia's own Constantine to put the barbarians in their place by conquest, by tribute, and by friendship. Yet the great ruler sowed the seeds of the empire's demise when, having defeated the barbarians of North-West Europe, he redeployed legions from the frontier garrisons to Constantinople and the East. In time, barbarians would be unable to resist the weakened frontiers of the western provinces and Britannia too would share the fate of the Western Empire.[48]

Who were the barbarians that besieged Roman Britain? Camden's two stories, the history of Britannia and the peopling of Britain, interact to produce an interesting answer. At first, of course, the barbarians were Britons, the native resistance to the Roman invasion and occupation. By the time of Constantine's wars they had become the 'Caledonians and Picts' of the 'remoter parts of Britain (that, as one says, are the witnesses of the sun's setting), and the people of the islands thereabouts'.[49] In Stilicho's day we know these invaders as Scots from Ireland as well as the 'barbarous Picts' and 'Saxon pirates'. As Claudian wrote of Stilicho's success: 'The seas are free, secur'd from Saxon power, / And Picts once conquer'd, Britain fears no more.'[50]

We reach a remarkable meeting of Camden's stories when he recounts events after Honorius withdrew the legions following Alaric's sack of Rome. Appealing for help against the predictable incursions of the Picts and Scots, Honorius sent letters of exhortation, instead of help:

[46] Camden, *Britannia* (1695), p. lxv.
[47] Camden, *Britannia* (1695), p. lxiv.
[48] Camden, *Britannia* (1695), pp. lxxi–lxxxiv.
[49] Camden, *Britannia* (1695), p. lxxvi.
[50] Camden, *Britannia* (1695), p. lxxxiv.

> The Britains animated by these letters of Honorious the Emperor, took up arms accordingly to defend their own cities; but being overpower'd by the Barbarians (who from all quarters came in upon them) they sent their earnest petitions again to Honorius to spare some assistance. Upon this he granted them one legion; which upon their arrival, soon routed a great body of the enemy, drove the rest out of the Province, and cast up an earthen wall between the Frith of Edinburgh and the Cluid ... [51]

The 'Britains' who appealed to Honorius in this account had to be a mixed group of Britons who lived within the province, Romans and their auxiliaries like the Dalmatians stationed at Alvana, and those peoples who intermixed and married to become what we now think of as Romano-Britons.[52] Gone were the warlike Britons of the early province, replaced by Picts and Scots-Irish. But what had become of those first Britons or 'Britains', whose name was now borne by a very different mixed collection of peoples? Part of the answer lies with the Picts and Scots – to whom we will return.

Honorius' aid proved to be fleeting. The legion returned to Gaul and the barbarians 'easily broke through this frontier, and with great outrage rov'd, plunder'd, and destroy'd every thing'. Another temporary respite followed under Valentinian, but Britain was caught in the empire's downward spiral. Camden constructed the story in distinctly moral terms capable of contemporary religious readings:

> The Empire fell down-right lame (as it were) and decrepit through the extremity of old age; and the Church was grievously pester'd with Hereticks, who spread their poysonous doctrines universally amidst the calamities of war. One of whom was Pelagius born here, who derogating from the grace of God, taught in this Island, That we might attain to perfect righteousness, by the merit of our own works.[53]

Camden continued his tale of Britain's destruction in a separate chapter after his analysis of Roman coins. He leaned heavily on the overwrought moralizing of the shadowy Gildas (c. fifth to sixth century), whose *De Excidio et Conquestu Britanniae* mourned the providential 'ruin and conquest of Britain'.[54] The 'duskish swarm of vermine, or hideous crews of Scots and Picts, somewhat different in manners, but all alike thirsting after blood' brushed aside the 'lazy' garrisons of the Wall and took 'all the North, and the remote parts of the Kingdom'.[55]

The Roman strain did not prove to be very robust. Intermingling with the Romans had tamed or exhausted the vigour of the old Britons, as Camden called on William of Malmesbury to explain:

> When the tyrants had left none but half foreigners in our fields, none but gluttons and debauchees in our cities; Britain, robb'd of her vigorous youth, and altogether

---

[51] Camden, *Britannia* (1695), pp. lxxxv–lxxxvi.
[52] Robin Fleming, *Britain After Rome: The Fall and Rise 400 to 1070* (London, 2010), pp. 22–38.
[53] Camden, *Britannia* (1695), p. lxxxvi.
[54] François Kerlouégan, 'Gildas', *Oxford DNB* at www.oxforddnb.com.
[55] Camden, *Britannia* (1695), p. ci.

uncultivated by the exercise of arts, became a prey to its neighbours, who gap'd after her destruction. For immediately after, many lost their lives by the incursions of Picts and Scots, many villages were burnt, and cities demolish'd, and all things turn'd topsy turvy by fire and sword.[56]

Heresy weakened the Britons, but cultural degeneration sapped their strength against the invading Scots, Picts, and Anglo-Saxons. Gildas once again supplied the more lurid details of Britons whose vices demonstrated 'a fondness for lyes and those that forge them, imbracing evil for good, and a veneration of lewdness instead of virtue, a desire of darkness rather than light, and entertaining Satan before an Angel of light'. In Gildas' apocalyptic telling, God sent the Picts, Scots, and plague to call the Britons to righteousness. The Britons ignored these scourges and God engineered a far worse one. The Britons were tricked into admitting the Saxons 'like so many wolves into the sheep-fold, to defend them from the northern Nations'.[57]

Camden could not resist closing his account of the Romans in Britain and the creation of a new nation of 'Britons' without once more poking fun at the British History. Reflecting on 'how many Colonies of Romans must be transplanted hither in so long time', Camden found it 'easie to believe that the Britains and Romans, by a mutual engrossing for so many years together, have grown up into one Nation'. For Camden, the lesson was obvious: 'So that I have oftentimes concluded it much more probable, that the Britains should derive themselves from the Trojans by these Romans' than any descendants of Brutus.[58]

Romano-Britons, Picts, and Scots

What awaited the Britons? They settled in Wales and Cornwall, 'miserably forc'd to seek a Country in their own native one' in remote regions 'fortified by nature with hills and æstuaries'. Like their Irish and Amerindian fellow travellers, the relocated Britons 'underwent such a weight of calamity as cannot to the full height of it be expressed … harrassed by a cruel war carried on far and near against them by the Saxons, Picts, and Scots'. According to Camden, the Saxons termed these inconvenient natives 'Britwales' and 'Cornweales'. Sequestered from 'the English by a trench of wonderful make, cast by King Offa', the warlike Welsh Britons retained their liberty until, in the words of Edward I, 'Divine Providence' delivered Wales and its inhabitants into his hands. For Camden, though, this only ushered in almost two hundred years of 'spight and hatred … between the two nations' until Henry VIII 'admitted them to the same laws

---

[56] Camden, *Britannia* (1695), p. lxxxvi.
[57] Camden, *Britannia* (1695), pp. ciii–civ.
[58] Camden, *Britannia* (1695), pp. lxxxvii–lxxxviii.

and liberties that the English have'. Overmatched by the Saxons, the 'Cornwalli' succumbed, despite resolute resistance.[59]

Yet the Britons did not simply disappear behind Offa's Dyke or the Tamar river to become the latter-day Welsh and the Cornish. Having kicked aside Geoffrey's British History, Camden next put the boot into tales of Pictish origins. Tacitus's account of Agricola's campaigns held the obvious answer to the question:

> For just as those Britains did, who in the Saxon invasion being loath to part with the liberty, withdrew and retreated to the west parts of the Island, Wales and Cornwall, full of craggy hills: so doubtless the Britains in the Roman war ... shifted to these northern parts, frozen by excess of cold, horrible in its rough and craggy places, and imbogued by the washing in of the Sea, and the fens in it; where they were defended not so much by their weapons, as by the sharpness of the air and weather, and grew up with the natives of the country into a populous nation.[60]

Camden seemed dismayed that anyone would believe that the Roman campaigns had left those retreating Britons 'without one remaining to propogate posterity; so that we must needs fill the place with foreigners from Scythia or Thrace?' Modern historians are equally sceptical.[61] Forcibly relocated by the Roman invasion, the Picts too emerged as a distinct people from among the first Britons.

Camden implicitly understood the process of ethno-cultural evolution around language, livelihoods, and customs and manners in all this. A static people and monoculture did not lie behind a convenient label like Briton. Just as he had for the Britons and Gauls, Camden built his explanation around an ethnographic analysis of 'manners, name, and language'. The Picts and Britons shared two obvious features: they did not exclude women from rulership and painted their bodies. 'Nor are these Barbarians (who so long infested the Romans by their sallies from the Caledonian wood) expressed by any other name in old Authors, such as Dio, Herodian, Vopiscus &c. than that of Britains,' Camden added. Nor would Camden let his readers forget that Severus had marked his victory against them by assuming the title *Britannicus Maximus*.

If they were indeed Britons, when did the name Pict come into use, and why? For Camden, it had originated about the time of Diocletian to distinguish them from their fellow Britons, 'who were confederate with the Romans and call'd Britains', while Pict was an obvious name for a people who still painted themselves. Camden admitted that the Pictish language did not offer a wealth of connections, 'because hardly a syllable of it is to be found in any Author', but accepted it as British on the basis of the scant evidence that did exist. For anyone who might wonder why the Picts had made war on their British brethren in the waning days of the empire, Camden reminded his readers that England's contemporary Irish subjects had found 'malicious and spiteful enemies' among 'their

[59] Camden, *Britannia* (1695), pp. cvii–cviii.
[60] Camden, *Britannia* (1695), p. cix.
[61] James E. Fraser, *From Caledonia to Pictland: Scotland to 795* (Edinburgh, 2009), pp. 43–58.

own fellow natives the Wild-Irish.'[62] Camden made an interesting connection to his own contemporaries who erroneously wrote that Caesar 'conquere'd the French in Gaul, and the English in Britain; whereas at that time there was then no such names in being'.[63] With that, Camden left his readers to choose between his 'conjectures' and Bede's second-hand stories of Picts from across the seas.

Camden had no doubt that he sailed into dangerous waters in accounting for the Scots. James VI's accession only gave urgency to disclaimers designed to ward off 'spiteful and ill-natur'd men' ready to 'misconstrue those things for calumny, which with all sincerity and plain-dealing I have here collected out of the antient Writers concerning the Scots'. Camden first clarified who his Scots were: 'the old, true, and genuine Scots only; whose posterity are those that speak Irish, who possess for a long way together that now called the West part of Scotland, and the Islands thereabouts; and are commonly termed Highland-men'.[64] For Camden, the traditional highland–lowland divide took on an ethnographic character whose origin could be found in his account of the peopling of Britain. James and his brethren were Scots in name only:

> For those more civilized, who inhabit the East part of the country, though they are adopted into that name, yet are not really Scots, but of the same German original with us English. This they cannot but confess, nor we but acknowledge; being called as well as we, by the aforesaid Highland-men, Sassones. Besides, they speak the same language that we do, namely the Saxon, with some variation in Dialect only; which is an infallible proof of the same original.[65]

Camden quickly defended himself from casting any aspersions and pledged his love for his new king and his subjects, the more so as 'men of the same blood and extraction ... and now much more, since by the favour of God we are united into one body under one sovereign head of England and Scotland; which may the Almighty sanctifie to the good, happy, prosperous, and peaceful state of both nations'.[66]

Camden made dangerous work of navigating these shoals. He went on to opine that Scottish origins (and etymology) were 'so wrapt up in mists and darkness, that even the sagacious Buchanan either did not discover it, or only discovered it to himself: for he has not answered the expectation of the world concerning him in this point'. James no doubt would have enjoyed this jab at the Scottish history of his now-dead but long-hated tutor, but it scarcely did credit to Buchanan's real achievements in differentiating 'between the various linguistic

[62] Camden, *Britannia* (1695), pp. cix–cxii.
[63] Camden, *Britannia* (1695), p. cxiv.
[64] Camden, *Britannia* (1695), p. cxiii.
[65] Camden, *Britannia* (1695), p. cxiii.
[66] Camden, *Britannia* (1695), p. cxiii.

communities in Britain'.[67] For James, the foundation of the Scottish kingdom, and his own *imperium*, lay in a particular tale:

> [This] Ile, and especially our part of it, being scantily inhabited, but by very few, and they as barbarous and scant of ciuilitie, as number, there comes our first King Fergus, with a great number with him out of Ireland, which was long inhabited before vs, and making himselfe master of the countrey, by his owne friendship, and force, as well of the Ireland-men that came with him, as of the countrey-men that willingly fell to him, hee made himself King and Lord, as well of the whole landes, as of the whole inhabitants within the same.[68]

For Camden too, Scottish origins lay across the North Channel, in Ireland and Carrickfergus, so named for 'that famous Fergus drowned there, who first brought the Scots out of Ireland into Britain'.[69] James's interest in Fergus ended there, with the conquest and foundation of the Scottish kingdom that had irrevocably established the sovereign supremacy of the king over his subjects, whatever their ethnic stripe. Camden's interest did not.

Camden praised his scholarly counterparts in Scotland for their ability to trace 'her Original from the highest steps of Antiquity, and do it both to their own honour, and that of their Country'. He proceeded to offer 'some short touches on those things which may afford them some light into the truth of it'. The crux of the matter was the origin of those Scots who had come out of Ireland. Were they Scythians who travelled to Ireland by way of Spain as Irish historians maintained? Certainly the ethnographic data in works of Strabo and Diodorus Siculus attested to the comparable barbarity of each, from blood oaths to weaponry. For Camden's part, he favoured a Gothic origin, suggesting that the Scots might be descended from the Goths driven out of Galicia by Constantine. Once more he turned to ethnographic markers to make the case. He likened Gael, Gaiothel, and the Gaiothlac languages to the Spanish Gallæci and possibly Goth. The dress and apparel of the highlanders, though, undoubtedly matched those 'formerly used by the Goths: as appears by Sidonius, who in his description of a Goth, has given you a fair draught of a Scotch Highlander'. The descriptions of both Gildas and Gerald of Wales added weight to the comparison.[70]

Camden's argument then took a turn toward an odd kind of British cultural imperialism: 'I would have the learned part of the Scotchmen consider, whether they are not descended from the old British Inhabitants of Ireland (for it is certain that the British formerly inhabited Ireland,).' According to Giraldus, Florilegus, and Asinius Quadratus, respectively, Gaidelach, Scot, and Almans all

---

[67] Roger A. Mason, 'From Buchanan to Blaeu: The Politics of Scottish Chorography, 1582–1654', in *George Buchanan: Political Thought in Early Modern Britain and Europe*, ed. Caroline Erskine and Roger A. Mason (Farnham, 2012), p. 29.

[68] King James VI and I, *Political Writings*, ed. Johann Sommerville (Cambridge, 1994), p. 73.

[69] Camden, *Britannia* (1695), p. 1015.

[70] Camden, *Britannia* (1695), pp. cxv–cxviii.

designated polyglot languages or peoples that 'arose from a medly of different men'. For Camden, Ireland was just such a melting pot of peoples and ethnic groups:

> Neither can it seem strange to any one, that so many nations should formerly crowd into Ireland, seeing that Island lies in the center between Britain and Spain, and very advantageous to the French Sea; and that in these eight hundred years last past, it is most certain from History, that the Norwegians, and Oustmans from Germany; and that the English, the Welsh, and the Scots out of Britain, have planted and settled themselves there.[71]

The original Britons must once have been among those peoples who crossed the seas to Ireland, a pattern imitated by their descendants in the many centuries that followed. Camden seemed to steer a surer course once the Scots had crossed into Britain. Their place among the barbarian tormentors of Britannia was easier to follow. The Scots 'provoked the Britains with continual skirmishes and ravages'.[72]

Camden's story moved to the creation of Scotland:

> [The] Scottish-state came not immediately to full growth, but continu'd a long time in that corner where they first arriv'd ... till at one and the same time they had almost quite routed the Picts, and the kingdom of Northumberland utterly destroyed by Civil Wars and the invasions of the Danes. For then all the north part of Britain fell under the name of Scotland, together with that inner country on this side the Cluid and Edinburgh Frith.[73]

Camden reminded his readers that Lothian was once part of the kingdom of Northumberland and a Saxon possession, with obvious ethno-cultural implications:

> By which means it comes to pass, that all the inhabitants of the East part of Scotland (called Low-land-men, as living Low) are originally Saxons, and speak English. But that such as live toward the West (called Highland-men from their high situation) are real Scots and speak Irish ... [74]

For good measure, Camden revised his highland–lowland topographical divide in terms that his king preferred: the Highlanders 'being mortal enemies of those Lowlanders that speak English'.[75]

This was the increasingly convoluted hodgepodge of conjectures that Camden wished his learned friends in Scotland to entertain. Scottish scholars seem to have agreed with Camden's self-deprecating suggestion that 'I am perfectly in the dark in this point: and have followed the truth (which has still fled from

---

[71] Camden, *Britannia* (1695), pp. cxviii–cxix
[72] Camden, *Britannia* (1695), p. cxxi.
[73] Camden, *Britannia* (1695), p. cxxi.
[74] Camden, *Britannia* (1695), p. cxxi.
[75] Camden, *Britannia* (1695), p. cxxi.

me) with much labour to no purpose.'[76] Instead, the great contest would be an etymological battle waged between the partisans of Buchanan and Llwyd, with Camden among Llwyd's supporters.[77] In Chapter 11 we will learn just how Scottish travellers and writers answered Camden's descriptions.

The Saxon wolf

God's greatest punishment for the Romano-Britons was not the fury of the Scots and Picts. Those peoples only announced God's first calls to righteousness. Inviting the Saxon wolf into the 'sheep-fold' proved to be the Britons' final undoing:

> At length, being mightily satisfied with the lands, customs, and plenty of Britain, and building upon the cowardize of the natives; under the pretence of ill pay and short diet, they enter into a league with the Picts, raise a most bloody war against their Entertainers, the Britains, in all parts put the frighted Inhabitants to the sword, wast their lands, raze their cities; and ... at length dispossess the Britains of the best part of the Island, and their hereditary estates. At which time (in a word) the miserable natives suffer'd whatever a Conqueror may be imagin'd to inflict, or the conquer'd fear.[78]

Band after band of Angles, Saxons, and Jutes poured out of Germany to engage and harass the Britons, but were these invaders the Britons' lasting doom? A definite 'shift away from cereals toward animal husbandry and grazing, and a tendency to develop a variety of regional patterns of farming that were better adapted to local conditions' followed the 'end of Roman administration', but this did not signify stagnation. Land clearance continued from 400 to 800, not least in Wales, the West, and lowland Scotland.[79] Regular contacts with continental Europe predated the Romans and outlasted them, along with trade and exchange between Britain, North Africa, and the Eastern Mediterranean.[80] Camden did not wholly embrace Gildas' narrative of apocalyptic punishment, but population, livelihoods, and trade did not feature in his account. Instead he told a kind of British redemption story in the chapters that followed.

Who, first of all, were the invaders? Camden spent some time identifying the homelands of the Saxons, Jutes, and Angles before moving on to his by-now characteristic ethnographic analysis. These English 'Fore-fathers', the Saxons, had

[76] Camden, *Britannia* (1695), p. cxix; William Ferguson, *The Identity of the Scottish Nation: An Historic Quest* (Edinburgh, 1998), pp. 120–43.
[77] Camden, *Britannia* (1695), p. cxix; Hugh Trevor-Roper, *The Invention of Scotland: Myth and History* (New Haven, 2008), pp. 33–72, alongside Jenny Wormald's review in *The Times Literary Supplement* (8 August 2008), pp. 11–12.
[78] Camden, *Britannia* (1695), pp. cxxii–cxxiii.
[79] Francis Pryor, *The Making of the British Landscape: How We have Transformed the Land from Prehistory to Today* (London, 2010), p. 211.
[80] Pryor, *British Landscape*, p. 226.

notable qualities, some of which continued to define Camden's fellow English. They were obviously a warlike nation but, according to Zosimus, they were 'the most valiant of all the Germans, both for greatness of soul, strength of body, and a hardy temper'. They once wore their hair close shaved except for a small patch above the crown. They wore loose linen garments with broad trim in several colours. England and its privateers might owe their maritime prowess to these Saxons, 'admirably skill'd in marine affairs; and by their constant piracies for so long, had inured themselves to the sea'. That said, there could be no doubt as to with 'what barbarity they prey'd upon our coasts'. Yet, among the Barbarians, the Saxons had an admirable quality, of sorts: 'of so much constancie and resolution were they (if a man may so call it,) that they would rather chuse to murther themselves, and throw away their lives, than be exposed to the contempt of others'. Like many barbarous peoples, the Saxons were inordinately superstitious, leaving them prey to everything from soothsayers to the neighing of horses in the search for guidance. According to the ancient sources, they worshipped Mercury or Wodan as their great god, they named the feast of Easter by their sacrifices to the goddess 'Eoster' in April, and venerated 'Herthus' as the Earth mother whose hand could be found in 'the affairs of men and nations'.[81]

Britain positively transformed these superstitious and warlike people: 'For in a very short time, they became so considerable, both for numbers, good customs, and large estates, that they were in a most prosperous and powerful condition, and their victory in a manner entire and absolute.' In turn, their encounters with the Saxons transformed the Britons: 'All the conquer'd, setting aside some few, who took refuge in the uncultivated Western parts, yielded themselves, and embraced their Laws, name, and language.'[82] However, the Britons, along with their cousins among the Picts and Scots-Irish, possessed a mark of civility unknown to the English-Saxons: Christianity. Camden chronicled these early Christian conversions, the work of 'Ninia or Ninianus the Britain', among the Britons in the Roman province and the missions by 'Columbanus, a Scot of Ireland, and a Monk also of singular holiness' to the peoples of the North.[83] Christianity proved to be the decisive element in transforming the English-Saxons into a great nation in Europe in the settled age of the Heptarchy (seven kingdoms). But it was not the Christianity of the Britons and their cousins that had the decisive impact.

Thanks to Augustine ('Austin' in Camden), 'the English Apostle' sent by Gregory the Great, the preaching of Christ banished 'heathenish profaneness' from among the English. The impact was immediate and decisive. No sooner had they been introduced to Christ, but the English 'laid out their utmost endeavours to promote it, by discharging all the duties of Christian Piety, by

---

[81] Camden, *Britannia* (1695), pp. cxxviii–cxxx.
[82] Camden, *Britannia* (1695), pp. cxxvii–cxxviii.
[83] Camden, *Britannia* (1695), pp. cxi–cxiii.

erecting Churches, and endowing them'. Indeed, 'no part of the Christian world could show either more or richer Monasteries' and 'even some Kings preferred a religious life before their very Crowns'.[84] The English became more than just pious; they promoted 'humane learning' with equal ardour. According to a German poet:

> Let this to Britain's lasting fame be said,
> When barbarous troops the civil world o'erspread,
> And persecuted Science into exile fled:
> 'Twas happy she did all those arts restore,
> That Greece and Rome had boasted of before:
> Taught the rude world to climb the untrod spheres,
> And trace th'eternal course of the stars.
> Nor Learning only, but Religion too,
> Her rise and growth to British soil doth owe ...
> 'Twas he [Alcuin] transported Britain's richest ware,
> Languages and arts, and kindly taught them here [in the realms of Charlemagne].[85]

One finishes these verses and imagines that Camden's English 'saved civilization' long before Thomas Cahill's Irish.

The foundation of Henry VIII's break from Rome and the Tudor royal supremacy lay in restoring the freedom of the *Anglicana Ecclesia*. According to Tudor ideology and mythology, this pure, primitive Church in Britain had existed under the imperial crown of English kings until the illegal expansion of papal jurisdiction over the realm. For Camden, as for Leland, the restored *Anglicana Ecclesia* was the legitimate descendant of the primitive Church, certainly not the corrupt dregs of popery – Celtic Christianity – among the Gaels of Ireland, Iona and the Western Isles, or the Highlands.

It was the fate of the Britons to join the English-Saxons or take refuge in Wales, Cornwall, and the Scottish uplands, clinging to their liberty and a marginalized, in time loathed, collection of customs and manners. Those Britons who followed the first course were redeemed from their corrupt state at the demise of Roman Britain. They joined in creating an English nation of renowned piety that nurtured and taught the foundations of civility. Thus we know the Britons' ultimate fate. But what of 'Britain'? Inevitably the rich expanse of the Angles' kingdoms (Northumberland, Mercia, and East Anglia) compared to those of the Jutes and Saxons in the Heptarchy helped to ensure that it was their name that would come to signify the whole. Among the seven kings, 'the Kings that were more powerful than the rest, were stiled the Kings of the English nation'. 'Then it was that the name of Britain fell into disuse in this Island;' continued Camden, 'and was only to be found in Books, being never heard in common talk.' The name and the power of the Angles may have been at the height of its

---

[84] Camden, *Britannia* (1695), pp. cxxxi–cxxxii.
[85] Camden, *Britannia* (1695), p. cxxxii.

glory, but 'such (according to the common revolution of things) were ready for a fall'.[86] Enter the Danes.

Britain in the Norse world

There are times when reading *Britannia* that you sense the lost possibilities for seeing the long historical complexity of the peoples of Britain. There are other times when we appreciate how much contemporary scholarship has moved on from the early modern period and its writers. Camden's treatment of the Danes is certainly one of those latter moments. For many today – visitors to York's Jorvik Centre or readers familiar with modern accounts of the Norse presence in Ireland – it seems easy enough to substitute the Danes for the English-Saxons in Camden's account: pirates and invaders who plundered the land and ravaged its people before deciding to settle permanently and establish long-term control and lasting prosperity.[87] But these are not Camden's Danes, the barbarians who swarmed out of Scandinavia and took to their oars only after appeasing the god Thor with a human blood sacrifice, the victim's brains dashed out by the blow of an ox yoke.[88]

After their first incursions, the Danes returned in force, 'making havock of every thing, and plundering over all England, they destroy'd Cities, burnt Churches, wasted the lands, and with a most barbarous cruelty drove all before them; ransacking and over-turning every thing'. They took the kingdoms of Mercia and East Anglia, together with a sizeable chunk of Northumbria, and settled down to receive the Danegeld, 'a heavy tax impos'd upon the miserable Inhabitants' to buy a settled, 'peaceful' occupation.[89] Between them, Alfred, Edward his son, and Athelstan cleared Mercia, East Anglia, and Northumberland and:

> [by] vigorous pursuit put the Danes into such a fright, that part of them quitted the kingdom, and the rest surrendered themselves. By the courage of those Princes was England deliver'd out of that gulph of miseries, and had a respite of 50 years from that bloody war.[90]

The 'cowardly spirit' of Aethelred, rather than pride, brought the English to grief once more, opening the door to the restoration of Danish power and tribute. In a truly biblical act of slaughter, the English conspired to murder all the Danes in the kingdom in one night, hoping to send a definitive message of defiance. Cnut answered with a new army of conquest before finally 'the Danish yoke was

[86] Camden, *Britannia* (1695), pp. cxxxiii–cxxxiv.
[87] Pryor, *British Landscape*, pp. 235–65.
[88] Camden, *Britannia* (1695), p. clii.
[89] Camden, *Britannia* (1695), pp. clii–cliv.
[90] Camden, *Britannia* (1695), pp. clii–cliv.

shaken off, and the government return'd to the English' at the death of Cnut's sons.[91]

The kingdom revived under Edward the Confessor, but not for long. Two centuries of Danish brutality had not been sufficient instruction for the English:

> The Clergy were idle, drouse, and ignorant; the Laity gave themselves over to luxury, and a loose way of living; all discipline was laid aside; the State, like a distemper'd body, was consum'd with all sorts of vice: but Pride, that forerunner of destruction, had of all other, made the greatest progress.

According to William of Malmesbury, English customs and manners bore witness to the people's pride and degeneracy. Their clothing hung no lower than mid-knee. Their heads and beards were shaved clean, save for moustaches. They loaded their arms with gold bracelets. Their skin was 'set with painted marks'. Rather than calling their flocks to righteousness, the clergy contented themselves with superficial learning and struggled even to 'hammer out the words of the Sacraments'.[92] Camden's Danes crossed the seas more than once to blast an English nation that gave in to vice, cowardice, and pride. They would not be the last ones to mete out punishment.

Norman Domesday

Taking into account the incursions by Franks/Gauls, Angles, Saxons, Jutes, and Danes, Camden concluded that providence had established the northern parts of Europe to be the place from whence men set out to 'make havock of France and Britain, and establish new kingdoms in them'. The Normans certainly fitted the bill, establishing themselves in Normandy and rapidly adopting 'French' customs and manners, including language, before acting as yet another providential punishment for the vice-ridden English. In chronicling so 'considerable a revolution in the British state', Camden offered *Britannia*'s readers a draft treatise composed when he was 'raw and younger' and 'had a design to write the history of our nation in Latin'. It is of course interesting that we are allowed a glimpse of the young Camden's literary designs. At the same time we see the impact of 1603 and James's accession. Camden framed the Norman conquest within the history of the Stuart *imperium* that he had come to see as a British state. This would be the defining context from which he closed his account.

The treatise of the budding Camden narrated the conquest, but what did the mature Camden think had been its impact? The initial effects of yet another conquest were predictable:

> William, as a token of his conquest, laid aside the greatest part of the English laws, brought in Norman customs, and ordered that all causes should be pleaded in French.

---

[91] Camden, *Britannia* (1695), pp. clii–cliv.
[92] Camden, *Britannia* (1695), p. cliv.

The English were dispossessed of their hereditary estates, and the lands and farms divided among his Soldiers; but with this reserve, that he should still remain the direct Proprietor.

The subjugation of the populace was indeed draconian – feudal obligations, castle building and garrisons, Domesday – but the long-term effects on the English were more complicated. In Camden's view, William 'made it his whole business to maintain the dignity of his government, and to settle the Kingdom with wholesome laws'. In doing so, the Conqueror confirmed many existing laws and added Norman laws that seemed most useful for his purposes.[93]

Camden had little to say about linguistic conquest here. Law-French was an undeniable legacy, but other French influences were ruled out when he trumpeted the survival of Anglo-Saxon languages among both the English and lowland Scots in earlier chapters. The Britons also provided cause for satisfaction in turning back the designs of the French-speaking Normans:

> [We] cannot but much admire and celebrate the divine goodness towards our Britains, the posterity of Gomer; who, though they have been conquer'd and triumph'd over successively by the Romans, Saxons, and Normans; yet hitherto they enjoy the true name of their Ancestors, and have preserv'd entire their primitive language, although the Normans set themselves to abolish it, making express laws to that purpose.[94]

Like their predecessors, the Normans failed to root out the language of the Britons – or the English.

The Normans accomplished something that none of their predecessors had, however. They successfully held the kingdom. While 'being seated in the midst of warlike Nations, they never made submission their refuge, but always arms'. How did Camden reconcile the Norman conquest with the continuation of the English nation? He used a nice sleight of hand to acknowledge their presence while writing them out of the story's longer narrative: 'Since that time [of Conquest], England has been equal for warlike exploits, and genteel Education to the most flourishing nations of the Christian world.' The Normans provided a timely and providential chastisement and a welcome dose of martial vigour.[95] Tristram Risdon, one of Camden's close readers and author of the *Survey of the County of Devon*, cited Domesday Book to define the relationship of the Anglo-Saxons and Normans as that of natives and conquerors: 'there was not a Hide of Land but the Conqueror knew the Value and the Owner ... And which was worse, the Natives violently disposed to reward his Soldiers with their Revenues, and expulsed some of them the Land.'[96] For Camden, though, it was the England of

---

[93] Camden, *Britannia* (1695), pp. clxi–clxii.
[94] Camden, *Britannia* (1695), p. xxvi.
[95] Camden, *Britannia* (1695), p. clxiii.
[96] Tristram Risdon, *The Chorographical Description, or, Survey of the County of Devon* (two volumes; London, 1714), I, pp. 132–3.

piety and humane learning, the England that blossomed from the first flowering of civility among the English-Saxons, which prevailed.

The changing face of humanity and *Britannia*

What went through Camden's mind as he fashioned and refashioned this complex narrative over successive editions? Seneca offered him what he took to be a fitting conclusion:

> From hence it is manifest, that nothing has continued in its primitive state. There's a continual floating in the affairs of mankind. In this vast orb there are daily revolutions: new foundations of cities laid, new names given to nations, either by the utter ruine of the former, or by its change into that of a more powerful party.

Camden had no doubt that this applied to his Britain and only the most obstinate reading would deny that this is the key to his account. It was an island once crisscrossed by primitive peoples. Of them 'there remains unto this day the Britains, the Saxons or Angles, with a mixture of Normans; and towards the North, the Scots'.[97]

Camden's Britain had also become a Stuart imperial Britain since he had first conceived *Britannia*: 'Whereupon the two Kingdoms of this Island, England and Scotland, which were long divided, are now in the most potent Prince, King JAMES, happily united under one Imperial Diadem.'[98] Like his fellow countrymen in the first years of James I's reign, Camden was conflicted over what this meant. One senses him working through the implications in *Britannia*. Camden concluded with an ominous observation by Nicephorus that returned to the theme of punishment from the North: 'As God very often sends terrors upon men from heaven ... So those Northern terrors are as it were reserved by God, to be sent out for a punishment, when, and upon whom the Divine Providence shall think fit.'[99] Were the Scots to be the next Northern terror visited upon the English nation? At least a few of Camden's countrymen in Parliament found them to be a beggarly pestilence. By the time the first English edition of *Britannia* appeared in 1610, there would be no love lost between the king of Scots and his English subjects in the House Commons, or, as James described it, the 'house of hell'.[100]

Camden read something else in the story of Britain's peoples. Camden felt that he had to set Gildas' apocalyptic narrative in an appropriate context for his readers and his times:

---

[97] Camden, *Britannia* (1695), p. clxiv.
[98] Camden, *Britannia* (1695), p. clxiv.
[99] Camden, *Britannia* (1695), p. clxiv.
[100] Elizabeth Read Foster, ed., *Proceedings in Parliament 1610* (two volumes; New Haven, 1966), II, pp. 101–3.

In reading these things, we ought not to be angry at honest Gildas for inveighing so keenly against the vices of his Countrymen the Britains, the barbarous outrages of the Picts and Scots, and the insatiable cruelty of our Saxon Ancestors. But rather being now, by engrafting or mixture for so many ages, become all of us one people, and civilized by religion and liberal arts, let us reflect upon what they were, and we ought to be; lest God likewise for our sins transplant other nations hither, that may root us quite out, or at least enslave us to them.[101]

These early chapters of *Britannia* relate an intense story of migrations and conquests, encounters and exchanges, triumph and destruction among a complex collection of peoples. Camden found in this history cause to call for the unity of hearts and minds so desperately sought by his king, perhaps through a shared Protestant faith or an understanding of Britain's multi-ethnic past, to be found in an example of liberal learning like *Britannia*. The peopling of Britain was both a cautionary tale and a hopeful meditation for its author.

Camden's journeys into the archives allowed him to tell this story of the peopling of Britain, stretching from its ancient inhabitants through to the Normans. We must remember that this vital story served only to introduce the much larger substance of *Britannia*: Camden's topographical surveys of England and Wales grounded in his own travels as well as the matching chapters covering Scotland and Ireland, realms to which he never travelled. It was on this material that Camden's reputation in *Britannia* was founded. It was also in these sections that we know Camden came closer than anyone else to producing a work that realized Leland's plans for a great civil history of Britain. Yet Camden understood from reading Seneca that the face of humanity and its affairs was forever changing. His *Britannia* was not the book Leland would have written in the 1540s. And, as we know, most of Camden's labours in the successive editions of *Britannia* from 1586 to 1607 went into expanding and improving the topographical sections. As humanity changed, so travel and discovery brought change to the story of Britannia and her peoples.

In 1693, with editions of the *Anglo-Saxon Chronicle* and Quintillian's *Institutio Oratoria* to his credit, the 'precocious antiquary' Edmund Gibson set out to gather the fruits of Camden's students and imitators for a new edition of *Britannia*.[102] That same year two proposals for publishing a new English translation by subscription were printed, including the names of confirmed subscribers. According to the sales pitch, English copies of *Britannia* were scarce and the price dear, especially for a translation deemed 'very ill'. Gibson undertook to revise and edit *Britannia*. The publishing end of the project was to be handled by the London printer Abel Swalle and the sharp bookselling brothers Awnsham and John Churchill. The printers promised a new translation by 'several Gentlemen of great Learning and Skill in the Antiquities of England', nicely set and printed

---

[101] Camden, *Britannia* (1695), p. civ.
[102] Brynley F. Roberts, 'Edward Lhuyd', *Oxford DNB* at www.oxforddnb.com.

on 'very good Paper', with the presumptuous additions of Philemon Holland from the 1610 edition exiled to the footnotes.[103]

Significant additions to the text were promised. 'All the discoveries that have been made in several Counties' by travellers since Camden's death would be added, as would the fruits of new journeys into the archives and the 'Histories of well nigh half the Counties of England'. Other planned additions included Thomas Smith's biography of Camden and expanded accounts of universities, coins, buildings, and the seats of the current nobility. There would be corrections as well, carefully placed in the margins outside Camden's original text. Perhaps the most elaborate and costly addition would be an entirely new set of maps. A second printed notice on 20 April 1693 duly informed subscribers that improved maps would require raising the book's price from 26s to 32s; an edition on larger paper was now offered, priced at 50s.[104] Thirty-two shillings did not make *Britannia* a cheap book, but the project was a viable concern and the first edition duly appeared in 1695. The most significant additions and corrections can be found in the topographic sections of *Britannia*, not in Camden's story of the peopling of Britain. Gibson decided to incorporate the additions by his fellow scholars after each original chapter and tied them into Camden's own with endnotes.

Why should this interest us? Reading between the lines of the two proposals we learn what had made Camden's *Britannia* inadequate by the 1690s. The proposal highlights the learning and skill of Gibson's team in the 'Antiquities of England' and remarks on the expansion of knowledge in surveys of 'well nigh half the Counties of England'. A century of local travel and study had revealed much that was new in England. Yet the focus on England is telling. Camden never travelled to Scotland or Ireland and his topographic surveys did not benefit from first-hand encounters with their peoples or those places. Wales was less problematic because Camden had travelled there, but it too had its shortcomings. Though the proposals showed no obvious plan for it, Gibson selected experts who could finally complete Camden's travels through Britain. He reassured readers:

> When I tell you, that the whole business of Wales was committed to the care of Mr Edward Lhwyd ... no one ought to dispute the justness and accuracy of his Observations. ... Nor can the additional Remarks in Scotland be question'd since they are grounded upon the authority of Sir Robert Sibbalds whose [works]. ... are a sufficient evidence how much he is master of the affairs of that Kingdom.[105]

---

[103] Anonymous, *New Proposals for Printing by Subscription, Cambden's Britannia* (WING C373A; London, 1693).
[104] Anonymous, *New Proposals for Printing by Subscription, Cambden's Britannia* (WING C373; London, 1693).
[105] Camden, *Britannia* (1695), Gibson's Preface.

Thomas Churchyard's attack against writers who pronounced on peoples and places they had never experienced at first hand could only have become a more pressing matter after a century of overseas travel, the veritable explosion of travellers on the Grand Tour, and the knitting together of Britannia's people and regions by better roads, canals, and bridges, the posts, and peace.[106]

Gibson's choice of lone experts – Lhuyd (Wales), Sibbald (Scotland), and Richard Cox (Ireland) – reminds us that Camden's most immediate impact on travel and ethno-topographical study was in England. The numbers of travellers and scholars eagerly writing micro-histories and descriptions of Scotland or Wales paled by comparison to those at work in England.[107] Indeed, the catalogues of manuscripts and books at the beginning of Gibson's *Britannia*, updated in later editions, make the point in the starkest terms.[108] Scotland, Wales, Ireland, and the British islands covered half a folio page, compared to four full pages for England. In the 1722 (second) edition, the number of works fairly exploded, approximately doubling in number for each nation, but English studies still outstripped the others combined. Still, this is a case of relative neglect, given the number of stand-in Morysons who travelled through Scotland, Cornwall, and Wales and the wealth of manuscript studies of the Welsh and Scottish localities from as early as the 1600s that were not listed in Gibson's additional reading.[109]

The 1695 edition of *Britannia* offers us an interesting opportunity, then. Gibson and his team conscientiously separated Camden's original from their own additions and corrections.[110] Side by side, Camden's original and the 1695 additions give us a window into the minds of late seventeenth-century scholars and travellers. As Camden had predicted, Britannia and her peoples had indeed changed in almost a century. But just what did Gibson and the others now feel compelled to add to Camden's story? Did the shortcomings look different, depending on which of Britannia's peoples were having their story retold? What do the changes tell us about how some travellers walking in the footsteps of Leland, Moryson, or Camden at the end of the seventeenth century

---

[106] John Leland, *The Itinerary of John Leland the Antiquarian* (nine volumes; Oxford, 1710–1712), VI, pp. 76–7.

[107] Stan Mendyk, *'Speculum Britanniae': Regional Study, Antiquarianism, and Science in Britain to 1700* (Toronto, 1989), pp. 82–113.

[108] Jan Broadway, 'A Convenient Fiction? The County Community and County History in the 1650s', in *The County Community in Seventeenth-Century England and Wales*, ed. Jacqueline Eales and Andrew Hopper (Hatfield, 2012), pp. 39–55.

[109] Lloyd Bowen, 'Fashioning Communities: The County in Early Modern Wales', *County Community*, pp. 78, 83.

[110] On the 1695 edition, Parry, *Trophies of Time*, pp. 331–57; Piggott, 'William Camden and the *Britannia*', pp. 22–6; Frank Emery, 'Edward Lhuyd, Edmund Gibson, and the Printing of Camden's *Britannia*, 1695', *The Library* 32.2 (1977), pp. 109–37; R. Mayhew, 'Edmund Gibson's Editions of *Britannia*: Dynastic Chorography and the Particularist Politics of Precedent, 1695–1722' *Historical Research* 73.182 (2000), pp. 239–61; Herendeen, *Camden*, pp. 507–8.

encountered, experienced, and thought about the peoples of Britain? Finally, could the encounter with multicultural Britain be captured within the confines of a single book such as *Britannia*? These questions become our focus for the rest of this book.

10

The Britannia of Edward Lhuyd

Born an illegitimate son of Bridget Pryse and Edward Lloyd in Shropshire, Edward Lhuyd gave up his father's Anglicized surname just before he turned thirty, around 1688. By then Lhuyd had added a fascination for natural history to his passionate devotion to Welshness, probably at the hands of his father's botanist-gardener Edward Morgan, himself associated with John Evelyn and the great naturalist John Ray. Lhuyd's earliest 'botanical activities are some notes apparently taken during a journey from [the family seat at] Llandforda to Cardiganshire'.[1] Jesus College, Oxford sparked Lhuyd's interests when he arrived in 1682. No influence may have been more important than joining Robert Plot's Philosophical Society. As Keeper of the Ashmolean, Plot 'conceived a plan to travel throughout Britain collecting materials towards the writing of a descriptive survey of the country ... [stimulated by] Pliny's *Historia Naturalis*, Leland, Camden, and the English chorographical tradition stemming from William Lambarde'.[2] Indeed, Plot deliberately aimed to augment and correct *Britannia* by travelling with the same wide-ranging remit and close attention to detail that Leland once had.[3]

Plot published his very detailed *Natural History of Oxfordshire* in 1674, by which he hoped to 'advance a sort of Learning so much neglected in England' by earlier generations: a close study of the natural world and its commercial possibilities.[4] Plot completed a similar volume for Staffordshire in 1686, while Lhuyd was one of his students. Lhuyd became Plot's assistant the following year and regular correspondence followed with Ray, Martin Lister, William Nicolson, John Aubrey, and other leading naturalists and scholars. Plot tasked him to prepare 'a catalogue of British fossils ... based on the museum's collections', but this fell by the wayside when Lhuyd succeeded Plot as Keeper of the Ashmolean in 1691. For his part, Plot embarked on journeys in Kent and Middlesex in the

---

[1] Brynley Roberts, 'Edward Lhuyd', *Oxford DNB* at www.oxforddnb.com; Frank Emery, *Edward Lhuyd F.R.S. 1660–1709* (Cardiff, 1971).
[2] A.J. Turner, 'Robert Plot', *Oxford DNB* at www.oxforddnb.com.
[3] *The Itinerary of John Leland the Antiquarian* (nine volumes; Oxford, 1710–1712), II, pp. 110–11, hereafter cited as *Itinerary of John Leland*.
[4] Robert Plot, *The Natural History of Oxfordshire* (WING P2586; Oxford, 1676), sig. b3b.

early 1690s. He died in 1696 before he could complete natural histories of either county, but his travels made him the ideal person to revise Camden's descriptions for Gibson.[5] By 1695, student and master – now colleagues – had shared in the common enterprise of revising *Britannia*. Perhaps better than any of Gibson's collaborators, Lhuyd captures the shortcomings of *Britannia* and the possibilities for its renewal a hundred years after its first publication.

Edward Lhuyd and the revision of *Britannia*

When Lhuyd accepted Gibson's commission, he provided an updated bibliography for readers. In the 1722 edition, produced after Lhuyd died in 1709, a short list of works about Wales included strange phenomena in coalmines, details of a recent swarm of locusts, and the medicinal springs of Glamorganshire, all from notices in *The Philosophical Transactions of the Royal Society*. Readers might also turn to a 'Manuscript of David Morganius, mentioned by Vossius', John Ray's account of silver smelting, Browne Willis's description of four Welsh cathedrals, Henry Rowlands' account of Anglesey (still in manuscript but finally published as *Mona Antiqua Restaurata* a year later), Dodderidge's *History* of the Principality, or Lhuyd's own *Archaeologia Britannica* published in 1707. The two works to which readers could turn who sought something more comprehensive and descriptive are familiar by now: Gerald's *Itinerary* (in Powel's 1585 edition) and Prise's description of Wales in Llwyd's *Cronica Walliae*.[6] Lhuyd's bibliography in 1695 looked radically different. It listed only three works: Gerald's *Itinerary*, Morgan's manuscript, and Owen's *Description of Pembrokeshire* in manuscript, thought then to be in the hand of Hywel Vaughan of Hengwrt.[7]

This paucity of descriptions compelled Lhuyd to undertake his own travels, a decision that led to run-ins with the 'money men'.[8] Abel Swalle arrived in Oxford in May 1693 to recruit experts, prompted by Gibson to seek out Lhuyd, thanks to the recommendation of William Nicolson, Gibson's collaborator for Northumberland.[9] He did not inspire confidence but Lhuyd agreed to revise the chapters on North Wales. The scope of the revisions and expenses dogged Lhuyd's negotiations with Swalle. In August, Lhuyd offered 'to doe all Wales & to take a journey speedily quite through it, for ten pounds in hand; and twenty

[5] Turner, 'Robert Plot'; Roberts, 'Edward Lhuyd'; Stan Mendyk, *'Speculum Britanniae': Regional Study, Antiquarianism, and Science in Britain to 1700* (Toronto, 1989), pp. 193–205.

[6] William Camden, *Britannia: Or a Chorographical Description of Great Britain and Ireland* (two volumes; London, 1722), I, 'Books and Treatises Related to the Antiquities of England'.

[7] William Camden, *Britannia: Or a Chorographical Description of Great Britain and Ireland* (London, 1695), 'A Catalogue of Some Books and Treatises Relating to the Antiquities of England', hereafter cited as Camden, *Britannia* (1695).

[8] *Life and Letters of Edward Lhuyd, Early Science in Oxford XIV*, ed. R.T. Gunther (Oxford, 1945), p. 198.

[9] Frank Emery, 'Edward Lhwyd and the 1695 *Britannia*', *Antiquity* 32 (1958), p. 179.

copies of ye book, when it shall be published: but he'll not come up farther than ye one half of it'. They appear to have settled on something like £25 and perhaps half as many complementary copies, overall close to the total value of Lhuyd's original demand.[10]

Lhuyd could call on a number of collaborators in North Wales to assist him, but a seven-week journey into South Wales was critical. 'I had but few acquaintances there, from whom I might receive any information', he wrote to his schoolmaster friend and collaborator in Ruthin, John Lloyd.[11] Lhuyd was candid with Lloyd and another collaborator, Richard Mostyn in Flintshire, about his frustrations with the booksellers:

> Mr. Swall and Mr. Churchill (who are my task-masters) did not require I should put myself to ye trouble & expences of a journey into Wales; for they care not how little is done for that country; their business being only to procure subscribers, which they have allready done to their satisfaction ... The truth is, the Booksellers concern'd in this new edition of Camden, are not willing to be at such charges with persons they employ, as to enable them to survey their respective Provinces.[12]

The Welsh prejudice was twofold. When Lhuyd saw the printed edition, he wrote that the 'undertakers put a trick upon us as to the maps of Wales; for when they told us in the proposals, they would give us a map of each county in England, it was generally understood that they comprehended Wales; but they have given us onely one map of north Wales and an other of South Wales'.[13] By contrast, John Speeds' *Theatre of the Empire of Great Britain* (1611) had finely etched maps for every Welsh county. The Welsh maps had been a running sore with Gibson since 1693, when Lhuyd threatened to 'withdraw his co-operation in correction of the [original] maps, feeling that the publishers were not interested in a thorough orthographic revision of the place-names'.[14] More than cost-consciousness and indifference were at work with Swalle and Churchill, though. By Lhuyd's estimation they wanted 'onely such additional notes as may render this edition preferable to any yt[that] hath been yet published.' The goal was not unrealistic. In the hands of local scholars, able to supplement them conveniently by their own journeys, the great number of English county histories made limited revisions palatable.[15] Not so for Wales. When Lhuyd's collaborator in Pembrokeshire and Carmarthenshire, Nicholas Roberts, first learned of

---

[10] *Life and Letters of Edward Lhuyd*, pp. 197–8, 246.
[11] *Life and Letters of Edward Lhuyd*, pp. 194–6, 198.
[12] *Life and Letters of Edward Lhuyd*, pp. 198, 207.
[13] *Life and Letters of Edward Lhuyd*, p. 259.
[14] Gwyn Walters and Frank Emery, 'Edward Lhuyd, Edmund Gibson, and the Printing of Camden's *Britannia*, 1695', *The Library* 32.2 (1977), p. 133.
[15] *Life and Letters of Edward Lhuyd*, p. 207.

Gibson's project in 1693, he vouched for the many mistakes and oversights in the original that demanded close attention and remedy.[16]

If underwriting Lhuyd's travels became a bone of contention, so did the scope of his additions. Lhuyd knew that Camden had little to say about certain counties in Wales and he assured local contacts that there was space for whatever they had uncovered before his visit or passed on afterward. Having learned in his correspondence with Nicolson, archdeacon of Carlisle, about shared etymology between Wales and the North of England, Lhuyd intended 'to observe ye method our ancestors used in nameing places', from castles and villages to rivers, mountains, and all manner of natural phenomena.[17] Inscriptions, folklore, artefacts, ruins, and all manner of antiquities also figured in Lhuyd's plans, although he admitted that time precluded any in-depth study of monuments.[18] 'As for miracles and ye old saints,' Lhuyd wrote, 'I'll meddle not with ym [them].'[19] His travels 'afforded little or no time to search after natural curiosities', though these too found their way into his additions, including fossils found in the Glamorganshire coal pits and the story of an inexplicable pestilence in Pembrokeshire.[20] Still, Lhuyd made major advances with his empirical precision and expansive identification of British cultural remains.[21]

Back in Oxford after his travels, Lhuyd wrote to Lloyd on St David's Day 1694 to report on the complications of drawing all this into a finished set of additions:

> Mr. GIBSON tells me now that they have not room for much additions; and that at his reviseing of all ye papers sent in, he must so dispose things as that the whole work shall appear uniform &c. w[hi]ch is contrary to ye agreement we made at first with the printers, and for that reason Dr EDWS would have me keep my papers, in order to print them apart. But since matters have gone so far, I am resolv'd they shall goe on for me, and therefore shall submit to their censure what I have collected.[22]

Lhuyd's bold determination to send his full additions wavered for fear that the booksellers would keep what they excised 'for a latin Edition or some other use' of their own.[23] White Kennett, responsible for Oxfordshire, quit the project and others began to voice complaints. Lhuyd consequently 'studied not to trouble them much with superfluities' in preparing his additions and asked Martin Lister to intercede with Churchill, having 'some authority with him'.[24]

---

[16] Emery, 'Edward Lhwyd and the 1695 *Britannia*', p. 180.
[17] *Life and Letters of Edward Lhwyd*, p. 192.
[18] *Life and Letters of Edward Lhwyd*, p. 255.
[19] *Life and Letters of Edward Lhwyd*, p. 196.
[20] *Life and Letters of Edward Lhwyd*, p. 204.
[21] Graham Parry, *The Trophies of Time: English Antiquarians of the Seventeenth Century* (Oxford, 1995), p. 354.
[22] *Life and Letters of Edward Lhwyd*, p. 27.
[23] *Life and Letters of Edward Lhwyd*, p. 230.
[24] *Life and Letters of Edward Lhwyd*, p. 239.

Good news arrived early in September, with page proofs of Cornwall forwarded by Gibson. Whereas 'I suspected all this while they would print but few Notes or Additions, I find by some counties I have seen, their Additions are almost as large as ye Text.'[25] Lhuyd wrote to Lister that ultimately Gibson 'has dealt very favourably with me, having printed all I sent, and also grav'd all the figures'.[26] Indeed, Gibson informed Lhuyd that he thought the additions 'without flattery, are done like a Gentleman & a scholar'.[27] In March 1695 Lhuyd sent John Lloyd his copy of *Britannia*, with evident satisfaction.[28]

Wales in Camden's *Britannia*

What was it that Lhuyd built on? Camden had gained some first-hand experiences in Wales and among the Welsh by the time that his 1594 edition appeared.[29] Given Camden's focus on British 'antiquity' and his scholarly predilections, the *Itinerarium Cambriae* stands side by side with classical and medieval sources. That Camden made good use of Leland's notebooks ensured that another great storehouse of personal observations found their way, at second hand, into *Britannia*. Outside Churchyard's verses, Camden's was the first systematic description of Wales to be built on significant first-hand experiences of the land and its peoples. The textual interactions of Gerald, Camden, and Lhuyd are a fascinating way to explore the experience of travel and the revision of *Britannia*.

Camden recognized that the boundary of Wales changed according to the fortunes of war with its neighbours. Logically for Camden, Britannia's story could not be told without Wales or the Welsh, but the formal incorporation of Wales within the Tudor *imperium*, 'engrafted' in the 1530s, still imposed a certain narrative.[30] Camden would not write, as Gerald had, with a foot in several cultural worlds. Lowland England and the Tudor regime would be Camden's norm, even if not an especially hostile one before the 1640s. Anglo-Welsh Union brought to the Welsh parliamentary representation, the unity and rigour of English common law, including the displacement of partible inheritance by primogeniture, and the end of purportedly fractious princes like Owain Glyn Dŵr. These 'laws and privileges' were needed in Wales.[31] The first inhabitants of South Wales were 'hardy, stout, warlike, averse to servitude, of great boldness and resolution (term'd by the Romans obstinacy and stubbornness) not to be wrought upon either by threats or kindness, and their posterity

[25] *Life and Letters of Edward Lhuyd*, p. 243.
[26] *Life and Letters of Edward Lhuyd*, p. 254.
[27] Quoted in *Life and Letters of Edward Lhuyd*, p. 11.
[28] *Life and Letters of Edward Lhuyd*, p. 259.
[29] George Owen, *The Description of Pembrokeshire*, ed. Dillwyn Miles (Llandysul, 1994), p. xxxvi.
[30] Camden, *Britannia* (1695), p. 574.
[31] Camden, *Britannia* (1695), p. 585.

have not degenerated in any of these particulars'.[32] These Welsh qualities, many of which Gerald noted, appeared differently to those writing within the Roman *imperium* or, in Camden's case, the Tudor *imperium*.

Camden turned south from Radnorshire, to Brecknockshire, and wrote that 'since nothing can be added in the describing of this small Province, to what the industrious Giraldus Cambrensis hath already written (who was Arch-Deacon hereof four hundred years since) I may do well for some time to be silent, and call him to my assistance'.[33] Gerald's assistance consisted of his topographic descriptions:

> [There is] a large Lake, which the Britains called Lhyn Savèdhan and Lhyn Savàdhan: Giraldus calls it Clamosum, from the terrible noise it makes, like a clap of thunder, at the cracking of the Ice. In English 'tis call'd Brecknockmere: it is two miles long, and near the same breadth, well stored with Otters, and also Perches, Tenches and Eels, which the Fishermen take in their Coracls.[34]

Camden ignored the humorous, ethnic one-upmanship between Milo Earl of Hereford and Lord of Brecknock, one Payn FitzJohn, and Gruffydd ap Rhys ap Tewdwr – Gerald's great-uncle – in the reign of Henry I:

> Earl Milo was chaffing Gruffydd about his claim to noble blood. ... 'There is an old saying in Wales,' he went on, 'that, if the rightful ruler of the land comes to this lake and orders the birds to sing, they all burst into song.' ... 'Well,' he [Gruffydd] answered, 'you now rule the country, so you had better be the first to speak to them.'[35]

The waterfowl covering the lake predictably ignored the two Anglo-Normans. Gryffudd prayed fervently and took his turn: '"If You have ordained that I should descend in direct line from the five princes of Wales, make these birds declare it in Your name." Immediately all the birds ... beat the water with their wings and began to sing with one accord and to proclaim him master.' Henry I's response, as reported by Gerald, may have been problematic for Camden, even with Elizabeth I's Welsh descent: '"I am not the slightest bit surprised. It is we who hold the power, and so we are free to commit acts of violence and injustice against these people, and yet we know full well that it is they who are the rightful heirs to the land."'[36]

Monmouth, now safely a part of England, could be cast in a positive light and Gerald's *Journey* served Camden well in that purpose. Even during Gerald's life it was a bountiful county, supplying its Welsh and English neighbours in times of need. Camden reported that the 'Inhabitants (saith Giraldus, writing of the time

---

[32] Camden, *Britannia* (1695), p. 574.
[33] Camden, *Britannia* (1695), p. 589.
[34] Camden, *Britannia* (1695), p. 590.
[35] Gerald of Wales, *The Journey Through Wales* and *The Description of Wales*, trans. Lewis Thorpe (London, 1978/2004), pp. 93–5.
[36] Gerald, *Journey*, p. 95.

when he liv'd) are a valiant and courageous people; much inured to frequent Skirmishes; and the most skilful archers of all the Welsh borderers'.[37] Camden gave the medieval Welsh their due from the safety of the Tudor present, but the abbey of St John the Baptist presented him with immediate problems. Just as for Leland, these sites could stand for an ancient Christianity of simple devotion and fervent piety, uncorrupted by papal jurisdiction that came in the van of Norman invaders. They could also be read as wounds on the religious landscape, thanks to the work of zealots or greedy 'reformers' under Henry VIII and Edward VI. Interestingly, Camden related Gerald's account of its founding in 'a place fit for true Religion, and most conveniently seated for canonical discipline'. However, he did not probe into Gerald's reflections about the abbey's decline, his meditations about human nature and corruption, or the debate concerning the piety of Benedictine and Augustinian rules – certainly fine grist for an evangelical reformer's mill. Perhaps it was simply a vanished world that Camden saw no need to engage with. Perhaps Camden cloaked his own feelings about the deliberate destruction of that world by what he left between the covers of Gerald's *Journey*. 'But enough of this, if not too much' was an ambivalent note for Camden to end on.[38]

Gibson continued the practice of italicizing major blocks of text that Camden had borrowed from his sources. In the case of Monmouthshire, the typeface difference gives us a vivid sense of how much material Camden had added from other sources, including information picked up during his own travels. He excerpted a good portion of Gerald's account of Roman Caerleon, but did not leave the evidence for the Roman presence at that: 'But in confirmation of the antiquity of this place, I have taken care to add some ancient Inscriptions lately dug up there; and communicated to me by the right reverend Father in God Frances Godwin, Lord Bishop of Llandaff, a lover of venerable antiquity.'[39] His own travels to Wales long ago completed, Camden relied on Bishop Godwin to supply him with new remains, a statue and the fragments of an altar unearthed by 'some labourers digging in a meadow' in 1602. The text included a reproduction of the inscriptions and drawings of the fragments. Camden closed his chapter with Monmouth's history of ethnic conflict. 'During the Saxon Heptarchy, this County was subject to the Mountain Welsh', but the Norman marcher lords pushed across the Wye, drove these particular Welsh back to the hills, and redrew the boundary forever.[40] The mountain Welsh did not merit either the pause or praise they received from Churchyard.

Camden created his description of Wales out of just this blend of first-hand observations, selections from classical, medieval, and contemporary sources, and

---

[37] Camden, *Britannia* (1695), p. 594; Gerald, *Journey*, pp. 112–13.
[38] Camden, *Britannia* (1695), p. 595; Gerald, *Journey*, pp. 96–102.
[39] Camden, *Britannia* (1695), p. 600.
[40] Camden, *Britannia* (1695), pp. 599–604.

the information of local contacts. Gerald's keen eye for details made his *Journey* an invaluable source. Sometimes Gerald's travels were the only material that gave Camden's descriptions the feel of a first-hand account. It is unlikely Camden visited the Isle of Barry in his travels through south Wales. Barry Island – now tied to the mainland by the docks of the Barry Railway Company – held a cave that almost foretold its industrial future: 'there is a narrow chink or chest, to which if you put your ear, you shall perceive such a noise as if Smiths were at work there. For sometimes you hear the blowing of the bellows, at other times the stroaks of the hammers; also the grinding of tools, the hissing noise of steel-gads, of fire burning in furnaces, &c.' For those who suspected the sea of producing the sounds, Gerald attested that they could be heard at any tide, whether the cave was wet or dry.[41] When Lhuyd revised this portion of *Britannia*, he denounced the story and produced an account from John Williams to explain how the sea and tides indeed produced the range of sounds.[42] In doing so, Lhuyd made good on Plot's old determination to uncover this mysterious island, emitting sounds fit for the 'Shop of Cyclops'.[43]

Camden relied on and engaged with Gerald's *Journey* in his description of Pembroke. He began with Gerald's topographic summary and added an appropriately patriotic note to the description of Milford Haven, reminiscent of Owen's: 'Nor is this Haven more celebrated for these advantages than for Henry the Seventh of happy memory landing here; who from this place gave England (at that time languishing with Civil Wars) the Signal of good hopes.' Gerald's own family hailed from Pembroke and he was one with 'those nobles Families in Ireland call'd Giralds, Giraldines, and Fitz-Giralds' by whom 'not only the Martitime parts of South-Wales were retain'd by the English, but also the Walls of Ireland reduced'. Camden also excerpted Gerald's account of the petrified tree trunks exposed by the great storm in Henry II's day, thinking it just possible that their burial might well date to the Deluge.[44]

There is a nice sense of the passage of years between the two travellers when it comes to the Flemish presence in Pembroke. Camden is very much in command of the story, expanding it, and, at times, refusing to bow to Gerald's account. The Flemings arrived thanks to the invitation of Henry I, 'when as the Sea, making breaches in their fences, had drown'd a considerable part of the Low-Countreys'. Camden contradicted the *Cronica Walliae*, reporting that they in fact spoke 'a language so agreeable with the English (which indeed has much affinity with Dutch) that this small Country of theirs is call'd by the Britains Little England beyond Wales'. Having brought the Flemings culturally and politically

[41] Camden, *Britannia* (1695), p. 611; Gerald, *Journey*, p. 125.

[42] Camden, *Britannia* (1695), pp. 616–17; Frank Emery, 'Edward Lhuyd and Some of His Glamorgan Correspondents: A View of Gower in the 1690s', *Transactions of the Honourable Society of Cymmrodorion* (1965), p. 65.

[43] *Itinerary of John Leland*, II, p. 108.

[44] Camden, *Britannia* (1695), pp. 629–30.

within the Tudor *imperium*, Camden allowed Gerald's description of their stout resolution, readiness to labour, and reputation as soothsayers, and inveterate conflicts with the Welsh. There is no doubt that Camden's sympathies lay with the Flemings, though:

> Moreover, the Flemings-way [road], which was a work of theirs (as they are a Nation exceeding industrious,) is seen here extended through a long tract of ground. The Welsh endeavouring to regain their old country, have often set upon these Flemings with all their power, and have ravag'd and spoil'd their borders; but they always with a ready courage defended their lives, their fortunes, and reputation.[45]

In Camden's telling, the Flemings were industrious people who had suffered at the hands of the Welsh. He called on William of Malmesbury's *Chronicle* to justify Henry I's use of the Flemings to vanquish the rebellion-prone Welsh and 'abate their pride' through colonization.[46] Camden silenced Welsh resistance, but Lhuyd answered back across the decades. He used Powel's edition of the *Cronica Walliae* to dismiss Camden's exaggerated account of the beleaguered Flemings who faced the wrath of the whole Welsh nation. Lhuyd knew well enough – he had read Gerald, too – that the Welsh seldom put aside local differences long enough to discover such unity of purpose.[47]

Caernarvonshire, home to the 'British Alps' of Snowdonia, left Camden searching for the proper ethno-topographical descriptions. Nature had raised the inner parts 'as if she would condense here within the bowels of the earth, the frame of this island' and 'made a most safe retiring place for the Britains in time of war'. Nonetheless, in what seems to be an un-credited borrowing from Gerald's *Journey*, Camden recounted the 'common saying among the Welsh, That the mountains of Eryreu would, in case of necessity, afford pasture enough for al the cattel in Wales.' As for Gerald's account of the two lakes atop Snowdon, with the wandering island and left-eyed fish, Camden refused to say more 'lest I might seem to countenance fables'. That said, Camden did not doubt the existence of the lakes, given the account of Gervase of Tilbury. Tilbury added his own peculiar spin on Snowdonia and its people, describing a springy boggy landscape across which the Welsh, 'by their agility', positively skipped and bounded in defiance of their enemies.[48]

It should be obvious that Camden had never travelled to Snowdonia and had no personal experience of its people. This perhaps explains what might be one of his most esoteric bits of archival digging. Camden turned to John of Salisbury's *Policraticus* (1159), who 'new-coin'd' the label 'Nivi-collini Britones' for the 'Snowdon-Britains' that stormed out of their hilltop and forest retreats to seize the lowlands. They vanquished, in John's phrase, 'our youth ... born to

[45] Camden, *Britannia* (1695), p. 631.
[46] Camden, *Britannia* (1695), pp. 630–1; Gerald, *Journey*, 141–2.
[47] Camden, *Britannia* (1695), p. 635.
[48] Camden, *Britannia* (1695), pp. 663–4.

consume the fruits of the earth, sleeping in daylight, postponing honourable duties for whoremongering', and the like.[49] Camden left Snowdon and its people with that moral trope and called on his readers to 'let us now descend from the mountains to the plains'. An approving account of the conquest and settlement of the coastal plain followed, including praise for the 'civility of the inhabitants' of Caernarvon proper, before Camden moved on to Anglesey.[50]

Mona, 'now Anglesey; which signifies the English-Island' was renowned, as Camden knew from Gerald, as the granary capable of feeding all Wales. Camden identified Holyhead and the western cape as a contact zone between Wales and Ireland, a 'common passage' for civilians and invaders alike as well as a place for migration and cultural exchange. With a hint of the period's prejudice, Camden reported that in late Roman times:

> some of the Irish Nation crept into this Island. For besides certain intrench'd Banks, which they call Irish Cottages; here is another place well known by the name of *Yn hericy Gwidil* [Irish stones], from some Irish, who under the conduct of one Sirigi, overcame the Britains there, as we read in the Book of Triades.[51]

Anglesey was one part of Wales that Lhuyd evidently did not reach during his whirlwind tour. He relied on his 'ingenious Friend', Rector John Davies of Newburgh, for additional details. Even so, Lhuyd would have none of this. He faulted Camden's linguistic skill and judgement: 'But I think we may not safely conclude from that name, either that the Irish had any settlement in these parts, or that there was any memorable action here betwixt that Nation and the Britains.' The Irish stones might be nothing more than grave markers and Lhuyd's own view of the Irish cottages made them out to be just 'some vast rude stones laid together in a circular order ... so ill shaped, that we cannot suppose them the foundations of any higher building: and as they are they afford no higher shelter or other conveniency for Inhabitants'.[52]

One senses that these were the moments when Camden's material, experiences, and contacts became inadequate to the task. He had much to say about Brecknock, Monmouth, Glamorgan, and Pembroke, but the rest pale by comparison. In some cases, Gerald simply offered him less guidance. Yet there was more to it than that. At no point did Camden draw explicitly on the *Description* rather than on Gerald's *Journey* and its ethnography. Camden may have reprinted Powel's 1584 edition of Gerald's works verbatim, but the only references to Powel's edition in *Britannia* are those in the additions by Lhuyd in 1695. Lhuyd's additions to Carmarthen, Cardigan, Montgomery, Caernarvon, Anglesey, Flintshire, even Glamorgan, all equalled or surpassed Camden's

---

[49] Camden, *Britannia* (1695), p. 664; John of Salisbury, *Policraticus*, ed. and trans. Cary J. Nederman (Cambridge, 1990), p. 113.

[50] Camden, *Britannia* (1695), pp. 664-6.

[51] Camden, *Britannia* (1695), pp. 664-6, 674-5.

[52] Camden, *Britannia* (1695), pp. 675, 677.

original. We know that Camden travelled to Wales, but no one reading *Britannia* – or the additions to the 1695 edition – would be convinced he that covered ground the way that Gerald or Leland had before him or Lhuyd later did.

Wales in Lhuyd's *Britannia*

Outside the well-travelled coastal lowlands of South Wales or the northern borders around Flintshire, Lhuyd had a lot of work to do to bring *Britannia* up to date. Lhuyd knew he was expected to check Camden's text and direct readers to specific additions using a system of endnotes. Beyond that, 'I knew not how far I might enlarge,' he wrote Gibson. Lhuyd felt that Gibson could have given him better guidance:

> I find upon perusal of Cornwall and those other Counties you have lately sent me, that the additional Notes on the English Counties are much more compleat than these, and somewhat in a different method. But my task was too large to be well perform'd by one hand, except more time had been allow'd. And having receiv'd no pattern for imitation, but only some general Instructions.[53]

Swalle, Churchill, and Gibson did not appreciate that what one scholar-traveller could accomplish with a single English county presented an enormous task for Lhuyd and his local collaborators.

Lhuyd called on an impressive, engaged network that included Robert Humphreys and Davies (Anglesey), Griffith Jones and Lloyd (Denbighshire), Mostyn (Flintshire), John Williams (Gower), Maurice Jones (Merioneth), and Alexander Forde, William Gambold, and Roberts (Pembrokeshire and Carmarthenshire).[54] Roberts received Lhuyd's exhaustive request for information and astutely realized that 'to answer all of them "would swell to a volume for each County"'.[55] Lhuyd limited the additions to only a fraction of Roberts's six folios of material.[56] He sensibly reconciled the abundance of material with the limits of the project: 'And whereas in some Counties I had Notes to add which did not refer at all to any part of the Text; I have inserted them after the Associations, with this mark ¶ prefixed. What I have added are generally observations of my own; and where they are not so, I have taken care to inform the Reader.'[57] Lhuyd's solution reflects how much he might have done with more time, and had he written without fear of what the booksellers would do with his material. To be fair, though, Lhuyd's willingness to take on the whole of Wales

[53] Camden, *Britannia* (1695), pp. 583–4.
[54] Emery and Walters, 'Edward Lhuyd', pp. 134–7; Frank Emery, 'A New Reply to Lhuyd's *Parochial Queries* (1696): Puncheston, Pembrokeshire', *National Library of Wales Journal* 10.4 (1958), p. 395.
[55] Emery, 'Edward Lhwyd and the 1695 *Britannia*', p. 180.
[56] Emery, 'Edward Lhwyd and the 1695 *Britannia*', p. 181.
[57] Camden, *Britannia* (1695), pp. 583–4.

had not been fully considered, if the pressures on informants to supply information and run-ins with Gibson over the production schedule are any indication.[58]

If we journey south-west with Lhuyd from his native Shropshire into
Radnorshire we can begin to appreciate the value of his personal encounters
with Wales and the Welsh. Lhuyd's additions explored the relationship of
certain peoples to the land. Attuned to natural history, Lhuyd explained cairns
and betrayed a talent for physical description:

> [Heaps of stones] are common upon mountains, in most (if not all) Counties of Wales,
> and are call'd in South-wales Karnen, and in North-wales Karned-heu. They consist
> of any such lesser stones from a pound weight to a hundred &c. ... confusedly piled
> up without any further trouble than the bringing them thither, and the throwing of
> them in heaps. On Plin Lhimmon mountain, and some other places, there are of these
> Karnedheu so considerably big, that they may be supposed to consist of no less than a
> hundred Cartloads of stones; but generally considered they are much less.[59]

The ethno-cultural meaning of these stone heaps was just as important as
their physical features.[60] They were not simply a Welsh phenomena, they 'are
also found in the North, and probably other parts of England; and are frequent
in Scotland and Ireland, being call'd by the same British name of kairn'. His
own observations seemed to confirm the common belief that these peoples
had built cairns as memorials to the dead, 'for that I have my self observed
near the summit of one of them, a rude stone monument (which I shall have
occasion to prove Sepulchral hereafter) somewhat of the form of a large Coffer
or Chest'. What removed all doubt from Lhuyd's mind was the on-going custom
in certain places to 'cast heaps of stones on the Graves of Malefactors and Self-
murderers'. Thus the Welsh called the worst traitors 'Karn-Vradwyr' and 'the
most notorious Thieves Karn-Lhadron'. Lhuyd even found the tradition among
the Romans, but concluded that it was of native origin because it was 'common
also in the Highlands of Scotland, and in Ireland, where their Conquests never
reach'd'. Christianity decisively affected this British cultural tradition, though.
These peoples had originally built cairns in memory of the best among them but
Christianity had turned an act of reverence into superstition and cairns into a
curse for malefactors.[61]

Camden repeated a local tradition that Brecknockmere – the lake with
the roaring ice – actually covered a city that has been swallowed up during an
earthquake. Working in the 1650s, John Aubrey recorded an account of the
legend from his kinsman Henry Vaughan and Thomas Williams. They reported
visible ruins in the form of squared stones and paved streets seen from a boat.

---

[58] Walters and Emery, 'Edward Lhuyd', pp. 114–15.
[59] Camden, *Britannia* (1695), p. 588. Gibson's editorial intervention with Lhuyd's text is
discussed in Walters and Emery, 'Camden's *Britannia*, 1695', pp. 117–32.
[60] Camden, *Britannia* (1695), p. 653
[61] Camden, *Britannia* (1695), p. 588.

They also cited Ptolemy's *Geographia* and the 'Antonine Itinerary'.[62] Lhuyd and Aubrey would collaborate throughout the 1690s on antiquities, folklore, and customs, but not over this story. 'All which I suspect as fabulous,' the naturalist in Lhuyd doubted upon reviewing Camden, 'and not worth any further notice, than as one of those erroneous traditions of the Vulgar, from which few (if any) Nations are exempted' and 'since no Histories inform us that any part of Britain was ever sensible of such calamities; I see no reason we have to regard these oral traditions.'[63]

Acceptable proof in the form of empirical evidence or recorded history nicely fits with the Lhuyd who would one day set Thomas Browne's *Pseudodoxia Epidemica* as a guide for debunking local traditions.[64] In it he explored the human capacity to believe nonsense and debunked commonly held beliefs across a vast range of topics, including mandrake roots that took the shape of humans, supposed truths received from the Bible, prejudicial stereotypes like the stench of Jews, and assumptions about 'blackness'.[65] The popular *Pseudodoxia* should provide travellers and scholars with a handy, standardized framework of folk beliefs to explore in their localities. Here was an empirical approach to cataloguing Welsh folk beliefs and assessing their superstition in an almost quantifiable manner.

Arriving in Glamorganshire, Lhuyd supplemented one of Camden's local informants, Mr J. Sanford. Lhuyd thought Kaerphyli rather more impressive than Sanford's report allowed, especially as a monument of Welsh or British antiquity: 'Kaerphyli-castle, probably the noblest ruins of ancient Architecture now remaining in Britain. For in the judgment of some curious persons, who have seen and compared it with the most noted Castles of England, it exceeds all in bigness, except that of Windsor.'[66] Lhuyd precisely detailed great chimneys, triangular pillars atop busts of men and women, and stately windows. He suggested that readers might judge 'whether this room was once a Chapel or Hall, &c. and also in some measure judge of the Antiquity of the place'. Lhuyd accepted the possibility that the ruin was Roman, as Camden reported, but its grandness might not be sufficient argument, considering that no other Roman artefacts had been found. Indeed, the only two coins found in the vicinity, one he received from the Aubrey and one purchased by Lhuyd himself, were neither Roman nor English, 'and therefore probably Welsh'.[67]

Before leaving Glamorganshire, Lhuyd decoded two standing stones near Margan abbey noted by Camden. He described the 'old British carving' that

[62] John Aubrey, *Monumenta Britannica or A Miscellany of British Antiquities [Parts One and Two]*, ed. John Fowles and Rodney Legg (Boston, 1980/81), p. 482.
[63] Camden, *Britannia* (1695), pp. 590, 592.
[64] Edward Lhwyd, *Parochial Queries* (WING L1947; Oxford, 1697), p. 2.
[65] Thomas Browne, *Pseudodoxia Epidemica, or, Enquiries into Very Many Received Tenents and Commonly Presumed Truths* (WING B5165; London, 1672).
[66] Camden, *Britannia* (1695), p. 613.
[67] Camden, *Britannia* (1695), pp. 610, 614-15; *Life and Letters of Edward Lhwyd*, pp. 206-7.

19 'The Great Hall of Caerphilly Castle, Glamorganshire' engraved by John Preston Neale (1814). Reproduced by permission of the Llyfrgell Genedlaethol Cymru/The National Library of Wales.

adorned the first and particularly noted a 'furrow or Canaliculus' down one side from top to bottom. Once again, a connection to peoples elsewhere in Britain suggested itself:

> [In] a Letter from the very learned and ingenious Dr James Garden of Aberdeen, to Mr J. Aubrey R.S.S. I found the Doctor had observ'd that amongst their circular stone-monuments in Scotland (such as that at Rolrich &c. in England) sometimes a stone or two is found with a cavity at on the top of it, capable of a pint or two of liquor; and such a Groove or small chink as this I mention ... [68]

Garden thought those stones might be used for the 'Libamina or liquid sacrifices' of the Druids. Because the Margan stone featured elaborate decoration, in contrast to the stones typically identified with the Druids, Lhuyd doubted that it had served such a purpose.[69]

Lhuyd tackled even the most esoteric details, thanks to his expertise and that of his local informants. He reported the discovery of an ancient golden torque found in a garden near Harlech castle in 1692 courtesy of Mostyn, and offered a long discussion of the prevalence of torques among the Britons. Aubrey had

[68] Camden, *Britannia* (1695), p. 618.
[69] Camden, *Britannia* (1695), p. 618.

already reported the find in his 'Monumenta Britannica', still unpublished, ironically, thanks to Gibson's *Britannia* exhausting the subscriber networks.[70] Current events also offered him the opportunity to describe a fiery phenomenon like a meteor shower that had consumed the corn, hay, and grass near Harlech and killed many cattle, sheep, horses, and goats. Both reports came by way of local informants, and Lhuyd's prolonged efforts to explain the fiery pestilence eventually involved him, Lister, Mostyn, and Lloyd in a debate about locusts and their toxic remains.[71] Having completed the additions, he hoped that Lloyd would accept the decision to leave in the unresolved account of 'ye prodigious fire ... for I was unwilling to omit wholy so strange and unaccountable a phœnomenon'.[72]

Lhuyd's labours came into their own in counties like Pembroke, Merioneth, and Caernarvonshire that Camden had not visited. Tipped off by John Lloyd, Lhuyd gained access to Owen's *Description* in manuscript via Hywel Vaughan.[73] Owen may have shared information with Camden, but his generosity evidently ended at sharing the actual *Description*. Thanks to it and an informant in Pembroke, Lhuyd added a discussion of round stone monuments that went by various names during his travels in Wales, including 'y Gromlech', 'Kromlecheu', and 'Kromlech'. He agreed that they were scenes of burials and idolatrous worship before Christianity, a phenomenon that flourished in the pagan Isles: 'we shall have little reason to doubt but that our Kromlech, as well as all other such circular Stone-monuments in Britain and Ireland (whereof I presume there are not less than 100 yet remaining) were also erected for the same use'.[74]

Once again James Garden enabled Lhuyd to connect the cultural traditions of Wales and Scotland across national boundaries:

I find that in several parts of that Kingdom [Scotland], they are call'd Chapels and Temples ... and did belong to the Drounich. Which word some interpret the Picts; but the Dr. suspects it might denote originally the Druids: in confirmation whereof I add, that a village in Anglesey is call'd Tre'r Driw, and interpreted the Town of the Druid.[75]

Lhuyd scoffed at those who imagined that the Danes had built the sites as seats of justice or for the election of kings. Here Lhuyd joined an existing conversation between Aubrey and Garden about bards and Druidical temples that lasted from 1692 to 1694.[76] Lhuyd thought them unlikely to be the work of 'such roving Pirats' rather than a settled population. More interesting, the

[70] Aubrey, *Monumenta Britannica*, p. 592; Michael Hunter, *John Aubrey and the Realm of Learning* (New York, 1975), p. 89, n. 8.
[71] *Life and Letters of Edward Lhuyd*, pp. 211, 218–25, 227–8, 233.
[72] *Life and Letters of Edward Lhuyd*, p. 243.
[73] *Life and Letters of Edward Lhuyd*, p. 199.
[74] Camden, *Britannia* (1695), p. 636.
[75] Camden, *Britannia* (1695), pp. 636–7.
[76] *The Occult Laboratory: Magic, Science and Second Sight in Late Seventeenth-Century Scotland, A New Edition of Robert Kirk's* The Secret Commonwealth *and others texts*, ed. Michael Hunter (Woodbridge, 2001), pp. 118–52, hereafter cited as *Occult Laboratory*.

history of migration and settlement was Lhuyd's chief argument against those claims, 'they'l want History to prove, that ever the Danes had any Dominion, or indeed the least Settlement in Wales or the High-lands of Scotland; where yet such Monuments are as frequent, if not more common, than in other places of Britain'.[77] Here he supported Garden's view (for Aubrey) 'that albeit the Danes made sundry descents into Scotland, yet they never had footing in it, much less were they master of it ... to make it probable that they were the builders of so many monuments dispersed over all the country'.[78] Any resemblance to Danish sites only testified to the kind of cultural diffusion associated with any religious belief system. Lhuyd had no doubt that one would find similar circles in remote parts of France, Spain, or Germany for that reason.[79]

Undoubtedly Lhuyd could have written much more about the natural history of Wales than either his remit from Gibson or the ordinary pattern of Camden's original allowed.[80] For Merioneth, Gerald provided the topographic description that made it the 'roughest and most unpleasant County of all Wales'. However, it was Camden who provided the corresponding ethnography that put its inhabitants in the company of other upland or highland peoples:

> The inhabitants, who apply themselves wholly to the breeding of cattel, and who feed on milke-meats, viz. butter, cheese, &c. ... are scarce inferior to any people of Britain, in stature, clear complexion, comeliness, and due proportion of limbs; but have an ill character amongst their neighbours for Incontinency [uncontrolled passions] and Idleness.[81]

There was no obvious reason for Lhuyd to supplement this discussion, but his naturalist interests prodded him. He disagreed sharply with Gerald's and Camden's characterization and fairly demanded that *Britannia*'s readers reconsider an unthinking view of the Welsh highlands:

> [It] may be answer'd (if that be worth notice) that for the pleasing prospect of a Country there is hardly any standard; most men taking their measures herein, either from the place of their own nativity and education, or from the profit they suppose a Country may yield. But if (as some hold) variety of objects makes a Country appear delightful, this may content with most; as affording (besides a sea-prospect) not only exceeding high mountains, and inaccessible rocks; with an incredible number of rivers, cataracts, and lakes: but also variety of lower hills, woods, and plains, and some fruitful valleys.[82]

Here was a prosaic echo of Churchyard at a time when the appreciation of topographical diversity and scenic beauty was beginning to take hold. More significantly, Lhuyd noted the contingent, constructed quality of aesthetic and

---

[77] Camden, *Britannia* (1695), p. 637.
[78] *Occult Laboratory*, p. 152.
[79] Camden, *Britannia* (1695), p. 637.
[80] Camden, *Britannia* (1695), pp. 638–42.
[81] Camden, *Britannia* (1695), p. 655.
[82] Camden, *Britannia* (1695), p. 657.

cultural sensibilities, seeing them as products of locale, learning, self-interest, or the like.

Lhuyd positively celebrated these Cambrian highlands for their fertility, beauty, and magnificence:

> These maintain innumerable herds of cattle, sheep, and goats; and are (in regard they are frequently fed with clouds and rains, and harbour much snow) considerably more fertil (though the grass be coarse) than the hills and ridges of lower Countries. Kader Idris is probably one of the highest mountains in Britain; and (which is one certain argument of it's height) it affords some variety of Alpine plants ... [83]

Lhuyd did take issue with Gerald's romantic image of Welshmen able to speak with one another between nearby mountaintops: 'I presume there are none such in nature: and am certain there are not any in Wales.' Yet in the context of *Britannia* and the use of Gerald's ethnography all of this implicitly called into question cultural assumptions associated with landscape, livelihoods, and distinctions of highland and lowland. Perhaps too there was something pointed in Lhuyd's association of the Welsh Dôl 'with the English Dale, so common in the North of England and Scotland'.[84]

Caernarvonshire allowed Lhuyd to be positively expansive. Indeed, so cursory was Camden's original account, not two full folio pages, that Lhuyd's five endnotes alone exploded into something twice that length. He took Camden's reference to the British Alps of Snowdon and ran with it, naming the different peaks, expanding the topographical description of individual mountaintops, and bringing in botanical and ichthyological insights from John Ray. Of Gerald's and Camden's two magical lakes, Lhuyd reported first-hand that one was actually a small pond with a little green patch near the bank that passed for the wandering island; the second contained plenty of trout and eels, but none of a monocular variety. Lhuyd uncovered a fascinating titbit that hinted at the locals' own origin folklore: 'I observ'd that the Inhabitants of these Mountains call any low Country Hendrev, which signifies the ancient habitation.' He accepted less readily their belief 'that the Irish were the ancient Proprietors of their Country' as well as Radnorshire and Brecknock. He could not fail to describe the Deluge-shells, as the ordinary Welsh named the black mussels 'peculiar to rapid and stony rivers ... common in Wales, in the North of England and Scotland, and some part of Ireland', that produced a slightly distorted variety of pearls.[85]

Camden found different qualities in the Welsh of Denbighshire as compared to those in Merioneth, perhaps because he had travelled personally into the county. The western portion was a thinly populated upland of bare and craggy hills, but 'the diligence and industry of the husbandmen hath long since begun to conquer the barrenness of the land on the sides of these mountains, as well

---

[83] Camden, *Britannia* (1695), p. 657.
[84] Camden, *Britannia* (1695), p. 657.
[85] Camden, *Britannia* (1695), pp. 667–74.

as other places of Wales'. The local Welsh cut the turf, dried and burned the clods, and fertilized the fields with the ashes. For Camden it was 'scarce credible' the quantities of rye they produced with this 'ancient' technique. In the Vale of Clwyd, Camden found the 'green meadows, the corn-fields, and the numerous villages and Churches ... afford us the most pleasant prospect imaginable'. The people were one with their location: 'the complexion of the inhabitants bright and chearful; their heads of a sound constitution; their sight very lively, and even their old age vigorous and lasting'. Denbigh was no Eden, though. Bleak mountains rimmed the valley to the east and the land had once suffered mightily, thanks to Welsh infighting and Anglo-Norman invasions, before Henry VIII created it as a county proper under the Union.[86]

Lhuyd left alone Camden's descriptions of the Welsh, preferring instead to concentrate, again, on the Druids, a fascination among contemporaries like Aubrey and Thomas Tanner (at work for Gibson on Wiltshire).[87] Lhuyd expanded Camden's discussion of the 'place call'd Kerig y Drudion, or Druid-stones' and debated the etymology of the word in relation to his own linguistic studies and the first-hand description of the place by a local informant. He weighed the evidence and agreed with the Druid connection, but the discussion 'put me in mind of a certain relique of their Doctrine, I have lately observ'd to be yet retain'd amongst the vulgar'. Lhuyd lamented the widespread persistence of erroneous and ridiculous opinions among the commoners, referring to Browne's *Pseudodoxia* for proof that superstition of all sorts was alive and well in Britain.[88] In this case, Lhuyd may have had cause for dismay:

> In most parts of Wales we find it a common opinion of the vulgar, that about Midsummer-Eve (tho' in the time they do not all agree) 'tis usual for snakes to meet in companies, and that by joyning heads together and hissing, a kind of Bubble is form'd like a ring about the head of one of them, which the rest by continual hissing blow on till it comes off at the tail, and then it immediately hardens, and resembles a glass ring; which whoever finds (as some old women and children are perswaded) shall prosper in all his undertakings.[89]

According to Lhuyd, glass beads or snake-stones were once used among the Druids, but he doubted whether these beads were they. The uncertainty drove Lhuyd in search of a definitive explanation during the rest of his travels.[90]

Camden gave a strong flavour of English imperialism to his account of the small, oblong border county of Flintshire. The area around Holywell, 'because it affords the most pleasant prospect, and was long since reduced by the English,

---

[86] Camden, *Britannia* (1695), pp. 679–82.
[87] Ronald Hutton, *Blood and Mistletoe: The History of the Druids in Britain* (New Haven, 2009), pp. 65–85.
[88] Camden, *Britannia* (1695), pp. 682–3.
[89] Camden, *Britannia* (1695), p. 683.
[90] *Life and Letters of Edward Lhuyd*, pp. 424, 430, 464.

was call'd by the Britains Teg-Eingl, which signifies Fair England'. When Henry II invaded this 'Fair England', Camden put his defeat at Cole-hill down to disorder in the ranks, a far cry from Gerald's account of a decisive Welsh victory or the bloody reprisals taken by the Welsh against Henry's forces when he sent raiding parties to Anglesey.[91] Camden took an unusual interest in Norman–Angevin imperialism in this account. The earls of Chester 'by light skirmishes with the Welsh as occasion and opportunity offer'd, were the first Normans that subdued this Country'. Kings of England consequently added the earldom of Chester to their crown for the dignity of the eldest son and vital strategic reasons: 'King Edward I. supposing it very advantageous, as well to maintain his own, as to bridle the Welsh; kept this and all the maritim parts of Wales in his own hands; and distributed the inland counties to his Nobles.' This was the work of an Angevin emperor, 'imitating herein the policy of Augustus Caesar, who himself undertook the charge of the outward and most potent Provinces'.[92]

Lhuyd was interested in none of this and his local contacts and travels through Flintshire directed his attention to etymology and place-names as well as natural history. He was particularly interested in the remains of leaves and shells found in coal pits and other locations. How to reconcile their type and structure with those commonly found in Britain brought Lhuyd into debates over the dispersal of plant and animal remains by the biblical flood.[93] He could not judge the matter based on his own findings and referred readers to a forthcoming 'Treatise of the origin of form'd Stones and other Fossils, from an ingenious person'. Finally, Lhuyd added an analysis of two pillars, thanks to the fieldwork and drawings of Richard Mostyn.[94] Just who had erected the monuments was an open question. Some of the symbols agreed with drawings of similar pillars in Plot's *Natural History of Staffordshire*. Lhuyd's old mentor concluded that the Danes had built the monuments, especially because of similarities to pillars with Runic inscriptions in Cumberland. However, the characters on Lhuyd's seemed 'nothing like the Runic'. The inscriptions were a mystery to Lhuyd, as was the monument's relation, if any, to a nearby barrow and the skulls and carcasses found there.[95]

Lhuyd turned a searching gaze on St Winifred's shrine at Holywell. He suggested that the powerful stream came not from a spring but from the work of miners who had diverted a 'subterraneous rivulet' as part of their common practice; the muddy, bluish quality of the water after a heavy rain seemed only to confirm the idea. Further, Lhuyd speculated that the miners had created

[91] Camden, *Britannia* (1695), pp. 688–9; Gerald, *Journey*, 189.

[92] Camden, *Britannia* (1695), p. 690.

[93] *Life and Letters of Edward Lhuyd*, pp. 381–98; Alexandra Walsham, *The Reformation of the Landscape: Religion, Identity, and Memory in Early Modern Britain and Ireland* (Oxford, 2011), pp. 376–9.

[94] *Life and Letters of Edward Lhuyd*, pp. 226, 230.

[95] Camden, *Britannia* (1695), pp. 689–94.

20   Detail from 'Flintshire' from John Speed, *Theatre of the Empire of Great Britain* (London, 1676). RB 204587 Huntington Library, San Marino, CA, reproduced by permission. Image produced by ProQuest as part of *Early English Books Online*. www. proquest.com

the rushing 'spring' long after Gerald's visit and that it had not then been a pilgrimage site or place of miraculous cures. 'For seeing we find that Author throughout the whole course of his Journey, was particularly curious and inquisitive about miraculous fountains, stones, bells, chains, &c.', why had Gerald provided no account of it, especially since he had lodged within a half a mile of the place? Writing to Mostyn while preparing his additions, Lhuyd took for granted 'that superstition and ignorance first gain'd them that reputation; which prejudice and bigotry has ever since maintain'd'.[96] He was somewhat less outspoken in *Britannia*, agreeing with Powel that St Winifred's miraculous well was the subsequent creation of monks. Camden originally noted the existence of St Winifred's well, its celebrated status, and the power of the stream, but nothing of its mystical or miraculous reputation. Camden found a fitting way to write popish or monkish superstition out of the story. By contrast, an empirical sense of truth drove Lhuyd to explain its natural properties. Both Camden and Lhuyd rejected the well's superstitious past, but did so from perspectives very much in keeping with their own times.[97]

Lhuyd's contribution to Gibson's *Britannia* ended with three appendices. He included a brief summary of the princes of Wales, beginning with Edward I's time, referring readers to the existing Welsh annals for the many generations of earlier princes. He then offered readers a handy plate illustrating twenty-nine different artefacts found in his travels, including pillars atop Mostyn, columns in Kaerphyli castle, and several fossilized leaves taken from the Neath coal pit in Glamorganshire. Finally, and quite appropriately, Lhuyd ended with a list of rare plants found in Wales.[98]

Lhuyd brought two sorts of additions to *Britannia*: material directly related to Camden's topics and first-hand observations that went beyond them. Lhuyd sometimes corrected or admonished Camden, but he principally offered readers new finds and expanded knowledge in the spirit of the original.[99] Having heard of one man who 'rails ag[ain]st Mr. Camdem with a great deal of Freedom', Lhuyd explained his own respect for Camden and the original *Britannia*: 'I look upon Mr. Camden to have been one of the most learned, judicious, and ingenious writers in his kind that ever England or perhaps any other countrey has produc'd; and therefore we must for our own credit treat him civilly.' Lhuyd was confident that 'what we can adde or correct, I make no question were he alive, but he would be thankful for it: for he seems to have been a man of very candid temper'.[100]

[96] *Life and Letters of Edward Lhuyd*, p. 232.
[97] Alexandra Walsham, 'Holywell: Contesting Sacred Space in Post-Reformation Wales', in *Sacred Space in Early Modern Europe*, ed. Will Coster and Andrew Spicer (Cambridge, 2005), pp. 211–32.
[98] Camden, *Britannia* (1695), pp. 699–702.
[99] Camden, *Britannia* (1695), pp. 603–10, 642–5.
[100] *Life and Letters of Edward Lhuyd*, p. 201.

Further travels through multicultural Britain

When he put the finishing touches to the Welsh additions, Lhuyd had bigger plans in mind. He wrote to Lister that if 'I gain any credit by this: its not unlikely but our gentry may be hereafter willing to encourage something more considerable'.[101] Gentry in Glamorganshire offered Lhuyd hopes that if 'the like encouragement would be allow'd from each county, I could very willingly spend the remainder of my days in that employment'.[102] But just what lifetime employment did Lhuyd have in mind? By May 1695 he was well on the way to developing this new project and he left us the outline in his *Design of a British Dictionary, Historical and Geographical; With an Essay, Entituled, Archaeologia Britannica: and a Natural History of Wales*.[103] Lhuyd's plans tell us much about how he thought Wales' story needed retelling and the determination to expand beyond the limitations of Camden's design in doing do.

The *Design of a British Dictionary* described three books. The first, Lhuyd's *Historical and Geographical Dictionary*, essentially combined the interest of Leland and Bale in 'all Persons memorable in the British History', the analysis of place-names, and a Camdenesque description of Wales itself.[104] The second book, *Archaeologia Britannica*, focussed on classical Britain and the Britons in four respects. First, Lhuyd proposed a comparison 'of the Modern Welsh with other European languages; more especially with Greek, Latin, Irish, Cornish, and American'. Lhuyd had caught the language bug around 1690, particularly after working with Ray.[105] Ray's linguistic studies were well known from his two books of English proverbs and his *Collection of English Words Not Generally Used*, an etymology that he divided on crude ethno-linguistic lines into two alphabetical catalogues 'as are proper to the northern, the other to the southern counties'.[106] Lhuyd brought a Welsh dimension to Ray's second edition, supplying him with a list of 'British Words parallel to some of the Northern Words in this Collection, from which probably the Northern Words may be derived'.[107] Cultural comparisons were not to be limited to linguistics, though. His second subject was to be a 'Comparison of the Customs and Traditions of the Britans, with those of other Nations'.[108] We can well imagine that Lhuyd would have produced something like Moryson's comparative ethnography, in this case designed to draw contrasts

---

[101] *Life and Letters of Edward Lhuyd*, pp. 239, 249.
[102] *Life and Letters of Edward Lhuyd*, pp. 269–70.
[103] Edward Lhwyd, *A Design of a British Dictionary* (WING L1944B; London, 1695); *Life and Letters of Edward Lhuyd*, pp. 269, 285–6, 291, 293, 298–9.
[104] Lhwyd, *Design for a British Dictionary*, p. 1.
[105] Roberts, 'Edward Lhuyd'.
[106] John Ray, *A Collection of English Proverbs* (WING R386; Cambridge, 1670); Ray, *A Collection of English Proverbs* (WING R387; Cambridge, 1678); Ray, *A Collection of English Words Not Generally Used* (WING R388; London, 1674).
[107] John Ray, *A Collection of Words Not Generally Used* (WING R389: London, 1691), sig. A6r.
[108] Lhwyd, *Design for a British Dictionary*, p. 2.

with and argue for continuities between the Britons and their European cousins. Other proposed sections testified to the continuing vitality of those subjects that most animated Camden and his readers: separate descriptions of the artefacts of British and Roman antiquity in Wales, from monuments and tombs to camps, coins, amulets, and fragments.[109]

Lhuyd proposed a third book, a detailed *Natural History* specific to Wales. He would use the classificatory framework of John Ray's *Synopsis* as a template for some observations, but the subjects ranged widely:

> A General Description of the Country, in respect of its Situation, and Quality of Soyl ... Meteors ... Comparative Tables of the Weather ... Also of the Sea, Rivers, Lakes, Springs, and Mineral Waters ... Description of the various sorts of Earths, Stones, and all Mineral Bodies ... Form'd Stones ... Of Plants: wherein we shall only take Notice of such as grow spontaneously in Wales, and have been rarely, or not at all, observ'd elsewhere in this Island: adding a Catalogue of such as are found in England, or Scotland, and have not been observ'd in Wales ... of Animals, in the same Method.[110]

This would hardly be a 'diversion' for Lhuyd's readers. As much as their labours provided certain intellectual starting points for Lhuyd's other projects, there are few hints in the works of Leland, Bale, Camden, or Moryson that the *Natural History* would be the essential final piece.

Lhuyd concluded that this scheme seemed 'most likely to find Acceptance amongst the Learned and Ingenious'.[111] In all this, Lhuyd called on the Welsh gentry, the great beneficiaries of political union, to assume the role once played by monasteries, bards and minstrels, and genealogical manuscripts in creating, nurturing, and preserving Welsh cultural life.[112] One reader of the *Design* thought the *Dictionary* and *Archaeologia* would be a lasting monument to Lhuyd and Wales: 'We shall then, I hope see our Ist planters as naked as they went, wthout ye imaginary dresse of mere art or fancy: then we shal see old citys & villages rise up from their ruines, with their ancient names & the etymologys of 'em.'[113] However, with so few local studies of Wales, Lhuyd and his fellow enthusiasts may have been ahead of the market, especially among the Welsh gentry asked to subscribe and testify their support. He explained to Lloyd that upon 'further consideration I think it more advisable to propose the antiquities of Wales &c. as my main aim and designe, than the Natural History, there being so few in our parts acquainted with this latter; and under the umbrage of that, to collect

[109] Lhwyd, *Design for a British Dictionary*, pp. 1–2.
[110] Lhwyd, *Design for a British Dictionary*, p. 2; *Life and Letters of Edward Lhuyd*, p. 308.
[111] Lhwyd, *Design for a British Dictionary*, p. 2.
[112] Richard Suggett and Eryn White, 'Language, Literacy, and Aspects of Identity in Early Modern Wales', in *The Spoken Word: Oral Culture in Britain, 1500–1800*, ed. Adam Fox and Daniel Woolf (Manchester, 2002), pp. 63–7; Richard Suggett, 'Vagabonds and Minstrels in Sixteenth-century Wales', in *Spoken Word*, pp. 138–72.
[113] *Life and Letters of Edward Lhuyd*, p. 287.

also all the materials I can for a Natural History'.[114] He later rejected the idea of publishing his findings yearly as diaries, a workable idea for a natural history, but 'the generality of subscribers are for the *Dictionary* and *Archaeologia* and very indifferent for the *Natural History*'.[115] Lhuyd accurately pegged his would-be subscribers and readers, even if his publication schedule set them the daunting task of engaging with the comparative study of the Celtic language families as a prelude to the books on customs and antiquities.[116]

Lhuyd explained his interest in comparative linguistics and ethnography in the dedication to the portion of *Archaeologia Britannica* published in 1707. Such a work would lead 'us to a Clearer Notion than we have had hitherto of the most Ancient Languages, and Consequently of the Origin of the First Colonies of these Kingdoms'.[117] Language and ethnography were, for Lhuyd, the keys to explaining Britain as a land crisscrossed and settled by migrants and defined by the cultural exchanges among them, not least exchanges revealed by the empirical, forensic study of words, idioms, place-names, and the like. Lhuyd shared this assumption with Camden. However, Lhuyd's *Design* marked a departure. By focussing on linguistics and ethnography, Lhuyd embraced topics at the forefront of travel and travellers' narratives that had, since Camden's era, acquired their own systematic approach and methods. Lhuyd recognized that Camden and others took 'notice of the Affinity of our British with the Celtic; but there being no Vocabulary extant of the Irish (or Ancient Scottish) they could not collate that Language therewith, which the Curious in these Studies, will now find to agree rather more than ours, with the Gaulish'.[118] Lhuyd defended the time spent travelling and collecting information precisely because meaningful comparative linguistics and ethnography demanded it.[119] Travel would be crucial for Lhuyd's work in a way that it had not been when Camden chronicled the settlement of Britain using classical and medieval sources.

The explosive growth in the study of natural history during the seventeenth century must be the greatest change from the intellectual world of the original *Britannia*. If the Society of Antiquaries defined the cultural context of the original *Britannia*, then the Royal Society and sister institutions like Plot's Philosophical Society devoted to the study of the physical world set the agenda for many of Camden's successors.[120] Lhuyd remarked on this in his additions to *Britannia*,

---

[114] *Life and Letters of Edward Lhwyd*, p. 285.

[115] *Life and Letters of Edward Lhwyd*, p. 299.

[116] Edward Lhwyd, *Archaeologia Britannica: Texts and Translations*, ed. Dewi W. Evans and Brynley F. Roberts (Aberystwyth, 2009), pp. 11–12.

[117] Edward Lhuyd, *Archaeologia Britannica ... Vol I. Glossography* (London, 1707), sig. b1v.

[118] Lhuyd, *Archaeologia Britannica*, sig. b2r.

[119] Edward Lhuyd, *A Compleat Translation of the Welsh Preface to Mr Lhuyd's Glossography, or his Archaeologia Britannica* (London, 1710?), pp. 11–13.

[120] Daniel Carey, 'Compiling Nature's History: Travellers and Travel Narratives in the Early Royal Society', *Annals of Science* 54 (1997), pp. 269–92; R.W. Frantz, *The English Traveller and*

noting that 'our Author confines himself not always to Antiquities and Civil History, but sometimes for the Reader's diversion, takes notice likewise of such occurrences in Natural History, as seem'd more especially remarkable'.[121] Such interests culminated in guides like the Royal Society's laborious and detailed instructions for travellers and observers of natural history, instructions for observing the 'Natives and Strangers' that rendered humanity (and cultural complexity) little more than another form of flora or fauna.[122] Plot included a catalogue of milestones and oddities in the life stages of humans in his study of Staffordshire.[123] For the next hundred years, the successors to Lhuyd, Plot, Sibbald, Aubrey, Boyle – Browne Willis, Richard Gough, Thomas Pennant – would achieve 'the comprehensive approach to parochial study first envisaged by the Baconian initiatives of the mid-seventeenth century, combining both the "curious" and the "useful" and concerned as much with the present as with the past'.[124]

If the *Design* was Lhuyd's standard for a complete description of Wales, there was only one way to achieve it:

> Now in order to the Performance of what is here propos'd, 'twill be necessary to travel Wales, at least four or five Summers; and likewise to make one Journey into Cornwal[l], and another into Ireland, or the Highlands of Scotland, for parallel Observations, as to their Language, their Names of Towns, Rivers, Mountains, &c.[125]

Why did he feel that travel was so necessary? It 'being certain,' he wrote, 'that the want of such actual Surveying, hath been in all Ages the occasion of much Error and Ignorance in Writings of this Nature'.[126] Lhuyd's emphasis on systematic, first-hand empirical examination emphasizes the social and intellectual reaction against casual observation, oral sources, and vulgar or untrained local contacts.[127] Thus he explained the importance of travel for would-be subscribers:

> It's well known, no kind of Writing requires more Expences and Fatigue, than that of Natural History and Antiquities: it being impossible to perform any thing accurately in those Studies without, without much Travelling, and diligent Searching, as well the most desert Rocks and Mountains, as the more frequented Valleys and Plains. The Caves, Mines, and Quarries must be pry'd into, as well as the outward surface of the

---

the *Movement of Ideas* (Lincoln, NE, 1934/1967), pp. 15–71; Mendyk, '*Speculum Britanniae*', pp. 114–35 and 146–69; Walsham, *Reformation of the Landscape*, pp. 357–76.
[121] Camden, *Britannia* (1695), p. 639.
[122] Robert Boyle, *General Heads for the Natural History of a Country, Great or Small; Drawn for the Use of Travellers and Navigators* (WING B3980; London, 1692), pp. 7–12.
[123] Mendyk, '*Speculum Britanniae*', p. 203.
[124] Adam Fox, 'Printed Questionnaires, Research Networks, and the Discovery of the British Isles, 1650–1800', *Historical Journal* 53.3 (2010), pp. 613–14; Frank Emery, 'English Regional Studies from Aubrey to Defoe', *Geographical Journal* 124.3 (1958), pp. 315–25.
[125] Lhwyd, *Design for a British Dictionary*, p. 2.
[126] Lhwyd, *Design for a British Dictionary*, p. 2.
[127] Woolf, *Social Circulation of the Past*, pp. 368–82; Emery, *Lhuyd*, pp. 19–29.

Earth; nor must we have less regard to the Creatures of the Sea, Lakes, and Rivers, than those of the Air and Dry Land.[128]

Travel and first-hand experiences were, then, the very core of Lhuyd's project. There is nothing remarkable in the need for travel if we think of Lhuyd writing his *Historical and Geographical Dictionary* or *Archaeologia Britannica* with their top-ographical descriptions and identification of the remains of classical antiquity. The same is true for the *Natural History*. As he explained to Lloyd when developing the project, 'there's no good to be done in't without repeated observations'.[129] Travel was not just essential for his study of the physical world, though. Lhuyd identified travel in Wales, Cornwall, Scotland, and, later, Ireland as critical, especially so that he need not rely on the accounts of others. Those journeys would be vital for the cultural comparisons – 'parallel observations', in Lhuyd's words – at the heart of his work, the linguistic analysis of the British tongue and the ethnographic comparison of the Britons with their neighbours.[130] As with Camden, understanding contemporary inhabitants of Britain naturally led back to the age or settlement, migration, and cultural exchange among its founding ethnic groups.

Travelling and labouring after this ambitious project may have brought Lhuyd to a premature end, but he certainly did not go it alone.[131] He spent almost eight months in Wales in 1696 and, along with his assistants and his protégé William Rowlands, spent 'the next four years travelling through Wales, northern Ireland, the Highlands of Scotland, and thence to Ireland, Wales again, Cornwall, and briefly to Brittany'.[132] Lhuyd built an impressive collaborative enterprise around his projects, not least in Gower.[133] He called on the experts and local informants who had helped him with *Britannia* and widened the circle, writing that 'corre-spondence as extensive as we can settle it, must be maintain'd with the Curious in these Studies'.[134] He also circulated printed questionnaires, bombarding the Welsh parishes with some four thousand copies of his *Parochial Queries* in 1697.[135] As the planning for his journeys reached the advanced stage, he sent the same *Queries* into Scotland.[136] The practice was well established. Lhuyd's own mentor, Plot, had adopted it when collecting material for his unpublished *Natural History*

[128] Lhwyd, *Design for a British Dictionary*, p. 2.
[129] *Life and Letters of Edward Lhuyd*, p. 270.
[130] *Life and Letters of Edward Lhuyd*, p. 270.
[131] Lhuyd recognized his subscribers and supporters in the published portion of *Archaeologia Britannica* and described some of his travels and assistants. Lhuyd, *Archaeologia Britannica*, p. clv.
[132] Roberts, 'Edward Lhuyd'; J.L. Campbell and Derick Thomson, *Edward Lhuyd in the Scottish Highlands 1699–1700* (Oxford, 1963), pp. xiv–xvl.
[133] Emery, 'View of Gower in the 1690s', pp. 59–114.
[134] Lhwyd, *Design for a British Dictionary*, p. 2.
[135] The figure is from Roberts, 'Edward Lhuyd'.
[136] *Life and Letters of Edward Lhuyd*, pp. 321–3.

of England and there is a direct connection between Lhuyd's queries and Thomas Machell's ground-breaking questionnaire sent through Westmorland in 1677.[137]

Lhuyd explained to recipients that his work would be extraordinarily difficult without their help and the *Design* could be improved by their responses. The importance of first-hand experience to would-be readers came through explicitly: 'Nor would I have any imagine, that by Publishing these Queries, I design to spare my self the least Labour of Travelling the Country, but on the contrary be assured, I shall either come my self, or send one of my Assistants into each Parish throughout Wales.' John Wallis, Edward Bernard, Lister, and Ray attached their names to a closing testimonial to Lhuyd's qualifications, orchestrated by Lhuyd himself.[138] Just for whom four thousand *Queries* were intended was also explained. They were directed to the gentry and 'better sort' in the first place, but Lhuyd asked them to 'communicate this paper where they think fit, amongst their Neighbours' including 'to those of the Vulgar, whom they judge Men of Veracity'.[139]

The questionnaire contained thirty-one queries methodically designed for the scope of Lhuyd's projects. Indeed, this 'methodising of observations' – in Lhuyd's words – became a central feature of travel and travel narratives in mid-seventeenth-century Britain.[140] Several queries stand out for their ethnographic content. One asked for the 'Customs, and peculiar Games and Feasts amongst the Vulgar' in the locality. Lhuyd was also interested in 'Vulgar Errors and Traditions, parallel with those treated of by the Learned and Judicious Author of *Pseudodoxia Epidemica*'.[141] Naturally, Lhuyd wanted information concerning words, phrases, uncommon names, and variations of dialect among the Welsh, especially on a regional basis. Writing as though he expected that some areas of Wales might appear like exotic lands apart, Lhuyd asked for the numbers and ages of any particularly 'Ancient Men and Women'. Finally, Lhuyd wanted observations in general on the 'Stature and Complexion [constitution] of the Inhabitants' with notes about exceptional cases, the strength or activity of particular men, and any antipathies to certain meats, drinks, or the like.[142]

Had Lhuyd completed the *Design* as laid out, he would have produced a remarkable description of Wales and a real achievement in ethnography. The *Design* would have brought together Lhuyd's and his assistants' complex and persistent encounters with Wales and the Welsh. Had Lhuyd's papers survived intact, their findings would have become a treasure trove of oral history and

[137] Robert Plot, *Quaer's to Be Propounded to the Most Ingenious of Each County in My Travels Through England* (WING P2589; Oxford, 1674?); Fox, 'Discovery of the British Isles', p. 603.
[138] *Life and Letters of Edward Lhuyd*, p. 319.
[139] Lhwyd, *Parochial Queries*, pp. 1, 3; *Life and Letters of Edward Lhuyd*, pp. 314–19, 325.
[140] *Life and Letters of Edward Lhuyd*, p. 270; Fox, 'Discovery of Britain', pp. 594–614; Justin Stägl, *A History of Curiosity: The Theory of Travel 1550–1800* (Amsterdam, 1995), pp. 47–170.
[141] Lhwyd, *Parochial Queries*, p. 2.
[142] Lhwyd, *Parochial Queries*, pp. 2–3.

collective memory. The responses to the *Queries* (1696) in Wales disappointed Lhuyd and left him wondering how well the Welsh honoured their country with their silence.[143] However, he received 170 replies to his *Queries*; R.H. Morris collected the bulk of them for publication by the Cambrian Archaeological Association (1909–11) and Frank Emery uncovered still others in the Bodleian.[144] What did local respondents recover and report to Lhuyd? We might consider the report from Gower.

The characterization of Pembroke as a little England beyond Wales carried through to Lhuyd's *Queries*. He asked his informants to report 'wherein doth the English of the Vulgar, in Pembrokeshire and Gowerland [the Gower Peninsula stretching west from Swansea], differ from that in the Western Counties &c. of England?'[145] Lhuyd's post-*Britannia* agent in Gower, John Hamon, did not disappoint.[146] Hamon's reply broke down the linguistic divisions between English and Welsh among the parishes in the hundred of Swansea. He reported that parishioners in the southern parts 'p[ro]nounce their words something like the West of England', while those in the north pronounced similarly and used the old words, but 'inclined more to the Welsh, and mixed some welsh words amongst their old English'. Linguistic distinctions and changes had become more pronounced on class lines, whereas 'in former times all people both highe & lowe did talke the old English'.[147] Lhuyd must have read with enthusiasm the glossary of 'The Old English of West Gower, which is now out of use'. It contained curious delights like Brothell (quick or speedy), Copped (saucy), Horvie (foul or dirty), Leechee leeke (like to like), Nim (take), Wathall and wixin (the waxing and waining of the moon), or whidame (grandmother).[148] These diverse people might vary in language and stature, 'but many of them [are] long livers, as well male as female', with many reaching their eighties and beyond.[149] Here was an interest in ethnography that looked past national boundaries to the rich cultural complexity of Britain's medieval past and those who had once studied it, like Gerald or Owen.

Those outside Lhuyd's collaborative enterprise and his correspondence could enjoy only the 'glossography' (comparative etymology) for the *Archaeologia Britannica*, published as a first volume in 1707.[150] For his fellow Welsh, to whom he addressed a Welsh preface, Lhuyd intended that the English would gain a

---

[143] *Life and Letters of Edward Lhuyd*, p. 352; Emery, *Lhuyd*, pp. 25–7.
[144] Frank Emery, 'A Map of Edward Lhuyd's *Parochial Queries in Order to a Geographical Dictionary*', *Transactions of the Honourable Society of Cymmrodorion* (1958), pp. 41–53; Emery, 'A New Reply', pp. 395–402; Emery, 'A New Account of Snowdonia In 1693 written for Edward Lhuyd', *National Library of Wales Journal* 18 (1973), pp. 405–17.
[145] Lhwyd, *Parochial Queries*, p. 2.
[146] Emery, 'View of Gower in the 1690s', pp. 76–81.
[147] Emery, 'View of Gower in the 1690s', pp. 107–8.
[148] Emery, 'View of Gower in the 1690s', pp. 106–7.
[149] Emery, 'View of Gower in the 1690s', pp. 92–3.
[150] *Life and Letters of Edward Lhuyd*, pp. 377–8.

proper understanding of the Welsh language and come to respect it as part of a venerable British cultural tradition.[151] He apologized for the more than ten years it had taken to publish just this much of his findings, but the projects could not be done right without the extensive travel in Wales, Scotland, Cornwall, and Brittany. Lhuyd defended his decision to publish the work as planned: 'I am very sensible that it had been less Expensive to the common People of Wales, Cornwall, Ireland and Scotland if I had given an Account of these Languages in so many distinct Books.' However, that was one sort of project and 'the collating of the original Languages of the isle of Brittain is another'.[152] The ethno-cultural comparisons became the essence of Lhuyd's projects once he had completed these journeys.

Lhuyd's was a project for scholars interested in cultural exchanges, 'written at the Command of some of the greatest Persons of Wales, and for no small Number of the learned Nobility and Gentlemen of England, who have a Curiosity of comparing with other Languages, the Irish, Cornish and Amorick, as well as the Welsh'. He expected to suffer at the hands of armchair critics in bookshops and coffee houses for taking the path of self-publication, but he knew whose opinion counted: 'None can be competent Judges of this, but Gentlemen of Wales or the Highlands of Scotland or of Ireland.' Indeed, he had great hopes that his friends in the Dublin Society would snatch up at least twenty of the two or three hundred to be printed.[153] By the time Lhuyd sent the *Archaeologia* to press, the total subscriptions came to several hundred.[154] Upon its publication in 1707, Lhuyd reported a hundred copies sent to Dublin, twenty taken by the bishop of Carlisle for Cumberland and Westmorland, and, with a nice nod toward the ethnic geography of Britain past and present, fifty sent 'amongst the novantique [new-old] northern Britans'.[155]

Confident of his scholarship Lhuyd may have been, but he could sense the greater design slipping from his grasp.[156] Two years later Lhuyd was dead and none of the successors whom he variously groomed over the years fulfilled his hopes by completing the project.[157] We gain a sense of what Lhuyd might have made of his ethnographic data and first-hand encounters from the letters he wrote during his travels.[158] His travels in Scotland are especially revealing. Lhuyd spent the autumn of 1699 in Scotland, sandwiched between journeys into Ireland. Interested in linguistics and artefacts of the British past, he concentrated

---

[151] *Life and Letters of Edward Lhuyd*, pp. 427–31, 474–87, 490–1.
[152] Lhwyd, *Translation of the Welsh Preface*, pp. 10–11.
[153] *Life and Letters of Edward Lhuyd*, p. 378.
[154] *Life and Letters of Edward Lhuyd*, pp. 489, 501, 504–6, 533.
[155] *Life and Letters of Edward Lhuyd*, pp. 535, 538.
[156] *Life and Letters of Edward Lhuyd*, p. 279.
[157] *Life and Letters of Edward Lhuyd*, pp. 293, 296, 314,
[158] *Life and Letters of Edward Lhuyd*, pp. 311–445. The best account of his journey to Scotland is Campbell and Thomson, *Lhuyd in the Scottish Highlands*, pp. xiii–90.

on western Scotland: 'Lhuyd travelled northwards on the road running along the west coast of Kintyre, and then through Knapdale and Lorne, crossing over to Mull by ferry and travelling down the Ross of Mull to reach Iona. After returning to the mainland, he travelled to Edinburgh by way of Inveraray, Dumbarton, and Glasgow.'[159]

Lhuyd prepared the ground in advance. While making final arrangements for his journeys in 1697, he sent Lister a parcel full of his Parochial Queries and asked him to forward them 'to the gentry and clergy in the Highlands of Scotland'. Lhuyd hoped that James Wallace (who investigated the Orkneys) and a Doctor Grey, with whom Lister was in touch in Scotland, would 'engage their friends if possible, to have answers to these queries ready by this time twelv-month' and supply him with the names of 'any gentleman or clergy-man amongst ye Highlands any thing studious of their own language and the antiquities of their countrey'. Sending Queries concerning Wales to Scotland was a tricky matter, though, as Lister pointed out. Still firmly focussed on producing the great description of Wales, Lhuyd replied that 'We must by no means think of changing ye word Wales for Scotland.'[160] In 1697 Lhuyd did not want to be drawn into writing an even larger description that included the Scottish highlands. Yet by the time he arrived in Scotland in 1699 his interests embraced much more.

Thus, as in Wales, clerics, schoolmasters, and trustworthy locals became Lhuyd's primary contacts.[161] In Glasgow and Edinburgh he made contact with faculty at the universities and met with two men at the centre of crucial networks of geographic knowledge, Robert Sibbald in Edinburgh and Robert Wodrow of Glasgow. Lhuyd reported to Lister in December 1699 that Sibbald 'shew'd me his MS De Aquatilibus Scotiae wch he has carried on for some years & is stil (as his occasions permit) dayly improving'. Lhuyd found Sibbald to be 'a gentleman no less obliging & communicative than learned and curious; has a tolerable collection of natural curiosities and a library of 8000 volumes'.[162] Sibbald, Wodrow, and other acquaintances became important agents for his investigations once he had left Scotland.[163]

By the time Lhuyd departed from Scotland in late 1699 he had settled on a set of questions that he asked his correspondents to investigate in his absence. Writing to Colin Campbell of Ardchatton from Glasgow, he made some eight queries. Most queries concerned linguistics, literary and oral culture, archaeological finds, and artefacts. One betrayed Lhuyd's interest in exploring the customs of the Highlands, asking for information about the 'peculiar Games

[159] Campbell and Thomson, Lhuyd in the Scottish Highlands, p. xvii.
[160] Life and Letters of Edward Lhuyd, pp. 321–3.
[161] Charles W.J. Withers, Geography, Science and National Identity: Scotland Since 1520 (Cambridge, 2001), p. 87.
[162] Life and Letters of Edward Lhuyd, p. 419.
[163] Campbell and Thomson, Lhuyd in the Scottish Highlands, p. xx; Withers, Geography, Science and National Identity, pp. 85–7.

EDWARD LHUYD

and customes, observ'd on set days throughout they year; and any other Fashions yt you know peculiar to the Highlands'. Lhuyd had already collected 'about three Sheets of the Customs and Rites of ye Highlands; wch ye famous Mr Boyl has procurd from some correspondent' and he wanted an account from Campbell against which to double-check them and 'our own few Observations made during our short stay'.[164]

Lhuyd hunted for manuscripts, artefacts, antiquities, botanical and mineral samples, and all manner of folklore in Scotland. Chests and boxes galore arrived in Oxford awaiting his return.[165] The letter to Lister gives us an idea of how his ethnographic interests grew with his travels. 'We sped well enough in ye Highlands as to some materials for ye *Archaeologia Britannica*: particularly we have been successful in meeting with several amulets of the Druids.' Lhuyd confirmed that 'Snake-buttons are ye same as describ'd in Denbigshire, *Camden*, by ye name of Adder-beads.' Lhuyd also learned that the Highland Scots used quartz pebbles to cure cattle that were elf struck: 'their opinion is that fayries, having not much power themselves, to hurt animal bodies, do sometimes carry away men in ye air, and employ them to shoot men, catle, &c. with bows and arrows'. He assumed that Lister had seen such arrowheads, the 'same chip'd flints ye native of New-England &c. head their arrows with, at this day'. Lhuyd also found several stone axes that he associated with Amerindian artefacts. Fascinated by the cultural parallels with peoples in the Americas, Lhuyd wanted Lister's help in determining how widespread this particular practice was: 'I never heard of them in Wales and would gladly be inform'd; whether you know of their being found in any part of England.'[166]

The 'Collection of Highland Rites and Customs' mentioned earlier gives us an idea about just how far Lhuyd probed into the cultural complexity of highland life. The Bodleian Library copy 'is found in a notebook that he evidently took with him to Scotland for his tour' and includes additional notes and comments.[167] Lhuyd made a copy from Sibbald's own; Sibbald took his copy from James Kirkwood, whose copy came from the lost original.[168] Lhuyd learned much about his primary interest, language, but from a distinctly ethno-cultural standpoint: 'Of their language, there are several Dialects, which make them to one another unintelligible, partly ridiculous. The purest Dialect is thought to be in Cantyre, Argyle & the Western Isles. Where they confine with the Lowlands they speak most corrupt. They can discern the countrey one is of by his Dialect.'[169] The language was not some primitive relic but 'both copious & significant', a near kin to Latin and French with some resemblance to Hebrew and Greek.

[164] Campbell and Thomson, *Lhuyd in the Scottish Highlands*, pp. 4–5.
[165] Emery, *Lhuyd*, p. 25.
[166] *Life and Letters of Edward Lhwyd*, pp. 419–20.
[167] *Occult Laboratory*, p. 35.
[168] *Occult Laboratory*, pp. 35–8.
[169] *Occult Laboratory*, p. 55.

387

It included translations of the Old and New Testaments, Psalms, and Knox's liturgy alongside a storehouse of its own proverbs and unique usages.[170] Lhuyd included among further notes at the end 'Every Shire in Scotland has a different dialect; but that of Mul is esteemed the purest Irish next unto Connacht Irish in Ireland.'[171]

Ticks and notes seem designed to confirm or clarify a report against Lhuyd's own observations or those of others. He noted the belted plaid worn by the better sort of women and the silver or brass broaches worn on the breast. However, he corrected a report that all common people typically wore rings of horn, brass, or silver: 'This is in the mainland not much in the Isles.'[172] Lhuyd must have harboured vivid memories of highland food and drink. The report read:

> In time of scarcity they launce their cows neck & make meat of their Blood; The Lochabermen when they Kil a Cow, hang up the whole carcase, & eat is as they need. When they are in the Hills they boyl their Flesh in the skin with a fire of the bones and other fuel. ... They (in the isles especially) have a way of drying their corn before it be threshen, by burning the straw & it together, keeping the corn very dextrously from being wronged with the Fire; then they grind it in Querns ... [173]

Lhuyd noted that people also added butter or milk to the blood sausage and the practice of hanging an entire animal 'is all over the Highlands'. He also knew better than to use 'skin' for 'Belly or Haggis'. The graddan corn described here caught the attention of every traveller to the Highlands and Isles, but Lhuyd added that this 'expeditious way of drying corn is frequently used in Kerry, Ireland'.[174] The people wrapped their cheeses in the pungent, salty ashes of burned seaweed. They likewise added the ash to butter, but not for salting, in Lhuyd's understanding.[175]

Lhuyd obtained a wealth of information covering buildings, monuments, bedding and sleeping, farming, fire and fuel, salt, hunting and fishing, trading and exchange, charms, diseases and cures, clans and names, war and feuds, trials, social degrees and distinctions, modes of address, bards and itinerant poets, music, feasts, hospitality, flitting or moving from one place to another, fear of thunder, fostering children, birth and baptism, death and burial, the computation of time, second sight and augury, dreams, and diverse religious practices and other superstitions. He engaged almost all of it in his notes. Lhuyd spotted an 'Ecclesiastic Doctrine of Penance' in the people's belief that God punished their sinful bodies with pain and long sicknesses, the better to satisfy God and

---

[170] *Occult Laboratory*, p. 55.
[171] *Occult Laboratory*, p. 75.
[172] *Occult Laboratory*, p. 56.
[173] *Occult Laboratory*, p. 58.
[174] *Occult Laboratory*, p. 58, nn. u, v, w.
[175] *Occult Laboratory*, p. 59, n. c.

purge their bodies before going to heaven.[176] Pregnant women made tiny slits in their petticoats at the sight of hares to ward off hare-lips in children.[177] At the Lord's Supper, they did not pass the bread from hand to hand 'but every one takes to himself'. Lhuyd queried 'whether the Presbyterians do this'.[178] Lhuyd's attention in all this ranged from the scholarly (language and linguistics) to the routine (food, livelihoods, social relations) to the exotic and mystical. His quest for linguistic information about the Highland Scots had grown into a deep curiosity about the complex ethno-cultural reality of their *pays*.

What Lhuyd found in Scotland did match the usual ethnic stereotypes. Perhaps being an outsider made it easier to own up to some first prejudices. A crude highland–lowland distinction faded before Lhuyd's actual experiences, as he explained in January 1700 to Thomas Molyneux in Dublin:

> It so happen'd that having travelled a hundred Miles in the Highlands [sic] to our Satisfaction we grew Luxurious of our good success and Curious to see the Lowlands and so advanced first to Glascoe and afterwards to Sterling and Edenborough we found a good deal of Civility and kindness as well in the highlands as the Lowlands And tho, the highlanders be represented both in England & Ireland Barbarous and Inhospitable we found em quite otherwise ... [179]

Lhuyd and his companions found the highland 'Gentlemen, men of good sense and breeding and the Comons a subtil inquisitive people and more civil to Strangers in directing them the way (the mean [main] occasion we had of their kindness) than in most other Counties [Countries].'[180] Earlier, in a letter to Richard Richardson, Lhuyd summed up his experiences among the Scots: 'In the High-lands we found the people every where civil enough; and had doubtless sped better as to our enquiries, had we had the language more perfect.'[181] Lhuyd offered the same assessment several months later in a letter to Henry Rowlands.[182]

In his letters to Molyneux and Rowlands, Lhuyd worked through an explanation for the origin and persistence of Highland stereotypes. Topography and cultural practices, especially customs and language, played crucial roles in the hostile ethnography:

> The main cause of their being reputed Barbarous I take to be no other than the Roughness of their Countrey as Consisting very much of barren mountains and Loughs and their retaining their antient habits and Customs and Language ... [183]

---

[176] *Occult Laboratory*, p. 68.
[177] *Occult Laboratory*, p. 69.
[178] *Occult Laboratory*, p. 71.
[179] Campbell and Thomson, *Lhuyd in the Scottish Highlands*, p. 6.
[180] Campbell and Thomson, *Lhuyd in the Scottish Highlands*, p. 6.
[181] *Life and Letters of Edward Lhuyd*, p. 423.
[182] *Life and Letters of Edward Lhuyd*, pp. 427-8.
[183] Campbell and Thomson, *Lhuyd in the Scottish Highlands*, p. 6.

Martin Martin, one of Lhuyd's contacts in Scotland, would shortly write virtually the same thing in his *Description of the Western Islands of Scotland* (1703) and we need hardly wonder if Lhuyd came by this view at first hand.[184] Lhuyd understood perfectly well that this mentalité affected ethnic identities and prejudices throughout Britain and Ireland, not just the Highlands of Scotland: 'on which account many Gent of good sense in England Esteem the the [sic] Welsh at this day barbarous & talk to much of wild Irish in this Kingdom'.[185]

Cultural isolation played a crucial role in reinforcing assumptions. Lhuyd wrote to Lister in December 1699 about his rambles through remote country that 'affoarded neither post nor carrier; as not having much communication (this time of year especially) with the cultivated parts of the kingdome'.[186] He also wrote to his fellow antiquarian Rowlands in March 1700 of having spent time 'in places quite remote from all correspondence, amongst the Hebrides, and other highlands of Scotland with whome their neighbours seem to have less commerce than they have with either of the Indies'.[187] Remoteness made these Scots a people apart and prevented others from – theoretically – experiencing the same reality that Lhuyd had during his travels. However, Lhuyd did not accept the differences entirely on their own terms. He explained to Rowlands that 'the main reasons of the contrary character I take to be their adhering too much to their antient customs, habit and language; whereby they distinguish themselves from all their neighbours; and distinctions always create mutual reflections'.[188] Lhuyd's observation echoed Elizabethan and Jacobean frustrations with Gaels in Ireland and Scotland who refused to accept lowland norms. The assumption of wilful difference would be at the centre of debates about 'improvement' in the century after Lhuyd's death, including Martin Martin's own estimation of improvement among the Hebrideans.[189]

Just another sort of highlander

Out of a hurried journey around Wales, Edward Lhuyd incorporated observations that directly added cultural complexity to Camden's description and moved beyond the original scope of *Britannia*. Lhuyd was an honest, diligent scholar and good natured according to his friends, but he suffered fools and time-wasters

---

[184] Martin Martin, *A Description of the Western Islands of Scotland*, ed. Charles W.J. Withers and R.W. Munro (Edinburgh, 1999), p. 205.

[185] Campbell and Thomson, *Lhuyd in the Scottish Highlands*, p. 6.

[186] *Life and Letters of Edward Lhuyd*, p. 418.

[187] *Life and Letters of Edward Lhuyd*, p. 427.

[188] *Life and Letters of Edward Lhuyd*, p. 428.

[189] Martin, *Description of the Western Islands*, pp. 200–3; Martin Rackwitz, *Travels to Terra Incognita: The Scottish Highlands and Hebrides in Early Modern Travellers' Accounts c. 1600 to 1800* (Münster, 2007), pp. 305–36.

badly.[190] We can find the origin of his *Design* for a proper description of Wales in the combination of travel, personality, and dealings with Swale, Churchill, and Gibson. The abundant natural history material for Flintshire suggests how much Lhuyd struggled to reconcile his interests in telling the story of Wales, the framework of Camden's original, and Gibson's imprecise instructions. When Lhuyd challenged the prejudices toward mountainous Merionethshire and its people, he articulated a very different aesthetic sensibility about topography and brought the world of the upland Welsh in from the margins. The first-hand encounter with antiquities, landforms, natural phenomena, villages and castles, and people fired Lhuyd's enthusiasm for travel. Ultimately, then, the strongest impression we get from reading Lhuyd's additions is how limiting and confining *Britannia* had become after his journey through Wales. Lhuyd's *Design* would have created a setting to let loose those interests.

Lhuyd was a creature of several worlds, the Welsh borders, Oxford, the Ashmolean Museum and Royal Society, the roads and byways of the Celtic Britons and their descendants. Involvement with Gibson's project propelled Lhuyd on a series of journeys where the engagement with cultural complexity became an essential, instinctive, defining part of who he was. Toward the end of his short life, from Oxford in May 1706, Lhuyd explained his linguistic and cultural motives in the Irish preface to the *Archaeologia Britannica*. For those who 'propose it were better to teach all manner of Persons in the three Kingdoms to speak English; I will readily agree with them in that, as being of universal advantage in order to promote Trade and Commerce'. But the architects of linguistic imperialism left the method and means to others. At the very least, Lhuyd argued, his dictionary of the British language could be a useful resource for those who aimed to bridge linguistic divides in creating a lingua franca for the Isles.[191] Like Gerald or John Taylor or Martin Martin, Lhuyd's multi-layered identity and life required self-reflection and direction.

In 1700, returning the books and papers he had borrowed from Thomas Tonkin, including a copy of Carew's *Survey of Cornwall*, Lhuyd could not help but remark that he and his party found the Cornish 'more suspicious and jealous ... than in any country we have travelled'.[192] His experience among the highland Scots had been different, even if he had set out with some of the usual anxieties: 'if it be the manner of the countrey (as some tel me) to knock men on ye head even for a threadbare suit of cloaths, I shall easily bridle my curiosity'.[193] Many highland travellers had been fed on these stereotypes, yet Lhuyd rose above them. For a Shropshire lad who delighted in his Welshness and found a home among the most learned in Oxford and metropolitan Britain and Ireland, Lhuyd

[190] Roberts, 'Edward Lhuyd'.
[191] Lhwyd, *Archaeologia Britannica: Texts and Translations*, p. 207.
[192] *Life and Letters of Edward Lhuyd*, p. 434.
[193] *Life and Letters of Edward Lhuyd*, p. 322.

achieved a remarkable disposition, thanks to his travels: 'As for coarse fare and hard lodging we are proof, being but an other sort of Highlanders our selves.'[194] Lhuyd and his friend William Nicolson had similarly associated North Wales with Cumbria as 'much of a piece' in the early 1690s.[195]

Few travellers ever identified so matter-of-factly with a world outside their own, but the commendatory poems that accompanied the first volume of the *Archaeologia Britannica* show that Lhuyd's sentiments did not exist in isolation. John Keill, the Edinburgh-educated natural philosopher and future Savilian professor of astronomy at Oxford, signed his contribution 'Scoto-Britannus'. His verse fused linguistic artefacts with upland topography and a hint of noble savagery: 'My delight is in ancient rusticity and in the rugged fragments of words which were once heard on these native mountains by my forefathers and ancestors, and even by those who begat those forbears.'[196] Edward Wynn of Anglesey adopted a similar poetic trick, writing to Lhuyd that 'your mind longs to march boldly over inaccessible paths and it brings forth arts unknown into the light ... the Celtic stock, fashioned by your books, claims the right to speak – according to the ancient norm – words ... such as struck and penetrated the ears of Caesar'.[197] Lhuyd and Colin Campbell met in Inveraray on what could only have been a cold day in December 1699. In the third person, Campbell summoned himself to praise Lhuyd:

> Though you be the accommodating, rustic Muse of the Bannae ['the higher mountains of Scotland and Ireland'], hoarse amid the melting snow ... and now slow of step because of grey-haired disuse, yet give voice to the public commendations which the skilled Lhwyd has deserved. Lhwyd too belongs to the Alps; he does not spurn the shepherd's pipe.[198]

Lhuyd experienced the cultural complexity of Britannia and its peoples in a compelling, unconventional manner only partly revealed to us across the centuries. Lhuyd and his work were as complicated as the cultures that he sought to experience and explain. Two Irish poets put limits on Lhuyd's cultural hybridity. John Balfe conceded, 'Although the busy Master Lhuyd is a foreigner, it is a fine thing to put Irish into print and to publish the traditions of the ancients.'[199] The farmer-poet Seán na Ráithíneach titled his work (translated), 'Though Edward was not a Gael' and referred to Lhuyd as 'an Sasaníoch' or 'that Englishman'. Still, he praised the 'excellence and intellect' with which 'This foreign hawk travelled hither and yon among the ordinary people with esteem

[194] *Life and Letters of Edward Lhuyd*, p. 322.
[195] Quoted in Emery, 'Edward Lhwyd and the 1695 *Britannia*', p. 179.
[196] Lhwyd, *Archaeologia Britannica: Texts and Translations*, pp. 68–9.
[197] Lhwyd, *Archaeologia Britannica: Texts and Translations*, p. 81.
[198] Lhwyd, *Archaeologia Britannica: Texts and Translations*, p. 75.
[199] Lhwyd, *Archaeologia Britannica: Texts and Translations*, p. 253.

for our ancient tongues' and expounded them in his dictionary.[200] Robert
Campbell, the Forester of Argyll, congratulated Lhuyd unreservedly:

> The ploughshare is put away and music is sung
> in the kingdom of Ireland every day;
> and a musical instrument is tuned
> in the pleasant lands of Scotland.
> The reason why I say that
> is that the splendid language of those countries,
> having been for a long time in slavery
> has now been freed from its bondage.[201]

Foreigner or not, Lhuyd would surely have agreed with Campbell that western
Scotland offered a pleasant prospect for a Welshman who was just another sort
of highlander.

[200] Lhwyd, *Archaeologia Britannica: Texts and Translations*, pp. 254–5.
[201] Lhwyd, *Archaeologia Britannica: Texts and Translations*, p. 89.

11

The Britannia of Robert Sibbald

In medieval Edinburgh, the Preaching Friar's Vennel led from the High Street to the Black Friary of the Dominican Monks founded by Alexander II. Here in 1588, in what was known by then as the Blackfriars Wynd, the earl of Bothwell pursued Sir William Stewart, cornered him in a cellar, and plunged a sword into his chest. The two men came to fatal blows days after Stewart challenged Bothwell to kiss his 'arse' during an argument in front of James VI.[1] Eighty years later, a Presbyterian zealot came within a hair's breadth of shooting dead the persecuting archbishop of St Andrews, James Sharpe, who kept his residence in the Blackfriars. The assassin lost his life after excruciating torture and two years' imprisonment on Bass Rock.[2]

How fitting that the man Edmund Gibson commissioned to revisit the Scottish chapters of *Britannia* should have been born in the storied Blackfriars in the tumultuous spring of 1641.[3] Young Robert Sibbald's family retreated to their estate in Fife during the 1640s. Tucked away in Fife, Sibbald began school in Cupar in 1650 before finishing his education at Edinburgh's Royal High School and going on to Edinburgh University, graduating M.A. in 1659. However, Sibbald witnessed the violence unleashed among the peoples of Britain and Ireland by religious bigotry and ethnic prejudice. For Oliver Cromwell, Charles I's final military defeat in 1648 signalled God's judgment on their great cause and the king was duly tried and executed as a man of blood in January 1649. Incensed at the execution of their shared sovereign by the English Parliament, the Scots proclaimed Charles Stuart king and crowned him Charles II at Scone in 1651. General William Monck, like Cromwell before him at the Battle of Dunbar, led the New Model Army into Scotland to punish the Scots. Sibbald watched in September 1651 as Monck destroyed Dundee in retaliation.[4] Perhaps

[1] Rob Macpherson, 'Sir William Stewart of Monkton', *Oxford DNB* at www.oxforddnb.com.
[2] James Grant, *Cassell's Old and New Edinburgh* (six volumes; Edinburgh, 1880-83), II, pp. 258-9.
[3] Charles W.J. Withers, 'Sir Robert Sibbald', *Oxford DNB* at www.oxforddnb.com; Roger L. Emerson, 'Sir Robert Sibbald, Kt, the Royal Society of Scotland and the Origins of the Scottish Enlightenment', *Annals of Science* 45 (1988), pp. 41-72.
[4] Withers, 'Robert Sibbald'.

as many as 1300 inhabitants paid with their lives.[5] The Scots were invited to consent to become part of a British Commonwealth in 1652, a union that was finally confirmed in 1654.

Robert Leighton, Principal of Edinburgh, steered Sibbald away from these deadly controversies. Sibbald left behind the decisive events of the fall of the Commonwealth and restoration of the Stuart monarchy when he departed for Leiden to study medicine in March 1660. Leiden brought Sibbald into contact with the pioneering naturalists of the Netherlands who had undertaken 'the systematic natural history of their equatorial colonies'.[6] He studied with Christian Marcgraf, brother to Georg Marcgraf and the author of *Historia Naturalis Brasiliae* (1648), which described 'the economy and culture of its Amerindians' alongside flora and fauna. According to Frank Emery, 'there was every chance for the young Scotsman (who had resolved "to goe abroad ... and see the world and know men") to hear of the regional work that proved so rewarding for natural historians'.[7] Sibbald returned to Edinburgh in 1662 and 'from this period he began to develop a deeper interest in natural history, geography, and antiquarianism, which were all to form parts of his vision for the creation of useful natural knowledge'.[8] He emulated the collection of useful knowledge advocated by Moryson, Marcgraf, and other travellers.

Sibbald's plans for a two volume 'Scottish Atlas' envisioned something much more than maps, topography, or descriptions of flora and fauna: 'Volume one, *Scotia Antiqua* (to be published in Latin), was to embrace the historical development of Scotland, the customs of the people and their antiquities. The English-language second volume, *Scotia Moderna*, would describe the country's resources as a work of contemporary chorography, on a county-by-county basis.'[9] Sibbald planned to cover the ethnographic details of the Scottish people, including 'peculiar Customs, Manners or Dispositions' among them. Like Lhuyd's *British Dictionary*, Sibbald's 'Atlas' would have resembled a Scottish *Britannia* with expanded emphasis on natural history and ethnography. When the two men met in 1699, they would have instinctively understood each other's burdens and ambitions. The two men's projects shared the same fate: they were never completed.

Sibbald owed a great deal to those Scots who accelerated their own century-long project to discover and master their country after the 1580s. Travellers and local scholars explored even the most remote reaches of Scotland, very much in the fashion of local historians like Carew, Dugdale, Lambarde, Burton, or

---

[5] *Historical Tales of the Wars of Scotland* (two volumes; Edinburgh, 1849), I, p. 340.
[6] F.V. Emery, 'Irish Geography in the Seventeenth Century', *Irish Geography* 3 (1957), p. 264.
[7] Frank Emery, 'The Geography of Robert Gordon, 1580–1661 and Sir Robert Sibbald, 1641–1722', *Scottish Geographical Magazine* 74.1 (1958), p. 6.
[8] Withers, 'Robert Sibbald'.
[9] Charles W.J. Withers, *Geography, Science and National Identity: Scotland Since 1520* (Cambridge, 2001), p. 72.

Pembrokeshire's Owen. Increasingly well travelled, humanist in outlook, and devoted to the cultural pedigree of family and estate, Scottish elites took serious interest in Scottish history, genealogy, chorography, and the production of useful knowledge in their capacities as local rulers and national figures.[10] Camden's *Britannia* and the accession of James VI to the English throne combined to give all of this a patriotic dimension: 'Scots were clearly not content to leave Camden's thin and patchy treatment as the sole authority on the northern kingdom' and 'there is a strong sense too of an ideological agenda aimed at countering the Anglocentricity of Camden's work and asserting the integrity of the Scottish kingdom'.[11] Scots like Timothy Pont, John Scot of Scotstarvit, James Balfour of Denmilne, the Aberdeenshire Gordons, and David Buchanan all put their feet, minds, and pens to the task of describing Scotland and its peoples in the first half of the seventeenth century. Maps, printed books, and manuscripts became the currency of their discoveries, supported by travel, scholarship, and the collection of documents and artefacts. They preserved those encounters in their libraries, collections, and circulating manuscripts (absent the take-off in subscription publication for such works in the London market).[12]

These travelling Scots decisively shaped one of the greatest scholarly projects of the seventeenth century, Willem and Joan Blaeu's *Atlas Novus*. The Amsterdam publisher Willem Jansson Blaeu began publication of the *Atlas Novus* in 1635. From their father's death in 1638, Joan and Cornelius took over the project, preparing and adding new volumes. Cornelius died in 1642 and Joan carried the project through to completion in 1658. He published a new edition of the *Atlas* between 1662 and 1665 in eleven volumes. It charted the known world in almost six hundred maps with Latin descriptions. Blaeu covered Scotland and Ireland in the fifth volume, published in 1654. In addition to forty-nine superb maps, most of them based on Pont's cartographic journeys, the *Atlas* included all of Camden's 'cursory' descriptions, excerpts from Buchanan's *Historia*, and new accounts designed to fill in gaps and provide coverage befitting a great nation. This stood in marked contrast to Blaeu's reductive fourth volume, which charted England simply using new engravings of the maps in John Speed's *Theatre of the*

[10] Keith M. Brown, *Noble Society in Scotland: Wealth, Family and Culture, from Reformation to Revolution* (Edinburgh, 2000), pp. 190–201, 205–10, 219–24; Withers, *Geography, Science and National Identity*, pp. 30–56; Michael Lynch, 'The Age of Timothy Pont', in *The Nation Survey'd: Essays on Late Sixteenth-Century Scotland as Depicted by Timothy Pont*, ed. Ian C. Cunningham (East Linton, 2001), pp. 26–34; Charles Withers, 'Pont in Context: Chorography, Mapmaking and National Identity in the Late Sixteenth Century', *Nation Survey'd*, pp. 139–48.
[11] Roger A. Mason, 'From Buchanan to Blaeu: The Politics of Scottish Chorography, 1582–1654', *George Buchanan: Political Thought in Early Modern Britain and Europe*, ed. Caroline Erskine and Roger A. Mason (Farnham, 2012), p. 42.
[12] James Raven, *The Business of Books: Booksellers and the English Book Trade 1450–1850* (New Haven, 2007), p. 105.

Empire of Great Britain alongside Speed's text and Camden's descriptions from *Britannia*.[13]

Blaeu's Scottish collaborators appropriated *Britannia*, answered Camden's biases, and supplanted his descriptions.[14] Travel and first-hand experience lay at the heart of their achievement and those journeys laid the foundation for Sibbald's own projects and his collaboration with Edmund Gibson when he 'inherited' many of his predecessors' manuscripts. Yet, while Blaeu's *Atlas Novus* may have been one of the century's most spectacular literary and artistic achievements, a multi-volume folio atlas in Latin was not a practical response to Camden's neglect: the first and only English edition of the *Atlas* of Scotland appeared in 2006, in a beautiful but unwieldy folio edition limited to six hundred copies.

Seventeenth-century Scots and their fellow Britons needed something else. Sibbald rather self-servingly criticized Blaeu's *Atlas* for being nothing more than a rehash of Buchanan's *Historia* with 'some few Scrapes out of Cambden, who is no friend to us in what he writeth'.[15] Sibbald's 'Scottish Atlas' and the invitation to revise *Britannia* became the means both to satisfy his own pretensions and to complete the 'patriotic' mission of Pont, Balfour, and the Gordons for a British audience. The rest of this chapter will examine how Sibbald did so, but first we must study the foundations those patriots laid for his ambitions.

Travels through multicultural Scotland from Pont to Blaeu

Walter Macfarlane, resident of the Canongate in Edinburgh and chief of the Macfarlanes of Arrochar, hired a scrivener, Alexander Taitt, to transcribe hundreds of topographical descriptions from as early as 1529 (John Benston's account of Orkney), carrying right through to 1744. A good deal of this material came into Macfarlane's 'Collections' by way of Sibbald's. These included the detailed accounts that Sibbald had obtained for his 'Scottish Atlas' using parochial questionnaires.[16] The generosity of James Gordon also benefited Sibbald's 'collections'. Gordon's father, Robert, Balfour of Denmilne, and Scotstarvit all worked from the 1620s to chart and describe Scotland, building on the travels and detailed cartographic work of the dead Pont.[17] With the exception

---

[13] Mason, 'From Buchanan to Blaeu', pp. 39–42.

[14] *Geographical Collections Relating to Scotland made by Walter Macfarlane*, ed. Arthur Mitchell and James Toshach Clark (three volumes; Edinburgh, 1906–1908), II, pp. 334–91, hereafter cited as *Geographical Collections*.

[15] Withers, *Geography, Science and National Identity*, p. 74.

[16] Withers, *Geography, Science and National Identity*, pp. 256–62.

[17] The complex working relationships are explained in Jeffrey C. Stone, *The Pont Manuscript Maps of Scotland: Sixteenth Century Origins of a Blaeu Atlas* (Tring, Hertfordshire, 1989), pp. 5–13; *The Blaeu Atlas of Scotland* (Edinburgh, 2006), pp. 11–15, hereafter cited as *Blaeu Atlas* (2006).

of Balfour's 'Topographical Descriptions' that Sibbald read and annotated, most of the materials that the Gordons had assembled for Blaeu's *Atlas* passed to Sibbald around 1683. Macfarlane put Taitt to work copying a good portion of Sibbald's 'collections' and added dozens of parish descriptions forwarded by local ministers to the Kirk authorities in the eighteenth century. When Macfarlane died in 1767, the Faculty of Advocates purchased his 'Collection' for its great library.

Macfarlane and Taitt laid the basis for a twentieth-century anthology of parish summaries and county histories, topographical measurements, records of anti-quarian sites and artefacts, genealogies, and accounts of natural wonders and exotic peoples that spanned an absolutely formative period in the discovery of Scotland. It has a shifting, mosaic quality about it: transcriptions of working notes and extracts drawn from 'original sources' that once existed only as manu-scripts, not a few of which are now lost. For example, Taitt copied a long extract from Sibbald's 'Topographic Notices' containing Robert Gordon's notes on the highlands and islands made in the 1640s. Much of what Gordon recorded came directly from Timothy Pont's notes of his travels, though Gordon 'commented, deleted, and amplified as he copied'.[18] What did the journeys through Scotland and encounters with its people look like as they passed through so many hands?

Cunningham, taking in the north-western half of modern-day Ayrshire, boasts one of Pont's only surviving topographic descriptions, based on his travels there between 1604 and 1608.[19] One senses that this is what the chapters in Leland's county-by-county civil history might have looked like. Pont's travels too may have found inspiration in similar demands for useful knowledge, first by a Presbyterian Kirk determined to plant a reformed ministry outside the lowlands and then by an imperial monarch, James VI and I, who needed to master the ethno-religious complexity of a united Britain and Ireland.[20] Pont began with etymology. He considered the locale's rich natural endowments, proof to think, with Buchanan, that it might well have signified a king's (Kuning, in Danish) habitation (Hamin). Cunningham had once been possessed by Edward de Balliol – a would-be king – and Richard de Morville, Constable of Scotland and a close confidant of Malcolm IV, who made good as a second-generation Franci (Anglo-Norman) transplant. David I, while earl of Huntingdon, settled de Morville's father, Hugh, in Northamptonshire and Rutland before making him a leading figure in his 'modernizing' regime as King of Scots after 1124.[21]

---

[18] *Geographical Collections*, II, p. xlv; Jeffrey C. Stone, 'Timothy Pont: Three Centuries of Research, Speculation and Plagiarism', in *Nation Survey'd*, pp. 8–10.

[19] Stone, *Pont Manuscript Maps*, p. 13; Stone, 'Timothy Pont', p. 6.

[20] Withers, 'Pont in Context', pp. 148–53.

[21] J. Fullarton, ed., *Topographical Account of the District of Cunningham, Ayrshire. Compiled About the Year 1600, by Mr. Timothy Pont* (Glasgow, 1858), pp. 1–2, hereafter cited as Pont, 'Cunningham'; Keith Stringer, 'Hugh de Morville' and 'Richard de Morville', *Oxford DNB* at www.oxforddnb.com.

Pont's topographic description witnessed to the first-hand familiarity that found its way into his map of Cunningham. He took pains to emphasize the nature and fertility of a land that fell by three degrees down to the sea. In the second degree, sandwiched between the hills of Renfrewshire and the coast, Pont found a 'deipe, fatt clayeish soyle, much enriched by the industrious inhabitants lymeing of their grounds'.[22] The long respite from foreign invasion gave Cunningham's inhabitants the peace in which to realize their talents:

> [It] is become verry ciuill and veill cultured; so that for the quantity it [is] marvelously veill beutified with goodly buildings and edifices of noble and gentlemen; and the duellings of the yeomanrie verry thick poudered ouer the face of this countrey, all for the most part veill and comodiously planted and garnished; so that one may vounder ho so small a bounds can containe so veill so maney people, hauing no trade to liue by bot their husbandry and the rent arraysing from the ground, except liuing on the sea coste by fischling.[23]

These people lived under the presbytery of Irvine, a hereditary bailiff (belonging to the earls of Eglinton), and the sheriff of Ayr. A most civil order by contrast to the battle of Lairgs in 1263, when the king of Norway apparently left sixteen thousand dead to water the soil with their blood. Reminiscent of Leland's lists in his *Itinerary*, Pont closed this part of the description with the dates of market fairs at parish churches and a list of the most notable hills and mountains.[24]

It is hard not to imagine the influence of Carew's *Survey of Cornwall* or Lambarde's *Perambulation of Kent* in the rest of Pont's 'Cunningham'. Pont laid out an alphabetical list of towns, parishes, towers, villages, hamlets, and houses of name and note with 'remembrances one [on] diuers of them'. The patchwork of cultures and *pays* that shaped Ayrshire comes through in these micro-descriptions. According to Pont, all those villages beginning with 'Achin' owed their names to the 'Irisch vord ... signifiing a fold, or manured croft of corne'. Ardrossen had a wonderfully complicated past. It took its name from 'ross in the ancient Brittich tongue [which] signifies a biland or peninsula'. The formidable castle boasted a cellar called the Wallace larder. It commemorated an atrocity. William Wallace had burned a house adjacent to the castle to trick the English garrison outside, where his 'veill armed companey gifs them a hote uelcome, and kills them euery mothers sone' afterward throwing the 'carcatches of thesse Englich' into the cellar.[25]

The story of Kilwinning reinforces Pont's sensitivity to cultural markers and exchanges. Kilwinning bore 'the name Vinnen of a certaine holy man so named,

---

[22] Pont, 'Cunningham', pp. 4–6.
[23] Pont, 'Cunningham', p. 6.
[24] Pont, 'Cunningham', pp. 7–8.
[25] Pont, 'Cunningham', pp. 9–10, 12, 26.

wich came from Irland, with certaine of his discipells and follouers and heir taught the gospell'. His notoriety owed much to 'superstitious posterity' and the 'vulgar credulous comons' who believed St Vinnen's well 'issewed of the tears of this Sant'. Pont returned here to Richard de Morville, but he betrayed less sensitivity to the complex family background than Leland might have. Pont identified him simply as a 'noble Englich man' who became a 'fugitiue from his auen countrey for the slaughter of Thomas Beckett'. De Morville was honoured with high office in Scotland and worked to safeguard his soul from Becket's murder by founding the abbey of Kilwinning.[26] Except it did not happen that way. The elder brother, Hugh, cut down Becket and Richard's piety seems to have been genuinely felt: 'On account of his generosity to Melrose and other good works, he was freed from his vow to found a Cistercian abbey by Pope Urban III.'[27] Pont's founding date of 1191 seems improbable, given Richard's death the year before, while the end date of 1591 probably marks the culmination of decades of dismemberment accelerated under the Kirk.[28]

Pont stood on firmer ground when he stuck to topography and focussed on the marks of civility among its inhabitants. This took two forms: the fair buildings that marked the countryside and livelihood gained from the land. The earl of Glencairn's salt works ensured that Saltcotes made good on its name. Pont regularly singled out nobles and gentry who planted their houses and precincts with gardens, orchards, and parks as if to confirm them as good subjects committed to peace and order in the localities. Hazelhead castle must have been exemplary: 'a stronge old bulding, enuironed with lairge ditches, seatted one [on] a loch, veill planted and comodiously beutified; the heritage of Robert Montgomery; laird therof. Famous it is for the birth of that renoned Poet, Alexander Montgomery.' Burnemouth signalled a new sort of civility as the birthplace of William Aird. As Pont noted, Aird was 'extraordinarily called' from his work as a mason to become a notable preacher and 'detector of the Romisch whoore in the begining of the reformatione of our church'.[29] In this Aird pursued a less 'cautious' path than Pont's father, Robert, proving to be a thorn in James VI's efforts to assert his supremacy over the Kirk in the 1590s.[30]

The painstaking detail that Pont poured into his maps carried over into his engagement with the *pays* through which he travelled and the marks of cultural complexity he found there. He may have muddled the details, but Pont knew that cultural complexity mattered and had to figure in his descriptions. Yet Pont often couched this complexity in reductive national terms – Irish, Scottish, or English. The generation that followed Leland helped to transform him into the father of English history. The 'patriotic' emphasis of travellers and writers

[26] Pont, 'Cunningham', p. 22.
[27] Stringer, 'Richard de Morville'.
[28] Pont, 'Cunningham', p. 23.
[29] Pont, 'Cunningham', pp. 13–14, 18, 30.
[30] Duncan Shaw, 'William Aird', *Oxford DNB* at www.oxforddnb.com.

like Pont, Balfour, the Gordons, and Scotstarvit sometimes similarly affected Scotland's cultural complexity. In this they followed the lead announced by the signatories to the Declaration of Arbroath, where 'what made them Scottish was not language or a native pedigree, but their obedience to the King of Scots'.[31] Alongside this ethno-royalism, Pont's generation recognized 'the importance of geography and mapmaking to national self-knowledge'. They fashioned 'a sense of national identity as geographically defined and constituted' through their travels and scholarship.[32] As Gordon of Straloch proclaimed in 1648, 'our Scotland is put on view and among the other regions of the world claims her place in the great and celebrated theatre of the famous Joan Blaeu'. This was no place to complicate national identities with Hugh and Richard de Morville or other Franci – Bruces, Stewarts, Balliols, Comyns – who added to the ethnic complexity of the Scotland ruled by David I, Malcolm IV, and William III.[33]

John Fullarton prepared Pont's 'Cunningham' for publication by the Maitland Club in 1858. Fullarton called on David Laing, the Scottish bibliophile and leading figure in both the Bannatyne Club and Scottish Society of Antiquaries, to supply a biographic sketch of Pont, accompanied by a short discourse on travel and discovery. For Laing, 'civilised strangers' who first visited a country provided the 'earliest intelligence'. John Hardying, Alexander Lindsay's *Rutter*, and the map that accompanied Lesley's *Historie* all played such roles. But Pont achieved something remarkable: the first maps constructed from actual surveys and 'accurate topographical accounts of the whole of the shires and districts of this country'.[34] For Fullarton, Laing, and others, Blaeu's *Atlas* was the monument to Pont's travels and discovery of Scotland.[35] In 1699 Sibbald similarly celebrated James Balfour's labours. Balfour 'travelled into foreign parts, in order to observe the manners of different nations', returning home to 'study the antiquities and history of his native country' for which 'he undertook various journeys through the different counties of Scotland'. The fruits of those journeys found a home in Balfour's 'common-place books' – what we know as his 'Topographical Descriptions' – from which 'he had begun to compose in Scots, a geographical description of the whole kingdom'.[36]

It might be possible to 'English' the de Morvilles, but the highlands and isles remained an exotic cultural realm even within a Scotland writ large. Sometime

[31] Dauvit Broun, 'Becoming a Nation: Scotland in the 12th and 13th Centuries', in *Nations in Medieval Britain*, ed. Hirokazu Tsurushima (Donington, 2010), p. 100.
[32] Withers, *Geography, Science and National Identity*, pp. 56, 68.
[33] A.D.M. Barrell, *Medieval Scotland* (Cambridge, 2000), pp. 12–41; Matthew Hammond, 'Introduction: The Paradox of Medieval Scotland', in *New Perspectives on Medieval Scotland 1093–1286*, ed. Matthew Hammond (Woodbridge, 2013), pp. 30–52.
[34] Pont, 'Cunningham', p. xxiv.
[35] Pont, 'Cunningham', pp. xx–xxvi.
[36] *The Historical Works of Sir James Balfour* (four volumes; Edinburgh, 1824–25), I, pp. xv, xxiv, xxv.

about 1630 Robert Gordon received a description to that effect from a local informant who travelled widely and spoke with many of the 'ancient men and woemen' of the region.[37] Topographic detail jostled with splashes of local colour in the account of this rugged but fertile region. Fishermen plying Loch Awe reportedly refused to fish for eels as 'bigg as ane horse', leaving them to 'ane ancient man' armed with a line 'bigg in greatness as a mans finger' and a hook to match; he hauled the beasts ashore and killed them with an iron pike. An anaesthetic herb grew along the rocky spine of Knapdale that made faint any man or woman who trod over it until a helping of meat restored the senses. The topography boasted still more exotic qualities north in Benderloch. In the cleft between two hills on the north side of Loch Crenan stood a chapel. It drew men and women from all parts on the morn before St Patrick's Day to drink from the fresh spring and cleanse their bodies of the past year's ailments. One of the lochs bounding Ardgore once sheltered its own 'Nessie' who devoured the country's ancient inhabitants. Along Loch Ness proper, Stratherrick was accounted a 'verie cold Countrey and eivill, fresh waters therintill [inside] being reid colloured running through Mosses'. Gordon's source evaluated scope for improvement. With great charge one might cut a canal between West and East Loch Tarbert and save the long journey round the Mull of Kintyre to the Sound of Bute and Clyde.[38] One wonders if either Gordon or Sibbald, into whose hands they eventually passed, knew what do with this grab-bag of details. Neither made use of them in their respective contributions to Blaeu's *Atlas* and Camden's *Britannia*.

By contrast, Gordon used his Aberdeenshire roots to good effect by composing detailed descriptions of Aberdeen and Banffshire. The draft descriptions survived to become part of Sibbald's papers and eventually MacFarlane's 'Collections'. The finished copies found their way into the 1662 edition of the *Atlas*. Gordon warned those born in a 'warmer air' that this 'temperate and healthy' region, bounded inland by the Spey, Tay, and Grampians, would strike them as chilly, though 'winters are mild beyond what one would believe from the latitude; it is surprising to foreigners arriving here, Danes, Prussians, Poles, since with them the earth for the whole winter lies hard and hidden under perpetual snow and solid ice'. For the chilly among them, Gordon reported that burnable peat came from the surface of the earth rather than riverbeds or marshes as in Belgium.[39] Gordon's observations reveal how the multinational shape of Blaeu's *Atlas* encouraged broader cultural comparisons than those that might be found in a description written primarily with a Scottish (Lesley, Buchanan) or British (Speed, Camden) context in mind. It connects these Scottish travellers

---

[37] *Geographical Collections*, II, pp. xxx–xxxi.
[38] *Geographical Collections*, II, pp. 148–50, 163, 172.
[39] *Blaeu Atlas* (2006), p. 93. The maps are accessible in the National Library of Scotland's digital collections at http://maps.nls.uk/atlas/blaeu/.

and writers to the cross-cultural perspective of Moryson and suggests that their national feeling or patriotic motives did not crowd out their long-standing Europeanism, whether among Parisian intellectuals like Boece or diasporic communities in Denmark and Poland.

Gordon had all of this in mind when he characterized the people of Banff and Aberdeen. The region yielded whatever its people could make of it, depending on their 'laziness or industry'. Dilatoriness robbed animals of hay for winter fodder, but Belgians and other inhabitants of the Low Countries offered a worse reproach: 'The sea is always open and available for navigation ... [and] is equally outstandingly full of fish, but the men from the dregs of the people who have applied themselves to this life practise it for daily needs, not to make money from business; hence while foreigners (especially Belgians) as we look on daily make great profits from catching herring and other fish, they seem to convict of laziness those whose study this should be.' Some of the better sort 'train in letters from their earliest years, and when grown up an education abroad is their pleasure', but too many refused to consider as well the life of a merchant. Their disdain and neglect contributed to a general poverty and want of employment that compelled too many Scots to 'equip themselves to bear arms', continuing a long tradition of serving abroad alongside Belgian, German, and French soldiers.[40]

For Gordon, there was all too much easy living among the landed gentry and their city counterparts. Gordon lamented: 'Parsimony was considered among the virtues by our ancestors, today through foreign contacts other customs have been imbibed – drunkenness, gormandising, luxury, which have brought poverty to many but have not been given up.'[41] Those who turned to Gordon's long account attached to the map of Fife found people who fully made good their potential: 'this most humane province produces civil, cultivated, kindly men, but second to none in carrying arms'. The Fife nobility nurtured 'the attractiveness and culture of the kingdom' as busy and productive lords. Local coal mines created employment, yielded an exportable commodity, and fuelled the sea salt works. The villages of east Neuk benefited from the active exploitation of the herring industry and the region profited from robust Continental trade. And, the ancient kingdom could boast St Andrews, 'not so long ago the metropolis of the whole kingdom in sacred matters' and still 'a dwelling of the Muses' thanks to its ancient university.[42]

The unflattering contrast between Fife and his native Aberdeen vexed Gordon. He felt a deep, personal obligation to describe the 'nature of the inhabitants' since, as he explained for readers, 'I owe my birth to these parts, I must speak modestly, and in this respect as elsewhere truth must be satisfied'. He

---

[40] *Blaeu Atlas* (2006), p. 93.
[41] *Blaeu Atlas* (2006), p. 93.
[42] *Blaeu Atlas* (2006), pp. 82–3.

found much to admire among 'his' people and their civility owed something to geography, cultural exchanges, and innate initiative:

> [Those] who have particular knowledge of these parts will admit that the inhabitants in gentler nature, trained judgement, and cultivation of mind and character excel all their neighbours, especially where this kingdom from here turns north and west. This is partly due to travels among foreigners, and to Aberdeen University, to which all who can gather from every side: from the mountain provinces to lay aside their native fierceness, others to take to a higher level the rudiments of piety and learning, and make themselves equal to public or private business in later life. If you look at the humbler sort and common people, they give themselves up to agriculture or the mechanical arts, which they practise scarcely successfully, yet some rise up.[43]

From the civility of learning, Gordon eventually moved on to the strange arrowheads, some with hooked barbs, that seemed to appear magically from one day to the next without digging or looking. He provided a drawing and reported that 'An upright and trustworthy man' found one of these so-called 'elf arrowheads' in the top of his legging. Lhuyd would have found these interesting along with Gordon's account of stone circles and megaliths, proof that there 'still remain traces of paganism, not in men's minds, but in places dedicated to cult'.[44] Between his impressionistic ethnography and the antiquarian and topographic details, readers of Blaeu's *Atlas* might have lamented not skipping ahead to Gordon's account instead of beginning with the rudimentary excerpts from Camden.

The 'farthest shore of Scotland' – as Blaeu termed it – benefited considerably from Gordon's labours and access to Pont's manuscripts, chiefly Ross, Sutherland, Caithness, Strathnaver, Moray and some smaller regions. Here were regions stamped with diverse cultural exchanges reaching back to the mists of time, and Gordon knew it. References to translations from 'the old language' abound while readers perhaps more used to the term 'gulf' needed a quick note that they are 'named throughout the whole kingdom by those who speak the old language "lochs"'.[45] Caithness bore the most obvious imprint of cultural exchange and the passage of time yielded something unique: 'But it should be noted that many place-names even today have a strange ring, whose origin has no reference to Scots, Irish, Danish, or Norwegian, but they seem of unknown, uncertain, and very ancient origin; such as Orbuster, Lybster, Robuster, Thrumster, and innumerable others. The popular speech today is a quite degenerate Scoto-Irish, sharing in both but satisfactorily reflecting neither.'[46] Fifty years later, Edward Lhuyd read the linguistic diversity and fruits of cultural exchange as distinctive dialects worthy of consideration rather than examples of degeneracy.

---

[43] *Blaeu Atlas* (2006), p. 93.
[44] *Blaeu Atlas* (2006), p. 94.
[45] *Blaeu Atlas* (2006), p. 100.
[46] *Blaeu Atlas* (2006), p. 108.

Gordon did not find Lesley's noble Scots in these regions but their degenerate offspring: 'to such an extent are the nature of the inhabitants blunted to the practice of a more civilised life (which is more common in cities), as they cling fast to their ancient language and old frugality. A correct judgment will attribute this to inertia rather than imitation of older generations.' Gordon might have had in mind Aberdeen itself or the likes of Arbroath, Stonehaven, or the villages of East Neuk when he idealized many 'opportunities for founding cities, very large, safe and capacious harbours; seas full of all kind of fish; fertile land, suited to crops and cattle; and rivers fitted for transportation'. All lay unfulfilled by the 'laziness' of inhabitants who 'grow up and grow old as masters in the same place … living off their cattle'. Anticipating the arguments of improvers in the next century, Gordon blamed the inhabitants for making themselves a people apart in a land scarcely known to 'foreigners, and even to Scots'. Indeed, 'some men equal to this task … set their minds to founding cities', but gave up the effort.[47]

Gordon's condemnation of the inhabitants in Caithness came after a more favourable account of Strathnaver. He made allowances for the limits of what one could accomplish in this mountainous region. 'The industry of the inhabitants, so far as it allowed by climate and soil,' he admitted, 'is employed on cattle' fatted and turned into dried beef for sailors, fishing, and iron mining and smelting. Indeed, Gordon wondered – perhaps with a verbal smirk toward the English – 'that the Danes, when they were subjugating England and raiding our kingdom, sought out rough and uncultivated places as these and looked for homes there'. Their descendants and others grew into a people that Gordon admired: 'strong, robust, tolerant of toil, cold, and heat, accustomed to frugality, and yet not of that roughness of character that the harshness of the region might seem to promise; but joyful in ingenious simplicity'. 'There is the same system of spirit and character in all the other neighbouring provinces,' Gordon continued, and it was 'common to all those regions which speak the old language, that as much as possible they venerate, cherish, and love their Lord, fight for him, in danger give up their lives with no reluctance' and patiently bear the customary burdens placed upon them. Caithness evidently changed Gordon's opinion. Elsewhere in his unpublished account of the Scottish polity he struck a different note from this seemingly impartial primer to Gaelic lordship. The first Scots brought tanistry, 'they being a rough, rude people, knowing litle of civilitie, but altogether barbarous, with armis ever in thair hands as is the use of the hielands even to this day'.[48] Moray prompted specific complaints that likewise expanded to define peoples throughout the region, from being hard drinkers of aqua vitae to the unimpressive architecture in a town like Elgin and the absence of nucleated villages as in England.[49] Gordon thus left readers with contradictory

[47] *Blaeu Atlas* (2006), pp. 108–9.
[48] *Geographical Collections*, II, p. 391.
[49] *Blaeu Atlas* (2006), p. 103.

ethno-cultural descriptions in his struggle to incorporate unique localities and communities within highland stereotypes.

More than any of Blaeu's Scottish collaborators, Gordon (and by extension Pont) gave real ethnographic substance to Scotland and its peoples. Blaeu could be an unresponsive collaborator, but Gordon knew theirs was vital work, considering what had been left undone:

> Our Boece, leaving the description of districts untouched, has turned aside to marvels, in most of which, as the truth has been thrown overboard, there is nothing marvellous. With Herodotus he all but ascribes our origin to the gods, so that some faults of his are disclosed in his history that have roused against him many writers who bore ill-will to us. And I wish that Buchanan, if I may be permitted to say it about so great a man, had kept what he has written in the first three books of his history separate, as a sort of supplement to the work itself, and had not indulged in such lofty conceits that even to foreign readers, he appears to have gone over from the historian to the partisan, passing the description of the kingdom rapidly and lightly by.[50]

Gordon obviously chafed at what he took to be the inadequacies of his predecessors and the lack of zeal among his contemporaries. He aimed by example to 'shake off the lethargy of our countrymen who are fitted to these studies' and push travellers and scholars to move beyond the history writing in which ethnography and topography had apparently been trapped for too long.[51] Gordon explained that 'However uninteresting these descriptions may perhaps appear to readers, as containing too little history, still, if they know the localities, or use the map, their aversion will be mitigated.'[52] For Gordon, the discovery of Scotland and its peoples demanded a deeper commitment to travel and first-hand experience among a much wider range of people. It demanded a new generation of Ponts. And, the fruits of their discoveries called for a new sort of presentation, in this instance Blaeu's great atlas.

Which brings us back to Sibbald. Gordon set a high standard for examining the cultural complexity of Scotland's localities, biases and all. His descriptions revealed the richness of peoples and cultures too easily homogenized or obscured by the familiar divisions of highland, lowland, and borders. James Gordon took possession of his father's papers – with the many transcriptions from Pont's own – and upon James's death in 1686, his neighbour David Gregory saw them safely into Sibbald's hands.[53] What did Sibbald do with this legacy when he took to revising Camden's *Britannia*? Did Sibbald embrace the particularities and fine-grained descriptions of the localities? Was it possible to accommodate the *pays* within his own ambitions and the expectations of Gibson and his backers in the

[50] *Geographical Collections*, II, p. 289.
[51] *Geographical Collections*, II, pp. 288–9.
[52] *Geographical Collections*, II, p. 289.
[53] Stone, 'Timothy Pont', p. 13.

new *Britannia*? Did he wish to do so? These questions frame the analysis that follows.

Contesting Camden's Scotland

Camden described Scotland with some hesitation. In the 1607 edition Camden asked for the 'liberty, with due respect to the Scottish Nation, in pursuance of my bold design of illustrating Britain, to prosecute my undertaking with their good leave; and drawing aside (as it were) the Curtains of obscure Antiquity, to point out, according to my ability, some places of ancient note and memory'. In Gibson's reading, Camden 'profess'd himself at a loss in the affairs of Scotland', which made it 'so much the more necessary to continue ... and add such things as seem proper and agreeable to the design'.[54] Camden created his description using the works of Ptolemy, Pomponius Mela, Fordun, Boece, Buchanan, and Lesley; only Mair seems to have escaped his interest or attention. He especially praised Fordun and Boece.[55] There might be something to say for having brought Buchanan and Lesley to a mainstream audience, given the prohibition against Buchanan's *Historia* and the Continental publication of Lesley's. Otherwise, Camden's Scottish chapters offer a thin, perfunctory topographic description punctuated by sites of memorable historical events drawn from his reading of the *Scotichronicon* and the other accounts. His only contemporary first-hand source was the Aberdeen poet John Johnston, Master of St Mary's College in the University of St Andrews. He authored '*Inscriptiones historicae regum Scotorum*, a sequence of Latin verses on the Scottish monarchs from Fergus to James VI, and *Heroes ex omni historia Scotica lectissimi*, a similar series of verses mostly on heroes of war'.[56] Both were available to Camden in Amsterdam editions (1602 and 1603) and he often called upon an apt selection from Johnston's poetry to improve on and capture the essence of a country he knew precious little about.

Camden admitted that his description was inadequate but believed the reign of James VI and I would change that:

> Thus have I run over Scotland more briefly than the dignity of so great a Kingdom deserves; nor do I at all doubt, but that some one hereafter may give a larger draught of it with a more exquisite pen, with more certainty and better information; since (as I said before) the greatest of Princes has now laid open to us these remote Countries, hitherto shut up.[57]

---

[54] William Camden, *Britannia: Or a Chorographical Description of Great Britain and Ireland* (London, 1695), pp. 881–3, hereafter cited as Camden, *Britannia* (1695).

[55] Camden, *Britannia* (1695), pp. 937, 940.

[56] J. Derrick McClure, 'John Johnston', *Oxford DNB* at www.oxforddnb.com; Angus Vine, *In Defiance of Time: Antiquarian Writing in Early Modern England* (Oxford, 2010), pp. 99–108.

[57] Camden, *Britannia* (1695), p. 950.

Of course Scotland had never been closed to its own travellers or European visitors, but Camden anticipated the rapid growth of travellers within Scotland – he knew of Pont's activities – as well as those who crossed the Tweed after 1603.

When Sibbald took his turn he wrote a competing description of Scotland. His focus was primarily topographical: a shire's location, geography with a smattering of natural history, important towns, castles, and other sites, livelihoods and economic practices along with notable families, historical events, or other matter of particular interest. He added information that eluded Camden (including ruins and would-be antiquities), corrected existing material as needed, and complemented what remained. He substantially expanded the account of Roman remains in Scotland. As with Camden, artefacts, inscriptions, and coins played their part. Sibbald's account of the Antonine wall, building on Pont's surveys, included an outline map of the fort at Airdoch, descriptions of ramparts and ditches, and an effort to explain the stages of the wall's construction.[58]

Overall, Sibbald's additions are never as impressive as Lhuyd's for Wales. He called on a number of local experts, but Sibbald did not undertake the kind of tour that Lhuyd had and the additions do not exceed the length of Camden's original. Oddly, the additions were placed in groups according to the ancient Latin tribal divisions (Gadeni, Selgovae, Novantes, Damnii, and Caledonii) used by Camden rather than the county-by-county endnotes elsewhere. The organization of the material may have been Gibson's. In November 1694, he complained to Arthur Charlett in University College, Oxford about the sorry state of the Scottish materials received.[59] What, then, did Sibbald set out to achieve that sets his Scotland apart from Camden's?

Despite the topographic dominance of the uplands and the importance of the pasture economy, Camden's 'Division of Scotland' followed ethno-cultural lines that relegated the highlands to second place: 'With respect to the manners and ways of living, it is divided into the High-land-men and Low-land-men. These are more civilized, and use the language and habit of the English; the other more rude and barbarous, and use that of the Irish, as I have already mentioned, and shall discourse hereafter.'[60] Writing twenty years after the first edition of Britannia, Camden removed borderers from Scotland's divisions. Those people, by 'the blessed and happy Union, enjoying the Sun-shine of peace on every side, are to be lookt upon as living in the very midst of the British Empire; and begin (being sufficiently tir'd with war) to grow acquainted with, and have an inclination to peace.'[61] Once Boece and Lesley took great pains to examine the cultural distinctiveness of the Border peoples. Camden and the Stuart *imperium* erased

[58] Richard Hingley, *The Recovery of Roman Britain 1586–1906: A Colony so Fertile* (Oxford, 2008), pp. 104–6.
[59] Frank Emery, 'Edward Lhuyd, Edmund Gibson, and the Printing of Camden's *Britannia*, 1695', *The Library* 32.2 (1977), p. 113.
[60] Camden, *Britannia* (1695), p. 885.
[61] Camden, *Britannia* (1695), p. 885.

them from the story, perhaps with lasting effect: we would be hard pressed to find much interest in the Borders among the travellers who followed Camden's lead across the Tweed. Linda Colley's eighteenth-century Britons owed a good deal to this same dynamic by which an imperial perspective hid or deliberately erased cultural complexity in Britain.[62]

Beginning with the Gadeni brought Camden and Sibbald through the Borders to Lothian and Edinburgh. Despite the sunlight of the Stuart *imperium*, the craggy hills and rocks of Tweeddale were 'inhabited by a warlike people, who by reason of so frequent encounters between the Scots and English in former ages, are always very ready for service and sudden invasions'.[63] Camden paused to note the noble Tweed and the abundance of wool produced in the Dale, but this was a county braced for war in his day and the noble families who fortified it for the crown received the most mention. The great marcher families like the Hepburns or Stewarts of Annandale, descended from Franci settlers, occupied most of Camden's description of the lands of the Selgovae in the western Borders.[64] Those of Nidisdale and Annandale were also a warlike people 'infamous for their depredations' in sallying across the Solway Firth to attack England. These rough people fished for salmon on horseback with spears and lived by stealing cattle. Camden called on Lesley – 'a Scotchman himself' – to explain. The raiders lay in wait for their prey under cover of darkness, seized their booty, and earned their reputations by their speed and skill in passing 'through those wild Desarts, crooked turnings, and deep precipices, in the thickest mists and darkness'. When they were captured, their natural 'persuasive Eloquence' could move authorities and adversaries alike to forgive their transgressions and admire their rough courage.[65]

Sibbald consigned the borderers' brutal nature and violent life to the past: 'The Inhabitants [of Dumfries] were a stout warlike People, in *former* times the bulwark of the Kingdom.'[66] He quickly passed on to topographic details, the better pasturage of Dumfries and the good corn land in the bottoms of Nidisdale.[67] Sibbald was deeply concerned for Scotland's economic improvement, especially writing during the hunger and dire economic conditions of the 1690s.[68] Understandably, he explained agricultural improvements in Tweeddale, especially Scotland's finest cattle and the abundance of wheat that allowed for local exports across the border to England. Peebles more typically produced oats and barley and Sibbald took Camden to task for not writing more about Selkirk,

---

[62] Linda Colley, *Britons: Forging the Nation 1707–1837* (New Haven, 1992), pp. 5, 17.

[63] Camden, *Britannia* (1695), p. 894.

[64] Camden, *Britannia* (1695), p. 905.

[65] Camden, *Britannia* (1695), p. 908.

[66] Camden, *Britannia* (1695), p. 909, emphasis mine.

[67] Camden, *Britannia* (1695), pp. 909–10.

[68] Emerson, 'Robert Sibbald', pp. 48, 52–3; Withers, *Geography, Science and National Identity*, p. 83.

whose once thick forests filled with deer had been destroyed by clearance. Peebles' 'Inhabitants have generally strong bodies, being sober and frugal in diet; and living mostly by feeding Cattle: whereby they do not only support themselves, but maintain a good Trade in England with their Wooll, Sheep, Cows, &c.'[69] Sibbald understood something about the Borders that Camden did not: the region contained 'some of the richest agricultural land of Scotland' and was fully populated and intensively farmed, despite the border conflicts.[70] Sibbald passed by the famous castle of Sanqhar and the border families that interested Camden. Instead he described a noble at one with the now-peaceful Borders: 'The Duke of Queensbury, who hath built a noble house at Drumlanerick, and is now adorning it with stately avenues, gardens, and Terras-walks.'[71] This was a far cry from the earl of Bothwell's Hermitage and its violent, lurid place in the history of Mary, Queen of Scots. Sibbald took the same approach in his account of the land of the Novantes in Galloway and Ayrshire, noting especially that 'it is very populous, and the Inhabitants of it are exceeding industrious'.[72]

Lothian, a region rich with a history of Anglo-Scottish conflict, was 'commended above any County in Scotland ... for its excellent Corn-lands, and civility' by Camden. He traced a route to Edinburgh from Seton through Borthwick, Newbottle, Dalkeith, and Musselburgh.[73] He described Edinburgh – 'called by the Irish-Scots Dun-Eaden' – as if rewriting a medieval chronicle:

> How Edenborough, by the vicissitudes of war, has been subject sometimes to the Scots, sometimes to the Saxons, who inhabited this Eastern part of Scotland, until it became wholly under the Scots Dominion in the year of our Lord 960, when the English Empire, under the convulsions of the Danish Wars, lay as it were expiring ... and what turns of fortune it felt afterwards: the Historians relate, from whom you are to be informed.[74]

Until they could put their hands on one of the standard accounts, Camden offered a poem by Johnston to would-be travellers. It recapped his own summary of Edinburgh's sights and ended on a lofty note:

> In the last borders of the Northern coast
> What rival land an equal sight can boast?
> These glories, Trav'ler, when at last you see,

[69] Camden, *Britannia* (1695), pp. 893–4, 899–901.
[70] Francis Pryor, *The Making of the British Landscape: How We have Transformed the Land from Prehistory to Today* (London, 2010), pp. 361–70.
[71] Camden, *Britannia* (1695), p. 910.
[72] Camden, *Britannia* (1695), pp. 909–16.
[73] Camden, *Britannia* (1695), pp. 895–7.
[74] Camden, *Britannia* (1695), pp. 897–8.

Say if you don't mistrust your wondring eye,
And think it transport all and extasy![75]

Sibbald improved on Camden considerably with current topographic information about Lothian and potted histories of its towns. There was no sign of Dunbar's lewd washerwomen, but he found lasting memories of Cromwell's inexplicable triumph with a handful of sickly soldiers, evidence of economic development in the form of salt-pans, and exports of broad cloth and herring. Contemporary civility erased the marks of war at Dunglas. What had once been destroyed in 1640 by the treachery of an English servant in the Earl of Haddington's entourage was 'now repaired, and adorned by Sir John Hall, the present possessor, with curious Gardens, spacious Courts, and a large and pleasant Avenue'.[76] This coast around Dunbar was 'the most fruitful of the Kingdom, especially in Wheat and Barley'. The same was true around Edinburgh proper, where coal, limestone, a sort of black marble, and copper could as well be found.[77] The legwork of predecessors like Pont handed Sibbald this sort of rich local description. It revealed life beyond the now sometimes superficial overviews of Boece, Lesley, or Buchanan. Sibbald learned and could document the industry and livelihoods of real Scots in his writing back against Camden.

Thirty years spent in Edinburgh served Sibbald well in his description of the 'chief City of the Kingdom of Scotland'. The Romans could not have made a better choice for a fortified site than the rock on which Edinburgh castle stood. It could not have been a coincidence that a marginal reference was inserted directing readers to Sibbald's rival John Slezer and his description of the castle. Abel Swalle published Slezer's *Theatrum Scotiae* in 1693, a project to which Sibbald was meant to contribute until he and Slezer fell out.[78] Sibbald brought his own eye and first-hand experiences to descriptions of the High Street (Royal Mile), churches like St Giles and the Tron Kirk, hospitals, or Charles I's parliament house. He must have known well the university founded by James VI, with its '3 Courts, adorned on all sides with excellent buildings, two lower, and one higher which is as large as both the other' and a library 'well stor'd with printed books and ... some Manuscripts: under which is the King's Printing-house'. Holyrood stood proudly at the far end of the High Street, along which one would find the College of Justice, the future Advocates Library – 'a Bibliotheque well

---

[75] Camden, *Britannia* (1695), p. 898.

[76] Camden, *Britannia* (1695), pp. 902–3; also Craig Statham, *Lost East Lothian* (Edinburgh, 2011), pp. 26–8.

[77] Camden, *Britannia* (1695), pp. 902–3.

[78] Camden, *Britannia* (1695), p. 903; John Slezer, *Theatrum Scotiae* (London, 1693), p. 7; Withers, *Geography, Science and National Identity*, p. 94. The prospects are accessible in the National Library of Scotland's digital collections at http://digital.nls.uk/slezer/.

Prospectus Civitatis EDINBURGENE a prædio DEAN dicto. The Prospect of EDINBRUGH from ŷ DEAN.

22   'Prospect of Edinburgh from ye Dean' engraved by John Slezer from Slezer, *Theatrium Scotiae* (Edinburgh, 1693). Reproduced by permission of the National Library of Scotland.

furnished with Books of Law and History' – and the Royal College of Physicians of Edinburgh founded by Sibbald himself and chartered by Charles II.[79]

The seventeenth century brought its own kind of modernity to Sibbald's Edinburgh. Some twenty years earlier the city magistrates, at great charge, brought 'one of the best Springs of Scotland into the City: which they did by leaden Pipes from a Hill at above 3 miles distance … [and] erected several stately Fountains in the middle of the High-Street to serve this town with water'. Sibbald's magistrates did their job well. The wellheads at the High Street, Lawnmarket, Netherbow, and Canongate served the city with water until the nineteenth century.[80] Yet Sibbald's distance from the histories of Boece and Lesley closed when he repeated the account of St Catherine's spring, even if he replaced its mystical aura with a medicinal one: 'The Oily Well … sends up along with the water an Oil or Balsom which swims upon it. 'Tis found by experience to be exceeding good not only for the cure of Scabs, but likewise of any pains proceeding from cold, as also for strengthening and putting life into any decaying part.'[81]

Linlithgow and its royal palace, with ranges built by one king each from James III to James VI, certainly received its due in Sibbald's telling as did nearby

[79] Camden, *Britannia* (1695), pp. 903–4; Withers, *Geography, Science and National Identity*, p. 71.
[80] See http://www.edinburgh-royalmile.com/interest/wellheads.html.
[81] Camden, *Britannia* (1695), p. 905.

Nidry Castle and its stone altar. Standing stones and camp remains found south of the town also represented an important addition. They too became part of Sibbald's project to elevate Scotland's status within *Britannia*.[82] Richard Hingley has detected this purpose in Sibbald's studies of the Roman presence in lowland Scotland, especially his *Historical Inquiries, Concerning the Roman Monuments and Antiquities in the North-Part of Britain called Scotland* (1707). Sibbald 'felt that the Romans with their "Guards", "colonies", and civility rather than the Picts or Caledonians, were the genetic and cultural ancestors of the Lowland Scots.' Thus, 'the Romans stayed long in this Country' and tutored Sibbald's ancestors in 'Arts and Policy ... they tamed their Fierceness, and brought them to affect a civil life'.[83] Eighteenth-century investigators might challenge Sibbald's reading, but for him the Antonine wall constituted 'a defence behind which the Roman cities and civility could flourish' long before Laing's Anglo-Normans brought civilization in their van.[84]

The Damnii once occupied Clydesdale, Renfrew, Lennox, and Stirlingshire. Gold and lapis lazuli dug in Crawford moor, the pollock and floating islands in Loch Lomond, and the craggy two-headed rock on which the mighty Dumbarton castle stood nearly exhausted Camden's description of the region. He called on one of Johnston's rhymes for a pithy, Protestant, and prosaic account of Glasgow:

> Not haughty Prelates e'er adorn'd thee so,
> Not stately Mitres cause of all thy woe,
> As Cluyd's muses grace thy blest abodes,
> And lift thy head among the deathless gods.
> Cluyd, great flood! for plenteous fish renown'd,
> And gentle streams that cheer the fruitful ground.
> But happy Glascow, Cluyd's chiefest pride,
> Glory of that and all the world beside,
> Spreads round the riches of her noble tide.[85]

For Sibbald, Glasgow demanded a description that recognized its place as, 'in respect of largeness, buildings, trade and wealth, the chief City in the Kingdom next Edinburgh'. He betrayed little personal familiarity with his neighbouring rival, though, and only the Tollbooth, St Mungo's cathedral, and the College received a mention. Of more interest were the remains of the Roman camp at Paisley and the evidence for two Roman roads in the vicinity, one to Falkirk and the other, perhaps, a terminus for Watling Street. Juggling antiquity and modernity, Sibbald added accounts of the commercial development of Clydeside, Greenock, the great herring fisheries, and Port Glasgow.[86]

[82] Camden, *Britannia* (1695), pp. 905–6.
[83] Quoted in Hingley, *Recovery of Roman Britain*, pp. 106–10.
[84] Hingley, *Recovery of Roman Britain*, pp. 106–10.
[85] Camden, *Britannia* (1695), p. 917.
[86] Camden, *Britannia* (1695), pp. 923–4.

Camden's last region, Caledonia, embraced the rest of Scotland as the land of the Picts, so named for 'that custom of painting their bodies', or the Caledonii as they were known to 'Classick Authors'. The Caledonii were one with their land:

> [A] people hardy, rough, unciviliz'd, wild and rustick, such as the Northern nations generally are; as observ'd to be of a fiercer temper from the extream coldness of their climate, and more bold and forward from their abundance of blood. And besides their clime, the nature of the country confirms it, which rises up every where in rough and rugged mountains; and Mountaneers are lookt upon by all as a hardy and robust sort of people.[87]

Camden found it interesting that the name 'Caledonii grew so common amongst the Roman writers, that they made use of to signifie all Britain, and all the Forests of Britain'. Caledonia also gave its name to that race of fierce, thick-maned bulls that pursued Robert the Bruce in the forests around Stirling, cousins to dogs so fierce that the Romans assumed they were 'brought over in cages of Iron.'[88]

Sibbald had no interest in Camden's tour through classical sources for the origins and meaning of Caledonii. He began methodically working his way through the shires, beginning with Fife. The pattern of his engagement with Camden's original continued much as before. Both men agreed on the productivity of Fife: grain, sea-coal, and great hauls of fish from a coast, in Camden's words, 'well planted with little towns, that breed good store of lusty Seamen'. Indeed, Camden used Johnston's verses to celebrate the industry of these lowland Scots. The elevation of St Andrews to metropolitan status out of the fourteenth-century conflicts between England and Scotland interested Camden, as did the noble families and seats of royal power, including Dunfermline and Falkland palace. Sibbald recounted the transfer of the hereditary shrievalty of Fife from the Sibbalds of Balgonie to the Rothes and lingered with some affection over Scotland's oldest university and the foundations of its three colleges (St Leonard's, St Salvator's, New College). Once again, 'stately houses of the Nobility and Gentry' replaced the remains of a more violent baronial Scotland.[89]

The contests for political control of Argyll with its many lochs and rocky coast interested Camden, from the arrival of the Scots from Ireland, a '3d Nation' to join the Britons and Picts, to the regal pretensions of the Lords of the Isles after its creation by James IV. Kintyre and Lorn were just continuations of the same topography and political narrative.[90] Sibbald gave his own patriotic account of the peopling of Argyll and the origins of the Scottish monarchy:

> formerly inhabited by the Horesti ... or Mountaineers, mentioned by Tacitus, viz. the true ancient Scots, who came from Ireland, and possessed themselves of the West-Isles,

[87] Camden, Britannia (1695), p. 925.
[88] Camden, Britannia (1695), pp. 925–6.
[89] Camden, Britannia (1695), pp. 927–30, 950–1.
[90] Camden, Britannia (1695), pp. 929–34.

and of these Countries. For distinction's sake, they were called the Northern Picts ... These two Counties, with the Western Isles, made up the Kingdom of the Scots, whilst the rest of Scotland was under the Romans and Picts. Afterwards, the whole Country came under one King, namely Kenneth the second, who was called Rex Scotorum.[91]

As for the people, Camden neatly blended Boece's heroic Scots and his own lowland prejudices:

These Parts are inhabited by a sort of people, barbarous, warlike, and very mischievous, commonly called Highland-men; who being the true race of the ancient Scots, speak Irish, and call themselves Albinnich. People they are of firm and compact bodies, of great strength, swift of foot, high minded, born as it were to exercises of War, or rather of robberies; and desperately bent upon revenge. They wear, after the manner of the Irish, strip'd Mantles of divers colours, with their hair thick and long; living by hunting, fishing, fowling, and stealing. In war, their armour is an iron head-piece, and a coat of Mail; their arms, a bow, barbed arrows, and a broad back-sword.[92]

Camden noted approvingly James's legislation from the 1580s, meant to curtail clanship among these people, 'what with plundering and murdering, they commit such barbarous outrages, that their savage cruelty hath made this Law necessary'.[93] Sibbald's response is telling of his efforts to rewrite the Scots. Sibbald dismissed Camden's details by reporting simply that the 'whole shire is mountainous, and the Inhabitants, who speak the Irish, live mostly by their hunting and fishing'. The only engagement with Camden was a marginal one, in which 'Plaids' was added for his cumbersome description of their mantles.[94]

Storied Perthshire presents another such contest. Camden found perhaps his best voice in this description:

Out of the very bosom of the Mountains of Albany issues the Tay, the greatest river in all Scotland, and rolls along thro' the fields, until widening it self into a Lake full of Islands, it there restrains its course. After this, kept within banks, it waters Perth, a large, plentiful, and rich country ... This Athol (to make a little digression) is infamous for Witches, but a country fruitful enough, having woody valleys, where once the Caledonian Forest (dreadful for its dark intricate windings, for its denns of bears, and its huge wild thick-maned bulls,) extended it self in former ages, far and near in these parts.[95]

Camden tracked the Tay to Dunkeld, home to the episcopal see and 'lookt upon by most as a town of the Caledonians' – Buchanan's account surfaces here. Ruthven demanded the condemnation of the plotters who briefly seized James, since 'the mentioning of such wicked generations, may be of use to caution posterity'. Scone and the stone of Scone, the coronation seat of Scottish kings

[91] Camden, *Britannia* (1695), p. 951.
[92] Camden, *Britannia* (1695), p. 934.
[93] Camden, *Britannia* (1695), p. 934.
[94] Camden, *Britannia* (1695), pp. 934, 952.
[95] Camden, *Britannia* (1695), p. 935.

since Kenneth, required creative treatment. What had been seized by Edward
I and taken to Westminster as the ultimate symbol of Scottish subjugation,
Camden turned into an object of almost Arthurian prophecy designed to herald
the Stuart succession: 'it hath now proved true' that 'where they find this stone
the Scots shall reign'.[96] There was little here for Sibbald to dispute or amend,
but he once again 'civilized' the spectre of the Caledonians or highland Scots.
Dunkeld, with its ruined cathedral, lay surrounded by 'pleasant woods, at the
foot of the Grampian hills' and acted as 'the chief Market Town of the Highlands; and is of late very much adorned with stately buildings, erected by the
Marquis of Athol'.[97]

The descriptions of Angus, the Mearns, and Aberdeenshire featured the
familiar duality, Camden's account filled out with historical events and the odd
verse from Johnston for topographic colour, supplemented by Sibbald's descriptions designed to offer a contemporary account of the people, their livelihoods,
and notable locations. One could thus find Camden's report of the foundation
of Aberdeen University, Johnston's poem praising the fine city and fertile countryside, and a long description of salmon – by law 'sold to the English for nought
but English Gold'.[98] Dundee, which Sibbald had seen destroyed at the age of ten,
was now a town 'adorned with excellent buildings of all sorts ... and a considerable trade with strangers' whose inhabitants 'are generally rich; and those who fall
into decay, have a large Hospital provided for them'.[99] Old and New Aberdeen
became yet another opportunity to describe Scots that were 'generally very civil
and polite'. The 'well bred' inhabitants lived in a city that exceeded 'the rest of
the Cities in the north of Scotland in bigness, trade, and beauty'. The built environment of the city was essential evidence, from 'large and stately' St Machars'
cathedral with its great, closed imperial crown for a steeple and the 'neatness
and stateliness' of King's College to streets paved with hard flint in the new
town or its city library. The many seats of the gentry and nobility stood alongside
great stone circles that seemed 'to have been places of worship in the time of
Heathenism', obelisks, and cairns that so fascinated Lhuyd in later years.[100]

Beneath Camden and Sibbald's Scotland

The character of both men's descriptions converged as they moved north
through Buchan, Elgin, and Inverness to Ross, Sutherland, and Caithness.
Each held to his particular elements and theme but they both became more

---

[96] Camden, *Britannia* (1695), pp. 935–8.
[97] Camden, *Britannia* (1695), p. 952.
[98] Camden, *Britannia* (1695), pp. 937–42.
[99] Camden, *Britannia* (1695), p. 952.
[100] Camden, *Britannia* (1695), pp. 952–5.

cursory in depth and detail.[101] Neither man wrote from experience. Camden had none and Sibbald's was confined to the east coast, Edinburgh, Fife, and Aberdeen. Camden's shortcomings are easier to understand. Sibbald's failure is less readily explained or credited, especially against snide comments about Blaeu's *Atlas* with its scrapings from Camden and Buchanan. Sibbald's additions often come off second best by comparison to the *Atlas Novus*. The additions to Berwickshire, possibly by Scotstarvit, and Sibbald's own tell a very similar story of Duns and its famous son, John Duns Scotus. However, only Blaeu's readers would learn that the fertile soils of the Mers nourished 'numerous inhabitants, in peace industrious, in war stout-hearted, who used to defend their possessions most bravely against the English'.[102] Among the 'Novantes', Sibbald noted the industrious people of Ayrshire and the great flocks of sheep kept by the people of Galloway.[103] But Kirkcudbright's minister, John Maclellan, had something more to say that would not have been out of keeping with Sibbald's efforts to 'civilize' the Scots of *Britannia*:

> The inhabitants are brave and warlike: certainly in the recent battle of Newburn on Tyne in England, a few Galloway cavalry ... gave an outstanding instance of their valour ... Formerly this people were ready to nourish discord, but have gradually learned by a more humane culture and reified religion to dispense with ferocity. The Gentry, ready with hand and counsel, are easily the equal of any in elegance of body and custom. The common people are of strong body and not wretched ability.[104]

In their descriptions of Scotland and its people, Blaeu's collaborators and Sibbald executed much the same project. They revised, updated, and added to Camden's *Britannia*. It would be unfair to suggest that readers interested in a more thoughtful and substantive description of Scotland and its peoples than Camden's should have stuck to Blaeu and ignored Gibson and Sibbald's new *Britannia*. For a vernacular audience Sibbald's important additions – and they were just that – played a vital role, especially for those who wished to see Camden's strengths in antiquarianism and chorography (regional description with an emphasis on ruling families and seats) extended to Scotland. Being separated by four decades, there was also no reason to think what had been accomplished in Blaeu's *Atlas* did not need revisiting.

If there is an explanation for the unflattering comparison with Blaeu's *Atlas* or, even, Lhuyd's additions about Wales, it emerges from Sibbald's working papers and archive. We know that Sibbald, the literal beneficiary of Pont's travels and the Gordons' labours, 'did not actively engage in direct observation ... Sibbald was the compiler of other's accounts, a personal "centre of calculation" situated

---

[101] Camden, *Britannia* (1695), pp. 941–58.
[102] *Blaeu Atlas* (2006), p. 61; Camden, *Britannia* (1695), pp. 901–2.
[103] Camden, *Britannia* (1695), pp. 915–16.
[104] *Blaeu Atlas* (2006), p. 71.

at the hub of a network of correspondents upon whose word he was reliant'.[105] He left the travelling and observation to local informants like John Adair and Martin Martin. His printed 'Advertisement' of 1682 solicited answers from people throughout Scotland to a comprehensive range of questions as well as specialized information from the nobility, clergy, gentry, burghs, and universities. Some sixty-five responses, often from clergy, survive among Sibbald's papers, including that of Reverend James Wallace, who went on to write his own *Description of the Isles of Orkney* in 1693. In following up responses to his 'Advertisement', Sibbald laid out a distinctly methodical approach for his respondents, asking them to tackle their locales parish by parish.[106] Many examples of parochial descriptions written for Sibbald or collected by him survived to be included in Macfarlane's *Geographical Collections*. We can contrast the differences between Sibbald's additions and the material with which he had to work by examining accounts of the border shires by John Ouchterlony and Andrew Symson. They give a nice sense of 'what might have been', had Sibbald exploited his informants better in revising *Britannia* or completed his 'Scottish Atlas'.

John Ouchterlony of Guinde or Guynd, some time after 1683, supplied Sibbald with a detailed account of the five presbyteries and fifty-some parishes in Forfarshire (Angus). Much of the description focussed on the local nobles, lairds, and ministers with their seats, livings, and general surroundings. The dating makes it impossible to know if Sibbald received this before or after his work on *Britannia* and it might have been collected for the 'Scottish Atlas'. As a practical matter it would have been impossible to include much of this information in either, but Ouchterlony framed his experiences according to the civility introduced by improving landholders and the coexistence of lowland and highland topography and ethnography.[107] The people of Forther parish might have stood in for many highland descriptions, except for Ouchterlony's matter-of-fact reporting. James Ogilvy, the Royalist earl of Airlie, held sway in the parish with its great glen and forests. According to Ouchterlony, 'the nature of the people and these of Blacklounans a highland place in the parish of Alithie consisting of diverse small heritors ... all one with the other highland men that you will get descrived to you in other places except that the Irish is not their native language for none speak Irish there except strangers that come from other partis, notwithstanding ... the Minister always preaches in the afternoon in the Irish toungue'.[108] No barbarity attached to these people. Instead it lay with the Danes and Scots who met centuries before at the battle of Panmure or the more

---

[105] Withers, *Geography, Science and National Identity*, p. 80.
[106] Withers, *Geography, Science and National Identity*, p. 71–84.
[107] *Geographical Collections*, II, pp. 25, 29, 35, 37–40, 43.
[108] *Geographical Collections*, II, p. 36.

recent depredations of avaricious townspeople who left Arbroath abbey the magnificent red stone ruin we now recognize.[109]

Such an account might have fired Sibbald's determination to wipe away the stigma of poverty attached to Scotland. A description he possessed before his work on *Britannia* seems hardly to have affected the additions. Andrew Symson, minister of Kirkinner and then of Douglas, started a description of Galloway in 1684 before he sought refuge in Perthshire for being on the wrong side when Presbyterian dissenters rose against James VII and II and the authoritarian Church of Scotland with its bishops.[110] Sibbald's *Advertisement* for his proposed *Scotia Antiqua & Scotia Moderna* in 1682 and appeal for information for the 'Scottish Atlas' in 1683 originally prompted Symson.[111] This ancient kingdom of the Britons boasted a diverse topography featuring abundant pastures and moorland, a jagged peninsular coastline with fertile coastal lowlands, numerous riverways, and a few notable hills. This topographic diversity and its thrusting place in the Irish Sea made Galloway a natural home to complex peoples and cultural practices. John Maclellan captured some of this for Blaeu and it became the ordinary stuff of Symson's first-hand experiences.

Nestled midway between the Dee and Cree rivers in the stewartry of Kirkcudbright, Monygaffe parish, much of it 'great hills, mountains, Rocks and Moors', held an important weekly mercat 'every Saturday, frequented by the Moormen of Carrick, Monnygaffe and other moor places, who buy there great quantities of meal and malt brought hither out of the parishes of Whitherne [Whithorn]'.[112] Travel was not easy across the length and breadth of this large parish and the weekly market brought the inhabitants together for the exchange of goods, news, and the like. The Restoration Kirk did not have the same effect. The upper part of the parish clearly needed its own church and it 'hath been endeavoured to get a Kirk erected there, but as yet that affair hath been unsuccessful and for any thing I know, will continue so to be, unless people concerned therein will learn to be more religious, which I fear, will not be in hast[e]'.[113] Irreligion took other forms in Monygaffe, like preserving the morality tale of the Piper and the Gout-well of Larg. The 'Piper stole away the offering left at this well (these offerings are some inconsiderable thing which the countrey people used to leave at well, when they come to make use of them towards any cure) but when he was drinking of ale, which he intended to pay with the money he had

[109] *Geographical Collections*, II, pp. 46–9.
[110] Clare Jackson, 'Andrew Symson', *Oxford DNB* at www.oxforddnb.com.
[111] Robert Sibbald, *Advertisement ... to Publish the Description of the Scotia Antiqua & Scotia Moderna* (WING S3721A; Edinburgh, 1682); Sibbald, *An Account of the Scotish Atlas, or, The Description of Scotland Ancient & Modern* (WING S3720; Edinburgh, 1683); *Geographical Collections*, II, p. 51.
[112] *Geographical Collections*, II, p. 69.
[113] *Geographical Collections*, II, p. 70.

taken away, the gout, as they say, seized him' and the well spurned his pleas for cure until he restored the offering.[114]

Wigton acted as a cultural crossroads too. The midsummer fair on St Albans day included the market for horses and young fillies, 'which the borderers from Annandale and places thereabout (the stile the Country calls them by, is Johnnies) come and buy in great numbers'.[115] This may be the earliest reference to 'Johnnies' being Scottish borderers, a good fifty years before Allan Ramsay's *Bonny Tweedside* matched the bonny lass with her johnny (as cited in the *Oxford English Dictionary*). Cattle too were serious business. A drover for the earl of Galloway once led a head of the great beasts into England, where mischief ensued, thanks to the standing prohibition of Irish cattle imports:

> [They] were seiz'd upon in England for Irish cattell and because the person to whom they were entrusted, had not witnesses ther ready at the precise hour to swear that they were seen calved in Scotland ... they were by the sentence of Sr J L and some others who knew well enough that they were bred in Scotland, knockt on the head and kill'd.[116]

All the blame for incivility, for a 'very hard measure' lay on the English official who perpetrated 'an act unworthy of persons of that quality and station'.[117]

Symson coloured his account of Galloway using scholarship, first-hand experience, and local informants. At one point he corrected the placement of Loch Merton 'in Speeds lesser Map', while local informers in Stranraver put him on to a remarkable artefact of the town's centuries-old contacts in the Irish Sea community – a sea-going connection that Symson repeatedly noted. Townsmen digging a water gate for the mill unearthed the remains of a ship. By the part of it dug out, 'my informers, who saw it, conjecture that the vessel had been pretty large, they also tell me that the boards were not joyned together after the usuall fashion of our present ships or barks as also that it had nailes of copper'. On to Kirkcolme, Symson's informants there reported on a powerful well, 'to which people superstitiously resort, to fetch water for sick persones to drink and they report that if the person's disease be deadly the well will be so dry that it will be difficult to get water, but if the person be recoverable, then there will be water enough'. All this and more Symson voluntarily composed for Sibbald. He completed the rest of the account based on Sibbald's parochial questionnaires for the 'Scottish Atlas'. Following the guidelines methodically, Symson reported on the nature of the country; products, plants, animals; forests, medicinal springs, parks, rivers; roads, bays, and ports available for commerce; monuments, forts, camps, battles; monasteries; noble houses; the nobility and gentry; religious divisions and officials.[118]

---

[114] *Geographical Collections*, II, pp. 70–1.
[115] *Geographical Collections*, II, pp. 72–3.
[116] *Geographical Collections*, II, pp. 78–9.
[117] *Geographical Collections*, II, p. 79.
[118] *Geographical Collections*, II, pp. 87, 93–4, 128.

The shire could not brag about its oats, but its people performed something almost wondrous with them. They laid the dry oats 'upon the Kiln flour [sic] in a circular bed about a foot thick, then being barefoot they go among it rubbing it with their feet (this they call Lomeing [loaming] of the corne), and by this means, the long beards and awnds are separated from the corne, and the corne made, as they terme it, more snod and easie to pass through the mill'.[119] When the oats arrived at the mill, 'the countrey people have the dexterity of making excellent and very hearty meal, I mean when they make it designedly and for their own use, shelling it in the Mill, twice and sometimes thrice, before they grind it into meal and they grind it not so small and fine, as they do commonly in other parts'. The hearty oatmeal 'abundantly satisfy themselves and furnish the Moorlands plentifully with victual, yea and oftentimes they vend and transport much thereof to other countreys'.[120] The local beer mixed with oats and roseager (bearded darnel) 'occasions strangers to find fault with our ale, although it do not much trouble the inhabitants ... providing there be not too great a quantity thereof'. Symson noted its 'narcotick' qualities, but might have been hard pressed to distinguish the symptoms of drunkenness from the dizziness, nausea, hallucinations, fainting, or seizures today associated with accidental ingestion of fungus-infected darnel.[121]

Sibbald requested one other sort of detail in his questionnaires: customs. Like the travellers who first discovered and sought to describe humanity in the Atlantic world, Symson understood that whatever he reported about livelihoods (and more) could not be separated from the 'customs' that defined the people of Galloway: 'concerning their particular customes &c. I have already given an account of their husbandry and occasionaly also of some other things'.[122] The ethnographer in Fynes Moryson would have had no trouble understanding what followed. The people commonly married on Tuesdays and Thursdays, as Symson knew at first hand. Their perfectly conventional burial practices included one odd – and sensible – custom: burning the bedstraw on which the deceased had lain. As great chewers of tobacco, 'let not a traveller want an ounce or two of Roll Tobacco in his pocket and for an Inch or two thereof, he need not fear the want of a guide ether night or day'. Barrelled whey sustained the populace in the winter months as a by-product of their cheese making. They knew how to tan hides with heather as well as bark. Symson explained precisely what sleeping rough meant here, stripping oneself naked and wrapping up in a blanket, sometimes outside – 'be the night never so cold and stormie' – keeping company with the cattle and sheep in their folds. Two dialect oddities stood out, dropping 'the letter H after T, as Ting for thing' and pronouncing 'V for W'. Veal was a rarity

---

[119] *Geographical Collections*, II, p. 102.
[120] *Geographical Collections*, II, p. 102.
[121] *Geographical Collections*, II, p. 103.
[122] *Geographical Collections*, II, p. 118.

on any table but a gentleman's. With a keener sense than their industrial-farming descendants, people understood that the distress caused to the cow by the absence of her calf interfered with natural milk production. They also thought it 'very ill husbandry' to sell a butchered calf that would yield a good deal more over its lifetime. Finally, the peculiarity of weights and measures in Galloway, at least some of which sprang from 'a debate betwixt the town and countrey' over the pints in a peck, demanded careful attention.[123]

Symson loved his work, and it showed. Again and again his talent for description brought Galloway and its people to life in all their complexity. Symson peeled away the veneer of national labels and stereotypes to reveal cultural complexity as real people lived and experienced it in the *pays*. His description is surely one of the most accomplished of its kind and stands out among its cousins preserved among Sibbald's papers. He reassured Sibbald that this rich account was 'from my own knowledge and observation'. He offered to aid any 'curious inquirer' from Carlisle, Glasgow, or Edinburgh as a first-hand guide to Galloway, 'affoording him my help and directions to travel to the principal places of this countery, yea and to Portpatrick itself (and thence to Ireland if he please)'. Still, Symson only finally transcribed his original account from 1684 in 1692 and sent it to Sibbald with some unspecified new details based on reports from informants.[124]

Sibbald expressed his satisfaction with Symson's work, yet made no obvious use of the description or many like it.[125] He offered *Britannia*'s readers little more than an account of Scotland shorn of the stereotypes with which they would have been familiar. Why? The most likely influence on Sibbald's approach was his plan for the 'Scottish Atlas'. Unlike Lhuyd, Sibbald accepted Gibson's commission when he was already fully engaged in writing his own, comprehensive description of Scotland. Why should he prejudice that project or pour his accumulated materials into *Britannia*? As Sibbald explained, 'I applyde myself to procure descriptions from those who resided in the Several Countreys and were most capable to do them and then I wrott myself.'[126] Indeed, Sibbald's attitude about travel and encounter harked back to Samuel Purchas, who had compiled *Purchas's Pilgrims* precisely so that others would not have to travel. 'It is certain that most of men have a great desire to travell,' Sibbald wrote in his overview of the *Scottish Atlas*, 'and it is certainly an inexcusable fault to be ignorant of what concerneth our own Countrey.' However, many could not travel, because of poverty or ill-health, and had to rely upon accounts like his. Thanks to those narratives, 'we can sitting at home view the whole Earth and Seas, and much sooner pass through them in our studies, than Travellers can do by their Voyages;

[123] *Geographical Collections*, II, pp. 118–22.
[124] *Geographical Collections*, II, pp. 127–8.
[125] Jackson, 'Andrew Symson'.
[126] Quoted in Withers, *Geography, Science and National Identity*, p. 80.

and so may, without hazard of being infected by the vices of Forreiners, improve our minds and reap all other Advantages from them'.[127] Nonetheless, it is hard not to think that the critical difference compared to Lhuyd's accomplishments lay in Sibbald's attitude to travel: he needed to get out of his study.

Sibbald completed two works: a partial description of Scotland in 1683 and a Scottish natural history, his *Scotia Illustrata* in 1684; he also repackaged earlier material into an expanded history of Fife and Kinross in 1710 and his *Description of the Isles of Orkney and Zetland* in 1711. Sibbald was in his his early forties when he accepted Gibson's commission; he lived for another thirty years without producing his own *Britannia* for Scotland. Admittedly, 'he lost many personal papers in a house fire on 20 March 1694 ... and financial difficulties forced him to sell a large proportion of his library in 1707–8'.[128] However, Sibbald's additions seldom exceeded Camden's original and pale by comparison to Lhuyd's. Sibbald had the information at hand to do more, but he cannot even be said to have improved on the details – the 'scrapings' from Camden and Buchanan – found in Blaeu's *Atlas Novus*. Sadly, then, *Britannia* was just a pause in Sibbald's real labours, sandwiched between his 'Scottish Atlas', plans for the Royal Society of Scotland, and involvement in other projects. Sibbald may have meant for the 'Scottish Atlas' to be his definitive work, an armchair traveller's delight built on the fieldwork of travellers like Symson, yet the revisions to *Britannia* were as close as he ever came.

Sibbald seems to emerge from all of this as a familiar type, the academic with a storehouse of knowledge but without the ability to make good on the promise of the raw material or to focus his intellectual designs. Sibbald missed an easy trick, the opportunity to refute cultural stereotypes and challenge simplistic, homogenous identities with descriptions of local reality and cultural complexity. Still, even a *Britannia* rewritten by Sibbald in his Canongate lodgings from a storehouse of material at hand had a vital purpose. Many of Sibbald's activities, his *Scottish Atlas*, the Royal College of Physicians of Edinburgh, dedicated efforts to found a Royal Society of Scotland, and the Scottish Society of Antiquaries, 'involved patriotic efforts to vindicate the honour of Scotland'.[129] Camden may have called Scotland 'a great kingdom' when writing after the accession of a Stuart king-emperor, yet it was still a poor relation and weak neighbour in his account. It becomes clear that Sibbald set out to redefine Scotland, to erase the stigmas of poverty and weakness, and to establish it on an equal footing with its neighbours. Within the pages of *Britannia* he succeeded.

We should not dismiss Sibbald's spirited assault on stereotypes of Scottish poverty and barbarity – or what he aspired to achieve with his 'Scottish Atlas' and the journeys of discovery that the project inspired. By contrast, having read

---

[127] Sibbald, *Scotish Atlas*, p. 3.
[128] Withers, 'Robert Sibbald'.
[129] Emerson, 'Robert Sibbald', p. 54.

both Gibson's 1695 and 1722 editions, Thomas Hearne was in no doubt as to whose additions deserved praise:

> But excepting what ye Learned Mr Llhuyd of ye Ashmolean Museum did there is nothing of any great moment appearing throughout the whole Book. ... And indeed I have often heard Mr Edward Lhuyd say that, tho' he was often importuned & sollicited to make Additions to, & Alterations in, w[ha]t he had done abt Wales, yet he would not add or alter anything, but yt [that], if w[ha]t he had done were reprinted, it should be done just as before. Upon which account I value the Ist Ed., looking upon Mr. Lhuyd's Account of Wales to be the very best Part of all the Additions.[130]

Hearne's praise for Lhuyd dismissed the work of Sibbald and two dozen collaborators who rewrote the descriptions of England. It is to the counties of England that we now journey.

---

[130] Quoted in *Life and Letters of Edward Lhuyd, Early Science in Oxford XIV*, ed. R.T. Gunther (Oxford, 1945), pp. 11–12.

12

England's Motley Breeds

John de Vere, Earl of Oxford, carried the sword of state in the grand procession to St Pauls that proclaimed the restoration of Henry VI before London's citizens. Eighteen months later, in April 1471, Oxford fled to Scotland after the battle of Barnet returned the Yorkist Edward IV to power. Oxford safely carried the Lancastrian cause into French exile. Great things awaited him after Henry Tudor defeated Richard III at Bosworth Field, thanks not a little to the mettle of Oxford and his men.[1] At best that would have been a dim prospect on the horizon when Oxford landed on rugged St Michael's Mount in Cornwall. He trusted 'to the natural strength of the place, fortyf'd himself ... and bravely defended it, tho' with little success' before his men answered the call of a full pardon for their crimes.[2]

For William Camden, Oxford's story was just one interesting feature of St Michael's Mount. Oxford's soldiers would have seen the remains of the chapel dedicated to the Archangel Michael, built by the earl of Cornwall after he had persuaded William the Conquer that a vision of Michael had been seen there. Camden remarked that others had 'pretended' the same vision, including Italian monks and the French at Mont St Michel. More believable for Camden were the artefacts found at the base of the mountain:

> within the memory of our Fathers, as they were digging for tinn, they met with spear-heads, axes, and swords, all wrap'd up in Linnen; of the same sort with those found long ago in Hircinia in Germany, and others lately found in Wales. For it is plain from the Monuments of Antiquity, that the Greeks, Cimbrians, and Britains, made use of brass-weapons, notwithstanding the ... medicinal virtue in them, which Macrobius takes notice of from Aristotle.[3]

Nested among the rocks below lived a red-billed crow 'found by the Inhabitants to be an Incendiary, and very thieving'. Camden related without scepticism that

---

[1] S.J. Gunn, 'John deVere', *Oxford DNB* at www.oxforddnb.com.
[2] William Camden, *Britannia: Or a Chorographical Description of Great Britain and Ireland* (London, 1695), p. 6, hereafter cited as Camden, *Britannia* (1695); Charles Ross, *Edward IV* (Berkeley, 1974), p. 192.
[3] Camden, *Britannia* (1695), p. 6.

'it often sets houses on fire privately, steals pieces of money, and then hides them'.[4]

The settling of Cornwall set the stage for Camden's description of a mountainous county – 'as if nature had design'd to arm it against the incursions of the sea'.[5] Camden quickly turned to the Cornish people and the literary jousts between Henry III's court poet, Henry d'Avranches, and his Cornish student Michael Blaunpayn or Michael the Cornishman. The two men traded exaggerated insults for public show and Michael's survived down to Camden's time.[6] According to Camden, d'Avranches 'play'd upon the Cornish-men, as the fagg-end of the world' while Michael responded 'in defence of his country' that in 'fish and tinn they know no rival shore' and Arthur always positioned his Cornish soldiers in the vanguard.[7] Camden agreed and added,

> Nor is Cornwall more happy in the soil, than it's inhabitants; who as they are extremely well bred, and ever have been so, even in those ancient times ... so are they lusty, stout, and tall: their limbs are well set; and at wrastling (not to mention that manly exercise of hurling the Ball) they are so eminent, that they go beyond other parts, both in art, and a firmness of body requir'd for it.[8]

Camden could not decide if this was the product of something unique to Cornwall or whether the fruitful westerly breezes made the Cornish 'lusty' like their westward-living Batavian and Aquitani counterparts. He thought this reputation might have been the occasion for stories of a race of giants in Cornwall.[9]

Camden scarcely missed a beat, entwining the complex peoples of Britain's past, laid out in the first section of *Britannia*, with its contemporary inhabitants, topography, and antiquarian remains in the county descriptions. Impressive testimony to Camden's lasting influence amongst local travellers and historians can be found in the score of talented collaborators whom Gibson recruited to bring the English counties to life.[10] They added their unique interests as scholars to Camden's original engagement with the cultural complexity of Britain. As Gibson observed,

> Whereas, the condition of places is in a sort of continual motion ... one who should attempt such a complete Description of a single Town, as might serve for all Ages to come, would see his Mistake by the experience of every year, every month, nay almost of

---

[4]   Camden, *Britannia* (1695), p. 6.

[5]   Camden, *Britannia* (1695), pp. 2–4.

[6]   Peter Binkley, 'Henry d'Avranches', *Oxford DNB* at www.oxforddnb.com; Binkley, 'Michael the Cornishman', *Oxford DNB* at www.oxforddnb.com.

[7]   Camden, *Britannia* (1695), p. 4.

[8]   Camden, *Britannia* (1695), p. 4

[9]   Camden, *Britannia* (1695), p. 4.

[10]   Camden, *Britannia* (1695), Gibson's Preface; Graham Parry, *The Trophies of Time: English Antiquarians of the Seventeenth Century* (Oxford, 1995), pp. 331–46.

every day. ... so that where an old Survey promises nothing but mean Houses, and poor Inhabitants, we are very often surpriz'd with handsom buildings and a wealthy people; and where we feed our selves with the hopes of finding every thing neat and splendid, we are entertain'd with nothing but rubbish and ruins.[11]

Gibson thus made his edition the fulfilment of Camden's original plan for a living description of Britannia. We can begin with Bishop Jonathan Trelawney of Exeter. Even though Trelawney opted to collect notices from local agents rather than traverse the rugged countryside of his diocese, he kept very much to the spirit of Gibson's project, that had Camden 'liv'd to this day, he had been still adding and altering; and had (no doubt) left his *Britannia* much more complete'.[12]

Jonathan Trelawney's Cornwall

Camden wrote of a land both ancient and modern, the stronghold of Britannia's oldest people, swept back by ancient invasions, and a contemporary fortress set against the incursions of the sea. The Tamar river divided Cornwall from the rest of England, yet Camden noted this nominal ethno-cultural boundary only in passing as he tracked the river's swift, violent course: 'For King Athelstan (who was the first King of England that entirely subdu'd those parts) made this the bound between the Cornish Britains and his own English, after he remov'd the Britains out of Devonshire, as we learn from Malmesbury.'[13] By contrast, the boundary was Bishop Trelawney's starting point.[14] What did that boundary mean for him? It must first of all have been a very personal one. Trelawney's father had been in the thick of Cornish royalism in the wars of the 1640s. He compounded with the Parliamentary victors to keep the family estate. The family became bedrock establishment figures with the return of the Stuart monarchs.[15]

Young Jonathan 'came under the influence of Dr William Jane, with whom he would remain close, an uncompromising defender of the restored Church of England'. Trelawney did not travel an easy road to preferment in the Church and ordinary concerns like money occupied him, especially upon inheriting his father's title, estate, and war debts in 1681. He became a fixture in the government of Cornwall and raised the county against the 'invasion' of Charles II's bastard son, James, Duke of Monmouth, when James, Duke of York came to the throne. Trelawney was elevated to the bishopric of Bristol, a stopping-off point to Exeter. He became one of the famous 'Seven Bishops' who defied James II's Declaration of Indulgence, which was designed to secure religious

[11] Camden, *Britannia* (1695), Gibson's Preface.
[12] Camden, *Britannia* (1695), Gibson's Preface.
[13] Camden, *Britannia* (1695), p. 13.
[14] Camden, *Britannia* (1695), p. 17.
[15] Andrew M. Coleby, 'Sir Jonathan Trelawney', *Oxford DNB* at www.oxforddnb.com.

and civil rights for his fellow Catholics. Trelawney managed that most devilish of balancing acts, taking a stand on principle for the Anglican Church as a loyal subject of a Catholic king. His reward was appointment to the see of Exeter in the final hours of James's regime. His translation was finally confirmed under William and Mary, even though he proved to be an uncompromising opponent of Protestant toleration.[16]

Trelawney, then, had deep ties to Cornwall and the established Church, a church that Cornishmen fought for in the 1640s as the restored Church of an ancient British Christianity once lost to papal corruption. Differences were much on Trelawney's mind when he composed his additions. He began: 'Cornwall, as by the situation 'tis in a manner cut off from the rest of England, so by its peculiar customs and privileges, added to a difference of Language, it may seem to be another Kingdom.'[17] Its position as a royal duchy and the importance of the Court of the Stannaries traditionally made Cornwall a jurisdictional anomaly. Trelawney thought it important to note the unique customs exemption for Cornish cloth first granted by Edward, the Black Prince and freedom to trade openly 'to all parts of the world, granted them by K. Charles I. in recompence of their Loyalty'. He was proud to include the letter of thanks sent by Charles I in September 1642, 'which begins thus; We are so highly sensible of the extraordinary merit of our County of Cornwall, &c, and concludes with an Order to have it read and preserv'd in every Church and Chapel throughout the whole County.' Finally, the Cornish preserved a customary right to take sea-sand inland in large quantities as fertilizer. Just how this sand improved the soil Trelawney was not certain, but he – like Lhuyd – turned to the expertise of John Ray. Ray suggested that it might have something to do an unusually heavy concentration of salty minerals.[18]

One might have expected Trelawney to sniff at thieving, fiery-footed crows or to debunk ancient saints. However, he recounted a story left to him by his predecessor, Bishop Joseph Hall, of a crippled man whose paralysis was cured by washing in St Maddren's well. Two other persons carried away bottles of the holy water after drinking from it and making offerings on Corpus Christi day. Within three weeks, strength began to return to their feeble legs. Another offering so improved them that one became a life-long fisherman and the other died fighting for Charles I. 'After this,' Trelawney explained 'the well was superstitiously frequented, so that the rector of the neighbouring Parish was forc'd to reprove several of his Parishioners for it.' The rector's tune changed when he accepted a dose of the water from a passing woman and found a cure for his

---

[16] Coleby, 'Sir Jonathan Trelawney'.
[17] Camden, *Britannia* (1695), p. 15.
[18] Camden, *Britannia* (1695), pp. 15–16.

distempered bowels.[19] Trelawney brought his own blend of reason and mysticism to the well:

> The instances are so near our own times, and too well attested, to fall under the suspicion of bare traditions or Legendary fables: And being so very remarkable, may well claim a place here. Only, 'tis worth our observation, that the last of them destroys the miracle; for if he was cur'd upon accidentally tasting it, then the Ceremonies of offering, lying on the ground, &c. contributed nothing; and so the virtue of the water claims the whole remedy.[20]

The stone circle of Boscawen-Un in West Penwith fascinated Camden and Trelawney. For Camden, the nineteen stones set in a circle and the centre stone were probably 'some trophy of the Romans under the later Emperors; or of Athelstane the Saxon, after he had subdued Cornwall'. Trelawney thought it 'worth the Reader's enquiry' to consider whether it was really a British sepulchral monument. Other stones standing on end served that purpose, including one 'particularly in Wales, observ'd by Mr Edward Lhwyd'.[21] Nearby the Wringcheese stones, so named for resembling a ring of cheese, stood the Hurlers. A century after Carew wrote of hurling, some local inhabitants called them hurlers 'out of a pious belief that they are men transform'd into stones, for playing at ball on Sunday'. Others thought a vengeful, Sabbatarian god had less to do with the matter, explaining the stones as either a battlefield monument or some sort of boundary marker. Trelawney gave a first-hand account that dismissed all three explanations. The Hurlers were 'oblong, rude and unhewen stones, pitch'd in the ground on one end, standing upon a down in three circles, the centers wereof [sic] are in a right line; the middlemost circle the greatest'. Thanks to Lhuyd's find, the bishop put them in the same category as the Boscawen-Un stones and decided that they were likewise the burial places of ancient Britons.[22]

Language simultaneously set Cornwall apart and bound it to Britain. Most inhabitants spoke English, but with a surprising feature 'observ'd by Travellers'. Theirs was 'more pure and refin'd than that of their neighbours, Devonshire and Somersetshire'. 'The most probable reason whereof,' Trelawney continued, 'seems to be this: that English is to them an introduc'd, not an original Language; and those who brought it in were the Gentry and Merchants, who imitated the Dialect of the Court, which is the most nice and accurate.' With the posh speech of their social betters may have come something else. The Cornish people's 'neat way of living and housewifery, upon which they justly value themselves above their neighbours, does possibly proceed from the same cause'.[23] Here English

---

[19] Camden, *Britannia* (1695), pp. 21–2.
[20] Camden, *Britannia* (1695), p. 22.
[21] Camden, *Britannia* (1695), pp. 5, 21.
[22] Camden, *Britannia* (1695), pp. 9, 23.
[23] Camden, *Britannia* (1695), p. 16.

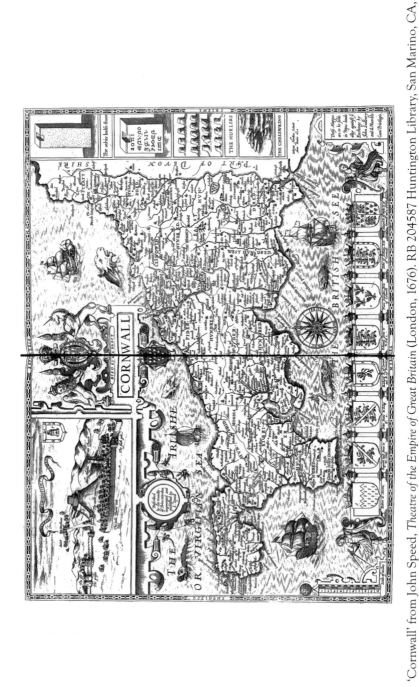

23 'Cornwall' from John Speed, *Theatre of the Empire of Great Britain* (London, 1676). RB 204587 Huntington Library, San Marino, CA, reproduced by permission. Image produced by ProQuest as part of *Early English Books Online*. www.proquest.com

distinguished the Cornish from their immediate neighbours yet brought them linguistically and culturally within the English-speaking mainstream.

This had clearly come at the expense of the Cornish language and Trelawney very nearly pronounced a requiem:

> The old Cornish is almost quite driven out of the Country, being spoken only by the vulgar in two or three Parishes at the Lands-end; and they too understand the English. In other parts the inhabitants know little or nothing of it; so that in all likelihood, a short time will destroy the small remains that are left of it. ... And indeed, it cannot well be otherwise; for, besides the inconveniences common to them with the Welsh (such as the destruction of their original Monuments, which Gildas complains of; and the Roman language breaking in upon them ... their language has some peculiar disadvantages.[24]

Interestingly, Trelawney wrote that the physical destruction of their 'Antiquity' accompanied the death of the Cornish language. His comment should give us pause before we assume that Camden and fellow antiquarians did not search the archives or did not scour Britain's fields for relics of the Classical past with a distinct awareness of Antiquity's cultural complexity.

For Trelawney, linguistic extinction was a cultural fate that the Cornish shared with their Welsh neighbours, only more so. Side-by-side translations of the Lord's Prayer allowed Trelawney to show the affinity between Cornish and Welsh that made their respective speeches mutually comprehensible but increasingly difficult to reconcile in writing. Religious change affected them very differently. Both might see Protestant reforms as the restoration of an ancient British faith they had uniquely helped to preserve. But the language of reform in Wales was Welsh, while in Cornwall it was English. 'The giving over of the Guirimears, i.e. great Speeches,' Trelawney explained, 'which were formerly us'd at the great Conventions of the people, and consisted of Scriptural Histories, &c.', certainly did not help. These gatherings must have been a sight, reminiscent of the Welsh eisteddfodau (mass gatherings entertained by musicians, poets, and artists). The Cornish met 'in the spatious and open downs, wherein there were earthen banks thrown up on purpose, large enough to enclose thousands of people, as appears by their shape in several places, which remains to this day'. Their loss, combined with increasing exchanges with English-speaking artisans, traders, and ministers, only speeded linguistic decline.[25]

Trelawney lamented the demise of Cornish and had a hand in trying to preserve some vestige of the native tongue. By his count, only three books could now be found in Cornish. One was an old vellum account of the passion of Christ, the 'Pascon agan Arluth', that appeared to date from the time of Richard III. In keeping with the uncorrupted purity of the Cornish faith, it 'positively

[24] Camden, *Britannia* (1695), p. 16.
[25] Camden, *Britannia* (1695), pp. 16–17.

determines against Transubstantiation'.[26] Translation of the 'Pascon' was the work of John Keigwin, a Cornish scholar with whom Trelawney worked: 'Keigwin's translation of "Pascon agan Arluth" was completed in 1682, that of William Jordan's "Creation of the world" was commenced in 1691 at the request of Jonathan Trelawney ... and the three dramas of the *Ordinalia* cycle were translated about 1695.' Keigwin left his mark with another member of Gibson's team. He 'translated some other Cornish pieces and assisted the linguist Edward Lhuyd with word lists as well as copies of these translations during and after the latter's visit to Cornwall in 1700.'[27] These losses of linguistic and cultural identity went hand in hand, yet Trelawney's preface to his revisions made Cornwall an altogether more distinct place within *Britannia* than it had been for Camden.

Kent: gateway to multicultural Britain

Across the south of England, in Kent, there was no hope of drawing such neat boundaries. As its skies would be for Kesselring's Luftflotte II and Dowding's Fighter Command in 1940, Kent was the battleground for Britain. The so-called Green Creek played host to the Danish fleet for many years. One company of these 'Northern men' under the command of Thorkell the Tall seized Archbishop Ælfheah of Canterbury as surety for a king's ransom due from Æthelred II, the Unready. Angry from waiting and insensible from drink, Thorkell's men murdered Ælfheah despite the warlord's desperate pleas to spare the archbishop's life. No fair language could 'soften the unbridled anger of his fellows, harder than iron and rocks; nor could it be appeas'd but by the effusion of innocent blood, which they presently and unanimously spilt, by pouring upon him Ox-heads, and showers of stones and sticks'.[28] For Camden, this sorry tale was one that made Greenwich notable.

The magnificent palace of Placentia, into which Humphrey, Duke of Gloucester, Henry VII, and Henry Howard, Earl of Northampton poured their time and money, also interested Camden. As well it should have. The 'greatest ornament by far that Greenwich has', he wrote, 'is our Elizabeth, who being born here by happy providence, did so enlighten Britain, nay, and even the whole world, with the rays of her royal virtues, that no praise can equal her merit'. Camden called on the verses of John Leland's river poem, the *Cygnea Cantio* to celebrate a keep 'like Jove's great palace pav'd with stars'.[29] Three Tudor stars were missing from Camden's account, however. Anne of Cleves, whom Henry had married at Placentia, his eldest child, Mary, born there like her sister, and the ill-fated Edward VI, who had taken his last breath within its walls. However,

---

[26] Camden, *Britannia* (1695), p. 17.
[27] Matthew Spriggs, 'John Keigwin', *Oxford DNB* at www.oxforddnb.com.
[28] Camden, *Britannia* (1695), p. 188.
[29] Camden, *Britannia* (1695), p. 189.

none of these made for either happy or politic reading in Camden's lifetime and it was not until Lhuyd's mentor, Robert Plot, revisited his journeys through Kent that the last two appeared for *Britannia*'s readers. Even then the doings of the Tudors did not interest Plot quite as much as did the great Observatory that stood at Greenwich, 'furnish't with all sorts of Mathematical Instruments fit for Astronomical Observations, such as Clocks, Telescopes, Quadrants, and a deep dry well for observation of the Stars in the day time; all which are most diligently and skilfully us'd by the learned Mr Flamsted, the King's Mathematician'.[30]

Time and history separated Camden's Kent from the county that Plot travelled through. For both men and their counterparts like John Aubrey, Britain's classical antiquity was born in Kent with the coming of Caesar.[31] Both men also faced a complication, as Camden wrote:

> I am now come to Kent; a country, indeed, which William Lambard, a person eminent for Learning and piety ... has been so lucky in his searches, that he has left but very little for those that come after him. Yet in pursuit of my intended method, I will run this over among the rest and lest (as the Comick Poet says) any one should suspect me to be a pilferer, I here gratefully acknowledge, that he was my Foundation and Fountain.[32]

Plot found himself in a similar situation, noting, of course, Lambarde's *Perambulation*, and also the competing 1659 descriptions by Richard Kilburne and John Philipot.[33] He admitted that 'one would think that little more could be said upon the subject', especially since Camden 'too spent some of the latter part of his life in this County', but Plot concluded that 'some things there are which have escap'd both the diligence of him and the rest' in the light of his own travels.[34]

Both Camden and Plot summarized the work of local experts and added smatterings of first-hand experience, but one theme dominated their treatment of Kent. Camden and Plot returned again and again to a land contested and settled by successive migrations and invasions. For Camden, then, the people who inhabited this rich, fertile county, 'very thick set with villages and towns', could 'at this day justly claim that commendation for humanity which Caesar bestow'd upon those in his time; not to mention bravery in war ... [so] that in their engagements among the rest of the English, the front of the battel was look'd upon to belong properly to them'. John of Salisbury's *Policraticus* came in handy for Camden in confirming their valour in the front ranks and William of Malmesbury was pressed into service as well: 'The country people and the

[30] Camden, *Britannia* (1695), pp. 214–15.
[31] John Aubrey, *Monumenta Britannica or A Miscellany of British Antiquities [Parts One and Two]*, ed. John Fowles and Rodney Legg (Boston, 1980/81), pp. 266–9.
[32] Camden, *Britannia* (1695), p. 185.
[33] Richard Kilburne, *A Topographie or Survey of the County of Kent* (WING K434; London, 1659); John Philipot, *Villare Cantianum, or, Kent Surveyed* (WING P1989; London, 1659).
[34] Camden, *Britannia* (1695), p. 213.

town-dwellers of Kent, retain the spirit of that ancient nobility, above the rest of the English; being more ready to afford a respect and kind entertainment to others, and less inclinable to revenge injuries.'[35] The noble qualities of ancient Britons overspread the island from John O'Groats to the White Cliffs, from the noble Scots of Fordun, Boece, and Lesley to heroic Kentish folk.

The 'Kentish Britains' who opposed Caesar's landing first established their reputation for valour, even if the Romans repulsed 'their horse and their chariots' with relative ease. Caesar and Tacitus were naturally Camden's chief sources for Roman Kent and he directed his readers to them. These bearers of antiquity 'quitted Britain' and much of Kent passed from the administrative authority of Vortigern to the Saxon warlord Hengist, thanks to his romantic links with Vortigern's daughter Rowenna. Or so Camden wrote. Plot found no mention of Rowena in the *Anglo-Saxon Chronicle* – perhaps he read Gibson's edition – and thought that battles at Aylesford and Crayford that killed some 4000 Britons were a more likely explanation. Plot's additions to Aylesford noted this again, as well as King Edmund Ironside's pursuit and defeat of the Danes there. Baldred was the last of these Kentish kings before the county came into the possession of Egbert and the West Saxons. They held the county until the Normans became the last invaders to successfully cross the Channel. According to Camden, the 'Kentish men carrying boughs before them, surrendered themselves to William the Conquerour at Swanscomb (a small village, where they tell us that Suene the Dane formerly encamp'd)'.[36]

Plot made himself something of a literary referee in his description, judging from among Camden's original, other studies of Kent, and his own travels and researches. One dispute that he weighed into concerned the tenure of gavelkind. According to Camden, the Kentish men surrendered 'upon condition they might have the Customs of their Country preserv'd entire, that especially which they call Gavel-kind'. Land held by gavelkind was divided into equal portions among the male heirs and, failing that, among the female heirs, even in cases of outlawry. In some two hundred dense pages, William Somner's 1659 *Treatise of Gavelkind* rejected Camden's claim, but Plot thought there must be something to the settlement with the Normans. 'For how else come they to retain their custom of Gavelkind,' retorted Plot, 'which once prevail'd all over Britain, as it does still in some parts of Wales? and why do the Heirs particularly in Kent, succeed to the Inheritance, tho' their Fathers suffer for felony or murder?'[37]

Maddeningly, Camden offered no other examples of the unique customs that the Kentish determined to preserve, but he must have sensed that they included much more than gavelkind. Customs that included legal privileges such as tax exemptions must have been an important element. 'So that what we

---

[35] Camden, *Britannia* (1695), pp. 185–6.
[36] Camden, *Britannia* (1695), pp. 186–7, 213, 218.
[37] Camden, *Britannia* (1695), pp. 187, 213.

find in an ancient Book is very true,' he concluded, 'tho' not elegantly written: The County of Kent urges that that County ought of right to be exempt from any such burthen because, it affirms that this County was never conquer'd as was the rest of England, but surrender'd it self to the Conqueror's power upon Articles of agreement, provided that they should enjoy all their liberties and free customs which they had, and us'd from the beginning.'[38] What might be most interesting in all this is Plot's connection between Welsh and Kentish practices. Partible inheritance often acted as a first cause in explanations for social disorder among peoples who practised it: Gaels in Scotland and Ireland, some Welsh, and Amerindians.[39] The absence of clanship perhaps set Kent apart for Camden and Plot, ensuring that its families who spurned primogeniture did not find themselves among lesser peoples in the scales of civility and barbarity.

The movement of peoples into and through it decisively shaped Kent. Though confused in his dating, Camden wrote that Æthelstan 'held a Meeting here of the Wise men of the Kingdom, and enacted Laws, in the year of our Redemption'.[40] While Camden had in mind an insular reconquest of England from foreign invaders, Æthelstan emerged in the early tenth century as a critical figure in the development of an Anglo-Saxon *imperium* in Britain. He triumphed at the battle of Brunanburh (927), responding to the invasion of Northumbria by a combined force that included a fleet assembled in Ireland by the exiled Danelaw king Olaf, the Britons of Strathclyde, and Constantine II of Scotland.[41] Æthelstan used the term 'imperator' in his 'claim to rule not just the English but all the peoples round about' and his use of royal charters became an institutional expression of those claims, including the 'witness lists with which they are supplied ... recording the presence of the Welsh and occasionally Scottish sub-kings, large numbers of ecclesiastics (abbots as well as bishops), and ealdormen from the Danelaw areas of England'.[42] With similar insularity, Camden also recorded the foundation of a Cluniac monastery in Faversham by King Stephen, 'who usurp'd the Crown of England' from Henry I's daughter the 'Empress' Matilda.[43] Indeed. But Stephen acted to seize and consolidate an Anglo-Norman *imperium* spanning the Channel.[44] Camden too betrayed the power of national labels to obscure and wash out cultural complexity.

Finding his way to Reculver, Camden remarked on the chalk pits, complete with columns, to be found along the coast. Just which of Kent's inhabitants were responsible eluded him. Pliny's description of the pits dug by Britons in the

---

[38] Camden, *Britannia* (1695), p. 187.
[39] Colin G. Calloway, *White People, Indians, and Highlanders: Tribal People and Colonial Encounters in Scotland and America* (Oxford, 2008), pp. 60–87.
[40] Camden, *Britannia* (1695), p. 195.
[41] Edward James, *Britain in the First Millennium* (London, 2001), p. 246.
[42] Sarah Foot, 'Æthelstan', *OxfordDNB* at www.oxforddnb.com.
[43] Camden, *Britannia* (1695), p. 195.
[44] David Carpenter, *The Struggle for Mastery: Britain 1066–1284* (Oxford, 2003), pp. 161–4.

county perfectly described those Camden found. Others might imagine that 'the English-Saxons might digg such holes for the same uses the Germans did, from whom they were descended'.[45] According to Tacitus, the Germans used the pits as a refuge from the cold or invaders and for storage, closing the opening with dung heaps in any case. By Camden's day Reculver had become a little country village notable for its monastery and pyramidal watchtowers.[46] Plot concluded that the Romans had built the latter, but the defensive focus of these 'Saxon Shore' forts is now open to question, along with the 'accepted view of fourth-century Britain trembling at the prospect of imminent attack from across the sea'.[47]

Plot thought that there was more to Reculver than met Camden's eye. The naturalist in him really put him on the scent. He thought the monastery's foundations must be those of an original Roman fort, while the chalk caverns and formations yielded evidence of intense activity:

> [Together] with the great quantities of Roman brick or tile; Opus Musivum, Coins, fibulae, Gold-wire, Ear-rings, Bracelets, &c. daily found in the sands ... all come from the landward upon fall or the cliffs, the terrene parts whereof being wash't away by the sea, these metalline substances remain likewise behind in the sands, whence they are constantly pick't out by the poor people of the place.[48]

Plot concluded that the place must have been of 'great extent, and very populous', given the quantities in which these artefacts were found. Further, he was confident that it had suffered some great devastation by fire or sword in the past, 'there being many patterns found of metals run together ... viz. of a piece of Copper and gold thus joyn'd in the melting'.[49] Perhaps it was with a nod to chalk, gold, and golf that Ian Fleming, a Kent resident, chose to set *Moonraker* and its explosive chalk cliffs, Auric Goldfinger's Reculver foundry, and the famous golf match between James Bond and Goldfinger at a thinly disguised Royal St George's, Sandwich.

Camden's history had to negotiate the break from Rome and the royal supremacy at Canterbury. Consequently, the city's splendour was bought with the 'pious superstition of former ages' and Camden made the martyred Archbishop Thomas Becket a troublesome priest:

> He was slain in this Church by the Courtiers, for opposing the King too resolutely and warmly by asserting the Liberties of the Church; was register'd on that account by the pope in the Kalendar of Martyrs, had divine hours pay'd him, and was so loaded with rich offerings, that gold was one of the vilest Treasures of his Shrine.[50]

---

[45] Camden, *Britannia* (1695), p. 196.
[46] Camden, *Britannia* (1695), p. 220.
[47] Francis Pryor, *The Making of the British Landscape: How We have Transformed the Land from Prehistory to Today* (London, 2010), p. 207.
[48] Camden, *Britannia* (1695), p. 220.
[49] Camden, *Britannia* (1695), p. 220.
[50] Camden, *Britannia* (1695), p. 198.

Camden used an account by Erasmus – 'who was an eye-witness' – of the accumulated riches to affirm 'that the name of Christ [to whom it was dedicated] was almost quite laid aside for that of S. Thomas'.[51] As if taking a page from Leland's methods for offering advice to the Church's supreme head, Camden closed the book on Becket's shrine:

> But King Henry 8. dispers'd all this wealth that had been so long in gathering, and drove out the Monks; in lieu whereof this Christ-Church has a Dean, Archdeacon, 12 Prebendaries, and 6 Preachers, whose business it is to sow the word of God in the neighbouring places.[52]

After James's accession Camden added a politic epilogue, praising the deceased Archbishop John Whitgift – 'extremely lamented by all good men', though certainly not evangelical Protestants and Catholics persecuted by the High Commission and ex officio oaths. Camden also praised the singularly courageous and prudent Richard Bancroft, no friend to either sort himself.[53]

For Plot, Canterbury was a city of great trade 'to which the Foreigners in it seem to have contributed very much'. Canterbury's newest residents had their own stories. 'They are partly Walloons, and partly French;' Camden explained, 'the first (being drive out of Artois, and other Provinces of the Spanish Netherlands, in the Reign of Queen Elizabeth, for adhering to the Reformed Religion) cam and settl'd here, and brought along with them the art of weaving silk, into this Kingdom.' Theirs now competed with the very best foreign silk. Recent French immigrants, Protestant refugees who had fled after Louis XIV's revocation of the Edict of Nantes, were 'numerous, and very industrious, maintaining their own poor, and living frugally' – no benefit tourists here. They joined with the Walloons to build 'a very great Congregation' in the stranger church near Canterbury Cathedral.[54] In Camden's time the centre of the cloth trade was elsewhere in Kent, in Cranbrooke, Tenderden, and Benenden, but the Flemings played the key role, invited by Edward III with 'promises of large rewards and grants of several immunities, to teach the English the cloath-manufacture, which is now one of the pillars of the kingdom'.[55]

Caesar, the Romans, and Leland's British bricks naturally pulled Camden toward Dover.[56] The cliffs prompted one of Camden's most unusual discussions, but apropos for a scholar so interested in the peopling of Britain. 'Give me leave to start a question here, not unworthy the search of any learned man that has a

---

[51] Camden, *Britannia* (1695), p. 198.
[52] Camden, *Britannia* (1695), p. 198.
[53] Camden, *Britannia* (1695), pp. 199–200.
[54] Camden, *Britannia* (1695), p. 221.
[55] Camden, *Britannia* (1695), p. 211. The story of the Canterbury Flemings and their counterparts can be explored across the essays in Nigel Goose and Lien Luu, eds, *Immigrants in Tudor and Early Stuart England* (Brighton, 2005).
[56] Camden, *Britannia* (1695), pp. 203–6, 222–3.

genius and leisure, Whether in this place where this narrow sea parts Gaul and Britain, there was ever an Isthmus or neck of land that joyn'd them?'[57] He began the investigation with classical sources that spoke to just such changes in the Earth's surface. Did not Pliny conclude that Cyprus had once been part of Syria? Virgil offered appropriate verses:

> When battering waves collecting all their force;
> Thro' solid land rug'd their impetuous course,
> While towns and fields on either side gave way,
> And let free passage for a narrow sea.[58]

Unfortunately, only one unknown author had been willing to venture that 'Once did the British touch the Gallick shore, Till furious waves the cliffs in sunder tore.' Some form of geological investigation was needed. Was the nature of the soil on both shores the same? At their narrowest point both coastlines rose to high rocks 'almost of the same matter and colour; which should hint that they have been broken through.' How deep were the straits? The Dover strait was 'scarce 25 fathoms', and much deeper on either side. Was the bottom sandy, hilly, or muddy, or did it feature shelves of land? 'I could not learn from the mariners that there are any such', except one shoal in mid-channel, Camden replied. The geological case was promising. Not so etymology, since Camden could not find any place on either shore that had a name in its 'ancient language of the place, from a breach, rent, separation, or such like'. Some of Camden's contemporaries argued that the landmasses must once have been connected, otherwise how had the first wolves released after the Great Flood multiplied and made their way into Britain and Ireland?[59] Camden was certainly right to ask the question. The two had been connected until rising sea levels and shifting landmasses had turned the isthmus between the chalk cliffs into salt marshes and, finally, an impassable barrier in the sixth century BCE.[60]

In many respects, Plot and Camden nicely complemented one another. Both travelled Kent and encountered its rich heritage and people at first hand. Both also wrote in the shadow of travellers who had explored the county with care and devotion. Each man had his own interests and emphases, but they told much the same story of this prosperous and storied county. A century did not divide Camden from Plot in the way that it perhaps did in the cases of Bishop Trelawney in Cornwall, Edward Lhuyd in Wales, or Robert Sibbald writing about Scotland. On one thing Plot and Camden agreed. If any part of Britain made it a crossroads of peoples and cultures, Kent did. With its complex history of migration and settlement, invasion and bloodshed, Kent was no rampart in a

[57] Camden, *Britannia* (1695), p. 206.
[58] Camden, *Britannia* (1695), pp. 206–7.
[59] Camden, *Britannia* (1695), pp. 207–8.
[60] Norman Davies, *The Isles* (London, 1999), p. 8.

fortress built by nature. Camden and Plot, Caesar and the Conqueror – and the first passengers aboard the Eurostar – knew that Kent was the gateway to Britain.

Migrations, settlements, and peoples apart in the 'English' heartlands

More than twenty collaborators made for lively and eclectic interventions in the descriptions of England. Richard Parsons took on Gloucestershire. Camden picked up echoes of primeval violence in the forest of Dean, formerly 'so thick with Trees, so very dark and terrible its shades, and various cross ways, that it rendred the Inhabitants barbarous, and embolden'd them to commit many outrages'. This infestation prompted an Act of Parliament under Henry VI, but discovery of rich veins of iron ore did more to clear the woods and improve the remaining natives. Parsons took up the story, though not without imparting a new kind of roughness to the forest dwellers:

> Here are several Fornaces for the making of Iron, which by the violence of the fire becomes fluid, and being brought to their forges, are beat out into Barrs of various shapes. The workmen are very industrious in seeking out the Beds of old cinders, which not being fully exhausted, are burnt again in the furnaces, and make the best Iron.

The great oak forest offered up its trees to the smelters, although Parsons thought war the worst affliction. It was once 'said to have been part of the Instructions of the Spanish Armada to destroy the timber', but 'what a foreign power could not effect, our own Civil dissensions did; for it went miserably to wrack in the Civil wars'.[61] With comments like this, it might not surprise us to learn that Parsons hunted dissenters with zeal or that his father steadfastly used the Book of Common Prayer throughout the 1640s and 1650s, despite nineteen weeks in a Cambridge gaol.[62] Camden closed his description of Gloucester with a long account of the wickedness of Richard III – it could not even be said of Richard, as it had of the malign Emperor Galba, that had he not reigned, he might still have been thought fit for the job. Camden apologized to his readers for this, 'I must not forget that I am a Chorographer, and so must lay aside the Historian.'[63]

Camden's description of Oxfordshire and the 1695 additions by the bishop of Peterborough, White Kennett, contained a heady dose of history and topography.[64] Below Eynsham the Evenlode carried the waters of the Cotswolds into the Isis, leaving 'nigh its own banks a great monument of Antiquity, a number of vastly great stones placed in a circular figure, which the Country-people call Rolle-rich stones'. The locals had a 'fond tradition that they were once men turn'd

[61] Camden, *Britannia* (1695), p. 232, 245.
[62] Suzanne Eward, 'Richard Parsons', *Oxford DNB* at www.oxforddnb.com.
[63] Camden, *Britannia* (1695), pp. 243–4.
[64] Laird Okie, 'White Kennett', *Oxford DNB* at www.oxforddnb.com.

24   The 'Rolle-rich Stones', Oxfordshire engraved by Johannes Kip, from William Camden, *Britannia: Or a Chorographical Description of Great Britain and Ireland* (London, 1695). From the private library of the author.

into stones'.[65] For the 1610 edition, Camden supplied a 'rudely' drawn image of the circle; it was redrafted with slightly increased detail for Gibson's edition. Both drawings seconded Camden's description of them as 'irregular and of unequal height, and by the decays of time are grown ragged'. A solitary windmill stood in the top right of each drawing, while the opposite corner depicted five standing stones outside the circle, reputed to be the knight companions to 'The King', the great solitary stone outside its east bound. The 1610 drawing included at least one person for perspective – of a sort – but the Dutch draughtsman Johannes Kip included three sets of travelling gentlemen exploring the circle in 1695. Kip drew one pair ambling through the circle proper, a second evidently remarking on two worn stones that came to just above their knees, and three men devoting real attention to the king's horsemen. These were scrutinizing travellers rather than solitary witnesses. Neither in 1610 nor in 1695 did these travellers match Camden's description of the local inhabitants, 'formerly such clowns and churls, that it past into a proverb, for a rude and ill-bred fellow, to be born at Hogs-Norton'.[66]

The conflicted relationship with Oxford University did not lead Camden to slight it. There were no clowns and churls to be found there, unless one counted the townspeople:

[65]   Camden, *Britannia* (1695), p. 254.
[66]   Camden, *Britannia* (1695), p. 253.

The City being thus adorn'd with beautiful buildings, many Students began to flock hither as to the common Mart of civility and good letters. So that learning here quickly reviv'd, chiefly through the care of the foresaid Robert Pulein ... And he met with such fortunate success in his endeavours, that in the reign of King John, there were three thousand Students in this place, who went away altogether, some to Reading, and some to Cambridge, when they could no longer bear abuses of the rude and insolent Citizens ... [67]

When town–gown relations settled down and the students returned, Oxford went from strength to strength. The papacy elevated it to the ranks of Paris, Bologna, and Salamanca with the title of university, 'offices in Church and State' were staffed by its learned fellows, and the collegiate system planted stately halls and schools throughout the city. Despite internal feuds among 'factions of Northern and Southern men', Oxford was recognized as 'the chief School in England, Scotland, Wales and Ireland'. Thomas Bodley's design for the re-foundation of the university library promised to crown Oxford's 'publick Arsenal of Wisdom'.[68]

As vice-principal of St Edmund's Hall, Kennett was more than happy to become lost in the university's history along with Camden. He could report that Bodley's design had grown into a great library, helped by new galleries and the legacy of Thomas Barlow, bishop of Lincoln in the 1650s. 'When one views the Catalogue of printed Books by Dr Hyde, and the other of Manuscripts by Dr. Bernard,' Kennett wrote triumphantly, 'he must admire the prodigious treasure, and neither envy Rome her Vatican, nor India her gold.' Not to be outdone were the Ashmolean, 'a neat and curious Edifice' filled with 'Natural and Artificial Curiosities', and the magnificent Sheldonian Theatre, protected by walls 'adorn'd with inestimable reliques of Grecian and Roman Antiquities'.[69]

Save for the Thames, the rest of Oxfordshire was hard pressed to find devoted attention from Camden or Kennett. In Camden's day Banbury was 'famous for making good Cheese' and the mischiefs the bishop of Lincoln brought on himself by 'his vain and expensive' building programme. According to Kennett,

While Philemon Holland was carrying on his English edition of this Britannia, Mr. Camden came accidentally to the Press, when this sheet was working off; and looking on, he found that to his own observation of Banbury being famous for Cheese, the Translator had added Cakes and Ale. But Mr. Camden thinking it too light an expression, chang'd the world Ale into Zeal; and so it pass'd to the great indignation of the Puritans of this town.[70]

Holland's 1610 edition certainly associated zeal, cheese, and cakes with Banbury. Gibson's edition excised the changes without even assigning them to the

---

[67] Camden, *Britannia* (1695), p. 259.
[68] Camden, *Britannia* (1695), pp. 259–62.
[69] Camden, *Britannia* (1695), pp. 273–5.
[70] Camden, *Britannia* (1695), p. 270.

footnotes with Holland's other interpolations.[71] Asked to update *Britannia* and supply its contemporary deficiencies, only a bishop who amused himself by associating Puritan zeal with popery would have bothered to relate this 'credible story' as an important addition.

* * * * *

Religious zeal and clericalism did not afflict a scholar who one would have thought belonged among Gibson's team. Today we appreciate the scale of John Aubrey's investigations. The imaginative qualities of mind that Aubrey brought to fieldwork, folklore, archaeology, place-names, pre-historic Britain and the quality of its peoples immediately engage readers of the posthumously published *Monumenta Britannica, Remaines of Gentilisme and Judaisme* and the *Naturall Historie of Wiltshire*.[72] But unorthodox ideas, something lacking by way of organizational skills, and a certain guardedness conspired to deflect publication in Aubrey's lifetime or involvement with the new *Britannia*.[73] With an echo of Fynes Moryson's troubles, Aubrey could not place his large, expensive 'Monumenta Britannica' with a publisher and suffered the misfortune of recruiting subscribers in 1693, just as Gibson's subscriptions were making the rounds. Awnsam Churchill eventually took on the manuscript, but neither he nor his descendants published it and it came to the Bodleian in 1836. Fearful of 'what snatching & catching there is of other mens discoverys', Aubrey eventually gave Gibson and his collaborators limited access to the 'Monumenta', including Thomas Tanner, who revised Wiltshire.[74] They made good use of it up to a point, but nothing in the additions does justice to how Aubrey engaged with the cultural complexity of Britain in his life and work.

Home to Avebury and Stonehenge, Wiltshire focussed Aubrey's fascination with monuments of Britain's ancient past. He made his name with the 'discovery' and investigation of Avebury (and later Stonehenge) as a Druid temple, along with the remains of camps, fortifications, pits, horns, and architectural designs. He defined natural history broadly, from soil quality to the human imprint of gardens, houses, fields, and the like. The experience of Britain's complexity and diversity across many fields seized his imagination and never let go.[75] But Aubrey warrants our attention for the deeply human quality of his investigations. For Graham Parry, he 'had a capacity to envisage the societies of the past as

[71] William Camden, *Britain or a Chorographicall Description of the Most Flourishing Kingdomes, England, Scotland, and Ireland* (STC 4509; London, 1610), p. 376, hereafter cited as Camden, *Britannia* (1610).
[72] Michael Hunter, *John Aubrey and the Realm of Learning* (New York, 1975), pp. 154–79.
[73] Hunter, *John Aubrey*, pp. 84–91.
[74] Quoted in Hunter, *John Aubrey*, p. 84.
[75] Hunter, *John Aubrey*, pp. 178–80, 192–6.

coherent systems inhabited by imaginable people, and his powers of empathy for the remote past were quite extraordinary for his time'.[76] I would go further. Aubrey directly linked the peoples who inhabited those past societies to their modern-day descendants. His omnivorous curiosity, his interest in customs and qualities, united the peoples of Britain, past and present.

Aubrey thrived on travel and encounter. They made his perspective anything but insular or parochial: 'My frequent journeys between south and north Wiltshire and the south part of Wales, have given me more opportunities than most men, to make remarks on this country: and particularly on Salisbury Plains.'[77] Particularly the Downs:

> [They] are the most spacious plaines in Europe, and the greatest remains that I can heare of of the smooth primitive world when it lay all under water. ... The turfe is of a short sweet grasse, good for the sheep, and delightful to the eye, for its smoothnesse like a bowling green, and pleasant to the traveller; who wants here only variety of objects to make his journey less tedious: for here is ... not a tree, or rarely a bush to shelter one from a shower.[78]

Aubrey wrote about his beloved Wiltshire within this broader ethno-topographic perspective, one that was British (and, elsewhere, Irish). His examination of longevity among the peoples of north and south Wiltshire, Montgomeryshire, Flintshire, Denbighshire, and Merionethshire duplicated an interest shared by travellers across the Isles and the centuries.[79]

Highland–lowland divides linked peoples as far away as Scotland and Wiltshire. Aubrey composed his *Remaines of Gentilisme and Judaisme* in the 1680s after 'searching classical authors for precedents for the folk-customs and superstitions he had long observed during his field-work'.[80] In 1694 he shared it with Edward Lhuyd, who reported finding it curious, ingenious, and rich in detail.[81] Ovid's precedent validated reports of Cromwell's soldiers that the 'Highlanders ate only oate-meale and water and milk' and did not have the wits to fish their abundant trout streams until the English taught them.[82] Poppies also led Aubrey back to Ovid, in a mishmash of notes in *Monumenta Britannica* on the diets of Britons, Welsh, and Scots, past and present. Aubrey's ancient Britons mixed poppies into their hearthstone cakes, while their modern counterparts in Wales still favoured hearth cakes (no report on the poppies). Hans Sloane and John Ray both provided information about another opiate, the dulse or edible seaweed consumed in coastal communities of Scotland, Ireland, and, infrequently,

---

[76] Parry, *Trophies of Time*, p. 277.

[77] Aubrey, *Monumenta Britannica*, p. 236.

[78] John Aubrey, *The Natural History of Wiltshire*, ed. John Britton (London, 1847), p. 107.

[79] Aubrey, *Natural History of Wiltshire*, p. 69.

[80] Hunter, *John Aubrey*, p. 83.

[81] John Aubrey, *Three Prose Works*, ed. John Buchanan-Brown (Carbondale, IL, 1972), p. 403.

[82] Aubrey, *Three Prose Works*, p. 285.

England. This led to other herbs that suppressed hunger, and mare's-milk cheese, taken from Pliny's account of the Britons' Scythian ancestors.[83] At least part of Aubrey's understanding of the early settlements and subsequent clashes and invasions in Britain through the Anglo-Saxons came from Buchanan's *Rerum Scoticarum Historiae*.[84]

Something of these rough, slow-witted Britons and their descendants could be found in the upland 'Indigenæ, or Aborigines' of north Wiltshire. Aubrey described them in the *Natural History of Wiltshire* as slow and dull, 'melancholy, contemplative, and malicious', with a sour humour, committed to 'little tillage or hard labour', and living 'chiefly on milke meates, which cooles their braines too much and hurts their inventions'.[85] Wiltshire had a highland–lowland divide of its own, albeit less stereotypical than that described for Scotland:

> On the downes, sc. the south part, where 'tis all upon tillage, and where the shepherds labour hard, their flesh is hard, their bodies strong: being weary after hard labour, they have not leisure to read and contemplate religion, but goe to bed to their rest, to rise betime the next morning to their labour.[86]

Soil and topography combined for other effects:

> As to singing voyces wee have great diversity in severall counties of this nation; and any one may observe that generally in rich vales they sing clearer than on the hills, where they labour hard and breathe a sharpe ayre. This difference is manifest between the vale of North Wilts and the South. So in Somersettshire they generally sing well in the churches, their pipes are smoother. In North Wilts the milkmayds sing as shrill and cleare as any swallow sitting on a berne [after Chaucer] ... [87]

Aubrey populated his landscape and descriptions with memorable locals met during his travels. George Newton, 'an ingenious man, who from a blacksmith turned clock maker and fiddle maker', assured Aubrey that iron ore from Send was the richest and best he had ever melted in his forge.[88] A north Wiltshire woman with the last name Shakespeare blamed the 'want of art' for the poor cheeses of Pertward and Lidyard, locales that otherwise sent their prized butter to London.[89] Aubrey betrayed a fondness for the delicious strawberries harvested by poor children in Colern woods.[90] The brewers of Salisbury made the best bottle ale in the nation, thanks to superior malt and water.[91] In Highworth, near

[83] Aubrey, *Monumenta Britannica*, p. 432.
[84] Aubrey, *Monumenta Britannica*, p. 27.
[85] Aubrey, *Natural History of Wiltshire*, p. 11.
[86] Aubrey, *Natural History of Wiltshire*, p. 11.
[87] Aubrey, *Natural History of Wiltshire*, p. 11.
[88] Aubrey, *Natural History of Wiltshire*, p. 21.
[89] Aubrey, *Natural History of Wiltshire*, p. 105.
[90] Aubrey, *Natural History of Wiltshire*, p. 50.
[91] Aubrey, *Natural History of Wiltshire*, p. 95.

Swindon, the locals made fuel bricks from compost, hay, and straw.[92] The loving mastery of traditional arts may explain a less praiseworthy feature of the men and women of Wiltshire. They resisted agricultural improvements and adopted them later than most.[93]

Aubrey's notes, jottings, and books open the world of the *pays*. He celebrated the sheep-shearings 'kept with good Cheer, and strong Beer' on the Downs after the fashion, in his telling, of the Roman Pastorum festa.[94] When Aubrey characterized the people's 'hard flesh' in north Wiltshire, he may have had in mind the Lott-Mead or field festival in Wanborough. Here the lord wore a garland of flowers and the mowers at one house always had 'a pound of beef and garlic for every man, according to that of Horace, "O dura messorum ilia!"', for the hard loins that come with reaping. In Latton, the people vouched that it took its name from the teaching of Latin, but Aubrey thought it had more to do with 'the British word Laith, which is a marasse [morass]', which well agreed with the place.[95] At Corston church, Aubrey found nothing that he deemed noteworthy. He explained:

> [The] modern zeal has been reforming hereabout. Surely this tract of land, Gloucestershire and Somerset, encline people to zeal. Heretofore nothing but Religious Houses, now nothing but Quakers and Fanatiques. It is a sour woodsere country [of spongy ground], and inclines people to contemplation. So, that, and the Bible, and ease, for it is now all upon dairy-grassing and clotheing, sett their witts a-running and reforming.[96]

Michael Hunter's superb study of Aubrey is surely right. He had a talent for recreating the past with grit, immediacy, and lively folk.[97] The peoples of Wiltshire and their counterparts throughout Britain were not exhibits trapped in time. Aubrey tied together past and present. They lived in his travels and imagination. More than coins and monuments and relics – the stuff of Camden and Tanner's Wiltshire – this cultural complexity, this glimpse of the *pays*, is what we lose by Aubrey's absence from Gibson's *Britannia*.

* * * * *

The small county of Bedfordshire gives us one of our few glimpses of Camden the traveller:

[92] *Wiltshire. The Topographical Collections of John Aubrey*, ed. John Edward Jackson (Devizes, 1862), p. 192.
[93] Aubrey, *Natural History of Wiltshire*, p. 103.
[94] Aubrey, *Three Prose Works*, p. 144; also Aubrey *Natural History of Wiltshire*, pp. 108–9.
[95] *Wiltshire. Topographical Collections*, p. 153.
[96] *Wiltshire. Topographical Collections*, p. 266.
[97] Hunter, *John Aubrey*, pp. 176–7.

We have not gone far from this place [Woburn abbey] (along by Hockley in the hole, a dirty road extreme troublesome to travellers in winter time; and through fields wherein are the best beans, yielding a pleasant smell, but by their fragrancy spoiling the scent of dogs, not without the greater indignation of the Hunters) till we ascend a white hill into Chiltern, and presently come to Dunstable, seated in a chalky ground, pretty well inhabited, and full of Inns.[98]

In the middle of Dunstable Camden found a stone cross – 'or rather a pillar' – with the arms of England, Castile, and Poitou engraved on it. The landmark commemorated the passage of Queen Eleanor of Castile's funeral train from Lincoln to Westminster in the time of Edward I. Nearby lay the Antonine encampment of Magioninium. There Longshanks's Norman predecessor Henry I 'planted a Colony that should be a curb to the insolence of Robbers (as the private History of the little Monastery, which he founded for such an ornament to his Colony, does plainly testifie.)'. Like their counterparts in Wales, Henry's subjects in Bedfordshire needed instruction in the ways of civility from their Norman rulers.[99]

Part of Camden's focus remained the waxing fortunes of civility and barbarity during the peopling of Britain. The Roman road was a reminder written on the face of Britannia: 'But when the Roman Empire in this land expir'd, and barbarism by degrees got ground, whilst the Saxon wars put all things in perpetual hurry, this great road, as all other things, lay quite neglected for a long time, until a little before the Norman Conquest, Leostan, Abbot of St Albans repaired and restor'd it.'[100] Whoever revised Hertfordshire for Gibson did not feel the need to improve on Camden's account of antiquity, restoring the county instead to its own times. Relying on John Norden's 1597 *Speculum* and map of Hertfordshire brought Hitchin, Hatfield, Burnt-Pelham, Stotford, Tibbalds, and Mergate into contemporary focus. Both Gibson's scholar and Camden agreed that Hertfordshire was 'well furnish'd with corn-fields, pasture-ground, meadows, little woods; and small but clear streams'. However, its importance as a gentry 'commuter belt' needed to be recognized, as anyone reading Thomas Fuller's *Worthies of England* would know. Those 'who have made particular enquiries into the affairs of this County, rather refer its flourishing condition to the main thorow-fares to and from London, which has been the cause of the improvement of their towns; and partly to the healthfulness of the air, which has induc'd several of the Gentry to settle in this Country, and given occasion to this saying, That they who buy a house in Hertfordshire, pay two years purchase for the air of it'.[101]

This Hertfordshire was a century and a world removed from that of Richard Lea, who helped himself to a font in Leith during the rough wooing of 1542–44

---

[98] Camden, *Britannia* (1695), p. 288.
[99] Camden, *Britannia* (1695), pp. 288–9.
[100] Camden, *Britannia* (1695), p. 302.
[101] Camden, *Britannia* (1695), pp. 291, 303.

and deposited it in the church of St Albans. Lea attached an inscription that read in part: 'Sir Richard Lea Knight saved me out of the flames, and brought me into England ... I who heretofore served only at the baptism of the Children of Kings, do now most willingly offer the same service even to the meanest of the English nation.' Once again turning to Fuller's *Worthies*, readers in 1695 were informed that the 'brazen Font, mention'd by Camden to have been brought out of Scotland, is now taken away; in the late civil wars, as it seems, by those hands which let nothing stand that could be converted into money'.[102]

Camden made his way through the Romano-British heartland of Middlesex and Essex in much the same fashion, but his turn toward the home counties of the Iceni in Suffolk, Norfolk, Cambridgeshire, and Huntingdonshire prompted an interesting intervention from Gibson's team. Gibson's collaborator questioned Camden's location of the Iceni and the neat identification of ethno-cultural complexity with conventional boundaries:

> Nor indeed can it be nicely determin'd: for how can we hope exactly to distinguish the bounds of the old British people; when all our ancient Authors, only deliver at large whereabouts such and such were seated, without ever descending to their particular limits? Besides most of the barbarous nations seem (according to their strength at different times) to have had dominions larger and narrower; especially in Britain, where there were so many Kings, we cannot imagine but they were now and then making encroachments upon on another.[103]

Rather than a confident belief that ethnicity could be mapped with precision, Gibson's collaborator suggested that the map of Britain represented a more cluttered reality of encounter, interaction, and hybrid identities. This treated Britain like the 'middle ground' of Amerindians, French traders, and British colonists of the Ohio Valley and Great Lakes.[104] Indeed, the boundaries drawn by kings and rulers obscured reality, 'since the bounds of the shire were set long after their time by King Alfred, who no doubt had rather an eye to the convenience of the Kingdom, than the exact limits of the Britains'.[105] Notional boundaries could obscure a very different local reality.

For the revised edition of 1722, Gibson called on the help of Thomas Tanner with Suffolk and Norfolk. We know that Tanner assisted Gibson in 1695 with Wiltshire, but not whether he had a hand in the earlier additions.[106] If they were the work of the same collaborator, the interest in cultural complexity carried only so far across the county line into Norfolk. For Camden, the soil of Norfolk

---

[102] Camden, *Britannia* (1695), p. 305.

[103] Camden, *Britannia* (1695), pp. 377–8.

[104] Richard White, *The Middle Ground: Indians, Empires, and Republics in the Great Lakes Region, 1650–1815* (Cambridge, 1991), pp. 50–93.

[105] Camden, *Britannia* (1695), p. 378.

[106] William Camden, *Britannia: Or a Chorographical Description of Great Britain and Ireland* (two volumes; London, 1722), sig. a2b.

varied from 'the fat, luscious', moist soil of the east to 'clayey and chalkey' deposits and 'poor, lean, and sandy' soil in western parishes. But there was one thing consistent: the goodly county produced inhabitants who were 'of a bright clear complexion; not to mention their sharpness of wit, and admirable quickness in the study of our Common-Law'. Norfolk had long been reputed 'the most fruitful Nursery of Lawyers; and even among the common people you shall meet with a great many, who (as one expresses it), if they have no just quarrel, are able to raise it out of the very quirks and niceties of the Law'. Gibson's collaborator readily agreed and Henry Spelman, native of Conghan, 'Oracle of Law, Patron of the Church, and glory of England' made the case. Indeed, Spelman's manuscript survey of Norfolk, which Speed relied upon in his *Theatre*, underpinned most of the additions in 1695, other than the rare plants taken in by the writer himself.[107]

'Tho Cambridge was consecrated to the Muses,' Camden wrote, 'yet it has not always escap'd the furies of Mars.' The Danes took up winter quarters there after the high season of plunder, 'when William I. determin'd to erect Castles in all parts, to be a curb to his new-conquer'd English'. Cambridge was not spared, and it suffered mightily in 'the Barons wars by those Out-laws from the Isle of Ely'. As for its most bitter conflicts: 'Here possibly some may secretly expect to hear my opinion concerning the antiquity of this University; but I'll not meddle in the case, nor am I willing to make any comparisons between our two flourishing Universities, which have none to rival them that I know of.'[108] Camden's successor did not take this charitably: 'Our Author … has hardly allow'd it so much compass, as the dignity of so famous an University and Nursery of Learning requires. So that 'tis no more than justice to be a little more particular upon their several Foundations, and the improvements that have been made upon them since his time, both in buildings and otherwise.'[109] Gibson's collaborator was good to his word in the additions, finding little space for anything but the university and – even more so – the rare plants of Cambridgeshire.[110]

Camden praised too sparingly Oxford's rival on the Cam, but the Fen country was like nothing he had seen in Oxfordshire. The great dykes and ditches pulled him away from the dons and colleges, Hingston, Brent-ditch, Seven-mile Dyke formerly called Fleam-Dyke or Flight-Dyke, Rech-Dyke named for the market town at its start, and the great Devil's Dyke, so called 'by the Common People, because they look upon it as a work of Devils rather than Men'.[111] The Fens were unique, a great expanse of precarious livelihoods earned in wary partnership with nature and the seasons:

---

[107] Camden, *Britannia* (1695), pp. 383–402.
[108] Camden, *Britannia* (1695), p. 406.
[109] Camden, *Britannia* (1695), p. 412.
[110] Camden, *Britannia* (1695), pp. 411–20.
[111] Camden, *Britannia* (1695), pp. 407–8.

All this Country in the winter-time, and sometimes for the greatest part of the year, is laid under-water by the rivers ... for want of sufficient passages. But when they once keep to their proper channels, it so strangely abounds with a rich grass and rank hey (by them call'd Lid) that when they've mown enough for their own use, in November they burn up the rest, to make it come again the thicker. About which time a man may see all the moorish Country round about of a light fire, to his great wonder. Besides it affords great quantities of Turf and Sedge for firing, Reeds for thatching; Elders also and other water shrubs, especially Willows either growing wild, or else set on the banks of rivers to prevent their overflowing ... [112]

Against this natural world, Camden had his doubts about the Fen drainage schemes already glimmering in the eyes of scheming courtiers and greedy projectors, thinking perhaps it was better, after the Oracle, 'Not to venture too far where heaven has put a stop.'[113]

For Camden this was a vivid landscape, cut deep by human hands, pockmarked with ponds, groves, fields, and hideaways, crossed by invaders, cut-purses, rebels, and outlaw barons. It was a peculiar land apart, and so were the people of the Fens:

The inhabitants in this and the rest of the fenny Country ... were call'd Girvii in the time of the Saxons; that is according to some mens explanation, Fen-men; a sort of people (much like the place) of brutish unciviliz'd tempers, envious of others, whom they term Upland-men, and usually walking aloft upon a sort of stilts: they all keep to the business of grazing, fishing, and fowling.[114]

The great cathedral of Ely rose above the Fens and the close air, 'a spacious, stately, and beautiful structure, but somewhat defac'd by shamefully breaking down the Noblemens and Bishops tombs'.[115] In 1695 the cathedral remained, but two 'very considerable improvements' had been made since Camden's time. Saintfoin, a kind of clover well suited to dry, barren ground, had been introduced and the Fen drainage about which Camden had been so sceptical – rightly so, to start – had transformed the landscape. The 'work was carry'd on at vast expence, but has at last turn'd to a double account, both in gaining much ground, and in mending the rest; and also in refining and clearing the air'.[116] Camden's Isle of Ely and the people, the 'Fen-men', who lived a life apart had passed away.

* * * * *

Camden turned to the Coritani, the people who took up 'a very large Tract of Ground in the Mediterranean parts of this Isle', meaning, by this unusual

---

[112] Camden, *Britannia* (1695), p. 407.
[113] Camden, *Britannia* (1695), p. 408.
[114] Camden, *Britannia* (1695), p. 408.
[115] Camden, *Britannia* (1695), pp. 410–11.
[116] Camden, *Britannia* (1695), p. 411.

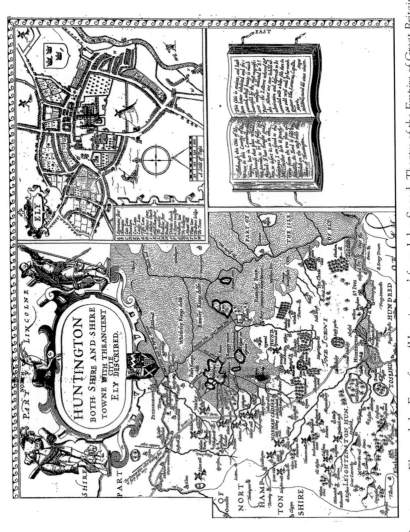

formulation, the counties of Northampton, Leicester, Rutland, Lincoln, Nottingham, and Derby. In some respects, this was the heartland of Camden's *Britannia*. The great ethnic migrations and conflicts scored the landscape. Camden could see this in Northampton: the town's castle and adjacent church dedicated to St Andrew built by the first earl, decay and neglect during the Saxon Heptarchy, its fiery destruction when 'the Dane with barbarous fury and outrage ravag'd all over England', survival under the Normans, valiant resolution down the centuries facing the ravages of baronial wars under John and Henry III, and one more conflict between Warwick the Kingmaker and Henry VI.[117] With good reason too, 'the Kings now and then held their Parliaments here, for the conveniencey of its situation, as it were in the very heart of England'. Indeed, the staples of English history played out in this heartland. Henry VII slew the tyrant Richard III at Market Bosworth in Leicestershire, 'the unfortunate and heroick' Mary, Queen of Scots lost her head at Fotheringhay – an incident that Camden wished could be forgotten or passed over in silence – and the brewers of Derby still produced the 'ancient and peculiar drink of the English and the Britains, very wholesome ... the cause, why some among us that drink ale live to the age of an hundred years'.[118]

Camden warmed to his subjects and readers throughout these chapters.[119] Arriving at Harborough, famous for its cattle fair, and Carleton in Leicestershire, Camden was positively chatty, and put off by the dialect of the locals: 'I know not whether it is worth relating, but most of the natives of this town, either from some peculiar quality of the soil, or water, or other unknown cause in nature, have a harsh and ungrateful manner of speech, with a guttural and difficult pronunciation, and a strange wharling in the utterance of their words.'[120] Gibson or his collaborator had something to add to this analysis of language and environment. Fuller's *Worthies* included an account of a Carleton native, a fellow of Trinity College, Cambridge who could not pronounce the letter 'r'. He 'made a speech of a competent length, with select words as to the matter, without any [r] therein. Which if true; he (no doubt) contriv'd it on purpose to prevent a deformity of pronunciation upon a frequent occurrence of that letter.' Presumably soil, water, or another natural element had nothing to do with this linguistic peculiarity and any difference apparently had fallen out of usage by Gibson's time, 'the present inhabitants, as they retain no remains of it in their speech, so neither in their memory, the most ancient among them knowing nothing of it'.[121]

One such matter concerned the settlement of the Jews in England and their expulsion. The clues began with a trove of coins and artefacts uncovered in Lindley, including a silver ring engraved in Arabic reading 'By Mahomet

---

[117] Camden, *Britannia* (1695), pp. 433–4.
[118] Camden, *Britannia* (1695), pp. 435, 444, 492, 494.
[119] Camden, *Britannia* (1695), p. 446.
[120] Camden, *Britannia* (1695), p. 443.
[121] Camden, *Britannia* (1695), pp. 449–50.

magnifie him, / Turn from him each hand that may hurt him.' William Burton conjectured that the money, rings, and other artefacts were 'the treasure of some Jew'.[122] What followed was a potted history of the Jewish presence in England, with a traditional emphasis:

> For that people flourish'd mightily in England a little after the Conquest, being encourag'd particularly by William Rufus; upon which they became very rich and flourishing. But their wealth in the succeeding reigns did them an injury; being miserably tortur'd by King John to make them discover and deliver up their hidden treasures. In 11th of Edw I. their Synagogues were all pluckt down; and in the 16th of the King, they were all banisht the Realm, to the number of 15000.[123]

The Lindley find must have been the treasure buried at the expulsion, with hopes that a changed climate under a new king would make it possible for the owners or their descendants to return and recover their possessions. As for the Arabic ring, it 'might be brought over out of Palestine or some of those Eastern Counties by some of the Jews'. The additions claimed that the ring acted as a marker of possession, just as in Ludgate a wall was found 'engraven with Hebrew Letters to this effect, This is the dwelling of Rabbi Moses, the son of the honourable Rabbi Isaac.'[124]

Antiquarian passion did not make Camden unthinkingly nostalgic. Crowland abbey, Lincolnshire, famous for its chronicle, was a case in point. Ghostly apparitions and beasts right out of medieval stories of monstrous races had once stalked Crowland:

> If out of the same Author I should describe the Devils of Crowland with their blubber lips, fiery mouths, scaly faces, beetle heads, sharp teeth, long chins, hoarse throats, black skins, hump shoulders, big bellys, burning loins, bandy legs, tail'd buttocks, &c. that formerly haunted these places ... you'd laugh perhaps at the story, and much more at my madness for telling it.[125]

Instead, Camden elected to describe a landscape that was haunting in its own right, since 'the situation and nature of the place is strange and different from all others in England'. Camden summoned up some of his most vivid first-hand descriptions:

> This Crowland lyes in the fenns, so enclos'd and encompass'd with deep bogs and pools that there is no access to it but on the north and east-side, and these by narrow Causeys. This Monastery, and Venice (if we may compare things of such different size and proportion) have the same situation. It consists of three streets, separated each from the other by water-courses planted with willows, built on piles driven into the bottom of the pool; having communication by a triangular bridge curiously built ...

---

[122] Camden, *Britannia* (1695), p. 452.
[123] Camden, *Britannia* (1695), p. 452.
[124] Camden, *Britannia* (1695), pp. 452–3.
[125] Camden, *Britannia* (1695), p. 461.

> Beyond the bridge ... stood formerly that famous Monastery, of very small compass, about which ... the ground is so rotten and boggy, that a pole may be thrust down thirty feet deep.[126]

Despite its forbidding location, the town was well inhabited and its people had adapted accordingly. The cowherds and milkmaids made their way to their distant flocks in boats, taking in a great catch of fish and ducks to boot. The right to take fish and fowl from the Fenland cost them £300 per annum to the king, but they had the better of the arrangement, netting as many as three thousand ducks at a time in August.[127] Both Camden's long, detailed original and its equally expansive counterpart in 1695 offered readers one of *Britannia's* strongest accounts.[128]

* * * * *

The bounds of Warwickshire, home to the Cornavi, did not present a regular outline, but the Avon divided it into two distinct topographies: the champaign ground to the south and east and the woodlands north and west of the river. The fields of corn and verdant pastures of the Feldon were best taken in from the delightful prospect atop Edgehill. Thomas Newsham, Gibson's expert in Warwickshire, did not conceal his disappointment with the county's renowned historian, William Dugdale. Between them, Dugdale's *Monasticon Anglicanum* and *Antiquities of Warwickshire* wrote the book on the county when they were published in the 1655 and 1656, respectively.[129] For Newsham, Dugdale spent too much time with 'excellent digressions of Monastic orders, consecrations of Churches, and such like' when he should have 'either in the body of his work, as such places lay in his way, or in the method which Dr. Plott has since us'd, making such Antiquities an Appendix'. Had Dugdale done so, 'we should probably have found the discoveries answerable to the appearance', but 'since we cannot compass the whole, let us be content with what we have; and accompany Mr. Camden to the several parts of the County'.[130] For Newsham, an ephemeral figure to be sure, Dugdale had not finished the story begun in *Britannia*, one of the few instances of such criticism for the county experts that followed Camden.

Warwick led Camden into a digression about the canny policies adopted by the Romans to meet the challenges of governing a multi-ethnic *imperium*. Britain was a perfect example:

---

[126] Camden, *Britannia* (1695), p. 461.
[127] Camden, *Britannia* (1695), p. 461.
[128] Camden, *Britannia* (1695), pp. 473–8.
[129] Graham Parry, 'The Antiquities of Warwickshire', in *William Dugdale, Historian, 1605–1686: His Life, His Writings and His County*, ed. Christopher Dyer and Catherine Richardson (Woodbridge, 2009), pp. 10–33.
[130] Camden, *Britannia* (1695), pp. 499, 509.

These troops were levied in Dalmatia: and here we may observe the political prudence of the Romans, who in their Provinces disposed and quart'red their foreign Troops in garrisons; with whom and the natives (by reason of the great diversity of language and humours) there could not likely be any secret combinations form'd against their Government. ... Whereupon it was, that from Africa the Moors, from Spain the Asturians and Vettones, from Germany the Batavians, the Nervii, Tungri, and Turnacenses; from Gaul, the Lingones and Morini, and from other parts the Dalmatians, Thracians, Alains, &c. were brought over to serve in Britain; as in their proper places we shall observe.[131]

Sent away from their own, mixed among others with whom they shared little by way of customs and language, these peoples learned obedience by incorporation within and conformity to the Roman *imperium*. Camden did not know that one day the British *imperium* would have its own parallel in the disproportionate numbers of Welsh, Scots, and Irish who became loyal agents of empire around the world.

Antiquity alone did not interest Camden in Warwickshire, any more than it did in the rest of *Britannia*. Leaving Kenilworth, Camden truly stepped back into his shoes as a traveller. He brought to life for his readers the sights, sounds, and cultural encounters that he remembered, and they are worth savouring:

For hence (that I may pursue the same course I did in my journey) I saw Solyhill, in which was nothing worth seeing beside the Church. Next, Bremicham, swarming with inhabitants, and echoing with the noise of Anvils (for here are great numbers of Smiths.) The lower part is very watery. The upper rises with abundance of handsome buildings: and 'tis none of the least honours of the place, that from hence the noble and warlike family of the Bremichams in Ireland had both their original and their name. From thence in the extreme point of this County northward, lies Sutton Colefield, in a foresty, unkind, and barren soil ... From hence going southward I came to Coleshull ... Lower in the middle of this woody country is seated Coventry, so called (as I conjecture) from a Convent ... 'Tis commodiously seated, large and neat; fortify'd with very strong walls, and adorn'd with beautiful buildings; amongst which two Churches of excellent Architecture stand together ... There is nothing in it of very great antiquity. That which seems to be the greatest monument, is the Religious-house or Priory, whose ruins I saw near these two Churches. This, King Canutus founded for Nuns ... [132]

Newsham updated some of this material, including the destruction of the city walls of Coventry at the order of Charles II. He found an opportunity at Coleshill to record – with perhaps the slightest gibe implied – that nearby Blith 'was purchas'd by Sir William Dugdale, and was his place of residence when he compil'd that accurate and elaborate work, his Antiquities of this County'.[133]

William Hopkins, who assisted Gibson with his edition of the *Anglo-Saxon Chronicle*, did not have any axes to grind with those who followed Camden into

[131] Camden, *Britannia* (1695), p. 501.
[132] Camden, *Britannia* (1695), p. 505.
[133] Camden, *Britannia* (1695), pp. 513–14.

ENGLAND'S MOTLEY BREEDS

Worcestershire. We might be tempted to neglect the unique importance of salt in the early modern Britain of Leland and Camden. It preserved food and made it more palatable, especially when the 'sell-by dates' had long passed. Camden started his description with the 'Wicci', who had inhabited Worcestershire in Bede's day, a people who owed their name to the valuable commodity:

> [It] may seem to be deriv'd from the Salt-pits, which the ancient English in their language nam'd Witches. For in this Country there are noble Brine-pits; and many Salt springs are ever and anon discover'd but are presently stopp'd up, because, as I learn from ancient writings, they are obliged, for the preservation of wood, to make Salt only in one place.[134]

'Nor let it be thought improbable that places should take their names from Salt-pits,' Camden explained further, 'seeing there are many instances hereof in all Countries; and our Ancestors the Germans ... firmly believed such places to be nearest Heaven; and that mens prayers are no where sooner heard by the Gods.'[135]

Inevitably, then, Camden picked up the story of Droitwich from where Leland and Harrison left off. Nature's bounty yielded three springs of the strongest brine, out of which was 'made the purest and whitest Salt'. Camden too noted that the saltpans were active for only part of the year, though it was Hopkins who parroted Harrison's complaint about the manipulation of the market. Environmental destruction did not escape Camden's view even if a veil of silence or indifference surrounded it: 'What a prodigious quantity of wood these Salt-works consume, though men be silent, yet Feckenham Forest, once very thick with trees, and the neighbouring woods, will by their thinness declare daily more and more.' Hopkins reported that the inevitable transition had been made by his time, for they 'now burn coal and not wood'.[136] Like the forest, superstition had evidently decayed in Droitwich:

> If I should say that Richard de la Wich, Bishop of Chichester, who was born here, did by his prayers obtain these Salt-springs, I am afraid some would censure me as very injurious to Divine Providence, and over-credulous of old wives fables. Nevertheless, so great was the pious credulity of our Ancestors, that they did not only believe it firmly themselves, and transmit it in writing to us, but also upon that account paid him honours in a manner divine; when for his skill in Canon-Law, and sanctity of life, he was solemnized for a Saint by Urban the fourth.[137]

Camden suggested that the credulousness that Leland and Harrison found in the inhabitants was a thing of the past, especially the baleful effects of the papal exploitation of the gullible.

134 Camden, *Britannia* (1695), p. 515.
135 Camden, *Britannia* (1695), pp. 515–16.
136 Camden, *Britannia* (1695), pp. 518, 524.
137 Camden, *Britannia* (1695), p. 518.

From Worcestershire, Camden's circuit through Britain took him into Staffordshire, the Welsh Borders, and Wales proper. In Shropshire and Cheshire, Camden and Gibson's collaborators recognized the 'middle ground' of the marches. Camden confessed that the story of encounter, violent or otherwise, and his determined interest in ethnic complexity threatened to overwhelm the description of a county like Cheshire. 'If I should particularly relate the skirmishes here between the Welsh and English in the beginning of the Norman times,' he explained of Chester, 'the many inroads and excursions, the frequent firings of the suburbs of Hanbrid beyond the bridge (whereupon the Welsh-men call it Treboeth, that is, the burnt town,) and tell you of the long wall made there by Welsh-mens skuls; I should seem to forget my self, and run too far into the business of a Historian.'[138]

Camden was not good to his pledge, though. He let a long passage from Lucian record Chester's place as a crossroads of people from the earliest times:

> [Chester] stood very convenient to receive the Roman Legions that were transported hither: and besides it was proper for watching the frontiers of the Empire, and was a perfect key to Ireland. For being opposite to the north parts of Ireland, it opened a passage thither for ships and mariners continually in motion to and again ... and on the south side with a harbour to ships coming from Gascoign, Spain, Ireland, and Germany ... [139]

Camden selected another passage from Lucian that made remarkably grandiose claims about Chester's place in the Roman *imperium*. The city was 'a spectacle exposed to the eye of all the world' with 'four gates answering the four winds; on the east-side it has a prospect toward India, on the west toward Ireland, and on the north towards greater Norway; and lastly, on the south, to that little corner wherein God's vengeance has confined the Britains ... and how they live to this day, their neighbours know to their sorrow'.[140]

Yorkshire beckoned once Camden had completed his description of Wales. He made a figurative allusion of some interest about the island's shape:

> Britain, which has thus far bulg'd out into several Promontories, coming gradually nearer, on one side to Germany, and the other to Ireland; does now (as if it were afraid of the breaking in of the Ocean) draw it self in on each side, retires farther from its neighbours, and is contracted into a much narrower breadth.[141]

Drawn in on itself this part of Britain might appear, but Yorkshire, the Lakes, and the North of England offered every bit as much evidence for migration and encounter as the rest of Britain. Yorkshire brought together every variety of people and exchange that interested Camden, from the ubiquitous presence

---

138 Camden, *Britannia* (1695), pp. 551, 559.
139 Camden, *Britannia* (1695), p. 559.
140 Camden, *Britannia* (1695), p. 559.
141 Camden, *Britannia* (1695), p. 703.

of the Romans and Danes to the imperial ambitions of the medieval Scottish monarchs who had played to England's disgruntled nobility.[142] Yorkshire received the attention of three experts for Gibson's edition who were themselves products of this mingling of peoples, albeit of a somewhat less violent kind. Dr Nathaniel Johnston, the 'whig Jacobite' son of Elizabeth Hobson and the transplanted Scotsman John Johnston, shared materials he collected for thirty years as part of his failed project to do for Yorkshire what Dugdale's *Antiquities* had done for Warwickshire.[143] The West Riding fell to another of Gibson's antiquarian colleagues, Ralph Thoresby of Leeds, friend of Thomas Kirke, who had penned the Weldonesque attack on the Scots in 1679 despite a relatively genial journey through Scotland. William Nicolson, a friend of Lhuyd, Thoresby, and Gibson, exercised a watching brief over the entire county. The Cumberland-born Nicolson rose to become, first, bishop of Carlisle and then the Church of Ireland bishop of Derry, publishing, to mixed reviews, three bibliographies between 1696 and 1724 covering England, Scotland, and Ireland.[144] These scholars, and John Burnsall of Hull, who tended to the East Riding, did not stray from Gibson's charge to update Camden. When Gibson adopted a different tack with his 1722 edition and integrated the additions with Camden's original text, there was little besides updated history and the inevitable list of rare plants to separate the work of Camden from his successors, other than the occasional brackets with which Gibson marked them.

Journeys north

Bannockburn, Pinkie, Dunbar, Solway Moss, and Flodden made any description of lowland Scotland as least partly an account of the battle for Scotland itself. From Yorkshire northward, Camden travelled through the lands over which the battle for England had been fought. He recorded that Northallerton was laid waste by the 'unheard of cruelty' of David I's ambitious design to push the Scottish border to Lancashire and the Tees. The king of Scots had been defeated at the battle of Standard, 'put to flight with such slaughter of his men, that the English themselves thought their revenge then at last sufficiently completed'.[145] The spectacular landscape and the engagements of Romans, Britons, Scots, Normans, and English fired Camden's imagination and defined this part of England for him. Yet Camden braced his 'antiquarian' readers for disappointment as they travelled toward Scotland:

---

[142] Camden, *Britannia* (1695), pp. 703–72.

[143] Mark Goldie, 'Nathaniel Johnston', *Oxford DNB* at www.oxforddnb.com.

[144] D.W. Hayton, 'William Nicolson', *Oxford DNB* at www.oxforddnb.com.

[145] Camden, *Britannia* (1695), p. 756.

I fear I shall be so far from satisfying the Reader, that I shall not satisfie my self. For after I had survey'd the far greater part of this County, I found but very few things as I had wish'd them; the ancient names seem'd to be every where so much obscur'd by Antiquity. However, not to seem wanting to this County, I will run the hazard of the attempt, hoping that that Divine assistance will not now fail me, which hath hitherto favour'd me.[146]

Camden no doubt had in mind his first visit to Salisbury Hall, the seat of the Talbots. He could make no sense of inscriptions on a wall that included a carved stone image of Cupid, except to think that 'many of the words are British names for places hereabouts'. The results were the same in 'the year 1603, when I came a second time to see this place, I met with an Altar the greatest and fairest that I ever saw'.[147]

Camden may have found the remains of antiquity harder to tease out as he travelled north, but it opened opportunities for him to investigate the complex history, culture, and interactions of the peoples he met and over whose lands he journeyed. Lancaster encapsulated the lasting effects of those encounters. The inhabitants 'more truly call [it] Loncaster, and the Scots, Loncastell, from the river Lon. Both its name at this day, and the river under it, in a manner prove it to be the Longevicum, where ... a Company of the Longovicarians, who took that name from the place, kept garrison'.[148] Romans, Scots, and English marked Lancaster's past and present when Camden arrived:

Tho' at the present the town is not populous, and the inhabitants thereof are all husbandmen (for the grounds about it ar well cultivated, open, flourishing, and woody enough;) yet in proof of its Roman antiquity, they sometimes meet with coins of the Emperors, especially where the Fryers had their cloyster: for there (as they report) stood the marks of an ancient city, which the Scots in a sudden inroad, in the year 1322, wherein they destroy'd every thing they could meet with burnt to the ground.[149]

Further along, at Furness, the whole tract except for the seaside was dominated by rocky, difficult uplands, 'among which the Britain's liv'd securely for a long time, relying upon the fortifications where-with nature had guarded them, tho' nothing prov'd impregnable to the Saxon Conquerors'.[150]

One topographic feature of the North stood out. The Pennines 'make themselves Umpires, and define the several Shires and Counties'. Where the mountains in Lancashire left off, barley and wheat were grown with some success and farmers reaped good oats from the valley bottoms.[151] So successful were the people of Lancashire at improving their sandy soils with marl (clay rich with

[146] Camden, *Britannia* (1695), p. 787.
[147] Camden, *Britannia* (1695), pp. 791–2.
[148] Camden, *Britannia* (1695), p. 795.
[149] Camden, *Britannia* (1695), p. 795.
[150] Camden, *Britannia* (1695), p. 795.
[151] Camden, *Britannia* (1695), pp. 788–9, 801.

organic matter) that Camden mused whether 'we may reasonably think Mankind rather to blame for their idleness heretofore, than the Earth for her ingratitude' where unimproved farmland was concerned. This was not idle praise. It spoke to the nature of Lancashire's people. 'But as for the goodness of this County,' Camden affirmed, 'we may see it in the complexion of the Natives, who are particularly well favour'd and comely.' Yet one wonders if Camden had his tongue in his cheek here or just made a spectacularly inapt observation in what immediately followed: 'nay, and if we will, in the Cattle of it too. For in the Oxen, which have huge horns, and proportionable bodies, you shall find nothing of that perfection wanting' by Mago the Carthaginian, author of a noted agricultural manual.[152]

Passing Chatmoss, Camden arrived at Holcroft, 'which gave both seat and name to the famous family'. Camden felt he had to explain this particular cultural practice: 'And this was a thing commonly practis'd heretofore, in other parts of England. Here are little Towns quite round (as also throughout this whole County, Cheshire, and other Northern parts) which have given names to families, and continue in the hands of those of the same name in this very day.' Camden added a very Elizabethan north–south prejudice about chivalry and nobility. Here in England 'these and such like families in the Northern Counties (that I may once for all observe it) as they rose by their bravery, and grew up more and more by their frugality, and the ancient self-contented simplicity'. By contrast, 'in the South parts of England, Luxury, Usury, Debaucheries, and Cheating have undone the most flourishing families in a short time: insomuch that many complain how the old race of our Nobility fades and decays'.[153] Here was a judgement with overtones of Boece or Lesley and the Earl of Essex's complaints about lost nobility, although for Essex it fed his hatred for the upstart family of William Cecil, the 'base pen clerk' who was among Camden's great patrons.[154]

Gibson's revisions in 1695 did not shed much new light on the antiquities that puzzled Camden, but he did make some important additions. Two of them would have appealed to eighteenth- and nineteenth-century readers who took up *Britannia* in an age of global capitalism and empire. Lancaster may have given its name to the county, 'yet Manchester, whether one consider Antiquity, number of inhabitants, or growth, seems to be more considerable'. An appropriate description of Lancashire – and Britain's – future industrial powerhouse followed:

> The Fustian-Manufacture, call'd Manchester-Cottons, still continues there, and is of late very much improv'd by some modern inventions of dying and printing; and this, with the great variety of other manufactures, known by the name of Manchester-wares,

---

[152] Camden, *Britannia* (1695), p. 787.
[153] Camden, *Britannia* (1695), pp. 788–9.
[154] Stephen Alford, *Burghley: William Cecil at the Court of Elizabeth I* (New Haven, 2008), pp. 316–18, 345–7.

renders not only the town it self, but also the parish about it, rich, populous, and industrious.[155]

In Camden's time Liverpool was 'the most convenient and frequented place for setting sail into Ireland'. It became only more so, but the Caribbean sugar economy transformed the city in a way that Camden could not have foreseen: 'To this (with their trade to the West-Indies, and the several manufactures in the parts adjacent) is probably owing the vast growth in the town of late years.'[156] Great changes were afoot, yet Gibson did not omit an account from Nicolson concerning cloudberries, the supposed 'dwarf mulberry' that Camden noted in passing at the crest of Pendle Hill. Nicolson reported that they actually grew 'plentifully on the boggy tops of most of the high mountains in both England and Scotland' as well in as Norway and other northern nations – including, one day, French Canada, where they are still made into a peaty-tasting liquor.[157]

* * * * *

Camden was drawn to Westmorland by the same natural beauty that eventually pulled generations of Romantics and their modern counterparts to the Lake District. It was apropos for naming practices in the region, for 'the North parts of England call wild barren places, such as are not fit for tillage, by the name of Mores'. At Levens and Betham he found waterfalls that 'tumbled headlong with a hideous noise'. The great falls literally spoke to the inhabitants: 'the neighbours draw certain prognostications of the weather: for when the Northern one has a clear sound, they promise themselves fair weather; but when the Southern, rain and mists'. Camden concluded a fairly cursory account of the southern part of the county before passing Windermere to Ambleside and points north in search of antiquities. The remains of the Roman station at Appleby kept his attention, where Reginald Bainbrigg lived, 'a very learned Gentleman, who courteously transcrib'd for me several ancient Inscriptions, and has remov'd some from his own garden'.[158] For his part, Bainbrigg, a local schoolteacher, wrote in 1600 to express his deep appreciation for Camden's project and his satisfaction that he and other local associates could make a tangible contribution to describing the antiquities and character of his little part of Britannia.[159]

Thomas Machell was less certain about Camden's accomplishment from the perspective of the 1690s. Machell was born near Appleby, at Crackenthorpe Hall, and counted Dugdale and Anthony Wood among his formative associates.

[155] Camden, *Britannia* (1695), pp. 798–9.
[156] Camden, *Britannia* (1695), pp. 790, 800.
[157] Camden, *Britannia* (1695), pp. 791, 799.
[158] Camden, *Britannia* (1695), pp. 805–7.
[159] Wyman Herendeen, *William Camden: A Life in Context* (Woodbridge, 2007), pp. 205–6, 307–8.

From his base at Kirkby Thore rectory, Machell laboured to produce an account of Westmorland in the style of Dugdale's *Antiquities*. To which end 'he travelled extensively, recording the heritage of his native county by direct observation, sketching buildings and heraldry, and noting inscriptions and information given him by local informants. He visited most parishes in northern Westmorland and, between 1691 and 1693, made three antiquarian journeys to the barony of Kendal, the southern half of the county.'[160] These journeys shaped his view of Camden's travels and description as partial and incomplete:

> For travelling from Lancaster, through the Barony of Kendal, to Workington in Cumberland, he met with little in his road, besides great mountains with here and there a Valley between, and so took an estimate of the whole from that part; imagining probably, that the more southerly corner was like to be as good at least, if not better than the rest. But had he gone northward he would have found reason to change his opinion ... And so far is it [the Barony of Westmorland] uncultivated, that it affords great plenty of arable ground; and those, good store of corn.[161]

Machell also questioned Camden's understanding of cultural traditions in the North: 'Nor do Mores in the northern parts signifie wild barren mountains, but generally Common of pasture ... [so] that in the Barony of Kendal (where they have most Mountains) there are few or no Mores, their Commons being call'd Fells.' Further, the mores were 'far from being uncapable of improvement, that most of them have been formerly plow'd'. All of this worked against a topographic etymology for 'Westmoreland' as the moorish land lying west of what 'Mr. Camden calls the English Apennine'.[162]

Machell's scholarly life seemingly led to this moment. In January 1677 he 'had printed the first questionnaire specifically intended to inform a county study and directed at the unit of the parish'.[163] Machell aimed to collect and compile these parish accounts into a commonplace book ready to answer his own questions and further researches in history.[164] The questionnaire set a standard that directly shaped those of Nathaniel Johnston (Yorkshire), Aubrey, William Molyneux (Ireland), Sibbald, and Lhuyd.[165] Its immediate significance lies in the title, *That the Northern Counties Which Abound in Antiquities and Ancient Gentry, May No Longer be Bury'd in Silence*. The situation and heritage of Westmorland and the North demanded attention. Machell called the gentry, clergy, and tenants 'of good Repute, Knowledge and Honesty' to honour their parish with as much information as they could gather. From the comprehensive list of queries, one

---

[160] Angus J.L. Winchester, 'Thomas Machell', *Oxford DNB* at www.oxforddnb.com.

[161] Camden, *Britannia* (1695), pp. 809, 811.

[162] Camden, *Britannia* (1695), p. 809.

[163] Adam Fox, 'Printed Questionnaires, Research Networks, and the Discovery of the British Isles, 1650–1800', *Historical Journal* 53.3 (2010), p. 599.

[164] Fox, 'Printed Questionnaires', p. 599.

[165] Fox, 'Printed Questionnaires', pp. 599–604.

could imagine John Leland circulating such a questionnaire. At least some of the questions would have allowed Machell to study the county's historical cultural complexity in its people and places: settlement; topography and livelihoods; games, sports and pastimes; the origins of local saints and associated customs; the histories of families and their landholdings; etymologies of street names; proverbs and peculiar customs.[166] How did Machell read the cultural complexity of Westmorland?

Like several of his colleagues who worked with Gibson, Machell died without ever completing his own project in 1698. He left his papers to his neighbour and fellow collaborator William Nicolson, who bound and deposited six volumes of 'imperfect, Raw and indigested' material in the chapter library at Carlisle; there they became a storehouse for scholars in years to come.[167] Machell's immediate legacy was to double Camden's description. He filled in essential gaps, both concerning antiquities and a description of the county and its inhabitants. He too had help, noting the assistance of Daniel Fleming of Ridal Hall, 'a great lover of ancient learning'. Following his opening critique he remarked on the heavy, castle-like fabric of noble houses in the county, 'for defence of themselves, their Tenants, and their goods, whenever the Scots should make inroads; which before the time of King James I. were very common'.[168] Following the Lune northward to its junction with the Birkbeck, Machell described the 'red stone about an ell high [approx. 45 inches], with two Crosses cut deep on one side'. Tradition had it that it was the 'Merestone between the English and Scots', but Machell would not commit, even though he reported that it stood about the same distance from Scotland as the 'Rere-cross upon Stane-more' that was erected for such a purpose. North to Tebay, and Machell also noted the fortified mount of Castle-bow designed to 'prevent also the Incursions of that people'.[169]

Machell performed his task with moments of asperity. He denied that Pendragon castle was 'a heap of great stones, in Mr Camden's time; when the walls, being four yards in thickness (with battlements upon them) were standing till the year 1660'. He disputed Camden's association of names and seats, suggesting that the Musgraves gave their name to the town and not the other way round, citing the word as the 'original' for offices like 'Landtgraff, Markgraff, Burggraff, &c. among the Germans'.[170] Appleby was a particular sore spot. Machell expanded the history of the town but also recounted in more detail the depredations of the wars with Scotland, noting with care the two occasions during the reigns of Henry II and Richard I when the town was burned. Centuries of

---

[166] Thomas Machell, *That the Northern Counties Which Abound in Antiquities and Ancient Gentry, May No Longer be Bury'd in Silence* (WING M127B; Oxford, 1677), pp. 1–3.

[167] Winchester, 'Machell'.

[168] Camden, *Britannia* (1695), p. 809.

[169] Camden, *Britannia* (1695), p. 811.

[170] Camden, *Britannia* (1695), pp. 811–12.

conflict and devastation literally redrew the face of Appleby, as Camden would have learned, had his investigations been more diligent:

> Since which, it never recover'd it self, but lay as it were dismember'd and scatter'd one street from another, like so many several villages; and one could not know, but by Records, that they belong'd to the same body. For which reason it is, that Mr. Camden mentions no more than Burgh-gate; whereas Bongate, Battle-burgh, Dungate, Scattergate, are all of them members of this ancient Town. Concerning the condition and misfortunes of this place, take this Inscription [reproduced in the text], placed in the Garden belonging to the School-house, amongst many others of Roman antiquity, collected by Mr. Bainbrigg, of whom our Author makes an honourable mention.[171]

The endowment of Bainbrigg's school mentioned by Camden 'was far short of what has been added since by some modern Benefactors'.[172]

Either by his own hand or Gibson's, Machell made an appearance in the text. He is mentioned in the description of Crackenthorpe Hall and praised for the careful collection and preservation of antiquities for his projected study. The Roman inscription at Crawdundalewaith, supplied to Camden by Bainbrigg, offered another opportunity to insert Machell personally into the text to criticize Camden: 'The Inscription ... is not altogether as Mr. Camden has represented it, being drawn from the very rock by the curious Mr Machel.' Machell produced his own images for the text and walked readers through Camden's – not, in his telling, Bainbrigg's – shortcomings. Other opportunities were taken for Machell to enter the text and improve Camden's original.

Britannia gave Machell too little scope to explore what he knew of cultural complexity in Westmorland. His parochial questionnaires and investigations since 1677 had yielded astonishing descriptions intended for a chapter on the nature and customs of the people, as we now know thanks to the illuminating work of Adam Fox.[173] Machell described a people at once kind, courteous, and hospitable, yet quick to avenge wrongs and averse to change or innovation. These were hardy types, in love with masculine pursuits, but sensible to the value of learning and schooling in a region peppered with free schools and chapels. 'In all,' according to Fox, 'his assessment was that a "scholar or a sol[d]jer they have in great reverence, but a pilfering theefe & a dastardly coward they hate above all things".'[174]

Lhuyd and John Hamon would later share Machell's focus on language and dialect. Machell 'thought that the dialect of Westmorland epitomized the inhabitants' resistance to innovation, believing ... [they] "speak in this county the Anglo Saxon an great purity, and tho they can doe otherwise yett they think

---

[171] Camden, *Britannia* (1695), p. 813.
[172] Camden, *Britannia* (1695), p. 813.
[173] Adam Fox, 'Vernacular Culture and Popular Customs in Early Modern England: Evidence from Thomas Machell's Westmorland', *Cultural and Social History* 9.3 (2012), p. 334.
[174] Fox, 'Machell's Westmorland', p. 334.

it pride and therefore will not be induced to correct it'".[175] This made for a curious kind of bilingual north–south divide: northerners could understand 'southern people' but the same could not be said of their southern counterparts with the dialects to be found in Westmorland and elsewhere.[176] Language, music, and memory open up much more complex cultural exchanges and assumptions than a simple binary divide, though. Lancashire, Yorkshire, and Scottish dialects reverberated through the county and surrounded Machell's birthplace at Appleby.[177] Seemingly no festivity in Westmorland omitted dancing to the sound of bagpipes, yet the boys' game 'Scotch and English' simultaneously preserved the imitation of long-dead warrior ancestors and instructed the lads in predatory arts that were increasingly irrelevant as the union of crowns aged.[178] Nonetheless, a decided anti-Scottish prejudice accompanied the game and lowland Scots were assumed to be both treacherous and cowardly.[179] Machell joins Lhuyd, Sibbald, and their colleagues, who found the bounds of *Britannia*, let alone reductive national labels, too restrictive for the complexity spread across the lands they traversed as well as the *pays* into which they entered.

The great middle grounds: Cumberland and Northumberland

Cumberland and Northumberland, the great meeting ground of peoples, cultures, and empires, inspired the very best efforts by Camden and Gibson: extensive scholarship, repeated first-hand observation, devoted collaborators, and, beginning with the 1610 edition, frequent plates, illustrations, and maps. All of Camden's interests were satisfied in these chapters, artefacts of antiquity and the early Christian past, the careful and engaging description of places seen at first hand, immersion in the world of the Roman 'frontier' and the Anglo-Scottish marches that succeeded it, and the intersection of topography and ethnography. Gibson had the help of Hugh Todd in Cumberland, another local antiquary with Carlisle connections. He was chaplain to Bishop Thomas Smith and appointed prebend in the cathedral when *Britannia* was published in 1695.[180] We could well count Todd among Gibson's collaborators who were most faithful to Camden's original design.

Careless readers may have thought they had turned to Camden's Welsh chapters with the opening description of Cumberland. Its name came from the inhabitants, 'who were the true and genuine Britains, and call'd themselves in their own language Kumbri and Kambri, and had 'in the heat of the Saxon

---

[175] Fox, 'Machell's Westmorland', p. 334.
[176] Quoted in Fox, 'Machell's Westmorland', p. 335.
[177] Fox, 'Machell's Westmorland', p. 335.
[178] Fox, 'Machell's Westmorland', pp. 340–1.
[179] Fox, 'Machell's Westmorland', p. 338.
[180] David J.W. Mawson, 'Hugh Todd', *Oxford DNB* at www.oxforddnb.com.

wars, posted themselves here for a long time'.[181] The encumbering lakes and mountains prompted approving comment from Camden:

> The Country tho' the Northern situation renders it cold, and the Mountains, rough and uneven, has yet a variety which yields a prospect very agreeable. For after swelling rocks, and the crowding mountains, big (as it were) with Metals (between which are Lakes stor'd with all sorts of Wild Fowl,) you come to rich hills cloath'd with flocks of sheep, and below them are pleasant large plans, which are tolerably fruitful.[182]

It is interesting that Camden found these uplands so much more agreeable than those of Merionethshire. He could not escape one associated prejudice, albeit applied to a maritime setting: 'The Ocean, also, which beats upon the shore, affords great plenty of the best fish and as it were upbraids the Inhabitants with their idleness, in not applying themselves closer to the fishing trade.'[183]

Camden nonetheless took to Cumbria, home to his Curwen ancestors. He – and Todd a century later – tackled matters small and large with evident delight:

> The one of these rivers, Esk, rises at the foot of Hardknott, a steep ragged mountain; on the top whereof were lately dug up huge stones and the foundation of a Castle, not without great admiration, considering the mountain is so steep that one can hardly get up it. Higher up the little brook Irt runs into the Sea; wherein the shell-fish, gaping and eagerly sucking in its dewy streams, conceive and bring forth Pearls, or (to use the Poet's name) Shell-berries.[184]

The inhabitants gathered up these shell-berries at low tide, but the local jewellers really profited, buying 'them of the poor people for a trifle' and selling 'them for a good price'.[185] Todd identified them as 'muscle pearls' and made a comment that suggested how much wider the intellectual horizons of the British *imperium* had grown in a century: they 'are frequently found in other rivers hereabouts; as also in Wales and foreign Countries. Sir John Narborough in his late Voyage to the Magellanick Straits, A.D. 1670 tells us, he met with many of them. Abundance of Muscles (says he, pag. 7) and many Seed pearls in every Muscle.'[186]

Camden arrived at St Bee's head. It was named for Bega, 'a pious and religious Irish Virgin, [who] led a solitary life there: and to her sanctity they ascribe the Miracles of taming a Bull, and a deep Snow that by her Prayers fell on Mid-summer day, and cover'd the valleys and mountains'.[187] Todd had no interest in tales associated with Irish virgins and instead discussed the endowment of a grammar school at St Bees by the devoted Protestant and local native Edmund Grindal. Grindal's zeal as archbishop of Canterbury had led to his suspension

---

[181] Camden, *Britannia* (1695), pp. 819, 840.
[182] Camden, *Britannia* (1695), p. 819.
[183] Camden, *Britannia* (1695), p. 819.
[184] Camden, *Britannia* (1695), p. 820.
[185] Camden, *Britannia* (1695), p. 820.
[186] Camden, *Britannia* (1695), pp. 840–1.
[187] Camden, *Britannia* (1695), p. 821.

by Elizabeth I and made him a figure best avoided for Camden. For Todd, he was the first in a line of important benefactors to St Bees, including the present bishop of Carlisle and John Lowther of Whitehaven.[188] Nearby stood Egremont castle, a keep rich with the history of this marcher county. It was once the seat of 'William de Meschines, upon whom King Henry the first bestow'd it, to hold by one Knight's Service, who should be ready upon the King's summons to serve in the wars of Wales and Scotland'. De Meschines 'left a daughter, the wife of William Fitz-Duncan, of the Blood-Royal of Scotland', through whom it eventually came to the Radcliffe earls of Sussex.[189]

Camden could not travel far without encountering the political and cultural middle ground that was Cumbria. Falling through the mountains near Newland, the Derwent 'spreads itself into a spacious Lake' that included three islands, one the seat of the Radcliffes, 'another inhabited by German miners', and the last (according to Bede) the hermitage of St Herbert. 'Upon the side of this,' Camden continued, 'in a fruitful field, encompass't with wet dewy mountains, and protected from the north-winds by that of Skiddlaw, lyes Keswick, a little market-town, formerly a place noted for Mines.' Even the topography here belied neat national or ethnic boundaries. Skiddlaw 'mounts up almost to the Clouds with its two tops like another Parnassus, and views Scruffelt, a mountain of Annandal in Scotland, with a sort of emulation'. The clouds that rose and fell between these admiring peaks foretold the weather, according to the local rhyme, 'If Skiddlaw hath a cap, Sruffel wots [knows] full well of that.'[190]

Cumbria was a middle ground long before the Anglo-Scottish wars. It was one of the great frontiers, better yet, contact points between the Roman *imperium* and its subject peoples and 'barbarian' neighbours. Camden and Todd were both driven to record and collect a wealth of descriptions and images to document the physical remains of that period and others. Todd described a 'large open vessel of greenish stone, with several little images curiously engraven upon it' that was uncovered near Cockermouth. Camden did not know if it was basin or font, from the images on it, but the parishioners of St Bridgets in Bridekirke now used it for the latter purpose. Three lines of 'strange Characters' (reproduced in the text) also puzzled Camden, especially 'what they mean, and to what nation they belong'. Some resembled the usual symbol to depict Christ in the time of Constantine, while others appeared to be Danish in character. He left the mystery for future scholars.[191]

Todd looked at the images and decided that they depicted Jesus's baptism by John the Baptist. For the meaning of the characters, Todd reproduced a letter from William Nicolson to William Dugdale,[192] originally written in November

---

[188] Camden, *Britannia* (1695), p. 841.
[189] Camden, *Britannia* (1695), p. 821.
[190] Camden, *Britannia* (1695), p. 822.
[191] Camden, *Britannia* (1695), pp. 823–4.
[192] Mawson, 'Hugh Todd'.

1685 and printed in the *Philosophical Transactions*. Nicolson concluded that the fabric was Christian but with runic inscriptions common to the pagan Saxons, and shared by them with the Danes. Nicolson explained that 'the Language of the whole seems a mixture of the Saxon and Danish Tongues; but that can be no other than the natural effect of the two Nations being jumbled together in this part of the World'. For Nicolson, this was not just an artefact of ancient cultures in contact, it was of immediate relevance to the people among whom he – somewhat unhappily – lived: 'Our Borderers, to this day, speak a leash [set of three] of Languages (British, Saxon, and Danish) in one; and tis hard to determine which of those three Nations has the greatest share in the Motly Breed.'[193] Not surprisingly, given his ethnographic interests, Aubrey included the letter in his account of Bridekirk in the *Monumenta Britannica*.[194]

What kind of people were these inhabitants of Cumbria and the Borders? Some of them were children of colonists. According to Camden, Carlisle flourished under the Romans and retained some of its magnificence under the kingdom of Northumbria even after 'the ravages of the Picts and Scots'. The Danes brought the history of this Carlisle to an end and 'it lay'd bury'd for about two hundred years in it's own ashes: till it began to flourish again by the favour and assistance of William Rufus'. Red William rebuilt the castle 'and planted there a Colony, first of the Flemings (whom, upon better consideration, he quickly remov'd into Wales) and then of English, sent out of the south'.[195] Or is that quite what happened? Todd's reading of the *Anglo-Saxon Chronicle* suggested a different story. He was confident that a transcription error had led Camden to mistake 'Husbandmen' for Englishmen, especially since 'before that time, the Inhabitants of Carlisle were English'. Further, what followed in the *Chronicle* 'strengthens the conjecture, expressing the errand upon which they were sent; viz. to cultivate those parts. To this Colony it is, that all the Records ascribe the first tillage that was known thereabouts.' Nonetheless, the settlement in 1092 was a key part of Franci imperialism in the North. Their descendants, including husbandmen from Lincolnshire, sparred with the Britons and Scots for control of Cumbria well into the thirteenth century.[196]

The 'Inhabitants on both sides, as living upon the Frontiers, are a swift, subtil, and nimble sort of Souldiers, as being inur'd to it by frequent skirmishes.'[197] The terrain over which the borderers skipped was captured visually in the 1610 edition and reproduced for 1695. A 'gaping, imperfect Inscription' depicted the rough terrain and wild foliage along the 'little river Gelt' at the time of its occupation by the second legion. The Gelt in turn emptied into the river 'Irthing, which runs

---

[193] Camden, *Britannia* (1695), pp. 840–1.
[194] Aubrey, *Monumenta Britannica*, p. 560.
[195] Camden, *Britannia* (1695), p. 833.
[196] R.R. Davies, *The First English Empire: Power and Identities in the British Isles 1093–1343* (Oxford, 2000), pp. 64–5, 145, 149, 158.
[197] Camden, *Britannia* (1695), p. 834.

with a violent and rapid stream along by Naworth-Castle'. At Naworth in 1570, several thousand retainers of Leonard Dacre rose in support of the Northern earls' schemes involving Mary, Queen of Scots. Lord Hunsdon and the soldiers of the Berwick garrison put them to flight and the sword.[198] Complementing Sibbald's rewriting of the Borders as a place of civility and improvement, Todd added an account of Naworth under the care of the Earl of Carlisle. It located Naworth firmly in an 'English' story of Britannia, though:

> Here is a Library, formerly well furnish'd with Books; and there are still many Manuscripts of value, relating chiefly to Heraldry and English History. In the Hall are the Pictures of all the Kings of England down from Saxon times, which were brought from Kirk-Oswald Castle when that was demolish'd about 100 years ago. In the garden-wall are a great many stones with Roman Inscriptions, which were collected and placed there by some of the Family.[199]

The respective descriptions conclude in a way that points up the contrast between Camden's interest in the ethnic hodge-podge that was his *Britannia* and Todd's Cumberland, located behind a clearly defined border separating England and Scotland. Todd added 'An Account of the Division of Cumberland by William the Conqueror amongst his Followers', a chronicle that offered little sense of the wider ethnographic context. Camden's was very different. Here we see that his story of the peopling of Britain was the interpretive foundation for first-hand experience with the British landscape and the marks left on it by its peoples: 'Upon the decay of Roman power in Britain, tho' this Country was cruelly harrass'd by the Scots and Picts, yet did it longest keep its original Inhabitants the Britains, and fell late under the power of the Saxons.' When 'the Danish wars had well nigh broke the Saxon government, it had its petty Kings, stil'd Kings of Cumberland, to the year of our Lord 946'.[200]

When Nicolson wondered which of the three nations – British, Saxon, or Danish – had left the greatest mark on the 'Motly Breed' of people in Cumberland, he needed to read further in *Britannia*. But read *Britannia* he did. It fell to Nicolson to update Cumberland's neighbour, Northumbria.

* * * * *

Alhough he ended his life as the Bishop of Kerry, Nicolson hailed from Great Orton in Cumbria and excelled at Queen's College, Oxford. Thanks to his aptitude for languages and the favour of Joseph Williamson, a fellow Cumbrian native and Secretary of State, Nicolson learned his German on the spot at Leipzig.

---

[198] Camden, *Britannia* (1695), p. 836; Wallace MacCaffrey, *The Shaping of the Elizabethan Regime* (Princeton, 1968), pp. 345–8; also Maureen M. Meikle, *A British Frontier? Lairds and Gentlemen in the Eastern Borders, 1540–1603* (East Linton, 2004).
[199] Camden, *Britannia* (1695), p. 844.
[200] Camden, *Britannia* (1695), p. 837.

He returned home to become 'the first holder of a lectureship in Anglo-Saxon studies established by Williamson at Queen's'. A deaconship drew Nicolson north to Carlisle in 1679 and a living in Torpenhow. Nicolson became an accomplished scholar and antiquarian in his remote living, becoming life-long friends with Edward Lhuyd and offering crucial encouragement to Lhuyd's involvement with *Britannia*.[201] Nicolson and Lhuyd shared many interests, including place-names, 'especially the Welsh elements in northern place-names'.[202] Nicolson completed 'witty' bibliographies of English, Scottish, and Irish histories and manuscripts between 1697 and 1724.[203] Nicolson took to his task of revising Camden's description with real care, but no doubt saw himself as the equal of the legendary author where Northumberland was concerned.

Even the most Anglocentric among Camden's contemporaries and readers would have been hard pressed to ignore the cultural hodge-podge that was Northumbria.[204] Camden's modern-day Ottadini were most distinctly descended from a certain topography and the cultural contacts that had occurred over it during many centuries:

> The Country it self is mostly rough and barren, and seems to have harden'd the very carcasses of its Inhabitants: whom the neighbouring Scots have render'd yet more hardy, sometimes inuring them to war, and sometimes amicably communicating their customs and way of living; when they are become a most warlike people and excellent horse-men. And, whereas they generally have devoted themselves to war, there is not a man of fashion among them but has his little Castle and Fort ... [205]

The fortified houses and castles were home to the barons who gave the North its unique political culture of prickly and sometimes over-mighty subjects. For both Camden and Nicolson, this 'was wisely done of our Ancestors, to cherish and support Martial Prowess, in the borders of the Kingdom'.[206]

Through the Tyne Valley and along the coasts, Camden found fruitful ground – 'with any tolerable husbandry' – but the rest of Northumbria was 'much more barren' and, unlike Cumbria, 'unviewly'. These unsightly grounds included wastes, mossy stretches, and mountaintop bogs that later lent their character and names to the rough people who inhabited them: nomads, moss-troopers and bog-trotters. The north Tyne began in the mountainous borders between England and Scotland and watered the valleys of Tyndale and Riddisdale, 'a valley too thinly inhabited by reason of the robberies', despite the policing of

---

[201] Hayton, 'William Nicolson'; Frank Emery, *Edward Lhuyd* (Cardiff, 1971), pp. 71–5.

[202] Edward Lhwyd, *Archaeologia Britannica: Texts and Translation*, ed. Dewi W. Evans and Brynley F. Roberts (Aberystwyth, 2009), p. 21.

[203] Hayton, 'William Nicolson'.

[204] William M. Aird, 'Northumbria and the Making of the Kingdom of the English', *Nations in Medieval Britain*, ed. Hirokazu Tsurushima (Donington, 2010), pp. 45–70.

[205] Camden, *Britannia* (1695), p. 847.

[206] Camden, *Britannia* (1695), pp. 847, 850, 870.

march wardens from both kingdoms. The two 'Dales breed most notable Bog-Trotters; and both have such boggy-top'd mountains as are not to be cross'd by ordinary horsemen'.[207] Across the valley, the river Rhead 'washes (or rather has almost wash'd away) another Town of venerable antiquity, now call'd Risingham; which in the old-English and high-Dutch languages signifies as much as Giants-Town, as Risingberg in Germany is Giants Hill'. Nicolson's German came in handy here, and he noted that Riese signified giant, but he doubted that the Saxons used the word or used it to refer to anything other than the high ground on which most villages were anciently placed before 'the Inhabitants drew down into the Valleys'. 'All over the Wasts (as they call them)' Camden explained, 'you see as it were the ancient Nomades; a Martial sort of people, that from April to August, lye in little Huts (which they call Sheals and Shealings) here and there disper'd among their Flocks.'[208] Camden returned to his interest in ethnography, but Nicolson followed Holland's 1610 translation in giving it a Scottish burr with the term shieling, commonly used to denote dwellings and smallholdings in Scotland.[209]

The greatest marker of a cultural frontier for travellers in Northumberland was the Roman wall.[210] For *Britannia*'s readers, 'the bounds of the Empire were seas, great rivers, mountains, desart and unpassable countries (such as this part affords) ditches, walls, empailures, and especially castles built in the most suspected places, whereof there are here great plenty of remains'.[211] Only first-hand observation and excavation could tackle the riddles of this imperial frontier. Camden's first-hand description of the Roman and Antonine walls, vallum, and military way stood for more than a century after his death.[212] It was a conversation across the decades to which Sibbald, Nicolson, and Gibson contributed, especially Gibson, who in 1708 and 1709 'travelled the whole length of the Wall except the part west of Carlisle' and produced a detailed account for the 1722 edition of *Britannia*.[213]

None of us who has viewed and walked the wall fail to be impressed by its might and the engineering – some of the plumbing and cisterns could certainly outperform the decaying remnants of Victoria's age. An image of fierce and woolly Scots almost inevitably comes to mind, staring out across the frontier at Housesteads. Yet the modern tendency to associate primitivism with

---

[207] Camden, *Britannia* (1695), pp. 848, 870–1.

[208] Camden, *Britannia* (1695), pp. 850–1, 870.

[209] Camden, *Britannia* (1610), p. 806; Ian D. Whyte, *Scotland Before the Industrial Revolution: An Economic and Social History c. 1050–c. 1750* (Harlow, 1995), pp. 42–5, 132–9.

[210] Richard Hingley, *The Recovery of Roman Britain 1586–1906: A Colony so Fertile* (Oxford, 2008), pp. 88–93.

[211] Camden, *Britannia* (1695), p. 849.

[212] Camden, *Britannia* (1695), p. 837–40.

[213] R.G. Collingwood, 'Hadrian's Wall: A History of the Problem', *Journal of Roman Studies* 11 (1921), pp. 48–50; Camden, *Britannia* (1695), pp. 857–8, 870, n. [d].

incompetence emphasizes the wall's impregnability and obscures a crucial feature of this frontier that Camden spotted. This was an imperfect and, in places, porous frontier. Indeed, we now know that farms, fields, and dry-stone walls marked both sides of the wall, revealing a 'farmed and domesticated landscape' that predated the Romans and served the forts and linked settlements around them.[214] Where the Irthing and the Tyne ran near to each other at Thirlwall, Camden 'saw large Mounts cast up within the wall, as design'd for watching the Country'. And watch carefully the sentries should have done, for this was a weak spot in the wall and Britannia's barbarian neighbours knew it: 'Here the Scots forc'd a passage ... the place was wisely enough chosen, as having no intercourse of rivers to obstruct their easie inroads into the very bowels of England.' Camden reproduced the account in Fordun's *Chronica Gentis Scotorum*, the 'Scotch Historian' whose 'book is not very common'.[215] According to Camden's selection,

> [The Scots] having conquer'd the Country on both sides of the Wall, began to settle themselves ... and summoning in the Boors [country people] (with the mattocks, pickaxes, wakes, forks, and shovels) caus'd wide holes and gaps to be made in it, through which they might easily pass and repass.[216]

Not quite the disastrous work of John Warburton, who surveyed and prescribed the demolition of whole sections of the Wall to build a new military way after 1745, but one that spoke just as strongly of Britannia as a contested middle ground.[217]

There was much more to Northumberland than ethnography and the wall. It was also a land rich in the history of early Christianity.[218] South, along the Tyne from St Oswalds lay Hexham, where, Camden reported, the first cohort of the Spaniards were garrisoned. The magnificent church was home to an episcopal see at the instance of Queen Etheldreda and lasted until the 'Danish wars prevailing'. According to Prior Richard's history, the church exceeded all the greatest monasteries in England because of the 'curious and most beautiful Fabrick' wrought by masons brought from Rome. Camden seemed too quick in adding that this was because the masons 'seemd' to vye with the Roman pomp'. Within the church Camden found the old tomb of a member of the Umfranvils, 'lying with his Legs across ... being, under that Banner, engag'd in the Holy War, for the recovery of the Holy-Land out of the Hands of the Mahometans'.[219] Still something of a High Church Anglican in the 1690s, Nicolson thought Camden

[214] Pryor, *British Landscape*, p. 186.
[215] Camden, *Britannia* (1695), p. 848.
[216] Camden, *Britannia* (1695), p. 848.
[217] Collingwood, 'Hadrian's Wall', p. 53; Hingley, *Recovery of Roman Britain*, pp. 133–9.
[218] Camden, *Britannia* (1695), p. 853.
[219] Camden, *Britannia* (1695), p. 854.

could have relayed more of the prior's account.[220] Particular descriptions of the walls, roof, ceiling, stairs, and pillars all made for interesting reading and led to the conclusion that 'no such stately structure was, at that time, to be met with on this side of the Alpes'.[221]

Camden composed one of the better capsule descriptions of Newcastle:

> 'Tis enoble'd by a Haven on the Tine, which is of that depth as to carry vessels of very good burthen, and of that security, that they are in no hazard of either storms of shallows. Its situation is climbing and very uneven, on the northern bank of the river, which is cross'd by a very fair bridge. As you enter the town from hence, you have, on the left hand the Castle overtopping you, and thereafter a very steep brow of a hill. On the right you have the Market-place, and the best built part of the Town; from which to the upper and far larger part, the ascent is a little troublesome. 'Tis beautified with four Churches: and defended by exceeding strong walls, wherein are seven gates, and a great many turrets.[222]

Here, and without acknowledgement, Camden reproduced Leland's explanation for the city walls, 'a very rich Burger carry'd off a prisoner by the Scots out of the middle of the town, first paid a round ransom for himself, and afterwards began the first fortifications of the place'.[223]

Camden's account would not serve modern readers badly, with the East Coast Main Line, Angel of the North, the Sage at Gateshead, and a few other tweaks. Even the Baltic Flour Mill was presaged by his comment that 'in spight of all the attempts of her enemies and the many neighboring thieves, that she is now in a most flourishing state of wealth and commerce'.[224] The famous Newcastle coals – 'to which so great a part of England and the Low Countries are indebted for their good fires' – made Camden return to his poet friend from Aberdeen, John Johnston. Johnston's verse suited Camden's purpose, though with a faint echo of the many attempts by Scottish kings to secure their southern border here at the Tyne:

> From her high rock great nature's work surveys,
> And kindly spreads her good through lands and seas.
> Why seek you fire in some exalted sphere?
> Earth's fruitful boom will supply you here.
> Not such whose horrid flashes scare the plain,
> But give enliv'ning warmth to earth and men. ...
> This place and Scotland more than Heaven can shew.[225]

---

[220] Hayton, 'William Nicolson'.
[221] Camden, *Britannia* (1695), p. 871.
[222] Camden, *Britannia* (1695), p. 856.
[223] Camden, *Britannia* (1695), p. 856.
[224] Camden, *Britannia* (1695), pp. 854, 871.
[225] Camden, *Britannia* (1695), p. 857.

It was Nicolson, though, who stood at a moment in time closer to what Newcastle would become:

> Both its Wealth and Commerce are wonderfully encreas'd since Camden's time. The Coal-trade is incredible; and for other Merchandice, Newcastle is the great Emporium of the northern parts of England, and of a good share of Scotland. The publick Revenue is also wonderfully advanc'd of late years ... [226]

Perhaps only to a modern reader does Nicolson's description of the subterranean coal fire at Fenham that lit up the night sky foretell Newcastle and the miners' fate under the blows of Thatcherism.[227]

Camden travelled north by way of Morpeth and Alnwick before reaching the sea at Dunstanburgh castle. He may have passed through Craster when it was notable for a stout fort rather than for oak-smoked kippers, moving on through coastal hamlets and fishing towns like Low Newton in the journey to Bamburgh castle. He found a castle down on its luck, much reduced during the Wars of the Roses and currently 'in a continual struggle with old Age, and the Winds; which latter has, through its large windows, drifted up an incredible quantity of Sea-sand in its several Bulwarks'.[228] Taking note of Holy Island, Camden turned inland toward the Till river valley. Chillingham castle and the Barony of Wooler played roles in the contest for supremacy in the North. In Henry III's reign, Wooler's Robert Muschamp was 'reckon'd the mightiest Baron in all these Northern parts', but his 'Inheritance soon after was divided and shared among women'. With a touch of *King Lear*, three daughters received three parcels each, dividing the great barony between the Scottish earl of Strathern, William de Huntercombe, and one Odonel de Ford. Nicolson seemed determined to fill out this relatively remote patch of Northumbria. He thought it worth mentioning the legend at Chillingham castle of the 'Chimney-piece with a hollow in the middle of it; wherein ('tis said) there was found a live Toad, at the sawing of the Stone'. Wooler evidently left a bad taste, though: it was a 'little inconsiderable Market-town, with a thatch'd Church, and some other marks of the Poverty of the Inhabitants. The advantages of a late Brief, upon a Fire here happen'd, may possibly raise it fairer out of its present Ashes.' More notable for Camden in this area was the field of Flodden. The English under the Earl of Surrey crushed a powerful Scottish army that surrendered its advantageous high ground and became caught in the marsh grass and mud at its bottom. James IV himself 'was found among the heaps of the slain' the next day.[229]

If a physical and mental wall separated the Scots and English as the Roman wall had once divided Romans from barbarians, it was the Tweed at Berwick. Yet just what sort of divide was it? At best it was only a nominal ethnographic

---

[226] Camden, *Britannia* (1695), p. 872.
[227] Camden, *Britannia* (1695), p. 872.
[228] Camden, *Britannia* (1695), pp. 860, 873.
[229] Camden, *Britannia* (1695), pp. 861–2, 873.

or cultural one.[230] Camden gave his readers a potted history, but captured the essence of Berwick:

> Being seated betwixt two mighty Kingdoms ... it has always been the first place that both Nations, in their wars, have had an eye on; insomuch, that ever since Edward the first wrung it out of the Scotch hands, the English have often retaken it as the Scots have ventur'd to seize it.[231]

For Camden, then, it was 'the last Town in England, and the best fortify'd in all Britain'. But history had moved far in a century. 'Berwick is now much out-done,' explained Nicolson, 'in strength and regular fortifications, by Portsmouth, Hull, Plymouth, and some other Forts in England; and is chiefly strong in the present Union of the two Kingdoms.'[232] Berwick's strength lay in the protection afforded by a peaceful union of England and Scotland, while Nicolson's strongholds marked the power of a British *imperium* whose focus had become decisively maritime and Continental since the 'Glorious' revolutions in both kingdoms.

Ethnographic assumptions had also changed, at least concerning the people of the North and the Scottish Borders. *Britannia*'s readers in 1695 accepted the assumptions that went with boors, freebooting moss-troopers, nimble bog-trotters, and nomads of the waste grounds. There is more to these words than meets the eye, though. That Gibson's readers found those terms at all is not due to Camden. For Camden, in the English translation of 1610, the moss-troopers who later reported on the Roman military way were actually 'Rank-riders or taking men of the borders'. The horsemen who crisscrossed the boggy ground were just that, 'notable light horsemen'. The boors from Scotland who went to work on the Roman wall with their pickaxes and hoes were simply 'Country people'. Only the nomads owed their story to Camden's time.[233]

It was Nicolson who supplied Gibson with the translation and thus turned Camden's original into terms with common currency for the late seventeenth century, terms with more obvious pejorative connotations.[234] English and lowland Scottish writers applied the term moss-trooper to borderers after 1650. They did so with a clear sense of their being lawless marauders who plagued the 'middle shires' of Stuart Britain. Bog-trotter was an even later term. It came into common use in the 1680s as a slur on the 'wild' Gaelic Irish and then became a catch-all racist nickname. For Samuel Johnson, the mosses of Scotland were no different than Irish bogs, hence moss-troopers and bog-trotters were one and the same. With hints of Fynes Moryson's conflation of the Irish and Arabs, bog-trotter found its way into the 1700 edition of Paul Rycaut's popular *History of the Turks*. Interestingly, the term did not appear in the newly translated

---

[230] Camden, *Britannia* (1695), p. 861.
[231] Camden, *Britannia* (1695), p. 863.
[232] Camden, *Britannia* (1695), pp. 863, 874.
[233] Camden, *Britannia* (1610), pp. 800, 802, 806.
[234] Camden, *Britannia* (1695), p. 865.

description of Merioneth, perhaps because of Lhuyd's careful treatment of the upland Welsh. By contrast, boor was a long-standing English word for peasants, husbandmen, and country people, but it also denoted rustic, rude peasants and came to be a common term for the peasantry of other nations.[235]

In 1695, then, ethnic prejudices found sharper definition in a manner that obscured a more contingent, open description by Camden. Nicolson had a different matter to take up with Camden, though. Camden turned to the travel narrative of Æneas Sylvius, Pope Pius II, for an ethnography that could capture something of the unique amalgam of peoples and cultures among 'the borderers in this Country'. 'Keen-witted, insinuating, the most agreeable of companions, devoid of all nice scruples', Æneas arrived in Scotland during the reign of James I (1406–37, though an English prisoner until 1424). His journey to Scotland complete, its precise purpose unclear, Æneas disguised himself as a merchant and made his way into England with a guide.[236] For Camden, Æneas' account was apropos to the borderers 'since their manners still continue the same'. In Berwick, Æneas was put up at the house of a local 'country-man, where he sup'd with the Curate of the place and his host'. He ate a meal of pottage, hens, and geese, but no bread or wine appeared.[237] From this point, the account begins to remind us of an explorer's discovery narrative:

> All the men and women of the town stock'd in as to some strange sight: and as our countrymen use to admire the Æthiopians or Indians, so these people star'd at Æneas, asking the Curate, what countryman he was? what his errand could be? and, whether he were a Christian or no? But Æneas being aware of the scarcity he would meet with on this road, was accommodated by a Monastery with a rundlet of red wine and some loaves of bread. When these were brought, they were more astonish'd than before, having never seen either wine or white bread. Big belly'd women, with their husbands, came to the table side, and handling the bread and smelling to the wine, beg'd a taste: so that there was no avoiding the dealing of the whole amongst them.[238]

If this was still an accurate description of the people for Camden in the late sixteenth century, it was nonetheless a far cry from the hospitable and wealthy Berwick of Moryson's experience in those same years.

Supper lasted well into the night when the curate, landlord, and boys of the household suddenly picked up and left, off 'to shelter themselves in a certain tower, at a good distance, for fear of the Scots, who (at low water us'd to cross the river in the night, and fall a plundering'. However, they left behind the women, and Æneas. Both 'wives and maids, were very handsom', but they were considered safe to leave behind, 'for they believe the enemy will not harm them; not looking upon whoredom as any ill thing'. In a different version, the meaning

---

[235] *Oxford English Dictionary*, 2nd edn (Oxford, 1989).
[236] P. Hume Brown, ed., *Early Travellers in Scotland* (Edinburgh, 1973), pp. 24–5, 28.
[237] Camden, *Britannia* (1695), p. 864.
[238] Camden, *Britannia* (1695), pp. 864–5.

is more straightforward, 'the women, they do not regard outrage done to them as any great misfortune'.[239] Thus was Æneas 'left alone (with only two Servants and a Guide) amongst a hundred women, who sitting in a ring, with a fire in the middle of 'em, spent the night sleepless, in dressing of hemp, and chatting with the Interpreter'. What conversations passed between Æneas and the women of Berwick went unrecorded until an explosion of barking dogs and gaggling geese sent them too into flight for fear of a Scottish raid. Æneas thought better of getting caught in the melee, more afraid of 'running out, and being unacquainted with the Country; he should be robb'd by the first man he met' than Scots he had just left across the Tweed. He kept 'close in his Bed-chamber (which was a stable) ... [until] both the women and guide return, acquainting them that all was well, and that they were Friends (and no Enemies) that were arriv'd'.[240] Camden did not carry the account as far as Æneas' arrival in Newcastle, where 'for the first time it seemed to him that he once more beheld civilization, and a country with a habitable aspect'.[241]

What Camden hoped his readers would learn about the manners of the borderers seems elusive: the exotic quality of bread and wine among a poor and remote people, the men's constant watchfulness against Scottish raids, and assumptions about the chastity or sexual proclivities of the Berwick women. One thing is certain. Nicolson did not appreciate Camden's use of Æneas' account: 'Whatever roughness Mr. Camden might fancy he saw in the Manners of the People of Northumberland, 'tis certain that the Description which Æneas Silvius gives of them is not their due at this day.' Point by point, Nicolson refuted Æneas' description as hopelessly outdated, along with Camden's own first-hand experiences that he thought it captured.[242] Their tables remained well stocked with hens and geese and now routinely included 'plenty of good bread and beer'.[243] Nicolson vented some real 'Northern' anger against what he took to be common prejudices among the Essex men of his own times:

> A Roundlet of Red-wine is a greater rarity in a Country-man's house in Middlesex, than on the borders of Northumberland; where you shall more commonly meet with great store of good Claret, than in the Villages of any other County in England. That wine is not the constant drink of the Country ought no more to be remark'd as a thing extraordinary, than that Yorkshire-Ale is not common in Italy.[244]

The borderers of Northumberland were not as either Æneas or Camden would have one believe. First, they were not a remote people set apart from their fellow subjects or the world at large: 'Strangers and Travellers are no novelties

[239] Hume Brown, *Early Travellers*, p. 29.
[240] Camden, *Britannia* (1695), p. 865.
[241] Hume Brown, *Early Travellers*, p. 29.
[242] Camden, *Britannia* (1695), p. 874.
[243] Camden, *Britannia* (1695), p. 874.
[244] Camden, *Britannia* (1695), p. 874.

to them; the Roads betwixt Edinburgh and Newcastle being as much frequented by such (of all Nations) as almost any others in the Kingdom.' They had not somehow been left behind by civility or progress. The 'Moss-Trooping Trade is now very much laid aside' and the local robberies came to no more than a small sum in any year. In Northumberland, 'mens persons are as safe, and their goods as secure, as in the most civiliz'd Kingdoms of Europe'. Nicolson turned the tables on the manners and behaviour of those in the South. In the North, whoredom was considered as scandalous a vice as anywhere, 'and it were our happiness if, in the Southern parts of the Kingdom, it were as little fashionable'.[245] Nicolson's neighbours were a people worthy to be esteemed and more faithful than most to his definition of the English character:

> In a word; the Gentry of Northumberland are generally persons of address and breeding, and preservers of the true old English hospitality in their Houses: And the Peasants are as knowing a people, and as courteous to strangers, as a man shall readily meet with in any other part.[246]

This was serious work for Nicolson, to blunt long-standing North–South prejudices. Even though he translated Camden's original using the pejorative terms of the age, Nicolson here put his own observations in place to challenge Camden's ethnography and experiences of the county. He did not want the people of Northumberland stereotyped, even if readers would learn that there were unsavoury characters like moss-troopers or superstitious folk in some parts.[247] Perhaps it was no accident, then, that his last addition to Camden's text concerned an outsider who came among the people of Northumbria and dealt badly with them:

> Bishop Walcher [of Durham] was a most vile oppressour and scandalous worldling. He bought the Earldom of Northumberland, and resolv'd to make the people pay for it. But, at last, being wearied with daily extortion, and reduc'd almost to beggary, they unanimously fell upon him and slew him, at a County-Court; which he used always to attend himself in person, the better to secure the Fees and other Perquisites.[248]

With a hint of reproach, Nicolson took a different view of, as Camden characterized it, this 'insurrection of the Rabble' against William the Conqueror's Lotharingian bishop: 'Their foreman gave the word; which most of our old Historians have thought worth the recording to posterity, "Short red, good red, slea ye the Bishop."'[249]

[245] Camden, *Britannia* (1695), p. 874.
[246] Camden, *Britannia* (1695), p. 874.
[247] Daniel Woolf, *The Social Circulation of the Past: English Historical Culture 1500–1730* (Oxford, 2003), p. 308.
[248] Camden, *Britannia* (1695), p. 874.
[249] Camden, *Britannia* (1695), p. 875; Henrietta Leyser, 'Walcher', *Oxford DNB* at www.oxforddnb.com.

Summa: Book Three

I decided to explore Camden's *Britannia* only in the latter stages of writing this book. I did so with some reluctance. I originally envisioned it fitting into the last chapter of the section about Fynes Moryson – in no more than a dozen pages! The accounts of Camden so often presented him as a dull, pedantic scholar and turned the label antiquarian into a prison suit.[250] *Britannia*, however widely read and definitive, superficially appeared to be a ponderous slog through the remains of antiquity, far removed from interactions with cultural complexity in the Britain of Camden's time. Quite the contrary. Far from being a dull scholar, Camden fairly leaps from the pages of *Britannia* as an engaged traveller and teacher, intent, wry, even spirited. The antiquarian label is accurate, but a profound injustice because of its failure to capture the breadth of Camden's intellectual pursuits. The topics he tackled are almost too tedious to list: archaeology, geology, and natural history, geography and topography, ethnography and anthropology, etymology, history, political economy and veiled religious commentary, even folklore and other miscellanea. Time and again Camden confessed to his inability to stay within narrow bounds or a carefully defined agenda for *Britannia*. Cornish giants thus found their way into the text even if he refrained from swamping the description of Cheshire with all its Anglo-Norman and Welsh encounters and a long wall built out of Welsh skulls.

Gibson's collaborators understood. Many spoke to Camden's eclectic work by their own additions. Some among them also pushed the bounds to include interests of their own, matters that Camden had left unattended, and topics that late seventeenth-century readers now expected. Richard Trelawney added a discussion of the Cornish language and its survival, but Edward Lhuyd remains the most dynamic case. Lhuyd determined after his travels to design his own great project to do for Wales what Camden had done for all of Britain. His pursuit of snakestones across Britannia and the Atlantic occupied no small amount of his interests or additions. Lhuyd's Scottish counterpart, Robert Sibbald, offered a unique wrinkle. The Scots who collaborated to produce the account of Scotland for Jean Blaeu's *Atlas Novus* set an impressive standard for the discovery of Scotland after the age of Buchanan and Lesley – or Camden. Despite the precedent of Blaeu's *Atlas* and his access to a wealth of information about the cultural complexity of Scotland, Sibbald's accomplishments seem more apparent than real. He composed a competing description of Scotland that virtually ignored Camden's own. He built on long-standing plans for a comprehensive description of Scotland and consciously removed the taint of poverty and incivility from England's northern neighbour and partner in Union. Neither Camden nor Sibbald rendered the rich, complex face of Scotland's people.

---

[250] Woolf, *Social Circulation of the Past*, pp. 180–2.

For Gibson and many of his collaborators, Camden's *Britannia* was an achievement that had lasted for more than a century and they took it up with due respect. Nonetheless, their own journeys into the archives and localities of Britain revealed shortcomings. Some responded matter-of-factly. For Lhuyd, Kaerphyli deserved a description that put it in the same league as Windsor, he shared Camden's affinity for inscriptions with a storehouse of examples from Carmarthenshire, and he gladly filled in the topographic details of Snowdonia. Robert Plot took up the task of adjudicating between the claims of Camden and William Somner about gavelkind and the 'treaty' with the Normans to preserve Kentish customs. Camden and White Kennett each used Oxfordshire's rivers to organize their descriptions, and one senses that both men could have spent many hours congratulating Oxford University on its beauty and greatness. The man who followed Camden through Cumberland did so with a real sense of intellectual partnership. Hugh Todd worked to decode the 'runic' inscriptions on the green stone basin at St Bridget's in Bridekirk with as much care as Camden had, and called on William Nicolson to really explore the cultural interactions that it represented. His competing account of William Rufus's colonization of Carlisle was matter of fact in suggesting that Camden's mistake arose from a flawed transcription of the *Anglo-Saxon Chronicle*.

Some corrected Camden with less deference. Lhuyd made subjugators of Camden's praiseworthy Flemish colonists, rejected the Irish presence in Anglesey as a consequence of faulty judgement and linguistics, and occupied his time in Flintshire with the remains of leaves and shells in coal pits rather than reflections on empire building. Kennett flattered his own religious prejudices in spending so much time explaining how zeal joined cakes and ale in the 1610 account of Banbury's notoriety. In contrast to Kennett and Oxford University, the individual who updated Cambridge thought that Camden's slight description positively detracted from the University's well-earned dignity and distinction. By the time Gibson's collaborator arrived in Leicestershire, the peculiar guttural speech of Carleton's inhabitants, if it existed in the first place, had passed away.

A few rode their own hobbyhorses through the additions. When Lhuyd identified himself as both Welsh and just another sort of Highlander, we appreciate that there must have been some annoyance with Camden's hostile character study of the people of Merionethshire. Westmorland presented two extremes, from the satisfaction that Reginald Bainbrigg found in helping Camden to illuminate his little plot of *Britannia*, to the sniping of Thomas Machell, for whom so little of Camden's description was sufficiently complete, properly evaluated, or correct. The Westmorland *pays* had a more complex story to tell. William Nicolson's work on Northumberland seemed to find an honest critical median. He utterly rejected Camden's ethnography as based on a faulty reading of both the people he encountered and Æneas Sylvius's narrative. Yet Nicolson's additions are manifestly the work of a dedicated local expert determined to build on Camden's foundations as his intellectual equal and to produce the best 'modern' account of Northumberland, even if that meant challenging prejudices both unthinking and deliberate.

None of these individuals, nor a single point of view, could possibly do justice to the cultural complexity of England and its people. *Britannia* tells us much about what Camden and his collaborators, along with Gibson and his, made of that complexity at either end of the seventeenth century. We see them grapple with the nature of a county or region's people quite often. Thus we find Trelawney self-consciously drawing the Cornish boundary at the Tamar, in contrast to Camden. We then see one of Gibson's contributors question Camden's assumption that one could locate Roman ethnic groups so closely according to county boundaries, especially boundaries drawn for political purposes centuries after the Romans. Coming full circle, Todd separated Cumberland and the borderers from Scotland with remarkable zeal at a time when the Union of crowns was almost a century old. For Camden, who lived on both sides of that Union, the Borders were nothing if not a meeting ground of peoples and cultural traditions.

Camden understood that *Britannia* would always be a work in progress and that others would follow his lead to new discoveries. As his 'Preface' from the 1607 edition made clear, some would accuse him of 'leaving out this or that little Town or Castle', but 'Somewhat must be left for the Labours of other Men.' John Leland's biographer made this a crucial lesson in 1772, that, in the words of the Kentish antiquary Robert Plot writing in the 1670s, 'a fair new building might be erected from what they had passed by'.[251] Camden had a strong sense of how the labours of other men would interact with his own:

> Inhabitants may better observe the particulars of the places where they live; and if they will inform me of any mistake, I will thankfully amend it; what I have omitted I will add; what I have not sufficiently explain'd I will explain better, when I am better inform'd: All I desire, is not to be censur'd out of Malice or a Contentious humour, which will ill become Men of Candour and Integrity.[252]

Camden reflected that a 'good Teacher' isn't someone who teaches everything, and leaves nothing for the invention of others. 'It is enough for me, that I have broken the ice; and I have gain'd my end, if I set others to work; whether to write more, or to amend what I have written.'[253] Lhuyd probably had good reason to think of Camden that 'what we can adde or correct, I make no question were he alive, but he would be thankful for it: for he seems to have been a man of very candid temper'.[254]

[251] *The Lives of Those Eminent Antiquaries John Leland, Thomas Hearne, and Anthony à Wood* (two volumes; Oxford, 1772), I, p. 66; *The Itinerary of John Leland the Antiquarian* (nine volumes; Oxford, 1710–12), II, p. 103.
[252] Camden, *Britannia* (1695), 'Mr. Camden's Preface'.
[253] Camden, *Britannia* (1695), 'Mr. Camden's Preface'.
[254] *Life and Letters of Edward Lhuyd, Early Science in Oxford XIV*, ed. R.T. Gunther (Oxford, 1945), p. 201.

Despite these debates and descriptions, we do not want to mistake *Britannia* for a thorough or particularly deliberate ethnographic description of Britain. We really find that in only two places. We encounter it in Camden's story of the peopling of Britain, but it was not Camden the traveller who wrote that account. In it we see first and foremost Camden the scholar, at home in the world of classical, medieval, and contemporary books and manuscripts. Only when Camden concluded with the four nations and began a sort of imaginative journey through the 'British Islands' did a more systematic ethnography emerge. Even then it was the additions to the Isle of Man that read like the ethnographies of foreign lands and peoples that had become commonplace by this point.[255]

It has remained easy to approach *Britannia* as an Anglocentric topography or antiquarian masterpiece. Geoffrey Elton, who later rubbished the 'non-existent history of ethnic minorities', numbered Camden's *Britannia* with the 'General surveys of England'.[256] It is no longer difficult to wonder at Elton's judgement. We might do well to revisit Colin Kidd's conclusions in *British Identities Before Nationalism*. Kidd wrote that 'the seventeenth and eighteenth centuries scarcely bear witness to any profounder sense of England as a multicultural nation' in his analysis of a 1731 panegyric, *South Britain*.[257] It read: 'Sprung from the Roman, Saxon, Norman Seed, / Blended with Britains, how they all unite, / And make the English so renowned in Fight.'[258] For Kidd, the peopling of England moved antiquarians only because 'ethnic diversity generated questions regarding the history of the English constitution'.[259] Neither conclusion stands against the intense, vigorous, and constant engagement with England's motley breeds by travellers and their narratives, from Leland through Camden and his successors.

Gibson's *Britannia* project puts paid to Anglocentric or narrow perspectives. Here was a British (and Irish) project in conception and execution, even with its biases. Every corner of Britain was represented on Gibson's team of travellers, writers, and experts. England prospered under the pens of Trelawney, Plot, Nicholson, Machell, and a host of others, including their unseen collaborators. Lhuyd worked with agents throughout Wales. Sibbald marshalled the documents and reports of Scots from the Borders to the Western Isles. Gibson's recruitment tapped into vibrant networks of specialized knowledge and interest that spanned the Isles (and beyond). In Trelawney, Plot, Lhuyd, Aubrey and Edmund Wyld, Nicholson, Sibbald, Martin, Wallace, and their associates (as well as Richard Cox and Thomas and William Molyneux in Dublin) we have overlapping associations of British–Irish experts pursuing related interests like botany, etymology, artefacts, improvement, and ethno-topographic description.

---

[255] Camden, *Britannia* (1695), pp. 1059–116.
[256] G.R. Elton, *England Under the Tudors*, 3rd edn (London, 1991), p. 434.
[257] Colin Kidd, *British Identities Before Nationalism: Ethnicity and Nationhood in the Atlantic World 1600–1800* (Cambridge, 1999), p. 77.
[258] Quoted in Kidd, *British Identities*, p. 76.
[259] Kidd, *British Identities*, p. 78.

Their varied collaborations predated Gibson's *Britannia*, furthered the renewal of Camden's account, or joined and expanded in the years that followed.[260] Indeed, Gibson's *Britannia* – in the fashion of the original – positively energized travellers, local scholars, intellectual networks, and learned societies across the Isles. They in turn made the eighteenth century, in Rosemary Sweet's words, 'the great age of county history'.[261] They also pursued projects, like the investigation of Druidry or economic improvement, designed 'to give the British, in an age of union, a better overview of their archipelago' and its imperial potential.[262] The curiosities, discoveries, and investigations of these polymaths and their eighteenth-century counterparts included the human complexity of Britain and Ireland, increasingly conceived as a complex cultural mosaic rather than a disjointed hodgepodge of successive settlers and migrations.[263]

Britannia prospered right through the eighteenth century, but not in quite the form in which Camden left it. Once Gibson had established the precedent, other editions followed, including Richard Gough's in 1789. As descriptions of Britain and its nations increased in number, variety, and specialization, *Britannia* became something less than Camden's account of multicultural Britain. It became – and largely remains – a topographic overview of classical ruins and remains. My own copy of Gibson's *Britannia* bears out its shrinking horizons. The volume once belonged to the massive library of John Ker, the third Duke of Roxburghe, famous for the *Roxburghe Ballads* and for whom the term 'bibliomania' was coined.[264] When Roxburghe's St James's library was broken up in 1812, Gough's edition raised a healthy £9.9s. By contrast, the 1695 *Britannia* sold for a paltry 9s., less than a third of its original price: Robert Morden's English county maps had been filleted out by someone who regarded *Britannia* as little more than a substitute atlas.[265] Many copies shared the same fate. I found my battered working copy via the ubiquitous AbeBooks for £260, almost a trifle compared to copies that fetch nearer £3000 with Morden's maps intact. Camden's story of

[260] *Life and Letters of Edward Lhuyd*, pp. 256-8, 330, 418, 431-33, 466, 534-5; F.V. Emery, 'Irish Geography in the Seventeenth Century', *Irish Geography* 3 (1957), pp. 268-73; *The Occult Laboratory: Magic, Science and Second Sight in Late Seventeenth-Century Scotland, A New Edition of Robert Kirk's* The Secret Commonwealth *and others texts*, ed. Michael Hunter (Woodbridge, 2001), pp. 21-8, 118-59, 205-15; Aubrey, *Monumenta Britannica*, pp. 29-30, 145-6, 160-1, 166-228, 496, 528, 550-61. Stan Mendyk, '*Speculum Britanniae': Regional Study, Antiquarianism, and Science in Britain to 1700* (Toronto, 1989), pp. 206-22 recovers such connections, particularly around Lhuyd, but the perspective is decidedly Anglocentric concerning English and Welsh figures, with a few Scots tacked on at the end.

[261] Rosemary Sweet, *Antiquaries: The Discovery of the Past in Eighteenth-Century Britain* (London, 2004), pp. xviii, 42-118.

[262] Ronald Hutton, *Blood and Mistletoe: The History of the Druids in Britain* (New Haven, 2009), p. 74.

[263] Sweet, *Antiquaries*, pp. 26-7, 119-230.

[264] Brian Hillyard, 'John Ker', *Oxford DNB* at www.oxforddnb.com.

[265] Robert H. Evans, *A Catalogue of the Library of the Late John Duke of Roxburghe* (London, 1812), p. 62 of the price list, sale items 8554 (Gibson's edition) and 8555 (Gough's edition).

multicultural Britain was well on its way to becoming Elton's survey of England or a collection of county histories.

In one vital respect, all the contributors to Gibson's project were being left behind as the encounter with multicultural Britain evolved. Leland and Moryson imagined that their own feet, eyes, and pens could encompass the complexity of the Tudor and Stuart dominions or a dozen dominions within one text. The generations that began with Camden and Pont and grew to embrace Blaeu and Sibbald understood that only many feet, eyes, and pens could produce a *Britannia*, *Atlas Novus*, or 'Scottish Atlas'. Travellers like Andrew Symson or Flintshire's Richard Mostyn (and their local contacts) became the critical figures in achieving such designs. But they also shattered those designs. Gough in his pique recognized what had happened. With his 1789 edition of *Britannia*, Gough aspired to update, correct, and augment the original (and Gibson's edition), but he was moved by another, very different consideration. Gough complained that 'now the rage to travelling about Britain is become so contagious ... every man who can write or tread makes a Pocket Britannia for himself or others'. His *Britannia* was intended to set straight the 'rude observations of every rambler' that followed in Camden's footsteps.[266] And, he most wanted to set readers of *Britannia* straight about antiquities and artefacts.[267]

Gough did not appreciate that the rude ramblers had been at work long before the 1780s in the person of Owen, Carew, Taylor, Symson, Mostyn, and dozens like them. Like John Worthington (c. 1649) and other seventeenth-century travellers, reading *Britannia* encouraged and guided Celia Fiennes in her great journeys of discovery around Britain beginning in 1697 and 1698.[268] Men and women like Fiennes wrote the final word on *Britannia* by their travels and by circulating their journals and diaries. The encounter with multicultural Britain had become theirs. When it passed into the hands of individual travellers like them, it renewed the possibilities for engaging with the cultural complexity that lay beneath the smothering power of familiar national labels or imperial Britons, to find the motley breeds not only of England but of Britain. That, however, is a story for another book.

---

[266] William Camden, *Britannia: Or, a Chorographical Description of the Flourishing Kingdoms of England, Scotland, and Ireland* (three volumes; London, 1789), I, p. vi.

[267] Hunter, *John Aubrey*, p. 203.

[268] *The Journeys of Celia Fiennes*, ed. Christopher Morris (London, 1947), pp. xxv, 42, 206; Woolf, *Social Circulation of the Past*, p. 152; Sweet, *Antiquaries*, pp. 309–31.

Reflection:
Painted with its 'Natives Coloures'

The Tudor historian and media personality David Starkey explained the riots that engulfed parts of England in the summer of 2011 in this way: 'The whites have become black. A particular sort of violent, destructive, nihilistic gangster culture has become the fashion and black and white boys and girls operate in this language together. This language which is wholly false, which is this Jamaican patois that has been intruded in England that is why so many of us have this sense of literally a foreign country.'[1] Starkey's fellow commentators on BBC *Newsnight* challenged his crass racial profiling, while others – including more than one hundred academics who signed an open letter to the BBC – wondered that anyone expected Starkey to offer thoughtful or informed comment in the first place. Starkey rejects both race and class as historical approaches, and later suggested that history teaching in British schools should reflect the dominance of its white monoculture, leaving immigrants to adjust.[2] Critics have long maintained that this version of 'Our Island Story' takes too narrow a view of British History for citizens in a multicultural society and interconnected world.

Implicit in the criticism is that Starkey should just stick to the Tudors, where questions of race–ethnicity and multiculturalism are not likely to trouble monocultural assumptions. It begs the question, when did Britain become multicultural? Post-war migration certainly changed the complexion of Britain and stoked the fears that prompted Enoch Powell's infamous 'Rivers of Blood' speech in 1968, forewarning (wrongly) the nation's descent into American-style race wars. Taking a longer view, perhaps Catholic or Jewish emancipation in the nineteenth century formally recognized a future of cultural diversity.[3] Yet for Leland, Lesley, Camden, Lhuyd, and their fellow travellers, multicultural Britain long predated the racialization of skin colour and post-colonial migrations. It embraced the island's first and successive settlers, the formation or identification of ethnic groups (Britons, Gaels, Picts, Scots, Welsh, Cornish, Romans, Angles,

---

[1] 'David Starkey on UK Riots', *Guardian* online, 13 August 2011. Weblinks for online articles and government documents are listed under electronic resources in the bibliography.
[2] 'David Starkey is Half Right About "Monocultural" Britain', *Guardian* online, 15 November 2011.
[3] Panikos Panayi, *An Immigration History of Britain* (Harlow, 2010), pp. 259–63.

Saxons, Jutes, Norse, Normans) and nations (English, Welsh, Scots, Irish, even British), and face-to-face encounters with the cultural complexity that lay beneath in the *pays*. Travellers painted Britain with native colours that were rich, vibrant, and, above all, complex.

The recovery of multicultural Britain through the experiences of Tudor and Stuart travellers speaks to how we study British History. The desire to escape insular narratives inspired Hugh Kearney to take a 'four nations' approach that gives due respect to the unique histories of the Irish, English, Welsh, and Scots and the interactions among them. Norman Davies massively expanded the detail, complexity, and curiosities of the four nations reattached to their European influences in *The Isles*; Andrew Marr, writing in the *Observer* in October 1999, a month before the book's publication, emphasized the challenge that Davies posed to the Tories' Europhobia and 'Little England' view of Britain under then-leader William Hague.[4] Robert Winder, in *Bloody Foreigners* (2004), wrote the story of a Britain that had 'absorbed migrants at a thousand points and times' in a pattern of resistance and accommodation.[5] Miranda Kaufmann's forthcoming (2016) *Black Tudors* promises to reveal the depth and breadth of a history virtually lost outside Peter Fryer's pioneering *Staying Power: The History of Black People in Britain* (1984).[6]

For the Tudors and Stuarts the dominant perspective on cultural complexity has been the New British History. Its practitioners explore the growth of a 'British state' and the institutional connections that bound together the 'three kingdoms' of the 'Atlantic Archipelago' (England and Wales, Ireland, and Scotland). An intense focus on the explosive consequences of religious pluralism within and across the four nations has yielded a history of ethno-religious conflict from Henry VIII right through to 1715. Lastly, scholars have devoted significant attention to the formation of distinct national identities as well as emerging notions of a supranational British identity.[7] Essential prods to the study of the peoples of Britain, Britishness, and empire in the early modern period came from John Pocock's 'plea for a new subject' in 1973, as well as Linda Colley's *Britons: Forging the Nation 1707–1837*.[8]

The benefits of shedding crude Anglocentric perspectives have been substantial, but the relative stability of national borders after 1450 encouraged a deceptive focus on nations and state building, identities, and three kingdoms

---

[4] Andrew Marr, 'A History Lesson for Wee Willie', *Observer*, 10 October 1999, p. 29.

[5] Robert Winder, *Bloody Foreigners: The Story of Immigration to Britain* (London, 2004), p. 6; also David Miles, *The Tribes of Britain: Who are We? And Where Do We Come From?* (London, 2005).

[6] Peter Fryer, *Staying Power: The History of Black People in Britain* (London, 1984), pp. 1–88.

[7] J.G.A. Pocock, *The Discovery of Islands: Essays in British History* (Cambridge, 2005), pp. 47–57.

[8] Pocock, *Discovery of Islands*, pp. 24–43.

at war.[9] Steven Ellis has hinted at the difficulty of recovering the complexity beneath the big picture of British state building:

> Within the British archipelago, the traditional organising principle for broad surveys is nation-centred, with separate grand narratives focussing on the rise of four nations, the consolidation of their respective national territories, and their sense of identify vis-à-vis other nations. Yet this practice tends to obscure the extent to which the four nations, and even to an extent their national cultures, were themselves influenced by the British pattern of state formation. Of course the same four nations inhabiting the British Isles in 1450 (some accounts would add the Cornish) still inhabited the same parts of the islands in 1660. In that sense there was continuity, but in the intervening two centuries the image, self-representation and cultural stereotypes of these nations had changed quite radically, as also had the actual population groups comprehended in each nominal nation.[10]

Hugh Kearney identified the pitfall another way when he wrote that 'what are normally regarded as four distinct "nations" appear more intelligible if they are seen ... in terms of "cultures" and "sub-cultures". Upon closer examination what seem to be "national" units dissolve into a number of distinctive cultures with their own perceptions of the past, of social status ... of religion and of many other aspects of life.'[11]

The late Rees Davies avoided these problems when he recovered the story of the Thames Valley Pipards, who settled at Ardee, north-west of Dublin, in the thirteenth century. They lived out the cultural encounters among English lowlanders like themselves, Anglo-Norman settler communities, and the Gaels.[12] Robert Bartlett's imaginative *Hanged Man* achieved much the same in its account of the Welsh rebel and future saint William Cragh. Cragh's execution and canonization are deeply enmeshed in the complex, hybrid society or 'middle ground' of Anglo-Norman-Welsh Gower.[13] Davies and Bartlett captured this complex medieval history, and did so with a deeply human touch, through the real lives of those who experienced it.[14] John Kerrigan's innovative *Archipelagic English* found a 'plethora of cultural as well as geopolitical interactions that drew many parts of the Stuart kingdoms into new relationships'.[15] Scott Oldenburg's recent

[9] Glenn Burgess, ed., *The New British History: Founding a Modern State 1603–1715* (London, 1999), p. 175.
[10] Steven G. Ellis and Christopher Maginn, *The Making of the British Isles: The State of Britain and Ireland 1450–1600* (Harlow, 2007), p. 375.
[11] Hugh Kearney, *The British Isles: A History of Four Nations*, 2nd edn (Cambridge, 2006), p. 9.
[12] R.R. Davies, *The First English Empire: Power and Identities in the British Isles 1093–1343* (Oxford, 2001), pp. 89–95.
[13] Robert Bartlett, *The Hanged Man: A Story of Miracle, Memory, and Colonialism in the Middle Ages* (Princeton, 2004).
[14] See also Robin Frame, *The Political Development of the British Isles 1100–1400* (Oxford, 1990); John Gillingham, *The Angevin Empire* (London, 2001).
[15] John Kerrigan, *Archipelagic English: Literature, History, and Politics 1603–1707* (Oxford, 2008), p. 13. For innovative work by literary critics, David J. Baker and Willy Maley, eds, *British*

analysis of literary texts challenges assumptions of English xenophobia and the self–other dichotomy in favour of a more complicated reality, including 'ideas about community founded on something other than common birthplace' or reductive national identities. He argues for genuine multicultural connections and solidarities among immigrants and English men and women forged out of shared religious commitments, economic interests, and domestic life.[16]

With the exception of religion there is still too little in the New British History of this 'mingling of peoples' and 'the conflict between, and creation of, societies and cultures'.[17] New investigations and creative approaches are needed. When Pocock called for an inclusive British History he did so as a New Zealander who felt that 'British entry into Europe' was forcing 'the negation of our historic existence as neo-Britains, and of any account of British history in which we had part'. Ironically, it spurred historians (including Pocock) to 'set about writing the history of New Zealand', including 'a history of the encounter between the settler and indigenous peoples, between *pakeha* and Maori, in which the imperial crown had not ceased to be a presence'.[18] That history of encounter and exchange, borderlands and middle grounds, better characterizes the rich medieval history of Davies or the work of colonial and imperial historians than the New British History of the Tudors and Stuarts.[19]

Travellers illuminate unique, typically first-hand experiences. Mair, Boece, Leland, Moryson, Camden, and many fellow travellers encountered, described, and constructed their multicultural Britain. They embodied a long tradition of engaging with and accepting – grudgingly or not – its cultural complexity. Throughout the period they had much in common with fellow Britons and other Europeans who thirsted for knowledge – factual or fanciful – of peoples in the Americas, Africa, and Asia. A few British travellers even united journeys at home and abroad. Fynes Moryson's storied travels in Europe and the Middle East equipped him to see the cultural complexity of the island to which he returned.

Identities and English Renaissance Literature (Cambridge, 2002); Mark Netzloff, *England's Internal Colonies: Class, Capital, and the Literature of Early Modern English Colonialism* (Houndmills, 2003); Philip Schwyzer and Simon Mealor, eds, *Archipelagic Identities: Literature and Identity in the Atlantic Archipelago, 1550–1800* (Aldershot, 2004); Schwyzer, *Literature, Nationalism and Memory in Early Modern England and Wales* (Cambridge, 2004).

[16] Scott Oldenburg, *Alien Albion: Literature and Immigration in Early Modern England* (Toronto, 2014), pp. 5, 15.

[17] Burgess, *The New British History*, pp. 3, 9; also Pocock, *Discovery of Islands*, pp. 294–5.

[18] Pocock, *Discovery of Islands*, p. 290.

[19] Notable attempts at the macro- and micro-history levels include Nigel Goose and Lien Luu, eds, *Immigrants in Tudor and Early Stuart England* (Brighton, 2005); Maureen M. Meikle, *A British Frontier? Lairds and Gentlemen in the Eastern Borders, 1540–1603* (East Linton, 2004); Mark Stoyle, *West Britons: Cornish Identities and the Early Modern British State* (Exeter, 2002); Stoyle, *Soldiers and Strangers: An Ethnic History of the English Civil War* (New Haven, 2005); Randolph Vigne and Charles Littleton, eds, *From Strangers to Citizens: The Integration of Immigrant Communities in Britain, Ireland and Colonial America, 1550–1750* (Brighton, 2001).

William Lithgow, in many respects a later counterpart to Moryson, excepting his unrestrained religious prejudices, completed his lost 'Surueigh of Scotland' after a decade of travel abroad between 1612 and 1621.[20] We appreciate that travel and first-hand experience had become an essential basis for experiencing Britain's own complex collection of peoples.[21] Commenting on the approach advocated in this book, the Tudor historian John Guy wrote in 2000: 'It all sounds very ambitious, but also very promising, and it is certainly the way British history has to develop if it is not to become ossified in the future.'[22] In 2005, referring to a journey 'north out of the arable lowlands of southern England' to the 'oceanic north' of the Orkney and Shetland islands, Pocock reflected: 'Britain, I saw, is an extraordinary island; and islands and archipelagos can contain more histories than can be easily seen together, or explained away.'[23] Travellers' journeys help us to recover those many histories by moving outside the established tracks of the New British History.

This book also points the way to a fresh look at the eighteenth century. Linda Colley's ground-breaking *Britons* transformed our view of the century by its focus on the construction of Britishness in the crucibles of war and empire. Colley approached nations as imagined communities (after Benedict Anderson) and wrote that if we accept that 'most nations have always been culturally and ethnically diverse, problematic, protean, and artificial constructs that take shape very quickly and come apart just as fast, then we can plausibly regard Great Britain as an invented nation superimposed, if only for a while, onto much older alignments and loyalties'.[24] The Britain of Leland, Lesley, Camden, and Gibson was such a place, 'much less a trinity of three self-contained and self-conscious nations than a patchwork in which uncertain areas of Welshness, Scottishness, and Englishness were cut across by strong regional attachments, and scored over again by loyalties to village, town, family and landscape. In other words, like virtually every other part of Europe in this period, Great Britain was infinitely diverse in terms of the customs and cultures of its inhabitants.'[25] Colley's imperial Britons did not spring from some blend of these peoples or the imposition of English hegemony over a Celtic periphery. Rather, they forged another identity from Protestant anti-Catholicism and hunger for the spoils of Empire that played out in contests with 'Others' in Europe and overseas.[26]

---

[20] Clifford Edmund Bosworth, *An Intrepid Scot: William Lithgow of Lanark's Travels in the Ottoman Lands, North Africa and Central Europe, 1609–1621* (Aldershot, 2006), pp. 23–174.

[21] William Cunningham, *The Cosmographical Glasse, Conteinyng the Pleasant Principles of Cosmographie, Geographie, Hydrographie, or Nauigation* (STC 6119; London, 1559), Preface, pp. 6, 72–5.

[22] Professional correspondence with John Guy, 9 November 2000.

[23] Pocock, *Discovery of Islands*, p. 55.

[24] Linda Colley, *Britons: Forging the Nation 1707–1837* (New Haven, 1992), p. 5.

[25] Colley, *Britons*, p. 17.

[26] Colley, *Britons*, p. 372.

Colley's Britons arose from particular historical circumstances that have now decisively passed away. It follows, then, that some of Britain's contemporary uncertainty can be explained by the collapse of this form of Britishness.[27] Colley took the occasion of the 2014 independence referendum in Scotland to revisit sources of 'union and disunion' within the political configurations of Britain and Ireland since 1707. Unities (shared islands with deep connections to the sea, notions of liberty, and royalism) within differences (national and regional complexities across languages, livelihoods, faith, politics, and identity) existed within shifting Atlantic, European, diasporic, and constitutional contexts that made historical understanding imperative and prognosticating the future positively foolhardy.[28]

This helps historians to investigate and explain contemporary uncertainties. Tudor and Stuart travellers and the rude ramblers with their pocket *Britannias* that so irritated Richard Gough in the 1780s point toward enlarged paths of historical understanding. Our travellers encountered the complex peoples over whom Britishness would be imposed or acted out. Further, when Tudor and Stuart travellers wrote about an island teeming with its own messy collection of peoples and cultures, they revealed something a good deal more permanent in Britain's long history than an imperial identity. Their island had been defined by the migration and settlement of peoples throughout its history. Theirs was a history of encounters, interactions, and exchanges, the division of the island – or Isles – into identifiable ethnic groups or nations, and the recognition of cultural complexity within. Their encounter with just one stretch of Britain's long multicultural past questions the preoccupation with the demise of a British imperial identity for understanding difficulties (or opportunities) associated with the cultural complexity of contemporary Britain. We now need parallel investigations of the peoples over whom Britishness rested and the interaction of multi-layered identities between 1707 and 1837.[29]

Let us return to Timothy Pont's Ayrshire (c. 1604–8) to consider how this might work.[30] John Fullarton developed his own take on Pont's 'Cunningham'

---

[27] Colley, *Britons*, p. 6.

[28] Linda Colley, *Acts of Union and Disunion* (London, 2014).

[29] Kathleen Wilson has implicitly done so with an emphasis on Englishness in the British imperial context and the instability of Britishness against competing layers of identity, difference, and belonging. Kathleen Wilson, *The Island Race: Englishness, Empire and Gender in the Eighteenth Century* (Abingdon, 2003), pp. 7, 43; also Adrian Hastings, *The Construction of Nationhood: Ethnicity, Religion and Nationalism* (Cambridge, 1997), pp. 61–3.

[30] Their massive increase and widespread dissemination again make travel narratives an obvious resource. Wilson, *Island Race*, pp. 208, n. 29. Examples of what might be accomplished include Malcolm Andrews, *The Search for the Picturesque: Landscape, Aesthetics and Tourism in Britain, 1760–1800* (Aldershot, 1989); Charles Batten, Jr, *Pleasurable Instruction: Form and Convention in Eighteenth-Century Travel Literature* (Berkeley, CA, 1978); Barbara Korte, *English Travel Writing from Pilgrimages to Postcolonial Explorations* (Houndmills, 2000); Ian Ousby, *The Englishman's England: Taste, Travel, and the Rise of Tourism* (Cambridge, 1990); Roxann

as he readied the description for publication in the mid–1800s. Fullarton read Pont's comments on agriculture and manufacturing as obvious evidence 'that extremely little change or progress in the arts of civil life ... had taken place ... from the long dreary medieval ages which had only come to be broken up in the preceding period'. When Pont wrote that rain made fertile Ayrshire waterlogged and 'verry troublesome to travellers', Fullarton replied that the 'important subjects of general inclosing, draining, and road-making, had scarcely as yet at all been thought of' there.[31] Fullarton reflected that 'Civilisation appears ever to have been migratory' and Scotland lay outside the history of civilization until 'the introduction of large bodies of Anglo-Saxon and Norman settlers' in the eleventh century brought 'feudal usages' and began to displace 'the aboriginal races' that held the land in common. The de Morvilles embodied this transformation in Cunningham. When the death throes of the Stuart dynasty ended in the defeat of the Jacobites in 1745, Scotland finally enjoyed 'a fair opportunity to devote herself to the pursuits of peaceful industry, or duly to attend to the amenities of civilisation'.[32]

Fullarton in 1858 appropriated Pont's travels and patriotic topography to support unionist assumptions and the 'civilizing mission' of the nineteenth century. That Fullarton did so reflects the importance that Scotland and Scots played in eighteenth-century Enlightenment theories of social evolution, the mania for improvement, and nascent environmentalism.[33] We see the same dynamic at work in the description of the Western Isles written by the Skye native Martin Martin in 1703, as well as in the 'agricultural' travels of Matthew and George Culley in England and Scotland between 1765 and 1798.[34] Theirs are just a few among many first-hand encounters with cultural complexity in the age of Colley's Britons. The language of observation, intelligence, and civilization applied to the travels of Pont reinforces how discoveries that took this form

---

Wheeler, *The Complexion of Race: Categories of Difference in Eighteenth-Century British Culture* (Philadelphia, 2000), pp. 176–286.

[31] J. Fullarton, ed., *Topographical Account of the District of Cunningham, Ayrshire. Compiled About the Year 1600, by Mr. Timothy Pont* (Glasgow, 1858), pp. x–xi, 6, hereafter cited as Pont, 'Cunningham'.

[32] Pont, 'Cunningham', pp. xiii–xx.

[33] Betty Hagglund, '"Not absolutely a native, nor entirely a stranger": The Journeys of Anne Grant', *Perspectives on Travel Writing*, ed. Glenn Hooper and Tim Youngs (Aldershot, 2004), pp. 41–53; Michael Hecter, *Internal Colonialism: The Celtic Fringe in British National Development 1536–1966* (Berkeley, 1975), pp. 79–123; Fredrik Albritton Jonsson, *Enlightenment's Frontier: The Scottish Highlands and the Origins of Environmentalism* (New Haven, 2013); Roy Porter, *The Creation of the Modern World: The Untold Story of the British Enlightenment* (New York, 2000), pp. 230–57; Charles W.J. Withers, *Gaelic Scotland: The Transformation of a Cultural Region* (London, 1988).

[34] Martin Martin, *A Description of the Western Islands of Scotland*, ed. Charles W.J. Withers and R.W. Munro (Edinburgh, 1999), pp. 200–8; *Matthew and George Culley: Travel Journals and Letters*, ed. Anne Orde (Oxford, 2002).

– cartography, topography, ethnography – advanced engagements with cultural complexity and the struggle for political or cultural mastery both at home and abroad, from Britons to Britain's agents of empire.[35] Consequently, Colin Kidd's determination to minimize some kinds of cultural complexity in comparison to others – among eighteenth-century Englishmen, customs, manners, and culture 'were subordinate considerations' to 'political, legal and ecclesiastical' institutions – deserves to be tested against the evidence of first-hand encounters.[36]

Marjorie Morgan in her *National Identities and Travel in Victorian Britain* (2001) examines national identities articulated by Britons during their travels in Europe and Britain proper, emphasizing 'that nations are forged both from within and from outside national borders'.[37] Travel in Europe or reference to political and abstract contexts encouraged travellers to imagine themselves as British. However, cultural and personal contexts or travel in Britain encouraged closer identification with English, Scottish, or Welsh nations. Morgan thus argues for the vital role of geographic context and the insufficiency of Britishness and empire – for Colley's Britons – in accounting for national identities among Victorians; the three, sometimes four, nations dominated the engagement with cultural complexity in Britain.[38]

Morgan's journey through more than one hundred travel narratives produces convincing and interesting patterns of engagement. Her sources also reveal instances when nations smother and abstract more complex realities. The Reverend Richard Trench travelled to Scotland in the 1840s: 'In Lancashire, he suddenly felt more southern than English, noting, "The language of the people … was to me, as a southern, almost like that heard in a foreign clime."'[39] Our anonymous traveller who purportedly encountered the lewd washerwomen of Dunbar in 1704 came to an analogous conclusion in attempting to surmount the linguistic differences in Lincolnshire. He wrote, 'I came to a Bridge, which the people here call Brigg; and I think the comon people of Lincolnshire speake more corruptly and awkwardlye then the comon people of any other county of England that I were ever in.'[40] The Anglo-Cornish traveller George Borrow

---

[35] Martin Rackwitz, *Travels to Terra Incognita: The Scottish Highlands and Hebrides in Early Modern Travellers' Accounts c. 1600 to 1800* (Münster, 2007), pp. 280–452; John Gascoigne, *Joseph Banks and the English Enlightenment: Useful Knowledge and Polite Culture* (Cambridge, 1994), pp. 119–49, 185–236; Colin G. Calloway, *White People, Indians, and Highlanders: Tribal Peoples and Colonial Encounters in Scotland and America* (Oxford, 2008); Margaret Connell Szasz, *Scottish Highlanders and Native Americans: Indigenous Education in the Eighteenth-Century Atlantic World* (Norman, OK, 2007); Jennifer Pitts, *A Turn to Empire: The Rise of Imperial Liberalism in Britain and France* (Princeton, 2005), pp. 25–58, 123–62.

[36] Colin Kidd, *British Identities Before Nationalism: Ethnicity and Nationhood in the Atlantic World 1600–1800* (Cambridge, 1999), p. 91.

[37] Marjorie Morgan, *National Identities and Travel in Victorian Britain* (Houndmills, 2001), p. 4.

[38] Morgan, *National Identities*, p. 206.

[39] Morgan, *National Identities*, pp. 215, 228.

[40] *The North of England and Scotland in MDCCIV* (Edinburgh, 1818), p. 17.

recounted in his *Wild Wales* (c. 1862) several experiences of north–south cultural and linguistic rivalries that would have surprised few Tudor and Stuart travellers.[41] Travel in Britain, more than in continental Europe, elicited these engagements. While Morgan finds that most 'collective imagining in travel journals did not focus on the local or regional realms' in this way, she nonetheless notes that the 'relationship between local and national identity is an area of study that has been largely ignored by British historians' in suggesting avenues for future research.[42] This deeper sense of cultural complexity, therefore, demands further attention. We might well seek it out as an essential corrective to homogenous national identities against which differences are lazily comprehended. Morgan found among her travellers that such a 'sense of [national] difference frequently produced hostile rather than forgiving feelings between people'.[43]

Tudor and Stuart travellers, then, open critical perspectives linking the medieval history of Rees Davies or Robert Bartlett and the ages of imperial Britons and Victorian nationals. Recovering the temporary quality of a British imperial identity or the complexity underlying a particular label can divert us from the easy path to stereotypes and hostility built around nations or ethnic groups, imperial nostalgia, and the false dichotomy of a monocultural metropole and diverse periphery. Comments like David Starkey's, or (as we will shortly see) the History curricula in schools, reveal just how alien the cultural complexity of Britain's past is to historians, teachers, students, and fellow citizens. Engagements with complexity in the Victorian period and Colley's long eighteenth century, the Tudors and Stuarts before them, or pre-Roman and medieval times may not provide specific guidance for addressing the contemporary challenges of multi-cultural Britain. Indeed, we would do well to avoid some of their responses and prescriptions. They do, however, bring into sharp focus an essential reality that helps to equip Britons for the task: the continuous making and remaking of Britain's cultural mosaic over many centuries is their 'burden of history' – and their opportunity.

* * * * *

How William Camden answered the question of when multicultural Britain began speaks to a pressing contemporary concern. In the decade during which I have worked on this book, xenophobia and race-baiting have become common fare in the daily news, from the whites-only Britain of the British National Party and the xenophobia of UKIP to the fear-mongering peddled by 'mainstream' politicians with ID cards, immigration quotas or points systems, and vans cruising

[41] Morgan, *National Identities*, p. 219; Ralph Griffiths, 'Wales', *Oxford Handbook of Holinshed's Chronicles*, ed. Paulina Kewes, Ian W. Archer, and Felicity Heal (Oxford, 2013), p. 690.
[42] Morgan, *National Identities*, pp. 216, 218.
[43] Morgan, *National Identities*, p. 210.

through London with billboards calling on immigrants to 'GO HOME OR FACE ARREST'.[44] All of this betrays a fundamental ignorance of Britain's past as a crossroads for the encounters and – sometimes – conflicts between peoples and cultures long before the *Empire Windrush* arrived at Tilbury in 1948 or Polish carpenters became ubiquitous joiners in Scotland after 2004. Some of this is wilful ignorance. Some of it must be thanks to the persistently homogenous and nostalgic histories to be found on television, web pages, and bookshelves.

By contrast, Education Scotland, the education department for the devolved government in Edinburgh, maintains a website devoted to the nation's history. On it you can link to topics in the history of twentieth- and twenty-first-century Scotland, including the 'New Scots'; this eventually links to an account of the close relationship between Scotland and Poland dating back to the fifteenth century and the long-term presence of Poles in Scotland.[45] The devolved government in Wales offers a comparable web presence for Welsh History, including the BBC's Huw Edwards narrating the story of Wales.[46] BBC History and the Historical Association also offer content with increasing sensitivity to the cultural complexity of Britain's history over many centuries and millennia, not just the imperial age or last century.[47]

This babel of voices in popular culture reflects and impacts on the uncertainty about what History ought to be taught in the classrooms of today's Britain.[48] In January 2011, the Secretary of State for Education in England, Michael Gove, initiated a review of the national curriculum for England and Wales. The national curriculum outlines curricula and standards for subjects taught in English and Welsh schools from ages five (Key Stage 1) to sixteen (Key Stage 4), including History. The History framework that emerged from the review process in 2012 and 2013 touched off a revealing debate about how History should be taught, as well as its broad aims in terms of content, skills, and applied learning after leaving school.

A good deal of management-speak pollutes the conversation – one of New Labour's more craven nods to market fundamentalism was to incorporate Education within the Department of Business, Industry, and Skills. However, Americans might be surprised by a central debate. Unlike the seemingly endless teaching of American History across several grade levels, there is little commitment to teaching British students a complete History of Britain. The

---

[44] Panayi, *Immigration History*, pp. 200–75; 'Immigration Bill Could Lead to Racism and Homelessness', *Guardian* online, 18 December 2013.

[45] http://www.educationscotland.gov.uk/scotlandshistory/.

[46] https://hwb.wales.gov.uk/itunesu/Pages/Story-of-Wales.aspx?lang=en.

[47] http://www.bbc.co.uk/history/british/ or http://www.history.org.uk/resources/general_resource_4714_117.html.

[48] A useful introduction to History teaching in English schools can be found in David Cannadine, Jenny Keating, and Nicola Sheldon, *The Right Kind of History: Teaching the Past in Twentieth-Century England* (Houndmills, 2011).

framework published in September 2013 aimed to rectify this situation by ensuring that all pupils

> know and understand the history of these islands as a coherent, chronological narrative, from the earliest times to the present day: how people's lives have shaped this nation and how Britain has influenced and been influenced by the wider world.[49]

Just what content would be taught to this end provoked some of the most spirited debate. To engage that debate, let us step back and examine the National Curriculum that Gove and his advisers believed desperately needed overhauling.

In March 2011, the Office for Standards in Education (Ofsted) issued 'History for All', a report assessing the strengths and weaknesses of History teaching based on reviews of 166 schools in England carried out between 2007 and 2010. It found that the 'view that too little British history is taught in secondary schools in England is a myth'.[50] Pupils studied a good deal of (undefined) British History and knew it well, though the inspectors found that 'the large majority of the time was spent on English history rather than wider British history'. Therefore, Ofsted called on the Department for Education to ensure the national curriculum led primary school students to understand history coherently and chronologically. It mandated that secondary students should study 'a significant amount' of History. Ofsted also recommended that secondary schools should 'ensure that pupils have a greater understanding of the history of the interrelationships of the different countries which comprise the British Isles'.[51] Ofsted clearly had in mind the changes to subject criteria for the General Certificate of Secondary Education (GCSE) and A Levels, the credentials for which students study who continue beyond the nominal school-leaving age of sixteen. The subject criteria for both credentials required that 'at least 25% of the syllabus has to cover "a substantial and coherent element of British history and/or the history of England, Scotland, Ireland or Wales".'[52]

What had the Ofsted inspectors found that prompted these recommendations? As a former secondary History teacher, I found the Ofsted report strangely encouraging. Unlike the dismal and hostile pronouncements that so often issue from 'inspectors' of US schools and their corporate and political partners in the 'reform' (privatization) movement, Ofsted repeatedly praised the very high quality of History teaching in English schools, the professional expertise and creativity of teachers, and the enthusiasm and sophisticated learning on the

---

[49] London, Department for Education (hereafter DfE), 'The National Curriculum in England: History Programmes of Study' (11 September, 2013).
[50] Manchester, Office for Standards in Education, Childrens' Services and Skills (hereafter Ofsted), 'History for All: History in English Schools 2007/10' (March, 2011), p. 6.
[51] Ofsted, 'History for All', pp. 7–8.
[52] Ofsted, 'History for All', p. 9.

part of students.[53] Teachers taught their subjects well and students learned thoroughly, enthusiastically, and with lasting effect. However, Ofsted identified one major area of concern with History for eleven- to fourteen-year-olds. Nearly half of the secondary schools visited from 2008 to 2010 had not planned and taught effectively the History curriculum as revised in 2007.[54]

The 2007 curriculum put multicultural Britain at the centre and laid out the importance of History with some feeling:

> History fires pupils' curiosity and imagination, moving and inspiring them with the dilemmas, choices, and beliefs of people in the past. It helps pupils develop their own identities through an understanding of history at personal, local, national, and inter-national levels. It helps them to ask and answer questions of the present by engaging with the past.[55]

The civic function of History was never in question.[56] It equipped students to 'take part in a democratic society' by encouraging 'mutual understanding of the historical origins of our ethnic and cultural diversity' and helping 'pupils become confident and questioning individuals'. Among the key concepts to be studied, then, was 'cultural, ethnic, and religious diversity'.[57] Teachers were asked to craft lessons that integrated broad overviews of history with thematic and in-depth studies. Subject content should draw on British, European, and World History from medieval to modern, but the emphasis – and, it must be said, genuine enthusiasm – lay with British History.[58] This no doubt reflected concerns for a socially inclusive Britishness that emerged in the last years of New Labour, especially in response to rising ethno-religious tensions following the Blair government's disastrous and unpopular involvement in the 'clash of civilizations' in Iraq, and the 7 July 2005 suicide bombings in London.[59]

What should this inclusive British History look like? The study of political power would set students on a Whig narrative charting the rise of constitutional

---

[53] Diane Ravitch, *Reign of Error: The Hoax of the Privatization Movement and the Danger to America's Public Schools* (New York, 2013). The impact of US-style reform in Britain has been examined by Melissa Benn in *School Wars: The Battle for Britain's Education* (London, 2011), pp. 85–178.

[54] Ofsted, 'History for All', pp. 48–9.

[55] London, Qualifications and Curriculum Authority (hereafter QCA), 'National Curriculum 2007' (2007), p. 111.

[56] Michael Gove's expert panel produced a dismal admin-speak successor in February 2013: 'A high quality history education equips pupils to think critically, weigh evidence, sift arguments, and develop perspective and judgment. A knowledge of Britain's past, and our places in the world, help us understand the challenges of our own time.' DfE, 'National Curriculum Framework' (February, 2013), p. 177.

[57] QCA, 'National Curriculum 2007', pp. 111–12.

[58] QCA, 'National Curriculum 2007', pp. 112–15.

[59] For example: http://news.bbc.co.uk/2/hi/uk_news/politics/4611682.stm; http://www.theguardian.com/politics/2007/feb/27/immigrationpolicy.race.

monarchy and parliamentary democracy, with a nod to protest movements, the rise of mass politics, and a civics lesson on the contemporary British polity. Traditional Anglocentric histories would fill the bill here unless innovative teachers took the lead in crafting something broader for their students. The study of social and cultural history (including religious change and diversity) as well as commerce and imperialism only implicitly called upon teachers to create lessons around diverse content. The explanatory notes accompanying the content prescriptions did a poor job of pointing the way, with some exceptions. They suggested that teachers should interrogate the British empire for its effects at home as well as 'the regions it colonised ... [and] its legacy in the contemporary world'.[60]

The new imperial history and work like Colley's *Britons* or Antoinette Burton's *Burdens of History: British Feminists, Indian Women, and Imperial Culture, 1815–1915* had clearly made some impact here, directly or indirectly. Keith Wrightson's *Earthly Necessities: Economic Lives in Early Modern Britain*, or a focus on Britain and Ireland's seventeenth-century struggles as conflicts fuelled by cultural and religious difference, would depend upon teachers who carried their university-level history into the classroom in an accessible fashion – or read our stand-in Morysons in Chapters 7 and 8.[61] National narratives have staying power and, as Daniel Woolf noted in 2003, only recently have historians 'reintegrated multiple community pasts into the national past', and then not 'without criticism from proponents of a basic curriculum in history that concentrates on the political and national, and tells the familiar story of the rise of Britain to greatness'.[62]

Just how multicultural British History would be under the 2007 curriculum was unclear, but two topics strove for it:

the different histories and changing relationships through time of the peoples of England, Ireland, Scotland and Wales
the impact through time of the movement and settlement of diverse peoples to, from and within the British Isles[63]

This is the history of Britain as sixteenth- and seventeenth-century travellers experienced it. In creating lessons and instructing pupils, teachers were expected to respect both the separate histories and identities of the four nations as well as their interconnectedness. In the case of immigrant Britain, teachers should focus

[60] QCA, 'National Curriculum 2007', pp. 115–16.
[61] Antoinette Burton, *Burdens of History: British Feminists, Indian Women, and Imperial Culture, 1815–1915* (Chapel Hill, 1994); Keith Wrightson *Earthly Necessities: Economic Lives in Early Modern Britain* (New Haven, 2000); Allan I. Macinnnes, *The British Revolution, 1629–1660* (Houndmills, 2005); Tim Harris, *Revolution: The Great Crisis of the British Monarchy, 1685–1720* (London, 2006).
[62] Daniel Woolf, *The Social Circulation of the Past: English Historical Culture 1500–1730* (Oxford, 2003), p. 296.
[63] QCA, 'National Curriculum 2007', p. 115.

on 'studying the wide cultural, social and ethnic diversity of Britain from the Middle Ages to the twentieth century and how this has helped shape Britain's identity'. Again, the personal and civic purposes were central: pupils should 'reach an informed understanding of, and respect for, their own and each other's identities. This can be linked with the study in citizenship of reasons for the recent migration to, from and within the UK.' The history of Britain as an immigrant nation defined by its cultural complexity provided an essential linkage to contemporary migration, laying the basis for a shared British History and citizenship.[64] It echoed Camden's call for unity around shared diversity in the Stuart *imperium*.

The 2007 national curriculum highlighted the essential 'opportunity' to study how the past had helped to 'shape identities, shared cultures, values and attitudes today'. In particular, History would help students to appreciate 'what people within a culture have in common as well as their diversity, appreciating that cultures are always changing as a result of contact with other cultures'. It ended on a rhetorical note, but there was some value in stating the obvious for those to whom it might not be self-evident: 'Studying the ways in which the past has helped to shape identities, shared cultures, values and attitudes today prepares pupils for life in a diverse and multi-ethnic society and in an increasingly interdependent world.'[65]

Ofsted found limited success in putting this into practice. The study of different histories and changing relationships among the peoples of Britain 'was not a strength in any of the schools visited and too many schools were giving this episodic and occasional coverage as part of larger investigations'. Inspectors cited the siege of Drogheda in 1649 as an example; it figured as 'part of a study on [Oliver] Cromwell with no real attempt to consider a wider British Isles perspective'. As for immigrant Britain, the study of 'the impact of the movement and settlement of diverse peoples through time: to, from and within the British Isles; too much work on multicultural Britain was at a low level'.[66] In other respects, History in schools enhanced students' sense of social responsibility, while some schools demonstrated excellent practice in developing their understanding of 'communities and cultures other than their own' and the 'historical roots of some contemporary issues'. The report quoted two students (years eight and nine) who aptly stated that 'Studying history stops people believing rubbish' and 'We need to know about the past as it helps us to respect people more.'[67]

If any of this concerned the Department for Education in 2011, it is not apparent from the review of the national curriculum and framework documents. If anything, they represent a significant retreat if not outright rejection of

---

[64] QCA, 'National Curriculum 2007', p. 115.
[65] QCA, 'National Curriculum 2007', p. 117.
[66] Ofsted, 'History for All', pp. 48–9.
[67] Ofsted, 'History for All', pp. 56–7.

multicultural British History. The framework of February 2013 may have been couched in terms of 'these islands' and the 'British people', but it reeks of the worst kind of American History that once included Amerindians only when the narrative reached Pocahontas and Custer or mixed in African-Americans only as victims (slavery, Civil War and Reconstruction, Jim Crow segregation), with a comforting nod to Civil Rights. Here the highly prescriptive subjects covering British History from the 'early Britons' to a twentieth century that included the 'Windrush generation' barely qualified as enriched English history: the Anglocentric narrative was spiced with multicultural Britain only during the wars of Edward I, the accession of James VI and I in 1603, and Home Rule for Ireland. As ever, 'the Enlightenment in England' hijacked Adam Smith and left his equally brilliant counterparts Adam Ferguson, Lord Kames, and David Hume behind; the devolution settlements in Wales and Scotland might never have happened – an obvious lost opportunity to link the retreat from an English empire at home with early Home Rule politics. Indeed, the stunning lack of sophistication betrays unquestioned assumptions at every turn, the most tired historical understanding, and no awareness of the teachers and students in action described by 'History for All'.[68] Ultimately, it reads like an exercise in faux expertise, simplistic nonsense dressed up in stilted management-speak; its final successor, in September 2013, simply gave up in favour of brevity.

The responses of the Historical Association (HA) and professors Peter Mandler and Arthur Burns on behalf of the Royal Historical Society (RHS) highlighted many problem areas.[69] (Here I should acknowledge that I am an HA member and RHS fellow.) Throughout, both responses emphasized the deeply flawed understanding of History as a discipline that assumes responsibility for more than the highly prescriptive rote learning of names, dates, and so-called hard facts. More to our purpose is the RHS response to one of the consultation form's more turgid questions: 'What impact – either positive or negative – will our proposal have on the "protected characteristic" group?' While decrying the overly political and English focus of the curriculum, here the RHS emphasized the importance of opportunities for greater study of World History as the better approach for modern Britain: 'If we accept that Britain is a multicultural nation, and we wish to signal to all its inhabitants that their history is taken seriously and given due regard, then the best way to do this is not through sometimes token efforts to teach English history as multicultural, but to give due space to the histories of all the peoples of the world in their own right.'[70] The response is constructive on both counts, but fails to recognize the possibility of a genuinely multicultural British History that is neither tokenistic nor parochial, especially

[68] DfE, 'National Curriculum Framework' (February, 2013), pp. 179–83.
[69] The Royal Historical Society and Historical Association have each made available facsimile copies of their completed version of the DfE 'Consultation Response Form'. Lacking pagination, I will cite the question answered when referencing the documents.
[70] RHS Consultation Response, question nine.

if it embeds Britain in global historical processes as this book does by linking travel, the discovery of humanity, and the encounter with cultural complexity.[71]

The HA response more openly challenged the Anglocentric narrative. It also warned against an insular focus on Britain, but recognized the importance of a multicultural curriculum. It objected to the notion that 'the British people have always been here as a distinct group; this is inaccurate' and noted the importance of the 'international perspective' for understanding 'the issues, events, and people that have shaped the history of Britain'.[72] The story of 'these islands' also needed work:

> This indicates a more inclusive approach toward Scotland, Wales and Ireland, which is to be welcomed, although this is not reflected in the content. It should also be pointed out that these islands have many stories to them, not just one as indicated in the draft. It is regrettable that concepts which clarify the importance of cultural, ethnic, and social diversity in previous versions of the national curriculum [2007] have been removed.[73]

The response decried the impact on the 'protected characteristics' groups and showed an instinctive feel for the realities of classrooms in a multicultural society:

> The white, Anglo-centric, male, political bias of the history curriculum will leave many behind. The attempts at inclusion of female and other diverse British histories are tokenistic. An example of this can clearly be seen in relation to Black British history. There is a long history of Black people in Britain. Records show that Black people have lived in Britain during the Roman period. However, the first time Black history in Britain is treated in the content is through Windrush. ... It also provides students with a skewed perception. In fact, immigration itself is poorly dealt with, being limited to their early settlers, Windrush, and East African Asians.[74]

The HA response demonstrates stronger focus on a multicultural British History in its own right, but it too spotlights World History as an essential corrective in traditional and insular British History. It remains implicitly juxtaposed with Europe and the world when the Association calls for many more opportunities to study an area of World History or another country 'for its own sake'.[75] The imaginative possibilities of a multicultural British History that is part of a curriculum based on shared historical processes alongside significant and telling discontinuities is unexplored. To be fair, though, the crudity of the draft curriculum, prepared without the expertise of 'teachers, subject associations,

---

[71] The same limitation in perspective can be found in Cannadine, Keating, and Sheldon, *Right Kind of History*, pp. 192, 200-1, 227-31.

[72] HA Consultation Response, question two.

[73] HA Consultation Response, question two.

[74] HA Consultation Response, question nine.

[75] HA Consultation Response, question three.

academics and history education specialists', and the follow-up consultation questions contained little scope for original or unconventional thinking.[76]

The February 2013 version of the National Curriculum garnered support from those, including David Starkey, who may have had little or no understanding of the 2007 curriculum and Ofsted's 'History for All' or found the old-time history a comfort. Simon Schama, celebrated for his multi-part BBC *History of Britain* and a proponent of narrative that gives meaning to past, present, and future, denounced Michael Gove's Anglocentric forced march through the high points of British History as '1066 Without the Jokes'.[77] Despite a spirited defence of the curriculum by Gove in May 2013, the Department for Education released a significantly revised National Curriculum in July.[78] It back-peddled on cramming endless facts into empty heads, in favour of teaching methods of historical inquiry, a flexible set of breadth and depth modules, and more World History. In his 'TeacherNetwork' column for the *Guardian*, Tim Taylor, a teacher in Norwich and visiting lecturer at Newcastle University, wrote that the worst excesses of the draft document had gone in favour of flexibility and clarity.[79] There was relief that teachers, historians, and advocates had actually moved an otherwise tone-deaf Tory coalition government and education minister. The HA replied on 7 July: 'We are particularly pleased to see world history reintroduced to the curriculum alongside the opportunity to study local history at all key stages. The revised curriculum removes much of the prescription giving greater scope for choice and respect for teachers' expertise.'[80] But what did it mean for multicultural British History?

The National Curriculum offered this revised (and still uninspiring) cut-and-paste version of its initial aims: students will 'know and understand the history of these islands as a coherent, chronological narrative, from the earliest times

---

[76] HA Consultation Response, question fourteen.

[77] http://www.telegraph.co.uk/culture/books/10146897/Simon-Schama-on-Michael-Gove.html.

[78] Michael Gove delivered the following at Brighton College on 9 May 2013: 'I have enjoyed reading – and hearing from – the different partisans. Those distinguished voices like Richard J Evans, David Priestland and David Cannadine who have, to various degrees, been critical. As well as those equally distinguished voices such as J.C.D. Clark, Jeremy Black, Anthony Beevor, David Abulafia, Niall Ferguson, Simon Jenkins, Andrew Roberts, Amanda Foreman, Simon Sebag-Montefiore, Chris Skidmore, David Starkey and Robert Tombs who have been, to various degrees, supportive. And I have particularly enjoyed listening to my friend and colleague Tristram Hunt who has, in various degrees, at various times, been both supportive and critical.' http://www.politics.co.uk/comment-analysis/2013/05/09/michael-gove-s-anti-mr-men-speech-in-full. The respective responses of Tristram Hunt and Richard Evans are 'History is Where the Great Battles of Public Life are Now Being Fought', *Guardian* online, 12 May 2013; 'The Mr Men Game', *New Statesman* online, 23 May 2013.

[79] 'Sshh, This New Primary History Curriculum is Really Rather Good', *Guardian* online, 16 July 2013.

[80] http://www.history.org.uk/news/news_1830.html.

to the present day: how people's lives have shaped this nation and how Britain has influenced and been influenced by the wider world'. This bit of bureaucratic word-smithing did not commit to more substantive multicultural British History, nor did the revised and reduced content suggestions. For now, the unrealized possibilities of the 2007 National Curriculum and the documented shortcomings highlighted in 'History for All' constitute the status quo for English students. Initial signs are not promising. A 2011 study noted that the 2007 revisions had asked teachers 'to address momentous historical events with an eye to current concerns about genocide and racial discrimination. These subjects were undeniably important, but they were complex and controversial, and the Historical Association issued a report noting that some teachers avoided them in the classroom, for fear of causing offence in local communities – or because in "all white" schools there was thought to be no need to discuss them.'[81] What of their counterparts in Wales and Scotland?

* * * * *

The National Curriculum nominally governs Wales, and Welsh students sit qualifying exams for (currently) A Levels beyond age sixteen. 'History in the National Curriculum for Wales' (2008) eschewed the content-heavy prescriptions of the draft 2013 National Curriculum. Instead, Key Stages 2 and 3 emphasized progressively outward-looking perspectives with the potential to link local complexity with Welsh, British, and international themes. Key Stage 2 students were expected to 'learn by inquiry about the ways of life of different people in these periods of history [early times to present], drawing on important developments, key events and notable peoples in their locality, Wales and Britain'. In this Key Stage students 'should be given' the opportunity to study daily life among the Iron Age Celts or the Romans, 'the Age of the Princes or in the time of the Tudors or in the time of the Stuarts', as well as changes in peoples lives in the nineteenth century and two contrasting periods in the twentieth. Key Stage 3 brought in opportunities to 'explore and interpret ... how the coming of the Normans affected Wales and Britain between 1000 and 1500' as well as 'the changes and conflicts in Wales and Britain between 1500 and 1700'.[82] This did not constitute the 'origins to present' narrative envisioned in the 2013 revision, but Welsh schools certainly offered pupils – albeit young ones – the opportunity to learn about their historic connections to the complex medieval and early modern Britain of Gerald, Churchyard, Owen, Taylor, and Lhuyd.

---

[81] Cannadine, Keating, and Sheldon, *Right Kind of History*, p. 201.
[82] Welsh Assembly Government, Department for Children, Education, Lifelong Learning and Skills, 'History in the National Curriculum for Wales' (2008), pp. 10–14.

GCSE and A Levels did not suggest the same possibilities because external qualification providers shaped the curriculum through examinations. These qualifications providers – testing companies, if you will – operate in England, Wales, and Northern Ireland and therefore reflect a History curriculum less sensitive to Welsh cultural complexity and nearly oblivious to a culturally complex past in England. As a November 2012 report by the Welsh Department for Education and Skills concluded, 'the time has come to develop a high-quality, robust and distinctive national qualifications system for 14- to 19-year-olds in Wales, and to support divergence between Wales and other parts of the UK where this is in the interests of learners in Wales'.[83] The Welsh DfE review recommended that a unified body called 'Qualification Wales' should establish and regulate the new system.[84]

The 'strengthened' GCSE examined by the Welsh Joint Education Committee (WJEC), the primary qualifications body in Wales's open market of providers, offered two routes for combining various units/examination papers. Those with obvious scope for multicultural History included (in chronological order):

- Changes in health and medicine, 1345 to the present day
- Changes in crime and punishment in Wales and England, 1530 to the present day
- The Elizabethan Age, 1558–1603
- Popular Movements in Wales and England, 1815–1848
- Wales and England in the early twentieth century, 1890–1919
- Depression, war and recovery in Wales and England, 1930–1951
- The Development of Wales 1900–2000
- The changing role and status of women in Wales and England, 1900 to the present day
- Developments in sport, leisure, and tourism in Wales and England, 1900 to the present day.

The modern history units offered a good deal of comparative and parallel history around topics and events; e.g. Chartism alongside the Merthyr and Newport Risings and the working conditions that fostered them.[85] Other modern history topics tended to be primarily English or Welsh without obvious comparisons or integration. The main economic and industrial developments from 1890–1919 emphasized Welsh industry and trades unionism, while the Great War's impact seems to homogenize the experience of Welsh and English alike, including the home front.[86]

---

[83] Welsh Government, Department for Education and Skills (hereafter WDfE), 'Review of Qualifications for 14 to 19-year-olds in Wales' (November, 2012), p. 4.

[84] WDfE, 'Review of Qualifications', pp. 5, 25–6, 38–44.

[85] Welsh Joint Education Committee (hereafter WJEC), 'GCSE in History' (2013), pp. 17–18.

[86] WJEC, 'GCSE in History', pp. 19–20.

'Wales 1900–2000' offered a solid history of twentieth-century Wales that would do well for any student, although the 'pressures on Welsh culture and society' were particularly inward looking and students seeking an explanation for the multi-ethnic character of, say, contemporary Cardiff would not have found it here.[87] A good deal depended on teachers, students, and examiners to unlock the possibilities of these papers. The rationale for the content did nothing to encourage a multicultural approach: 'the social, cultural, religious and ethnic diversity of the various societies' was included and examined only 'where appropriate'.[88] Which brings us to the 'Elizabethan Age, 1558–1603'. Wales and the Welsh make a token appearance as they are acted upon by the Tudor state in 'How Wales was treated' under the Elizabethan religious settlement.[89] This is the Tudor Wales of Starkey's white monoculture, rather than Churchyard's distinctive Welsh men and women or Owen's cultural crossroads.

Only with A Levels do Welsh students aged sixteen to nineteen have the opportunity to move beyond these sporadic points of cultural contact or token inclusion of Wales into an Anglocentric or unionist frame. WJEC made explicit the aim for students to 'acquire an understanding of different identities within society and an appreciation of social, cultural, religious and ethnic diversity through the study of aspects of British and non British history'.[90] Here a set of narrative period studies covered the History of Wales and England from 1483 to 1980 while in-depth studies included the early modern units 'Wales and the Tudor State c. 1529–1588' and 'Rebellion and Republic 1629–1660'. The period studies covering the Tudors and Stuarts read a good deal like enriched English History with Welsh additions that served a traditional English narrative.

The Tudor narrative centred on the rise and development of Tudor kingship and carried over much of the GCSE bias.[91] The Stuart topics may be worse, an English narrative of Parliament, civil war and regicide, Restoration, Glorious Revolution, and the rise of party politics that feels as old as Snowdon. Worse than letting the Whig narrative stand on its own may be the inclusion of a topic focussed on the 'main changes and developments in the relationship between England and her Celtic neighbours' of Ireland, Scotland, and Wales.[92] Even Tudor and Stuart English travellers had the good grace to acknowledge a cultural divide in Scotland between the Gaedhealtacht and the lowlands, however crudely they conceived it. The in-depth unit 'Rebellion and Republic' does not signal even this much awareness, let alone the ethno-cultural complexities of Mark Stoyle's *Soldiers and Strangers*. The 'roles of Ireland, Scotland and Wales

---

[87] WJEC, 'GCSE in History', pp. 33, 45–6.

[88] WJEC, 'GCSE in History', p. 9.

[89] WJEC, 'GCSE in History', pp. 28–9.

[90] WJEC, 'AS GCE in History/A Level GCE in History', p. 9, hereafter cited as 'GCE in History' (2012).

[91] WJEC, 'GCE in History' (2012), pp. 16–19.

[92] WJEC, 'GCE in History' (2012), p. 22.

in the Civil Wars' are sandwiched into a topic focussed on the 'relationship between Crown and Parliament, c. 1629' and reductive outlines of Charles I's personal rule and the experiment in republicanism.[93] The other in-depth unit on Wales and the Tudor state enriches the GCSE outline, but still takes a very Westminster-centred approach to the Acts of Union and religious revolution; the socio-economic unit focussed very directly on Welsh society thus reads more like a rupture in the narrative than an essential part of it.[94]

Hard on the heels of revising the National Curriculum, the DfE in London initiated a review of GCSEs to bring the qualifications into line.[95] GCSE specifications should include a 'substantial and coherent element of British history and/or the history of England, Scotland, Wales or Ireland' with at least one in-depth study chosen from the medieval, early modern, or modern periods; a world history unit from one of these same three periods; a comparative or thematic unit that draws on all three time periods. In order to promote chronological breadth, the British and World History units could not come from the same time period, although at the expense of directly integrating Britain within shared historical processes and ruptures at the global level. As with the existing GCSEs, much depends on the creation and examination of content, including the incorporation of primary sources and good secondary analyses. Overall, these frameworks are not supportive of teachers or students interested in a dynamic and challenging multicultural British History. Perhaps matters are different in Scotland?

* * * * *

The Curriculum for Excellence (CfE) is Scotland's newly integrated programme of instruction aimed at creating successful learners, confident individuals, responsible citizens, and effective contributors. CfE emphasizes student capabilities from ages three to eighteen across eight curricular areas. This creates a blizzard of experiences and outcomes, much of the time couched in the stifling jargon of an assessment culture run amok. Indeed, such emphasis on capabilities, outcomes, and assessments makes it hard to focus on subject content including History, which is part of the integrated Social Studies curriculum along with Geography and whatever constitutes Modern Studies. Subject content matters, but less for its own sake than as the vehicle to deliver capabilities and achieve outcomes. The framework comes with 'organisers' that structure the subject matter:

[93] WJEC, 'GCE in History' (2012), pp. 50–1.
[94] WJEC, 'GCE in History' (2012), pp. 48–9.
[95] DfE, 'History GCSE Subject Content and Assessment Objectives' (June, 2013), pp. 3–4.

- people, past events and societies
- people, place and environment
- people in society, economy and business.[96]

When the newly elected prime minister of Australia, Tony Abbot, declared Australia 'open for business' on 7 September 2013, he staked out his coalition's business-friendly agenda. Ahead of the 2014 referendum on Scottish independence, the devolved government seemed determined to send a similar message with the emphasis on education as preparation for the workforce and the creation of an entrepreneurial society.[97] Precious little in the matrix of experiences and outcomes on this topic has anything to do with a multicultural society, except to 'describe the main features of a democracy and discuss the rights and responsibilities of citizens in Scotland' or explain the differences in rights and responsibilities between Scotland and 'a contrasting society'.[98] The stadial theory of social evolution, pioneered by Lord Kames and Adam Smith and used to justify re-engineering colonial societies, finds echoes in the second topic when it associates environmental relationships with 'social and economic differences between more and less economically-developed countries and ... the possibilities for reducing these differences'.[99] The opportunity to understand how cultures emerged from the adaptation to different environmental imperatives offers some basis for cultural comparison; such an outcome would readily resonate with virtually any traveller's account of early modern Scotland and its cultural zones.

The thematic focus creates opportunities to understand cultural complexity and apply it to the history of multicultural Britain when students come to the study of people, past events, and societies. From an early stage, students are expected to 'use evidence to recreate the story of a place or individual of local historical interest'. More advanced students will have to 'explain why a group of people from beyond Scotland settled here in the past' and discuss the impact. They would also learn to 'explain the similarities and differences between the lifestyles, values and attitudes of people in the past by comparing Scotland with a society in Europe or elsewhere'. In the latter stages students can integrate the three outcomes by demonstrating: 'I have investigated a meeting of cultures in the past and can analyse the impact on the societies involved.' This 'meeting of cultures may result from, for example, conflict, conquest, exploration or discovery, the expansion of power or migration'.[100] If teachers pursued these learning outcomes by integrating rich content from the histories of Scotland, Britain, and the wider world, students might well achieve something significant

---

[96] Education Scotland, 'Curriculum for Excellence: Social Studies Experiences and Outcomes' (undated), hereafter cited as 'CfE Social Studies Outcomes'.
[97] 'CfE Social Studies Outcomes', p. 1.
[98] 'CfE Social Studies Outcomes', p. 13.
[99] 'CfE Social Studies Outcomes', p. 9.
[100] 'CfE Social Studies Outcomes', p. 18.

as members of a multicultural society. They might indeed be able to affirm, 'I have developed a sense of my heritage and identity as a British, European or global citizen and can present arguments about the importance of respecting the heritage and identity of others.'[101] (One would like to replace 'or' with 'and' in the enumeration of citizenships.)

In contrast to Ofsted's 'History for All', Education Scotland's November 2012 report 'Social Studies 3–18' gives little evidence of what these experiences look like in classrooms occupied by teachers and students. Instead the report drowns readers with assessment discourse.[102] Not so when we consider the Scottish Higher and Advanced Higher examinations that students typically sit at seventeen and eighteen.[103] At both levels, History consists of three units with associated topics and question sets: Scottish, British, and European/World. Scottish topics for the Higher cover the wars of independence (1249–1328), the age of reformations (1542–1603), the treaty of Union (1689–1740), migration and Empire (1830–1939), and the impact of the Great War (1914–1928). The British topics for the Higher aim to integrate Scottish and English History under church, state, and feudal society (1066–1406), the century of revolutions (1603–1702), Britain 1851–1951, Britain and Ireland 1900–1985; the Atlantic Slave Trade is oddly inserted here. Topics for European/World History range from the Crusades (1071–1204) through the American or French Revolutions, German or Italy from 1815–1939, Russia 1881–1921, Twentieth Century America, ending with appeasement and the road to war (1919–1939) and the Cold War. The Advanced Higher carries over some of this content and adds new topics. The Scottish wars of independence (1284–1357), a more expansive Scotland from Union to Enlightenment (1707–1815), Germany (1918–1939), and Britain (1938–1951) are joined by Northern Britain from the Iron Age to 1034, the Italian Renaissance, the US Civil War, the modernization of Japan (1840–1920), South Africa: Race and Power (1902–1984), the Spanish Civil War, and Russia from the Czars to Stalinism (1914–1945). All of these build on the Social Studies curriculum in History at National levels four and five.[104]

For those who support a coherent narrative for school History, this topical approach must prove frustrating. It certainly lacks possibilities for helping Scottish students to understand the history of Scotland or Britain as a narrative of cultural encounters and exchanges over a longue durée. They will not find anything comparable to Neil Oliver's comprehensive and intelligently conceived

[101] 'CfE Social Studies Outcomes', pp. 2–4.
[102] Education Scotland, 'Social Studies 3–18' (September, 2012), second in a series of regular reports on the impact of CfE on students.
[103] Beginning with 2013–14, the HNC or Higher National Certificate and HND or Higher National Diploma are being phased in as replacements.
[104] Scottish Qualifications Authority, 'Higher History Course Support Notes' and 'Advanced Higher Course Support Notes'.

ten-part BBC *History of Scotland* (2008).[105] Connections between the existing topics are not straightforward. The 1951 end date for the study of modern Britain rules out a meaningful engagement with post-war migration, the contemporary face of Britain, or what Bashir Maan called the 'New Scots'.[106] Lost too are the dynamic linkages that might have been made with two promising multicultural topics, early Northern Britain to 1034 or the Scottish experience of migration and empire in the nineteenth and early-twentieth centuries.

The practical consequences for contemporary multicultural Scotland and Britain are not hard to find. The devolved government in Edinburgh struggled with the race-baiting immigration policies of the Labour government in the early 2000s: the Scottish economy needed a more liberal immigration policy. The 'One Scotland' initiative – making Scotland 'no place for racism' – likewise ran up against the broader political cynicism of race politics. Social Studies and History will not measurably help Scottish students to understand why the devolved government continues to stake out a different position in response to immediate need, let alone that this might be more consistent with Scottish and British History than the xenophobia coming from Westminster.[107] Individual units offer prospects to encourage the cultural sensitivity and openness aimed for by certain learning outcomes in the CfE, but a broad sense of Scotland and Britain's multicultural past appears to be an unlikely result.

Like their Welsh and English counterparts, Scottish students sit exams to obtain advanced qualifications. In their 2013 Highers, students answered one question each from British History and European/World History, followed by a special-topic question that required the evaluation of gobbets from primary and secondary sources. In the first section, one question examined whether the desire to develop 'law and order' drove the centralization of monarchy under David I and the Angevin emperor Henry II – no rehashing of Henry and Becket here. The gobbets covering the treaty of Union (1707) had a timely value.

'Migration and Empire' brought a not quite integrated sense of Scotland's multicultural history within the United Kingdom and empire. Students interrogated two sources for the 'experience of Irish immigrants in Scotland', evaluated another for the contribution of Scots to the growth and development of the empire, and set their 'recalled knowledge' against a final source for the social and cultural impact in Scotland of immigrants.[108] The examiners surely missed a trick

---

[105] Neil Oliver, *A History of Scotland* (London, 2009).

[106] Bashir Maan, *The New Scots: The Story of Asians in Scotland* (Edinburgh, 1992).

[107] http://www.scotland.gov.uk/Topics/People/Equality/18934.

[108] The last source came from T.M. Devine's account of Italian immigrants in his *Scottish Nation 1700–2000* (London, 1999), pp. 486–7, 512–18. In 2001, J.G.A. Pocock praised Devine's history, but included it among insular narratives. He faulted Devine for not addressing English immigrants in Scotland, a story often told in reverse with accounts of Scottish migration to England. 'Since this new [British] history was originally offered as a replacement for a history which was that of the English state and the provinces of its empire,'

with an excerpt from James Hunter's *Glencoe and the Indians*, one of a growing number of books linking Scottish migration to the encounters, exchanges, and dispossessions between Scots and Amerindians in North America. Students were asked to determine only if the excerpt sufficiently covered the reasons why Scots left their homeland, not whether some of those same Scots who suffered at the hands of 'improving' landholders did not perpetrate comparable outrages in North America.[109] Examiners lost the opportunity to ask students to link and scrutinize the imperial project abroad and at home.

The Advanced Higher followed a similar format. Students choosing early Britain might have answered this prompt: '"Britain received a third tribe, namely the Irish (the Scotii)." How valid is this view of the origin of the Scots?' A Part II question challenged students to explain the usefulness of an extract from Samuel Johnson's *Journey to the Western Isles of Scotland* in documenting social change in eighteenth-century Scotland rather than the cultural encounters for which Johnson had no shortage of sensitive, pithy, and prejudiced observations and comments.[110] As for their counterparts in England and Wales, coursework and examinations only modestly sought out Scottish students' understanding of a multicultural British (or Scottish) past.

* * * * *

Richard J. Evans, Michael Gove's bête noire and the retired Regius Professor of Modern History at Cambridge who demolished the Holocaust denials of David Irving, chose to emphasize the possibilities of the revised national curriculum in England (and Wales). Evans particularly welcomed the recognition 'that children are not empty vessels to be filled with patriotic myths' and that the possibilities for 'young people to develop a sense of citizenship' depended upon being 'able and willing to think for themselves. The study of history does this.'[111] Making his case, Evans rebuked traditional Anglocentric narratives and mono-cultural assumptions, reaffirmed the ideal of a multicultural society, and linked patriotism to a narrative of migration, encounter, and settlement over the longue dureé of Britain's history. Evans's points are worth considering in the light of current practice in schools.

Evans asked how Gove could concoct a coherent chronological narrative when 'the historical development of Scotland, Ireland – and, up to a point, Wales too – was in may ways different from that of England up to the seventeenth century and in some respects well beyond it'. Whether they crossed ethno-cultural

---

Pocock explained, 'we now need to get past a stage in which it is that of the latter peoples with the English left out.' Pocock, *Discovery of Islands*, pp. 289, 297.

[109] http://www.sqa.org.uk/pastpapers/papers/papers/2013/H_History_all_2013.pdf.

[110] http://www.sqa.org.uk/pastpapers/papers/papers/2013/AH_History_all_2013.pdf.

[111] 'Michael Gove's History Wars', *Guardian* online, 13 July 2013.

boundaries with sensitivity or with reductive stereotypes in mind, the British travellers studied here would certainly have understood Evans's point. Adults who complain that children grow up knowing little or nothing about the English Civil War only demonstrate how far removed they are from understanding the 'the civil wars throughout Britain' in the seventeenth century. With hindsight, travellers from 'south of the border' like William Brereton or William Howells knew full well, once the wars of the three kingdoms began, that, in Evans's phrase, the 'crucial, indeed pivotal role was played by the Scots Covenanters, who kicked the whole thing off'. Evans echoes one of the axioms of the New British History, giving 'due recognition not just to the interconnectedness of past events in England, Wales, Scotland and Ireland but also to their relative autonomy too. Britain in this sense has always been a multicultural society, and we should celebrate that fact.' In attendance when Starkey claimed that Britons outside London lived in a white monoculture, Evans called on his Welsh roots: 'My parents were unquestionably white, but they grew up in a part of Britain where they first learned English at school, and spoke another language entirely in everyday conversation. The fact they attended Welsh-language services at a Calvinist Methodist chapel and not the English-language Church of England did not alter their British identity one bit.' Of Starkey's monoculture, so easily disposed of with resort to Leland or Camden or Lhuyd, Evans wrote simply 'This is patently untrue, and what's more, skin colour has nothing to do with it.'

The 2012 Olympics demonstrated how little Gove and his supporters really understood either modern Britain or British History. For Evans (and Hugh Mair, whose reflections he cites), the games offered 'vindication of people's ability to feel British patriotism while holding on to many of the customs, beliefs, and values particular to minorities'. The impact of immigration throughout Britain's history plays a vital role in explaining this. Evans cites Barbara Roche, a Labour immigration minister, who called Britain 'a country of immigrants. Originally there was no one here. People came and the only difference is how long ago.' In polite form, Roche underscored a brilliantly scathing cartoon by Martin Rowson aimed at race-baiting immigration debates in the final years of New Labour (2008). In his cartoon, titled 'A Vision of Britain, uncorrupted by the vile stain of Immigration!', Rowson depicts a vicious, feral animal sitting in a godforsaken, rain-swept landscape reading a tabloid that announces a tidal wave of Picts, Celts, Angles, Saxons, Jutes, Vikings, Normans, and French. The creature snarls 'Stuff orf aht of it, ya stinkin' humans!'[112]

For a verdict on those 'ancient' migrations, Evans turned to Barry Cunliffe's *Britain Begins*, quoting 'The islanders have always been a mongrel race and we are the stronger for it.' Tudor and Stuart travellers might not have agreed on who among their immigrant ancestors made them stronger, but they would not have needed a tutorial in the layers of cultural complexity that migrants brought

---

[112] http://www.theguardian.com/cartoons/martinrowson/0,7371,1186035,00.html.

to Britain or the 'motley breeds' to be found there as a result. A school that followed their lead or – more realistically – the call of historians and teachers like Evans would stand a chance of improving on the one-quarter of English schools that inadequately linked the study of 'British History' with the goal to 'enhance pupils' sense of social responsibility'.[113] Ultimately, the insularity of History betrays a failure to make good either the scope for or the necessity of a multicultural approach to one's own history and the essential linkages to be made with British, Imperial, and World History.

* * * * *

Tudor and Stuart travellers create paths to historical understanding that contest ignorance or indifference. Martin Martin and William Stukeley help us to appreciate that these too have a long pedigree. Martin's much-quoted preface to his *Late Voyage to St. Kilda* (1698) chided myopic Britons, disengaged from the 'undiscovered country' at home:

> If we hear at any time a description of some remote corner in the Indies cried in our streets, we presently conclude we may have some divertisement in reading of it; when in the meantime, there are a thousand things nearer us that may engage our thoughts to better purposes, and the knowledge of which may serve more to promote our true interest, and the history of Nature.[114]

Stukeley, the traveller and natural philosopher who helped to refound the Society of Antiquaries in 1718, believed 'that a more intimate knowledg of Brittan more becomes us' and hoped that his *Itinerarium Curiosum* (1724) would 'rouse up the spirit of the Curious among us, to look about them and admire their nativ furniture'.[115] Stukeley took aim at Britons who used their Continental grand tours to walk in the footsteps of antiquity and others who simply lacked curiosity about home.

Martin and Stukeley got it wrong. Britons trained their gazes on Britain itself as a place to be discovered centuries before Stukeley's myopic lament. From at least Gerald of Wales in the twelfth century Britons scrutinized 'home' with much the same degree of intensity as travellers gave to continental Europe, the Holy Land, and faraway islands. They cast the same curious, questioning, sometimes hostile gaze on their near neighbours in Holywell or multi-ethnic London that was trained on the Indus valley or the patchwork quilt of peoples in Jerusalem and Istanbul. The stories of British travellers to the Levant or Mysore or the Mohawk valley before 1700 disrupt many comfortable assumptions about

---

[113] Ofsted, 'History for All', p. 56.

[114] Martin, *Description of the Western Islands*, p. 236.

[115] William Stukeley, *Itinerarium Curiosum Or, An Account of the Antiquitys and Remarkable Curiositys in Nature or Art, Observ'd in Travels Thro' Great Brittan* (London, 1724), p. 3.

513

white men's burdens and the clashes of civilizations. But so do the journeys and accounts of early modern Britons who painstakingly studied their own island at first hand as if it too was a strange, undiscovered country.

Geoffrey Elton fundamentally misunderstood Britain's history when he called Camden's *Britannia* a general survey of England and rubbished the 'non-existent history of ethnic minorities'.[116] The travellers studied here underscore the untenable position taken by Elton and his successors. Indeed, the demographic red herring – 'white Anglo-Saxon' and its other incarnations – becomes not just irrelevant but deceptive when compared to the recognition of and interest in cultural complexity among Tudor and Stuart travellers. English dominance within Britain did nothing to dampen enthusiasm for exploring cultural complexity in England itself, let alone beyond the Tudor heartland. There was nothing tokenistic, false, distorted, or 'politically correct' about doing so. Examining the varieties, complexities, and distinctions among the peoples whom travellers encountered took on the quality of an obsession.

The winter 2015 issue of *The Historian*, the popular magazine of the Historical Association, included an article about medieval foreigners in England. Mark Ormrod previewed the database 'England's Immigrants 1330–1550', freely available online.[117] Readers learned that 'at least one person in every hundred was a foreigner', the same proportion of the population occupied by the clerical orders that so colour our image of medieval England.[118] The reality of the encounters and interactions tends to escape us, but the pattern seems to be one of broad toleration alongside suspicion and moments of hysteria. 'In spite of a quite explicit sense of Englishness evident at least by the fourteenth century,' explains Ormrod, 'notions of nationality were much more inclined to fragment into local particularism. The English vernacular did not use the word "foreigner", but rather "stranger"; and this term, significantly, was applicable as much to people from other parts of England as it was to those from beyond the seas.'[119] Camden closed *Britannia* by quoting Seneca on the changing faces of humanity, the Shropshire native Edward Lhuyd described himself as just another sort of 'Highlander' the more he travelled into and identified with the Scottish Gaedhealtacht, and William Nicolson puzzled over the relative influences of British, Danish, and Saxon in the language spoken by the motley breed of English in Cumbria. Whether viewed from the fourteenth, seventeenth, or twenty-first centuries, the homogenous, Anglocentric place beloved by traditional historians or nationalist politicians did not exist.

---

[116] G.R. Elton, *England Under the Tudors*, 3rd edn (London, 1991), p. 434; Panayi, *Immigration History*, p. 210.

[117] www.englandsimmigrants.com.

[118] Mark Ormrod, 'Friend or Foe? Foreigners in England in the Later Middle Ages', *The Historian* 124 (2015), p. 14.

[119] Ormrod, 'Friend or Foe?', p. 17.

The national curricula in England, Wales, and Scotland have yet to provide a focussed or sustained challenged to this particular form of historical ignorance and breeding ground for racism. This book makes it more difficult to sustain such ignorance in one of the most storied and popular periods of British History, the Tudors and Stuarts. For Shakespeare's John of Gaunt, England may have been an island walled in like a stone set in a silver sea. Some today might wish to live in similar isolation and geographic ignorance. But neither the mentality nor the topography would have made any practical sense to the travellers who encountered Britain when Shakespeare penned *Richard II*. The instinct and passion among Britons to discover and rediscover their native land at first hand is a bright, vivid thread woven into the fabric of the island's long history. It is a profound complication for Shakespeare's Gaunt and for those today who would mute or scrub out its colour. The travellers of Tudor and Stuart Britain demand that the island's history be rewritten in a more honest and complicated manner, painted indeed with, in John Leland's words, its 'natives coloures'.

Bibliography

Manuscript sources

British Library, London
Sloane MS 3228, 'Journey to the Holy Land' by an anonymous Scottish traveller, 1655–6.

National Library of Scotland, Edinburgh
MS 2506, printers' manuscript of *The North of England and Scotland in MDCCIV* (Edinburgh, 1818)
MS Tyn.316, copy of *An Itinerary Written by Fynes Moryson* (1617) owned and annotated by the earl of Haddington.

National Library of Wales, Aberystwyth
MS 22880B, 'Notebook of James Matthew Thompson'.

Published primary sources[1]

Anonymous, *New Proposals for Printing by Subscription, Cambden's Britannia* (London, 1693).
——, *The North of England and Scotland in MDCCIV* (Edinburgh, 1818).
Aubrey, John, *The Natural History of Wiltshire*, ed. John Britton (London, 1847).
——, *Wiltshire. The Topographical Collections of John Aubrey*, ed. John Edward Jackson (Devizes, 1862).
——, *Three Prose Works*, ed. John Buchanan-Brown (Carbondale, IL, 1972).
——, *Monumenta Britannica or A Miscellany of British Antiquities [Parts One and Two]*, ed. John Fowles and Rodney Legg (Boston, 1980/81).
B., E., *A Trip to North-Wales Being a Description of the Country and People* (London, 1701).
[Bale, John], *The Laboryouse Iourney [and] Serche of Iohan Leylande, for Englandes Antiquitees Geuen of Hym as a Newe Yeares Gyfte to Kynge Henry the Viij.* (London, 1549).
[Balfour, James], *The Historical Works of Sir James Balfour* (Edinburgh, 1824–25).

---

[1] The catalogue numbers from A.W. Pollard and G.R. Redgrave, *Short-Title Catalogue of Books Printed in England, Scotland and Ireland and English Books Printed Abroad 1473–1640* (STC) and D.G. Wing, *Short-Title Catalogue of Books Printed in England, Scotland and Ireland, Wales and British America and of English Books Printed in Other Countries 1641–1700* (WING) are cited in the footnotes.

Barlow, Roger, A Brief Summe of Geographie, ed. E.G.R. Taylor (Hakluyt Society; London, 1932).

[Bellenden, John] Heir Beginnis the Hystory and Croniklis of Scotland (London, 1540).

The Blaeu Atlas of Scotland (Edinburgh, 2006).

Bodin, Jean, Method for the Easy Comprehension of History, trans. Beatrice Reynolds (Columbia, 1945).

[Boorde, Andrew], The Fyrst Boke of the Introduction of Knowledge made by Andrew Borde, ed. F.J. Furnivall (London, 1870).

Bower, Walter, Scotichronicon, ed. D.E.R. Watt (nine volumes; Aberdeen/Edinburgh, 1996–2000).

Boyle, Robert, General Heads for the Natural History of a Country (London, 1692).

Brennan, Michael G., ed., The Origins of the Grand Tour: The Travels of Robert Montagu Lord Mandeville (1649–1654) William Hammond (1655–1658) and Banaster Maynard (1660–1663) (London, 2004).

Brereton, William, 'Travels in Holland, the United Provinces, England, Scotland and Ireland', Remains Historical and Literary Connected with the Palatine Counties of Lancaster and Chester (London, 1844).

Brome, James, An Historical Account of Mr. Rogers's Three Years Travels over England and Wales (London, 1694).

——, An Historical Account of Mr. Brome's Three Years Travels over England, Scotland, and Wales (London, 1700).

Brooke, Ralph, A Discoverie of Certaine Errovrs Pvblished in Print in much Commended Britannia 1594 (London, 1599).

Brown, P. Hume, ed., Early Travellers in Scotland (Edinburgh, 1973).

Browne, Thomas, Pseudodoxia Epidemica, or, Enquiries into Very Many Received Tenents and Commonly Presumed Truths (London, 1672).

Buchanan, George, Ane Detectioun of the Doingis of Marie Quene of Scottis (London, 1572).

——, The History of Scotland (London, 1689).

Burton, William, The Description of Leicestershire (London, 1622).

Camden, William, Britannia, siue Florentissimorum Regnorum Angliae, Scotiae, Hiberniae, et Insularum Adiacentium (London, 1607).

——, Britain or a Chorographicall Description of the Most Flourishing Kingdomes, England, Scotland, and Ireland (London, 1610).

——, Britannia: Or a Chorographical Description of Great Britain and Ireland (London, 1695).

——, Britannia: Or a Chorographical Description of Great Britain and Ireland (two volumes; London, 1722).

——, Britannia: Or, a Chorographical Description of the Flourishing Kingdoms of England, Scotland, and Ireland (three volumes; London, 1789).

Carew, Richard, A Survey of Cornwall (London, 1602).

Carley, James P., ed., The Libraries of Henry VIII (London, 2000).

Chandler, John, John Leland's Itinerary: Travels in Tudor England (Stroud, 1993).

Childrey, J., Britannia Baconica: Or The Natural Rarities of England, Scotland, & Wales (London, 1660).

Chope, R. Pearse and Alan Gibson, eds, *Early Tours in Devon and Cornwall* (Newton Abbot, 1967).

Churchyard, Thomas, *Worthines of Wales* (London, 1587).

[Culley, Matthew and George], *Matthew and George Culley: Travel Journals and Letters*, ed. Anne Orde (Oxford, 2002).

Cunningham, William, *The Cosmographical Glasse, Conteinyng the Pleasant Principles of Cosmographie, Geographie, Hydrographie, or Nauigation* (London, 1559).

Davies, John, *A Discouerie of the True Causes Why Ireland was Neuer Entirely Subdued* (London, 1612).

D'Avity, Pierre, *The Estates, Empire and Principalities of the World* (London, 1615).

Doddridge, John, *The History of the Ancient and Moderne Estate of the Principality of Wales, Dutchy of Cornewall, and Earldome of Chester* (London, 1630).

Evans, Robert H., *A Catalogue of the Library of the Late John Duke of Roxburghe* (London, 1812).

[Fiennes, Celia], *The Journeys of Celia Fiennes*, ed. Christoper Morris (London, 1947).

[Fordun, John of], *Johannis de Fordun Scotichronicon* (Oxford, 1722).

——, *John of Fordun's Chronicle of the Scottish Nation*, ed. William F. Skene (two volumes; Burnham-on-Sea, 1993).

Foster, Elizabeth Read, ed., *Proceedings in Parliament 1610* (two volumes; New Haven, 1966).

Fullarton, J., ed., *Topographical Account of the District of Cunningham, Ayrshire. Compiled About the Year 1600, by Mr. Timothy Pont* (Glasgow, 1858).

Geographical Collections Relating to Scotland Made by Walter Macfarlane, ed. Arthur Mitchell and James Toshach Clark (three volumes; Edinburgh, 1906–1908).

Gerald of Wales, *The Journey Through Wales* and *The Description of Wales*, trans. Lewis Thorpe (London, 1978/2004).

——, *The History and Topography of Ireland*, trans. John J. O'Meara (London, 1982).

Hadfield, Andrew, ed., *Amazons, Savages, and Machiavels: Travel and Colonial Writing in English, 1550–1630* (Oxford, 2001).

Harrison, William, *The Description of England*, ed. George Edelen (Ithaca, 1968).

Herodotus, *Histories* (New York, 1910/1997).

Historical Tales of the Wars of Scotland (Edinburgh, 1849).

[Holinshed, Raphael], *The Firste Volume of the Chronicles of England, Scotlande, and Irelande* (London, 1577).

Hughes, Charles, *Shakespeare's Europe* (London, 1903).

James VI and I, *Political Writings*, ed. Johann P. Sommerville (Cambridge, 1994).

Jobson, Richard, *The Golden Trade* (London, 1623).

John of Salisbury, *Policraticus*, ed. and trans. Cary J. Nederman (Cambridge, 1990).

[Jonson, Ben] *Ben Jonson*, ed. C.H. Herford and Percy Simpson (eleven volumes; Oxford, 1952–61).

Kew, Graham, *The Irish Sections of Fynes Moryson's Unpublished Itinerary* (Dublin, 1998).

Kilburne, Richard, *A Topographie or Survey of the County of Kent* (London, 1659).

Lambarde, William, *A Perambulation of Kent* (London, 1576).

——, *Dictionarium Angliæ Topographicum & Historicum. An Alphabetical Description of the Chief Places in England and Wales* (London, 1730).

Leedham-Green, E.S., *Books in Cambridge Inventories* (two volumes; Cambridge, 1986).

Leland, John, *Cygnea Cantio* (London, 1545).

—, *The Itinerary of John Leland the Antiquarian* (nine volumes; Oxford, 1710–12).

—, *The Itinerary of John Leland*, ed. Lucy Toulmin Smith (five volumes; Carbondale, IL, 1964).

Leslie, John, *The Historie of Scotland*, ed. E.G. Cody (two volumes; Edinburgh, 1885–95).

Lithgow, William, *Totall Discourse of the Rare Aduentures, and Painefull Peregrinations of Long Nineteene Yeares Trauayles* (London, 1632).

Lhuyd, Edward, *A Design of a British Dictionary* (London, 1695).

—, *Parochial Queries* (Oxford, 1697).

—, *Archaeologia Britannica ... Vol I. Glossography* (London, 1707).

—, *A Compleat Translation of the Welsh Preface to Mr Lhuyd's Glossography, or his Archaeologia Britannica* (London, 1710).

—, *Life and Letters of Edward Lhwyd*, ed. R.T. Gunther, *Early Science in Oxford XIV* (Oxford, 1945).

The Lives of Those Eminent Antiquaries John Leland, Thomas Hearne, and Anthony à Wood (Oxford, 1772).

Llwyd, Humphrey, *Cronica Walliae*, ed. Ieuan M. Williams (Cardiff, 2002).

Loomba, Ania and Jonathan Burton, eds, *Race in Early Modern England* (Houndmills, 2007).

Machell, Thomas, *That the Northern Counties Which Abound in Antiquities and Ancient Gentry, May No Longer be Bury'd in Silence* (Oxford, 1677).

Major, John *A History of Greater Britain as Well England as Scotland*, trans. Archibald Constable (Edinburgh, 1892).

Mason, Roger A. and Martin S. Smith, eds, *A Dialogue on the Law of Kingship among the Scots: A Critical Edition and Translation of George Buchanan's* De Iure Regni apud Scotos Dialogus (Farnham, 2004).

Martin, Martin, *A Description of the Western Islands of Scotland*, ed. Charles W.J. Withers and R.W. Munro (Edinburgh, 1999).

Meyer, Albrecht, *Certaine Briefe, and Speciall Instructions for Gentlemen, Merchants, Students, Souldiers, Marriners, &c. Employed in Seruices Abrode* (London, 1589).

More, Thomas, *Utopia*, ed. Edward Surtz (New Haven, 1964).

Morgan, Richard and Hywel Wyn Owen, *Dictionary of the Place-Names of Wales* (Llandysul, 2008).

[Moryson, Fynes], *An Itinerary Written by Fynes Moryson ... Containing His Ten Yeeres Travell Throvgh the Twelve Dominions of Germany, Bohmerland, Sweitzerland, Netherland, Denmarke, Poland, Italy, Turky, France, England, Scotland, and Ireland* (London, 1617).

—, *An History of Ireland, from the Year 1599, to 1603* (Dublin, 1735).

—, *The Itinerary of Fynes Moryson in Four Volumes* (four volumes; Glasgow, 1907).

Norden, John, *Speculis Britaniæ Pars The Description of Hartfordshire* (London, 1598).

The Occult Laboratory: Magic, Science and Second Sight in Late Seventeenth-Century Scotland, A New Edition of Robert Kirk's The Secret Commonwealth *and others texts*, ed. Michael Hunter (Woodbridge, 2001).

Ogilby, John, *Britannia, Volume the First, or, An Illustration of the Kingdom of England and Dominion of Wales by a Geographical and Historical Description of the Principal Roads Thereof* (London, 1675).

Owen, George, *The Description of Pembrokeshire*, ed. Dillwyn Miles (Llandysul, 1994).

Owen, Hywel Wyn and Richard Morgan, *Dictionary of the Place-Names of Wales* (Llandysul, 2008).

Palmer, Thomas, *An Essay of the Means How to Make Our Trauailes, into Forraine Countries, the Most Profitable and Honourable* (London, 1606).

Pevsner, Nikolaus, *The Buildings of England: Worcestershire* (Harmondsworth, 1968/1977).

Philipot, John, *Villare Cantianum, or, Kent Surveyed* (London, 1659).

Plot, Robert, *Quaer's to be Propounded to the Most Ingenious of Each County in My Travels through England* (Oxford, 1674).

—, *The Natural History of Oxfordshire* (Oxford, 1676).

Price, John, *Historiae Brytannicae Defensio* (London, 1573).

Rastell, John, *A New Iuterlude and a Mery of the Nature of the .iiii. Element* (London, 1520).

Ray, John, *A Collection of English Proverbs* (Cambridge, 1670).

—, *A Collection of English Words Not Generally Used* (London, 1674).

—, *A Collection of English Proverbs* (Cambridge, 1678).

—, *A Collection of Words Not Generally Used* (London, 1691).

R[ichards], W[illiam], *Wallography: or The Britton Describ'd* (London, 1682).

Risdon, Tristram, *The Chorographical Description, or, Survey of the County of Devon* (London, 1714).

Sibbald, Robert, *Advertisement ... to Publish the Description of the Scotia Antiqua & Scotia Moderna* (Edinburgh, 1682).

—, *An Account of the Scotish Atlas, or, The Description of Scotland Ancient & Modern* (Edinburgh, 1683).

Slezer, John, *Theatrum Scotiae* (London, 1693).

Spenser, Edmund, *A View of the State of Ireland*, ed. Andrew Hadfield and Willy Maley (Oxford, 1997).

Stewart, William *The Buik of the Croniclis of Scotland*, ed. William B Turnbull (London, 1858).

Stow, John, *A Survey of London*, ed. Charles Lethbridge Kingsford (two volumes; Oxford, 1908).

Stuart Royal Proclamations Volume I: Royal Proclamations of James I 1603–1625, ed. James F. Larkin and Paul L. Hughes (Oxford, 1973).

Stukeley, William, *Itinerarium Curiosum Or, An Account of the Antiquitys and Remarkable Curiositys in Nature or Art, Observ'd in Travels Thro' Great Brittan* (London, 1724).

Taylor, John, *The Carriers Cosmographie* (London, 1637).

—, *A Short Relation of a Long Iourney Made Round ... Wales* (London, 1653).

Tours in Scotland 1677 and 1681 by Thomas Kirk and Ralph Thoresby, ed. P. Hume Brown (Edinburgh, 1892).

Trapnel, Anna, *Report and Plea or A Narrative of Her Journey from London into Cornwall* (London, 1654).

Williams, Roger, *The Hirelings Ministry None of Christs* (London, 1652).

Worcestre, William, *Itineraries*, ed. and trans. John H. Harvey (Oxford, 1969).

Secondary sources

Abulafia, David, *The Discovery of Mankind: Atlantic Encounters in the Age of Columbus* (New Haven, 2008).

Aird, William M., 'Northumbria and the Making of the Kingdom of the English', in Tsurushima, *Nations in Medieval Britain*, 45-70.

Alford, Stephen, *Burghley: William Cecil at the Court of Elizabeth I* (New Haven, 2008).

Anderson, Benedict, *Imagined Communities* (London, 1983/1991).

Andrews, Malcolm, *The Search for the Picturesque: Landscape, Aesthetics and Tourism in Britain, 1760-1800* (Aldershot, 1989).

Archer, Ian, 'The Nostalgia of John Stow', in Smith, Strier, and Bevington, *The Theatrical City*, 17-34.

Armitage, David, *The Ideological Origins of the British Empire* (Cambridge, 2000).

Baker, Alan R.H. and Mark Billinge, eds, *Geographies of England; The North-South Divide, Material and Imagined* (Cambridge, 2004).

Baker, David J. and Willy Maley, eds, *British Identities and English Renaissance Literature* (Cambridge, 2002).

Barber, Sarah and Steven G. Ellis, eds, *Conquest and Union: Fashioning a British State 1485-1725* (Harlow, 1995).

Barrell, A.D.M., *Medieval Scotland* (Cambridge, 2000).

Bartlett, Robert, *Gerald of Wales 1146-1223* (Oxford, 1982).

——, 'Medieval and Modern Concepts of Race and Ethnicity', *Journal of Medieval and Early Modern Studies* 31.1 (2001), 39-56.

——, *The Hanged Man: A Story of Miracle, Memory, and Colonialism in the Middle Ages* (Princeton, 2004).

Bartley, J.O., *Teague, Shenkin and Sawney: Being an Historical Study of the Earliest Irish, Welsh and Scottish Characters in English Plays* (Cork, 1954).

Batten, Jr., Charles, *Pleasurable Instruction: Form and Convention in Eighteenth-Century Travel Literature* (Berkeley, CA, 1978).

Beckett, Margaret J., 'The Political Works of John Lesley, Bishop of Ross (1527-96)' (Ph.D. thesis; University of St Andrews, 2009).

——, 'Counsellor, Conspirator, Polemicist, Historian: John Lesley, Bishop of Ross 1527-96, *Records of the Scottish Church History Society* 39 (2009), 1-22.

Beer, Barrett L., *Tudor England Observed: The World of John Stow* (Stroud, 1998).

Benn, Melissa, *School Wars: The Battle for Britain's Education* (London, 2011).

Berghoff, Hartmut et al., eds, *The Making of Modern Tourism: The Cultural History of the British Experience, 1600-2000* (Houndmills, 2002).

Bhaba, Homi K., *The Location of Culture* (London, 1994).

Bietenholz, Peter G. and Thomas B. Deutscher, eds, *Contemporaries of Erasmus* (three volumes; Toronto, 1985-87).

Black, Jeremy, 'The Grand Tour', in Myers and Harris, *Journeys Through the Market*, 65-91.

Borm, Jan, 'Defining Travel: On the Travel Book, Travel Writing and Terminology', in Hooper and Youngs, *Perspectives on Travel Writing*, 13-26.

Bosworth, Clifford Edmund, *An Intrepid Scot: William Lithgow of Lanark's Travels in the Ottoman Lands, North Africa and Central Europe, 1609-1621* (Aldershot, 2006).

Bowen, Lloyd, 'Representations of Wales and the Welsh during the Civil Wars and Interregnum', *Historical Research* 77 (2004), 358–76.

—, 'Fashioning Communities: The County in Early Modern Wales', in Eales and Hopper, *County Community*, 77–99.

Braddick, Michael, *State Formation in Early Modern England c. 1550–1700* (Cambridge, 2000).

Bradshaw, Brendan, Andrew Hadfield, and Willy Maley, eds, *Representing Ireland: Literature and the Origins of Conflict 1534–1660* (Cambridge, 1993).

Brayshay, Mark, 'Royal Post-horse Routes in England and Wales: The Evolution of the Network in the Later-sixteenth and Early-seventeenth Century', *Journal of Historical Geography* 17.4 (1991), 373–89.

—, 'Waits, Musicians, Bearwards and Players: The Inter-urban Road Travel and Performances of Itinerant Entertainers in Sixteenth and Seventeenth Century England', *Journal of Historical Geography* 31.3 (2005), 430–58.

Brennan, Michael G., *English Civil War Travellers and the Origins of the Western European Grand Tour* (London, 2002).

Brett, Caroline, 'John Leland, Wales, and Early British History', *Welsh Historical Review* 15 (1990–91), 169–82.

Broadie, Alexander, *The Shadow of Scotus: Philosophy and Faith in Pre-Reformation Scotland* (Edinburgh, 1995).

Broadway, Jan, *'No Historie So Meete': Gentry Culture and the Development of Local History in Elizabethan and Early Stuart England* (Manchester, 2006).

—, 'A Convenient Fiction? The County Community and County History in the 1650s', in Eales and Hopper, *County Community*, 39–55.

Brotton, Jerry and Lisa Jardine, *Global Interests: Renaissance Art between East and West* (Ithaca, 2000).

Broun, Dauvit, 'Attitudes of Gall to Gaedhel in Scotland before John of Fordun', in Broun and MacGregor, *Mìorun Mòr nan Gall*, 49–82.

— and Martin MacGregor, eds, *Mìorun Mòr nan Gall, 'The Great Ill-Will of the Lowlander'?: Lowland Perceptions of the Highlands, Medieval and Modern* (Glasgow, 2009).

—, 'Becoming a Nation: Scotland in the 12th and 13th Centuries', in Tsurushima, *Nations in Medieval Britain*, 86–103.

—, *Scottish Independence and the Idea of Britain: From the Picts to Alexander III* (Edinburgh, 2013).

Brown, Keith M., *Noble Society in Scotland: Wealth, Family and Culture, from Reformation to Revolution* (Edinburgh, 2000).

Burgess, Glenn, ed., *The New British History: Founding a Modern State 1603–1715* (London, 1999).

Burke, Peter, 'A Survey of the Popularity of Ancient Historians 1450–1700', *History and Theory* 5.2 (1966), 135–52.

Burns, J.H. and Mark Goldie, eds, *The Cambridge History of Political Thought 1450–1700* (Cambridge, 1991).

—, 'George Buchanan and the Anti-monarchomachs', in Mason, *Scots and Britons*, 138–58.

Burrow, John, *A History of Histories* (New York, 2008).

Burton, Antoinette, *Burdens of History: British Feminists, Indian Women, and Imperial Culture, 1815–1915* (Chapel Hill, 1994).

Calloway, Colin G., *White People, Indians, and Highlanders: Tribal Peoples and Colonial Encounters in Scotland and America* (Oxford, 2008).

Cameron, Jamie, *James V: The Personal Rule 1528–1542* (East Linton, 1998).

Campbell, Bruce M.S., 'North–South Dichotomies, 1066–1550', in Baker and Billinge, *Geographies of England*, 145–74.

Campbell, J.L. and Derick Thomson, *Edward Lhuyd in the Scottish Highlands 1699–1700* (Oxford, 1963).

Campbell, Mary B., *The Witness and the Other World: Exotic European Travel Writing, 400–1600* (Ithaca, 1988).

Cannadine, David, ed., *What is History Now?* (Houndmills, 2002).

——, Jenny Keating, and Nicola Sheldon, *The Right Kind of History: Teaching the Past in Twentieth-Century England* (Houndmills, 2011).

Canny, Nicholas, *Europeans on the Move: Studies in European Migration, 1500–1800* (Oxford, 1994).

——, *Making Ireland British 1580–1650* (Oxford, 2001).

Capp, B.S., *The Fifth Monarchy Men: A Study in Seventeenth-century English Millenarianism* (Totowa, NJ, 1972).

Carey, Daniel, 'Compiling Nature's History: Travellers and Travel Narratives in the Early Royal Society', *Annals of Science* 54 (1997), 269–92.

Carley, James P., 'John Leland in Paris: the Evidence of his Poetry', *Studies in Philology* 83.1 (1986), 1–50.

——, 'Harrison and Leland', in Kewes, Archer, and Heal, *Holinshed's Chronicles*, 187–201.

Carpenter, David, *The Struggle for Mastery: Britain 1066–1284* (Oxford, 2003).

Carr, A.D., 'Inside the Tent Looking Out; The Medieval Welsh World-View', in Davies and Jenkins, *From Medieval to Modern Wales*, 30–44.

Chaney, Edward *The Evolution of the Grand Tour* (London, 1998).

Chonaill, Bronagh Ní, '"The Welsh, you know, are Welsh": the Individual, the Alien, and a Legal Tradition', in Tsurushima, *Nations in Medieval Britain*, 75–85.

Colley, Linda, *Britons: Forging the Nation 1707–1837* (New Haven, 1992).

——, *Acts of Union and Disunion* (London, 2014).

Collingwood, R.G., 'Hadrian's Wall: A History of the Problem', *Journal of Roman Studies* 11 (1921), 37–66.

Collinson, Patrick, 'John Stow and Nostalgic Antiquarianism', in Merritt, *Imagining Early Modern London*, 27–51.

Coster, Will and Andrew Spicer, eds, *Sacred Space in Early Modern Europe* (Cambridge, 2005).

Cowan, Edward J. and Richard Finlay, eds, *Scottish History: The Power of the Past* (Edinburgh, 2002).

Cramsie, John, 'Commercial Projects and the Fiscal Policy of James VI and I', *Historical Journal* 43.2 (2000), 345–64.

——, *Kingship and Crown Finance under James VI and I 1603–1625* (Woodbridge, 2002).

——, 'The Philosophy of Imperial Kingship and the Interpretation of James VI and I', in Houlbrooke, *James VI and I*, 43–60.

Cunningham, Ian C., ed., *The Nation Survey'd: Essays on Late Sixteenth-Century Scotland as Depicted by Timothy Pont* (East Linton, 2001).

Cust, Richard, 'Catholicism, Antiquarianism and Gentry Honour: The Writings of Sir Thomas Shirley', *Midland History* 23 (1998), 40–70.

Dalrymple, William, *White Mughals: Love and Betrayal in Eighteenth Century India* (Harmondsworth, 2003).

Davies, Norman, *The Isles* (London, 1999).

—, *Vanished Kingdoms: The Rise and Fall of States and Nations* (New York, 2012).

Davies, R.R., *The British Isles 1100–1500: Comparisons, Contrasts, and Connections* (Edinburgh, 1988).

—, *Domination and Conquest: The Experience of Ireland, Scotland and Wales 1100–1300* (Cambridge, 1990).

—, 'The Peoples of Britain and Ireland 1100–1400 I. Identities', *Transactions of the Royal Historical Society Sixth Series* 4 (1994).

—, 'The Peoples of Britain and Ireland 1100–1400 II. Names, Boundaries and Regnal Solidarities', *Transactions of the Royal Historical Society Sixth Series* 5 (1995).

—, 'The Peoples of Britain and Ireland 1100–1400 III. Laws and Customs', *Transactions of the Royal Historical Society Sixth Series* 6 (1996).

—, 'The Peoples of Britain and Ireland 1100–1400 IV. Language and Historical Mythology' *Transactions of the Royal Historical Society Sixth Series* 7 (1997).

—, *The First English Empire: Power and Identities in the British Isles 1093–1343* (Oxford, 2001), 113–71.

— and Geraint H. Jenkins, eds, *From Medieval to Modern Wales; Historical Essays in Honour of Kenneth O. Morgan and Ralph A. Griffiths* (Cardiff, 2004).

—, 'The Identity of "Wales" in the Thirteenth Century', in Davies and Jenkins, *From Medieval to Modern Wales*, 45–63.

—, *Lord and Lordship in the British Isles in the Late Middle Ages* (Oxford, 2009).

Dawson, Jane E. A., 'Anglo-Scottish Protestant Culture and Integration in Sixteenth-century Britain', in Ellis and Barber, *Conquest and Union*, 87–114.

—, *Scotland Re-formed 1488–1587* (Edinburgh, 2007).

DeMolen, Richard L., 'The Library of William Camden', *Proceedings of the American Philosophical Society* 128.4 (1984), 326–409.

Devine, T.M., *Clanship to Crofters' War: The Social Transformation of the Scottish Highlands* (Edinburgh, 1994).

—, *The Scottish Nation 1700–2000* (London, 1999).

Dew, Nicholas, 'Reading Travels in the Culture of Curiosity: Thévenot's Collection of Voyages', *Journal of Early Modern History* 10.1&2 (2006), 39–59.

Dewald, Carolyn and John Marincola, eds, *Cambridge Companion to Herodotus* (Cambridge, 2006).

Dolan, Brian *Exploring European Frontiers; British Travellers in the Age of Enlightenment* (Houndmills, 2000).

—, *Ladies of the Grand Tour* (London, 2002).

Dorsch, T.S., 'Two English Antiquaries: John Leland and John Stow', *Essays and Studies 1959* (London, 1959), 18–35.

Driver, Felix, *Geography Militant* (Oxford, 2001).

Duffy, Eamon, *The Voices of Morebath: Reformation and Rebellion in an English Village* (New Haven, 2001).

Dyer, Christopher and Catherine Richardson, eds, *William Dugdale, Historian, 1605–1686: His Life, His Writings and His* County (Woodbridge, 2009).

Eales, Jacqueline and Andrew Hopper, eds, *The County Community in Seventeenth-Century England and Wales* (Hatfield, 2012).

Ellis, Steven G. and Sarah Barber, eds, *Conquest and Union: Fashioning a British State 1485–1725* (Harlow, 1995).

— and Christopher Maginn, *The Making of the British Isles: The State of Britain and Ireland 1450–1600* (Harlow, 2007).

Ellison, James, *George Sandys: Travel, Colonialism and Tolerance in the 17th Century* (Woodbridge, 2002).

Elsner, Jas and Joan-Pau Rubies, eds, *Voyages and Visions: Towards a Cultural History of Travel* (London, 1999).

Elton, G.R., *The Tudor Constitution* (Cambridge, 1960).

—, *England Under the Tudors*, 3rd edn (London, 1991).

Emerson, Roger L., 'Sir Robert Sibbald, Kt, the Royal Society of Scotland and the Origins of the Scottish Enlightenment', *Annals of Science* 45 (1988), 41–72.

Emery, Frank, 'A Map of Edward Lhuyd's *Parochial Queries in Order to a Geographical Dictionary*', *Transactions of the Honourable Society of Cymmrodorion* (1958), 41–53.

—, 'A New Reply to Lhuyd's Parochial Queries (1696): Puncheston, Pembrokeshire', *National Library of Wales Journal* 10.4 (1958), 395–402.

—, 'Edward Lhwyd and the 1695 Britannia', *Antiquity* 32 (1958), 179–82.

—, 'English Regional Studies from Aubrey to Defoe', *Geographical Journal* 124.3 (1958), 315–25.

—, 'Edward Lhuyd and Some of His Glamorgan Correspondents: A View of Gower in the 1690s', *Transactions of the Honourable Society of Cymmrodorion* (1965), 59–114.

—, 'The Geography of Robert Gordon, 1580–1661 and Sir Robert Sibbald, 1641–1722', *Scottish Geographical Magazine* 74.1 (1958), 3–12.

—, *Edward Lhuyd F.R.S. 1660–1709* (Cardiff, 1971).

—, 'A New Account of Snowdonia in 1693 written for Edward Lhuyd', *National Library of Wales Journal* 18 (1973), 405–17.

— and Gwyn Walters, 'Edward Lhuyd, Edmund Gibson, and the Printing of Camden's *Britannia*, 1695', *The Library* 32.2 (1977), 109–37.

Erskine, Caroline and Roger A. Mason, eds, *George Buchanan: Political Thought in Early Modern Britain and Europe* (Farnham, 2012).

Estabrook, Carl B., *Urbane and Rustic England: Cultural Ties and Social Spheres in the Provinces, 1660–1780* (Manchester, 1998).

Everitt, Alan, *Landscape and Community in England* (London, 1985).

Ferguson, William, *The Identity of the Scottish Nation: An Historic Quest* (Edinburgh, 1998).

Fitzmaurice, Andrew, *Humanism and America: An Intellectual History of English Colonisation, 1500–1625* (Cambridge, 2003).

Fleming, Robin, *Britain After Rome: The Fall and Rise 400 to 1070* (London, 2010).

Ford, Judy Ann, 'Marginality and the Assimilation of Foreigners in the Lay Parish Community: the Case of Sandwich', in French, Gibbs, Kümin, *The Parish in English Life*, 203–16.

Forte, Angelo, Richard Oram, and Frederik Pederson, *Viking Empires* (Cambridge 2005).

Fox, Adam, *Oral and Literate Culture in England 1500–1700* (Oxford, 2000).

——, 'Printed Questionnaires, Research Networks, and the Discovery of the British Isles, 1650–1800', *Historical Journal* 53.3 (2010), 593–621.

—— and Daniel Woolf, eds, *The Spoken Word: Oral Culture in Britain 1500–1850* (Manchester, 2002).

——, 'Vernacular Culture and Popular Customs in Early Modern England: Evidence from Thomas Machell's Westmorland', *Cultural and Social History* 9.3 (2012), 329–347.

Fradenburg, Louise Olga, *City, Marriage, Tournament: Arts of Rule in Late Medieval Scotland* (Madison, WI, 1991).

Frame, Robin, *The Political Development of the British Isles 1100–1400* (Oxford, 1990).

Frantz, R.W., *The English Traveller and the Movement of Ideas 1660–1732* (Lincoln, NE, 1967).

Fraser, James E., *From Caledonia to Pictland: Scotland to 795* (Edinburgh, 2009).

French, Katherine L., Gary G. Gibbs, and Beat A. Kümin, eds, *The Parish in English Life, 1400–1600* (Manchester, 1997).

Fryer, Peter, *Staying Power: The History of Black People in Britain* (London, 1984).

Fuller, Mary C., 'Making Something Fit of It: Questions of Value in the Early English Travel Collection', *Journal of Early Modern History* 10.1&2 (2006), 11–38.

Gadd, Ian and Alexandra Gillespie, eds, *John Stow (1525–1605) and the Making of the English Past; Studies in Early Modern Culture and the History of the Book* (London, 2004).

Games, Alison, *The Web of Empire: English Cosmopolitans in an Age of Exploration 1560–1660* (Oxford, 2008).

Gascoigne, John, *Joseph Banks and the English Enlightenment: Useful Knowledge and Polite Culture* (Cambridge, 1994).

Gillingham, John *The Angevin Empire* (London, 2001).

Given-Wilson, Chris, *Chronicles: The Writing of History in Medieval England* (London, 2004).

Goldstein, R. James, *The Matter of Scotland: Historical Narratives in Medieval Scotland* (Lincoln, NE, 1993).

Goose, Nigel and Lien Luu, eds, *Immigrants in Tudor and Early Stuart Britain* (Brighton, 2005).

Grafton, Anthony, 'Humanism and Political Theory', in Burns and Goldie *Cambridge History of Political Thought 1450–1700*, 9–29.

Gransden, Antonia, *Historical Writing in England II: c. 1307 to the Early Sixteenth Century* (Ithaca, 1982).

——, *Legends, Traditions and History in Medieval England* (London, 1992).

Grant, James, *Cassell's Old and New Edinburgh* (Edinburgh, 1880–83).

Greenblatt, Stephen, *Renaissance Self-Fashioning: From More to Shakespeare* (Chicago, 1980) .

—, ed., *New World Encounters* (Berkeley, 1993).

Griffiths, Paul and Mark S.R. Jenner, eds, *Londinopolis: Essays in the Cultural and Social History of Early Modern London* (Manchester, 2000).

Griffiths, Ralph, 'Wales', in Kewes, Archer, and Heal, *Holinshed's Chronicles*, 679–94.

Guy, John, *Tudor England* (Oxford, 1988).

—, ed., *Tudor Monarchy* (London, 1996).

—, 'Tudor Monarchy and Its Critiques', in Guy, *Tudor Monarchy*, 78–109.

—, 'Thomas Cromwell and the Intellectual Origins of the Tudor Revolution', in Guy, *Tudor Monarchy*, 213–33.

—, *My Heart is My Own: The Life of Mary Queen of Scots* (London, 2004).

—, *A Daughter's Love: Thomas and Margaret More* (London, 2008).

Habib, Imtiaz H., *Black Lives in the English Archives, 1500–1677* (Aldershot, 2008).

Hadfield, Andrew, *Spenser's Irish Experience: Wilde Fruite and Salvage Soyl* (Oxford, 1997).

—, *Literature, Travel, and Colonial Writing in the English Renaissance 1545–1625* (Oxford, 1998).

Hadfield, Andrew and John McVeagh, eds, *Strangers to That Land: British Perceptions of Ireland from the Reformation to the Famine* (Gerard's Cross, 1994).

Hadfield, Andrew, Brendan Bradshaw, and Willy Maley, eds, *Representing Ireland: Literature and the Origins of Conflict 1534–1660* (Cambridge, 1993).

Hagglund, Betty, '"Not absolutely a native, nor entirely a stranger": The Journeys of Anne Grant', in Hooper and Youngs, *Perspectives on Travel Writing*, 41–53.

Hammond, Matthew H., 'Ethnicity and the Writing of Medieval Scottish History', *Scottish Historical Review* 85.1 (2006), 1–27.

—, ed., *New Perspectives on Medieval Scotland 1093–1286* (Woodbridge, 2013).

Harris, Michael and Robin Myers, eds, *Journeys Through the Market: Travel, Travellers and the Book Trade* (Folkstone, 1999).

Harris, Oliver, '"Motheaten, Mouldye, and Rotten": The Early Custodial History and Dissemination of John Leland's Manuscript Remains', *Bodleian Library Record* 18.5 (2005), 460–501.

Harris, Tim, *Revolution: The Great Crisis of the British Monarchy, 1685–1720* (London, 2006).

—, *Rebellion: Britain's First Stuart Kings, 1567–1642* (Oxford, 2014).

Hastings, Adrian, *The Construction of Nationhood: Ethnicity, Religion and Nationalism* (Cambridge, 1997).

Heal, Felicity and Henry Summerson, 'The Genesis of the Two Editions', in Kewes, Archer, and Heal, *Holinshed's Chronicles*, 3–12.

Hecter, Michael, *Internal Colonialism: The Celtic Fringe in British National Development 1536–1966* (Berkeley, 1975).

Helgerson, Richard, *Forms of Nationhood: The Elizabethan Writing of England* (Chicago, 1992).

Herendeen, Wyman, *William Camden: A Life in Context* (Woodbridge, 2007).

Highley, Christopher, *Catholics Writing the Nation in Early Modern Britain and Ireland* (Oxford, 2008).

Hill, Christopher, *The English Bible and the Seventeenth Century Revolution* (Harmondsworth, 1993).

—, *Liberty Against the Law: Some Seventeenth-Century Controversies* (Harmondsworth, 1996).

Hingley, Richard, *The Recovery of Roman Britain 1586–1906: A Colony so Fertile* (Oxford, 2008).

Hoak, Dale, ed., *Tudor Political Culture* (Cambridge, 1995).

Hodgen, Margaret T., *Early Anthropology in the Sixteenth and Seventeenth Centuries* (Philadelphia, 1964).

Hooper, Glenn and Tim Youngs, eds, *Perspectives on Travel Writing* (Aldershot, 2004).

Hornblower, Simon and Anthony Spawforth, eds, *The Oxford Classical Dictionary* (Oxford, 1996).

Hoskins, W.G., *Provincial England: Essays in Social and Economic History* (London, 1963).

Houlbrooke, Ralph, ed., *James VI and I: Ideas, Authority, and Government* (Aldershot, 2006).

—, 'England', in Kewes, Archer, and Heal, *Holinshed's Chronicles*, 629–48.

Hutton, Ronald, *Blood and Mistletoe: The History of the Druids in Britain* (New Haven, 2009).

Islam, Said Manzurul, *The Ethics of Travel: From Marco Polo to Kafka* (Manchester, 1996).

Jackson, Clare *Restoration Scotland 1660–1690: Royalist Politics, Religion, and Ideas* (Woodbridge, 2003).

James, Edward, *Britain in the First Millennium* (London, 2001).

Jardine, Lisa, *Worldly Goods: A New History of the Renaissance* (London, 1996).

— and Jerry Brotton, *Global Interests: Renaissance Art between East and West* (Ithaca, 2000).

Jasanoff, Maya, *Edge of Empire: Lives, Culture, and Conquest in the East 1750–1850* (New York, 2005).

Jenkins, Geraint H., ed., *The Welsh Language before the Industrial Revolution* (Cardiff, 1997).

Jenner, Mark S.R. and Paul Griffiths, eds, *Londinopolis: Essays in the Cultural and Social History of Early Modern London* (Manchester, 2000).

Jones, J. Gwynfor, 'The Welsh Language in Local Government: Justices of the Peace and the Courts of Quarter Sessions c. 1536–1660', in Jenkins, *The Welsh Language*, 181–206.

Jonsson, Fredrik Albritton, *Enlightenment's Frontier: The Scottish Highlands and the Origins of Environmentalism* (New Haven, 2013).

Kearney, Hugh, *The British Isles: A History of Four Nations* (Cambridge, 2006).

Keating, Jenny, David Cannadine, and Nicola Sheldon, *The Right Kind of History: Teaching the Past in Twentieth-Century England* (Houndmills, 2011).

Kelley, Donald R., *Faces of History: Historical Inquiry from Herodotus to Herder* (New Haven, 1998).

Kendrick, T.D., *British Antiquity* (London, 1950).

Kerrigan, John, *Archipelagic English: Literature, History, and Politics 1603–1707* (Oxford, 2008).

Kew, Graham, 'Shakespeare's Europe Revisited: The Unpublished *Itinerary* of Fynes Moryson (1566–1630)' (Ph.D. thesis; Birmingham University, 1995).

Kewes, Paulina, Ian W. Archer, and Felicity Heal, eds, *Oxford Handbook of Holinshed's Chronicles* (Oxford, 2013).

Kidd, Colin, *Subverting Scotland's Past: Scottish Whig Historians and the Creation of an Anglo-British Identity, 1689–c.1830* (Cambridge, 1993).

——, *British Identities Before Nationalism: Ethnicity and Nationhood in the Atlantic World 1600–1800* (Cambridge, 1999).

——, *The Forging of Races: Race and Scripture in the Protestant Atlantic World, 1600–2000* (Cambridge, 2006).

Knecht, R.J., *Renaissance Warrior and Patron: the Reign of Francis I* (Cambridge, 1994).

Korte, Barbara, *English Travel Writing from Pilgrimages to Postcolonial Explorations* (Houndmills, 2000).

Langton, John, 'South, North, and Nation: Regional Differences and Consciousness in an Integrating Realm, 1550-1750', in Baker and Billinge, *Geographies of England*, 137-43.

Letts, Malcolm, *As the Foreigner Saw Us* (London, 1935).

Levine, Joseph M., *Humanism and History: Origins of Modern English Historiography* (Ithaca, 1987).

Levy, F.J., 'The Making of Camden's *Britannia*', *Bibliothèque d'humanisme et Renaissance* 26.1 (1964), 70-97.

——, *Tudor Historical Thought* (San Marino, CA, 1967).

Liebersohn, Harry, *The Travelers' World* (Cambridge, MA, 2006).

Loomba, Ania, *Shakespeare, Race, and Colonialism* (Oxford, 2002/2009).

Lord, Peter, *Words With Pictures: Welsh Images and Images of Wales in the Popular Press, 1640-1860* (Aberystwyth, 1995).

Loxley, James, 'My Gossip's foot voyage', *Times Literary Supplement* 5554 (11 September 2009), 13-15.

Lynch, Michael, *Scotland: A New History* (London, 1991).

——, 'The Age of Timothy Pont', in Cunningham, *The Nation Survey'd*, 26-34.

Maan, Bashir, *The New Scots: The Story of Asians in Scotland* (Edinburgh, 1992).

MacCaffrey, Wallace, *The Shaping of the Elizabethan Regime* (Princeton, 1968).

McCann, Franklin T., *The English Discovery of America to 1585* (New York, 1952).

McClendon, Muriel C., Joseph P. Ward, and Michael MacDonald, eds, *Protestant Identities: Religion, Society, and Self-Fashioning in Post-Reformation England* (Stanford, 1999).

MacDonald, Michael, Muriel C. McClendon, and Joseph P. Ward, eds, *Protestant Identities: Religion, Society, and Self-Fashioning in Post-Reformation England* (Stanford, 1999).

MacDougall, Norman, *James IV* (East Linton, 1997).

McFarlane, I.D., *A Literary History of France: Renaissance France 1470-1589* (London, 1974).

——, *Buchanan* (London, 1981).

MacGregor, Martin, 'Gaelic Barbarity and Scottish Identity in the Later Middle Ages', in Broun and MacGregor, *Mìorun Mòr nan Gall*, 7-48.

McGurk, John, *The Elizabethan Conquest of Ireland: The 1590s Crisis* (Manchester, 1997).

Macinnes, Allan I., *The British Revolution, 1629-1660* (Houndmills, 2005).

MacLean, Gerald, *The Rise of Oriental Travel: English Visitors to the Ottoman Empire, 1580–1720* (Houndmills, 2004).

——, *Looking East: English Writing and the Ottoman Empire Before 1800* (Houndmills, 2007).

McLeod, Wilson *Divided Gaels: Gaelic Cultural Identities in Scotland and Ireland c. 1200–c.1650* (Oxford, 2004).

McRae, Andrew, *God Speed the Plough: The Representation of Agrarian England 1500–1600* (Cambridge, 1996).

——, *Literature and Domestic Travel in Early Modern England* (Cambridge, 2009).

Maczak, Antoni, *Travel in Early Modern Europe* (Oxford, 1995).

Maginn, Christopher and Steven G. Ellis, *The Making of the British Isles: The State of Britain and Ireland 1450–1600* (Harlow, 2007).

Maley, Willy, Brendan Bradshaw, and Andrew Hadfield, eds, *Representing Ireland: Literature and the Origins of Conflict 1534–1660* (Cambridge, 1993).

—— and David J. Baker, eds, *British Identities and English Renaissance Literature* (Cambridge, 2002).

Mancall, Peter C., 'Introduction: What Fynes Moryson Knew', *Journal of Early Modern History* 10.1&2 (2006), 1–9.

——, *Hakluyt's Promise: An Elizabethan's Obsession for an English America* (New Haven, 2007).

Mapstone, Sally and Juliette Wood, eds, *The Rose and the Thistle: Essays on the Culture of Late Medieval and Renaissance Scotland* (East Linton, 1998).

Marshall, Peter, 'Religious Ideology', in Kewes, Archer, and Heal, *Holinshed's Chronicles*, 411–26.

Mason, Roger A., ed., *Scots and Britons: Scottish Political Thought and the Union of 1603* (Cambridge, 1994).

——, *Kingship and the Commonweal: Political Thought in Renaissance Scotland* (East Linton, 1998).

——, 'From Chronicle to History: Recovering the Past in Renaissance Scotland', in Suntrup and Veenstra, *Building the Past*, 53–66.

——, 'From Buchanan to Blaeu: The Politics of Scottish Chorography, 1582–1654', in Erskine and Mason, *George Buchanan*, 13–48.

—— and Caroline Erskine, eds, *George Buchanan: Political Thought in Early Modern Britain and Europe* (Farnham, 2012).

——, 'Civil Society and the Celts: Hector Boece, George Buchanan and the Ancient Scottish Past', in Cowan and Finlay, *Scottish History*, 95–119.

——, 'Scotland', in Kewes, Archer, and Heal, *Holinshed's Chronicles*, 647–62.

Matar, Nabil, *Islam in Britain 1558–1685* (Cambridge, 1998).

——, *Turks, Moors and Englishmen in the Age of Discovery* (New York, 1999).

——, ed., *In the Lands of the Christians: Arabic Travel Writing in the 17th Century* (London, 2002).

Mather, James, *Pashas: Traders and Travellers in the Islamic World* (New Haven, 2009).

Mayer, Thomas F., 'On the Road to 1534: the Occupation of Tournai and Henry VIII's Theory of Sovereignty', in Hoak, *Tudor Political Culture*, 11–30.

Mayhew, R., 'Edmund Gibson's Editions of *Britannia*: Dynastic Chorography and the Particularist Politics of Precedent, 1695-1722', *Historical Research* 73.182 (2000), 239-61.

Mealor, Simon and Philip Schwyzer, eds, *Archipelagic Identities: Literature and Identity in the Atlantic Archipelago, 1550-1800* (Aldershot, 2004).

Meikle, Maureen M., *A British Frontier? Lairds and Gentlemen in the Eastern Borders, 1540-1603* (East Linton, 2004).

Mendyk, Stan, 'Early British Chorography', *Sixteenth Century Journal* 17.4 (1986), 459-81.

—, *'Speculum Britanniae': Regional Study, Antiquarianism, and Science in Britain to 1700* (Toronto, 1989).

Merritt, J.F., ed., *Imagining Early Modern London: Perceptions and Portrayals of the City from Stow to Strype, 1598-1720* (Cambridge, 2001).

Miles, David, *The Tribes of Britain: Who are We? And Where Do We Come From?* (London, 2005).

Moir, Esther, *The Discovery of Britain: The English Tourists 1450-1850* (London, 1964).

Molyneaux, George, 'Why Were Some Tenth-Century English Kings Presented as Rulers of Britain?', *Royal Historical Society Transactions* 21 (2011), 59-91.

Morét, Ulrike, 'Gaelic History and Culture in Mediaeval and Sixteenth-Century Lowland Scottish Historiography' (Ph.D. thesis; University of Aberdeen, 1993).

Morgan, Marjorie, *National Identities and Travel in Victorian Britain* (Houndmills, 2001).

Morton, Graeme, *William Wallace: Man and Myth* (Stroud, 2004).

Myers, Robin and Michael Harris, eds, *Journeys Through the Market: Travel, Travellers and the Book Trade* (Folkstone, 1999).

Netzloff, Mark, *England's Internal Colonies: Class, Capital, and the Literature of Early Modern English Colonialism* (Houndmills, 2003).

Ohler, Norbert, *The Medieval Traveller* (Woodbridge, 1989).

Oldenburg, Scott, *Alien Albion: Literature and Immigration in Early Modern England* (Toronto, 2014).

Oliver, Neil, *A History of Scotland* (London, 2009).

Orme, Nicholas, 'Popular Religion and the Reformation in England: A View from Cornwall', in Tracy and Ragnow, *Religion and the Early Modern State*, 351-75.

Ormrod, Mark, 'Friend or Foe? Foreigners in England in the Later Middle Ages', *The Historian* 124 (2015), 12-17.

Orwell, George, *The Road to Wigan Pier* (London, 1937).

Ousby, Ian, *The Englishman's England: Taste, Travel and the Rise of Tourism* (Cambridge, 1990).

Pagden, Anthony, *The Fall of Natural Man: The American Indian and the Origins of Comparative Ethnology* (Cambridge, 1982).

—, *Lords of All the World: Ideologies of Empire in Spain, Britain and France c. 1500-c.1800* (New Haven, 1995).

Palmer, Patricia *Language and Conquest in Early Modern Ireland: English Renaissance Literature and Elizabethan Imperial Expansion* (Cambridge, 2001).

Panayi, Panikos, *An Immigration History of Britain* (Harlow, 2010).

Parry, G.J.R., 'William Harrison and Holinshed's Chronicles', *Historical Journal* 27.4 (1984), 789–810.

—, *A Protestant Vision: William Harrison and the Reformation of Elizabethan England* (Cambridge, 1987).

—, 'John Stow's Unpublished "Historie of this Iland": Amity and Enmity amongst Sixteenth Century Scholars', *English Historical Review* 102.404 (1987), 633–47.

—, 'Trinity College Dublin MS 165: The Study of Time in the Sixteenth Century', *Historical Research* 62 (1989), 15–33.

—, *The Trophies of Time: English Antiquarians of the Seventeenth Century* (Oxford, 1995).

—, 'The Antiquities of Warwickshire', in Dyer and Richardson, *William Dugdale*, 10–33.

—, 'Harrison's "Chronology" and Descriptions of Britain', in Kewes, Archer, and Heal, *Holinshed's Chronicles*, 93–110.

Patterson, Annabel, *Reading Holinshed's Chronicles* (Chicago, 1994).

Petrina, Alessandra, 'A view from afar: Petruccio Ubaldini's *Descrittione del Regno di Scotia*', unpublished paper presented to the 'Thirteenth International Conference on Medieval and Renaissance Scottish Language and Literature' (Padua, 2011).

Piesse, A.J. ed., *Sixteenth-century Identities* (Manchester, 2000).

Piggott, Stuart, *Ruins in a Landscape: Essays in Antiquarianism* (Edinburgh, 1976).

—, 'William Camden and the *Britannia*', in Richardson, *English Local History*, 12–29.

Pitts, Jennifer, *A Turn to Empire: The Rise of Imperial Liberalism in Britain and France* (Princeton, 2005).

Pocock, J.G.A., *The Discovery of Islands: Essays in British History* (Cambridge, 2005).

Porter, Roy, *The Creation of the Modern World: The Untold Story of the British Enlightenment* (New York, 2000).

Power, M.J., 'John Stow and His London', in Richardson, *English Local History*, 30–51.

Pratt, Mary Louise, *Imperial Eyes: Travel Writing and Transculturation* (London, 1992).

Pryor, Francis, *The Making of the British Landscape: How We have Transformed the Land from Prehistory to Today* (London, 2010).

Quadflieg, Helda, '"As mannerly and civill as any of Europe": Early Modern Travel Writing and the Exploration of the English Self', in Hooper and Youngs, *Perspectives on Travel Writing*, 27–40.

Quinn, D.B., *England and the Discovery of America* (New York, 1974).

Rackwitz, Martin, *Travels to Terra Incognita: The Scottish Highlands and Hebrides in Early Modern Travellers' Accounts c. 1600 to 1800* (Münster, 2007).

Ragnow, Marguerite and James D. Tracy, eds, *Religion and the Early Modern State: Views from China, Russia, and the West* (Cambridge, 2004).

Raven, James, *The Business of Books: Booksellers and the English Book Trade 1450–1850* (New Haven, 2007).

Ravitch, Diane, *Reign of Error: The Hoax of the Privatization Movement and the Danger to America's Public Schools* (New York, 2013).

Richardson, Catherine and Christopher Dyer, eds, *William Dugdale, Historian, 1605–1686: His Life, His Writings and His County* (Woodbridge, 2009).

Richardson, Glenn, *Renaissance Monarchy: The Reigns of Henry VIII, Francis I and Charles V* (London, 2002).

Richardson, R.C., ed., *The Changing Face of English Local History* (Aldershot, 2000).

Robb, Graham, *The Discovery of France: Historical Geography from the Revolution to the First World War* (New York, 2007).

Roberts, Michael, '"A Witty Book, but mostly Feigned": William Richards' *Wallography* and Perceptions of Later Seventeenth-century England', in Schwyzer and Mealor, *Archipelagic Identities*, 153-65.

Rood, Tim, 'Herodotus and Foreign Lands', in Dewald and Marincola, *Cambridge Companion to Herodotus*, 290-305.

Ross, Charles, *Edward IV* (Berkeley, 1974).

Rowse, A.L., *The England of Elizabeth* (London, 1950).

Royan, Nicola, 'The *Scotorum Historia* of Hector Boece: A Study' (D.Phil. thesis; Oxford, 1996).

——, 'The Relationship Between the *Scotorum Historia* of Hector Boece and John Bellenden's *Chronicles of Scotland*', in Mapstone and Wood, *Rose and the Thistle*, 136-57.

Rubin, Miri, 'What is Cultural History Now?', in Cannadine, *What is History Now?*, 80-94.

Said, Edward, *Orientalism* (London, 1978).

——, *Culture and Imperialism* (New York, 1993).

Salway, Peter, *Roman Britain* (Oxford, 1984).

Scarfe, Norman, *To the Highlands in 1786: The Inquisitive Journey of a Young French Aristocrat* (Woodbridge, 2001).

Scattergood, John, 'John Leland's *Itinerary* and the Identity of England', in Piesse, *Sixteenth-century Identities*, 58-74.

Schwyzer, Philip, *Literature, Nationalism and Memory in Early Modern England and Wales* (Cambridge, 2004).

——, 'Archipelagic History', in Kewes, Archer, and Heal, *Holinshed's Chronicles*, 593-607.

—— and Simon Mealor, eds, *Archipelagic Identities: Literature and Identity in the Atlantic Archipelago, 1550-1800* (Aldershot, 2004).

Selwood, Jacob, *Diversity and Difference in Early Modern London* (Farnham, 2010).

Sharpe, Kevin, *Sir Robert Cotton 1586-1631: History and Politics in Early Modern England* (Oxford, 1979).

Sheldon, Nicola, David Cannadine, and Jenny Keating, *The Right Kind of History: Teaching the Past in Twentieth-Century England* (Houndmills, 2011).

Shrank, Cathy, *Writing the Nation in Reformation England 1530-1580* (Oxford, 2004).

Smith, Anthony D., *The Ethnic Origins of Nations* (Oxford, 1986).

Smith, David L., Richard Strier, and David Bevington, eds, *The Theatrical City: Culture, Theatre and Politics in London 1576-1649* (Cambridge, 1995).

Spawforth, Anthony and Simon Hornblower, eds, *The Oxford Classical Dictionary* (Oxford, 1996).

Spufford, Margaret, *Small Books and Pleasant Histories: Popular Fiction and its Readership in Seventeenth-Century England* (Cambridge, 1981).

Stägl, Justin, *A History of Curiosity: The Theory of Travel 1550–1800* (Amsterdam, 1995).

Statham, Craig, *Lost East Lothian* (Edinburgh, 2011).

Stepan, Nancy, *The Idea of Race in Science: Great Britain 1800–1960* (Basingstoke, 1982).

Stone, Jeffrey C., *The Pont Manuscript Maps of Scotland: Sixteenth Century Origins of a Blaeu Atlas* (Tring, Hertfordshire, 1989).

—, 'Timothy Pont: Three Centuries of Research, Speculation and Plagiarism', in Cunningham, *Nation Survey'd*, 1–26.

Stoye, John, *English Travellers Abroad 1604–1607* (New Haven, 1989).

Stoyle, Mark, '"Pagans or Paragons?": Images of the Cornish during the English Civil War', *English Historical Review* 111.441 (1996), 299–323.

—, *West Britons: Cornish Identities and the Early Modern British State* (Exeter, 2002).

—, *Soldiers and Strangers: An Ethnic History of the English Civil War* (New Haven, 2005).

Suggett, Richard, 'The Welsh Language and the Court of Great Sessions', in Jenkins, *The Welsh Language*, 153–80.

— and Eryn White, 'Language, Literacy, and Aspects of Identity in Early Modern Wales', in Fox and Woolf, *The Spoken Word*, 52–83.

—, 'Vagabonds and Minstrels in Sixteenth-century Wales', in Fox and Woolf, *Spoken Word*, 138–72.

Summerson, Henry, 'Sources: 1587', in Kewes, Archer, and Heal, *Holinshed's Chronicles*, 77–92.

Suntrup, Rudolf and Jan Veenstra, eds, *Building the Past = Konstruktion der eigenen Vergangeheit* (Frankfurt/New York, 2006).

Suranyi, Anna, *The Genius of the English Nation: Travel Writing and National Identity in Early Modern England* (Newark, DE, 2008).

Swett, Katharine W., '"Born on My Land": Identity, Community, and Faith Among the Welsh in Early Modern London', in McClendon, Ward, and MacDonald, *Protestant Identities*, 249–65.

Swift, Roger, ed., *Irish Migrants in Britain, 1815–1914* (Cork, 2002).

Szasz, Margaret Connell, *Scottish Highlanders and Native Americans: Indigenous Education in the Eighteenth-Century Atlantic World* (Norman, OK, 2007).

Taylor, E.G.R., *Tudor Geography 1485–1583* (London, 1930).

—, *Late Tudor and Early Stuart Geography 1583–1650* (London, 1934).

Thomson, Derick and J.L. Campbell, *Edward Lhuyd in the Scottish Highlands 1699–1700* (Oxford, 1963).

Tracy, James D. and Marguerite Ragnow, eds, *Religion and the Early Modern State: Views from China, Russia, and the West* (Cambridge, 2004).

Trench, Richard, *Travellers in Britain: Three Centuries of Discovery* (London, 1990).

Trevor-Roper, Hugh, *The Invention of Scotland: Myth and History* (New Haven, 2008).

Tsurushima, Hirokazu, ed., *Nations in Medieval Britain* (Donington, 2010).

Verdon, Jean, *Travel in the Middle Ages* (South Bend, IN, 2003).

Vigne, Randolph and Charles Littleton, eds, *From Strangers to Citizens: the Integration of Immigrant Communities in Britain, Ireland and Colonial America, 1550–1750* (Brighton, 2001).

Vine, Angus, *In Defiance of Time: Antiquarian Writing in Early Modern England* (Oxford, 2010).

Walsham, Alexandra, *Providence in Early Modern England* (Oxford, 1999).

——, 'Holywell: Contesting Sacred Space in Post-Reformation Wales', in Coster and Spicer, *Sacred Space in Early Modern Europe*, 211–32.

——, *The Reformation of the Landscape: Religion, Identity, and Memory in Early Modern Britain and Ireland* (Oxford, 2011).

——, 'Providentialism', in Kewes, Archer, and Heal, *Holinshed's Chronicles*, 427–42.

Walters, Gwyn and Frank Emery, 'Edward Lhuyd, Edmund Gibson, and the Printing of Camden's *Britannia*, 1695', *The Library* 32.2 (1977), 109–37.

Ward, Joseph P., Muriel C. McClendon, and Michael MacDonald, eds, *Protestant Identities: Religion, Society, and Self-Fashioning in Post-Reformation England* (Stanford, 1999).

Warneke, Sara, *Images of the Educational Traveller in Early Modern England* (Leiden, 1995).

Warnicke, Retha M., *William Lambarde: Elizabethan Antiquary 1536–1601* (Chichester, 1973).

Wheeler, Roxann, *The Complexion of Race: Categories of Difference in Eighteenth-Century British Culture* (Philadelphia, 2000).

White, Richard, *The Middle Ground: Indians, Empires, and Republics in the Great Lakes Region, 1650–1815* (Cambridge, 1991).

Whyte, Ian D., *Scotland Before the Industrial Revolution: An Economic and Social History c. 1050–c.1750* (Harlow, 1995).

——, *Migration and Society in Britain 1550–1830* (Houndmills, 2000).

Williams, Clare, *Thomas Platter's Travels in England 1599* (London, 1937).

Williams, Glanmor, *Recovery, Reorientation and Reformation: Wales c. 1415–1642* (Oxford, 1987).

——, *Owain Glyndwr* (Cardiff, 1993/2005).

——, 'Unity of Religion or Unity of Language? Protestants and Catholics and the Welsh Language 1536–1660', in Jenkins, *The Welsh Language*, 207–33.

Williams, Penry, *The Later Tudors: England 1547–1603* (Oxford, 1995).

Williams, William H.A., *Tourism, Landscape, and the Irish Character* (Madison, WI, 2008).

Williamson, Arthur, 'An Empire to End Empire: The Dynamic of Early Modern British Expansion', *Huntington Library Quarterly* 68 (2005), 223–52.

Williamson, James A., *The Voyages of the Cabots and the English Discovery of North America under Henry VII and Henry VIII* (London, 1929).

Wilson, Kathleen, *The Island Race: Englishness, Empire and Gender in the Eighteenth Century* (Abingdon, 2003).

Winder, Robert, *Bloody Foreigners: The Story of Immigration to Britain* (London, 2004).

Withers, Charles W.J., *Gaelic Scotland: The Transformation of a Cultural Region* (London, 1988).

——, *Geography, Science, and National Identity: Scotland Since 1520* (Cambridge, 2001).

——, 'Pont in Context: Chorography, Mapmaking and National Identity in the Late Sixteenth Century', in Cunningham, *Nation Survey'd*, 139–54.

Wood, Andy, *The Memory of the People: Custom and Popular Senses of the Past in Early Modern England* (Cambridge, 2013).

Woolf, D.R., *Reading History in Early Modern England* (Cambridge, 2000).

——, *The Social Circulation of the Past: English Historical Culture 1500–1730* (Oxford, 2003).

Wrightson, Keith, *Earthly Necessities: Economic Lives in Early Modern Britain* (New Haven, 2000).

Zacher, Christian K., *Curiosity and Pilgrimage: The Literature of Discovery in Fourteenth-Century England* (Baltimore, 1976).

Electronic resources

Department for Education (London)

https://www.education.gov.uk/consultations/index.cfm?action=conResults&consultationId=1881&external=no&menu=3 'National Curriculum Framework' (February, 2013).

https://www.gov.uk/government/publications/national-curriculum-in-england-history-programmes-of-study/national-curriculum-in-england-history-programmes-of-study 'The National Curriculum in England: History Programmes of Study' (11 September, 2013).

https://www.gov.uk/government/uploads/system/uploads/attachment_data/file/206146/GCSE_History__final.pdf 'History GCSE subject content and assessment objectives' (June, 2013).

Education Scotland

http://www.educationscotland.gov.uk/Images/social_studies_experiences_outcomes_tcm4-539891.pdf 'Curriculum for Excellence: Social Studies Experiences and Outcomes' (undated).

http://www.educationscotland.gov.uk/Images/SocialStudies3to18_tcm4-731894.pdf 'Social Studies 3–18' (September, 2012).

The Guardian online

http://www.guardian.co.uk/uk/video/2011/aug/13/david-starkey-whites-black-video?INTCMP=ILCNETTXT3487 'David Starkey on UK Riots' (13 August 2011).

http://www.guardian.co.uk/politics/blog/2011/nov/15/david-starkey-monocultural-britain?INTCMP=SRCH 'David Starkey is Half Right About "Monocultural" Britain' (15 November 2011).

http://www.theguardian.com/uk-news/2013/dec/18/uk-immigration-bill-homelessness-racism-mps 'Immigration Bill Could Lead to Racism and Homelessness' (18 December 2013).

http://www.theguardian.com/commentisfree/2013/may/12/niall-ferguson-british-history-parochial 'History is Where the Great Battles of Public Life are Now Being Fought' (12 May 2013).

http://www.theguardian.com/teacher-network/2013/jul/16/new-primary-history-curriculum 'Sshh, This New Primary History Curriculum is Really Rather Good' (16 July 2013).

http://www.theguardian.com/books/2013/jul/13/michael-gove-teaching-history-wars 'Michael Gove's History Wars' (13 July 2013).

The Historical Association

www.history.org.uk/file_download.php?ts=1366214217&id=11761 'National Curriculum Consultation Response' (2013).

New Statesman online

http://www.newstatesman.com/politics/uk-politics/2013/05/mr-men-game 'The Mr Men Game' (23 May 2013).

Office for Standards in Education (OFSTED)

http://www.ofsted.gov.uk/resources/history-for-all 'History for All: History in English Schools 2007/10' (March, 2011).

Oxford Dictionary of National Biography

www.oxforddnb.com.

Qualifications and Curriculum Authority (QCA)

https://media.education.gov.uk/assets/files/pdf/h/history%202007%20programme%20of%20study%20for%20key%20stage%203.pdf 'National Curriculum 2007'.

The Royal Historical Society

www.royalhistoricalsociety.org/Reform%20of%20NC%20Response%20form%20 (11%20April%202013%20final).pdf 'National Curriculum Consultation Response' (2013).

Scottish Qualifications Authority

http://www.sqa.org.uk/sqa/47923.html 'Higher History Course Support Notes'.
http://www.sqa.org.uk/sqa/48466.html 'Advanced Higher Course Support Notes'.

Welsh Education

http://learning.wales.gov.uk/docs/learningwales/publications/130424-history-in-the-national-curriculum-for-wales-en.pdf 'History in the National Curriculum for Wales' (2008).

http://wales.gov.uk/docs/dcells/publications/121127reviewofqualificationsen.pdf 'Review of Qualifications for 14 to 19-year-olds in Wales' (November, 2012).

http://www.wjec.co.uk/uploads/publications/18260.pdf 'GCSE in History' (2013).

http://www.wjec.co.uk/uploads/publications/15726.pdf 'GCE in History' (2012).

Index

STUDIES IN EARLY MODERN CULTURAL, POLITICAL AND SOCIAL HISTORY